THE GERMAN CINEMA BOOK

THE GERMAN CINEMA BOOK

Edited by
Tim Bergfelder, Erica Carter
and Deniz Göktürk

bfi Publishing

First published in 2002 by the
British Film Institute
21 Stephen Street, London W1T 1LN

The British Film Institute is the UK national agency with
responsibility for encouraging the arts of film and television
and conserving them in the national interest.

Cover image: *Bildnis einer Trinkerin* (Ottinger, Ulrike, 1979)
Set by Fakenham Photosetting, Norfolk
Printed in the UK by St Edmundsbury Press, Suffolk

British Library Cataloguing-in-Publication Data
A catalogue record for this book is available from the British Library

ISBN 0–85170–946–x (pb)
ISBN 0–85170–945–1 (hb)

Contents

Preface and Acknowledgments

During the two years that preceded the completion of *The German Cinema Book*, the collection has been transformed from a few pages of rough notes, to a five-part survey that we hope will be of value both to specialist scholars of German cinema, and to general readers who share our own enthusiasm for exploring the wealth of the German-speaking countries' multi-faceted contributions to film. For their contributions to this project, the editors would like to thank the following: first, our contributors, whose good humour in the face of a sometimes uncompromisingly demanding editorial triumvirate has been greatly appreciated, as has their willingness to place their knowledge and expertise in the service of this book. Second, we would like to thank colleagues in the School of Modern Languages at the University of Southampton, the Departments of German and Film and Television Studies at the University of Warwick, and the Department of German Studies at the University of California, Berkeley, for their support and encouragement. For translation and editorial assistance, we are especially grateful to Robert Kiss. Seán Allan, Joseph Garncarz, Iris Kehr, Lutz Koepnick, Peter Latta, Richard Parker and Martin Pumphrey who have lent their expertise at crucial points. At the BFI, we are indebted to Sophia Contento for help with illustrations, as well as to our editor Andrew Lockett, for inviting us to embark on this project, and for his sustained commitment to writing on German film.

This book could not have taken its current shape without financial support for translation and bibliographical research from the Arts and Humanities Research Board, the British Film Institute and Popular European Cinema (PEC) 3 at the University of Warwick. For invaluable assistance with illustrations, we wish finally to thank BFI Stills, the Stiftung Deutsche Kinemathek, the University of Warwick Library (Harmssen Collection), Bildarchiv Preussischer Kulturbesitz, the Export-Union of German Cinema (London branch, UK) and the Munich Stadtarchiv.

Notes on Contributors

Tim Bergfelder is Senior Lecturer in Film Studies at the University of Southampton. He has published on aspects of German, British and European cinema history in various journals and edited collections, and is currently completing a monograph on European co-productions and popular German film genres of the 1960s, *International Adventures* (Berghahn, forthcoming).

Hans-Michael Bock is Head of the film-historical research centre CineGraph in Hamburg, and is series editor for the publishers edition text und kritik, Munich, and Berghahn, Oxford and New York. His publications as author and editor include: *CineGraph: Lexikon zum deutschsprachigen Film* (edition text+kritik, 1984); *Paul Leni: Grafik, Theater, Film* (Deutsches Filmmuseum, 1986); *Das Ufa-Buch* (Zweitausendeins, 1992, co-ed. with Michael Töteberg); and *Recherche: Film* (edition text+kritik, 1997, co-ed. with Wolfgang Jacobsen).

Erica Carter is Reader in German Studies at the University of Warwick. She has lectured and written extensively on German cultural and cinema studies; her publications include *How German is She? Postwar West German Reconstruction and the Consuming Woman* (University of Michigan Press, 1997) and *Dietrich's Ghosts: Stars in Third Reich Film* (BFI, forthcoming).

Horst Claus is Reader in German Cinema at the University of the West of England, Bristol. He is co-author of *Reclams Lexikon des deutschen Films* (Reclam, 1995). He is currently writing a monograph on the director Hans Steinhoff, and has restored several of Steinhoff's silent films.

Thomas Elsaesser is Professor of Art and Culture at the University of Amsterdam. His many publications on German cinema as author and editor include: *New German Cinema: A History* (BFI and Macmillan, 1989); *A Second Life: German Cinema's First Decades* (with Michael Wedel, Amsterdam University Press, 1996); *Fassbinder's Germany. History, Identity, Subject* (Amsterdam University Press, 1996); *The BFI Companion to German Cinema* (with Michael Wedel, BFI, 1999); *Weimar Cinema and After. Germany's Historical Imaginary* (Routledge, 2000) and *Metropolis* (BFI, 2000).

Claudia Fellmer is a PhD student at the University of Southampton, currently completing a thesis on stars in GDR cinema. She has presented several papers on this subject at conferences in Britain and the United States.

Joseph Garncarz is *Privatdozent* in Film Studies at the University of Cologne. His main subject of study is German film history and he has published widely on this topic in journals and edited collections. His PhD thesis on film versions was published as *Filmfassungen* (Lang, 1992). He is currently working on two books, *On the Origins of Cinema: Film in German Variety Theatres and Travelling Shows, 1895–1924* and *German Cinema: A Comprehensive History*.

Ian Garwood is a lecturer in Film and TV Studies at the University of Glasgow. His current research interests are film music, issues in film narration, alternative cinemas and post-1960s German cinema. He has written on film music for a number of journals and anthologies.

Deniz Göktürk is Associate Professor in German at the University of California, Berkeley. Her research interests include transnational cinemas and multiculturalism. She has published numerous articles on these subjects, and the monograph *Künstler, Cowboys, Ingenieure: Kultur- und mediengeschichtliche Studien zu deutschen Amerika-Texten 1912–1920* (Wilhelm Fink, 1998).

Marie-Hélène Gutberlet is a technical assistant at Frankfurt/Main University, and is currently completing her doctoral thesis 'Auf Reisen: Afrikanisches Kino', which focuses on aspects and contexts of reception. She is co-editor of the anthology *Afrikanisches Kino* (Horlemann, 1997). She has published and organised conferences and retrospectives on African, Black and Experimental Cinema.

Malte Hagener is a research assistant at the University of Amsterdam. He is the editor of *Als die Filme singen lernten. Innovation und Tradition im Musikfilm, 1928–1938* (edition text+kritik, 1999) and *Geschlecht in Fesseln. Sexualität zwischen Aufklärung und Ausbeutung im Weimarer Kino, 1918–1933* (edition text+kritik, 2000).

Sabine Hake is Professor of German at the University of Pittsburgh. She is the author of *Passions and Deceptions: The Early Films of Ernst Lubitsch* (Princeton University Press, 1992), *The Cinema's Third Machine: Writing on Film in Germany, 1907–1933* (University of Nebraska Press, 1993), *Popular Cinema of the Third Reich* (University of Texas Press, 2002) and *German National Cinema* (Routledge, 2002).

Jan-Christopher Horak is Curator at the Hollywood Entertainment Museum. Previously, he was Director of Archives and Collections at Universal Studios; Director of the Munich Filmmuseum; and Senior Curator at the George Eastman House. His many publications include: *Making Images Move: Photographers and Avant-Garde Cinema* (Smithsonian Institution Press, 1997); *Berge, Licht und Traum. Dr. Arnold Fanck und der deutsche Bergfilm* (Bruckmann Verlag, 1997); *Lovers of Cinema. The First American Film Avant-Garde 1919–1945* (University of Wisconsin Press, 1995); *The Dream Merchants: Making and Selling Films in Hollywood's Golden Age* (George Eastman House, 1989); *Anti-Nazi-Filme der deutschsprachigen Emigration von Hollywood 1939–45* (MAKS Publikationen, 1984); *Fluchtpunkt Hollywood. Eine Dokumentation zur Filmemigration nach 1933* (MAKS Publikationen, 1986, expanded 2nd edition); *Helmar Lerski – Lichtbildner. Fotographien und Filme 1910–1947* (Das Museum, 1982); and *Film und Foto der zwanziger Jahre* (Württembergischer Kunstverein, 1979).

Anton Kaes is Chancellor Professor of German and Film Studies and currently chair of the German Department at the University of California, Berkeley. His major publications include: *Expressionismus in Amerika: Rezeption und Innovation* (Max Niemeyer, 1975); *Kino-Debatte: Literatur und Film*, ed. (Max Niemeyer, 1978); *Weimarer Republik: Texte und Dokumente zur deutschen Literatur 1918–1933*, ed. (an expanded version, *The Weimar Republic Sourcebook*, co-edited with Martin Jay and Edward Dimendberg, was published by the University of California Press in 1994); *Deutschlandbilder: Die Wiederkehr der Geschichte als Film* (edition text+kritik, 1985); and *From Hitler to Heimat: The Return of History as Film* (Harvard University Press, 1989). In 2000, his book on Fritz Lang's *M* appeared in the BFI Classics series. He is also co-editor of the first history of German film, *Geschichte des deutschen Films* (Metzler, 1993). Professor Kaes is currently working on a cultural history of cinema in the Weimar Republic, tentatively entitled: *Shell Shock: German Cinema after the Great War*, forthcoming from Princeton University Press.

Frank Kessler is a professor of Film and Television History at Utrecht University (the Netherlands). He is the author of numerous articles on film history and theory, one of the founders and editors of *KINtop – Yearbook of Early Cinema*, and co-editor of *Mapping Modernity. Silent Cinema and the Networks of Modern Life* (forthcoming).

Robert J. Kiss teaches in the Department of German Studies at the University of Warwick, where he recently completed a PhD on *The Doppelgänger in Wilhelmine Cinema (1895–1914): Modernity, Audiences and Identity in Turn-of-the-Century Germany* (2 vols, 2000). He is a contributor to *Journeys of Desire: European Actors in Hollywood*, ed. Alastair Phillips and Ginette Vincendeau (BFI/Slatkine, 2002), and also works as a freelance translator specialising in cinema-related texts.

Peter Krämer teaches Film Studies at the University of East Anglia, Norwich. He has published essays on American film and media history, and on the relationship between Hollywood and Europe, in numerous journals and edited collections. Together with Alan Lovell, he co-edited *Screen Acting* (Routledge, 1999). He is currently working on *The Big Picture: Hollywood Cinema from Star Wars to Titanic*, to be published by the BFI, and *The New Hollywood: From Bonnie and Clyde to Star Wars* (for Wallflower Press).

Martin Loiperdinger is Professor of Media Studies at the University of Trier, and co-editor of *KINtop – Yearbook of Early Cinema*. His research interests include: history of visual media; the art of projection; early cinema; and film and politics. He has published numerous articles, and worked on some television features on film history up to the 1960s. His book publications include *Rituale der*

Mobilmachung – der Parteitagsfilm 'Triumph des Willens' von Leni Riefenstahl (Leske + Budrich, 1987) and *Film Schokolade: Stollwercks Geschäfte mit lebenden Bildern* (Stroemfeld/Roter Stern, 1999).

Stephen Lowry is Professor of Media and Communication Studies at the Hochschule der Medien, Stuttgart. Publications include *Der Filmstar* (Metzler, 2000), *Pathos und Politik: Ideologie in Spielfilmen des Nationalsozialismus* (Max Niemeyer, 1991) and articles on film theory and film history. He is co-editor of the journal *montage/av.*

Johannes von Moltke is an assistant professor for Film/Video Studies and German Studies at the University of Michigan. He has published on the New German Cinema and German popular culture, and is currently completing a book on the role of *Heimat* in German film history.

Julian Petley lectures in Media and Communications Studies at Brunel University. He is the author of *Capital and Culture: German Cinema 1933–45* (BFI, 1979) and a contributor to *Anglo-German Attitudes* (Avebury, 1995). He has curated various seasons on German cinema at the National Film Theatre and the Goethe Institutes in both London and Dublin. He is currently writing a book on media censorship in contemporary Britain for Routledge.

Ulrike Sieglohr is Senior Lecturer in Film, Television and Radio Studies at Staffordshire University. Her many publications include *Focus on the Maternal: Female Subjectivity and Images of Motherhood* (Scarlet Press, 1998) and, as editor, *Heroines without Heroes: Reconstructing Female and National Identities in European Cinema, 1945–51* (Cassell, 2000). Her current research concerns 'The Poetics of Exile'.

Marc Silberman is Professor of German at the University of Wisconsin, Madison. He has written on and translated texts by Heiner Müller and Bertolt Brecht. He is the author of *German Cinema: Texts in Context* (Wayne State University Press, 1995), and is currently working on East German cinema of the 1950s and 60s.

Michael Töteberg is Director of the Media Rights Department at the Rowohlt Publishing House in Reinbek, and contributor to *CineGraph: Lexikon zum deutschsprachigen Film* (edition text+kritik, 1984). His many publications as author and editor include: *Fritz Lang* (Rowohlt, 1985); *Das Ufa-Buch* (Zweitausendeins, 1992, co-ed. with Hans-Michael Bock); *Metzler Filmlexikon* (Metzler, 1995); *Szenenwechsel: Momentaufnahmen des jungen deutschen Films* (Rowohlt, 1999); and *Fassbinder* (Rowohlt, 2002). He has also edited collections of writings by Wim Wenders, Edgar Reitz and Rainer Werner Fassbinder, and published annotated editions of screenplays, as well as numerous books on individual films.

Eva Warth is a professor of Film and Television Studies at the University of Bochum. She is the author of *The Haunted Palace. E. A. Poe und der amerikanische Horrorfilm 1909–1969* (WVT, 1990), co-author of *Never-Ending Stories. Soap Opera and the Cultural Production of Meaning* (WVT, 1992) and co-editor of *Remote Control. Television, Audiences, and Cultural Power* (Routledge, 1989). Forthcoming are: *Mapping Modernity. Silent Cinema and the Networks of Modern Life* and *Gender and Silent Cinema.*

Introduction

Germany can look back on as long a film history as any other country, and yet, more often than not, its cinema has seemed ambivalent even in its achievements. The disasters of German history this century have left their mark on the cinema, and even more so on the image and idea we have of it.

(Thomas Elsaesser).[1]

Classical histories

Thomas Elsaesser's quote above succinctly summarises the difficulties, both methodological and ideological, of writing a history of German cinema. German film has been assigned, whether justifiably or not, an almost unique place in the canon of world cinemas, accompanied by its own set of critical parameters and modes of evaluation, which aim, on the whole, to explain particularly the excesses of German history (rather than the norms) through the images of the national film culture. Attempts at 'normalising' this history, even at the localised level of film culture, frequently elicit the suspicion of dubious intentions, and can be seen as supporting the exculpation and moral relativisation of Germany's past.

One could argue that Germany's fractured political history throughout the twentieth century makes it next to impossible to trace a national film history in straightforwardly linear terms, since the very definition of Germanness has to negotiate not only continuities, but also a plethora of different cultural, ideological and geographical contexts and ruptures across different periods. A film history that acknowledges such differences has to take into account, for example, the fertile influence of German-speaking cultures from Eastern Europe, or from areas which have always had a distinct or separate national identity (i.e. Austria, Switzerland), not to mention wider transnational and transcultural connections. It needs to counterpoint the rabid nationalism of the 1930s and 40s with the cosmopolitan legacy of Jewish diaspora and exile, and to chart the ideological divisions and boundaries of the Cold War, as well as the re-emergence of a more multi-cultural conception of Germanness in recent years. It is precisely this indeterminacy of, and competing claims about, what 'German' means across not always overlapping cultural, historical, national and linguistic definitions that have left their mark on the understanding of German film history. Before we outline some of the ways in which these indeterminacies may be used productively as a marker of German cinema's richness and diversity, it is necessary to provide a brief account of how these contradictions have been resolved traditionally.

It is notable that, while there are a large number of publications on a variety of aspects of German film, there have until recently been few comprehensive accounts of German film history in its entirety. Studies written prior to the 1950s, such as Oskar Kalbus' *Vom Werden deutscher Filmkunst* (1935) or H. H. Wollenberg's *Fifty Years of German Film* (1948), provide necessarily partial and largely anecdotal narratives from a contemporary point of view, though Kalbus' book provides a fascinating insight into how national film history was retrospectively constructed during the Nazi period.[2] Since then, selected moments in German film history, most notably Weimar, Nazi and the New German Cinema of the 1970s, have received an enormous amount of scholarly attention, both in Germany and elsewhere, which in turn has facilitated a commonly held perception that German cinema can be defined and understood almost exclusively through an isolated engagement with these three historical periods.

From the 1970s to the mid-90s, the exploration of Weimar, Nazi and New German Cinema ran parallel to evolving critical paradigms in film analysis. Thus, one can chart a development from Roger Manvell and Heinrich Fraenkel's *The German Cinema,* the three-volume encyclopaedia *Klassiker des deutschen Stummfilms, Klassiker des deutschen Tonfilms* and *Der neue deutsche Film*,[3] and Frederick Ott's *The Great German Films: From Before World War One to the Present*,[4] with their emphasis on 'masterpieces' and auteurs, to the more sophisticated theoretical arsenal which informs Eric Rentschler's *German Film and Literature* and Marc Silberman's *German Cinema: Texts in Context*. Yet the historical focus on Weimar and New German Cinema remained mostly undisputed irrespective of critical methodology.[5] Wolfgang Jacobsen, Anton Kaes and Hans-Helmut Prinzler's *Geschichte des deutschen Films* can be seen as the first attempt to provide a more comprehensive history of German film, covering the nine decades of German cinema from its beginnings through to the 1980s.[6] But even here, a rather disjointed history emerges; indeed the editors argue in their introduction that German film historiography may best be compared with 'working on a building site'.[7] In similar vein, Sabine Hake cautions in the introduction to her *German National Cinema* against attempts to homogenise a 'national cinema striving for internal coherence and unity that, in fact, can and will never be achieved'.[8]

Such comments need to be read against the background of a selectively condensed, yet teleologically ideal narrative, which has dominated the perception of German cinema for decades, both within Germany itself, and even more strongly abroad. This narrative charts German cinema from mostly undistinguished (hardly known and barely explored) beginnings to its first peak of artistic excellence in the Weimar period, producing outstanding masterpieces, and individual auteurs such as Fritz Lang and F. W. Murnau. For the Third Reich, the narrative's emphasis shifts from a discussion of artistic merit to an analysis of filmic effects, and of the institutional underpinnings of a politically compromised culture industry. For the period between 1945 and 1962, there are two possible variations to the narrative, sometimes, and somewhat paradoxically, used in conjunction. According to the first version (the 'legacy-of-fascism' argument), German cinema is unable to shake off the ideological heritage of the Nazi period, and stifles innovation and democratisation. In the second version (the 'media imperialism' argument), Hollywood assumes near-complete control over German production, distribution and audiences. Thus, film histories concerned with the exploration of German cinema's national representability tend to fast-forward fairly rapidly to the Oberhausen manifesto in 1962, which initiates the New German Cinema, constituted as the culmination of Germany's struggle for cultural legitimisation. It is no coincidence that what is omitted in this narrative are not only entire decades of film production, but also a tradition in German cinema which is centred on popular genres and stars.

Critical paradigms

One reason why the conception of German cinema around notions of the national and art has proved so persistent and persuasive is that it complements commonly held ideas and stereotypes of German identity and culture which remain in circulation both abroad and in Germany itself. Because German cinema (and culture more generally) has often been exclusively defined as 'high culture', the notion of a popular German cinema is, particularly outside Germany, difficult to imagine, possibly even eliciting ridicule and disbelief.

Aesthetic notions of Germanness have focused instead on the perception of German culture as caught between the poles of austere intellectualism and romantic melancholy. Hence the attempt to incorporate Weimar cinema into, and legitimise it through, the legacy of nineteenth-century German romanticism which, for example, characterises Lotte Eisner's approach in her well-known *The Haunted Screen*.[9] This is the same approach by which German cinema has been appropriated in Germanist and art history curricula all over the world as an annex to, or illustration of, particular art canons and literary traditions.

For the detractors of German culture, on the other hand, intellectualism and romanticism have frequently been seen as synonymous with impenetrability and morbid pessimism. It was, for example, the alleged morbidity of German culture that led Sergei Eisenstein in the 1920s to denounce expressionist cinema as a 'barbaric carnival of the destruction of the healthy human infancy of our art'.[10] Similar stereotypes persist elsewhere; thus, the directors of the New German Cinema, as Thomas Elsaesser has argued, fashioned and came to embody, both at home and abroad, the clichéd image of either the brooding and tortured Teutonic genius or the disenchanted and enigmatic intellectual mandarin (Rainer Werner Fassbinder and Werner Herzog are the most prominent exponents of the former type, Alexander Kluge represents the latter).[11] The notion that German audiences are an amorphous mass, prone to the influences of totalitarianism and capitalism, perpetuates the popular belief abroad that the German 'nation' (understood as a racially unified entity) represents an unpredictable collective force, bound together by blood and soil. The dissenting, individualist and resistant high culture of the New German Cinema, on the other hand, provides an alternative notion of German identity, and can be seen to signal an ethically and aesthetically enlightened nation which has addressed, and morally overcome, its past. It is no coincidence that, for the past thirty years, the films of the New German Cinema have been used by successive West German governments and their agencies abroad (such as the Goethe Institutes) to promote the Federal Republic and its culture.

While these notions of Germanness relate to wider public perceptions, stereotypes and strategies of cultural promotion, in discourses on German cinema they are critically legitimated by specific theoretical paradigms. Perhaps the most influential among these is linked to the Critical Theory of the Frankfurt School. Originating in the 1920s as a loose grouping of cultural critics and social scientists, the Frankfurt School comprises a rather disparate body of work and figures such as Theodor Adorno, Max Horkheimer, Herbert Marcuse, Leo Lowenthal, and the more distinctly independent Walter Benjamin and Siegfried Kracauer. As both Marxists and Jews, the founding members of the Frankfurt School fled Germany in the 1930s, but continued to write trenchant critiques of capitalist ideology in their (mostly North American) exile. Adorno was among the few who returned to Germany after the war, and who triggered a renaissance of the School's ideas among a younger generation of German academics.

It is however the School's first generation, and particularly the work of Adorno, Horkheimer and Kracauer, which has been taken up in debates on German film, if however, as we argue below, in a somewhat selective fashion across different decades. Adorno's notion of the culture industry as an inescapable system and all-pervasive expression of capitalist ideology, and the notion of high culture as a possible (though not necessarily guaranteed) site of resistance, had a profound impact on critical discourses on German cinema as well as on the ethos and practice of many German film-makers in the 1970s. Indeed, Adorno's conception of history as a dialectical process can be seen to have almost turned into its parody in some historical narratives of German cinema, where dark ages are overcome in decisive breaks through heroic struggles, culminating in the soundly emancipatory movement of the New German Cinema. Notably, Adorno himself was far more pessimistic with regard to cultural change, perceiving mass culture and high art as 'two halves of a whole that do not add up'.[12]

Adorno's critical stance crucially also dictated until recently the terms by which popular German film was discussed. For Adorno, capitalist production was all-encompassing and irredeemable, and its specific political contexts and cultural manifestations to some extent inter-changeable or merely incidental. Adorno's disdain for mass culture extended from American jazz music, radio, advertising and Hollywood films to post-war German commercial cinema. On the latter he opined that 'what is repulsive about Daddy's cinema is its infantility, its industrially activated regression'.[13] For Adorno, mass audiences could only be understood as misled victims, trapped, but also complicit in their own domination unless they transcend their role as consumers. 'Popular' culture in the sense of a relatively autonomous domain or tradition is thus not only no longer possible in the age of the culture industry; the very claim for its existence becomes an act of critical collusion: 'the culture industry is not the art of the consumer, but rather the projection of the will of those in control onto their victims'.[14] In the past, discourses on German cinema have often echoed this dictum by discussing the German film industry, market and audience as a relatively unified and coherent system of capitalist domination and oppression, whether this power is exerted at a national level or through global media imperialism. This critical framework has resulted in a contradictory evaluation of the German film industry, which has been frequently condemned both for its capitalist 'essence' and for its failure or inefficiency as a capitalist industry, evidenced for example in the often cited derisory term 'Bavarian cottage industry' for post-war German film production.[15]

Siegfried Kracauer's *From Caligari to Hitler*, meanwhile, provided the theoretical framework by which the culture industry could be seen to intersect with more specifically national characteristics.[16] His well-known thesis was that German cinema of the 1920s and early 30s textually prefigured and anticipated the Nazi dictatorship, and that it projected an innately German psychological proclivity towards authoritarian social and political structures. In Kracauer's analysis of the ideological function and effects of filmic narratives and styles, textual features were not only seen to reflect national formations and developments. By creating homologies between narratives and styles and a particular national trajectory, cinema became the supreme agency and medium in constructing national identity, exemplifying what Patrice Petro has described as an endemic critical conflation of 'narrative and national identity, national identity with subject, and all three terms with male subjectivity and male identity in crisis'.[17]

Crucially, what distinguishes Kracauer from Adorno is the former's rejection of high culture as a possible remedy. During the 1920s, Kracauer perceived lowbrow forms of entertainment and the function of cinema as a public sphere in rather ambivalent terms, and assigned them at least a progressive potential in contributing to a wider change in social relations. As we argue below, it is thus Kracauer's writings from the Weimar period that have been taken up by recent revisionist historians of German cinema. In *From Caligari to Hitler*, by contrast, it is precisely the bourgeoisification of cinema as a social institution, and the high cultural aspirations of Weimar films, which for Kracauer facilitate, articulate and promote a dominant national psychological disposition towards totalitarianism.

Kracauer's linkage of cinema and nation in *From Caligari to Hitler* remained largely unquestioned for a long time. Moreover, either as an explicit methodology or as an implicit reference point, his thesis not only informed later studies of Weimar cinema and the Nazi film industry. It has also been instrumentalised to virtually collapse all of German cinema's history into a privileged causal relationship between issues of nationhood (or its dominant psychological dispositions) and cinema's narrative and stylistic conventions. Hence the preference for historical periods which are overdetermined in their political and national symbolism (Weimar, the 'Third Reich', the 1970s), and the simultaneous neglect, or forced integration, of those periods (e.g. Early Cinema, the 1950s) and cultural manifestations (popular genres, stars, audience diversity) which threaten to expose the perceived homogeneity of German national cinema (and the nation itself) as a fiction.

The new film history: institutions and sites

Critical approaches to German cinema have, in sum, often been constricted by the double ideological bind of, on the one hand, a Marxism that situates film within the culture industry as an ineluctable matrix of capitalist mass manipulation, and on the other, a theory of nation in which film becomes the morally compromised product of a national culture tainted with fascism's historical stain.

Recent years, however, have witnessed crucial historiographical shifts. The emergence of a new German film history has occurred in part through the institutionalisation in Germany and elsewhere of film studies as a scholarly (albeit not always an academic or university) discipline. In Britain and the US, post-1968 curriculum reform, coupled with higher education expansion from the 1960s on, produced a climate of innovation out of which academic film studies was born. In the German-speaking countries, by contrast, film studies was slower to gain academic legitimacy. As this present collection demonstrates, research in

German film history is currently flourishing; yet it is not at all uniquely the universities that provide the institutional focus for this burgeoning field. In Germany itself, university film research and teaching occur often still on the fringes of other, related disciplines – theatre and literary studies, media sociology, the history of art, cultural studies, cultural history – with few of the integrated programmes that might engender an academic community with its own methodologies, theories or research agendas. Alongside the activities of the *Gesellschaft für Film- und Fernsehwissenschaft* (Society for Film and Television Studies), whose annual conferences and news bulletin provide an important focus for current efforts to 'consolidate [film studies] theory and research into an autonomous discipline', it is around Germany's network of film archives and independent research centres that film-critical and historical activity regularly coalesce.[18] The commitment to film scholarship and research in each of Germany's four major film museums (in Potsdam, Munich, Frankfurt and Berlin) finds expression, first, in a prolific publications output: thus the *Filmmuseum Berlin* and *Filmmuseum Potsdam* together boast current lists totalling over seventy monographs and edited collections, alongside the Berlin museum's two journals, *FilmGeschichte* and *FilmExil*. Second, the museum sector often provides the best umbrella for such grand-scale research as (to take just one instance) a recent collaboration between the Goethe University of Frankfurt and the *Deutsches Filminstitut* (DIF, or German Film Institute, the research arm of the Frankfurt Film Museum) on a project designed to produce a social history of contemporary German film. DIF publications from that venture will complement such existing gems as the Institute's annotated database of 1920s and 30s documents from the Berlin film censor, as well as its CD-Rom filmography of the top one hundred German films from 1895 to 1998.[19]

Important critical studies emanate, finally, from a handful of smaller independent research centres funded largely from federal cultural budgets to act as catalysts for regional, national and international research on German film. The Hamburg-based *CineGraph* is especially active in this regard. *CineGraph*'s annual conference and publications series have established the centre as a key instigator in the rediscovery of popular directors and genres from Early German and Weimar film, as well as of German cinema's interactions with other European film cultures.[20] Contributions to *CineGraph*'s edited collections from British and non-German continental European scholars signal, moreover, a commitment to cross-cultural scholarly exchange that has been a characteristic feature of German film history in recent decades. Contemporary scholarship on European national cinemas is often a dual- if not a multi-language pursuit, whose practitioners pursue triangular careers publishing, researching and lecturing across (at least) continental Europe, North America and the UK.[21] In German film history, alongside international conferences that include *CineGraph*'s annual symposia, the US German Studies Association conferences, the Pordenone and Bologna festivals, and the occasional Popular European Cinema conference series initiated at the UK University of Warwick in 1989, transnational scholarly connections are sustained in the first instance by journals with an editorial commitment to Anglo/US-German exchange. North American and British titles wrestle in this context with the chronic underfunding of translation in a linguistically insular publishing world. The US-based *New German Critique* has the most sustained record of an editorial policy that has overcome that hurdle to publish regular overviews and translations of key texts from the history and theory of German film. Recent special issues from generalist film studies titles, moreover, including *Seminar*, *Camera Obscura* and *Screen*, may indicate a growth of Anglo-American interest in German film theory and critical history: an interest that has yet, however, to match the openness of those journals' German and Austrian counterparts towards critical dialogue with film studies in an Anglophone frame.[22] The peppering of German-language journals and edited collections with English-language contributions in the original or translation has fostered a climate of intellectual bi- (if not yet multi-) culturalism, and created a scholarly canon whose key texts derive from both sides of the German–English language divide. Thus it is that Heike Klippel, in her 1997 survey of film theory in the Federal Republic of Germany, is so at ease locating as seminal to that survey works by UK- or US-based scholars; here then, Teresa de Lauretis, Stephen Heath, Claire Johnston and Judith Mayne appear alongside Adorno, Benjamin and Kracauer as the precursors of a now culturally hybrid film-theoretical canon.[23] Thus it is too that a rash of late-1990s German star studies adopted methodologies from, and/or republished in German, key theoretical and critical texts from star studies in the UK and North America; or that feminist film studies in the German-speaking world have been engaged for two decades at least in a critical dialogue with Anglo-American psychoanalytical theories of gendered spectatorship (theories which, however, often resist accommodation within the cultural-philosophical and phenomenological traditions that regularly frame German feminist studies of gender and film[24]).

The new film history: theories and methods

There is of course (thankfully) no single methodology or theory uniting the rich array of new film histories that have emerged from recent decades of cross-European and transatlantic scholarly exchange. It is, however, possible to specify prevailing tendencies. The first is the recourse in much recent historiography to micro-archival studies of often hitherto neglected periods and objects of study. In that leftist corner of German film history that saw cinema as a tool of cultural-industrial mass deception in Adorno and Horkheimer's sense, a trend towards revisionist studies based on differentiated analysis of archival sources became visible from the early 1980s on. The legitimation crisis experienced in western Marxism following capitalism's neo-liberal regeneration in the early 1980s, and the collapse of state socialism as an apparently viable alternative after 1989, provoked in German film history a new awareness of classical Marxism's unreliability as a founding paradigm: an awareness visible in methodological shifts in the arena of industry history in particular. Thus for example such writers as Klaus Kreimeier and Wolfgang Mühl-Benninghaus moved from earlier accounts of what Mühl-Benninghaus had described in orthodox Marxist terms as 'state monopoly capitalism' in German film industries, to more methodologically pluralist accounts, in Kreimeier's case of The Ufa studios, in Mühl-Benninghaus', of Germany's transition from silent film to sound, seen now through the lens of an 'interdisciplinary media history'.[25]

A second effect of the events of 1989 relates less to critical orthodoxies and framing methods, than to a material expansion in the field of objects available for film-historical study. As Horst Claus elaborates in this volume, the years since German unification in 1990 have seen a gradual opening of archives in the former GDR and other ex-Warsaw pact states. That archival renaissance has in the first instance triggered a reassessment of East German film history from 1945 to 1990. DEFA histories, as Claus notes, have shifted emphasis in recent years from accounts of GDR film as the mirror of a largely successful state dictatorship, to histories that foreground that cinema's role in negotiating and reworking what were in fact the profound contradictions and tensions in GDR state socialism. The recourse to archival material as the basis for a revised history of GDR film has, moreover, provoked a rethinking of post-war German film history *tout court*. In such works as Sabine Hake's *German National Cinema*, or Katie Trumpener's *Divided Screens: Postwar Cinema in East and*

West, the story of post-1945 German cinema is no longer told as a necessarily bipolar narrative of separate development, but rather in terms of a network of occasionally distinct, but also occasionally overlapping, East–West cross-currents and interrelations.

The return to the DEFA archives is, moreover, also a symptomatic development from a period that has seen a renewed emphasis across all domains of cinema history on empirical archival research as a basis for broader historiographical reconceptualisations. The film historian Herbert Birett became an early exemplar of that trend when he used his exhaustive archival studies of early German cinema to develop insights into shot length as the basis for comparative analyses of early film.[26] Birett's catalogues of early silents in distribution during film's 'lost era' before 1911 stand, moreover, alongside such works as *CineGraph*'s regularly updated biographical film lexicon, as well as an expanding range of catalogues and 'checklists' of film collections and documentary resources at the regional, national and international archives and museums, as indispensable resources for a new film history that seeks to recover lost periods, film texts and cinema personnel from historical oblivion.[27]

But it is not only in their minute archival preoccupations that practitioners of the new German film history have diverged from predecessors schooled in 1970s and 80s ideology critique. The break with Frankfurt School Marxism has also involved a shift in conceptualisations of the audience, seen now no longer as the passive victim of mass manipulation, but as one among a plurality of social actors in the complex process of the historical construction of film-cultural values, ideologies and meanings. Helmut Korte, for example, draws on both Anglo-American cultural studies and the literary reception aesthetics of Iser and Jauss as resources for a rethinking of late Weimar film history from the perspective of audience reception.[28] Korte's focus on reception as what he terms film history's 'most significant social dimension' is reproduced by Joseph Garncarz when, in a series of groundbreaking essays, he uses such sources as audience polls and box-office records to question numerous film-historical orthodoxies, including the myth of Hollywood's enduring stranglehold on German markets, and of German cinema as devoid of an indigenous star system that might be fit to challenge star images Hollywood-style.

Feminism and film

The combination of archival research with a re-theorised focus on reception is especially prevalent in feminist histories of German film. Feminist film historians are familiar enough with the necessity to search hidden corners (archives, autobiographies, diaries, oral histories, forgotten scholarship) for data that might assist in their larger project of the reinscription in film history of a gendered perspective. Hence, for example, the enthusiastic reception within German feminist film history of Emilie Altenloh's previously critically neglected sociological study of pre-First World War film audiences, *Zur Soziologie des Kino (A Sociology of the Cinema).*[29] That work's painstaking reconstruction of audience trends in one Wilhelmine town famously helped undermine the argument prevalent in pre-feminist studies that it was working-class men who were the primary audience for early film. Altenloh's portrait of a pre-war audience finely differentiated in class terms, and including at all social levels a preponderance of women, laid the foundations, moreover, for a burgeoning of feminist studies from the late 1980s on that used Altenloh's reception data as one source for a gendered reconceptualisation of pre-First World War and Weimar film.

Importantly, though, the work of such writers as Miriam Hansen, Heide Schlüpmann or Patrice Petro has not been confined to the empirical recuperation of women 'hidden' or suppressed from existing histories of German film.[30] Certainly, their engagement with Altenloh has led these writers to identify archival investigations of female audiences as one building-block in the feminist rewriting of a gendered history of German film. German feminist film historians share, then, with many English-speaking film scholars the perception that it is reception history that offers the richest territory for the mapping of gender in film.[31] At the same time, however, feminist film historians raise an issue that has been pivotal in the recent development of the wider field of German film history when they caution against a conflation of empirical research with empiricism *tout court.* Empiricist epistemology, as Jackie Stacey has commented, contains pitfalls for feminist film history in its grounding of *all* knowledge in 'the unmediated observable truth of experience'.[32] While 'experience' certainly remains a central category for feminist histories of all kinds, feminist epistemologies, in contrast to empiricism, tend to share a 'critical stance in relation to … objectivity', and to assert the legitimacy of political engagement and particularism.[33] Feminist film history, then, struggles to reconcile two conflicting imperatives: the desire on the one hand to restore to film historiography empirically grounded accounts of women's cinematic experience, and on the other, to sustain the more speculative analytical mode demanded by feminism's political-theoretical commitments.

The new German film history and Weimar theory

It is this dual focus on social experience and cultural politics that perhaps explains why feminist film historians have been prominent in the re-engagement in recent years in both Anglophone and German 'new film history' with a Marxist film-critical canon that predates Adorno and Horkheimer's *Dialectic of Enlightenment*, and eschews that work's pessimism regarding cinema's relation to larger structures of politics and power.[34] Adorno and Horkheimer's work, like Kracauer's contemporaneous *From Caligari to Hitler*, was written in a post-war spirit of despair over the collapse of cultural values represented by fascism's triumph in Italy and Germany, and in particular by genocide against the Jews and other minorities under the Third Reich. Since that mid-twentieth-century moment, however, successive post-fascist political emergencies have led some among Adorno and Horkheimer's Frankfurt School descendants to rethink those writers' end-of-Enlightenment pessimism, and to call for a productive re-engagement with media cultures in general, and in particular with film. Hans-Magnus Enzensberger is significant in this context, as is the film-maker, theorist and cinema activist Alexander Kluge, whose utopian aspiration for the 1960s West German movement known as the Young German Cinema was that it might help realise the Enlightenment cultural legacy by functioning as what Stuart Liebman calls 'a paradigm of operations in a radically open and democratic public sphere'.[35]

Kluge's own contributions to that project included his 1966 *Abschied von Gestern* (*Yesterday Girl*), which became the first post-war German film to win a significant international prize when it was awarded the Silver Lion at the 1966 Venice Film Festival. Yet it is not Kluge's resolutely difficult (post-)modern film practice that renders most urgent a revision of Adorno and Horkheimer's culture industry thesis. Rather, it is mainstream cinema's extraordinary capacity for technological innovation, diversification and change that most clearly undermines those writers' vision of the culture industry's reproduction of the eternal same. Digital technology and the globalisation of the cultural industries have triggered what Marc Silberman in this volume terms 'a restructuring process of the entire communications domain' (p. 171). In this context, those film historians who aspire to sustain into a digital age 1970s and 80s film studies activist commitments have begun to revisit theoretical work which, like that of Adorno and Horkheimer, conceptualises cinema as the product of a

specific formation of capitalist modernity, yet, unlike those writers, deploys the category of 'modernity' as a dynamic socio-political concept that is 'capable of connecting [film] art with major vectors of social change'.[36]

The antecedents of such a dialectical view of modernity are traced in much recent theoretical work to the Weimar period, and to the theoretical writings on film of, among others, Siegfried Kracauer, Walter Benjamin, Rudolf Arnheim and Béla Balázs. The critical rediscovery of Weimar film theory began in the mid-1960s with the German publication of Kracauer's *Theory of Film*, as well as his *The Mass Ornament*, a volume of essays deriving from the period preceding the author's North American exile, and published during his time as a critic for the progressive *Frankfurter Zeitung*. Kracauer's essays – a collection of (often polemical) engagements with the phenomena of Weimar modernity (including street maps, hotel lobbies, dance halls and, of course, cinema) – were complemented in 1984 with the republication of the film-critical writings of the Hungarian-born Balázs, followed at the end of the decade by Walter Benjamin's collected works.[37]

Embedded in these new editions were key film-theoretical works: Kracauer's essays on film reception in his 'Little Shop Girls at the Movies' essay, as well as his writings on the 'mass ornament' and the 'cult of distraction'; Balázs on silent cinema's revisualisation of the human condition in his 'Visible Man' (*Der sichtbare Mensch*, orig. 1924; Benjamin on history and memory in modernity, or on the democratisation of art in 'the age of mechanical reproduction'. Two decades on, German film studies' engagement with the theoretical paradigms those essays develop has produced a series of important critical commentaries, including a 1987 special issue of *New German Critique* on Weimar film theory; Sabine Hake's 1993 study of Balázs, Kracauer and Rudolf Arnheim in her survey of German silent cinema criticism and theory, *The Cinema's Third Machine*; a monograph on Kracauer by the feminist film theorist Gertrud Koch; Massimo Locatelli's *Béla Balázs: Die Physiognomik des Films* (*The Physiognomy of Film*); and various exegeses of Walter Benjamin on film.[38]

Aside from these author-based studies, moreover, the impact of Weimar film theory has been felt in significant realignments in the focus of German film-historical enquiry and critical debate. What contemporary historians take first from Balázs, Kracauer, Arnheim and Benjamin is their common understanding of cinema as a dynamic cultural force whose historical significance resides in its production of new subjective modes, and thus of historical subjects specific to particular moments in modernity's development. For Balázs, for instance, specified elements of film language (his concern is especially with close-up and montage) create a 'technology of seeing and showing' that is not only historically unprecedented, but that also fosters historically new subjectivities and identities. What Balázs terms the 'substrate of development' that is produced by the new poetics of film is nothing less than 'the human individual (der Mensch) in her/his social being'.[39] Arnheim, analogously, takes a detour through Gestalt psychology to argue that 'shape and color, sound and words are the means by which man [sic] defines the nature and intention of his life'.[40] Kracauer's phenomenology of perception, by contrast, is more rigorously dialectical. For him, the perceptual and experiential modes film helps engender – in particular 'distraction' (Zerstreuung) as the peculiar mode of (in)attention that mass cultures demand – produce what Thomas Elsaesser has described as 'a specifically modern form of self-estrangement, which signalled not only the end of bourgeois notions of the individual, but also of its critiques in the name of the authentic self'.[41]

The rediscovery of a body of 1920s and 30s critical writing that aimed radically to historicise the new perceptual modes to which the moving image and cinema cultures gave rise has provided fertile territory in more recent decades for a reconceptualised history of the relation between subjectivities, cultural identities and German film. Released from the methodological stranglehold of, on the one hand, a social psychology that read German film as the mimetic reflection of what the Kracauer of From Caligari to Hitler had termed the 'psychological dispositions' of a nation, and on the other hand, an Anglophone film-psychoanalytical tradition that all too often saw film as reproducing universal Oedipal structures of visual pleasure and sexual difference, scholars have begun to map a history that relates German film to specific psychic formations developed through film audiences' encounters with modernity's characteristic film-textual and cultural forms. This new 'psychological history' of German film includes not only the feminist corpus referenced above, but recent revisionist histories of Weimar film in general. Anton Kaes' Shell Shock: Film and Trauma in Weimar Germany, for instance, shares with Thomas Elsaesser's Weimar Cinema and After the guiding perception that German film of 1918–33 must no longer be read as the expression of a transhistorical national unconscious, but rather as the vehicle for a plurality of 'historical imaginaries' deriving from a multiplicity of quintessentially modern experiences: modern trench warfare in Kaes' case, in Elsaesser's 'the metropolitan cityscape, the popular mass media, the ephemeral stimuli of autonomous spaces and the surface effects of neon light or shop windows'.[42]

Both Kaes and Elsaesser acknowledge a debt to Weimar film theory as what Kaes terms a 'shield', both against the 'extreme formalism' of 1970s and 80s Anglophone film analysis, and the 'essentialism' and 'determinism' associated with Kracauer's From Caligari to Hitler as 'the master narrative for the critical study of [Weimar] film'.[43] Weimar cultural critique, especially as represented by the Kracauer of the 'mass ornament' and related essays, has been similarly influential in post-1990 studies of Third Reich film. Especially significant have been the writings of the film critic Karsten Witte (who edited Kracauer's essays for their post-war publisher, suhrkamp). The US film historian Eric Rentschler thus locates his own 1996 study of Third Reich film, Ministry of Illusion. Nazi Cinema and its Afterlife, in a line of descent that reaches back to Kracauer and Benjamin, but refracts their writings through the later work of Witte, whose analyses of the 'structures of experience' encoded in Third Reich film's visual and aural signs are cited by Rentschler as a seminal influence on his own studies of the 'form, address and appeal of Nazi films'.[44]

Historiographical shifts beyond Weimar theory

The rediscovery of the Weimar Kracauer, and the concomitant displacement of his 1947 From Caligari to Hitler, are, however, only part of a larger process that has begun to unhook German film historiography from its anchorage in a political master narrative of nation. Weimar film theory emerged in response to a modern cinema whose production modes, film styles and popular appeal derived as much from German film's relation to international as to national film-cultural, political and economic developments. In contemporary German film history, the rediscovery of German cinema's international dimension has occurred not only through Weimar theory, but also, for example, as a result of what we noted above was the internationalisation of German film history itself as a scholarly discipline. It is such 'legendary' cross-national events as the 1990 Pordenone Film Festival, for instance, that have been most instrumental in triggering an awareness that 'film production and cinema exhibition up to World War I were a highly international business, making nonsense of an idea of national cinema that does not ... take note of tendencies in other major film-producing countries, such as France, Denmark, Italy, and of course the United States.'[45] That perception of Germany's cinematic internationalism is reinforced by recent scholarship on émigré and exile cinemas (in which context the important work of Jan-

Christopher Horak merits special mention); by studies on Hollywood's relations with German cinema from, among others, Thomas Saunders, Markus Spieker and James Morrison; and finally by recent work that resituates post-1990 German cinema within the context of global cultural industries and systems of representation.[46]

Alongside, finally, the relocation of German cinema within a broader history of cultural identities in modernity, as well as its re-siting in the context of international markets, transnational migrations and image flows, German film history's re-encounter with Weimar theory has helped trigger a third methodological realignment within the discipline. For Kracauer and Balázs certainly, but perhaps most centrally for Benjamin, it was film's status as the early twentieth century's foremost popular art that lent the medium crucial cultural-political significance. In what we identified above as the transcultural discursive field that is German film studies, a cross-fertilisation between Weimar film theory and Anglophone film studies is notable in particular in relation to Benjamin's 'Artwork' essay, whose famous aspiration for cinema that it might contribute to broader processes of mass cultural democratisation finds echoes especially in Anglophone cultural studies, with its similar vision of popular cultures as forces for social transformation. Benjamin is often cited, then, alongside such figures as Janice Radway or Stuart Hall, as mutually influential in engineering a shift in film-historical focus from German cinema as a cultural field organised around modernist aesthetics and major *auteurs*, to German cinema as a popular cinema with nationally specific genres, star systems, film styles and narrative forms.[47] The *CineGraph* collections cited above as the foremost examples of contemporary historiography on popular genres are joined in this context by critical star studies to constitute an emergent critical-historical canon that, as Sabine Hake has argued, displaces German film history's conventional 'symptomatic readings of a few canonical films and film directors', and explores instead 'the genres, the audiences, and the stars ... that constituted German cinema ... often in opposition to the demands of art cinema and political cinema'.[48]

As German national cinema, moreover, has come to be seen as the site of multifarious interrelations among a diverse array of popular-cultural texts whose audiences are, equally, highly differentiated according to socio-economic grouping and cultural identity, so too film historiography has begun to shift to encompass a more differentiated vision of film's place within cultures of nation. The *Wende* (turning point) of 1989–90 in any case necessitated a rethinking of post-war German 'national' cinema in terms

of developments at least partially shared across the inner German border between the FRG and GDR. Post-war labour migration from Germany's East and South, moreover, has provoked a rethinking of German nationhood in terms of longer histories of migration, minority cultural assimilation and/or the denigration and persecution of 'alien' elements: histories that in turn demand (as Deniz Göktürk and Marie-Hélène Gutberlet argue elsewhere in this volume) a rethinking of German cinema as a transnational and multi-ethnic cultural space.

Project of this book

It was against the backdrop sketched above – in the context, that is, of a renewed film-historical engagement in recent decades with film-theoretical issues, and a concomitant remapping of the contours of national cinema in Germany – that this present volume was conceived and its structure developed. Previous collections on German cinema had often been organised chronologically into movements and periods: Wilhelmine and Weimar Cinema, the Third Reich, post-war popular cinema, the New German film, DEFA and post-*Wende* German film. In our view, however, the approaches outlined above raised question marks over a periodisation that assumes a synchronicity between German film history's ruptures and breaks, and the caesurae of German political history. Certainly, the vicissitudes of German film history have to an extent been determined by turning points in the larger history of nation – 1917/18 was not only the moment of the monarchy's collapse and the founding of the first republican democracy on German soil, but also the beginning of film-industrial consolidation with the founding of Ufa in 1917; similarly, film historians ignore at their peril the relation between the Nazi takeover in 1933, and the functionalisation of film to ideological ends that was a central feature of 1930s and 40s German film. Nonetheless, a film history grounded as much in culture as in politics must trace film-historical continuities as well as ruptures, discontinuities as well as convergences between cinema and the politico-economic history of the German nation.

To that end, we have organised this volume in thematic sections designed to enable the reader to perceive the continuities of German cinema across different decades, while painting concise portraits of individual historical cases and moments, aesthetic movements or representational systems. At the same time, each of the book's five thematic sections, 'Popular Cinema', 'Stars', 'Institutions and Cultural Contexts', 'Cultural Politics' and 'Transnational Connections' follows an internal chronological order that

recalls German film history's more conventional periodisa-
tions. The substantial bibliography that follows pursues the
same dual logic of synchrony and diachrony through the
organisation of its various sections. Following introductory
sub-sections on works of film reference, general histories,
film historiography and film theory and criticism, the bibliography presents an overview of works covering the thematic concerns of the 'new German film history' (genres,
stars, migration, exile and transnational connections),
before proceeding to works organised under German film
history's classical period headings from the Wilhelmine
period to the present day. A resources section detailing CD-
Rom and online data sources, as well as addresses for
sources of film, video, DVD and related materials, completes
a volume that we hope offers a panorama of both established and more recent tendencies in German film history,
presents German cinema in its rich diversity and provides a
comprehensive resource for further research and debate.

Notes

1 Thomas Elsaesser, 'The German Cinema as Image and
    Idea', in Ginette Vincendeau (ed.), *Encyclopedia of European
    Cinema* (London: Cassell/BFI, 1995), p. 172.
2 Oskar Kalbus, *Vom Werden deutscher Filmkunst,* 2 vols
    (Altona-Bahrenfeld: Cigaretten-Bilderdienst, 1935); H. H.
    Wollenberg, *Fifty Years of German Film* (London: Falcon,
    1948).
3 Roger Manvell and Heinrich Fraenkel, *The German
    Cinema* (London: J. M. Dent, 1971); Ilona Brennicke and
    Joe Hembus, *Klassiker des deutschen Stummfilms
    1910–1930* (Munich: Goldmann, 1983); Christa
    Bandmann and Joe Hembus, *Klassiker des deutschen
    Tonfilms 1930–1960* (Munich: Goldmann, 1980); Robert
    Fischer and Joe Hembus, *Der neue deutsche Film,
    1960–1980* (Munich: Goldmann, 1981).
4 Frederick W. Ott, *The Great German Films: From Before
    World War One to the Present* (Secaucus, NJ: Citadel, 1986).
5 Eric Rentschler (ed.), *German Film and Literature:
    Adaptations and Transformations* (London and New York:
    Methuen, 1986); Marc Silberman, *German Cinema – Texts
    in Context* (Detroit: Wayne State University Press, 1995).
6 Wolfgang Jacobsen, Anton Kaes and Hans-Helmut Prinzler
    (eds.), *Geschichte des deutschen Films* (Stuttgart and
    Weimar: Metzler, 1993).
7 Ibid., p. 7.
8 Sabine Hake, *German National Cinema* (London and New
    York: Routledge, 2002), p. 3.
9 Lotte H. Eisner, *The Haunted Screen: Expressionism in the
    German Cinema and the Influence of Max Reinhardt*
    (Berkeley: University of California Press), 1969; originally
    published in France in 1952 under the title *L'écran
    démoniaque.*
10 Sergei Eisenstein, 'Griffith, Dickens, and the Film Today',
    reprinted in Thomas Elsaesser (ed.), *Space, Frame,
    Narrative. An Early Cinema Reader* (Norwich: University of
    East Anglia, 1986), p. 260.
11 Thomas Elsaesser, *New German Cinema A History*
    (London: BFI and Macmillan, 1989).
12 Theodor Adorno and Max Horkheimer, 'The Culture
    Industry: Enlightenment as Mass Deception', in Simon
    During (ed.), *The Cultural Studies Reader* (London and
    New York: Routledge, 1993), p. 29.
13 Theodor Adorno, *The Cultural Industry: Selected Essays
    on Mass Culture* (London and New York: Routledge, 1991).
    p. 154.
14 Ibid., p. 160.
15 Timothy Corrigan, *New German Cinema: The Displaced
    Image* (Austin: University of Texas Press, 1983), p. 2.
16 Siegfried Kracauer, *From Caligari to Hitler: A Psychological
    History of the German Film* (Princeton, NJ: Princeton
    University Press, 1947).
17 Patrice Petro, *Joyless Streets: Women and Melodramatic
    Representation in Weimar Germany* (Princeton, NJ:
    Princeton University Press, 1989), p. xviii.
18 Joseph Garncarz and Thomas Elsaesser, 'Film Theory', in
    Thomas Elsaesser and Michael Wedel London: (eds.), *The
    BFI Companion to German Cinema* (BFI, 1999), p. 103.
19 Deutsches Institut für Filmkunde, *Die deutschen Filme.
    Deutsche Filmographie 1895–1998. Die Top-100.* (Frankfurt:
    Deutsches Institut für Film, 1999 [CD-Rom]. See also the
    DIF webpage at http://www.deutsches-filmmuseum.de for
    details of its censorship database.
20 Among the many *CineGraph* publications are monographs
    on directors such as Reinhold Schünzel, Joe May and
    Richard Oswald, as well as collaborative publications with
    edition text+kritik on Anglo-German, Danish-German,
    Franco-German and German-Russian co-operations in the
    1910s and 20s. See the bibliography, pp. 265–7, for further
    details. *CineGraph* also publishes, under the editorship of
    Hans-Michael Bock, the indispensable *CineGraph: Lexikon
    zum deutschsprachigen Film,* a comprehensive and regularly
    updated biographical register of German film personnel,
    English-language extracts from which are available via the
    CineGraph webpage.
21 Though there has to date been little work that extends the axis
    of German film-historical debate to Africa and Asia, it is worth
    noting one important recent exception, John E. Davidson's
    Deterritorializing the New German Cinema (Minneapolis and
    London: University of Minnesota Press, 1999).

22 *Seminar: A Journal of Germanic Studies*, vol. 33, no. 4 (1997); special issue on recent German film. *Camera Obscura*; no. 44 (2000); special issue on post-Wall German cinema: *Screen*, vol. 43, no. 2 (2001); special issue on Emilie Altenloh.

23 Heike Klippel, 'Nach 1968. Filmtheorie in der Bundesrepublik Deutschland', in Hans-Michael Bock and Wolfgang Jacobsen (eds.), *Recherche Film: Quellen und Methoden der Filmforschung*, (Munich: edition text+kritik, 1997), pp. 83–98.

24 Cf. e.g. translations of extracts from the work of Jackie Stacey and Janet Staiger in Werner Faulstich and Helmut Korte, (eds.), *Der Star. Geschichte, Rezeption, Bedeutung* (Munich: Wilhelm Fink, 1997); also Stephen Lowry and Helmut Korte, 'Das Phänomen Filmstar', in idem, *Der Filmstar* (Stuttgart and Weimar: Metzler, 2000), pp. 5–30. On feminist film theory: Claire Johnston's seminal 'Women's Cinema as Counter-Cinema' was published in German in 1977 as 'Frauenfilm als Gegenfilm', *Frauen und Film*, 11, 1977, pp. 10–18. Laura Mulvey's 'Visual Pleasure and Narrative Cinema' appeared as 'Visuelle Lust und nar-ratives Kino', in Gislind Nabakowski, Helke Sander and Peter Gorsen (eds.), *Frauen in der Kunst* (Frankfurt am Main: suhrkamp, 1980), pp. 30–46. An early and influential exploration of the relation between feminist film theory and Weimar phenomenology was Patrice Petro's *Joyless Streets*. For a development of feminist film theory via Nietzschean cultural philosophy, see Heide Schlüpmann, 'Die Wiederkehr des Verdrängten. Überlegungen zu einer Philosophie der Filmgeschichte aus feministischer Perspektive', *Frauen und Film*, 56/7, pp. 41–58.

25 Klaus Kreimeier, *Kino und Filmindustrie in der BRD Ideologieproduktion und Klassenwirklichkeit nach 1945* (Kronberg: Scriptor, 1973) and idem, *Die Ufa-Story: Geschichte eines Filmkonzerns* (Munich and Vienna: Hanser, 1992). For Wolfgang Mühl-Benninghaus, compare his *Zur Rolle des staatsmonopolistischen Kapitalismus bei der Herausbildung eines Systems von Massenkommunikation zwischen 1900 und 1933. Überlegungen zum Zusammenhang von Ökonomie und Kultur*, Diss. phil. Humboldt-Universität Berlin/GDR, 1997, with his later *Das Ringen um den Tonfilm: Strategien der Elektro- und der Filmindustrie in den 20er und 30er Jahren* (Düsseldorf: Droste, 1999).

26 Herbert Birett, 'Alte Filme. Filmalter und Filmstil: Statistische Analyse von Stummfilmen', in Elfriede Ledig (ed.), *Der Stummfilm: Konstruktion und Rekonstruk-tion* (Munich: Verlegergemeinschaft Schaudig, 1988), pp. 69–88.

27 Cf. e.g. Hans-Michael Bock (ed.), *CineGraph: Lexikon zum deutschsprachigen Film* (Munich: edition text+kritik, 1984); Michael Wedel (ed.), *German Cinema, 1895–1917: A Checklist of Extant Films in International Archives* (Amsterdam: University of Amsterdam, 1995); Elke Schieber (ed.), *Die Sammlungen des Filmmuseums Potsdam: Bestandsübersicht* (Potsdam: Filmmuseum, 2001); *Findbücher zu Beständen des Bundesarchivs* (Koblenz/Berlin: Bundesarchiv-Filmarchiv, 1971ff).

28 Helmut Korte, *Der Spielfilm und das Ende der Weimarer Republik: Ein rezeptionshistorischer Versuch* (Göttingen: Vandenhoeck & Ruprecht, 1998).

29 Emilie Altenloh, *Zur Soziologie des Kino* (Jena: Eugen Diederichs, 1914). The second part of Altenloh's study appears in English translation as 'A Sociology of the Cinema', in *Screen*, 42, no. 3, 2001, pp. 249–93.

30 See e.g. Miriam Hansen, 'Early Silent Cinema: Whose Public Sphere?', *New German Critique*, 29; 1983, pp. 147–84: Heide Schlüpmann, *Unheimlichkeit des Blicks: Das Drama des frühen deutschen Kinos* (Basel/Frankfurt am Main: Roter Stern, 1990); Sabine Hake, *The Cinema's Third Machine: Writing on Film in Germany, 1907–1933* (Lincoln, NE, and London: Nebraska University Press, 1993), esp. ch. 3: Patrice Petro, op. cit.

31 Cf. e.g. Jackie Stacey, *Star Gazing. Hollywood Cinema and Female Spectatorship* (London and New York: Routledge, 1994); Janet Staiger, *Interpreting Films. Studies in the Historical Reception of American Cinema* (Princeton, NJ: Princeton University Press, 1992).

32 Stacey, op. cit., p. 74.

33 Cf. Sandra Kemp and Judith Squires, 'Epistemologies', in eadem (eds.), *Feminisms* (Oxford: Oxford University Press, 1997), p. 142.

34 Cf. in this context Jackie Stacey's comments on Walter Benjamin in Stacey, op. cit., pp. 232ff: also Schlüpmann, op. cit., Petro, op. cit., Hansen, op. cit., and Gertrud Koch, *Kracauer zur Einführung* (Hamburg: Junius, 1996, trans-lated as *Kracauer: An Introduction* [Princeton, NJ: Princeton University Press, 2000]).

35 Stuart Liebman, 'Why Kluge?', *October*, 46, Autumn 1988, p. 15. See also Oskar Negt and Alexander Kluge, *Öffentlichkeit und Erfahrung. Zur Organisationsanalyse von bürgerlicher und proletarischer Öffentlichkeit* (Frankfurt am Main: suhrkamp, 1972). For a summarising review, see Eberhard Knödler-Bunte, 'The Proletarian Public Sphere and Political Organisation', *New German Critique*, 4, Winter 1975, pp. 51–75.

36 Alison Butler 'New Film Histories and the Politics of Location', *Screen*, 33, no. 4, Winter 1992, pp. 413 and 426.

37 Kracauer's *Theory of Film* was first published in English in 1960 (New York: Oxford University Press), then in German

as *Theorie des Films* (Frankfurt am Main: suhrkamp, 1964). See also Siegfried Kracauer, *Das Ornament der Masse* (Frankfurt-am-Main: suhrkamp, 1977), available in English as *The Mass Ornament: Weimar Essays* (Cambridge, MA, and London: Harvard University Press, 1995); Béla Balázs, *Schriften zum Film, I (1922–1926) II (1926–1931)* (Berlin, Munich and Budapest: Henschel, Hanser and Akadémia Kiadó, 1984); Walter Benjamin, *Gesammelte Schriften* (Frankfurt am Main: suhrkamp, 1980).

38 *New German Critique*, 40, Winter 1987, special issue on Weimar film theory: Sabine Hake, *The Cinema's Third Machine*; Gertrud Koch, op. cit.; Massimo Locatelli, *Béla Balázs: Die Physiognomik des Films* (Berlin: Vistas, 1999).

39 Béla Balázs, *Der Geist des Films* (Halle and Saale: Knapp, 1930), p. 6.

40 This is Arnheim's post-war summary of the position he outlines in his 1933 *Film als Kunst*. The quote is taken from the 1957 English-language edition *Film as Art* (Berkeley: University of California Press), p. 6.

41 Thomas Elsaesser, 'Cinema – The Irresponsible Signifier or "The Gamble with History": Film Theory or Cinema Theory', *New German Critique*, 40, Winter 1987, p. 89.

42 Thomas Elsaesser, *Weimar Cinema and After: Germany's Historical Imaginary* (London and New York: Routledge, 2000). Anton Kaes' *Shell Shock* was published in 2002 by Princeton University Press.

43 Anton Kaes, 'German Cultural History and the Study of Film', *New German Critique*, 65, Spring/Summer 1995, p. 49.

44 Eric Rentschler, *The Ministry of Illusion: Nazi Cinema and its Afterlife* (Cambridge, MA, and London: Harvard University Press, 1996); also Karsten Witte, *Lachende Erben, Toller Tag: Filmkomödie im Dritten Reich* (Berlin: Vorwerk 8, 1995). Translations from Witte include his 'Visual Pleasure Inhibited. Aspects of the German Revue Film', *New German Critique*, 24–5, Autumn/Winter 1981/2, pp. 238–63, and various posthumously published translations in a special issue of *New German Critique*, 74, 1998. A more extensive review of revisionist histories of Third Reich film is provided by Erica Carter, 'The New Third Reich Film History', *German History*, 17, no. 4, 1999, pp. 565–83.

45 Thomas Elsaesser, 'Early German Cinema: A Second Life?', in idem. and Michael Wedel (eds.), *A Second Life: German Cinema's First Decades* (Amsterdam: Amsterdam University Press, 1996), p. 12.

46 Cf. e.g. Jan-Christopher Horak, *Fluchtpunkt Hollywood: Eine Dokumentation zur Filmemigration nach 1933* (Münster: MakS, 1984); Thomas Saunders, *From Berlin to Hollywood: American Cinema and Weimar Germany* (Berkeley: University of California Press, 1994); Markus Spieker, *Hollywood unterm Hakenkreuz: Der amerikanische Spielfilm im Dritten Reich* (Trier: Wissenschaftlicher Verlag, 1999); Joseph Garncarz, 'Hollywood in Germany. The Role of American Films in Germany, 1925–1990', in David W. Ellwood and Rob Kroes (eds.), *Hollywood in Europe. Experiences of a Cultural Hegemony* (Amsterdam: VU University Press, 1994); James Morrison, *Passport to Hollywood. Hollywood Films, European Directors* (Albany: SUNY Press, 1998). On the period since 1990, see Peter Krämer and Malte Hagener in this volume.

47 Walter Benjamin, 'The Work of Art in the Age of Mechanical Reproduction', in Hannah Arendt (ed.), *Illuminations* (New York: Schocken, 1969).

48 Hake, op. cit. (2002), p. 1.

PART ONE

POPULAR CINEMA

Introduction

Tim Bergfelder

Throughout the twentieth century and beyond, German cinema has shared with most other European film cultures and Hollywood a long-established tradition of popular genres, whose continuous as well as prolific production dates back to the earliest days of cinema. Yet for reasons outlined in our general introduction, the history of German popular cinema remained for some time unwritten, or otherwise subjected to derision or ideological suspicion. Thus, unlike in the contexts of British or Hollywood cinema, where indigenous popular genres have frequently been celebrated both by critics and audiences at large as a legitimate expression of national culture, in German cinema a deep chasm has existed almost from the beginning between a critical orthodoxy for which the very term 'popular' is suspect (hence what Jan-Christopher Horak terms in his contribution the 'bias against genre'), and a national audience which shows a remarkable enthusiasm for, and loyalty to, popular genre traditions.

Three separate, if mutually reinforcing, factors have contributed to this critical repression. The first factor originates, as we have argued, in the disdain of an indigenous cultural elite for what is dismissed either as an insufficiently elevated manifestation of national culture or as an irredeemable expression of capitalism (or both). Second, popular German cinema has often been ill-equipped to meet expectations from outside Germany, partly because of established perceptions of what German cinema should and should not be, and partly owing to national differences in popular traditions (buttressed by specific cultural contexts and references) that do make some genres less amenable to travel abroad. Hence the often limited distribution and success of popular German films beyond the indigenous market; witness in particular, as Jan-Christopher Horak's contribution in this section documents, the long-standing hostility towards, and incomprehension of, German comedy among foreign critics and audiences. The third contributing factor is the

notion that the only original and authentic version of popular cinema (at least within the western context) is Hollywood, and that any national manifestations of popular genres (particularly in Europe, where audiences have always experienced indigenous and Hollywood films simultaneously) can only pass as pale imitations.

Looking at the generic output of the German film industry over the last century, one finds indeed many genre formulae familiar from Hollywood and elsewhere (if not always employing the same categories in Germany itself): comedy, musicals, melodrama, crime thrillers, war films, historical epics, Westerns, horror films and science fiction, to name but a few. There are also a number of often temporary genres for which one cannot immediately determine a foreign equivalent, at least in their specific conventions, such as the post-First World War *Aufklärungsfilm* (sex education melodramas, providing often lurid, yet sometimes progressive exposés on issues such homosexuality and prostitution, see Robert Kiss' contribution in this section), 'Doctors' films' (a melodrama sub-genre particularly popular in the 1940s and 50s), or the post-Second World War 'rubble' cycle (existential and highly stylised dramas set against urban ruins).[1] Finally, there is one genre which appears in its iconography to be exclusively defined, indeed overdetermined, by its Germanness, the *Heimatfilm*, a genre which spans the entire history of German cinema in many permutations.

One could be tempted to divide this plethora of different genres according to their perceived national representability or uniqueness, which might locate the *Heimatfilm* with its iconic German locations at one end of the spectrum, and the German Western (with its obvious reference to, and faked representation of, the American Wild West) at the other. On closer inspection though, such rigid classifications are difficult to maintain. For example, while exploring the *Heimatfilm*'s specific characteristics in his essay in this section, Johannes von Moltke argues that the *Heimatfilm* is essentially a spatial genre, and is at its core as concerned with wider, and often supra-national, constructions of modernity as other spatial genres elsewhere, such as the Hollywood Western, film noir, or the British 'heritage' film. This argument not only allows von Moltke to establish illuminating connections and similarities beyond national specificity, but also to draw productively on an Anglophone critical tradition of genre analysis which eschews the ideology critique traditionally associated with evaluations of the *Heimatfilm*.

Conversely, a closer study of the German Western reveals a genre inflected both by national discourses and international influences that is far from being just an inauthentic version of the superior Hollywood original. As Deniz Göktürk has shown, the earliest German Westerns in the 1910s in fact evolved in parallel to the development of their US counterpart.[2] They drew in equal part on Hollywood iconography, and on indigenous literary and filmic narratives about America which predate the conventionalisation of the Hollywood Western as a genre, and which reflected on the social and psychological repercussions of German mass emigration to America during the nineteenth and early twentieth centuries. Thus, the focus in the early German Western is frequently to explore the dichotomies of 'home' and 'abroad', mapped onto the transatlantic division between European/German traditions and national roots and American modernity, cosmopolitanism and uprootedness. The later German Westerns in both West and East Germany in the 1960s, too, articulate their very specific takes on the genre, in the former case in a negotiation of an increasingly global and consumer-oriented society of spectacle and tourism, in the latter in an anti-imperialist revision of the American frontier myth.[3]

What this suggests is that rather than being, as has often been claimed, parochial and introspective, popular German cinema and its audiences have frequently engaged in an active dialogue and exchange with other cultures and global concerns. This is perhaps not surprising given the international diversity of, and particularly the presence of Hollywood in, the German film market. In any event, a critical exploration of German cinema's dialogic dimension, and particularly its negotiation of self vs other, emerges as a far more productive approach to German popular genres than the presumption of stable national characteristics, or charges of plagiarism. Indeed a number of contributors to this section analyse their generic case studies through an investigation of both their cultural and historical specificity (which includes an acknowledgment of both dominant and marginal cultural groups and discourses), and their relationship to international contexts.

Jan-Christopher Horak points out that while indigenous German comedy may not have been successful with foreign audiences, the imprint that German-Jewish exiles such as Ernst Lubitsch, Billy Wilder and Henry Koster have left on Hollywood, and on international conventions of film comedy, has been immense. Importantly, Horak locates the American success of such directors (and the renaissance of their work in Germany since the late 1960s) in their shared heritage of German-Jewish comedy, which demonstrates that the cultural exchange between German and international cinema can be reciprocal. Tim Bergfelder's contribution on German adaptations of British crime novels, and generic conventions more generally, also charts a cross-cultural discourse which facilitated German audiences to negotiate conceptions of national belonging through an engagement and identification with an imagined cultural other, at a time when the very idea of national identity was in question. In Robert Kiss' contribution on queer German cinema, very ostensibly about notions of self other, a cross-cultural dialogue is traced predominantly in the often uneven and precarious but also sometimes mutually enriching interactions between a dominant culture and a specific marginal social group, articulated mostly through the conventions of popular cinema.

Another emphasis that runs through many of the contributions in this section is the importance accorded to popular cinema's intertextual connections with, and indebtedness to, other media, in particular, but not exclusively, 'lowbrow' literary fiction. Thus, von Moltke traces the *Heimat* genre from its late nineteenth-century origins in novels by best-selling authors such as Ludwig Ganghofer and Ludwig Anzengruber, to its latest incarnation on television. Horak's contribution determines the dual influence of working-class Jewish stage farces and regional, especially Bavarian, folk theatre as crucial for the conventionalisation of German film comedy. Bergfelder sees the development of the German crime film as inseparably intertwined with the industrial and promotional strategies of mass publishing, which fostered a cross-fertilisation of different art forms and media. Kiss' essay too references a plethora of literary, scientific and journalistic intertexts, ranging from best-selling autobiographies, mainstream pulp novels and political pamphlets, to homoerotic vampire fiction distributed through subscription-only gay publications.

Finally, all of the contributions in this section articulate the realisation that a clear-cut division between popular and art cinema is very often difficult to uphold, given their frequent overlaps and interdependencies. Thus von Moltke discusses the New German anti-*Heimat* film of the 1970s as simultaneously rejecting and still drawing on the genre's conventions. Horak describes how modernism and popular traditions in regional culture coalesce in the work of comedians such as Karl Valentin and Herbert Achternbusch. Bergfelder equally charts the adoption of generic conventions and iconography of lowbrow sources into the work of modernist playwrights, painters and film directors. Indeed one should not forget that many of the most esteemed *auteurs* of the Weimar period worked with explicitly lowbrow sources: witness the productive and only superficially incongruous collaboration of Fritz Lang and the pulp novelist and screenwriter Thea von Harbou.[4] Kiss too connects esteemed classics of a national art cinema with more popular antecedents, while tracing the continuous appeal and influence of popular genres and stars for later generations of gay audiences and independent queer film-makers, such as Rosa von Praunheim. In summary what this section aims to achieve in the historical and cultural diversity of its individual case studies, as well as in the shared themes and questions we outlined above, is not only to reinstate popular German cinema as a rich field of study, but also to challenge preconceived notions of what both 'popular' and 'German' mean.

Notes

1   See, e.g., Robert Shandley, *Rubble Films: German Cinema in the Shadows of the Third Reich* (Philadelphia: Temple University Press, 2001).

2   Deniz Göktürk, *Künstler, Cowboys, Ingenieure: Kultur- und mediengeschichtliche Studien zu deutschen Amerika-Texten 1912–1920* (Munich: Wilhelm Fink, 1998). See also her 'Moving Images of America in Early German Cinema', in Thomas Elsaesser and Michael Wedel (eds.), *A Second Life: German Cinema's First Decades* (Amsterdam: Amsterdam University Press, 1996), pp. 93–100.

3   On the West German Westerns, see Tassilo Schneider, 'Finding a New *Heimat* in the Wild West: Karl May and the German Western of the 1960s', in Edward Buscombe and Roberta E. Pearson (eds.), *Back in the Saddle Again. New Essays on the Western* (London: British Film Institute, 1998). On DEFA's Westerns, see Gerd Gemünden, 'Between Karl May and Karl Marx: The Defa *Indianerfilme* (1965–1985)', in *Film History*, 10 (1998), pp. 399–407.

4   Reinhold Keiner, *Thea von Harbou und der deutsche Film bis 1933* (Hildesheim: Olms, 1991).

1

Evergreens: The *Heimat* Genre

Johannes von Moltke

The 1950s in perspective

Second only to Nazi cinema, which has recently become the object of sustained critical re-evaluations, the 1950s arguably remain the quintessential 'bad object' of German film historiography. Unlike the cinema of virtually any other era, the decade of the 1950s yielded no significant *auteurs*, harboured few compelling institutional developments other than a perennial economic crisis, and produced hardly a stylistic experiment worth mentioning. Worst of all – particularly when measured against the international success stories of Weimar and the New German Cinema – the 1950s seem singularly detached from contemporary developments beyond the German borders: German cinema, it appears, was never as parochial as during the 1950s. In its effort to stake its claim on a market heavily influenced by American films and Allied distributors, the German film industry had turned inward. This protectionist strategy for product differentiation was matched by a proliferation of titles that appealed to a peculiarly German sense of the local: *Heimatglocken* (*Bells of the Heimat*, 1952), *Heimatland* (*Homeland*, 1955), *Sohn ohne Heimat* (*Son Without a Heimat*, 1955), *... und ewig ruft die Heimat* (*... and the Heimat Calls Forever*, 1956), *Lied der Heimat* (*Song of Heimat*, 1957), *Heimweh* (*Homesick*, 1957), *Heimatlos* (*Homeless*, 1958), *Einmal noch die Heimat sehn* (*To See the Heimat Once More*, 1958) – these are just some of the *Heimat*-compounds that appeared on theatre marquees during the decade. As such, they were symptomatic of a much broader obsession with the notion of *Heimat*, a term usually translated as 'home' or 'homeland', but with considerably more connotative baggage than any available translation. As a focal point for a wide range of discourses, the notion of *Heimat* functioned as one of the decade's most prominent 'keywords'. The production and reception of the *Heimatfilm* as arguably the decade's 'key genre' is both a symptom of this cultural constellation and one of its constitutive elements.[1]

In Anglo-American criticism, the *Heimatfilm* of the 1950s enjoys the curious status of a genre that is 'at the same time famous and virtually unknown'.[2] As if further proof were needed for the parochialism of 1950s German film production, the films remain external to the experience of the critics, let alone a broader public beyond the German borders.[3] On the other hand, for German film and (especially) television audiences, mention of the *Heimatfilm* will still conjure up a fairly stable set of plots and images, consisting of picturesque Alpine landscapes or herds of sheep roaming the northern plains, of morally upstanding men and girlish women clad in traditional dress (*Trachten*) trying to track down the sinister poacher whose self-serving obsession threatens the fabric of the local community. Additional associations might include the repeated integration of (pseudo-)traditional *Volksmusik*, whether as part of the plot or as the non-diegetic soundtrack; lengthy inserts of Alpine flora and fauna, often on the whimsiest motivation; the appeal to forms of humour and values allegedly held by the country folk who people these films; and perhaps even individual stars, or starring couples such as Sonja Ziemann and Rudolf Prack, or Anita Gutwell and Rudolf Lenz.

The persistence of these images in the German media landscape for more than half a century is telling – both for what it says about the function of *Heimat* during the 1950s and in terms of what it reveals about the lasting, if irritating, cultural relevance of the first post-war decade at the turn of the millennium. Scholarship on the *Heimatfilm* has focused mainly on the former issue, arguing that the *Heimatfilm* provided its historical audiences with a series of remote and archaic places where they could heal the wounds of war and take a 'holiday from history'.[4] Drawing on the work of Siegfried Kracauer in particular, a number of critics have advanced a psychological history of the genre that emphasises its nostalgic, escapist and anti-modern tropes. Kracauer's influential book *From Caligari to Hitler* not only provided a useful model for correlating film and society, but also appeared to offer the appropriate categories for naming the dominant 'psychological dispositions' to be gleaned from the (*Heimat*) films of the 'Adenauer era'. As in the years leading 'from Caligari to Hitler', these dispositions comprised a willingness to retreat into a shell, to submit to authority and to glorify petit-bourgeois existence.[5] The corresponding ideology critique of the *Heimatfilm* sees the genre as the epitome of the culture industry, arguing that it served to obfuscate political realities by offering its 'consumers' false escapes into non-existent, pre-modern idylls, thus aligning them with the reactionary ideology of the decade.[6]

While such approaches have yielded crucial insights into the ideological functions of mass culture, their totalising claims leave little room for historical or textual detail. Where the latter is addressed, in turn, questions of history and ideology tend to disappear altogether. Thus, the only study to date that looks at a broad sample of films in any detail suffers from a largely quantitative and strikingly ahistorical approach, designed to define the 'trivial' character of the *Heimatfilm*.[7] Only recently have scholars begun to re-evaluate such totalising approaches to the cinema of the 1950s in general, and to the *Heimatfilm* in particular, focusing on the potential for 'subversion' contained in the landscapes of these films.[8] Accordingly, they have argued for the need to interrogate the 'gaps, ellipses and silences' which riddle the films of the *Heimat* genre, and which call for detailed attention to the workings of film form, reception, and the institutional contexts in which the *Heimatfilm* was able to thrive.[9] As Erica Carter rightly suggests, we should view the cinema of the 1950s 'as a vehicle not for blind manipulation but for the airing of ambiguities, tensions, and contradictions'.[10]

In keeping with the spirit of these recent revisions, this article reconsiders the production of *Heimat* in German cinema. Given the fact that the notion of *Heimat*, for all its proliferating meanings, always connotes a sense of place, I argue that the *Heimatfilm* needs to be understood as a 'spatial genre' in the sense in which this notion has been applied to the Western with its emphasis on landscape and the frontier, or to the explorations of the urban landscape in film noir. With its persistent foregrounding of regional and provincial spaces, of recurrent types of landscapes, and

of an ideologically loaded notion of the local, the *Heimatfilm* has mobilised particular images of 'place' which, upon closer inspection, become legible as responses to the ongoing transformation of space in modernity. In order to study the ideological function of those responses, I draw on recent work in cultural geography on the transformation of space, which, in the words of David Morley, 'insists on the necessity of rethinking our sense of place in the context of the transformations and destabilisations wrought both by the forces of economic globalisation and by the global media industries'.[11] Such an approach allows us to see how the *Heimatfilm* has served to imagine, if not facilitate, various processes of social, technological and spatial modernisation *within* the ostensibly bounded realm of the local. Even as the remote settings of the *Heimat* genre, like the term *Heimat* itself, seem custom-made for a retreat to a much earlier moment in the history of modernisation, the genre continually produces ideological compromise formations aimed at 'harmonising' the contradictions between the local and its variously defined 'others'. A closer look at the genre reveals that the spaces of *Heimat* remain profoundly ambivalent, bearing traces of both the pastoral and the industrial, the local and the global, the traditional and the modern.[12]

These ambiguities are particularly evident in the historical context of the 1950s, when the *Heimatfilm* provided an ideological space that would contain competing claims on the reconstruction of German national identity – from an unmastered but ever present Nazi past, through the integration of entire populations expelled from the East, to the momentous transformations that lurked underneath everyday talk of 'normalisation' and an 'economic miracle'. However, the habitual conflation of the *Heimatfilm* with the Federal Republic of the 1950s obscures some important film-historical continuities, as well as the fact that concern with the increasingly permeable boundaries of the local is by no means limited to this particular national and historical context. In a broader perspective, neither the *Heimatfilm* nor the decade's cinema as such are bookended neatly by the Nazi – and/or 'rubble' – years on the one hand, and by the dawn of the New German Cinema on the other. Rather, the *Heimatfilm* functions in a longer film-historical *durée*, as it constantly re-articulates cinematic as well as social and cultural obsessions that exceed the narrow scope of the 1950s. To treat the *Heimatfilm* merely as a brief 'holiday from history' for the first post-war decade is to reify the genre at the expense of a more detailed look at historical continuities, internal contradictions and different 'uses' of the *Heimatfilm*.[13] Given the generic hybridity even of those films which have long served as the prototypes of the genre – the first fifteen minutes of *Schwarzwaldmädel* (*Black Forest Girl*, 1950), for example, come straight out of an Ufa *Revuefilm* – it would thus be misleading to impose an essentialised, ahistorical generic unity on the *Heimatfilm*. Its coherence is better grasped in pragmatic and discursive terms, much in the way Andrew Higson has recently defined the British 'heritage film'. Like notions of 'heritage' in Britain, *Heimat* discourses 'have always informed particular currents within the national film culture, surfacing more visibly at some times than at others'.[14] We must therefore begin by expanding the historical focus of our inquiry and take a long shot of the developments before and after the 1950s ; only then can we cut in to a close-up on the productions of that era, which continue to inform the overall 'image' of the *Heimatfilm* for most viewers.

Continuities

As Eric Rentschler has rightly suggested, 'the *Heimatfilm*, by dint of its persistence throughout the entire span of German film history, acts as a seismograph, one that allows us to gauge enduring presences as they have evolved over the last eighty years.'[15] Even a cursory glance at the genre's history reveals a set of striking personal, narrative, stylistic and 'pragmatic' continuities dating back at least to the period between 1910 and 20. Thus, given the flourish of discursive activity around the question of *Heimat* in various political, cultural and literary movements from the turn of the century,[16] it was only a matter of time before the nascent medium of cinema tapped this discourse. By 1912, we find at least one writer explicitly demanding that the 'cinematograph' be impressed to the 'service of *Heimatkunst*',[17] and it has been suggested that the label '*Heimatfilm*' was already common currency during the First World War.[18] Even where the films have not survived, titles such as *Heimatliche Scholle* (*Homestead*, 1910), *Heimkehr* (*Homecoming*, 1911), *Heimat und Fremde* (*Home and Away*, 1913) or *Wenn die Heimat ruft* (*When the Heimat Calls*, 1915) testify to one aspect of early cinema's affinity with *Heimat* discourse.[19] In addition, literary texts which had already been produced and received within the generic framework of *Heimatliteratur* soon served as source material for repeated adaptations, among them the work of Ludwig Ganghofer and Ludwig Anzengruber, or Wilhelmine von Hillern's best-selling *Die Geier-Wally* (*Vulture-Wally*, 1875).

Indeed, reviewing the first adaptation of *Die Geier-Wally* which was first published in 1921, a critic already complained that 'one can't bear to see any more Tyrolean farms, peasants' huts, open air dance floors and village

inns.' The slight exasperation with which the reviewer lists the film's 'overused motifs' (if only to applaud their artful treatment by director E. A. Dupont and set designer Paul Leni) testifies to the familiarity of a quasi-generic iconography. By the early 1920s, in other words, the *Heimatfilm* had already begun to enter cinematic discourses and practices, with trade papers reporting the founding of a production company named 'Ostmärkischer Heimatfilm' in 1926, or the premiere of a 'great German *Heimatfilm*' in 1927.[20] This is not to say, however, that the cinema's imbrication with *Heimat* discourses had already yielded institutionalised definitions of a *Heimat* genre. Indeed, while it is tempting to assume that the *Heimat* genre would soon flourish in the blood-and-soil climate of Nazi ideology, the attribution of generic labels even during the 1930s and 40s was not as consistent as retrospective filmographies suggest.[21] However, the term *Heimatfilm* was clearly available to reviewers and the industry alike.[22]

While such considerations of labelling and terminology are important in a historical or 'pragmatic' conception of the genre, particular qualities that we tend to associate exclusively with the *Heimatfilm* of the 1950s already appear in different guises before that decade. Upon closer inspection, three aspects of *Heimat* discourse in particular share a long tradition prior to the 'classical' period of the *Heimatfilm* in the 1950s, providing some of the historical co-ordinates along which to plot otherwise latent generic continuities. These include, first, the repeated involvement of the same *personnel*, such as the director Hans Deppe, the composer Giuseppe Becce, or the producer Peter Ostermayr, who literally personified one variant of the *Heimatfilm* for half a century.[23] Second, as Ostermayr's career plainly suggests, there is an astonishing continuity of basic *texts* to be adapted over and over again: Ostermayr acquired the rights to the best-selling novels of Ludwig Ganghofer in 1920 and managed to exploit most of these wildly popular Alpine texts at least three times – producing his first 'Ganghofer series' in the early 1920s, then remaking the same films as an independent producer for Ufa between 1934 and 1940, and finally producing another set based on the same novels during the 1950s, now in widescreen and colour. With further adaptations by Harald Reinl and Hans W. Geissendörfer in the 1970s, the Ganghofer novels provide a textual backbone for the *Heimat* genre that spans virtually the entire twentieth century. In a similar vein, Uta Berg-Ganschow has rightly identified *Die Geier-Wally* as an 'evergreen' of the *Heimat*-genre:[24] a 1988 film of that title by Walter Bockmayer is a queer send-up of the version produced by Ostermayr in 1956, which, in turn, was

Die Geier-Wally (1921), top left, *Die Geier-Wally* (1940), top right, *Die Geier-Wally* (1956), bottom left, *Die Geier-Wally* (1988), bottom right. (Images courtesy of Stiftung Dt. Kinemathek)

already a remake of a 1940 remake by Hans Steinhoff of E. A. Dupont's original 1921 adaptation of Wilhelmine von Hillern's novel from 1875.

Ostermayr liked to refer to his productions as 'landscape-bound films' that performed 'cultural work for the Bavarian *Heimat*'. This link between location and *Heimat* represents a third vector along which to map articulations of the *Heimatfilm* throughout German film history. Thus, the emphasis on Alpine and rural landscape that has been taken to characterise the *Heimatfilm* clearly has antecedents, particularly in the cycle of films known as '*Bergfilme*' ('mountain films'). Usually attributed to the pioneering efforts of its 'inventor' Arnold Fanck, the cinematic fascination with Alpine landscapes already forms a staple of early cinema; recent research into the early non-fiction film in particular has revealed a veritable obsession with landscapes and travel.[25] In this respect, Fanck's career is also exemplary in that it leads directly from the early 'view' aesthetic through its gradual dynamisation by way of

technical innovations and heroic stunts, to its more or less successful (in)fusion with fictional narration in *Der heilige Berg* (*The Holy Mountain*, 1925/6), *Der Kampf ums Matterhorn* (*Battle for the Matterhorn*, 1928), or *Stürme über dem Montblanc* (*Avalanche*, 1930). Fanck's fetishisation of camera technique throughout his work evokes the formal 'exhibitionism' of an early 'cinema of attraction'.[26] Like the explicit acknowledgement of the camera's presence in that earlier mode, Fanck's virtual personification of the camera-as-mountaineer serves to mediate the ostensibly unmediated experience of the Alps: drawing on a romantic rhetoric of the Alps as a space of the sublime, uncontaminated by traces of modernity, the *Bergfilm* simultaneously populates and popularises that space.[27]

While it is true that the *narrative* function of nature shifts from the *Bergfilm* to the *Heimatfilm* proper (where it is generally 'pacified', but remains an 'excessive' backdrop to the melodramatic plot), the staging of natural landscapes for spectacle and at the expense of narrative remains a staple of both the *Berg-* and the *Heimatfilm*.[28] Both, in turn, also tie in with the earlier, non-fictional forms mentioned above by virtue of a shared overlap with the emerging culture of tourism. The history of the 'tourist view' in (German) cinema, in other words, would lead from the proto-travelogues of the first two decades, through the *Bergfilm* and the increases in Alpinism during the 1920s and 30s,[29] to the rediscovery of Alpine landscapes in both the *Heimatfilm* and the *Wirtschaftswunder* of the 1950s, when average citizens were again spending up to a month's income on vacations every year.

If these examples begin to suggest the continuity of cinematic uses of *Heimat* well before the 1950s, it is equally important to bear in mind the 'genre redefinitions' and 'genre repurposings' (Altman) that prolong the history of the *Heimatfilm* into the present. Just as Thomas Elsaesser and Eric Rentschler recently interrogated the sometimes disconcerting *contemporaneity* of cinematic legacies that date back to Weimar and the Nazi era,[30] we ought to dwell on the 'afterlife' of the 1950s at the turn of the century as well. Thus, reincarnations of the *Heimatfilm* have included continued remakes and re-releases from the 1970s onward,[31] joined by the unbroken series of rebroadcasts on television since the early 1980s. If these developments principally index a logic of repetition and pastiche, others have worked to sustain the genre through renewal and critique, as in the case of the so-called 'new' or *Anti-Heimatfilm*.[32] Peter Fleischmann's *Jagdszenen aus Niederbayern* (*Hunting Scenes from Lower Bavaria*, 1969) stands as the first example of a wholesale 'repurposing' of the genre, and a number of notable Young German film-makers from Rainer Werner Fassbinder to Volker Schlöndorff followed suit. In the eyes of the young *Autoren* who imaginatively inherited the genre from the Ostermayrs and Deppes of 'Papa's Kino', the *Anti-Heimatfilm* – while aesthetically and ideologically distinct from the 'classical' 1950s *Heimatfilm* – explicitly worked within the tradition that the *Autoren* were keen to subvert. This return to the genre in the context of the social movements of the late 1960s, in other words, had as much to do with a nascent 'new regionalism' and a 'renaissance of the *Heimat* feeling'[33] as it did with the established popularity of the *Heimatfilm* itself – a potential which the young film-makers felt the need to tap, given the poor home box-office of their internationally successful productions.

While few, if any, of these productions actually managed to cash in on the genre's popular appeal, Edgar Reitz apparently found the right mixture of nostalgia and critique in his successful TV mini-series *Heimat* (1984). As a film that self-consciously signalled its generic (and national) lineage with its choice of title,[34] Reitz's *Heimat* crystallised aspects of the genre's development from the 1950s through the 80s. Both the overwhelming popularity of this series with a domestic television audience (garnering ratings of up to 26 per cent) as well as the scandalised reactions by critics and scholars which followed owed much to Reitz's decision to face the problem and the genre of *Heimat* as a compromised but stubborn popular cultural formation head-on. As one of the major cultural events of the decade, Reitz's film successfully fused the popular but allegedly 'uncritical' *Heimatfilm* of the 1950s with the vehemently critical but unpopular *Anti-Heimatfilm* of the 1960s and 70s, thus maximising the audience appeal of his series.[35]

Meanwhile, there seems to be no shortage of *Heimat* productions elsewhere. Wherever we look, German audiovisual culture is saturated with images which only a few decades ago would have been attributed to the *Heimatfilm* proper. On the one hand, the genre still provides the template for the production and reception of films made for theatrical release, such as *Die Siebtelbauern* (*The Inheritors*, 1998) or *Viehjud Levi* (*Jew-Boy Levi*, 1999). Perhaps more to the point in a 'pragmatic' view of genre history, though, the *Heimatfilm* appears to have found a new home and new 'users' on television. Gerhard Bliersbach dates this return to the 1950s to the evening of 9 September 1980 when the public station ARD launched a series entitled '*Heimatfilme*' by broadcasting the 1951 version of *Grün ist die Heide* at prime time.[36] A random sampling of public and commercial programming would confirm the continued massive presence of 1950s cinema in German televisual 'memory' – whether in the form of semi-annual reruns of the *Sissi* trilogy (1955–7) starring Romy Schneider, or *Die Trapp-Familie* (*The Trapp Family*, 1956); *Heimat*-bound soaps such as *Schwarzwaldklinik* (*Black Forest Hospital*); almost nightly prime-time broadcasts of *Volksmusik*-shows that have inherited the iconography of the *Heimat* genre (such as *Musikantenstadl* [*Musicians' Village*], or *Kein schöner Land* [*No Country More Beautiful*]);[37] regular instalments of *Zauberhafte Heimat* (*Magical Heimat*) and *Heimatgeschichten* (*Tales from the Heimat*) from varying German-speaking regions on public television; or the commercial viability of the *Heimatkanal* marketed by Leo Kirch's pay-TV 'Premiere World', which offers a continuous mix of 1950s *Heimatfilme*, television series such as *Der Bergdoktor* (*The Mountain Doctor*) and the occasional *Volksmusik*-show on a twenty-four-hour basis.

The continuing presence of *Heimat*-programming on all channels begs the question of the *reasons* for the genre's continuity. In other words, what functions have this genre and its attendant discourses served that have distinguished them from other genres and discourses, thereby ensuring their continued viability? To study the *Heimatfilm* as a popular genre in this sense is to investigate the history and the social concerns to which it responds, which it reworks in terms of its formal construction, and to which it has been able to provide very flexible imaginary solutions. As I suggested above, those social concerns are to be sought particularly in the transformations of space brought about by processes of modernisation. In order to trace some of the ways in which the *Heimatfilm* has responded to these issues, I want to return from the pragmatic historical continuities of the genre to the question of its historical functions during the 1950s.

Nostalgic modernisation: *Heimat* in the rear-view mirror

At the end of *Wenn die Heide blüht* (*When the Heath is in Blossom*, 1960; dir. Hans Deppe), a *Heimatfilm* so overburdened with generic stereotypes as to border on the self-reflexive, we witness the establishment of two couples in the genre-typical countryside. The preceding plot has revolved around Rolf, an ageing peasant's prodigal son, who originally fled his native village for America, but who comes to realise that his rightful place is back home, as the heir to his father's estate. This realisation is reinforced by the romantic sub-plot, in which Rolf is torn between Sonja, the daughter of the local game warden, and Vera, an itinerant singer whom Rolf meets on the ocean liner that carries him back to Germany. The distinction between these two women condenses the film's governing dichotomies of local versus foreign, traditional versus modern, rooted versus mobile, rural versus urban; as variations on the theme of *Heimat* versus *Fremde*, they predetermine Rolf's choice and the film's outcome. Along with a series of misunderstandings, the happy ending thus apparently settles these dichotomies as well, and the prodigal son is united with Sonja, who has just been chosen as *Heidekönigin* (queen of the heath) at the local pageant. Vera on the other hand is forced to realise that Rolf has learned his *Heimat* lesson and has decided to stay for ever in the provincial idyll he once scorned; she leaves for Hamburg in her car, accompanied by her persistent but innocuous suitor, Dr Erdmann. As the two of them drive away, Vera's convertible is brought to a temporary halt by the inevitable herd of sheep roaming the heath. They pause before this idyllic scene, and Vera adjusts the rear-view mirror to touch up her lipstick. In a tight close-up, the camera aligns us with her gaze into the mirror where we see the kiss between Rolf and Sonja that seals the narrative.

The shot which frames the 'legitimate' couple in the rear-view mirror of the convertible is brief, but odd enough in its composition to stand out in the otherwise conventional closing sequence of *Wenn die Heide blüht*. Without making any claims on directorial intention, I would suggest that this closing is emblematic of some central generic concerns of the *Heimatfilm*. For this particular shot doubly refracts the viewer's gaze: on the one hand, we see Rolf and Sonja, ostensibly the very incarnation of *Heimat*, belonging, and continuity at the film's end, precisely through the desiring eyes of the woman who moves *outside* the space of *Heimat*, partaking in its spectacle as a tourist at best. In this regard, Vera's gaze doubles that of the predominantly urban audience to whom the *Heimatfilm* was addressed, and whom the genre undoubtedly helped to recruit as clients for the newly revived German tourist economy – for like the *Heimat* movement before the turn of the century, the *Heimatfilm* of the 1950s conveys an 'essentially urban attitude toward the out-of-doors'.[38] In addition, the fact that Vera's gaze is relayed through the mirror of a parked car evokes the spectator's situation in front of a screen. As the couple leaves in the convertible, the film comes to a close, and the viewer, too, leaves the cinema with a backward glance. Inasmuch as it explicitly, if almost imperceptibly, references the discursive framework of its exhibition, the *Heimatfilm* offers a highly mediated and distinctly modern experience of an ostensibly archaic idyll. In the experience of the urban movie-goer, but also of West German society at large, caught in the momentous transformations of the *Wirtschaftswunder*, *Heimat* exists only as a myth. That myth, incarnated in *Wenn die Heide blüht* by

Wenn die Heide blüht (1960) (Courtesy of Stiftung Dt. Kinemathek)

the union of Rolf and Sonja at the film's end, promises its own perpetual regeneration precisely when it is about to recede into the distance, superceded by the trappings of modernity. As Eric Rentschler remarks, 'it is only after *Heimat* ceases to be taken for granted that the notion is articulated'.[39] In their obsession with the logics of *Heimat*, the films of the genre function similarly to ritualise the passing of a moment when *Heimat* was still taken for granted.

Significantly, the films perform this function *not* simply by imagining Heimat as 'an uncontaminated space, a realm of innocence and immediacy'.[40] To suggest, as many have, that the *Heimatfilm* is quintessentially an escapist genre, is to overlook the fact that the escape routinely contains elements of the world *from* which viewers were allegedly escaping. In particular, if *Heimat* in the *Heimatfilm* is simply conceived as an escape from modernity, this does not account for the fact that the modern is not 'outside' of *Heimat*, it is part of it. With remarkable consistency, various modern 'contaminations' reach well into the plots of the films; and while the narration is ostensibly structured to exorcise the tropes of the foreign, 'American', urban, hyper-modern, mobile and/or disembedded 'other' from the space of *Heimat*, the films' manifest message is often complicated on the more formal level by a more dialectical logic of tradition and change: rather than holding modernity at bay, the *Heimatfilm* ultimately helps to *naturalise* its effects.[41]

This is precisely why the genre was so successful during the period of the *Wirtschaftswunder*, whose effects it made available *within* the space of *Heimat*. As in the *Bergfilm*, which had showcased the Alpine sublime as an object of technological (including cinematographic) mastery, the spaces we encounter in the *Heimatfilm* of the 1950s are 'remote' only in a superficial sense; upon closer inspection they are regularly suffused with traces of technological and social modernisation, yielding a sort of 'industrialised provincialism'.[42] Hence, films like those of the *Immenhof* series (e.g. *Die Mädels vom Immenhof* [*The Immenhof Girls*, 1955], *Ferien auf Immenhof* [*Vacation at Immenhof*, 1957]), *Gruß und Kuß vom Tegernsee* (*Greetings from Tegernsee*, 1957) or *Ferien vom Ich* (*Holiday from the Self*, 1952) which all explicitly negotiate a tourist plot, offer vistas of a new service economy. Austrian productions such as *Das Lied von Kaprun* (*The Song of Kaprun*, 1955) sing the praises of one of the country's biggest engineering projects of the time, the Hohentauern dam. The comings and goings in films like *Schwarzwaldmädel*, *Die Landärztin* (*Lady Country Doctor*, 1958), or *Wenn die Heide blüht* showcase the most up-to-date and stylish modes of transportation; indeed, the films' obsession with mobility in the allegedly

static, enclosed boundaries of *Heimat* suggests a far more complicated dialectic of inside and outside than the standard readings of the term (and the genre) would allow. Thus, when the female doctor Petra Jensen arrives in the Bavarian village of Kürzlingen on a motor scooter in *Die Landärztin*, Paul May's film significantly does not use this constellation to prove the superiority of traditional ways of life over the lifestyle and professionalism of the urban intruder. Nor, of course, does it engage in a full-scale attack on Kürzlingen's patriarchal provincialism. Rather, in chronicling Petra's gradual integration into the community as well as the latter's grudging acceptance of her professional skill, the film asks its audience to entertain the idea of *Heimat* as a compromise formation, a space in which the urban reaches the local and modernity meets tradition. The undeniable political conservatism of such films, then, consists not in an anti-modern stance, but in the selective embrace of the modern and in the mythologisation of modernisation as a process that ultimately does not threaten the underlying sense of continuity and *Gemeinschaft*. This ideological paradox, which we might describe as a project of nostalgic modernisation, lies at the heart of the *Heimat* genre in German cinema.

No place like home: topographies of *Heimat*

Needless to say, these negotiations of tradition and modernity serve to hide the erosion, or absence, of precisely the pre-modern, 'safe', 'uncontaminated', or otherwise mythologised sense of place that the term *Heimat* is often taken to convey. In advancing an ideology of nostalgic modernisation custom-made for the *Wirtschaftswunder*, the *Heimatfilm* elaborates a generic topography of the local onto which we may map not only a retrograde provincialism, but the effects of modernisation as well. Traditionally, it would seem, *Heimat* is by definition a *limited* terrain, if not 'necessarily small' as one of the many sociologists concerned with the question of *Heimat* in the 1950s saw it.[43] Whether we approach the issue with nostalgic sentimentality or with scorn, *Heimat* appears at first as a bounded space, onto which one cathects either warm feelings of *Gemütlichkeit* or a claustrophobic sense of being trapped. Correspondingly, Willi Höfig singles out the 'closed system of the *Heimat*-world' as one of the defining characteristics of the genre, stressing the ways in which these films police the boundaries that separate this system from the transitory world 'outside'.[44] This definition of *Heimat* as a 'closed' space, fenced off

against the *Fremde* as its irreconcilable 'other', is still prevalent in most readings of the genre and its films. It attributes
to the *Heimatfilm* the production of place along the lines
criticised by Doreen Massey when she glosses 'the most
common formulations of the concept of geographical
place' in human geography. Like *Heimat*, these notions of
place are designed to evoke stasis and nostalgia, and an
'enclosed security'. Like the *Heimatfilm*, such formulations
represent an attempt to 'fix the meaning of places, to
enclose and defend them: they construct singular, fixed and
static identities for places, and they interpret places as
bounded enclosed spaces defined through counterposition
against the Other who is outside'.[45]

Such definitions of place are both conceptually simplis-
tic and politically reactionary – both of which has been
said more than once of the *Heimatfilm* as a genre, too. As
Massey has repeatedly pointed out, a more circumspect
view of our sense of the local would need to account for the
fact that 'it is precisely … the presence of the outside
within which helps to construct the specificity of the local
place'.[46] While such a view resonates especially with the
reconfiguration of spatial regimes under current conditions of 'globalisation', it holds true as well for the history
of modernisation throughout the twentieth century, which
saw the increasing 'disembedding' of local place.[47] One of
the 'consequences of modernity', as Anthony Giddens
defines them, consists in the fact that 'the very tissue of
spatial experience alters, conjoining proximity and distance in ways that have few close parallels in prior ages'.[48]
The advent of modernity, Giddens argues, 'increasingly
tears space away from place by fostering relations between
"absent" others . . . locales are thoroughly penetrated by
and shaped in terms of social influences quite distant from
them'.[49]

Such a view of modernisation as a profound transformation of our sense of place can begin to explain some of the
recurrent ambiguities of the *Heimatfilm*. It allows us to see
the fetishisation of camera technique and of (communications) technology in some of Fanck's films not as a contradiction to the director's quasi-religious veneration of
nature; rather, the isolation of the protagonist on the
mountain top and his connection to the world below via
radio, aeroplane and telegraph are two aspects of the same
process by which nature and the sublime are (re-)produced
under conditions of modernity. Similarly, the retreat to the
provinces in the *Heimatfilm* of the 1950s is no longer
simply a flight from post-war urban rubble, let alone from
social and economic reconstruction; to the degree that the
ostensibly remote spaces of the *Heimatfilm* are suffused
with tropes of mobility – whether in terms of expulsion

and displacement or motorisation and tourism – the place
of *Heimat* itself is transformed, its promise of stability a
mere compensation for a series of more profound destabilisations that have long since occurred. For all its nostalgic,
if not reactionary politics, the study of the *Heimatfilm* thus
requires conceptually more nuanced terms than those
available in the literature on the topic; terms which can
account for the films' often phantasmagoric constructions
of place, for their manifest obsession with questions of displacement and mobility, and for the 'distanciated relations'
that structure the local.

Not only does such a framework allow us to re-view
some of the *Heimat*-'evergreens' in a new light that can
help to elucidate the reasons for their longevity; in
addition, relocating the *Heimatfilm* in a cultural geography
of modernisation permits us to draw connections between
the 'local' case of West Germany in the 1950s and *its* distant
others. Only if we open up such larger perspectives can we
avoid matching the ostensible parochialism of that era's
cinema on the methodological level. For in such a perspective, the *Heimatfilm* is hardly the only response to the spatial consequences of modernity. While the British heritage
film might be seen as a similar – if later – reaction, as I have
already suggested, other traditions and genres open up
alternative vistas on the same underlying issues. A comparative look to the eastern half of Germany during the
1950s, for example, reveals a striking renegotiation of
Heimat as DEFA grapples with the transformation of the
local, of rural communities and of agricultural production
under socialism.[50] Likewise, the negotiation of the frontier
myth and of national space in the American Western provides an intriguing point of comparison with respect to the
question of how the cinema has mediated and responded
to changing spatial configurations. Finally, a broader view
of the media themselves as agents of spatial transformation
can help to explain why, in recent years, the *Heimat* genre
has flourished not so much in the cinema, but rather on
television, a medium which Raymond Williams famously
described as one of 'mobile privatisation'.[51] If television can
supply us with the experience of 'simultaneously staying
home and imaginatively . . . going places',[52] what better
medium, then, to host a genre that gives us the experience
of imaginatively staying home and simultaneously going
places?

Notes

1 In his study of the German *Heimatfilm* from 1947 to 1960,
   Willi Höfig assigns one in five films produced during those
   years to the genre, with 1952 and 1956 yielding record

percentages (33 per cent and 36 per cent respectively). *Der deutsche Heimatfilm 1947–1960* (Stuttgart: Enke, 1973), p. 166.

2 Tassilo Schneider, 'Genre and Ideology in the Popular German Cinema: 1950–1972' (diss. University of Southern California, 1994), p. 144.

3 This is not to say that they are unavailable. In the US, for example, the German Language Video Center in Indiana-polis has specialised in producing NTSC copies of canonic (and not-so-canonic) works from the 1930s to the 50s.

4 Schmieding takes this term from the historian Hermann Heimpel to describe the function of the *Heimatfilm* and other popular films from the 1950s in *Kunst oder Kasse: Der Ärger mit dem deutschen Film* (Hamburg: Rütten und Loening, 1961).

5 Cf. Barbara Bongartz, *Von Caligari zu Hitler – von Hitler zu Dr. Mabuse? Eine 'psychologische' Geschichte des Films von 1946–1960* (Münster: MakS, 1992); Bärbel Westermann, *Nationale Identität im Spielfilm der 50er Jahre* (Frankfurt am Main: Peter Lang, 1990); Gertraud Steiner, *Die Heimat-Macher: Kino in Österreich 1946–1966* (Vienna: Verlag für Gesellschaftskritik, 1987); and Gerhard Bliersbach, *So grün war die Heide: der deutsche Nachkriegsfilm in neuer Sicht* (Weinheim: Beltz, 1985).

6 Indeed, when Adorno reconsiders the chapter on the culture industry in *Dialectics of Enlightenment* from the point of view of the 1950s, he exemplifies the workings of the culture industry by referring to the *Heimatfilm* in particular: cf. Theodor W. Adorno, 'The Culture Industry Reconsidered', in Stephen Bronner and Douglas Kellner (eds.), *Critical Theory and Society: A Reader,* (New York: Routledge, 1989), p. 132; cf. also Klaus Kreimeier, *Kino und Filmindustrie in der BRD: Ideologieproduktion und Klassenwirklichkeit nach 1945* (Kronberg: Scriptor, 1973).

7 Cf. Höfig, *Der deutsche Heimatfilm.* As a counterpart to Höfig's resolutely synchronic approach, a project at the University of Tübingen yielded what is arguably the first and only attempt at tracing the genre's historical development, even at the risk of forfeiting a coherent theoretical framework. Cf. Ludwig-Uhland-Institut, Projektgruppe deutscher Heimatfilm (directed by Wolfgang Kaschuba), *Der deutsche Heimatfilm: Bildwelten und Weltbilder* (Tübingen: Tübinger Vereinigung für Volkskunde e.V., 1989).

8 Fritz Göttler, 'Westdeutscher Nachkriegsfilm: Land der Väter', in Wolfgang Jacobsen, Anton Kaes and Hans-Helmut Prinzler (eds.), *Geschichte des deutschen Films,* (Stuttgart and Weimar: Metzler, 1993), p. 197.

9 Heide Fehrenbach, *Cinema in Democratizing Germany: Reconstructing National Identity after Hitler* (Chapel Hill: University of North Carolina Press, 1995), p. 152.

10 Erica Carter, *How German is She? Postwar West German Reconstruction and the Consuming Woman* (Ann Arbor: University of Michigan Press, 1997), p. 179.

11 David Morley, *Home Territories* (New York and London: Routledge, 2000), p. 5.

12 In stressing the ambivalence of the *Heimatfilm*, my goal is not to exculpate, let alone 'celebrate', the 1950s as a misunderstood decade of subversion; nor do I intend to suggest that we re-evaluate the decade by reading it 'against the grain' in the manner of certain strands of French *auteur* criticism that began to rehabilitate 'conservative' Hollywood directors *during* the 1950s. Given the political climate of restoration coupled with the progressivist economic ethos of the *Wirtschaftswunder*, the ambivalence of the *Heimatfilm* is hardly subversive; as I argue below, that ambivalence serves instead to define its *selective* embrace of modernisation and thus its specific form of cultural and political conservatism.

13 In arguing against the ahistorical treatment of genre, I am drawing on Rick Altman's proposal for a 'pragmatic' approach to genre that synthesises theoretical and historical concerns. Cf. Rick Altman, *Film/Genre* (London: BFI, 1999).

14 Andrew Higson, 'The Heritage Film and British Cinema', in Andrew Higson (ed.), *Dissolving Views: Key Writings on British Cinema* (New York: Cassell, 1997), p. 237.

15 Eric Rentschler, *West German Film in the Course of Time* (New York: Redgrave, 1984), p. 104.

16 For two excellent studies of the *Heimatbewegung*, cf. Celia Applegate, *A Nation of Provincials: The German Idea of Heimat* (Berkeley: University of California Press, 1990) and Alon Confino, *The Nation as Local Metaphor: Württemberg, Imperial Germany, and National Memory 1871–1918* (Chapel Hill: University of North Carolina Press, 1997); on the *Heimatkunst* movement and the *Heimatroman*, cf. Karlheinz Rossbacher, *Heimatkunstbewegung und Heimatroman: Zu einer Literatur-Soziologie der Jahrhundertwende* (Stuttgart: Klett, 1975).

17 Dr Wilhelm Spickernagel, 'Der Kinematograph im Dienste der Heimatkunst', in *Hannoverland. Parteilose Zeitschrift für die Pflege der Heimatkunde und des Heimatschutzes unserer niedersächsischen Heimat*, vol. 6 (1912), p. 234.

18 Walter Freisburger, *Theater im Film: eine Untersuchung über die Grundzüge und Wandlungen in den Beziehungen zwischen Theater und Film* (Emsdetten: Lechte, 1936); although Freisburger's claim has yet to be substantiated, the proliferation of *Heimat*-titles during the war years in particular does suggest at least some proto-generic patterns of repetition and recognisability.

19 The synopsis for *Heimatliche Scholle* telegraphs the genre's

syntax and semantics: 'Drama. Son of a peasant turns to crime in the city. Returns home.' For this and other titles see Herbert Birett's invaluable website 'Quellen zur Filmgeschichte' at http://www.unibw-muenchen.de/campus/Film/wwwfilmbi.html

20 Cf. 'Wer kennt den "Ostmärkischen Heimatfilm" ', in *Film-Kurier*, vol. 8, no. 246, 20 October 1926, and 'Die heutige Berliner Uraufführung', in *Film-Kurier*, vol. 9, no. 180, 2 August 1927.

21 Karl L. Kraatz's *Deutscher Film Katalog: Ufa, Tobis, Bavaria 1930–45* (Frankfurt-am-Main: Transit-Film, n.d.), for instance, lists thirty-nine '*Heimatfilme*' for the period from 1930 to 1945. However, the filmography is incomplete and the classificatory scheme somewhat arbitrary, and one is tempted to surmise that the generic rubrics are determined far more by the present of the 1950s than by the pragmatic contexts of their production and reception in the 1930s and 40s.

22 Thus, in 1932, critics identified the first version of *Grün ist die Heide* as an 'explicit *Heimatfilm*', and Hans Deppe's *Heideschulmeister Uwe Karsten* (1933) was reviewed as a wholesome '*Heimatfilm*' that would exemplify the German sound film's 'mission' to achieve the 'trinity' of 'German Man [and] German song in the German landscape' (quoted in Oskar Kalbus, *Vom Werden deutscher Filmkunst*, vol. 2 [Altona-Bahrenfeld: Cigaretten-Bilderdienst, 1935], p. 58). Peter Ostermayr's productions of Ganghofer adaptations were also marketed by Ufa as '*Heimatfilme*'.

23 Giuseppe Becce supplied the music for Fanck and Trenker, and continued to orchestrate majestic images of nature in the films of the 1940s and 50s. Harald Reinl, who also set out working with Fanck, advanced to become one of the most prolific directors of the *Heimatfilm* from the 1950s well into the 70s. Other significant personal continuities would necessarily include Hans Deppe, the 'King of the *Heimatfilm*', who, after a career as an actor, debuted as a director in 1934 with the first version of *Ferien vom Ich* (*Holiday from the Self*); he tops Höfig's list of '*Heimatfilm*-Directors', having contributed ten films to the genre between 1947 and 1960, and fourteen more during his career before 1947.

24 Uta Berg-Ganschow, 'Der Widerspenstigen Zähmung', in *Frauen und Film*, no. 35, 1983, pp. 24–8.

25 Cf. Tom Gunning, 'Before Documentary: Early Nonfiction Film and the "View" Aesthetic', in Daan Hertogs and Nico de Klerk (eds.), *Uncharted Territory: Essays on Early Nonfiction Film* (Amsterdam: Nederlands Film Museum, 1997), p. 15.

26 Cf. Tom Gunning, 'The Cinema of Attraction: Early Film, its Spectator, and the Avant-Garde', originally in *Wide Angle*, vol. 8, nos. 3/4, 1986, pp. 63–70.

27 Cf. Eric Rentschler, 'Mountains and Modernity: Relocating the *Bergfilm*', in *New German Critique*, no. 51, Autumn, 1990, pp. 137–61.

28 For arguments concerning the distinction between the treatment of nature in the *Bergfilm* and the *Heimatfilm*, cf. Horak, 'Träume vom Wolkenmeer und einer guten Stube', in *Berge, Licht und Traum: Dr. Arnold Fanck und der deutsche Bergfilm* (Munich: Bruckmann, 1997), p. 30; also Thomas Jacobs, 'Der Bergfilm als Heimatfilm. Überlegungen zu einem Filmgenre', in *Augen-Blick*, no. 5, 1988, pp. 19–30.

29 Cf. Christian Rapp, *Höhenrausch: Der deutsche Bergfilm* (Vienna: Sonderzahl, 1997).

30 Cf. Eric Rentschler, *The Ministry of Illusion: Nazi Cinema and its Afterlife* (Cambridge, MA, and London: Harvard University Press, 1996) and Thomas Elsaesser, *Weimar Cinema and After: Germany's Historical Imaginary* (London and New York: Routledge, 2000).

31 Cf. 'Die Heimatfilm-Welle rollt wieder', in *Konkret*, no. 42, 15 November 1973, pp. 18 and 19; and Kai Krüger, 'Im Kino darf wieder geweint werden', in *Die Zeit*, 16 February 1973.

32 Cf. Eric Rentschler's chapter 'Calamity Prevails over the Country. Young German Filmmakers Revisit the Homeland', in *West German Film in the Course of Time*, pp. 103–28; and Daniel Alexander Schacht, *Fluchtpunkt Provinz: der neue Heimatfilm zwischen 1968 und 1972* (Münster: MakS, 1991).

33 Cf. Wilfried von Bredow and Hans-Friedrich Foltin, *Zwiespältige Zufluchten: Zur Renaissance des Heimatgefühls* (Bonn: Dietz, 1981). Also Jürgen Bolten, 'Heimat im Aufwind. Anmerkungen zur Sozialgeschichte eines Bedeutungswandels', in Hans-Georg Pott (ed.), *Literatur und Provinz: Das Konzept 'Heimat' in der neueren Literatur* (Paderborn: Schöningh, 1989), pp. 23–38.

34 The series' title was originally to be 'Made in Germany'.

35 On Reitz's *Heimat* cf. most recently Rachel Palfreyman, *Edgar Reitz's* Heimat: *Histories, Traditions, Fictions* (Oxford and New York: Peter Lang, 2000).

36 Cf. Bliersbach, *So grün war die Heide*, p. 33.

37 On these shows, see Georg Seeßlen's acerbic remarks in 'Reichsparteigag und Bauernstube: Eine Volksmusiksendung im Jahr 1985', in *VolksTümlichkeit: über die Gnadenlose Gemütlichkeit im neuen Deutschland* (Greiz: Weisser Stein, 1993), pp. 19–45.

38 Applegate, *A Nationa of Provincials* p. 71. Rural audiences predictably had much greater qualms about the *Heimatfilm*'s lack of authenticity, and were clearly *not* the genre's intended audience. Willi Höfig quotes a 1951 survey in which *Schwarzwaldmädel*, one of the prototypes

of the *Heimatfilm* of the 1950s, topped the audience ranking of then current films; the only dip in the film's popularity was in the *Schwarzwald* itself. Höfig, *Der deutsche
Heimatfilm*, p. 74, n. 414.

39 Rentschler, *West German Film in the Course of Time*, p. 105.

40 Rentschler, *The Ministry of Illusion*, p. 74.

41 Cf. Georg Seeßlen, 'Der Heimatfilm. Zur Mythologie eines
Genres', in Christa Blümlinger (ed.), *Sprung im Spiegel:
Filmisches Wahrnehmen zwischen Fiktion und Wirklichkeit*
(Vienna: Sonderzahl, 1990), pp. 343–62.

42 Cf. ibid., p. 349.

43 Oskar Köhler, 'Heimat', in *Staatslexikon*, Bd. IV (Freiburg,
1959); quoted in Bredow and Foltin, *Zwiespältige
Zufuchten*, p. 26.

44 Höfig, *Der deutsche Heimatfilm*, p. 388.

45 Doreen Massey, 'A Place Called Home?', in *New Formations*,
no. 17, 1991, p. 12.

46 Ibid., p. 13.

47 Anthony Giddens, *The Consequences of Modernity* (Stanford,
CA: Stanford University Press, 1991), p. 18. Giddens defines
'disembedding' as the ' "lifting out" of social relations from
local contexts of interaction and their restructuring across
indefinite spans of time-space', ibid., p. 21.

48 Ibid., p. 140.

49 Ibid., pp. 18f.

50 Relevant films for such a comparison include, among
others, such diverse productions as Konrad Wolf's often
disavowed debut, the musical *Einmal ist keinmal* (*Once is
Never*, 1955), Cold War propaganda such as *Das verurteilte
Dorf* (*The Condemned Village*, 1952), Kurt Maetzig's epic
chronicle of post-war reconstruction in the provinces,
Schlösser und Katen (*Castles and Huts*, 1957), or Artur
Pohl's drama about the integration of 'resettlers'
('*Umsiedler*') from the East, *Die Brücke* (*The Bridge*, 1949).

51 Cf. Raymond Williams, *Television, Technology, and Cultural
Form* (London: Fontana, 1974).

52 Sean Moores, quoted in David Morley, 'Bounded Realms:
Household, Family, Community, and Nation', in Hamid
Naficy (ed.), *Home, Exile, Homeland: Film, Media, and the
Politics of Place* (New York and London: Routledge, 1999),
p. 159.

2

German Film Comedy

Jan-Christopher Horak

The bias against genre

In the narrative of German film history the very term German comedy seems to be an oxymoron. Germans are known for tragedy, for their love affair with death, not for comedy. But the Germans also have an inferiority complex vis-à-vis comedy. As early as 1912, a Berlin film journalist stated plainly that the Germans were short of comical ideas.[1] Ludwig Thoma, the well-known German playwright and editor of the humoristic magazine *Simplicissimus,* noted a few years later that 'One would be better served to save one's tears for the "grotesque, merry, fits of laughter producing" mirth, which Berlin film companies hope do justice to humour.'[2] In the mid-1920s, it was a critic in *Der Kinematograph* who complained that 'German cinema has had to do without comedies for quite a while, making do with foreign humour which does not always match German tastes.'[3] Later classical film historians damned silent German comedy for supposedly being nothing more than faint reproductions of superior French and American films. As Siegfried Kracauer wrote from his exile in New York in *From Caligari to Hitler,* 'they themselves [the Germans] were incapable of producing a popular comedian'.[4] Meanwhile, non-German historians, like Robert Brasillach/Maurice Bardeche, René Jeanne/Charles Ford, Jerzy Toeplitz and Roger Manvell, ignore German comedy altogether. While Georges Sadoul devoted space to early comedy, complimenting popular comedians such as Oscar Sabo, Anna Müller-Linke, Guido Herzfeld and Ernst Lubitsch, he couldn't suppress an ironic sneer when he stated that German film comedies have their own particular character, and that non-Germans consider them to be heavy and boring.[5]

While foreigners attribute German humourlessness to a perceived national characteristic, the German bias against film comedy runs deeper, its roots buried in the intellectual disdain for genre cinema in general. As Thomas Elsaesser has pointed out, this attitude against genre is based in part on the German intelligentsia's overwhelming preference for art cinema.[6] How else to explain a canonical periodisation of German film history which privileges *The Cabinet of Dr Caligari* (1919) and German expressionism as the beginning of German cinema, then moves directly to Nazi propaganda cinema, before valorising the New German Cinema of Fassbinder, Herzog and Wenders? But who outside Germany knows Otto Waalkes? Thus, while the foreign view turns a national stereotype into the explanation for comedy's invisibility in the narrative of German film history, film comedy has occasioned fits of self-loathing in German critics.

However, the edifice has been crumbling, not just in the area of genre studies, but in terms of viewing German film history holistically as a series of continuities in personnel, political and aesthetic ruptures, and generic conventions. In the past decade, serious research has taken German film comedy beyond popular film literature, integrating it into academic film history.[7] Genre in German cinema has become a contested site of film-historical discourse; genre, and with it comedy, is now perceived as an ideological control mechanism for the ruling class or as a discourse potentially capable of subverting the institutional status quo.

Writing of early German film comedy, Thomas Brandlmeier notes that the genre is embedded in the German entertainment industry's tendency to take taboo-breaking issues and transform them into affirmative, likeable and ordinary pleasures.[8] Brandlmeier hypothesises an ur-German fear and loathing of physical comedy (having to do with shame of the body) and the prevalence of an affirmative laughter that supported normative behaviour and branded outsiders as foreign and other.[9] However, American comedies were also often xenophobic, utilising racial stereotyping, even while they allowed for the undermining of social norms, so that even while German comedies may have been deeply conservative and conformist, this does not preclude them from also transporting subversive moments.

In *The BFI Companion to German Cinema*, Elsaesser and Wedel postulate in their notes on German film comedy 'strong elements of subversive, grotesque, and surrealist humour'.[10] Examples abound, as will be demonstrated below. Furthermore, German cinema was not devoid of physical comedy, as Ernst Lubitsch, Karl Valentin, Arnold Fanck, Felix Bressart, or Heinz Erhardt demonstrate. It is also at least debatable that physical comedy is inherently subversive given conservative examples of physical comedy, whether Fanck and Erhardt or Harold Lloyd and Leo McCarey. However, Brandlmeier's argument that the suppression of the carnivalesque in classical German theatre caused its comedy's normative tendencies is worth further exploration.

It is a fact that the German film industry produced thousands of comedies, many of which have yet to be preserved, let alone historically evaluated. As Elsaesser and Wedel note, German comedies are the bread and butter of the German film industry, regardless of the period.[11] German comedy's status as a linchpin of the film industry's economy, its popularity in the mass medium, makes it particularly susceptible to ruling-class scrutiny. Given its institutional basis, then, and the particular circumstances of German history in the twentieth century, film comedy has been a barometer for the winds of political change, as have other genres to a greater or lesser degree.

Inscribed within the history of a society that spent much of the twentieth century under the shadow of a fascist episode, German comedy is qualitatively different from American, French or Italian comedy. While these national cinemas functioned under more or less democratic albeit capitalist ideological systems, German comedy was subject at different moments in history to liberal capitalist regimes and authoritarian dictatorships. During the *Kaiserzeit* and Weimar period, comedies could be liberating, risking transgressions of social and sexual taboos, thus allowing audiences to experience moments of subversive pleasure. National Socialism under Adolf Hitler, however, brought with it the codification of norms devised to maintain the political, social and moral status quo, including the rigorous suppression of sexual desire. Unlike capital in other countries, which allowed genre cinema in the interest of box-office to construct ambiguous ideological narratives, monopoly capitalism under German fascism displayed zero tolerance for subversive discourses. Such norms enjoyed a long afterlife in post-war Germany.

Both Elsaesser and Brandlmeier champion Ernst Lubitsch for his Jewish physical comedy and sexualised heroes, and this may be a key to formulating a critical view that explores the discourse surrounding sexuality as an indicator of ideological content, giving us a more complex view of the socio-political history of German film comedy. This essay will argue that German comedy's potential for subversion was deeply influenced by the German-Jewish cultural symbiosis; not just Lubitsch, but numerous other comedians working in that tradition. The Holocaust obliterated that culture, and it took a generation for Germany's film industry to recover, once again allowing it to discover gender relations as a motor for comedy. Interestingly, the West German reception of Lubitsch and Billy Wilder accompanied the first sex comedies by Young German filmmakers in the late 1960s, and certainly influenced subsequent German film comedy, as the traditions of Weimar and its exile cinema once again entered German cultural consciousness.

Early cinema and Weimar

According to Gerhard Lamprecht's catalogue, *Deutsche Stummfilme*, which is by no means a complete record of German film production in the 1910s, the Berlin and Munich film industries released over fifty feature-length comedies in 1914, and over forty in 1915; in 1928 the industry released over forty comedy features, approximately 25 per cent of the total output. Taking into consideration the countless shorts being produced, it becomes clear that comedies were big business in the silent era. Ernst Lubitsch alone starred in or directed thirty-one comedies from 1914–18.[12] Heinrich Bolten-Baeckers turned out over twenty comedies in the 1913–15 period and would continue comedy production into the mid-1920s. Starring Leo Peukert (as Professor Rehbein), Anna Müller-Lincke, or Herbert Paulmüller, the 'BB Films' were popular not only in Germany, but supposedly throughout Europe.[13] The rotund Leo Peukert seems to have been one of the most popular silent film comedians before and during the First World War, although virtually none of his films survive.[14] Appearing in such films as *Leo, der Aushilfskellner* (*Leo, the Substitute Waiter*, 1913), *General von Berning* (1914) and *Das Patentschnappschloss* (*The Patented Lock*, 1915), Leo Peukert, like Ernst Lubitsch, Guido Herzfeld, Ernst Matray and Anna Müller-Lincke, developed a particular style of comedy, which had its origins in the working-class (Jewish garment) districts of East Berlin. Anna Müller-Lincke specialised in straitlaced wives, difficult mothers-in-law and silly mothers, German *Hausfraus* all, the scourge of Prussian manhood.

A completely different kind of comedy was practised by *Volkskomiker*, Bavarian comedians whom Lubitsch successfully parodied in *Mayer auf der Alm* (*Mayer in the Alps*, 1913), *Mayer aus Berlin* (*Mayer from Berlin*, 1919) and *Kohlhiesels Töchter* (*Kohlhiesel's Daughters*, 1920). The best-known of these comedians was Karl Valentin, although Valentin was also a modernist. Konrad Dreher starred in films such as *Der Tyrann von Mückendorf* (*The Tyrant of Mückendorf*, 1915). Another comedian in this 'Bavarian' vein was Arnold Rieck, whose boorish professors and small-town teachers, figures of authority unmasked, were extremely popular.

Finally, Dr Arnold Fanck, a director more commonly known for his melodramatic *Bergfilme*, also directed Bavarian comedies. In *Der grosse Sprung* (*The Big Leap*, 1927), Leni Riefenstahl (a goat shepherdess) and Luis Trenker (as the village idiot) romp in the Alps as happy peasants, while Hans Schneeberger plays the millionaire from Berlin. Unlike the Lubitsch parodies, though, the confrontation between city and country is seen from the perspective of the nature-wise peasants. Filled with ironic references to Fanck's previously deadly serious work, as well as moments of genuine grotesque humour and physical comedy, *The Big Leap* was both a commercial and critical success for Ufa.[15]

After the introduction of sound, Fanck remade one of his silent films as a *Bergfilm* comedy, *Der weisse Rausch* (*The White Ecstasy*, 1931), again starring Riefenstahl, this time as a city girl transposed to the country. Sans narrative, psychology and meaningful dialogue, the film was pure physical comedy, with forty skiers participating Keystone Cop-like in a race through the mountains, while two carpenters from the flatlands of Hamburg (extremely tall and short) learn to ski, wearing their traditional north German garb. It was also a huge commercial success, although at least one Berlin critic characterised the film as an advertisement for ski tourism.[16] Interestingly, both films sublimate sexuality into the physicality of the ski race – Riefenstahl is shown as a surrogate mother in *The Big Leap*, presaging the Nazi's mother fixation – and are never anti-authoritarian in the manner of American slapstick, even though Fanck's comedies can claim a refreshing sense of the physical.

The most radical German comedian was Karl Valentin. Valentin's character's extreme attempts to be normal in an authoritarian society, his obsessive pursuit of a normality which cannot be attained, pointed to the dehumanising character of socially defined conformity. His social deformity is expressed physically, specifically in the comedian's extremely awkward relationship to his own body. Valentin's visual humour indeed draws much of its power from his inability to come to terms with the physicality of his corpus. The physical world presents him endless challenges in which he willingly engages, but which ultimately bring him to his knees, despite his continuous struggles.

Valentin's body is awkwardness incarnate: tall and extremely thin, all skin and bones, the image of an anorexic, his arms and legs and feet extended much too far in every direction. His extremities are accentuated by pencil-like fingers and an elongated nose which extends conspicuously from the sharp features of his face. His undernourished visage and hollow eyes are framed by very short cropped hair, slicked back, and his too large and protruding ears.[17] His visual foil is the well-fed short Liesl Karlstadt, who emphasises Valentin's lack of bulk. Valentin and Karlstadt's comedy emphasises the grotesque, the abnormal in the everyday, the continual struggle of little people in an unjust world. In their comic universe, order always seems to degenerate into chaos. Order is only a chimera, an illusion upheld for the comfort of the ruling classes. The discrepancy between illusion and reality, and the frustration of the disenfranchised in attempting to cope with that difference, thus leads more often than not to physical violence, to the infliction of pain. Indeed, Valentin's comedies are filled with violence against himself and others. In both cases, the comedy is based on the audience's pleasure in seeing a person physically hurt, an experience encapsulated by the German word *Schadenfreude*, which is untranslatable in all its socio-psychological repercussions, but loosely connotes the joy in seeing another's misfortunes; a scopic regime connected to the sadistic rather than the erotic.

Ernst Lubitsch also has his sadistic moments (often directed at the poor Margarete Kupfer), but that tendency is mitigated by the joy of sex. Significantly, his work in Germany has in the past been described as completely inferior to his 'sophisticated' American films. Lotte Eisner's condescending tone is audible when she places Lubitsch's German comedies in the tradition of the 'nonchalant, rather cynical humor of the Konfektion, the Jewish lower middle class engaged in the ready-made clothing trade', degrading his comedy as one of 'oafish effects' and 'Central European vulgarity'.[18] Could it be that Eisner, herself a product of a completely assimilated German-Jewish haute bourgeoisie, was embarrassed by the ethnicity of Lubitsch's humour?[19]

Hermann Thimig and Ossi Oswalda in Ernst Lubitsch's *Die Puppe* (1919)

Ernst Lubitsch's comedy is not only specifically German-Jewish, but has its origins in a wholly different tradition from that of the classical theatre described by Brandlmeier, namely Jewish farces and low comedy, as practised by the Berlin Herrnfeld Theatre and touring companies from the *stetl*.[20] Lubitsch's Jewish petit bourgeois heroes in films such as *Der Stolz der Firma* (*Pride of the Firm*, 1914) and *Schuhpalast Pinkus* (*Shoe Palace Pinkus*, 1916) are unabashed social climbers, con-men who start as apprentices and end up succeeding in business by marrying the boss's daughter. Short-circuiting the ideologically prescribed path to riches via the sweat of labour and diligence, they embrace sexual desire, turning social norms upside down in the process. Similarly, the Ossi Oswalda comedies, *The Oyster Princess* (1919) and *I Don't Want to Be a Man* (1919), reveal Lubitsch giving free rein to the id beyond all socially defined propriety. The expression of sexual desire thus becomes itself an act of subversion, breaking down class barriers and the social order.

Jewish humour also informed the comedies of Max Mack (*The Tango Queen*, 1913), and in the 1920s the work of Richard Eichberg, Wilhelm Thiele and (later) Billy Wilder. Eichberg, who had specialised in detective melodramas earlier in his career, began a successful series of light sex comedies, including *Die keusche Susanne* (*Innocent Susanne*, 1926) and *Das Girl von der Revue* (*The Revue Girl*, 1928). Situated in Lubitsch's East Berlin fashion district, Eichberg's *Der Fürst von Pappenheim* (*The Earl of Pappenheim*, 1927) featured Curt Bois cross-dressing in a comedy as wild as Berlin's *Kurfürstendamm* in the 1920s. Thiele's knack for light comedy (*Hurrah! ich lebe!* [*Hurrah! I'm Alive*, 1927]) took him into the sound period as Ufa's most successful musical comedy specialist with films like *Die Drei von der Tankstelle* (*Three from the Petrol Station*, 1930) and *Die Privatsekretärin* (*The Private Secretary*, 1931). Wilder's career blossomed with scripts for *Ihre Hoheit befiehlt* (*Her Highness Commands*, 1931) and *Madame wünscht keine Kinder* (*Madame Wants No Children*, 1933). Curt Wilhelm's *Man braucht kein Geld* (*You Don't Need Money*, 1931), Alexis Granowsky's *Die Koffern des Herrn O. F.* (*The Suitcases of Mr O. F.*, 1931) and

Fritz Kortner's *Der brave Sünder* (*The Well-Behaved Sinner*, 1931) all have an anarchic streak to them, both cynical and sentimental, typically Wilder (his detractors would assert decades later), but also characteristically Jewish.

The bottom falling out of the capitalist world order brought an element of angst to Germany's Depression comedies, not dissimilar to Jewish fears of the next pogrom. Suddenly, German middle-class values concerning order were called into question. In German cinema, honourable citizens become drifters, willing to do anything to get their personal economies back into shape, even if it meant lying, stealing and cheating.[21] In both *Man braucht kein Geld* and *Die Koffern des Herrn O. F.* the rumour that an American millionaire has come to town is enough of a promise to get people working again. In *Der brave Sünder* it is every man for himself, as two lowly white collar workers travel to Vienna with a packet of money, only to lose it time and again, while sinking into infantile and regressive states that reveal the storm beneath the calm, orderly surfaces of their souls. Significantly, as in Lubitsch, erotic desire and monetary exchange are interchangeable.

The highest paid film actor in Weimar Germany in the period 1930–33 was the German-Jewish comedian, Felix Bressart. Starring in no fewer than eighteen comedy vehicles between 1930 and 1933, Bressart plays the clerk who unwittingly sows chaos wherever he goes, e.g. in *Der Herr Bürovorsteher* (*Mr Office Manager*, 1931). Bressart uses his seemingly awkward body like a square peg in a round hole. Others may storm ahead, but Bressart twists and turns with uncertainty, simultaneously turning semantics and syntax inside out. In *Drei Tage Militärarrest* (*Three Days Arrest*, 1931), a film belonging to the popular (right-wing) sub-genre of army recruit comedies (*Kasernenhofkomödien*), Bressart's anarchic hero subverts any intended conservative propaganda.[22]

Felix Bressart (left) in *Der Herr Bürovorsteher* (1931)

Hitler forced Bressart into exile, like countless other German Jews. He would become a favourite of Ernst Lubitsch in his American films (*Ninotchka* [1939], *The Shop Around the Corner* [1940], *To Be or Not to Be* [1942]), playing essentially his established character, albeit in supporting roles. Bressart, and the subversive comedy tradition he represents, thus belongs to a German exile cinema which constitutes the missing half of German cinema history as previously written for the period 1933–50.[23] Not surprisingly, film comedies were German exile cinema's most popular genre, just as they had been in Weimar. In some host countries, for example the Netherlands and Hungary, German émigrés made only comedies, while in France and England their comedies are a distinct minority. Another continuity between pre-1933 comedy and German exile cinema was their tendency towards light comedy, even while catering to national tastes and thematising the experience of exile: *La crise est fini* (*The Crisis is Over*, 1934, dir. Robert Siodmak, France), in which a group of actors are suddenly homeless when their theatre closes; *Peter* (1934, dir. Henry Koster, Austria), in which a homeless girl must dress as a boy to get a job; *100 Men and a Girl* (1937, dir. Henry Koster, USA), in which out-of-work musicians band together; and *The Captain of Kopenick* (1941, dir. Richard Oswald, USA), about a 'stateless' ex-con with the perfect flim-flam, are cases in point. So too is Max Ophuls' *Komodie om Geld* (*Comedy About Money*, 1936), a film made in the middle of the world-wide Depression, which satirises the obsessive quest for money. A master of ceremonies comments on the story, as though life were really a cabaret: a bank messenger loses an enormous amount of money, is however acquitted by a jury, and goes on to head an international financial institution, where he loses even greater sums of money, driving him to the brink of suicide. In the end, everything is brought back to order, so that the daughter can finally marry her poor friend. Although identified as a so-called 'Jordaan film', a typical Dutch comedy from the working-class district of Amsterdam, the film's 'rags to riches to rags story' narrative not only closely resembled the fate of many émigrés, but owed an equally strong debt to German-Jewish comedy. In particular, the hero who bungles his way to success seems more *Schlemihl* than *Staatsmann*.

While Anglo-American criticism has postulated a schism in the films of Lubitsch, Wilder and Henry Koster, I would argue for continuities between their German and subsequent American careers. All three worked with exiled German scriptwriters in America. All three maintained large circles of German-speaking friends, despite public statements that they no longer spoke German. Koster's team included exiles Joe Pasternak (producer) and Felix Jackson (writer), and they saved Universal by importing the German *Backfisch* (teenage girl) character with which they had created successful comedies in Germany and Hungary, and morphing her into the all-American girl, Deanna Durbin.[24] The subversive moment is glimpsed in the other, encapsulated in the slightly kinky relations her pre-pubescent characters entertain with elderly men and father figures.

Fascism and its aftermath

With the forced emigration of German Jewry, including countless actors, writers and directors, Joseph Goebbels' Propaganda Ministry was happy to have a 'racially purified German' comedy be the only game in town. Reinhold Schünzel would be among the last to leave. Schünzel carried Lubitsch's torch, after the latter had gone to Hollywood in the mid-1920s. In fact, Elsaesser's catalogue of character traits for Schünzel's comic persona (both as actor and director) is applicable to both Lubitsch and Jewish humour: preference for narratives of 'impersonations, mistaken identities, role reversals, harmless contricks and deceptions … the nature of erotic desire around exchange and substitution'.[25] Elsaesser goes on to analyse Schünzel's *Hallo Caesar* (1926), a film that reverberates with associations of American slapstick comedy and the cinema of attractions, as well as early German cinema 'numbers' programmes, while creating a self-conscious parody of the film industry and a comedy of erotic exchange values. Klaus Kreimeier, on the other hand, focuses on Schünzel's thoroughly evil and perverse villains (which Elsaesser sees as the criminal twin of Schünzel's comic persona). He also highlights Schünzel's sound era comedies, which subversively undercut gender definitions in *Viktor und Viktoria* (1933) and *Amphitryon* (1935), and fascist pomp and circumstance in *Land der Liebe* (*Land of Love*, 1933).[26] While the last film was banned, leading to Schünzel's speedy exile to Hollywood, the first two were produced under Goebbels' nose (and were successful), no mean trick given Schünzel's status in Nazi Germany as a so-called 'half-Jew'.

Just how much the German cinema industry lost can be gauged by the fate of a Robert Thoeren film story, which the scriptwriter sold to a French company in his first year of exile, *Fanfare d'amour* (*Fanfare of Love*, 1935). It was remade in 1951 in Germany as *Fanfaren der Liebe* by Kurt Hoffmann (Schünzel's former Aryan assistant), who learned little from his master, turning it into a harmless comedy. It was a fellow German exile, Billy Wilder, who took the gender-bending story and transformed it into *Some Like It Hot* (1959).

German film historian Karsten Witte argues that film comedy in the Third Reich, far from being harmless entertainment, as many historians have claimed,[27] actively propagandised fascist ideology. Indeed, comedy functioned to make German film audiences emotionally pliable for a propagandistic consensus constructed across all media discourses. Through a double aesthetic strategy of separation and integration, politically and morally unacceptable characters are separated from the social fabric, while characters who represent the rigorous institutionalisation of fascism's class and gender norms are integrated into the community.[28] Witte also notes that visual comedy, as utilised in American films, is morphed into verbal humour, thus subjecting it to tighter ideological control. Comedy's mission is to distract audiences from the reality of war, allowing Germans a moment of respite from the bombings and mounting casualties. Furthermore, film comedy under fascism uses faux transgressions as safety valves for pent-up aggression against the state, thus better harnessing support for the war effort.

To test this hypothesis, one need look no further than the career of Heinz Rühmann, arguably the most popular German film comedian from the 1930s through the 50s. Rühmann's star persona (see Stephen Lowry in this volume) defined the prototypical German 'everyman', surviving three political systems from Weimar to Bonn, through an ambiguous mixture of constancy and opportunism, mediocrity and insolence. Mimicking the 'little man' whose humanity supposedly shines through despite repeated setbacks, Rühmann's less attractive characteristics included an authoritarian *Weltanschauung*, e.g. in *Quax, der Bruchpilot* (*Quax, the Crash Pilot*, 1941) and *Feuerzangenbowle* (*Hot Spiced Punch*, 1944). As Stephen Lowry has noted, Rühmann, while seemingly subverting established order, is always simultaneously looking for loopholes in the system, in order to grab a bit of power for himself, thus re-integrating him into the status quo.[29] In a number of his post-war films the actor plays tragicomic figures who are portrayed as victims of an inhuman political system. Rühmann thus continues as a figure of identification for the German middle class in the Federal Republic, transforming perpetrators into victims, allowing them to repress their culpability for the Holocaust.

Rühmann also demonstrates a streak of infantilism in many of his roles that seemingly runs through much German comedy after 1933, yet without the subversive potential such infantilism brings to American comedy (Harry Langdon, Stan Laurel). Infantilism here is a signifier for the repression of sexuality in favour of faecal humour. Case in point: Heinz Erhardt. The most popular comedian of the 1950s, Erhardt was an overweight, older actor who specialised in downtrodden and infantile husbands/fathers, trapped in an anal stage of development. Invariably lower middle class, Erhardt's characters, whether in *Witwer mit fünf Töchtern* (*Widower with Five Daughters*, 1957) or *Der Haustyrann* (*The Domestic Tyrant*, 1959), are losers rather than social climbers, conformist rather than subversive and completely unerotic. He struggles against children and wives, vainly attempting to establish authority and control through law. While the collective trauma of a 'lost' war may partially explain Erhardt's socio-psychic make-up, how is it that Ernst Lubitsch or Fatty Arbuckle could exude an erotic aura, though neither of them were conventionally attractive, while German comedians from Rühmann to Hans Moser to Heinz Erhardt are emasculated as well as infantile? One answer may be that Nazi culture allowed women only one role, that of mother, thus banishing any sexual discourse from the cinema. Furthermore, sexual desire is completely repressed in Nazi cinema, as I have argued elsewhere, since it invariably weakened men in their resolve to sacrifice themselves for the Fatherland and is thus associated with the feminine.[30]

The shadow cast by the sexual politics of the Third Reich reaches deep into the post-Second World War era in Germany, beyond Erhardt and the commercial cinema of the 1950s. In *Otto – Der Film* (1985) and *Otto – Der neue Film* (1987), Otto Waalkes plays a character from East Frisia whose citizens are thought to be dumb and dumber. Tall and skinny with long blonde hair, Otto's comic persona is that of an adult with the mind of an eight-year-old, who prances like a bunny and is obsessed by faecal humour. His ideas about sex are strictly pre-pubescent. In *Otto – Der neue Film*, Otto chases after an empty-headed sexpot, but realises in the film's final frames that the ugly duckling that he knows not only loves him, but will bring him domestic bliss, and thus return metaphorically to him the absent mother.

An abnormal attachment to the mother, precluding any form of sexuality, whether homoerotic or heterosexual, is also the subject of one of the most popular films of the 1980s, Loriot's *Oedipussi* (1988). Directed by and starring Vicco von Bülow, better known as the cartoonist and humorist Loriot, *Oedipussi* concerns a furniture salesman well into his fifties, who seemingly cannot separate himself from his overbearing mother, even after he finally meets a woman who interests him erotically. She, too, still lives at home, so that both are trapped in an endless childhood, leading to repeated failed attempts at sexual contact. While

the film takes much of its comic energy from an exact observation of German petit bourgeois mores and morality, the film fits into the pattern of German conformist comedy: the film's happy end has the couple on holiday in Italy with mother (literally and figuratively) in the driver's seat.

Rediscovering lost traditions

In the late 1960s German cinema discovered sex and comedy, leading to a boom in semi-pornographic films and sex comedies, the latter made by Peter and Ulrich Schamoni, May Spils, Maran Gosov, Franz-Josef Spieker and Klaus Lemke, among others. Comedies such as Ulrich Schamoni's *Alle Jahre wieder* (*Next Year, Same Time*, 1967), Spieker's *Wilde Reiter GmbH.* (*Wild Rider Co.*, 1967) and Maran Gosov's *Engelchen* (*Angel Baby*, 1968) were often financially successful, causing them to be derided by 'serious' critics like Enno Patalas. They objected to the fact that these films openly referenced American genre formulae, were unabashedly vulgar and, in contrast to the New German Cinema of Fassbinder *et al.*, supposedly lacked an *Autoren* point of view.[31] May Spils' *Zur Sache Schätzchen* (*Go For It, Baby*, 1968), however, not only received positive reviews from *Filmkritik's* Peter W. Jansen, but was also credited with 'a precise sense of wordplay, as one only finds in Yiddish'.[32] In tune with the sexual revolution of the 1960s, comedies like *Engelchen* rode the wave of *Aufklärungsungsfilme* (sex education films), while simultaneously creating intelligent parodies of such films. *Engelchen*, which spawned several sequels, including Gosov's *Bengelchen liebt kreuz und quer* (*Sex Adventures of a Single Man*, 1968) and Michael Verhoeven's *Engelchen macht weiter – hoppe, hoppe reiter* (*Up the Establishment!*, 1968), captured not only the *Zeitgeist* of Munich's free-wheeling Schwabing district, but also exploded German bourgeois notions of morality. While such sex comedies were few and far between, they did indicate a sea change both in terms of a less repressed attitude towards a discussion of sexual relations and the development of narratives which eschewed conformist paradigms.

Herbert Achternbusch, meanwhile, became the heir to Karl Valentin's cloak, although many of Achternbusch's films seem more depressing than comic. Lionised by German critics, Achternbusch has failed to make an impression abroad, possibly because Achternbusch's comedy, like that of Valentin, is one of stasis rather than movement, and passivity and powerlessness in the face of crushing social norms, rather than manic activity. Achternbusch's characters are passive-aggressive, whether the last Indian in a sanatorium in *Der Kommantsche* (*The Commanche*, 1979) or Christ returned to Bavaria in *Das Gespenst* (*The Ghost*, 1982) or a soldier returning from the Second World War forty years late in *Heilt Hitler!* (*Cure Hitler!*, 1986). Faced with the deadening ordinariness of German contemporary society, they flee into madness or drink, occasionally striking out wildly in desperate acts of violence. Achternbusch's negative reception abroad is compounded by his use of primitive aesthetics, eschewing classical narrative address, or any logic of character or plot, while hinging narratives on a pun or a metaphor.[33]

If Achternbusch represents a return to the subversive comedy of Valentin, then shifts in post-war reception, especially of the American comedies of Lubitsch and Wilder, represented a partial recuperation of German film comedy traditions. In the late 1960s, Ernst Lubitsch and Billy Wilder were rediscovered by young German audiences with no memory of fascism or the plight of the exiles. The Berlin Film Festival in 1968 presented a first serious Lubitsch retrospective, followed in the subsequent two to four years by the West German television premiere of much of Lubitsch's American work, in particular *The Shop Around the Corner*. The reception of Wilder's American films began slightly earlier with regular commercial screenings and reviews in *Filmkritik*, and the huge commercial

success of the re-release of *One, Two, Three* (1961) in the early 1980s. At the same time, other German exiles, including Max Ophuls, received regular screenings at the Munich Filmmuseum, where Doris Dörrie and Herbert Achternbusch were regulars among the audience, while the Saarbruecken Film Festival named its comedy prize after Ophuls, a native son. Bernhard Moeller has recently argued that the viewing habits of Germans in the last quarter of the twentieth century have been heavily influenced not only by the comedies of Billy Wilder, but by American comedies in general.[34]

Indeed, both the cinematic return of the exiles and Young German sex comedies prepared the ground for the *Beziehungskomödie* (relationship comedy) boom of the 1990s, with nods to Frank Ripploh's *Taxi zum Klo* (*Taxi to the Toilet*, 1980) and Doris Dörrie's *Männer* (*Men*, 1986). While the sex comedies proved that all German audiences were willing to deal with previously repressed content, Lubitsch and Wilder demonstrated to the youngest generation of film-makers that sex comedies could also be elegant, rather than vulgar. Ripploh's happily homosexual hero, who hops from bed to bed (just before AIDS put a stop to the party), and the heroine in Dörrie's communal flat who seeks her pleasure where she finds it, opened the field for a new generation of post-New German Cinema directors, such as Sönke Wortmann, Rainer Kaufmann and Detlev Buck. As a result, German film comedy had a sudden revival in the last ten years of the twentieth century, turning not only into box-office gold, as it has done consistently through the decades, but also gaining a measure of respect abroad. Gone are the neutered comedians of the past; *ménage à trois* and hetero/homoerotic complications are the order of the day in films like *Der bewegte Mann* (*Maybe, Maybe Not*, 1994), *Stadtgespräch* (*Talk of the Town*, 1995), *Männerpension* (*Jailbirds*, 1996), and *Rossini* (1997). The latest entry, *Mädchen, Mädchen* (*Girls, Girls*, 2001), an American-style teenage comedy about three girls trying to have their first orgasm, has earned over DM20 million at the German box-office. The degree to which these films are actually subversive, rather than merely being pleasant entertainments for a liberated generation that no longer considers sex a taboo, is a subject for further research. In any case, this new generation of film-makers was born after the Second World War, without direct memory of German fascism, yet is cogniscent of German and Jewish film traditions.

On the other hand, the new Millennium has also brought us *Harte Jungs* (*Just the Two of Us*, 2000), *Der Schuh des Manitu* (*Manitou's Shoe*, 2001), and *Feuer, Eis und Dosenbier* (*Fire, Ice and Beer in Cans*, 2002), which

Horst Buchholz in Billy Wilder's *One, Two, Three* (1961)

have been characterised as 'trash comedies about the sexual frustrations of German men'.[35] The second named film brought a whopping eleven million visitors into German cinemas, raising the country's market share to 18.4 per cent, and making it the most successful German film of all time. The trend to vulgar, adolescent sex comedy refers us back to Brandlmeier's dictum that while French farces visualised the upending of illicit sex, German film parodied erotically unsuccessful husbands, attempting to engage in legitimate sex.[36] And indeed the pubescent faecal humour of *Harte Jungs* demarcates German film comedy as a continuously contested site in German film history.

Thus, while the academic reception of German film comedy was initially hindered by a bias against genre and the belief that conformist discourses dominated the genre, recent research presents a more diverse picture. Within the context of a national cinema, German comedy's discontinuities are to be sought in the country's turbulent political history, the latter causing the erasure from history of a vibrant cultural phenomenon: the German-Jewish heritage. Only through the symbolic reunification with that tradition has German comedy been able to move forward towards the creation of a revived German film comedy tradition.

Notes

1 Siegfried Kracauer, *From Caligari to Hitler* (Princeton, NJ: Princeton University Press, 1947), p. 21. Kracauer is referring to an article by Balduin Möllhausen, 'Der Aufstieg des Films', in *Ufa-Blätter* (Berlin), 1921.

2 Ludwig Thoma, 'Das Kino' (1915), reprinted in Fritz Güttinger (ed.), *Kein Tag ohne Kino: Schriftsteller über den Stummfilm* (Frankfurt am Main: Deutsches Filmmuseum, 1984), p. 329. Trans. by Jan-Christopher Horak.

3 Review of *Die gefundene Braut* (1825, Rochus Gliese), quoted in Illona Brennicke and Joe Hembus, *Klassiker des deutschen Stummfilms 1910–1930* (Munich: Goldmann, 1983), p. 186.

4 Kracauer (1947), p. 21.

5 Georges Sadoul, *Storia Generale del Cinema. Il Cinema Diventa Un'Arte* (Turin: Giulio Einaudi editore, 1967), p. 686.

6 Thomas Elsaesser, 'Reinhold Schünzel and *Hallo Caesar* (1927)', in Jörg Schöning (ed.), *Reinhold Schünzel* (Munich: edition text+kritik, 1990).

7 Parts of this essay first appeared in 'Ridere da Sentirsi male. Il Cinema comico Tedesco e Karl Valentin / Laughing Until it Hurts: Karl Valentin and German Film Comedy', in Paolo Cherchi Usai and Lorenzo Codelli (eds.), *Prima di Caligari.*

Cinema tedesco, 1895–1920 (Pordenone: Le Giornate del Cinema Muto, 1990); German trans. 'Schadenfreude: Deutsche Filmkomödien und Karl Valentin', in *Kintop*, no. 1, 1992.

8 Thomas Brandlmeier, 'Frühe deutsche Filmkomödie, 1895–1917', in Hans-Michael Bock and Wolfgang Jacobsen (eds.), *Der komische Kintopp* (Hamburg: Cinegraph FilmMaterialien 10, 1997), p. 27; a shorter version of this essay appears in English in Thomas Elsaesser (ed.), *A Second Life. German Cinema's First Decades* (Amsterdam: Amsterdam University Press, 1996), pp. 103–13.

9 Brandlmeier (1997), pp. 32ff.

10 See Thomas Elsaesser and Michael Wedel, *The BFI Companion to German Cinema* (London: BFI, 1999), p. 55.

11 Ibid, pp. 55f.

12 See Wolfgang Jacobsen's filmography in Hans-Helmut Prinzler and Enno Patalas (eds.), *Lubitsch* (Munich: C. J. Bucher Verlag, 1984).

13 Friedrich von Zglinicki, *Der Weg des Films* (Berlin: Rembrandt, 1956), p. 347. Bolten-Baeckers had set up one of the earliest German film studios in 1906 in Berlin-Steglitz and distributed films in France through Gaumont.

14 Oskar Kalbus, *Vom Werden deutscher Filmkuns,* vol. 2 (Altona-Bahrenfeld: Cigaretten-Bilderdienst, 1935), p. 35.

15 See Jan-Christopher Horak, *Berge, Licht und Traum. Dr. Arnold Fanck und der deutsche Bergfilm* (Munich: Bruckmann, 1997), pp. 35–6.

16 Ibid., p. 45.

17 In many ways, Valentin's body resembles a caricature, a comic drawing from the books of Wilhelm Busch, e.g. the haggard tailor Böck from the *Max und Moritz* stories. See 'Max und Moritz. Eine Bubengeschichte in sieben Streichen' (1865), in Wilhelm Busch, *Samtliche Werke. Band III* (Munich: Verlag Braun & Schneider, 1943), pp. 29–35.

18 Lotte Eisner, *The Haunted Screen: Expressionism in the German Cinema and the Influence of Max Reinhardt* (Berkeley: University of California Press, 1969), p. 79.

19 A corrective to this view has been Sabine Hake, *Passions and Deceptions: The Early Films of Ernst Lubitsch* (Princeton, NJ: Princeton University Press, 1992).

20 See Peter Sprengel, *Populäres jüdisches Theater in Berlin von 1877 bis 1933* (Berlin: Verlag Haude und Spener, 1997).

21 See Hans C. Blumenberg, 'Der Aufstand der Bürovorsteher', in *Die Zeit*, no. 36, 29 August 1980. See also Karsten Witte, 'Katastrophen unter der Normaluhr', in *Die Frankfurter Rundschau*, no. 221, 23 September 1980, p. 9.

22 Mid-year 1931, Bressart announced to the German press that he would no longer play in military comedies, due to their ideological content. See Wolfgang Jacobsen, 'Felix

Bressart', in *CineGraph: Lexikon zum deutschsprachigen Film* (Munich: edition text+kritik, 1984ff).

23 See Jan-Christopher Horak, 'In der Fremde. Exilfilm 1933–1945', in Hans-Helmut Prinzler, Wolfgang Jacobsen and Anton Kaes (eds.), *Geschichte des deutschen Films* (Stuttgart and Weimar: Metzler, 1993); English trans. 'German exile cinema, 1933–1950', in *Film History*, vol. 8, no. 4, December 1996.

24 See Jan-Christopher Horak, 'Three Smart Guys: How a Few Penniless German Émigrés Saved Universal Studios', in *Film History*, vol. 11, no. 2, 1999.

25 Elsaesser (1990).

26 Klaus Kreimeier, 'Der Grossstadtgauner', in Thomas Koebner (ed.), *Idole des deutschen Films* (Munich: edition text+kritik, 1997), pp. 80–81.

27 See e.g. David Stewart Hull's *Film in the Third Reich* (Berkeley: University of California Press, 1969).

28 Karsten Witte, *Lachende Erben, Toller Tag: Filmkomödie im Dritten Reich* (Berlin: Vorwerk 8, 1995), p. 48.

29 Stephen Lowry, 'Der kleine Mann als Star', in Koebner (1997), pp. 267ff.

30 See Jan-Christopher Horak, 'Eros, Thanatos, and the Will to Myth: Prussian Films in German Cinema', in Bruce Murray and Christopher Wickham (eds.), *Framing the Past: The Historiography of German Cinema and Television* (Carbondale: University of Southern Illinois Press, 1992).

31 Peter Schamoni once spent several hours at the Munich Filmmuseum complaining to me about my predecessor's treatment of his and his brother's films, when Patalas was a critic and later head of the Filmmuseum.

32 Ponkie, *Münchner Abendzeitung*, quoted in Robert Fischer and Joe Hembus, *Der neue deutsche Film 1960–1980* (Munich: Goldmann, 1981), p. 42.

33 The only extended discussion in English of Achternbusch is Gerd Gemünden's chapter on the director in *Framed Visions. Popular Culture, Americanization, and the Contemporary German and Austrian Imagination* (Ann Arbor: University of Michigan Press, 1998).

34 Hans-Bernhard Moeller, 'Zur deutschen Filmkomödie der Generation nach 1968', in *Monatshefte*, vol. 93, no. 2, Summer 2001, p. 196. While I believe that Moeller's thesis is essentially correct, I think the argument demands further research. In particular, one needs to account for why German audiences were more immune to American comedies in the 1920s, 30s and 50s, when certainly such films were a heavy presence on German screens. I would hypothesise that American consumer culture became all-pervasive in post-Second World War Germany, making German audiences more susceptible to American comedy forms.

35 Brandlmeier (1997), pp. 32f.

36 Marianne Wellershoff, 'Fummeln, stammeln, rammeln in *Der Spiegel*, no. 11, 11 March 2002, p. 250.

3

Extraterritorial Fantasies: Edgar Wallace and the German Crime Film

Tim Bergfelder

> The international currency enjoyed by the detective novel is related both to the internationalism of its representation of society, and to an absence of national specificity in the genre's structure and principal themes – an absence that is reflected in the uniformity of the detective novel in different national contexts. There is, however, a national specificity in the detective novel's differing shades and tones, and it is certainly no coincidence that it is the highly civilised Anglo-Saxons who have identified the genre's very type and produced its clearest models.[1]

I begin my discussion of the German crime film with the above quote from Siegfried Kracauer's 1925 study of the detective novel for a number of reasons. Kracauer is, of course, best remembered today for his 1947 study *From Caligari to Hitler*, which provided an enduring template for the analysis of German and other national cinemas and their genres, by suggesting analogies between film narratives and characters and the collective psychology of a nation.[2] The Kracauer of 1925, by contrast, seems to conceive of an international circulation of thematic motifs and genres, which are re-interpreted in different nuances according to specific cultural needs and historical contexts. This suggests a different methodology, and a less fixed notion of national cultures, from the one that *From Caligari to Hitler* employs. It was Kracauer, again in 1947, who saw German cinema as temperamentally incapable of producing a properly native version of the crime genre, aping Anglo-Saxon conventions instead.[3] By now, this is a well-worn verdict frequently levelled at many other European-made popular genres, seen as inferior copies of

their Hollywood counterparts, and often castigated for eschewing their 'duty' of properly reflecting their national context. As my discussion will show, the German crime film was indeed frequently an extraterritorial genre, centred on a transnational imaginary or fantasy (very often featuring Britain, or a particular version thereof, as its emblematic location or reference point). Rather than dismissing such fantasies for their stereotypes, their inauthenticity or their escapism, I propose that these fantasies provide not only clues as to how constructed and constantly shifting any notions of national identity are, but more specifically how identity formations are negotiated through an engagement and sometimes identification with an imaginary idea of the foreign. After all, what if not also a projective fantasy of the foreign informs Kracauer's comment above about those 'highly civilised Anglo-Saxons'?

In the following pages my aim is not to provide a comprehensive historical survey of the German crime film (for which there is no space here). Instead I hope to illuminate a number of historical continuities, ruptures and detours both in the thematic development and the audience appeal of the genre, focusing on its enduring fascination with Britain. Specifically, I ground my conception of the genre's transnational fantasies in terms of German cinema's relationship with other forms of cultural consumption such as popular literature, critical and public discourse; but also in terms of the genre's visual as well as narrative codes and influences. As a case study I look at the German reception and adaptation of Edgar Wallace, not only as a prime example of the intertextual connections indicated above, but also because his work and persona in some respect 'became' German, or at least embodied a particularly German idea of Britain.

Outside Germany, British crime novelist Edgar Wallace (1875–1932) has not received much critical attention in recent years, and he is no longer a household name even among avid readers of crime novels. In studies of the history of British crime fiction, he is mostly acknowledged as a prolific author of formulaic pulp novels in the 1910s and 20s, interesting for the evolution of the genre only insofar as Wallace, in his tireless self-promotion and through his diversification into journalism, theatre, cinema and politics, provides the very prototype of the twentieth-century best-seller author *cum* media celebrity.[4] Thus, outside observers of the enduring appreciation of Edgar Wallace in Germany have been puzzled about why post-war German cinema audiences and readers remained so attached to Wallace's old-fashioned tales about gothic mansions, foggy and gaslit London streets, and incorruptible Scotland Yard inspectors.

In his heyday, Edgar Wallace was often perceived as a quintessentially British phenomenon, yet a great part of his success, both during his lifetime and even more after his death, depended on his works' distribution in other national markets, including Europe and the United States. In Germany, Wallace had caught on by the mid-1920s. As in Britain, the Wallace boom in Germany branched out from publishing into theatre and cinema. Max Reinhardt staged *The Ringer* as *Der Hexer* in Berlin in 1926,[5] and between 1927 and 1934, five Wallace novels were adapted for the German screen.[6] After a hiatus during the Nazi period, Wallace again rose to prominence after the war, and experienced a peak in popularity during the 1960s, when Wallace adaptations became the bread and butter of the commercial film industry. As Malte Hagener points out in his contribution to this volume, even today the German film industry holds up the Wallace cycle of the 1960s as a model producers should emulate. As recently as the mid-1990s, a German TV channel commissioned and transmitted a new series of Wallace adaptations.

In order to understand this success, and particularly its longevity, it is necessary to look more generally at the development of the crime genre in Germany, and how Wallace fitted into this context. Detective novels, both in indigenous and foreign variants, in book form or as dime novels, had been published widely in Germany since the turn of the century. British crime fiction, particularly Sir Arthur Conan Doyle's Sherlock Holmes stories, provided the main model for, and influence on, the genre, and German crime authors frequently imitated the style of British novels. German cinema had already adopted the crime film formula in the early 1910s, resulting in serials featuring fictional detective heroes with English names such as 'Stuart Webbs' or 'Joe Deebs'.[7] Sebastian Hesse and Heide Schlüpmann, among others, have argued that these early detective serials were instrumental not only in establishing a commercially powerful symbiosis between the film industry and mass publishing, but also in providing, through their narratives' enlightened rationality, emancipatory fictional alternatives to the repressive class and gender hierarchies of Wilhelmine society.[8] Kracauer suggested in a similar vein that the Germans' 'deep-founded susceptibilities to life abroad enabled them . . . to enjoy the lovely myth of the English detective'.[9]

An English influence, however, was not only evident in what were commonly perceived as lowbrow cultural forms. Indeed, an iconography of crime, as Maria Tatar has documented, became pervasive during the Weimar years, cross-fertilising commercial entertainment and the artistic avant-garde.[10] Central to this iconography was the figure of Jack the Ripper. Bertolt Brecht, for example, refashioned the seventeenth-century London of John Gay's *Beggar's Opera* into the Victorian underworld of *Die Dreigroschenoper*, which was famously adapted for the screen by G. W. Pabst in 1931, and whose anti-hero Mackie Messer (Mack the Knife) was at least in part modelled on Jack the Ripper folklore. Frank Wedekind's stage tragedy *Erdgeist*, filmed in the Weimar period as *Pandora's Box* (1929) by Pabst, featured Jack the Ripper as a lethal avenger of male insecurities, a figure, at least in Pabst's version, that seems to suggest a German masculinity torn apart by the social and psychological legacies of World War one. Jack the Ripper mythology moreover provided the template through which the Weimar period's real-life serial killers (for example, Hanover-based Fritz Haarmann,[11] who dismembered, and drank the blood of his young male victims, or Peter Kürten from Düsseldorf, who killed over thirty-five women and children) were framed and sensationalised in the tabloid press. This discourse in turn resurfaced in the disturbingly ubiquitous, and frequently misogynist, representations of mutilation, murder and sexual aggression in Weimar pictorial art (George Grosz, Otto Dix), as well as in films such as Fritz Lang's *M* (1931), which not only documented the psychopathology of a paedophile killer (given great pathos by Peter Lorre's performance), but also the paranoid public and media response to such individuals.[12]

Compulsive serial criminals can of course be prominently found elsewhere in Weimar cinema, albeit in more fantastical guises: thus films such as *Das Cabinet des Dr Caligari* (*The Cabinet of Dr Caligari*, 1920), *Nosferatu* (1922), or *Dr Mabuse der Spieler* (*Dr Mabuse the Gambler*, 1922) can be seen as both drawing on and subverting the conventions of the detective formula, in that the genre's traditional agents of order are either rendered unreliable, implicated in the crimes, or turn out to be passive and ineffectual bystanders, giving full rein to the urges and drives of pathological criminals. One should be careful not to arrive too quickly (as Kracauer famously did) at neat explanations as to how this diverse array of serial killers, sex crimes and subverted narrative formulae reflects a perceived collective German psychology. Thomas Elsaesser has suggested with regard to the Expressionist classics above that these texts functioned to some extent as highly self-reflexive, and almost proto-post-modernist, commentaries on the formulae and conventions they were using, and should therefore not be seen as an unmediated reflection of Weimar social realities.[13] Similarly one could argue that the popular detective serials of the 1910s and 20s invited a pleasurable recognition less of psychological or social motivations, than of (often internationally circulating) generic attractions, and of familiar visual, performance and narrative codes which were often imported wholesale from British literary conventions. That German audiences were well versed in these codes is evident in the success of numerous crime parodies of the time on stage, and in film and book form, which crucially relied on the audience's generic foreknowledge.

There are a number of reasons why the end of the Weimar crime boom in publishing, theatre and cinema was a direct result of the political takeover by the Nazis. Jewish publishing houses, such as Wallace's German representative Goldmann, found themselves the target of the Nazis' policy of 'Aryanisation'; their Jewish management and owners were disowned and had to flee persecution. Alongside theatre and the film industry, publishing came under the control of Nazi ideological directives. Dime novels were banned, possibly because their circulation was difficult to control.[14] While a number of foreign crime novels continued to be published in Germany at least until the late 1930s, the main priority of publishers now rested with promoting a new nationalist literature. Similarly, crime thrillers became an almost insignificant aspect of German film production after 1933, and where they were made at all, any potentially disturbing social comment was avoided through the format of the crime-comedy (a good example is *Der Mann, der Sherlock Holmes war* [*The Man Who Was Sherlock Holmes*, 1937], which tells the story of two impostors impersonating Holmes and Watson). The Nazis' ideological hostility towards crime fiction is well documented. Acknowledging the fact that crime thrillers continued to be read surreptitiously by a large number of Germans, Nazi academic Erich Thier perceived this situation as 'not without danger',[15] since

the detective novel is a specific product of a bourgeois society in its capitalist, Western and Anglo-Saxon variant. . . . Bourgeois societies are, by their very nature, susceptible to crime . . . They thus differ from other forms of national communities that are based on power and honour, faith and loyalty, labour and achievement . . . The prevalence of the detective novel in Germany is therefore comparable to the invasion of an alien mentality.[16]

Interestingly, Thier offers here a similar argument, albeit from a very different ideological perspective, to Kracauer's 1925 analysis of the genre, namely that the figure of the detective, and the emergence of a crime genre more generally, are dependent on the social context of a liberal democracy, exemplified primarily by Great Britain. Although the United States equally qualifies as a capitalist Anglo-Saxon society, American conventions (e.g. the iconography of the urban, ethnic gangster, disseminated by Hollywood in the early 1930s) appear to have influenced the German understanding of the genre to a lesser extent during this period. Having thus established an explicit connection between Britishness and crime fiction, it is not surprising that one of the few German crime films produced during the war, *Dr Crippen an Bord* (*Dr Crippen On Board*, 1942), was conceived as a vehicle for anti-British propaganda. What is clear, however, and what even Thier's study has to concede rather grudgingly, is that the appeal of crime fiction was and remained widespread even in totalitarian Germany, despite a shortage of supply during the Nazi years, and despite ideological attempts to discredit the genre, and to discourage its distribution.

After 1945 the boom in crime fiction (though initially not in crime film genres) resumed in West Germany, and the number of crime novels in circulation rose rapidly throughout the 1950s.[17] By the mid-1950s, Edgar Wallace had become once again one of the most widely read and distributed novelists in Germany. Goldmann resumed its pre-war promotional strategies by re-issuing Wallace novels in paperback, in its series 'Rote Krimis' (Red Crime Thrillers). Series such as the Rote Krimis helped re-integrate popular literature within a framework of consumer culture, and Goldmann's aggressive, and unashamedly populist, marketing was chiefly responsible for the renewed crime boom in the 1950s. It attracted not only readers already familiar with Wallace from the 1920s, but also, and perhaps more importantly, a younger generation. As an easily available and inexpensive consumer product, the Rote Krimis were not only a sign of increased consumer choice, but more generally they provided confirmation of West Germany's new confidence and worldliness.

Robin Smyth has suggested some of the reasons why Wallace increasingly fell out of favour with post-war British tastes, and why he could appeal in particular to non-British readers:

> what is chiefly disappointing on rereading the books is that there is so little authentic London atmosphere. . . . Perhaps that is one reason why he comes over better in translation where readers are less exacting about such details . . . Despite the obvious efforts to be modern his plots are comfortably old-fashioned and Gothic and steeped in wish-fulfilment.[18]

Wallace's nostalgia for the past (from a German perspective, significantly, a pre-Nazi past), his disregard for authenticity and his eagerly proclaimed modernity certainly fitted existing patterns of cultural production and reception in Germany. It was precisely the duality of tradition and social progress (seen in contrast to the stagnation of social achievements in Germany) with which German Wallace readers had connected in the 1920s, and which finds an echo in Kracauer's previously noted pronouncements about the Germans' 'deep-founded susceptibilities' for the 'highly civilised Anglo-Saxons'. It was the same susceptibilities that Nazi ideologues worried about and tried to suppress. By the 1950s, however, West Germany was promoting a new sense of a national as cosmopolitan (i.e. European) identity, and of the country's normality vis-à-vis other nations as a *bona fide* social democracy. In this context, Wallace came to epitomise the 'classic crime novelist', as the guarantor of essentially nostalgic pleasures. His public persona (circulated through book cover photographs of the author in wide-brimmed hat, and with a long cigarette holder) was marketed in Germany as quintessential 'Englishness'. However, this notion of Englishness did not carry the same associations of longing for social progress as it had before the war, but was redefined in line with West Germany's new sense of self-worth.

Despite the popularity of classic crime fiction in the 1950s, the West German film industry rarely ventured into this genre until late in the decade. In the early post-war years, there had been a number of attempts to revive the format, including *Mordprozess Dr Jordan* (*The Murder Trial of Dr Jordan*, 1949), *Epilog – Das Geheimnis der Orplid* (*Epilogue – The Orplid Mystery,* 1949), *Fünf unter Verdacht* (*Five Suspects*, 1949), or *Der Fall Rabanser* (*The Rabanser Case*, 1950), but these films remained exceptions among indigenous productions increasingly dominated by the *Heimatfilm*. For a return to Weimar's obsession with sex crimes and serial killers one has to look even harder in the cinematic output of the 1950s: both Peter Lorre's *Der Verlorene* (*The Lost One*, 1951) and Robert Siodmak's *Nachts wenn der Teufel kam* (*At Night When the Devil Came,* 1957) featured serial killers, and indeed reminded contemporary critics of Lang's *M*. This reminder, however, may have proved too uncomfortable, not least because both films suggested analogies between their pathological protagonists and the collectively condoned or perpetrated crimes of the Nazi period. They thus explicitly challenged West Germany's ideology of a political 'zero hour', of a national reinvention after 1945. While Siodmak's film at least found some critical acclaim, former *M* star Lorre's only directorial effort, a stylish and melancholy film set in a bleak post-war German wasteland, was almost completely ignored. The only other German serial-killer film of any impact was *Es geschah am hellichten Tag* (*It Happened in Broad Daylight*, 1959), directed, like the other two examples, by a returning émigré, Ladislao Vajda.

West German television, by contrast, discovered the police and detective format early on, one of the most successful series in the 1950s being *Stahlnetz* (*Net of Steel*), which focused on the daily routine of an urban police precinct. Indeed, over the next decades the German crime genre, and particularly its variant the cop show, would increasingly find its central outlet on television.[19] The lack of indigenous crime films in the 1950s is all the more surprising in view of the fact that foreign crime films were regularly shown on West German screens, and with great success. Under the headline 'Is the German crime film dead?' one newspaper reported that

> a great many foreign crime films have appeared in German cinemas . . . In the English examples, good old Scotland Yard has made a welcome reappearance. In recent years these foreign films have attracted an increasing number of admirers.[20]

The apparent appeal of 'good old Scotland Yard', the success of crime films on television, and changing cinema audience demographics by the late 1950s, made Edgar Wallace and his reassuringly generic and foreign (rather than socially realist and German-centred) understanding of crime an obvious choice for the German film industry. In 1959 Danish producer Preben Phillipsen's company Rialto ventured into the genre once again, having secured a deal to make Wallace films for the German market.

Rialto's first two Wallace films, *Der Frosch mit der Maske/Frøen* (*The Masked Frog*, 1959) and *Der rote*

Kreis/Den blodrøde cirkel (*The Crimson Circle*, 1960), were nominally Danish-German co-productions, shot largely in Danish studios, with an almost exclusively German cast and crew. After the success of the first two films, Phillipsen relocated his production base, first to Hamburg (where *Die Bande des Schreckens* [*The Terrible People*, 1960] and *Der grüne Bogenschütze* [*The Green Archer*, 1960] were shot), and then to Berlin. Many of the Wallace films, particularly in the early and mid-1960s were among the top-grossing films in Germany.[21] Between 1959 and 1972 Rialto produced thirty-two Wallace films. *Das Rätsel des silbernen Halbmonds* (*The Mystery of the Silver Crescent*, 1971) was the last in the series released theatrically in Germany, after which the series' back catalogue was sold off to television, where the Rialto films are constantly repeated even today.

While the Wallace series, unlike the detective serials of the 1910s and 20s, never had one consistent main hero, there were nevertheless a number of continuities. Almost all the crimes depicted in the series had financial motives, and were frequently linked to internecine family feuds over inheritance matters. These feuds were fought out in labyrinthine settings, such as country mansions with hidden doors, mazes, or traps, or subterranean hideouts in London's underworld, all of which could equally have featured as backdrops for the detective serials of the 1910s. The British netherworlds of the German Wallace films were inhabited respectively by crude stereotypes of the British working and upper classes (the latter portrayed with their tongues firmly in cheek by a gallery of eminent German stage actors, including Elisabeth Flickenschildt, Charles Regnier and Wolfgang Kieling), whereas modernity was invariably associated with a white-collar middle class, embodied by an efficient, upwardly mobile and morally unambiguous young Scotland Yard detective. The use of such stereotypes is revealing in what it can tell us about German perceptions of Britishness at the time and what the appeal of this imagined Britishness may have been. It displays a great deal of incomprehension of the real dynamics of the British class system, but it also points to a preferred version of Britishness which cherishes its most idiosyncratic, irreverent and non-conformist qualities, exemplified by the films' roll-call of eccentric aristocrats, dotty old ladies and Dickensian rogues.

In terms of narrative conventions, methodical crime detection played a subordinate, almost irrelevant part in the Wallace series. The films specialised in convoluted subplots, while the final uncovering of the criminal mastermind seemed to happen by mere coincidence. Many films ended abruptly without providing sufficient explanations or motivations. While the basic narrative set-up of the series rarely changed, differentiation manifested itself in increasingly bizarre villains and murder methods. Victims harpooned by killers in diving suits, drug-peddling nuns and homicidal gorillas (a nod less to Wallace than to Edgar Allan Poe's *The Murders of The Rue Morgue*) were among the more surreal inventions of the series. Perhaps the most iconic presence of the cycle, however, was the actor Klaus Kinski in his pre-Herzog incarnation, whose manic portrayals of deranged characters provided a virtually unique reinvention of Weimar performance style in post-war German cinema, and who articulated the otherwise repressed legacy of Peter Lorre's child killer, Conrad Veidt's somnambulist and Haarmann's real-life vampire. As if to underline their referentiality to, and reverence for, the Weimar period, the Wallace films also frequently featured veteran stars such as Lil Dagover and Fritz Rasp.

In critical writing on the genre, the predominant strategy to explain the German Wallace phenomenon has been the recourse to post-war Germany's political landscape, and its textual manifestations in the films themselves. Jack Edmund Nolan, one of the first Anglophone critics to take note of the Wallace film series in 1963, commented that 'the Wallace films evidently displace the tensions in a country which has only a wall between it and the People's police'.[22] Nolan saw the Wallace films promoting

> the socially dangerous idea that successful enterprises are conducted by likeable master criminals who can be stopped only by other criminals. And running through them is a faint tone of anti-Americanism and a heavier rumble of anti-British feeling.[23]

While Nolan does not expand on what exactly constitutes anti-Americanism and anti-British feelings in the Wallace

Echoes of Weimar cinema in *Der rote Kreis* (1960)

films, his Kracauer-inspired link between narrative patterns and national history has nevertheless stuck. Robin Smyth, writing on the German Wallace phenomenon in *The Observer* in 1982, equally concluded: 'Why has Germany kept the Edgar Wallace flame alive? Probably because Germany is, as it evermore insistently proclaims, an Angst-ridden society.'[24]

Other critics have offered different analogies between the Wallace films and their perceived national and social context. Norbert Grob has interpreted the films as expressing the conservative political consensus of the early to mid-1960s, an evaluation shared by other German film critics.[25] In Grob's reading, which is diametrically opposed to Nolan's perception of 'likeable master criminals', the violence with which the forces of law and order in the Wallace films dispatch their criminal adversaries anticipates and mirrors the repressive actions by the state authorities against non-conformist elements in German society by the end of the decade.

Apart from the reductive perception of cinema audiences such reflectionist approaches entail, what is equally problematic is the way in which narrative (defined almost exclusively in terms of plot and character development) is prioritised over the genre's visual characteristics, its *mise-*

Klaus Kinski

en-scène, the formal traditions it draws on, and its actual mode of circulation and reception. Tassilo Schneider has rightly suggested that 'the key to an understanding of the popular German cinema after World War II is not to be found in sociological content analysis'.[26] For Schneider, popular genres such as the Wallace series provided 'imaginary solutions to ideological contradictions',[27] and he argues that

> the moving in and out of popularity of particular genres, and the displacement of one genre by others at particular points in history, can give access to changes in the terms through which audiences related to and understood the social relations and positions that structured the environment in which they found themselves.[28]

Unlike Nolan, Smyth and Grob, Schneider sees the Wallace films as the cultural product of a society precisely not characterised by consensus or homogeneity, but instead by social tensions and conflicting ideological discourses. Like Nolan, Smyth and Grob, however, Schneider locates the interaction between the genre and its social context primarily at the level of plot and character development. Thus, the series' 'ruthless speculators, power- and money-hungry entrepreneurs, and corrupt officials' represent for Schneider the conflict in 1960s German society between a new economic elite and a disenfranchised underclass, while the cycle's 'sexually aggressive, revengeful and greedy female protagonists' are seen to reflect fraught gender relations, and more specifically, German women's uncertain position in the 1960s between 'liberation and instrumentalisation'.[29] In such characterisations, the Wallace films enact for Schneider 'a concerted return of the repressed',[30] resulting in 'violent but helpless expressions of paranoia'.[31]

It is important to note that Schneider's analysis is couched in an explicit comparison between the Wallace series and American film noir. One may wonder, however, how productive this link is. As for the Wallace films' *mise-en-scène* and cinematography, one can certainly identify continuities not just from film noir, but perhaps more directly from Weimar cinema. The well-known devices of chiaroscuro lighting, angled compositions, emblematic sets, and stylised performances are all frequently employed in the Wallace films (which may be due, at least in part, to a continuity of studio personnel and production practices from the late 1920s to the 60s).

What is striking about Schneider's reading, however, is the complete absence in his discussion of the series' endemically self-reflexive, parodic, or comic elements and

Eddi Arent (right) in *Der rote Kreis* (1960)

characters which were frequently foregrounded in contemporary German reviews, and which constituted a significant appeal of the series. Foremost among these elements were the clownish antics of comedian Eddi Arent, who, as a regular supporting actor in the series, provided the farcical counterpoint to Kinski's demonic characters. Commenting on the films' eclectic blend of horror, crime and comedy, German critic Joe Hembus said that the series 'presented itself with a certain self-ironic pride as if it had succeeded in growing bananas in a Prussian allotment'.[32] Like film noir, the Wallace films featured narratives that bordered on incomprehensibility, but unlike film noir, this incomprehensibility was not motivated by protagonists' mental or social disorientation, or disempowerment. Unlike film noir, with its fatalism, its relentless narrative drive towards a predetermined ending, and consistently pessimistic outlook, the Wallace films were the cinematic equivalent of a 'House of Horrors' theme-park ride. As in the silent 'cinema of attractions', and more specifically, as in early German cinema's detective serials, generic conventions and

character stereotypes were blatantly foregrounded, with only minimal investment in psychological realism or cause-and-effect chains to drive the narratives. Sabine Hake has more recently argued that 'the performative and representational excess and the ironic self-awareness in the Edgar Wallace films have contributed to their enduring status as (postmodern) cult movies.'[33]

For German audiences in the 1960s, I would suggest, the Wallace series articulated a very particular and, despite the films' frequently macabre narrative content, pleasurable fantasy about England and London, a fantasy grounded both in established generic expectations (which in some cases reach back to, as I have argued, as early as the 1910s), and in the interrelationship with other forms of cultural consumption. The Wallace cycle envisaged Britain as a site of distraction, escape, and adventure – to the point where location and settings became one of the series' main attractions. It constructed a topography of Britain, and more specifically of London, which fragmented urban space into distinct units, such as a gothic underworld, famous tourist landmarks (Big Ben, the Tower, Tower Bridge), as well as more contemporary and seedy attractions (such as Soho strip clubs, which, like many other ingredients of the German Wallace cycle, do not feature in the original novels). These fragmented attractions found their aural equivalent in the films' psychedelic soundtracks, liberally plundering any conceivable international musical style, from weirdly overdubbed mambos to rock'n'roll and Stockhausen. In this respect, the Wallace films created visual and aural hierarchies and dichotomies between a 'hip' and attractively modern metropolis ('swinging London'), and a dark British netherworld which was locked in a distant past, exemplified alternately by a Jack-the-Ripper East End, or by gothic mansions of the 'haunted house' variety. How much this particular topography solidified into a distinctive imaginary space can be gauged from the fact that the very few films in the series which were actually shot on real locations in Britain were perversely rejected by German audiences for their 'inauthenticity', i.e. for their deviation from the genre's established visual codes and (largely fake) settings.[34]

The cultural imagination shared by the films and their audiences was characterised simultaneously by an obsession with a more distant past and by a forward-looking attitude, a strange form of 'progressive nostalgia' which bracketed the white spot of an absent present and recent past. I would argue that this skewed temporality may well explain the phenomenal success of these cultural forms. The Wallace series was able to provide distractive pleasures at least in part because its historical and cultural reference point was a period untainted by German national guilt, and more generally, by memories of the Second World War. Twenty years after the German bombing of London, and the destruction of German cities by the RAF, the Wallace cycle promoted less, as Nolan assumed, anti-British feelings, than a new, if rather forced, normality in international relations, which drew equally on pre-war cultural interactions, and on the changing socio-political landscape of post-war Europe. The simultaneously modern and quaintly old-fashioned Britain the Wallace cycle portrayed was reassuringly a place in which the Second World War had never happened. As the failure of crime films with a more recognisably German setting in this period suggests, it was the imaginary as well as codified space of the Wallace films which provided its audiences a temporary and pleasurable escape from the constrictions of a troublesome and often repressed national identity through the processes of impersonating, and identifying with, a largely fictitious cultural other. The series' eagerly proclaimed cosmopolitanism, and its fantasy Britain created in German

studios inhabited by German actors masquerading as British characters, transformed national identity into a generically coded commodity. In other words, the Wallace cycle both disavowed its contemporary national context, yet reified it within the parameters of an internationally proliferating consumer culture.

That the pleasures of the 'Anglophile' German crime film thus depended ultimately less on a reflection or consolidation of a real or stable national referent (whether German or British), but precisely on its loss, diffusion and generic reinvention, was noticed even abroad. Puzzled by a German cinema which mostly bypassed German contemporary reality altogether (other examples include the popular Karl May Westerns, shot in Yugoslavia as a surrogate nineteenth-century Arizona, and featuring multinational casts), the British journal *Films and Filming* commented on Germany's genre patterns in the 1960s:

> West German filmmakers are almost succeeding . . . in destroying German nationalism. So far as many of them are concerned these days, no such race seems to exist.[35]

Notes

1 Siegfried Kracauer, 'Der Detektivroman. Ein philosophischer Traktat, 1922–1925', reprinted in Kracauer, *Schriften 1*, (Frankfurt: suhrkamp, 1971), pp. 103–04. Trans. by Erica Carter.

2 Siegfried Kracauer, *From Caligari to Hitler: A Psychological History of the German Film* (Princeton, NJ: Princeton University Press, 1947).

3 Ibid., pp. 20–21.

4 Margaret Lane, *Edgar Wallace. The Biography of a Phenomenon* (London: Hamish Hamilton, 1938). See also Jens-Peter Becker, *Sherlock Holmes und Co. Essays zur englischen und amerikanischen Detektivliteratur* (Munich: Goldmann, 1975), pp. 15–27.

5 Robin Smyth, 'Wurst Wallace', in *The Observer*, 14 February 1982.

6 For a complete list of Wallace adaptations, see Florian Pauer, *Die Edgar Wallace Filme* (Munich: Goldmann, 1982).

7 See e.g. Karen Pehla, 'Joe May und seine Detektive. Der Serienfilm als Kinoerlebnis', in Hans-Michael Bock and Claudia Lenssen (eds.), *Joe May. Regisseur und Produzent* (Munich: edition text+kritik, 1991), pp. 61–73; Tilo Knops, 'Cinema from the Writing Desk: Detective Film in Imperial Germany', in Thomas Elsaesser and Michael Wedel (eds.), *A Second Life: German Cinema's First Decades*

(Amsterdam: Amsterdam University Press, 1996), pp. 132–42; Sebastian Hesse, 'Kult der Aufklärung. Zur Attraktion der Detektivfilm-Serien im frühen deutschen Kino (1908–1918)', in Corinna Müller and Harro Segeberg (eds.), *Die Modellierung des Kinofilms* (Munich: Wilhelm Fink, 1998), pp. 125–53.

8 Hesse, op. cit., pp. 127–9. For a similar argument on the emancipatory qualities of early German genre cinema, see also Heide Schlüpmann, *Die Unheimlichkeit des Blicks. Das Drama des frühen deutschen Kinos* (Basel and Frankfurt-am-Main: Stroemfeld/Roter Stern, 1990); Robert J. Kiss, *The Doppelgänger in Wilhelmine Cinema (1895–1914): Modernity, Audiences and Identity in Turn-of-the-Century Germany*, unpublished PhD thesis, University of Warwick, 2000; and the contribution by Frank Kessler and Eva Warth in this volume.

9 Kracauer, *From Caligari to Hitler*, p. 20.

10 Maria Tatar, *Lustmord. Sexual Murder in Weimar Germany* (Princeton, NJ: Princeton University Press, 1995).

11 Haarmann's story has been filmed twice in recent decades: Ulli Lommel's *Die Zärtlichkeit der Wölfe* (*The Tenderness of Wolves*, 1973) and Romuald Karmakar's *Der Totmacher* (*Deathmaker*, 1995).

12 Anton Kaes, *M* (London: BFI Film Classics, 2000).

13 Thomas Elsaesser, 'Social Mobility and the Fantastic: German Silent Cinema', in James Donald (ed.), *Fantasy and the Cinema* (London: BFI, 1989), pp. 23–38; see also his *Weimar Cinema and After Germany's Historical Imaginary* (London and New York: Routledge, 2000).

14 Peter Nusser, *Der Kriminalroman* (Stuttgart: Metzler, 1980), p. 118.

15 Erich Thier, 'Über den Detektivroman', 1940, reprinted in Jochen Vogt (ed.), *Der Kriminalroman. Band II* (Munich: Wilhelm Fink, 1971), p. 483.

16 Ibid., pp. 484–5.

17 Nusser, op. cit., p. 9.

18 Smyth, op. cit.

19 Over the decades, highly popular series such as *Der Kommissar* (*The Inspector*), *Derrick*, *Tatort* (*Scene of the Crime*) and *Der Alte* (*The Old One*) have consolidated the format as one of the most enduring mainstays of German television programming up to this day. It is worth noting that what crucially distinguishes these formats from the English-influenced detective and crime films is not only their resolutely national (and in many cases explicitly regional) setting, but also their shift in emphasis from a fantasy about the foreign to a fantasy of class, gender and age. The *Tatort* series in particular works with clearly iden-tifiable German locations (shot in gritty realism), the use of local dialects, often proletarian tough heroes and narratives that touch on sensitive social issues. Series such as *Derrick* and *Der Alte*, on the other hand, are morality plays invari-ably set in nouveau riche suburban environments, rife with deceptive social appearances, and generational and gender conflicts.

20 Ralph G. Bender, 'Ist der deutsche Kriminalfilm tot?', in *Westfälische Rundschau*, 30 January 1960.

21 Joseph Garncarz, 'Hollywood in Germany. The Role of American Films in Germany', in David Ellwood and Rob Kroes (eds.), *Hollywood in Europe. Experiences of a Cultural Hegemony* (Amsterdam: VU University Press, 1994), pp. 126–7.

22 Jack Edmund Nolan, 'West Germany's Edgar Wallace Wave', in *Films in Review*, vol. xiv, part 6, 1963, p. 378.

23 Ibid., p. 379.

24 Smyth, op. cit.

25 Norbert Grob, 'Das Geheimnis der toten Augen. 13 Aspekte zum deutschen Kriminalfilm der sechziger Jahre', in Hans-Peter Reimann, Rudolf Worschech (eds.), *Abschied von Gestern: Bundesdeutscher Film der sechziger und siebziger Jahre* (Frankfurt: Deutsches Filmmuseum, 1991), pp. 72–97. See also: Georg Seeßlen, 'Edgar Wallace. Made in Germany', in *epd film*, vol. 6, June 1986, pp. 31–5.

26 Tassilo Schneider, 'Somewhere Else: The Popular German Cinema of the 1960s', in *Yearbook of Comparative and General Literature*, no. 40 (Indiana: Indiana University Press, 1992), pp. 81–2.

27 Tassilo Schneider, 'Finding a New *Heimat* in the Wild West: Karl May and the German Western of the 1960s', in Edward Buscombe and Roberta E. Pearson (eds.), *Back in the Saddle Again: New Essays on the Western* (London: BFI, 1998), p. 157.

28 Ibid., p. 153.

29 Ibid., pp. 153–4.

30 Ibid., p. 153.

31 Ibid., p. 155.

32 Robert Fischer and Joe Hembus, *Der neue deutsche Film 1960–1980* (Munich: Goldmann, 1981), p. 196.

33 Sabine Hake, *German National Cinema* (London and New York: Routledge, 2002), p. 153.

34 Equally unsuccessful were those Edgar Wallace B-film pro-ductions that were made at around the same time by the British Merton Park studios, only a handful of which were distributed in Germany.

35 Robin Bean, 'Sex, Guns and May', in *Films and Filming*, vol. 11, part 6, 1965, p. 52.

4

Queer Traditions in German Cinema

Robert J. Kiss

This contribution aims to outline a brief history of 'queer' – that is to say, of narratives, characters and enigmatic moments that have challenged, confronted and confounded the str(i/u)ctures of heteronormativity – across all periods of German cinema. This overview does not seek to be exhaustive, but rather is intended to highlight a range of significant queer traditions in German film.

Central to this survey is a focus on three distinct paradigmatic modes of thinking queer that have informed German cinema in distinct ways at different times: as will be shown, each has asserted itself most when it has been able to intersect with public sexual sub-cultures. The first paradigm is that of 'sexual intermediacy', a concept deriving from nineteenth-century sexology, which posits the existence of a third sex (comprising and conflating androgynes, hermaphrodites, homosexuals, transsexuals and transvestites) between male and female gender, and informs the majority of films produced before the 1960s. Second, the notion of queer sexualities as 'unheimlich' (or 'uncanny') resonates especially through numerous so-called Weimar Expressionist works. Third, there is the category of 'schwul': a pejorative term reclaimed by gays in post-1968 identity politics, which nevertheless – as various New German films testify – accommodates a considerable degree of slippage into other queer realms.

As well as attempting to showcase the rich history of queer in German cinema, I seek briefly to highlight how various German film-makers since the 1970s have consciously referenced and synthesised elements from the above three distinct(ive) paradigms, thus acknowledging, celebrating and canonising these as a particular heritage of German 'queer traditions'.

Interrupting gender binaries: sexual intermediacy on the Wilhelmine and Weimar screen

Researchers of gay and lesbian film have long venerated *Anders als die Andern* (*Different from the Others*), a successful *Aufklärungsfilm* (sexual enlightenment film) produced when censorship was briefly suspended in 1919–20, as the first work of cinema in which homosexuality is placed 'centrally, unambiguously and positively'.[1] Directed by Richard Oswald, *Anders als die Andern* was co-scripted by and featured Berlin sexologist Dr Magnus Hirschfeld. Like the emancipatory organisation he founded in 1897, the *Wissenschaftlich-humanitäres Komitee* (Scientific-Humanitarian Committee), the film sought to present homosexuality as a natural phenomenon rather than an illness, and thus to counter hostile social attitudes in general, and more specifically, Paragraph 175 of the German penal code, which punished with up to five years' imprisonment 'unnatural sexual acts between persons of the male sex'.[2]

Anders als die Andern focuses on violin virtuoso Paul Körner (Conrad Veidt), whose romance with his pupil Kurt (Fritz Schulz) is cut tragically short by Franz (Reinhold Schünzel), a blackmailer who ensnares homosexuals with threats of exposure under Paragraph 175. Franz duly exposes Paul, leading to the latter's imprisonment, loss of all offers of employment following his release, and ultimately his suicide. Prior to this, lengthy flashbacks detail other episodes of Paul's social exclusion. The film stresses throughout that Paul represents but one of innumerable innocents whose nature cannot be altered, and whose chances of happiness and fulfilment are extinguished solely by 'uninformed' social attitudes and the effects of Paragraph 175.

Reinhold Schünzel and Conrad Veidt in *Anders als die Andern* (1919)

However, as Richard Dyer and Alice Kuzniar have observed, several central sequences of *Anders als die Andern* cannot be adequately contained within or explained by the category of 'homosexuality', and point instead to other queer sexualities.[3] For example, Paul first encounters the blackmailing Franz at a transvestite ball, where we see men in dresses and make-up and women in suits – in which context it is worth noting that one of the film's performers is the lesbian dancer Anita Berber, a mainstay of Weimar nightlife who first popularised the cross-dressed tuxedo and monocle look that would later become associated with Marlene Dietrich. Meanwhile, in a fantasy sequence (missing from extant prints), a sword bearing the legend '§175' is shown hanging over vast columns of male, female and androgynous figures – even though the law pertained only to male homosexuals.

Returning to contemporary sources, it becomes evident that these representations are bound up in the paradigm of 'sexual intermediacy' ('*sexuelle Zwischenstufen*'), which maintained the existence of a third sex 'between' men and women. This intermediate category had originated (in print at least) in the work of nineteenth-century theorists such as Johann Ludwig Caspar and Karl Heinrich Ulrichs, who suggested that male and female attributes were present in random distribution in all human beings, and that while in most cases one set of attributes predominated – facilitating the fixing of male or female gender – there also existed numerous individuals in whom the blend (whether physical, psychological or behavioural) was more ambiguous, resulting in their 'in-between-ist' status as members of a third sex. By the beginning of the twentieth century, these ideas enjoyed wide currency not only in medico-scientific circles, but also in both popular and sub-cultural discourse, so that many German homosexuals, transvestites, androgynes and other queer types now readily identified – and were likewise popularly referred to – as 'sexual intermediates'.

This increased currency was in no small part due to the publicising efforts of Hirschfeld and his *Wissenschaftlich-humanitäres Komitee*, whose first campaign pamphlet, *Was soll das Volk vom dritten Geschlecht wissen?* (*What Should the People Know of the Third Sex?*), sold some 30,000 copies between 1902 and 1904 alone, and whose quarterly journal, published from 1899 to 1923, bore the telling title *Jahrbuch für sexuelle Zwischenstufen* (*Yearbook for Sexual Intermediates*).[4] As in *Anders als die Andern*, Hirschfeld's demands for the abrogation of Paragraph 175 were throughout couched within a broader debate about sexual intermediacy that presented homosexuality as merely one of a panoply of possible articulations of third-sex identity.

Considering Wilhelmine and Weimar cinema in terms of 'sexual intermediate' rather than specifically 'gay and lesbian' representation yields numerous examples of films which, as Kuzniar has concluded, 'at the very least … seem to say that single-gendered identity and single-vectored desire are restrictive and inhibiting'.[5] For example, in the comedy one-reeler *Aus eines Mannes Mädchenzeit* (*From a Man's Time as a Girl*, 1913), Wilhelm Bendow stars as an effeminate youth who gains employment in women's clothing as a cook. The film confounds stable gender (and sexual) identities at every turn. As a 'man', Bendow minces and pouts while running his hands over his chest to signify 'feminine' curves. As a 'woman', he adopts the phallic epithet Lydia Bratwurst ('Lydia Fried-Sausage') and indulges in male-coded behaviour such as taking snuff. During his transformation from male to female garb, Bendow holds up and derides each item of attire – from a man's starched dickey to a woman's brassiere – as simply a bizarre fashion creation rather than an intrinsic marker of gender. Furthermore, the romantic advances made towards Lydia by 'her' businessman employer (Rudolf Senius) – which, significantly, 'she' does little to resist – are at once heterosexual in motivation and outward appearance, yet homosexual in terms of reception and audience knowledge. Similarly, Lydia's deep kisses with a maid – who grows disgusted only upon discovering that Lydia is a man (!) – constitute a challenging amalgam of hetero- and homo-paradoxes.

There need be little doubt that works like *Aus eines Mannes Mädchenzeit* were open to (and indeed invited) sexual intermediate readings. For one thing, the Berlin head-censor Karl Brunner informed Kurt Tucholsky in 1913 that he objected to the evident 'basis in perversity' of such cross-dressing comedies.[6] In the case of *Aus eines Mannes Mädchenzeit* in particular, its star Wilhelm Bendow already enjoyed substantial appeal as a performer in Berlin nightclubs and theatres with a largely 'sexual intermediate' clientele – the sorts of locale familiar from the writings of Christopher Isherwood.[7] Meanwhile, the film's title was a play on that of a widely read sexual intermediate autobiography, *Aus eines Mannes Mädchenjahren* (*From a Man's Girlhood Years*), which contained an afterword by Hirschfeld. This narrative of a pseudo-hermaphrodite would itself go on to be filmed as an *Aufklärungsfilm* during the censor-free period at the beginning of the Weimar Republic, advertised with promises of 'splendid scenes that capture the full tragedy of sexual intermediacy'.[8]

The existence of a Berlin 'scene' did not escape general attention, and consequently, sexual intermediate imagery 'queers' numerous mainstream books and films, as a signifier of the modern metropolis. In the detective comedy *Wo ist Colleti?* (*Where is Colleti?*, 1913), for example, we see that the audience at the Kammerlichtspiele cinema on Potsdamerplatz is composed almost entirely of men in dresses; in *Nächte der Weltstadt* (*Cosmopolitan Nights*, 1926), androgynously attired women dance together; and in Fritz Lang's *Dr Mabuse, der Spieler* (*Dr Mabuse the Gambler*, 1922) and *Das Testament des Dr Mabuse* (*The Testament of Dr Mabuse*, 1933), cross-dressed men and women serve as shorthand for a decadent urban milieu. Recent restorations of Lang's *Metropolis* (1927) likewise include twenty precious frames showing (in close-up) a woman in top hat and tails, staring lustfully at the semi-naked dance of the 'false' Maria in the Yoshiwara nightclub – thereby (re)queering a sequence that has traditionally been discussed in terms of heterosexual male scopophilia.

The *Hosenrolle*, or narrative of a woman who assumes male attire, is of course another celebrated trope of Wilhelmine and Weimar cinema, stretching from Asta Nielsen in *Jugend und Tollheit* (*Youth and Folly*, 1912) through to Ossi Oswalda in *Ich möchte kein Mann sein* (*I Don't Want to Be a Man*, 1919), and on to arguably the most extreme gender b(l)ender of them all, Reinhold Schünzel's *Viktor und Viktoria* (*Victor and Victoria*), in which Renate Müller plays a woman who takes on the identity of a (male) female impersonator. As Dyer and Kuzniar have demonstrated, these works are rich with allusions to sexual intermediacy, and engage in playful deconstructions of gender and sexuality wherein ostensibly heterosexual male characters (and audience members?) find themselves attracted towards other visually male figures.[9] At the same time, as Daniela Sobek observes, the coded actions and behaviours in these films open up performative spaces 'affording women spectators … possibilities for identification on the path to lesbian self-discovery'.[10] With their images of women moving in traditionally male spheres, these films can be seen also to engage with the contemporary women's movement, in which regard it is interesting to note that many commentators considered the perceived masculinisation of new women to have rendered them also members of a third sex – an argument put forward in perhaps its most unadulterated form in Ernst von Wolzogen's 1900 novel *Das dritte Geschlecht* (*The Third Sex*).[11]

It is profitable to consider Leontine Sagan's *Mädchen in Uniform* (*Girls in Uniform*, 1931), traditionally regarded as the foundation stone of lesbian film-making in Germany, from this viewpoint also, since contemporary critical reception was directed both at its portrayal of the awakening same-sex feelings between Manuela (Hertha Thiele) and her boarding-school mistress Fräulein von Bernburg (Dorothea Wieck), *and* at the film's perceived feminism – the fact that it was directed by a woman and focused on the experiences and psychology of female central characters. Here too, homosexuality is fixed within the third sex paradigm, as Manuela's declaration of love comes only after she performs a *Hosenrolle* in her school play. While lesbianism, unlike male homosexuality, was not specifically legislated against – because it was feared that such a posture might give credence to the notion that women had sexual desires[12] – lesbians nevertheless regularly faced social exclusion and conservative vitriol. The absence of a legal framework against which to battle is, however, of significance for *Mädchen in Uniform*: for unlike *Anders als die Andern*, the film is not beholden to any expository *Aufklärungsfilm* agenda, but can instead undertake a naturalistic representation of burgeoning romance, leading to Manuela and von Bernburg's tender(ly photographed) kisses amid warmly lit sets.[13]

Hermann Thimig and Renate Müller in *Viktor und Viktoria* (1933)

Uncanny sexuality and 'The Closet of Dr Caligari'

While the above works represented sexual intermediacy relatively directly, other Wilhelmine and Weimar films – and in particular numerous of the so-called 'Expressionist masterpieces' – can be seen to have allegorised the ambivalent social construction of queer sexualities within the realm of the *unheimlich* (uncanny), as monstrous but beautiful 'othernesses' that interrupt hegemonic constructions of normality. Without wishing to invoke a knee-jerk *auteurism*, it is nevertheless striking that many of these works were directed by or starred people who lived outside the heterosexual, or who otherwise had connections – like Conrad Veidt and Richard Oswald – to overtly sexual intermediate films. This implies some degree of contemporary awareness or perception of parallels between the social exclusion and pathologisation of these narratives' fantastic monsters and those living queer sexualities.

Substantial evidence can be located in primary sources on sexual intermediacy to support such a viewpoint. For example, several anonymous donors to Hirschfeld's *Wissenschaftlich-humanitäres Komitee* during its first year of campaigning signed themselves 'Dorian Gray',[14] thereby allying themselves to what Harry Benshoff has subsequently termed 'the quintessential imagery of the monster queer – that of a sexually active and attractive young man who possesses some terrible secret which must perforce be locked away in a hidden closet'. As Benshoff continues, it is consequently unsurprising that the poster (the film itself is lost) to *Das Bildnis des Dorian Gray* (*The Picture of Dorian Gray*, 1917) – scripted and directed by Richard Oswald – depicts Dorian as an effeminate fop with his hands on his hips, who sports both make-up and jewellery, and thereby references the 'sexual intermediate' category.[15]

Similarly, Richard Dyer has pointed to a preponderance of vampire fiction and imagery in the 'male culture' (i.e. gay) magazine *Der Eigene* between 1896 and 1931 – dwelling on not altogether unwilling male 'victims' of vampire counts and the male–male contact that vampire 'attacks' facilitate – that might be referred to in situating comparable imagery in *Nosferatu* (1922), directed by Friedrich Wilhelm Murnau.[16] The gay Murnau and his partner Hans Ehrenbaum-Degele were indeed subscribers to *Der Eigene*, and it has been suggested that Murnau may well have anonymously authored certain of these homoerotic eulogies to young men 'with beautiful throats', prototypes of *Nosferatu*'s Hutter (Gustav von Wangenheim) at the mercy of Count Orlok (Max Schreck).[17]

Kuzniar, meanwhile, has highlighted various queer aspects of *Das Cabinet des Dr Caligari* (*The Cabinet of Dr Caligari*, 1920) relating to the figure of Cesare, who resides literally in a closet, and is played by Conrad Veidt just a couple of months after his starring role in *Anders als die Andern*. Drawing on Richard Murphy's assessment of Cesare's appearance and position within the narrative as 'simultaneously passive and active, innocent and evil, and peculiarly androgynous', Kuzniar suggests that his character may be read as an approximation of the social construction of sexual intermediates at this time: a powerful yet conflictual paradox whose unintelligibility within and challenging of normative systems leads simultaneously to denial and over-representation, exclusion and empowerment.[18] Thomas Elsaesser also suggests that *Caligari* may be seen as a fantastic representation of the enforced lifestyle of sexual intermediates – living unsuspected by day as esteemed members of society, while leaving their closets at night as third sex 'monsters'. In particular, Elsaesser cites a comment made by American screenwriter Anita Loos about her 1927 visit to Berlin: 'Any Berlin lady of the evening might turn out to be a man; the prettiest girl on the street was Conrad Veidt.' From here, Elsaesser ironically concludes: '*Caligari*, Anita Loos might have added, was probably using his dummy-double Cesare to model clothes rather than commit nocturnal crimes.'[19]

Another recurrent narrative in numerous Expressionist films is that of two men (presented as mad scientists or alchemists driven by 'unholy' goals) engendering life together – a life which itself turns out to be monstrously queer, as in *Homunculus* (1916) or the various adaptations of Hanns Heinz Ewers' 1912 novel *Alraune* (two in 1918; 1928; 1930). Kracauer already discusses these narratives' queerness in *From Caligari to Hitler*:

> [A]bnormal traits are presented as the result of abnormal origins. But the postulate of such origins is actually a poetic subterfuge rationalizing the seemingly inexplicable fact that these heroes are, or feel themselves to be, different from their fellow creatures. What makes them different? Homunculus formulates the reason of which the Golem is only obscurely aware: 'I am cheated out of the greatest this life has to offer!' He hints at his inability to offer and receive love. … Rodin's much-stressed friendship with him adds a touch of homosexuality that rounds out the picture. … Alraune's family resemblance to Homunculus is apparent.[20]

Kracauer here seems to be implying, through his choice of wording about being 'different from their fellow creatures', a direct linkage between these works and *Anders als die Andern*, which he discusses shortly afterwards in *From Caligari to Hitler*. In this way, fantastic and naturalistic works alike can be seen to have showcased and responded to the very visibility of queer sexualities that characterises this early part of the twentieth century in Germany – while at the same time throughout acknowledging that this visibility by no means effected any cessation of widespread social scrutiny and disapprobation.

Dissonant voices in Third Reich cinema

Under National Socialism, not only tens of thousands of gay men (facing a much intensified version of Paragraph 175), but also lesbians, transvestites and other queer types deemed to contravene Aryan precepts were forced into emigration or exterminated in concentration camps. Against this backdrop, it seems all the more important to stress that queer presences and sensibilities did on occasion manage to assert themselves on the Third Reich screen, thereby disrupting – however momentarily – the regime's totalising efforts.

At the very beginning of the Third Reich, before Goebbels and his propaganda machinery had fully taken charge, it was still possible for unambiguously queer works to appear – *Viktor und Viktoria*, for example, was in fact released *after* Hitler's accession to power. However, a shift in attitude was soon in evidence, with the follow-up to *Mädchen in Uniform*, Frank Wisbar's *Anna und Elisabeth* (*Anna and Elisabeth*, 1933) – again starring Hertha Thiele and Dorothea Wieck – now 'aim[ing] to show how sick and twisted [lesbian] relationships are'.[21]

Nevertheless, some queer avenues remained. Famously, Zarah Leander's portrayals of socially excluded women tirelessly battling adversity in the hope of a miracle[22] found identification not only with mainstream, but also subcultural spectators including gay men, lesbians and – as became clear later, through their impersonations of Leander – transvestites. Leander's songs from these films likewise communicated melancholic yet tirelessly hopeful sentiments through lyrics such as '*Kann denn Liebe Sünde sein?*' ('Can Love be a Sin?') and '*Davon geht die Welt nicht unter*' ('The World Won't Go Under'), and these struck a similar chord with queer audiences. It should be noted that Leander's lyricist, Bruno Balz, was a gay man (one of several in Leander's entourage) who was freed from incarceration in 1941 in order that he continue to pen her lyrics. Kuzniar furthermore suggests that Leander's deep voice – whose 'masculine' timbre was often commented upon – as

Star postcard of Zarah Leander (1938)

well as her tall, broad-shouldered figure endowed her with certain androgynous qualities to which German queer audiences might have related.[23]

It is noteworthy also that Wilhelm Bendow – the Berlin 'scene' star of *Aus eines Mannes Mädchenzeit* – managed, somehow, to maintain a career as a character actor, appearing in around fifty films during the Third Reich. Bendow's androgynous characteristics seem far more pronounced than those of Leander, as he displays (and plays up) his thin, diminutive frame, effete gestures and camp voice (described by one critic in 1932 as 'his lightly powdered manner of speaking')[24] in works like *Der schüchterne Casanova* (*The Shy Casanova*, 1936) or *Meine Freundin Josefine* (*My Girlfriend Josefine*, 1942). It is Bendow also who plays one of Nazi cinema's few *unheimlich*, otherworldly creatures, the moon-man in *Münchhausen* (1943). Significantly, the narrative asserts that moon-people have detachable heads, and so Bendow enters the film carrying his moon-wife's head in his hands, thereby appearing as a bizarre, fantastic medley of male and female bodies.

Third Reich cinema furthermore contains numerous works promoting same-sex political organisations, like the Nazi land girls in *Ich für Dich, Du für mich* (*Me for You, You for Me*, 1934), and body culture, as in the opening to the second part of Leni Riefenstahl's *Olympia* (1936), in which naked male athletes glisten together in a sauna. While these images are clearly intended as representations of Nazi social organisation – and should by no means be interpreted as further positive examples of queer visibility – they are nevertheless so intensely homosocial or homoerotic that they frequently seem almost to transcend into the homosexual. In this regard, it is perhaps worth considering that Adolf Brand, the publisher of *Der Eigene*, had as early as 1916 been acquitted of distributing male pornography on the grounds that his photographs were 'artistic, scientific and eugenical ('*rassenhygienisch*'),' while Nicolas Kaufmann, director of the most celebrated pre-Nazi body culture film, *Wege zu Kraft und Schönheit* (*Ways to Strength and Beauty*, 1925), was a gay man who belonged to Hirschfeld's *Wissenschaftlich-humanitäres Komitee*.[25] While this perspective cannot hope to offset the overriding hatred for all things queer that characterises this period – after all, both Brand and Kaufmann managed to survive in Germany after 1933 only by obscuring their sexuality – this cultural heritage of '*über*-homosociality' nevertheless illuminates intriguing inconsistencies in the heteronormative configuration of sexual identity within National Socialism.

Stifled queer visions of the 1950s

In queer history, the early post-war years may seem like little more than an adjunct to the conditions of the Third Reich, with both West and East Germany adopting (and actively prosecuting under) versions of Paragraph 175. If queer characters appear in films of this period, then they do so fleetingly, as in Peter Pewas' *Straßenbekanntschaft* (*Passing Acquaintance*, 1948), which contains a single shot of two foppish, make-up-wearing men running hand in hand from a dance floor. Such a moment seems revealing only in that it acknowledges the continued existence of a queer culture, but one so stifled that it can scarcely be articulated. At the same time, it should be remembered that *Straßenbekanntschaft* is an anti-syphilis *Aufklärungsfilm*, so that this solitary image is located squarely within the context of sexual disease and the 'scourge' of promiscuity. Likewise, Kuzniar observes that while Zarah Leander starred in a further seven films and continued to enjoy a strong sub-cultural following at her concerts, 'the extent to which gay life was closeted during this period also cannot be underestimated; admiration for Leander was … hardly a public banner for gay pride, and it was only post-Paragraph 175 that her audiences became more openly gay.'[26]

During the 1950s, a number of sanitised remakes of Weimar 'classics' managed to excise the queer content of the originals almost completely. Thus, Arthur Maria Rabenalt's *Alraune* (*Unnatural*, 1952) replaces lesbianism with a journalistic exposé of abortion and artificial insemination, while the 1957 version of *Viktor und Viktoria*, as Daniela Sobek notes, 'degenerates into a burlesque about the German economic miracle'.[27]

There is one film of this period, though, in which queer characters feature centrally and unambiguously – Veit Harlan's Paragraph 175 *Aufklärungsfilm*, *Anders als Du und ich* (*Different from You and Me*, 1958). However, Harlan had been the Third Reich's star-director of *Jud Süß* (*Jew Süss*, 1940), and since he co-scripted *Anders als Du und ich* with former Nazi sexual researcher Hans Giese, it is perhaps unsurprising that the finished work should present queer images constructed as, essentially, the anti-images of contemporary straight society.

In Harlan's intended version of the film, Boris (Friedrich Joloff) is a dealer in modern art – thereby immediately connecting him (and by association, homosexuality) with National Socialist notions of 'degenerate art' – whose French acquaintances cannot comprehend why Germany maintains the discriminary Paragraph 175. The mother of a young man whom Boris had 'seduced' seeks to blackmail him with threats of exposure under the dreaded Paragraph, but Boris instead exposes her for having committed procuration (of a servant-girl to 'straighten out' her son). While the mother goes to prison, Boris finds sanctuary in Italy. This dubious narrative implies that it is impossible for gay men to live in 1950s Germany, so they should probably go somewhere else 'where these things are understood'. However, this version of *Anders als Du und ich* was rejected – as too liberal! – by the West German film industry's regulatory body, the FSK, and this original cut was shown only in Austria and Switzerland. In the version released in the Federal Republic, Boris' French friends do not complain about the discriminary Paragraph at all, and in the end, Boris fails to flee to Italy and is instead captured and imprisoned by the Federal authorities (thus emphasising that *all* 'sexual miscreants', from procurers to homosexuals, will find their condign punishment).[28]

What remains significant about *Anders als Du und ich* is that Harlan prefigures various (immeasurably queerer) directors of the post-1968 cinema, who looked back to the pre-Nazi period for queer traditions to synthesise within their own emancipatory works. Harlan's point of reference is clearly Richard Oswald's *Anders als die Andern*, whose narrative of blackmail he adapts, and whose title he alludes to (after a heteronormative fashion). Furthermore, Harlan's work fully espouses the 'sexual intermediate' category from its 1910s model, bedecking its 'gay' male characters in jewellery and make-up, and repeatedly referring to them as members of *Das dritte Geschlecht* (*The Third Sex*), under which title the film also played.

(Un)fixing queer identities in post-1968 cinema

The emergence of a substantial gay movement in West Germany began around 1969, following the toning down of Paragraph 175 (a law that would not be struck absolutely until 1994). Establishing itself within the framework of post-1968 student politics, this movement was both confrontational and political, configuring gays as a radical group that could overcome encrusted socio-cultural structures. One of the movement's slogans crystallises this confrontational-revolutionary spirit: '*Brüder und Schwestern, warm oder nicht, Kapitalismus bekämpfen ist unsere Pflicht*' ('Brothers and sisters, whether poofs or not, our duty is to fight capitalism').

Notably, it was a film that functioned as one of the principal catalysts in initiating a wide-ranging discussion of homosexuality in West Germany, Rosa von Praunheim's *Nicht der Homosexuelle ist pervers, sondern die Situation, in der er lebt* (*It is Not the Homosexual Who is Perverse, but the Situation in Which he Lives*, 1971), whose cinematic release was swiftly followed by television screenings in 1972 and 1973.[29] Employing shocking images and language to inflame a response from gays and straights alike, *Nicht der Homosexuelle* presents various episodes in the life of a young gay man, Daniel (Bernd Feuerhelm), taking in a seemingly endless cavalcade of gay stereotypes ranging from body-worship and fashion-consciousness to cottaging and cruising. The film seeks simultaneously to illuminate – in unflinching close-up – the social peripheries within which gays are confined and constructed in hetero-centred society and, as Kuzniar puts it, to 'refut[e] … the homosexual's easy legibility', through the displaying of a wide array of distinct yet interwoven gay identities.[30]

The German term for 'gay' used throughout *Nicht der Homosexuelle* is '*schwul*', which, as Kuzniar comments, is employed on no fewer than ninety occasions and at this time constituted an extremely striking and confrontational usage (for the film's American screenings, von Praunheim correspondingly translated '*schwul*' as '*faggot*').[31]

Interestingly, the possible significations of '*schwul*' at points transcend homosexuality, as for example during one extended sequence in which Daniel visits a transvestite club. This tendency recurs throughout post-1968 German 'gay and lesbian'-identified cinema, implying that '*schwul*' regularly connotes more than its lexicographical definition.

For instance, although von Praunheim (Germany's most prolific queer *auteur*, with over fifty films to his name) has never ceased to label himself a '*schwul* filmmaker', his oeuvre embraces not only male and female homosexuality, but also transsexual activism, as in *Vor Transsexuellen wird gewarnt* (*Transsexual Menace*, 1996), camp diva-dom, as in his paean to songstress Evelyn Künneke, *Ich bin ein Antistar* (*I am an Anti-Star*, 1976) and male-to-female transvestism, as in his film about (and featuring) East German transvestite Charlotte von Mahlsdorf, *Ich bin meine eigene Frau* (*I Am My Own Woman*, 1992).[32] The latter addresses androgyny also, since von Mahlsdorf is played for much of the running-time by act(or)(ress) Ichgola Androgyn. Here, one could also cite the use of 'unrealistic' (i.e. bearded) male-to-female drag in Frank Ripploh's *Taxi zum Klo* (*Taxi to the Toilet*, 1980), presented as an act of radical '*schwul*' confrontation;[33] while in Werner Schroeter's *Der Tod der Maria Malibran* (*The Death of Maria Malibran*, 1971), one of the '*schwul*' lesbians is played by male-to-female transvestite Candy Darling;[34] and so forth.

On the one hand, it might be argued that such instances of 'slippage' into other queer sexualities are by no means unique to German '*schwul*' cinema, but can be found in 'gay and lesbian' films of all nationalities, as signifiers of what Dyer has termed a 'solidarity of outsiderdom'.[35] On the other, it should not be overlooked that these 'slippages' run parallel to another tendency within German '*schwul*' cinema, that of mobilising allusions to a positive gay and lesbian past, which almost without exception means Wilhelmine and Weimar notions of sexual intermediacy and the *unheimlich*. In this way, the definitional boundaries of '*schwul*' may be being actively reconfigured (whether consciously or otherwise) through interaction with these earlier queer traditions. Thus it is perhaps unsurprising that Ulrike Ottinger – one of the vanguard of lesbian filmmakers in New German Cinema – should at the same time as resurrecting Dr Mabuse (as a woman) confront us with innumerable androgynous characters in her *Dorian Gray im Spiegel der Boulevardpresse* (*Dorian Gray in the Mirror of the Yellow Press*, 1984), or that von Praunheim should present androgyny as '*schwul*' in his *Caligari*-esque *Horror Vacui* (1984), as well as in *Anita: Tänze des Lasters* (*Anita: Dances of Vice*, 1987), his biopic about Anita Berber, the celebrated Weimar lesbian dancer featured in *Anders als die Andern*. Significantly, in the only major work from the GDR (where gay groups were outlawed completely until 1985),[36] Heiner Carow's *Coming Out* (1989), the central character's titular coming out as '*schwul*' commences during a re-enactment of the drag ball from *Anders als die Andern* with the addition of 1980s disco lights and music, and at which Charlotte von Mahlsdorf and another androgynous figure crying '*Es gibt überhaupt keine Weiber mehr!*' ('There are no more women at all!') are present.

In von Praunheim's recent production *Der Einstein des Sex* (*The Einstein of Sex*, 2000), meanwhile, he goes so far as to (re)define '*schwul*' literally *through* the figure of Magnus Hirschfeld, whose campaign work and same-sex romances the film depicts. The *unheimlich* tradition was invoked throughout the film's publicity also, which stressed that Hirschfeld is played by Friedl von Wangenheim, whose father Gustav had been the vampire's homo-desired prey in Murnau's *Nosferatu*. Thus, German '*schwul*' cinema, enacting its own distinctive retro-mode, can be seen consistently to re-invent both itself and the referents of its texts, as it renegotiates their signification through earlier queer traditions.

German cinema: a panoply of queer(s)

In the above, I have attempted to outline a few reasons why it may be more productive and apt to think of German *queer*, rather than German *gay and lesbian* cinema. Historically, the 'sexual intermediate' paradigm has precluded gay 'exclusivity' by locating homosexuality firmly *within* (as opposed to *alongside*, as so often in the British-American tradition) a broader range of queer sexualities. Even within cinema that terms itself '*schwul*', the retro-mode has in recent years helped to maintain (and perhaps also reactivate) the influence of these diversifying 'third-sex' notions. Hopefully, the sample of queer films (representing barely the tip of the iceberg) in this overview has been sufficiently broad to indicate that 'queer' is intended here to signify a sensibility, presence or mood that can show up in any number of settings in German cinema, and that it is not simply a new 'designer label' for a monolithic canon of predetermined 'masterpieces'. Queer, as I have used it here, and as other writers have employed it in connection to (and in connecting with) German cinema, is challenging, empowering and refreshing precisely because of the rich multiplicity of its forms and voices.

Notes

1 Richard Dyer, *Now You See It: Studies on Lesbian and Gay Film* (London and New York: Routledge, 1990), p. 7.

2 Hermann Schmitt (ed.), *Strafgesetzbuch für das Deutsche Reich*, 9th edn (Munich: C. H. Beck, 1907), p. 79.

3 The section that follows draws especially on Dyer, op. cit., pp. 17–22; Robert J. Kiss, 'From a Man's Time as a Girl: Male Sexuality and the *Rockrolle*', in *The Doppelgänger in Wilhelmine Cinema (1895–1914): Modernity, Audiences and Identity in Turn-of-the-Century Germany* (University of Warwick, PhD thesis, June 2000), vol. 1, pp. 231–77; and Alice A. Kuzniar, *The Queer German Cinema* (Stanford, CA: Stanford University Press, 2000), pp. 21–7.

4 Sales figure in Magnus Hirschfeld, *Die Homosexualität des Mannes und des Weibes* (Berlin: Louis Marcus, 1914), p. 974.

5 Kuzniar, op. cit., p. 35.

6 Kurt Tucholsky, 'Verbotene Films', *Die Schaubühne*, vol. 9, no. 40, 1913, p. 952.

7 See especially Wilhelm Bendow and Marcellus Schiffer, *Der kleine Bendow ist vom Himmel gefallen* (Berlin: Efra-Verlag, n.d. [1925]).

8 Cited in Friedrich von Zglinicki, *Der Weg des Films* (Berlin: Rembrandt, 1956), p. 561; and cf. N. O. Body, *Aus eines Mannes Mädchenjahren*, 4th edn (Berlin: Gustav Riecke, n. d. [1907]).

9 See especially Kuzniar, op. cit., pp. 31–56.

10 Daniela Sobek, *Lexikon lesbischer Frauen im Film* (Munich: Belleville, 2000), pp. 5–6.

11 Robert J. Kiss, 'Give Me Your Trousers or I'll Shoot!: Female Gender and the *Hosenrolle*', in op. cit., vol. 1, pp. 180–230.

12 John Fout, 'Sexual Politics in Wilhelmine Germany: The Male Gender Crisis, Moral Purity, and Homophobia', *Journal of the History of Sexuality*, vol. 2, no. 3, 1992, p. 394.

13 Cf. Dyer, op. cit., pp. 27–46.

14 Andreas Sternweiler and Hans Gerhard Hannesen (eds.), *Goodbye to Berlin? 100 Jahre Schwulenbewegung* (Berlin: rosa winkel, 1997), p. 43.

15 Harry M. Benshoff, *Monsters in the Closet: Homosexuality and the Horror Film* (Manchester and New York: Manchester University Press, 1997), pp. 20–1.

16 Richard Dyer, 'Children of the Night: Vampirism as Homosexuality, Homosexuality as Vampirism', in Susannah Radstone (ed.), *Sweet Dreams: Sexuality, Gender, and Popular Fiction* (London: Lawrence and Wishart, 1988), p. 48; and cf. idem, op. cit., p. 20.

17 Loy Arnold, Michael Farin and Hans Schmid, *Nosferatu: Eine Symphonie des Grauens* (Munich: Belleville, 2000), pp. 52f.

18 Kuzniar, op. cit., pp. 30–1, and citing Richard Murphy, 'Carnival Desire and the Sideshow of Fantasy: Dream, Duplicity and Representational Instability in *The Cabinet of Dr Caligari*', *Germanic Review*, 66, 1991, p. 50.

19 Thomas Elsaesser, *Weimar Cinema and After: Germany's Historical Imaginary* (London and New York: Routledge, 2000), p. 99, and citing Anita Loos, *A Girl Like I* (New York: Viking, 1966), p. 128.

20 Siegfried Kracauer, *From Caligari to Hitler* (Princeton, NJ: Princeton University Press, 1947), pp. 32–3 and 154.

21 Dyer, *Now You See It*, p. 44.

22 Cf. Erica Carter's piece in this volume.

23 Kuzniar, op. cit., pp. 57–69. It is worth noting that Bruno Balz's name already carried substantial appeal among queer audiences, since he had been a popular celebrity on the Weimar 'scene'. Cf. Sternweiler and Hannesen, op. cit., p. 104.

24 Cited in Erich Plümer (ed.), *Wilhelm Bendow – Schauspieler und Kabarettist* (Einbeck: Gebrüder Börner, 1984), p. 19.

25 Sternweiler and Hannesen, op. cit., pp. 53 and 124–25.

26 Kuzniar, op. cit., p. 59.

27 Sobek, op. cit., p. 289.

28 See especially Sternweiler and Hannesen, op. cit., pp. 260–1.

29 Ibid., pp. 279–81.

30 Kuzniar, op. cit., p. 12.

31 See especially ibid., pp. 99–103; and Dyer, *Now You See It*, pp. 216–22.

32 Kuzniar, op. cit., p. 257; and cf. Rosa von Praunheim, *50 Jahre pervers* (Cologne: Kiepenheuer & Witsch, 1993).

33 Cf. Dyer, op. cit., pp. 227–8.

34 Cf. Kuzniar, op. cit., pp. 118–31.

35 Dyer, op. cit., p. 266.

36 See especially Jürgen Lemke, *Gay Voices from East Germany* (Bloomington: Indiana University Press, 1991).

PART TWO

STARS

Introduction

Erica Carter

We noted in our general introduction how German film history has developed as a culturally hybrid discipline whose impetus derives both from nationally specific, and from international historiographical developments. The star case studies that follow serve to an extent as an illustration of that general trend. Contemporary star studies in German film history take, broadly speaking, two distinct forms. On the one hand, much post-war German-language scholarship, from Enno Patalas' early sociological studies, to more recent overviews by Werner Faulstich, Helmut Korte, Stephen Lowry, or Claudia Lenssen, situates German stars in the context of a Hollywood-dominated western cinema whose nationally based star systems are seen to display broadly similar social-industrial structures and representational conventions.[1] Thus when Lowry, Korte or Lenssen, for instance, include as seminal to German studies of stardom such figures as James Dean, Elizabeth Taylor, or Brigitte Bardot, they not only underscore the significance of international stars in forming nationally distinctive audience tastes and preferences. At the same time, Lowry and Korte, for example, insist that German cinema, at least throughout its studio period under Ufa, boasted a star system that mirrored that of Hollywood both in terms of its institutional apparatus (which included a highly developed film and fan press, advertising and merchandising via star postcards, photographs, cigarette cards and so on), and in its apparent replication of Hollywood models of star representation.[2]

This recognition of the German star system's international dimension, moreover, has run in tandem with an enthusiastic engagement with Anglophone star analysis as a resource for methods and approaches to the study of German-speaking stars. Alongside the work of such writers as Christine Gledhill, Richard de Cordova or Jackie Stacey, Richard Dyer's seminal book *Stars* in particular is regularly cited as having 'laid the groundwork for star analysis within film studies' from the late 1970s on.[3] In that study,

Dyer drew on sociological and semiotic methodologies to elaborate a paradigm for the textual analysis of stars as social phenomena, images and signs.[4] The rich promise this work held out for German as well as UK- or US-based star studies was that the semiotic analysis of stardom as 'a complex configuration of visual, verbal and aural signs' could yield insights not only into the 'meaning' of stars, but also the social and ideological function of their image.[5] It is in pursuit of just that promise that Stephen Lowry sets out below to explore Heinz Rühmann's capacity to manage or magically resolve social contradictions between desires for rebellion, and authoritarian social norms. Dyer's emphasis on the function of stars as both normative and alternative or oppositional social types is similarly reproduced in Anton Kaes' study of Paul Richter as an embodiment of German nationhood, as well as in Malte Hagener's account of Til Schweiger as a model of 'new man' masculinity German-style.

Yet a second tendency in contemporary German star studies is less indebted to Anglophone studies that locate Hollywood as 'the dominant paradigm of both mainstream cinema and stardom'.[6] In recognition of the shortcomings of a critical paradigm that constructs European star systems merely as pale shadows of their Hollywood equivalents, historians and film analysts have begun to explore what Joseph Garncarz has termed the 'nationally distinctive' elements of German star systems from the early silents on.[7] Against visions of a Hollywood cultural imperialism that imposes a singular model of stardom on European industries, Garncarz, along with such writers as Knut Hickethier and, in contributions below, Malte Hagener and Claudia Fellmer in particular, have insisted on the national specificity of German star systems in (at least) three areas. At the level of the industry, first, German stars were never as seamlessly integrated as their US contemporaries into the mass production machinery of the studio system. Writers on early German cinema (including Frank Kessler and Eva Warth in this volume) have traced the history of German film stars to the early 1910s–20s, when the emergence of the long (narrative) film as cinema's primary textual mode, as well as changing practices of exhibition and reception, produced the rudiments of a star system. When Ufa emerged as Germany's prototypical studio in 1917, however, that system's distinction from Hollywood was evident in both the economic and cultural status afforded to Ufa stars. The corporation was in any case slow to adopt a Hollywood-style industrial mode that located both films and stars as standardised commodities within a mass production system. As Thomas Elsaesser has noted, the structuring of the early Ufa around the so-called 'director-unit system' gave directors an unparalleled degree of artistic control at all production stages.[8] But the relatively loose contractual arrangements with stars that were a further characteristic of the Ufa production mode (stars usually worked freelance or on short-term contracts) situated German stars also as creative artists in a pre-mass manufacturing mode. Dependent on the one hand for their livelihood on the studios, major stars at least were also 'free' to exercise a degree of control over their roles and star image. The most powerful among them, including the pair generally viewed as German national cinema's first stars, Asta Nielsen and Henny Porten, exploited their status to establish production companies in which their artistic control was assured. Both major and minor figures, moreover, bolstered both their income and their public profile with theatre work. Throughout the 1920s and 30s, the majority of film actors and actresses were theatre-trained, and often garnered their greatest acclaim for stage performances, not roles on screen.[9]

The significance of theatre in the construction of star images is, then, a second element that has historically distinguished German stars at least from Hollywood (though not from other continental European stars). Early film stars, including, alongside Asta Nielsen, such figures as Albert Bassermann and Emil Jannings, were drawn from a stable of theatre-trained actors already prominent as stars within highbrow and/or popular theatre. Even under the 'Third Reich' (a period that arguably marked the heyday of a US-style film star system in Germany), the absence until the late 1930s of Hollywood-style screen actor training meant that many of the idols of popular genre cinema cut their professional teeth on the bourgeois stage. Thus the very diverse talents of, among others, Renate Müller, Werner Krauss, Marlene Dietrich, Paula Wessely and Willy Fritsch were trained initially in stage technique under the theatre director Max Reinhardt. Other stars of the period hailed from more popular performance traditions, includ-

ing operetta (Zarah Leander), variety (Hans Albers) and revue (Lilian Harvey, La Jana, Marika Rökk): popular forms arguably now superseded by a television medium that, as Malte Hagener notes below, has become a third important media site, alongside theatre and film, for the construction of images for German cinema stars.

Yet even today, Hagener continues, a theatrical background remains paramount for German stars, since 'a "proper"… acting education is [considered] indispensable for an actor to be recognised critically'. As Knut Hickethier has observed, then, the 'multimediality' that characterises German star images derives its specificity to a significant degree from the interpenetration of film and, latterly, television star systems with theatre.[10] The recourse to theatre as a training ground and source of cultural legitimacy highlights, moreover, a third feature that has traditionally contributed to the 'national distinctiveness' of German cinema stars. As Claudia Fellmer observes in her contribution below, one key characteristic of stardom is 'the fluctuation between ordinariness and extraordinariness in a given star image'. As Fellmer's study of the former GDR actor turned international star, Armin Mueller-Stahl, further suggests, however, there is an element of national specificity to the terms on which the extraordinary and the ordinary are understood. In the German context, it has become something of a historiographical truism to say that the country's late political development as a nation-state-contributed to the overvaluation in Germany of culture as the repository of collective values, and especially the values of nation. In that context, and even after German political unification in 1871, cultural practitioners – including actors and actresses in theatre and film – often occupied a privileged socio-cultural position as emblems of national cultural prowess and excellence. Hence, arguably, the perceived imperative for German stars to display excellence in the established arts, especially theatre. The 'extraordinariness' of German stars, in other words, is often defined, not only by their perceived virtuosity in theatrical performance, but by extension, by their perceived capacity to embody the cultural values of nation.

For Anton Kaes below, this is precisely the function afforded to the star of Fritz Lang's *Nibelungen* (1924), Paul Richter, whose body in performance, Kaes claims, 'carried connotations of a strong and young national body', and thus offered one among numerous sites (alongside, for instance, sports and body culture) on which, through representations of the perfect body, 'the nation could come into representation'. Erica Carter traces similar efforts in Third Reich film press discourse around Marlene Dietrich to re-anchor this wayward émigré star in the symbolic body of the nation. In Dietrich's case, those efforts were as futile as they proved in relation to such later 'prodigal daughters' as Romy Schneider or Hildegard Knef, both objects of a similar ambivalence when they left the country and thereby renounced what Schneider herself deprecatingly termed their status as 'German national heritage'.[11]

What Romy Schneider, like Kaes and Carter, identifies here as specific (and in her case, specifically constricting) about German constructs of stars as extraordinary figures is their boundedness within discourses of nation. That there is a national specificity too in the versions of 'ordinariness' historically purveyed by German star systems is evident from contributions below by Stephen Lowry and Claudia Fellmer. For both writers, 'the ordinary' emerges as a category rooted in particular masculine and class-based cultural norms. Stephen Lowry thus locates the comedian Heinz Rühmann as the classical representative of 'the basic petit-bourgeois habitus and norms that made up a central moment of cultural continuity in ... German society throughout the twentieth century'. Fellmer's study of Mueller-Stahl, by contrast, situates the actor, at least in his early GDR years, as emblematic of a state socialist construction of the film star as normative icon of the working class. Fellmer's discussion of Mueller-Stahl's definition within East German star discourse, not as 'star', but as *Publikumsliebling* ('audience darling'), offers illuminating insights into the ways in which DEFA harnessed a longer German tradition that situated film stars as national icons, and placed that tradition in the service of the SED regime's broader project to establish the GDR as a culturally autonomous nation.

Yet what must finally be stressed in any study of German stars is the ambivalence that surrounds their status as national emblems. As writers on stars from Edgar Morin to Alexander Walker, Richard Dyer and beyond have observed, the star is a quintessentially modern formation in which surface appearance and stylistic excess are privileged over 'natural' beauty and spiritual essence. The star's preoccupation with surface sits uneasily, however, with a German nationalism that, in its most conservative forms at least, has conventionally vilified what are seen as unhealthy modern obsessions with appearance and visual sensation. It is, then, in the first instance the modernism of the star image that places star systems in tension with traditional German discourses of nation.

A second source of stars' ambivalence within national discourse relates to issues of sexuality and gender. Both male and female star images are regularly invested with qualities of gender ambiguity and sexual excess – disruptive elements indeed in nationalist iconographies that locate men as patriarchal heroes, and women as mothers to the nation. The qualities of glamour, cosmopolitanism and internationalism, moreover, that attach conventionally to stardom further destabilise cinematic discourses that situate film stars as embodiments of nation. It was a particular paradox of Third Reich film, for instance, that its most favoured screen idols were exotic foreigners. The Dutch operetta star Johannes Heesters, the Swedes Zarah Leander and Kristina Söderbaum, the Russian *grande dame* Olga Tschechowa and Marika Rökk, the 'heart-with-paprika' Hungarian revue queen,[12] are but the most prominent of many actors and actresses who certainly answered the Nazis' demand for stars of international standing and pan-European appeal, yet whose 'foreignness' stood in tension with Third Reich aspirations for a cinema rooted in national values and German excellence. Moreover, as a comparison between the cases of Dietrich and Meuller-Stahl below demonstrates, it was not only in the 1930s and 40s that the contradiction between the national and the international in star images has surfaced as a source of trouble in German discourses of star reception. Émigré stars in particular, though admired for their international reputations, continue today to be perceived in certain contexts as threatening the integrity of an identity as 'German' star. As Claudia Fellmer comments, Mueller-Stahl's 'Germanness', for instance, has been most loudly celebrated at home at those moments when his ethnically diverse roles (in his recent films, often as Eastern Europeans and/or Jews) threaten to 'dismantle' the 'Germanness' for which he is lauded domestically, and replace it with a shiftless identity caught in flux between the 'homeland culture', and a diasporic or transnational condition.

The case of émigré stars, in other words, highlights the more general necessity to understand star images within German 'national' cinema as temporary, and occasionally defensively constructed formations of a national film culture that struggles to sustain a distinctive identity in international markets, as well as among audiences closer to home. German star studies, it might be argued, must concern themselves therefore neither exclusively with Hollywood models that German cinema is assumed to have adopted wholesale, nor uniquely with indigenous film-cultural traditions. More fruitfully – and this is certainly the route taken by the contributions below – star analyses might set out to trace the historically variable processes of cultural differentiation that situate German star images within and between national and international markets and systems of cinematic representation.

Notes

1 See Enno Patalas, *Sozialgeschichte der Stars* (Hamburg: Schröder, 1963); Werner Faulstich and Helmut Korte (eds.), *Der Star. Geschichte, Rezeption, Bedeutung* (Munich: Wilhelm Fink, 1997); Claudia Lenssen, *Blaue Augen, Blauer Fleck. Kino im Wandel von der Diva zum Girlie* (Berlin: Parthas/Filmmuseum Potsdam, 1997); Stephen Lowry and Helmut Korte, *Der Filmstar* (Stuttgart: Metzler, 2000).

2 Lowry and Korte, op. cit., p. 259.

3 Christine Gledhill, *Stardom. Industry of Desire* (London: Routledge, 1991), p. xiv. See also Richard Dyer, *Stars*, 2nd edn (London: BFI, 1998); Jackie Stacey, *Star Gazing: Hollywood cinema and female spectatorship* (London: Routledge, 1994); Richard de Cordova, *Picture Personalities: The Emergence of the Star System in America* (Urbana: University of Illinois Press, 1990).

4 Dyer, op. cit, pp. 1ff.

5 Ibid., p. 34.

6 Gledhill, op. cit., p. xiii.

7 Joseph Garncarz, 'The Nationally Distinctive Star System of the Weimar Republic'. Unpublished paper, delivered at the 3rd Popular European Cinema Conference ('PEC3: The Spectacular') at the University of Warwick, March 2000.

8 Thomas Elsaesser, *Weimar Cinema and after: Germany's historical imaginary* (London and New York: Routledge, 2000), p. 120.

9 Joseph Garncarz, 'The Nationally Distinctive Star System'; also Walter Freisburger, *Theater im Film. Eine Untersuchung über die Grundlage und Wandlungen in den Beziehungen zwischen Theater und Film* (Emsdetten: Lechte, 1936), p. 9.

10 Knut Hickethier, 'Vom Theaterstar zum Filmstar. Merkmale des Starwesens um die Wende vom neunzehnten zum zwanzigsten Jahrhundert', in Werner Faulstich and Helmut Korte (eds.), op. cit., p. 47.

11 Romy Schneider, quoted in an interview with the feminist journalist Alice Schwarzer in Alice Schwarzer, *Romy Schneider. Mythos und Leben* (Cologne: Kiepenhauer & Witsch, 1998), p. 100.

12 'Heart with Paprika' is the title of Marika Rökk's autobiography: see Marika Rökk, *Herz mit Paprika: Erinnerungen* (Frankfurt-am-Main: Ullstein, 1991).

5

Siegfried – A German Film Star Performing the Nation in Lang's *Nibelungen* Film

Anton Kaes

Posing for the nation

A primordial mountain range. A painted rainbow arches over it, linking heaven and earth, Gods and mortals. Fritz Lang's *Siegfried*, the first part of his two-part Nibelungen film of 1924, begins with this chimerical still image, setting the stage for a story that is not of this world. A long shot of gigantic tree trunks, dwarfing the few Neanderthal men visible in the distance, reinforces our first impression that we have entered the territory of legends and fairy-tales. Cut to a medium close-up of a hairy, ape-like creature pushing bellows to fan flames for a smithy. These three shots – the mythic rainbow, the primal forest and the primitive, dark-skinned, barely human being – prepare us for the first glimpse of the hero of the film, thrown in stark relief against these surroundings. Bathed in dazzling white light, Siegfried (or more precisely, Paul Richter playing Siegfried) poses in a moment of frozen time, ethereal and majestic, resembling a statue of a young Greek god.

Shot from a low angle to make him look like a sculpture, the image is indeed reminiscent of classical monuments, harking back to Greek art and foreshadowing the Nazis' appropriation of it. Only ten years later, Arnold Breker, the most famous among Nazi sculptors, produced a series of public statues of oversized naked bodies posing similarly with sword or torch in hand. Richter does not act here in the conventional sense; he *poses* for the camera, displaying his naked torso and looking down his bare muscular arms to his sword which is at first outside the frame. His eyes are directed at his extended arms, his slightly angled face in self-absorbed concentration, hard and rigid in maximum tension, reminiscent of body-building poses. Strong backlighting sculpts his body. The act of his posing is underscored by the camera's cut to an onlooker, the dwarf Mime, Siegfried's mythical guardian and teacher, who provides the intended reaction of awe and wonderment. Siegfried is presented as the bodily foil to Mime: tall vs stunted; erect and upright vs lying and crouching; hairless vs hairy; groomed and taut vs unkempt and slovenly; nude vs covered; white and clean vs dirty and squalid; blond Aryan superman vs the debased and abject dark other. Mime, played by Georg John, acts as the primitive, reduced to watching the shining hero with a mixture of jealousy and dread. The camera cuts back and forth between them; they do not share the same frame. In an unexpected, unsettling cut the camera suddenly switches to a position slightly behind Siegfried, capturing his back, a subtle foreshadowing of his only vulnerable spot, as we later find out.

The motionless posing is followed by vigorous activity. Siegfried begins to forge his sword with exaggerated vehemence, surrounded by heavy billows of smoke and sculptured by strong lighting from overhead, from the back and the sides. The smoke – an old theatrical effect often employed in productions of Wagner's *Ring* – adds to the magical quality of the hero of unknown origins, half-god, half-human, outside of time and space, carefree soul and warrior. Smoke also gives light a palpable presence, making it visible. The lighting alone valorises the notion of the unique and special character of the hero, it gives a radiant glow to his bodily contours, it brings out the texture of his

Nibelungen Part 1: Siegfried (1924)

naked skin and lends the translucent image a sense of depth. It even seems to illuminate the onlooker. In his posing, Richter follows earlier pictorial representations of Siegfried as a mythical figure. He performs 'Siegfried' according to visual representations and iconographic conventions (from sculpture to paintings and book illustrations) that existed for more than a hundred years – this is an iconography the film can assume the audience to know. Acting itself does not signify in a vacuum but partakes of, and draws on, a discursive force-field shared by film-maker and audience alike in 1924. This force-field consists of a myriad of aesthetic and political representations and discourses relating Siegfried to the German nation. In what follows I want to explore how film actors become identified with their nation, how they bring the national into representation, and how, in turn, the nation shapes an actor's role and identity. Let us first look at the cultural moment of 1924, which largely determined the perceptions of both

actor and nation, as well as the paratextual framework within which Richter's embodiment of Siegfried 'made sense'. [1]

Myth as mission

When *Siegfried*, the long-anticipated new film by Fritz Lang finally opened on 14 February 1924, it was more than a cultural event. It was brazenly political. Gustav Stresemann, Germany's Foreign Minister, and numerous other politicians as well as delegates from German industry and commerce were in attendance. The widely covered spectacle turned these officials themselves into actors who performed their roles as representatives of the nation; they provided the national framework within which a cultural product like the *Nibelungen* – Germany's quintessential national epic – could resonate. Newspapers had written for weeks about the filmic adaptation of the 'German Iliad' whose production had consumed two full years. Costing 8 million marks, it was the most expensive European film ever made before *Metropolis* topped this record three years later. A sixty-member symphony orchestra played an original score by Gottfried Huppertz, emulating the *leitmotif* structure of Richard Wagner's *Ring des Nibelungen* (1876). Cinema itself seemed to have arrived at the pinnacle of high culture after having being denigrated (especially in Germany) as a disreputable and frivolous form of commercial mass culture for more than two decades.

Lang and Thea von Harbou, who co-wrote the screenplay, used the undisputed cultural capital of the *Nibelungenlied* to raise the artistic stakes of the new medium by a few notches. They could build on the special brand of artistic, i.e. *auteur*ist, cinema that had sprung up in Germany since the days of Paul Wegener's *Der Student von Prag* (*The Student of Prague*, 1913) or Lang's own *Der müde Tod* (*Destiny*, 1921) – films that deliberately set themselves apart from the mass entertainment cinema that thrived in Germany as everywhere else. While this popular cinema soon developed an international set of narrative strategies and visual tropes, high art tended to draw on national folk-tales and historical legends. D. W. Griffith's highly acclaimed masterpiece, *The Birth of a Nation* (1915) and Abel Gance's *Napoleon* (1928) demonstrate that the nexus of artistic aspiration and national discourse was not confined to Germany.

When Lang and his wife decided to film the *Nibelungen*, the ultimate German folk-tale and national epic, they placed their film in a long history of literary and dramatic adaptations that had dramatically increased at the end of the First World War. In 1924, it would have been nearly impossible to watch a film about the Nibelungen without being already familiar with both the story and the character of Siegfried.[2] Since its rediscovery in the middle of the eighteenth century and its glorification at the height of German romanticism, the epic had become mandatory reading in school. It was a favourite among illustrated children's books, and it comes as no surprise that Lang took his major design ideas from Carl Otto Czeschka's illustrated *Nibelungen* edition for children, published in 1909. The epic had also inspired numerous dramatic adaptations, with Friedrich Hebbel's two-part play *Die Nibelungen* (1860) and Richard Wagner's four-part opera, *Der Ring des Nibelungen* being the most famous. Thea von Harbou, who had played Kriemhild as a young girl in a school production of Hebbel's *Nibelungen*, also published a popularised prose version of the saga, *Das Nibelungenbuch*, which appeared as a 'tie-in' in 1924 with illustrations from the film.[3] It was also widely known that Hindenburg and

Hitler, after the defeat of the German army in 1918, had likened Germany to the figure of Siegfried, claiming that Germany was betrayed by the home front and stabbed in the back just like Siegfried was. In popular memory from the romantic period to the First World War, Germany was identified with Siegfried. Siegfried was Germany. Germany was Siegfried.

Billed as a *Monumentalfilm*, the *Nibelungen*'s premiere resembled that of an opera with orchestra, curtain and long applause at the end of the film. The director as well as the actors appeared on stage to take bows and receive flowers. At a banquet afterwards, Stresemann expressed the hope that the Nibelungen film would unite the German people and build a bridge to other nations. Stresemann's speech (published in the next day's papers) confirmed the film's serious political and ethical mission. His words echoed a chorus of voices that had preceded the film's premiere and pre-structured its reception. Lang himself, a Viennese who had become a German citizen only in 1924, openly confessed his trepidation about making the Nibelungen saga into a movie, fearing that he might be accused of trivialising what he repeatedly called the 'sacred national epos' of his new homeland. On the day of the film's premiere, as if to underscore the gravity of the undertaking, Lang and Thea von Harbou laid a wreath at the grave of Frederick the Great. More than simply a public relations stunt, this act of remembrance illustrated the nationalistic milieu in which the film was seen and discussed, a milieu that saw a mythical link from the *Nibelungenlied* via Fredrick the Great to the Nibelungen movie. Indeed, the film begins with a dedication: 'To the German people'. The film's goal, according to Thea von Harbou, was to instil in the 'great, exhausted and overworked German people' a desire for a collective identity based on a mythical national narrative.[4] Following Wagner's project of his *Ring* cycle which was designed to reconstitute a national community that had been lost, Lang's *Nibelungen* indeed promised a renewed sense of national identity and pride at a moment of crisis.

In early 1924, when *Siegfried* opened, German society was deeply split and traumatised by its military defeat in the First World War and the failed revolution, by the harsh and seemingly unjust terms of the Versailles Treaty, and by a string of political assassinations and hyperinflation, which had destabilised the middle class. The *Nibelungen* responded to these multiple traumas by offering a radical shift in perspective – from history to myth: by rejecting the present, eternal values would emerge, values that would not only relativise the misery of the post-war period but indeed would transcend them in myth. The film took up the challenge of re-inscribing images of a founding myth for Germany (however problematic this myth was in light of the fact that it ends in total destruction). The political and cultural stakes seemed higher than in any previous German film.

An Aryan Tarzan

How did the German audience in 1924 come to identify the actor Paul Richter as Siegfried? As in all cinema dealing with history and myth, the film had to make use of iconic references already in circulation and known to the viewers. In this case a century-old history of visual representations of Siegfried existed in the arts (from sculpture to paintings and book illustrations) as well as on stage. Images of Siegfried as a mythical young hero abounded especially during and after the War. In order to be recognisable as Siegfried, Richter had no choice but to model his looks and habitus after previous portrayals of Siegfried. In this sense, Paul Richter does not act, but rather 'enacts' a script given to him by prior representations; he had to play to the images that were already known before he embodied the role. This may be the reason that a contemporary critic could speculate as follows:

> I do not know whether Fritz Lang had thought of filming the eternal national epic of the Germans before he met Paul Richter. It would be reasonable to think that only the acquaintance with this young actor who was to offer such a perfect incarnation of young Siegfried gave him the idea.[5]

In the historical moment of 1924, the body of Richter (or is it the body of Siegfried?) became a corporeal metaphor for the nation.

Siegfried's signature hair, the long blond wavy mane that crowns Richter's head as if sculpted, and his pale skin defined, in the racialist discourse of the time, ideals associated with the Aryan race and its supposed superiority. The blond hair was a semiotic marker dear enough to Thea von Harbou to wax poetic even in the screenplay: 'His hair, of the lightest blond and flowing like a golden stream, is brushed backwards from the forehead. He has the habit of tossing it back with wild vigor when it falls, fair and fine as it is, onto his forehead.'[6] In addition to special lighting effects a chemical was used to make Richter's hair shimmer and enhance Siegfried's dazzling blondness. Camera angles, framing and montage further constructed the predominance of its white hero over the dark-skinned *Untermensch*, described in the screenplay as resembling a

'gorilla with depraved face and bristly hair'. In stark contrast to him, Siegfried appears as an apotheosis of whiteness, in terms of its racial implications immediately recognisable to the viewer of 1924 as an ideal image of Germanness.

Béla Balázs in his 1924 book *Der sichtbare Mensch oder die Kultur des Films* (*Visible Man or the Culture of Film*), which appeared in the same year as the *Nibelungen*, had already argued in a surprising and troubling passage that the future of cinema would show the domination of the white race because cinema emanated from Europe and America, spreading the white man's vision of man across the globe.[7] Movies played a major role in this dissemination of white dominance, according to Balázs, to the extent that actors from the white West embodied ideals of white beauty. The whiteness of Siegfried's skin is stressed by his white clothes and further intensified by the snow-white horse on which he rides away from his underlit habitat – a white knight in search of adventure and love, in battle against the treacherous darkness that surrounds him.

Whiteness, as Richard Dyer's study *White* has shown, possesses a range of connotations that all play into the image of our hero: untouched purity, virtue, innocence, chastity and finally death.[8] The film shows Siegfried as a guileless, impetuous young hero marked for death from the beginning. Lang stages what the audience already knows: thus the preponderance of posing. Action in this film is condensed into pregnant moments of great visual power in which time seems to stand still.

Richter's half-naked torso, displayed in his posing, also conjures up a rush of associations that relate the iconic mythical figure to the cultural moment of 1924. Being unfettered by clothes signalled freedom and strength but also a position untouched by class and status consciousness – his half-naked body puts him in visual contrast to the courtly Burgundians who wear formal attire that displays prestige and wealth, but also covers up and hides secrets. In physical terms, Siegfried has less in common with the Burgundians than with the emblem of natural man, Tarzan, who appeared on screen as early as 1918 and became widely popular in Germany in the Weimar Republic. In 1924, four volumes of William Rice Burroughs' serial novel about Tarzan's adventures were published in German translation, prompting the conservative critic Otto Koischwitz to complain about a veritable 'Tarzan epidemic'.[9] Siegfried's natural state as the noble savage who sets out to get his Kriemhild (as Tarzan gets his Jane) makes him appear ignorant of the treacherous world of civilisation and thus vulnerable.

The representation of the actor's sculpted torso and the pose he strikes in the very first shot are also reminiscent of the iconography of Weimar's *Körperkultur*. Inadequately translated as 'body culture', *Körperkultur* had become a popular movement that promoted the training of the body, along with health, beauty and strength. It may not be a coincidence that in the same year that *Siegfried* opened, the former military officer Hans Surén published a small illustrated book on body-building, entitled *Der Mensch und die Sonne* (*Man and Sun*).[10] Enjoying phenomenal success, with numerous editions throughout the 1920s, it became later seamlessly absorbed into the Nazi ideology of the strong body. (In his 1936 edition, Surén added the subtitle 'Arisch-olympischer Geist' ('Aryan-Olympian Spirit'). Surén's book contains, in addition to a stylistically overwrought hymn to sunlight and instructions for nude bathing and gymnastics, a large number of pictures of men and women, most of them nude or half-nude, in various poses reminiscent of Siegfried's physique. In his preface, Surén reminded the nation of the importance of physical strength, stating there could be no national strength without strong bodies. Surén's emphasis on the patriotic dimension of gymnastics had a long history, dating back to Friedrich Ludwig Jahn's belief, in the early nineteenth century that only well-trained bodies are capable of defending the nation.[11] Also Nietzsche's glorification of the heroic body as an antidote to decadence and degeneration was widely known at the time. In 1924, the well-toned body of the actor that played Siegfried carried connotations of a strong and young national body, of an effulgent national community. Lang's film anchors national identity in the body of the actor.

Only a year after the Nibelungen film, Ufa promoted a full-length documentary on German body culture entitled, *Wege zur Kraft und Schönheit* (*Ways to Strength and Beauty*), one of its most popular *Kulturfilme*, which also linked physical beauty and prowess to the regeneration of the community. Twelve years later, Leni Riefenstahl would perfect the analogy between the athlete's body and the national body in her two-part *Olympia* film. Sports and body culture had become the site where the nation could come into representation – after the national spirit was no longer allowed to express itself in military form.

Nevertheless the Nibelungen film does begin with Siegfried forging a weapon, a sword more precise and more powerful than has ever been seen. The energetic production of this sword alludes to the German fantasy of gaining a *Wunderwaffe* (miracle weapon) in the last desperate years of the war. The film underscores the fantasmagoric quality of this miracle weapon in a trick sequence when the sword cuts a bird's feather tumbling through the air into two halves. The precision of the sword is paralleled by the pre-cision of the camera that miraculously captures this feat in slow motion. This obtrusive shot – a throwback to an earlier cinema of attractions – stops the action for a moment and diverts attention away from the actors. It none-too subtly suggests that for Lang the actors are part of a larger design; we are not seeing a narrative that is driven by characters as agents. There are two crosscuts to Siegfried, one showing his face filled with worry and anguish, the other with youthful laughter after the sword has passed the test. In both instances the gestures are exaggerated in an acting style that unapologetically derives from the pictorial school. This type of acting, as Lea Jacobs and Ben Brewster have recently shown, was guided by studying statues and painting and by copying poses from the other arts.[12] Given the weight of iconographic tradition that the film has to carry, it is not surprising that most of the acting in the film is pictorial, even though there are scenes, for instance between Siegfried and Brunhilde, that oscillate between the pictorial and a more modern style that relies on small restrained gestures and subtle facial expressions.

Making a star

Siegfried is played by the Viennese Paul Richter, who was trained, like almost all German-speaking film stars, as a stage actor before he joined the film industry. He may have caught Lang's eye in his role as the British officer Mac Allen in Joe May's 1921 *Monumentalfilm*, entitled *Das Indische Grabmal* (*The Indian Tomb*), where he played the romantic love interest of the wife of the Maharaja (played by Conrad Veidt), a colonial fantasy of an Indian woman falling in love with an adventurous, dashing white Englishman. After a smaller role as the rich playboy Edgar Hull in Lang's 1922 *Mabuse*, he was cast by Lang as Siegfried, a role that overshadowed the rest of his career. Endowing it with an air of youthful invincibility and vitality, he soon became identified with his role. Broad-shouldered, blond, blue-eyed and athletically built, he also was cherished as a male sex symbol in the 1920s, much adored by female admirers as well as by Weimar's homosexual community. Similar to Ramon Novarro and Rudolph Valentino, he represented eternal youth and self-confidence, but radically different from them, he did not have the exotic appeal of ethnic otherness. On the contrary, Richter was stylised as the ultimate embodiment of immaculate Nordic whiteness. (Or was he exotic in his own right by being such an ultra-pure specimen of the Aryan race in a nation that in reality looked not half as Aryan as the racial theorists claimed?)

Richter had to compete for star status with Conrad Veidt, his demonic counterpart. While Richter personified the naive and energetic idealism of German youth in its pre-war prime, Veidt symbolised repression, mystery and unappeasable desire. Unlike Richter, Veidt played complex and self-destructive characters: the homosexual in *Anders als die Andern* (Different from the others): the somnambulist zombie in *The Cabinet of Dr Caligari* who defies his master; and the enigmatic love-lorn Indian ruler in *The Indian Tomb*, where he plays opposite Paul Richter. The two actors are a study in contrast: Veidt uses his tall and slim, stiffly erect body with a hitherto unknown intensity, his gestures are sparse, signifying pitiless self-control in his jealous rage; while Richter's athletic body is unrestrained and hyperactive in his pursuit of the Indian woman. Veidt's facial features look ascetic and strained, with taut veins traversing his temples; Richter's expression in contrast is spontaneous, rash, impulsive, adolescent.

Richter was known to be an avid mountain climber, athlete, hunter and friend of nature. After Siegfried he played romantic roles as adventurer and lover until, in 1934, he was cast as a forest ranger in Hans Deppe's *Schloss Hubertus*, an early *Heimatfilm*. Here he lorded over nature, forests and heaths, and made young women fall in love with him. His roles varied only slightly from the Nazi period to the 1950s when he was featured in such fully-fledged *Heimatfilme* as *Das Schweigen im Walde* (1955), *Wetterleuchten um Maria* (1957) and his last role in 1958, *Der Schäfer von Trutzberg*.) It is not a coincidence that Richter was cast in over thirty films in roles that required an authentic and authoritative 'German look', because the *Heimatfilm* plot usually hinges on the valiant defence of *Heimat* against those who do not belong and therefore pose a threat to the community. Siegfried's naive heroism and German rectitude in the face of all perils around him is thus replayed numerous times, though almost comically scaled down from the heroic-mythical to the melodramatic domestic.

It was part of the *Nibelungen* publicity campaign to build up Paul Richter as a German counterpart to Rudolph Valentino, who had become in Hollywood the object of female and male desire. While Valentino represented the slightly decadent and sensuous Latin lover, Paul Richter played the upstanding and virtuous Nordic alternative. In 1925, a small book on Paul Richter was published by a Viennese press, ninety pages long with illustrations, which carried the identification between role and actor in its very title: *Paul Richter: Jung-Siegfried, der Held* (*Paul Richter: Young Siegfried, the Hero*).[13] It contained a biography of Paul Richter, an adulatory essay on him as a 'Mensch und

Künstler' ('Man and Artist'), another panegyric essay, 'Paul Richter, mein Gatte und Partner' ('Paul Richter, my Husband and Partner'), written by his wife, the actress Aud Egede Nissen, and, finally, a section on Paul Richter and his audience, in which fan mail is reproduced. In addition, we are treated to photos of him as a three-year-old and as a young stage actor; we also see him rowing, playing tennis, swimming, mountain climbing and boxing – a whole section is dedicated to him as a sportsman. In his own six-page essay, entitled 'What I Have to Say about my Profession', he tries hard to demystify his role as star by insisting that film acting, far from being glamorous, is instead exhausting work, dangerous and hazardous to one's health. He complains about the strong lights that ruin one's eyesight, the heat generated in the studio, the make-up that cannot be removed, and the sheer physical peril into which directors put their actors. (It is true that Richter's knee cap was shattered when the artificial dragon's tail inadvertently hit him during the filming of *Nibelungen*, an incident which stopped the production for six months.) He also emphasises the labour and danger involved in acting – a true German star who sacrifices his well-being in the name of art and for the fatherland.

As the 1925 volume makes clear, the audience played a large role in constructing the figure of Siegfried. Richter was flooded with fan mail from admiring women and men. Besides the usual private questions – the favourite one being whether he used a wig to produce this sculpted blond hair – there are also touching testimonies as to the function of his role as Siegfried. A letter from England, dated 15 February 1925, was sent by a former soldier who was heavily wounded in the trenches and suffering from nervous disorders and spells of amnesia. The soldier's wife explains in an accompanying note that he, Richter, represented to her crippled husband what he once was and could have been had he not been wounded. 'You will understand that it is difficult to stand apart from life when one is only 26 years old. But my husband is kind and patient even though he often has great pains.'[14] She asked for pictures of him as Siegfried to remember the film that made such an impression on this British war veteran. We can assume that this letter was selected by the editor of the book to attest to the global appeal of this national epic and to demonstrate the healing and regenerative power of the Nibelungen film.

This small book dedicated to Richter as an actor pursues contradictory goals. On the one hand it asserts a parallelism, even symbiosis, between the actor's personality and Siegfried's character, while on the other it tries to rescue Richter from being eternally bound to this one role.

A biography of Richter would have to be different from that of other actors, a certain Hugo Rappart claims in this book, because in Paul Richter's case 'hardly ever was an artist similarly identified with his role as he was with his Siegfried'.[15] He claims that the mythical figure of Siegfried as created by Richter shares a number of characteristics with the actor's personality, especially his sunny disposition. The motto of the book, printed as facsimile of Richter's handwriting, declares: 'I thank with all my heart whoever liked my Siegfried because he shows that he understood my experience as he understands purity, happiness and sunshine.'[16] This triad of 'Reinheit, Glück und Sonne' is meant to sum up Siegfried's character as well as Richter's private life. It is therefore no surprise that his biographer pronounces:

> Paul Richter *was* Siegfried. . . . the personification of the radiant and, despite his tragic end, happy human being. A joyful young man, whose life abounds with eternal sunshine. The personification of youth, sun, happiness, and love. … Richter had given cinema a new type which found in Siegfried its most perfect representation: the young, radiant human being. That is the reason why he became an idol of youth which found a role model in him worthy of emulating.[17]

The repetitive invocation of youth and happiness as the traits of a German hero betrays the strain in this creation of a male star who is young and appealing, not sinister like Werner Krauss or Conrad Veidt (in *The Cabinet of Dr Caligari*) or tragic like Emil Jannings (in *Der letzte Mann* [*The Last Laugh*], 1924). Richter's acting persona combined the chiselled features of Greek statues, the toned physique associated with German *Körperkultur*, the blond hair of the Aryan race and, most emphatically, the adventurous and aggressively idealistic and anti-modern spirit of the organised German youth movement, which according to one of its chroniclers, Walter Laqueur, was a 'microcosm of modern Germany'.[18]

For the audience of 1924, Richter's acting in *Siegfried* invoked the adolescent but misguided, even lethal, idealism of the German youth movement. Since the audience knew that two million German youths had been senselessly killed in battle less than a decade before (and since they also knew how the film would end), Richter's posing at the beginning of the film had the effect of giving the audience a moment to behold German youth as it had once flourished before the War ended it all. In this way, the beginning already was the end.

Notes

1 I am referring to Genette's use of 'paratext' which covers all the representations (promotional statements, interviews, debates, reviews, etc.) that surround a text and shape its reading. The premise is that no text exists or signifies in abstraction. See G. Genette, *Paratexts: Thresholds of Interpretation* (New York: Cambridge University Press, 1997).

2 On the reception history of the *Nibelungenlied* in the Weimar Republic, see G. Hess, 'Siegfrieds Wiederkehr: Zur Geschichte einer deutschen Mythologie in der Weimarer Republik', *Internationales Archiv für Sozialgeschichte der deutschen Literatur*, 6 (1981), pp. 1–144; H. Münkler and W. Storch, *Siegfrieden. Politik mit einem deutschen Mythos* (Berlin: Rotbuch Verlag, 1988).

3 Thea von Harbou, *Das Nibelungenbuch* (Munich: Drei Masken Verlag, 1924).

4 Harbou, 'Vom Epos zum Film', in *Reklame-Broschüre der Ufa-Decla*, 1924, p. 9.

5 Anon., *Paul Richter: Jung-Siegfried, der Held* (Vienna: 'Mein Film'-Buch und Zeitungsverlag, 1925), pp. 39f.

6 *Siegfried–Drehbuch*, Collection Adalbert von Schlettow. Quoted with permission from Filmmuseum-Deutsche Kinemathek. (My translation.)

7 B. Balázs, *Der sichtbare Mensch oder die Kultur des Films* (Vienna and Leipzig: Deutsch-österreichischer Verlag, 1924), pp. 32f.

8 See R. Dyer, *White* (London: Routledge, 1997), pp. 207ff.

9 See O. Koischwitz, 'Die Tarzan-Epidemie', *Eckart*, 1 (October 1924), pp. 21f. Koischwitz reports that the popularity of the translated novels was such that even a parody had appeared in German. After deploring the reading public's bad taste, the author tries to account for the phenomenal success of the Tarzan books in Germany (four volumes appeared in 1924): 'It is not only sensationalism that is satisfied but also, if only darkly unconscious and debased, the dreamlike longing of an epoch that is tired of culture [*kulturmüde*].' He speaks of 'an epoch which seeks in fantasy the liberation, denied in real life, from the pressure of a prison-like culture', an epoch which 'lends the natural and unmediated life of animals and savages a spiritual ideal to aspire to' (p. 22).

10 H. Surén, *Der Mensch und die Sonne* (Stuttgart: Dieck & Co, 1924). See also the telling titles of his subsequent books: *Volkserziehung im dritten Reich: Manneszucht und Charakterbildung* (Stuttgart: Franckhsche Verlagshandlung, 1934); *Gymnastik der Deutschen: Rassenbewusste Selbsterziehung und Charakterbildung* (Stuttgart: Franckhsche Verlagshandlung, 1938).

11 See S. Goltermann, *Körper der Nation: Habitusformierung und die Politik des Turnens 1860–1890* (Göttingen: Vandenhoeck & Ruprecht, 1998).

12 B. Brewster and L. Jacobs, *Theatre to Cinema* (New York: Oxford University Press, 1997), pp. 85 ff.

13 Anon., *Paul Richter*, op. cit.

14 Ibid., p. 86.

15 Ibid., p. 5.

16 Ibid., p. 3.

17 Ibid., pp. 17 and 21.

18 W. Z. Laqueur, *Young Germany: A History of the German Youth Movement* (New York: Basic Books, 1962), p. xi.

6

Marlene Dietrich – The Prodigal Daughter

Erica Carter

On 28 March 1933, Joseph Goebbels gave his first speech as Reich Propaganda Minister to film industry representatives. Addressing what he dubbed the artistic failings of late Weimar cinema – its low-life themes, its social realism, its distance from popular taste – Goebbels drew international comparisons, most famously with Eisenstein's *Battleship Potemkin* (1925) (which he described as 'unparalleled as film art'), but also with Edmund Goulding's 1927 Anna Karenina portrait, *Love*, in which Greta Garbo played the title role. Of her performance, Goebbels said the following: 'Garbo has proved that there is such a thing as a special art of film. This film is no surrogate for theatre or stage performance. There precisely *is* an art that belongs to film alone.'[1] Goebbels' claim, then, is that it is, among other things, stars and the quality of their performance that give film its distinctive artistic quality. Especially significant is what Goebbels deems the absence of star quality among German screen actors of the period: instead he names as his model of stardom Greta Garbo, a European idol long since lost to Hollywood cinema.

This equation of stardom with Hollywood has a long tradition in German star discourse. The very term 'star' is an Anglicism in German; and even the most recent film-critical studies often share a vision of Hollywood as the dominant model for German stardom.[2] Two key assumptions underpin this perception. Hollywood is claimed, first, to have held undisputed sway in European film markets since the late 1910s, and thus to represent the dominant economic model for mainstream cinema in general, and star systems in particular. The second assumption is a cultural one, and relates to Hollywood's presumed status as the primary film-cultural paradigm around which European national cinemas have articulated the meanings and values of stardom. Goebbels' comments on Garbo are

a case in point; for she figures here as the epitome of a Hollywood stardom that 1930s German film cannot yet emulate.

Yet there are reasons to relativise this vision of an unchallenged Hollywood hegemony. Economically, certainly, Hollywood's penetration of German film markets has rarely been matched by exports in the opposite direction; indeed as Geoffrey Nowell-Smith has observed, film exports to Hollywood from Europe in general remained negligible throughout the twentieth century. Even economically, however, there are grounds to assume what Nowell-Smith terms a 'dual', not a one-way relation. As he notes, Hollywood's rise to European market dominance was periodically interrupted through the twentieth century: by the coming of sound, for instance, and the concomitant surge in demand for indigenous language productions; or by state-orchestrated protectionism – import quotas and stringent censorship that, in Germany, began as early as the First World War and extended with increasing severity through the Third Reich.[3] Recent reception histories of the period from Weimar to the 1990s, moreover, show how audience demand has provided a further counterweight to Hollywood dominance. Joseph Garncarz uses trade press statistics on the top ten films from 1925 on to estimate for the Weimar period that German films accounted for over 75 per cent of box-office revenue from top films, as opposed to just over 15 per cent for Hollywood titles. A similar picture emerges for the 1950s, when German films among the top ten attracted over four times the box-office revenue of their Hollywood competitors.[4]

Garncarz' work is illuminating, too, for its challenge to notions of Hollywood star models as universally dominant. His studies of Weimar stars echo previous scholarship on early cinema in demonstrating both the persistent popularity of such 'home-grown' talent as Charles Willi Kayser or Claire Rommer, and the rooting of that popularity in national cultural traditions.[5] What distinguished Weimar's 'nationally distinctive star system', argues Garncarz, was both the artisanal economic model on which it depended (until well into the 1940s, stars worked predominantly as freelancers, rather than, as in Hollywood, under long-term contract to a single studio[6]), and its organisation around nationally specific cultural values and taste codes. As Garncarz notes, Weimar stars' differentiation from Hollywood was realised 'by a discourse on art (not) private lives'; hence the paucity of press coverage, in this period and later, of stars' intimate personal lives, as well as the emphasis on their actorly prowess, their status as artists of genius and their attachment to theatre as the 'culturally dominant medium'.[7]

The work of Garncarz and others suggests that in studying German stardom, we should abandon binary models of one national cinema's subservience to Hollywood, and conceive that relation instead as a two-way process of translation between culturally specific representational modes, values and norms – a process that shifts in different historical moments and locations. Our focus here is on the early years of the Third Reich: a period of special interest in the history of German cinema's negotiation with stardom Hollywood-style. That Hollywood remained for the greater part of the 1930s not only Germany's chief rival on the domestic market, but also the most coherent example of a cinema whose success Germany wished to duplicate is evidenced by import and distribution data from the period. Although foreign imports fell after the Nazi takeover, Hollywood films retained a significant presence in Germany throughout the 1930s. In 1933, they made up over two-thirds of foreign film imports (sixty-five of a total of ninety-two films imported that year).[8] Even by 1936, the proportion remained at around 50 per cent, though import controls had by this stage reduced total imports to around seventy of the 200 films required annually to fill exhibitors' programmes.[9]

Hollywood's continued success on German markets produced what Markus Spieker terms a characteristic 'dualism' in responses from party ideologues and the German industry. Goebbels' desire for an American-style 'media modernity' was balanced, Spieker suggests, against the anti-Americanism he inherited from the cultural nationalism of Weimar and earlier. That ambivalence was mirrored by an industry that admired Hollywood's technical brilliance, while excoriating its shallowness and low artistic ambition.[10] The star system in particular provoked ambiguous responses from both industry and regime. On the one hand, their awareness of stars' role in drawing audiences is evident in numerous interventions by the Propaganda Ministry into casting decisions, or in the privileges accorded to stars (high salaries, invitations to social events with prominent Nazis, etc.).[11] That stardom was problematic, however, for both industry and state is evidenced by the ambivalence surrounding stars in film commentary of the 1930s. The cinema owners' trade paper, *Film-Kurier*, commented in early 1933 that it was merely a 'love of beauty and glamour' that produced audience adulation of major stars.[12] By 1935, it was by contrast polemicising against the 'monstrosity' of stardom, or, in a 1937 piece, bemoaning the detrimental effects of 'star mania' on 'individuals and artists of a serious nature'.[13]

Film-Kurier's comments draw in part on that conception of the artist-star identified above as a long-standing feature of star discourse in Germany. Their vehemence derives, however, from circumstances particular to National Socialism. The Nazi takeover was followed by rapid moves towards state control of film through *Gleichschaltung*, increased censorship, and eventual nationalisation (see Julian Petley in this volume). Film was seen here, then, as a vehicle for the state-orchestrated assertion of a racist cultural nationalism that was only incipient in German cinema pre-1933. Nazi cinema's simultaneous aspiration to European market dominance, however, necessitated a commitment to internationalism associated heretofore primarily with Hollywood directors, film styles and stars.

The ramifications of that tussle between national and international ideologies, values and cultural forms are traced in what follows through a discussion of stars and stardom in Third Reich film. Exploring first the specific (racialised) inflection given to Weimar's 'nationally distinctive star system' under National Socialism, I move on then to consider the German reception of Marlene Dietrich after 1933. As an émigré in Hollywood, courted throughout the early 1930s by a German industry hungry for major stars, Dietrich found representation in German star discourse both as an embodiment of the national values the domestic industry sought to assert, and of the internationalism after which it (often unsuccessfully) strove.

Stars, character and personality

German star discourse, as we saw above, has often eschewed the preoccupation with private lives that provides the backbone of Hollywood star–audience relations. Under National Socialism, the public display of private intimacies was especially frowned upon, since it fostered an individualism considered antipathetic to fascism's collectivist ideals. That collective ethos was further buttressed by Nazi cinema's commitment to an ensemble aesthetic which was already pervasive before 1933 in German popular film. As the illustrated weekly *Filmwelt* observed in 1937, 'It is not the star who is the most important figure, but the film and the totality of its artistic significance ... It is a crime against art for the star to use his power to undermine the integrity of the total work of art'.[14] That anti-individualism was embedded, moreover, in the aesthetic structure of Third Reich narrative cinema. Writers on Third Reich film have often claimed that it aped Hollywood's narrative conventions; and indeed, much German genre film deployed the narrative strategies of classical Hollywood style: universal narrative motivation, the concealment of the film text's fabricated nature, and the management of time and space to support narrative causality.[15]

German film style departed from Hollywood, however, in at least one important sense. David Bordwell writes of classical Hollywood film that it accords centrality to character construction, since it is on the psychological plausibility of characters that narrative development depends.[16] In Third Reich film, by contrast, psychological depth is regularly abandoned in favour of the fabrication of ideal types: the soldier hero, the self-sacrificial mother, the masculine model of racial health. Recurrent features of visual and narrative organisation contribute to that location of types, not characters, as the aesthetic centre of Third Reich film. German narrative film of the 1930s and 40s is notable, for instance, for its preference for static camera and the long takes. The dominant shot is the medium close-up; in dialogue sequences, the two-shot and the long take prevail over close-ups and point-of-view editing. It is, moreover, not only this characteristically cautious use of camera and montage that mute character interaction and development. The heavy reliance on dialogue as a means of subjective expression – as opposed, for example, to *mise-en-scène* elements (lighting, décor, gesture, etc.) – situates Third Reich style in a realist tradition that eschews emotional ambivalence in favour of the supposed clarity of the spoken word.

A number of visual and narrative features in 1930s and 40s German cinema suppress, then, the psychological depth that is integral to character development in Hollywood realism. Indeed, this rejection of character was made explicit in numerous disquisitions on film acting under National Socialism. The actor-director Paul Wegener, for instance, commented in a 1934 speech that film roles must be 'shaped by the actor from the depths of his human essence'. The creative process, Wegener continued, gained shape 'not on the basis of ... pre-given stylistic principles. Instead, it grows from the mystical depths ... of that personality that slumbers at the complex subjective core of genuine talent'.[17] The Romantic conception of 'personality' as a subjective core that finds unmediated expression in film art surfaced repeatedly in 1930s film theory. The term differed from Hollywood ideas of character in a number of aspects. Most important was its rooting not in bourgeois humanist ideas of character as the product of personal experience and development (the classic vehicle for that humanist vision being the *Bildungsroman*). Instead, Third Reich film borrowed from race theory a vision of personality as a socio-biological essence identifiable by physical type. As the *Reichsfilmintendant* and director of the anti-Semitic documentary *Der ewige Jude* (*The Eternal Jew*, 1940), Fritz Hippler, wrote in his *Betrachtungen zum Filmschaffen* (*Considerations on Film Art*, 1942), 'that there is a correspondence between character and external appearance is evident not only from modern psychological research; it is also part of ancient and deeply rooted folk wisdom'.[18] This *völkisch* vision had various implications for the representation of character in German film. The division of human beings in Nazi race theory into physical and racial types made it the filmmaker's task to reflect that 'natural' appearance on film. Film commentators in any case made much of the status of the photographic image as a physical trace of human reality; thus for Hippler, film was 'more fundamentally rooted in its material origins than any other category of art'.[19] This notion of an organic unity between the film image and its referent in turn produced a distrust of stylisation or visual excess – melodramatic acting style, expressionist lighting, extravagant costume – since these were conceived as forms of masquerade that obscured the essence of racial type. Witness Hippler again on film acting and costume:

> What is ... primarily at stake in film is not so much the art of acting style, but rather the representation of personal types ... The *nouveau riche* or the metropolitan individual ... wear masks, even when going about their everyday business. Since they have a sense of being constantly under observation, they never show his true face, but strike poses [which] may even appear genuine, despite their use of masquerade.[20]

Here, the association of actorly stylisation with metropolitan modernity is the source of its denigration. Elsewhere, the masquerade is linked to other forms of social and racial deviation: with Jewishness, for example, or with feminine licentiousness. Most interesting for our purposes, however, is the identification by Nazi film commentators of stylistic excess as a key feature of Hollywood stardom: a feature, moreover, that they find distasteful because it infringes the norms of a racially defined national film aesthetic.

Why Dietrich?

In February 1934, Joseph Goebbels revisited a favourite theme: 'If German film is one day to conquer the world, then it must appear again as *German* film; it must put into representation our specific essence, our qualities, our character, our virtue – and if you wish, our weaknesses too . . .'[21] Goebbels' caveat – 'and . . . our weaknesses too . . .' – acknowledges the tension between his imperialist wish for a revitalised German film industry that will displace Hollywood in its ability to 'conquer the world', and the *völkisch*-nationalist aspiration for films expressive of German essence. Until mid-decade, moreover, only one figure on the international stage combined the qualities of Germanness with the world stature that Goebbels demanded. That figure was Marlene Dietrich; and her success as a German star in Hollywood makes her an illuminating figure for any study of 1930s Germany's negotiation of Hollywood stardom. Karsten Witte has noted how Third Reich cinema cultivated a new generation of stars, each partially modelled on a Hollywood alter ego – Adolf Wohlbrück on Clark Gable, Lilian Harvey on Claudette Colbert, Marika Rökk on Eleanor Powell, Zarah Leander on Dietrich and Garbo. In a dynamic of incorporation and disavowal that was characteristic of Third Reich film's 'Germanicised Americanism', each of these figures adopted

Desire (1936)

symbolic elements of the star image of their Hollywood other, while at the same time repudiating those features that transgressed German aesthetic and ideological codes.[22]

Though the same dynamic is visible in Dietrich, she is a different case, since she embodies in a single star image both the characteristic qualities of Hollywood stardom, and of both an actual and (in her films) a fictional German identity. Though Dietrich lived mainly in Hollywood after emigrating in 1930, she retained German citizenship until 1939, and cultivated a screen persona to which her 'Germanness' was integral. In the twelve films Dietrich made between 1930 and 1939, her origins were most explicitly referenced in four early Austro-German roles, as a Viennese prostitute in *Dishonored* (1931), a cabaret artiste in *Blonde Venus* (1932), a German peasant girl in *Song of Songs* (1933) and a Prussian princess in *The Scarlet Empress* (1934). In other films from this period, signifiers of Dietrich's German ethnicity – her accent, her visual and performance style – were harnessed to less specific representations of European identity; thus in her role as the cabaret singer Amy Jolly in *Morocco* (1930), for example, her national origins are unclear, as they are also in her part as Madeleine the fallen woman – 'Shanghai Lily' – in *Shanghai Express* (1932).

By 1935, the more diffuse Europeanness suggested by these three roles had displaced Dietrich's Germanness entirely, and she began exploring new personae culled from the length and breadth of the European continent. Beginning with her role as the seductress Concha Perez in *The Devil is a Woman* (1935), she now became, variously, a Parisian jewel thief (*Desire*, 1936), a Russian countess (*Knight without Armour*, 1937), a French convent-school graduate (*The Garden of Allah*, 1936), an English diplomat's wife (*Angel*, 1937) and finally the barroom queen 'Frenchie' in *Destry Rides Again* (1939).

In the German press, the capacity of this German-yet-international star to transcend the boundaries of nation was often proudly celebrated. Her penchant for boundary transgression was evident not only in her screen roles, but in her actual geographical mobility; thus the gossip columns admired the ease with which she traversed cities and continents, appearing now in Los Angeles, now New York, then Paris, Cannes, London. In film reviews, Dietrich's capacity to embrace the world was underscored with metaphors of spatial expansion; thus in *The Scarlet Empress*, a 'chapter of world history' was said to be used to create her role;[23] in *Desire*, she becomes the 'great actress' free to explore 'the full range of her talents';[24] and in a *Film-Kurier* feature on fans and stardom, the fervour of Dietrich's fans is explained by her capacity to represent 'beauty *unbounded*'.[25]

Dietrich's capacity for world conquest, evident in the trope of geographical mobility that surfaced in narrative constructions of her life as a star, made her, then, an ideologically appropriate figure for German audience identification; for her image addressed precisely those desires for geographical expansion that Goebbels articulates in the quote above. More problematic, however, was the association within Dietrich's star image between her traversing of geographical boundaries, and other forms of border transgression. In gender terms, first, Dietrich hovered on the border between masculinity, femininity and a more androgynous identity. Her husky vocal delivery suggested gender transgression, as did the men's suit she wore, perhaps most dazzlingly on-screen in *Morocco* and *Blonde Venus*, but off-screen too, where she became a fashion leader in early 1930s cross-dressing. If Dietrich flouted gender convention, moreover, then her transgression of sexual codes was yet more evident. Her early Hollywood films with von Sternberg only once explicitly referenced the lesbian desires she had publicly celebrated in Berlin, most famously in an alleged affair with the cabaret artiste Claire Waldoff. In a legendary cabaret scene in *Morocco*, Dietrich did kiss a female audience member full on the lips; but from this point on, her screen characters were limited to a heterosexual identity. Nonetheless, her multi-valent sexual desires were repeatedly emphasised – by references to her former prostitution in *Dishonored*, for instance, tales of her past as fallen woman in *Shanghai Express*, or of extra-marital liaison in *Blonde Venus*, *The Scarlet Empress* and *The Devil is a Woman*.

Perhaps the most prominent source of outrage among German commentators, however, was the suggestion of racial mixing in Dietrich's screen persona. From *The Blue Angel* (1930) on, Dietrich's gender and sexual transgressions were brought into association in her films with an implied slippage across ethnic identities. When Emil Jannings as *Blue Angel*'s Immanuel Rath awakes for the first time in Lola Lola/Dietrich's bedroom, his initial encounter is not with Dietrich, but with the black doll that became, as her daughter Maria Riva later revealed, Dietrich's 'good-luck charm' throughout her life, and a regular presence in her films.[26] Traditionally, the doll is for girls and women a powerful figure of identification; thus Dietrich's capacity to put herself in the place of the black other is already suggested by the black playmate that is an apparently incidental element of *mise-en-scène* in *The Blue Angel*. The suggestion here of mobile ethnicity is reinforced in Dietrich's later films. In *Morocco*, Dietrich as Amy Jolly is fascinated by local women who form liaisons with Foreign Legion men, then trail them, even into battle, and remain ever attentive to their needs. Though Dietrich at first scorns such primitive subjection, she herself 'goes native' in the final sequence, discarding high-heeled shoes to join the peasant women in their pursuit of soldier lovers across the desert.

Clearly, then, Dietrich's star image infringes the norms of racial and sexual purity around which Third Reich ideologies of identity were articulated. But to read her image in purely ideological terms would be to miss what Dietrich reveals of the specifically cinematic issue of Hollywood stardom and its problematic reception in Germany. *Of course* Dietrich was reviled in the German press – for her 'American' flirtations with gender and sexual ambiguity, or her supposed racial degeneracy. At the same time, however, as late as 1936, her film *Desire* could still be ecstatically reviewed in the German press; indeed the continuation of at least a smattering of sympathetic reporting on Dietrich until late-decade bespeaks a continued fascination with her image in Nazi Germany. It was not Dietrich's star image *per se* that was damned, then; indeed her excessive qualities, the 'boundlessness' of her beauty, were recognised as star attributes that German film might wish to emulate (and later did, most centrally in the star construction of Zarah Leander as the Third Reich's principal film diva). The crucial ideological issue was rather the extent to which star quality could be harnessed, its ambivalences managed and its excesses regulated to meet demands for a specifically German star mode of the kind articulated above by such Nazi fellow travellers as Hippler and Wegener.

Richard de Cordova has observed that it is in discourses of reception that what he terms this 'work of regulation' occurs. For Cordova, the star system involves 'a strict regulation of … knowledge produced about the actor': a knowledge circulated and managed across a range of media forms, including the trade and popular film press, advertising, newsreels and so on.[27] Under the Third Reich, of course, that regulation was orchestrated by the state via stringent media censorship, including the outlawing in 1936 of critical film reviewing in favour of apologetic 'film contemplation' (*Filmbetrachtung*). In that context, a study of the press reception of Dietrich can help reveal which elements of her version of Hollywood stardom were deemed ideologically assimilable to Third Reich star discourse – and which rejected. In what follows, therefore, an analysis of Dietrich coverage in the film press and other sources is used to explore three strategies in the 'regulation' of her image in post-1933 Germany. The first strategy involved a repudiation of Dietrich's capacity for masquerade: a capacity considered to offend the personality aesthetic underpinning star construction in Third Reich film. Second, constraints on the masquerade were imposed in part through the privileging in reception discourses of linear narrative over visual spectacle (my example here is Frank Borzage's *Desire*). Third and finally, Dietrich's image was 'managed' through the rescripting of her personal life as a story of return to home and father/mother Germany: a story that returned Dietrich also to a symbolic place as an icon not of Hollywood, but of German nation.

From masquerade to narrative: *The Devil is a Woman* and *Desire*

I suggested above that a Romantic conception of personality as expressive of inner essence was central to Third Reich film aesthetics. By contrast, the Hollywood star system can be characterised as modernist in its foregrounding of the split between the star's private and public personae: a split therefore between the self and its image, identity and representation. Unsurprisingly therefore, it was in those films that emphasised Dietrich's status as image that she was most reviled by German critics. *The Devil is a Woman* is a case in point. The film was in any case politically dubious in the Third Reich context, since its plot circulated around a Spanish republican (Cesar Romero), who wins the heart of Dietrich as the seductress, Concha Perez. *The Devil*'s deviant propensities were evident, too, in its bizarrely disjointed scripting by John dos Passos – a figure already suspect in Germany for his left politics and literary experimentalism. But it was the film's visual style that attracted the greatest opprobrium. Like many of von Sternberg's films, *The Devil* was reviled for its 'emptiness' and 'lack of meaning'. This was a film in which visual signifiers were released from their 'real' referents; thus Dietrich's image was split, fragmented, rendered unrecognisable as it became 'two (kilo)metres of lipstick-laden lips on screen, amongst a sea of garlands and massed balloons'.[28] But the image was not only fractured, released from the 'illusion of wholeness' that Linda Schulte-Sasse has suggested was pivotal to Third Reich representations of identity.[29] Dietrich is divorced too from the 'soul' that should infuse her; she is the 'shadow of a costumed vamp' in a film with a 'corpse-like absence of soul'.

Echoing Hippler's condemnation of modern acting style as masquerade, reviews of *The Devil*, then, deplore Dietrich's departure from her 'essence' as an emblem of German identity. Coverage of a subsequent film, *Desire*, by contrast, reveals a Dietrich still worthy of redemption. *Film-Kurier* enthuses:

The Devil is a Woman (1935)

> No longer is Dietrich the centre of some techno-aesthetic experiment à la Sternberg. Here, she plays a role that … has a genuine beginning and end, a meaning and a content – a comedy role whose possibilities are recognised and exploited so convincingly that it is towards her above all that applause at the end of the film is directed.[30]

In *Desire*, then, Dietrich's image is seen as rescued from the ambivalences characteristic of the masquerade, and anchored instead in narrative and character. In many ways, too, the review was accurate. Borzage (as *Film-Kurier* also notes) abandons von Sternberg's disruptive use of un-motivated star close-up in *The Devil*; similarly, Dietrich's capacity for masquerade, drawn upon in von Sternberg's films to heighten the ambiguity of her image, is both nar-ratively motivated, and negatively valued. Dietrich in *Desire* plays a jewel thief, the success of whose mission (she steals a priceless pearl necklace) depends on her capacity for disguise. That redemption is possible only when the masquerade is relinquished is emphasised in the film's dénouement, when Dietrich dons a demure A-line skirt and workaday jacket to confess her crime to her would-be fiancé, Tom Bradley (Gary Cooper). Earlier in the film, too, the threat of the masquerade – its capacity to destabilise identity – has been deflected by its comedic treatment. In

the opening sequences, Dietrich's ability to pull off her crime depends on her disguise as the wife of two men, a psychiatrist and a jeweller. A subsequent scene, in which the two confront each other, each convinced that Dietrich is the other's wife, is not only among the film's funniest; it is also noticeably lengthy – as if it took this long to defuse the threat to symbolic order represented by Dietrich's slip-page across identities.

Dietrich the prodigal daughter

Film press responses to *The Devil* and *Desire* rehearse, then, both that denunciation of the star-image-as-mask, and the desire for stars' integration into aesthetic totalities (the totality of the actorly ensemble, or of well-made narrative) that I identified earlier as a characteristic of Third Reich star aesthetics. A third strategy in the regulation of Dietrich's star image is revealed, moreover, by press treat-ment of the continuing uncertainty over Dietrich's future return to Germany.

Dietrich was, of course, but one of a host of film per-sonnel who entered Hollywood in successive waves of Weimar emigration. Her contemporaries, émigrés who tried their luck in Hollywood from the late 1920s on, included such major figures as Emil Jannings; Lil Dagover, the *grande dame* of German Expressionism; and Lilian Harvey, the Anglo-German actress who chirruped her way to stardom in the 1930 musical *Die Drei von der Tankstelle* (*The Three from the Filling Station*).

What distinguished Dietrich was her refusal to return. Jannings, despite winning an Academy Award for his per-formance in von Sternberg's *The Last Command* (1928), came back after only three years (1926–9) to renew his reputation as one of Germany's foremost actors of stage and screen. Dagover's 1932 Hollywood sojourn was still briefer, yielding only one engagement, despite her distin-guished history in such films as *Das Cabinet des Dr Caligari* (*The Cabinet of Dr Caligari*, 1919), or *Der Müde Tod* (*Destiny*, 1921). Harvey's comeback was the German remake of Frank Capra's *It Happened One Night* (1934), *Glückskinder* (*Lucky Kids*, 1936), which re-established her as one of Germany's premier musical comedy stars (until she fled the country for good in 1939).

The contrast with Dietrich was stark. Although a regu-lar visitor to Europe throughout the 1930s, she never crossed the border to Germany; indeed it was not until 1944/5 that she would return, this time as an American cit-izen and US army entertainer. Nonetheless, from 1933 on, the film press regularly speculated on Dietrich's return. Until mid-decade at least, the trade journal *Film-Kurier*, for instance, regularly (mis)reported Dietrich's supposedly imminent German visits, beginning with a confident announcement in January 1933 of Dietrich's plans for a February trip.[31] That those plans were shelved was not finally confirmed until July of the same year, in a report that noted irritably that Dietrich would shortly be visiting Cannes (and could thus, by implication, make a detour to Germany without difficulty).[32] By July 1934, when Dietrich was reported to have called off a planned Viennese tour, the journal's rancour was evident; thus for the first time, 'Marlene' became 'Frau Dietrich' in an article that noted with injured irony that 'already last year, Frau Dietrich noticeably omitted to grace her German homeland and us un-modern Berliners with her presence.'[33]

The piece displays many of the narrative and stylistic features of what was at this stage still a recurrent news story of Dietrich's imminent return. Defending the star against attacks in the German popular press, *Film-Kurier* declares, 'Though we never try to obscure … the emptiness of her performance, its … vapid quality, we (believe that) "God is glad of the repentant sinner …" And Marlene Dietrich is a beautiful sinner indeed.'[34]

The biblical allusion – 'God is glad of the repentant sinner' – situates Dietrich as a prodigal daughter whose offences will be forgiven, if only she comes home. In post-1933 Germany, of course, it was not primarily in Christianity that this prodigal return was ideologically located, but in Nazi myths of ethnic unity. The return to the *Reich* of all ethnic Germans was a key feature of Nazi racial policy: hence Adolf Hitler's comment in *Mein Kampf* that, 'People of the same blood should be in the same *Reich*. The German people will have no right to engage in colonial policy until they shall have brought all their children together in one State.'[35] *Mein Kampf*'s phrasing is typical of fascist nationalism in its use of a key melodramatic trope – the child's return to the mother – to articulate the racial ideology of *Heim ins Reich*. The image of the prodigal daughter, and the narrative of her return, were, moreover, recurrent features of contemporary German film melodrama. Detlef Sierck/Douglas Sirk's early feature *Schlußakkord* (*Final Chord*, 1936) tells the story of an émigré mother who returns to Germany seeking reunion not only with her child, but – through her romance with a prominent conductor – with German cultural tradition. That same year, one of German cinema's rising stars, Marika Rökk, scored a hit with *Und Du, mein Schatz, fährst mit* (*Come Too, My Love*, 1936) the tale of an operetta-singer-turned-variety-star who abandons an American career in favour of wifely duties in her German home. The formula was perfected in the Zarah Leander vehicle and

box-office blockbuster *Heimat* (1938). Based, like Dietrich's *Song of Songs*, on a novel by Hermann Sudermann, *Heimat* achieves the resolution that Dietrich's narrative refused; for here, as one contemporary review put it, 'Zarah Leander is … the great figure of homecoming, a woman who fled … her paternal home …, then endured the bitterest personal sacrifices before … returning to the home she has always loved and never forgotten …'[36] The contrast, both with Dietrich's films, and with her biography, is stark. In almost none of her films does narrative resolution involve homecoming. The final frame of *Morocco*, for instance, shows Dietrich disappearing across the horizon to begin life as a desert vagrant. Similarly, though the dénouement of *Shanghai Express* returns Dietrich to her British lover, there is no suggestion that they will now leave China for less exotic European climes.

Press commentary on Dietrich, by contrast, resists her films' territorial dispersion of her image by reasserting the fantasy of her imminent journey home. The fantasy character of Dietrich commentary is most evident in its use of the conventions of film melodrama to cover the life of the star. Contemporary reportage has regular recourse to the great melodramatic motifs: desire (Germany's for Dietrich); transgression (hers, in Hollywood); guilt (Dietrich is a 'beautiful sinner'); redemption (achieved by her return home). Those motifs are embedded, too, in the classical narratives of family melodrama: Dietrich is the 'child'[37] who has sinned; her German audience a 'loyal' public that will 'forgive its favourites much; for it takes more than a single error for one who is truly loved to fall out of favour'.[38]

Towards the end of the decade, hopes of Dietrich's return were fading; and when the familial reunion that was the desired conclusion to her story was finally revealed as unattainable, German press responses were couched in the bitter irony of an Oedipal desire that, once rebuffed, turns to sadism. Thus in December 1937, *Film-Kurier* for the first time satirised Dietrich, in the following vein:

> Marlene Dietrich has announced her willingness to make a film for *Tobis* next year, provided that, along with her not inconsiderable fee, she is granted the following conditions: 1) that she receives the title of professor, 2) that no-one answers her back, 3) that her hats be exhibited in Ufa's education department …[39]

Two years after *Film-Kurier*'s embittered caricature, Dietrich took US citizenship, Germany went to war, and the dream of the star's return was shelved. Yet it did not die, nor indeed did the ambivalences Dietrich elicited in

German discourses of nation. In post-war West Germany, the star's wartime absence was widely and perversely interpreted as an attack on German integrity; thus like many returning émigrés, she met pervasive hostility when she visited the country for a 1960 cabaret tour. The smear campaigns that accompanied Dietrich throughout that visit were the final nail in the coffin of her relation to Germany; she returned only in death, to be buried in 1992 in her native Berlin. As Gertrud Koch has observed, moreover, even that return was fraught with difficulty: there were few prominent guests at her funeral, and a planned public ceremony was cancelled in view of 'vox pop … voices … that still consider Dietrich a "traitor"'.[40]

Dietrich's status as a political irritant in post-war Germany has been matched by a continuing difficulty in the cinematic assimilation of her image. Josef Vilsmaier's 2000 biopic, *Marlene*, is a case in point. In a manner uncannily akin to Third Reich representations of the star, the film relies upon a pedestrian narrative realism that suppresses the polysemic sensuality of her image. As one reviewer put it, *Marlene* is little more than an 'insipid chronicle of showcase episodes patched together with the glue of … embarrassing sentiment'.[41] Most extraordinarily, Vilsmaier's film, in fabricating as the object of Dietrich's 'true love' a German officer involved in the resistance, revives the 1930s fantasy of Dietrich's symbolic belonging to an ethically unsullied German nation. Even after her death, then, it seems that Dietrich's star image lives on as a disruptive element in cultural nationalist fantasies of Germany as aesthetic totality and/or integrated nation: a source of trouble that can find a place only within those traditions in German cinema that refuse (unlike Vilsmaier's film) to suppress those ambiguities that are the hallmark of stardom Dietrich-style.

Notes

1 Quoted in Gerd Albrecht, *Der Film im Dritten Reich. Eine Dokumentation* (Karlsruhe: DOKU-Verlag, 1979), p. 27.

2 See for instance Christine Gledhill, 'Introduction', in Gerd Albrecht (ed.), *Stardom. Industry of Desire* (London and New York: Routledge, 1991), p. xiii. Richard Dyer's study, *Stars*, 2nd edn (London: BFI, 1998) similarly takes Hollywood as its principal model, as do Stephen Lowry and Helmut Korte, who argue in their co-authored volume *Der Filmstar* (Stuttgart and Weimar: Metzler, 2000) – a work greatly indebted to Dyer – that Germany had a Hollywood-style star system at least through the period of Ufa's dominance (pp. 259–72). Studies of early cinema often present a less Hollywood-centric view: see e.g. Knut

Hickethier, 'Vom Theaterstar zum Filmstar. Merkmale des Starwesens um die Wende vom 19. Zum 20. Jahrhundert', in Werner Faulstich and Helmut Korte (eds.), *Der Star. Geschichte, Rezeption, Bedeutung* (Munich: Fink, 1997), pp. 29–47.

3 Geoffrey Nowell-Smith, 'Introduction', in idem and Steven Ricci (eds.), *Hollywood and Europe. Economics, Culture, National Identity 1945–95* (London: BFI, 1998), pp. 1–3.

4 Joseph Garncarz, 'Hollywood in Germany. Die Rolle des amerikanischen Films in Deutschland: 1925–1990', in Uli Jung (ed.), *Der deutsche Film: Aspekte seiner Geschichte von den Anfängen bis zur Gegenwart* (Trier: Wissenschaftlicher Verlag, 1993), p. 172.

5 Joseph Garncarz, 'Warum kennen Filmhistoriker viele Weimarer Topstars nicht mehr?', *montage/av*, vol. 6, no. 2, (1997), p. 67.

6 Idem, 'The Nationally Distinctive Star System of the Weimar Republic', unpublished paper, delivered at the 3rd Popular European Cinema Conference at the University of Warwick, March 2000. On Third Reich stars, see Andrea Winkler-Mayerhöfer, *Starkult als Propagandamittel* (Munich: Ölschläger, 1992); also – specifically on contractual arrangements – Boguslav Drewniak, *Der deutsche Film 1938–1945* (Düsseldorf: Droste, 1987), esp. p. 150.

7 Garncarz, 'The Nationally Distinctive Star System of the Weimar Republic'. On stars and the discourse of film art under National Socialism, see Erica Carter, *Dietrich's Ghosts: Stars in Third Reich Film* (London: BFI, forthcoming).

8 'Das Band, das uns verbindet. Tatsachen und Anmerkungen über den ausländischen Film in Deutschland', *Film-Kurier*, 1 January 1934.

9 'Liquidiert Amerika seine deutschen Niederlassungen?', *Film-Kurier*, 17 June 1936. US imports were yet more stringently controlled after 1939 in retaliation against alleged anti-German sentiment in numerous films, including Warner Bros.' *Confessions of a Nazi Spy*. Some US films remained in distribution until well into 1940, but by 1941, the import and exhibition ban was total.

10 Markus Spieker, *Hollywood unterm Hakenkreuz: Der amerikanische Spielfilm im Dritten Reich* (Trier: Wissenschaftlicher Verlag, 1999), p. 45.

11 See Gerd Albrecht, *Nationalsozialistische Filmpolitik: Eine soziologische Untersuchung über die Spielfilme des Dritten Reichs* (Stuttgart: Enke, 1969), chs. 8 and 11; also Winkler-Mayerhöfer, op. cit., pp. 91ff.

12 'Ein Wort über die Star-Verehrung', *Film-Kurier*, 12 January 1933.

13 'Das Starunwesen, Seine Folgen und möglichen Gegenmaßnahmen', *Film-Kurier*, 1 January 1935; 'Filmkünstler im kleinen Kino', *Film-Kurier*, 3 March 1935.

14 *Filmwelt*, no. 21, 25 March 1937.

15 See David Bordwell, 'The Classical Hollywood Style', in David Bordwell, Janet Staiger and Kristin Thompson, *The Classical Hollywood Cinema. Film Style and Mode of Production* (London: Routledge, 1985), pp. 1–84.

16 Ibid., pp. 12–18.

17 'Paul Wegener sprach in der Lessing-Hochschule über die Schauspielkunst', *Film-Kurier*, 22 December 1934.

18 Fritz Hippler, *Betrachtungen zum Filmschaffen* (Berlin: Hesse, 1942), p. 91.

19 Ibid., p. 6.

20 Ibid., p. 82.

21 Reichminister's address, 9 February 1934, cited in Oskar Kalbus, *Vom Werden deutscher Filmkunst*, vol. 2 (Altona-Bahrenfeld: Cigaretten-Bilderdienst, 1935), p. 102.

22 Karsten Witte, *Lachende Erben, Toller Tag: Filmkomödie im Dritten Reich* (Berlin: Vorwerk 8, 1995), p. 112.

23 'Geänderte Pläne von Marlene Dietrich', *Film-Kurier*, 5 April 1934.

24 'Sehnsucht', *Film-Kurier*, 3 April 1936.

25 'Ein Wort über die Star-Verehrung', *Film-Kurier*, 12 January 1933.

26 Maria Riva, *Marlene Dietrich* (London: Bloomsbury, 1992), p. 71.

27 Richard de Cordova, 'The Emergence of the Star System in America', in Christine Gledhill, op. cit., pp. 10 and 28.

28 All quotes from 'Die Spanische Tänzerin', *Film-Kurier*, 29 June 1935.

29 Linda Schulte-Sasse, *Entertaining the Third Reich: Illusions of Wholeness in Nazi Cinema* (Durham and London: Duke University Press, 1996).

30 'Sehnsucht', *Film-Kurier*, 3 April 1936. On Dietrich and masquerade, see also Mary Ann Doane, *Femmes Fatales. Feminism, Film Theory, Psychoanalysis* (New York and London: Routledge, 1991).

31 'Paramount klagt gegen Marlene', *Film-Kurier*, 3 January 1933.

32 'Marlenes Pläne. Kein Besuch in Deutschland?' *Film-Kurier*, 15 January 1933.

33 'Marlene Dietrich befindet sich nicht in Wien', *Film-Kurier*, 4 July 1934.

34 Ibid.

35 Adolf Hitler, *Mein Kampf* (London: Hutchinson, 1976) (German original 1925/6), p. 17.

36 Felix A. Dargel, ' "Heimat" ' im Ufa-Palast', reproduced in Gerd Albrecht (ed.), *Die großen Filmerfolge* (Ebersberg: Edition achteinhalb, 1985), p. 32.

37 'What have they done to you, my child?' is the pathetic question that concludes *Film-Kurier*'s review of *The Devil*, 29 June 1935.

38 'Fussnoten. Natürlich zieht Marlene', *Film-Kurier*, 3 July 1935.

39 'Knapp und witzig', *Film-Kurier*, 31 December 1937.

40 Gertrud Koch, 'Exorcised. Marlene Dietrich and German Nationalism', in Pam Cook and Philip Dodd (eds.), *Women and Film. A Sight and Sound Reader* (London: Scarlet Press, 1993), p. 11.

41 Hellmuth Karasek, 'Der ungeliebte Engel', *Der Spiegel*, 25, 2000, p. 246.

7

Heinz Rühmann – The Archetypal German

Stephen Lowry

Heinz Rühmann was both the leading star of the twentieth century in Germany and virtually unknown outside his own country. Although in the 1960s he did appear in a Hollywood movie, Stanley Kramer's *Ship of Fools* (1964), as well as in several European co-productions, this had little effect on his career. He was, and remained, a specifically German movie star. Moreover, he was one of the best-known and best-liked stars in Germany for much of the time from his breakthrough to stardom in the early 1930s until today, making over a hundred movies, many of which are still shown regularly on TV.

Heinz Rühmann's popularity may seem even stranger outside Germany if one looks at his image and the movies he made. They do not correspond to any of the usual clichés of German cinema as heavy, soul-searching drama. He was never one of those tortured expressionist protagonists, and during the Nazi period, when his star status really became established, he never appeared as a nationalist hero or a fated genius. In his appearance – small, with round cheeks and a pointed nose – and his way of acting – agile, often pouting or with a cheeky, but boyish smile[1] – Rühmann was not the least bit soldierly and did not even make a convincing romantic lead. Instead, his popularity was firmly based on his portrayal of the 'little man' in numerous light comedies.

Still, Heinz Rühmann was indisputably the leading German star and as such is typical of German national cinema. Its domestic success has always been based to a large part on comedies which have not exported well and thus not shaped its international reputation. In this respect, comedies, and Rühmann as the genre's leading exponent, are more culturally specific and representative than the art-house movies or the Nazi propaganda films that have seemed so Germanic to the rest of the world.

At home, Rühmann was regarded as a 'people's actor' (*Volksschauspieler*), and even as a 'German as God might have dreamt of him'.[2] His reputation rested on his role as the petit bourgeois hero, the 'little man', and – later in his career – as a representation of the 'eternally human'. This image enabled him to succeed during the Nazi period as well as during the 'economic miracle' of the 1950s. It also allowed him to be useful within the ideological system of Nazi cinema and – perhaps less paradoxically than might first seem – later to be remodelled into an emblem of the integrity of the 'average man' under a repressive regime.[3] His role as a German 'everyman' led him to be seen explicitly as an icon of the national self-image. Celebrations of his film work – and of the image he represented – began in 1940 when he was granted the title of 'state actor' (*Staatsschauspieler*) by the Nazis, continued with numerous prizes as the most popular actor in the 1950s and 60s, and included honours from the city of Munich, the Bavarian state and the highest order granted to civilians by the German federal government.

The following discussion of Rühmann's career and films locates some reasons for his popularity, and situates it in its historical context. Rühmann's star image is presented here as a relatively constant cinematic representation of the basic petit bourgeois habitus and norms that made up a central moment of cultural continuity in all parts of German society throughout the twentieth century. Rühmann is an image of conformity to middle-class social values, be it those of the Nazi fellow travellers (*Mitläufer*) or the closed-minded mentality in the Adenauer period. This point is illustrated by an exploration of the development of Rühmann's image, particularly of how his roles and the film narratives unfold similar models of integration into the status quo of the respective period.

Rühmann presented an image of normality, but as a star, his image had to be attractive enough to work as a box-office magnet. While much closer to the audience than the more heroic stars, he was still a very special 'little man', one who succeeds, who always lands on his feet, who holds his own through comic repartee. In this way, he imbued his embodiment of the 'man on the street' with the specific, larger-than-life individuality of a movie star.

German cinema's star system – like any other – worked as a system of differences. It was set up to serve economic interests, and that meant that it had to offer a broad range of stars to appeal to the tastes of various audiences. Rühmann was primarily a comic actor, and thus his image was essentially different from the leading character actors of the Weimar and Nazi periods such as Heinrich George, Werner Krauss, and Emil Jannings, as well as from romantic leading men like Willi Forst, Willy Birgel, Willy Fritsch, Gustav Fröhlich, and Viktor Staal, or adventurous heroes like Hans Albers. All were popular stars, and each of them represented a facet of how contemporary culture defined masculine ideals. What distinguishes Rühmann from the others was the continuity and longevity of his image. While the older ideals and traditional identities represented by character actors and heroes became obsolete, Rühmann's image of the 'little man' proved able to adapt to the new situation of restoration and the economic miracle in the 1950s. He filled a comic slot alongside another version of petit bourgeois masculinity, the upright young men in the Heimatfilme predominately played by Rudolf Prack.

Rühmann's star image of the 'little man' represents one way German society tried to harmonise modernisation and notions of more traditional life forms from the 1930s onwards. Rühmann shows the adaptation of the Kleinbürger to modernism. This was an overarching development of German society on its late and crisis-ridden way towards modernity. The technological and social dystopias of Weimar cinema, and the reactionary, anti-modernist strain of Nazism were two extreme reactions against that development. Rühmann's films are figurations of the other, more continuous and longer-term adaptation to social modernisation in the forms of private life, middle-class materialism and social conformity.

Rühmann's career

Rühmann's career began on the stage. He developed his typical acting style when he had to play a bit part as a waiter: feeling that this was below him, he delivered his lines in the chopped-off, monotone way that became his trademark. His first film role came in 1926, but it was not until 1930 that he made his breakthrough in the popular musical comedy Die Drei von der Tankstelle (The Three from the Filling Station). At first, his youthful élan seemed to predestine him to play the comic sidekick for actors like Willy Fritsch, Hans Albers, and Max Pallenberg. However, he soon took on leading roles and quickly advanced to star status.[4] By the mid-1930s he was appearing in as many as six movies per year, most of which did very well at the box-office. In parts adapted from stage comedies such as Der Mustergatte (A Model Husband, 1937) or specially created for films, Rühmann solidified his image.

Rühmann was highly successful with the public, but his career ran into trouble when he came under pressure from the Nazi authorities because of his Jewish wife. After he divorced her in 1938, he was back in good standing and was given his own production unit within the Terra studio. In 1940 he was named 'state actor'. During the war he appeared in some of his greatest box-office successes, including Die Feuerzangenbowle (The Hot Wine Punch, 1944), which was not only the most successful film comedy during the entire Nazi period, but has retained its popularity until today.

After the war, Rühmann went through a career slump, largely because the public did not accept him in the period of so-called rubble films. He had to wait until 1953 to make a comeback, but then regained star status immediately, again playing the 'little man'. Rühmann gradually established a reputation as a character actor, emphasising the human strengths and weaknesses of his roles in films like Der Hauptmann von Köpenick (The Captain from Köpenick, 1956) and Der brave Soldat Schwejk (The Good Soldier Schwejk, 1960). Nevertheless, attempts to cast him against his type, for example in a satire about the Nazi period, Der Schulfreund (The Schoolmate, 1960), or as a rigidly moralist police inspector in Es geschah am hellichten Tag (It Happened in Broad Daylight, 1958), tended to fail for the broad public. It wanted to see Rühmann in his 'typical' roles and misread such seriously meant ones as humorous.[5] Performance on stage (for instance in Waiting for Godot) and TV (Death of a Salesman) furthered his image as a serious actor, but his best-liked films continued to be comedies. With increasing age he became a 'legend in his own time' and a fatherly version of the 'eternal human', reading Christmas stories on TV and appearing on talk shows. With his extremely long career and the high degree of continuity in his image, Rühmann came to represent 'the' German star in popular consciousness (an image also played upon in his last screen role in Wim Wenders' In weiter Ferne, so nah! [Far Away So Close, 1993]). Heinz Rühmann died in 1994 at the age of 92, with obituaries in all the media acclaiming him as a great actor and human being. A popular magazine, Bunte, summed up:

Der Mustergatte (1937)

We loved Heinz Rühmann. We loved him because, in a time of flexing muscles, a time of horrible crimes and horrible bravery, he did not play the great hero, but the crafty little loser. This was no hero, no oath of allegiance become human, no 'man of destiny'. Instead, he represented the casually sauntering German. … He was quick-witted, humorous, funny, and wise – and that is how we wish to keep him in mind.[6]

Others went further:

With his wonderful films he drove away our everyday worries. He took us by the hand and carried us away to the land of smiles. Heinz Rühmann was a star, but always remained one of us. Simple. Modest. He brought us much happiness.[7]

No one smiled as roguishly, no one reached as many ears with a soft, almost broken voice. … Heinz Rühmann is dead, but in the hearts of millions he will live on.[8]

The Nazi period

The formative years for Rühmann's image were the 1930s. Thus, his rise as a star coincided with the period of the National Socialist takeover and consolidation of power and his most successful films were made during the War. He was a major star of Nazi cinema, and was quite typical of it, since for the most part the films of this period were not propaganda, but entertainment with latent ideological content.

Although Rühmann later kept his private life out of public sight and gained the image of a reticent, unpretentious person, in the 1930s and 40s, his 'private' life was very much part of his star persona, closely linked to his on-screen image. While studio publicity and star build-up was not as extensive and planned in Germany as in Hollywood, the public was well informed about its stars.[9] They knew all about Rühmann's hobbies – cars and aeroplanes. A movie magazine even ran a contest, asking readers to send in ideas for a movie in which Rühmann could play a pilot, offering a flight with him in his private plane as a prize. At the time, when the pilot was still one of the new heroes of technical modernity (and of course of the Nazi war effort), this lent Rühmann's image a dynamic and daring side, compensating his more humble role as the 'little man'. The marriage to his second wife, the actress Hertha Feiler, was well publicised in magazines and a book prizing them as a model couple.[10] In general, writers stressed similarities between Rühmann and his screen persona and emphasised his 'authenticity', saying he played himself. While that is exaggerated, he did play an unchanging kind of character that became synonymous with 'Rühmann'.

There are recurring patterns in the characters and plots of Rühmann's movies, especially 'integration in power structures' and 'the petit bourgeois run astray'. Both deal with social integration, using the narrative, the protagonist and Rühmann's image to work through and re-affirm middle-class identity, the social hierarchy and – as Sabine Hake has stressed[11] – a particular form of masculinity.

Rühmann's best-known movie, *Die Feuerzangenbowle*, shows how the character becomes integrated into structures of authority.[12] This film tells the story of a debonair author who had been educated by a private tutor and never gone to school. Fired by a wager and the hot wine punch of the title, he decides to disguise himself as a pupil and go to school. In doing so, he becomes not only increasingly childish – playing pranks on the teachers – but also more 'natural' and 'human'. He discards his cosmopolitan affectations and becomes 'himself': spontaneous, boyish and 'normal'. Significantly, he also discards his sophisticated, liberated and sexy, but cold-blooded and manipulative lover, trading her in for a wholesome and even maternal schoolgirl. The schoolboy pranks which are the source of most of the humour in the film and which might seem to suggest rebellion against the teachers, are just a necessary step in the character's search for his identity. They never really threaten authority. Instead, they just re-affirm the 'natural' superiority of the Rühmann character, culminating in his triumph at the end, when he parodies one of the teachers and makes fools of the entire faculty. However, this is no rebellion, as is made clear when he reveals his real identity as a best-selling author, complete with doctoral diploma and a high income. His youthful jokes are a necessary part of his socialisation. They integrate him into the school class, and by extension the *Volksgemeinschaft*, the Nazi notion of a corporative community, simultaneously affirming his natural position in life and society. This narrative process also reconfirms Rühmann's star image, peeling away the 'false' traits that the character first shows to re-establish his identity as an ordinary, but special, 'little man'.

A similar process structures many of Rühmann's films, including another wartime success, *Quax, der Bruchpilot*

(*Quax, the Crash Pilot*, 1941). Here the central character, a proper but insecure employee in a travel bureau, wins pilot's lessons in a contest. In flight school it is not just flying that he has to learn – though his apparent lack of skill quickly earns him the nickname 'Quax, the crash pilot' – but rather discipline, courage and above all comradeship. His 'civilian' attitudes (he acts like a tourist demanding first-class service) can be seen as a humorous protest against the military-style discipline of flight school or even as a satire of Nazi reality. However, the potentially 'subversive' force of comedy is quickly redirected into an affirmation of the status quo: when 'Quax' gives up his affectations and his false individualism, he is able to become 'one of the boys' and even proves to be a naturally talented pilot. In doing so, he wins the affection of the girl and of his paternally authoritarian flight instructor. Again, the infantilisation of the figure – Rühmann plays several scenes with the instructor like a child expecting punishment or begging for affection – and his submission to power are shown as the way to gain identity and even authority: in the end he is a flight instructor himself. Voluntary subordination proves to be the first step towards identification with and assumption of authority.

The second pattern – the petit bourgeois run astray – structures several of Rühmann's films in the 1930s. The humour in these 'comedies of errors' is primarily based on class differences and mistaken identities. In films like *Pipin der Kurze* (*Pipin, the Short*, 1934), *Die Umwege des schönen Karl* (*Handsome Karl's Roundabout Ways*, 1937) and *Der Gasmann* (*The Meter Man*, 1941), lower middle-class protagonists unexpectedly become wealthy or involved in high society. This goes to their heads, they begin living a life of luxury, and fall for previously unattainable women. Along the way, they lose their family and friends, along with their own 'true' identity. But fate catches up with them and they return to their old life and its values. Here, too, a process of education structures the story: the philistine, who dreams of riches and social status, gets a chance to live out his fantasies, only, of course, to find that they do not bring him happiness. Thus, the film's (happy) ending rigidly reconfirms his class and personal identity, which at first was not truly secure.

An interesting example of this storyline is found in *Die Umwege des schönen Karl*, which tells of a small-town waiter who dreams of making it big, goes to Berlin in the time of the Weimar Republic, and through a series of mishaps is mistaken for a member of high society.[13] While still a waiter, he also becomes involved in the world of business and politics, falls in love with the daughter of the head of the 'Liberal Economic Party', estranges himself from the girl who loves him, and at the same time – to finance his double life – starts betting on horse races and becomes embroiled in the underworld. In the end he is forced to return ruefully to his former position and to his fiancée, renouncing the big city, politics and the upper class, which have by then been denounced as hypocritical and morally worthless.

This movie is interesting in that it parodies 1920s German film style to attack Weimar politics and society. Many of the film's comic – and ideological – effects result from the contrasts it builds up between the various characters and the social classes they represent. The plot firmly re-establishes middle-class identity and values, not only because the protagonist must learn to embrace them as his own, but because they prove themselves against all the other characters, classes and milieus. The class discourse is paralleled by a corroboration of conventional gender roles: the Rühmann character must not only renounce his dreams of social climbing, but with them his sexual fantasies regarding the upper-class woman. She is shown to be more neurotic than erotic and to be quite willing to sacrifice her feelings for him in favour of her social standing. In the end, he recognises the qualities of his wholesome and loyal middle-class fiancée and remorsefully returns to her. Thus the film addresses various desires, only to redirect them in the course of the story into conventional channels, while at the same time hooking up to elements of Nazi discourse such as *völkisch* anti-capitalism and the defamation of democracy. The ideological work in the text was effective in part because of Rühmann's function as actor and star embodying the 'little man'.

By the early 1930s it was possible to build Rühmann films around his stable and popular star image. An author writing in 1940 described the typical scheme of Rühmann films as follows:

> [Rühmann is] always the little man who wants to break out of his routine life, but who can't seem to manage it. Until one day, on his own or because of someone else, he gets involved in something that forces him to be a hero despite himself. Through this, he, the man with inferiority complexes, regains his self-confidence, so that he can now consciously make use of his capabilities, and in the end he always emerges as the winner who gets the girl. That is how the public views 'its' Heinz Rühmann, and that is how it will get to see him. …[14]

Articles from that period generally emphasise Rühmann's human qualities, his childish aspects (including both bashfulness and audaciousness), and the quiet side of his humour, which takes the sting out of it. His image and roles are characterised by contradictory traits. He is the little man, but he is a winner; he is shy, but self-assertive; he is rebellious and impertinent, but subordinate, well behaved, and at times downright servile in the face of authority. His relationship to power – both his subservience and his readiness to lord it over others – may appear quite unpleasant today, but must have seemed normal to the contemporary audience.

Rühmann's image, together with the typical narrative patterns, accounts for much of his popularity, and for the ideological effects of his films. His appearance and acting style did much to shape his image and the social, personal and gender roles associated with it. His slight stature, round cheeks, sharp nose and ready smile contributed not only to his comic effects, but also to the impression of a friendly and modest person. Quick and apparently spontaneous facial expressions and body movements displayed energy and youthfulness. His way of walking seemed particularly characteristic, leading one critic to refer to him as the 'nonchalantly sauntering German'.[15] Small exaggerations in his facial expressions gave the impression of childishness, of emotions not quite under adult control, and thus more natural and truer than is usual. Shyness, joy and anger become visible in his fidgeting, postures, expressions and way of talking. His body, as well as his manner of speaking and throwing away lines, presented a kind of casualness that seemed modern and natural, especially in contrast to the formal social conventions and soldierly rigidity often seen at the time (however, Rühmann does sometimes integrate aspects of a more 'military' way of speaking – chopped off, 'telegraphic' diction, gruffness, etc. – especially when he is trying to assert his 'manliness'). Thus, the Rühmann characters had an aspect of youthful informality and even impudence that made up part of their attractiveness, even if they now seem conventional and stuffy.

Rühmann's characters' bashfulness could quickly turn into fearful submissiveness, or into arrogance and authoritarianism. In his bodily presence and his strangely pressed voice, sometimes mumbling, stammering, or breathlessly rushing ahead, the little man shows not only a certain naturalness and nonchalance, but also his insecurity and at times deep-seated inhibitions.[16] Sex appeal is one thing he never has. When he tries to be a 'ladies' man', what is most clearly discernible is his fear of women, which can quickly turn into outright misogyny. Even when married or in love, the Rühmann characters seem strangely asexual and inhibited.[17] Just as his relationship to authority oscillates between childish rebellion and submissiveness, his relationship to women is governed by a mix of boyish inhibitions and paternalistic arrogance.

The 'little man' in the 1950s

While Nazi cinema always attracted attention as propaganda and recent studies have developed a more complex 'different take' on it,[18] the German cinema of the 1950s has generally been ignored or regarded as insignificant.[19] Here, too, although no one would claim that the films are artistic masterpieces, a new evaluation is overdue. While the conventional view is that of saccharine films and a stuffy, prudish society, seen historically, the 1950s were a time rife with social conflicts, although many of them stayed under the surface. In Germany, the rapid shift from economic recovery to a new wave of social and economic modernisation coincided with a new youth culture,[20] first steps in the direction of the sexual revolution and a shift from class politics towards a depoliticised, affluent society. Furthermore, the question of national identity was a constant, though often indirectly expressed theme throughout German culture. While the films may seem idyllic and essentially meaningless, they are forms of widely based popular culture (1956 marked the all-time high point of German cinema attendance) that forcefully exhibit West Germany's imaginary process of finding its own identity as a modern society. Thus Rühmann's comedies work through many of the same problems as the *Heimatfilme*. Both genres revolve around questions of belonging to a community that was redefining itself between the poles of Americanism and whatever 'Germanness' could still mean, between traditional life forms and consumerism, between hierarchical community (*Gemeinschaft*) and modern social mobility.[21]

Briefträger Müller (1953)

That Rühmann advanced to star status again in the 1950s is hardly a coincidence. His first major hits in this period were *Keine Angst vor großen Tieren* (*Don't Be Afraid of Wild Beasts/Bigwigs*, 1953) and *Briefträger Müller* (*Postman Müller*, 1953), which re-established him in the public's mind as the archetypal German little man, now involved with finding his place in the working world and a society increasingly involved with wealth and status. Throughout the 1950s and 60s, Rühmann played similar roles, often with a fatherly touch, in movies like *Wenn der Vater mit dem Sohne* (*When Father and Son …*, 1955), *Vater sein dagegen sehr* (*It's Tough to Be a Father*, 1957), *Der Lügner* (*The Liar*, 1961) and *Max, der Taschendieb* (*Max, the Pickpocket*, 1961).

In all these films, he portrayed essentially the same kind of character as in the 1930s and 40s. Moreover, the familiar narrative patterns of his older films also often recur. For example, *Keine Angst vor großen Tieren* tells the story of a typical Rühmann protagonist having to grow up and take on authority, while *Briefträger Müller* repeats the pattern of the philistine gone astray.

Emil Keller, the hero of *Keine Angst vor großen Tieren*, is anything but heroic. Instead, he lets his boss, his landlady and almost everyone else intimidate him. Brief moments of impudence just underline his inability to assert himself openly. He meekly accepts his subordinate position in life until he falls in love with his boss's secretary, when he is forced to try to be a 'real man' in front of her and stand up to the boss. However, his attempts to overcome his fears repeatedly fail. His hopes rise when he is mentioned in his uncle's will. However, the inheritance turns out not to be riches but three circus lions. Keller, despairing of ever improving his position, tries to hang himself in the circus cage, but mistakenly lets the lions into the ring. Suddenly, he rises to the occasion, cracks the whip and tames the lions. As the film programme describes it: 'When he leaves the cage after his lonely victory he is completely transformed. He has experienced the power of the will – a power that he will now try out in dealing with people.'[22] His new self-assured, 'manly' behaviour lets Keller overcome his boss and win the woman. Thus in the end he gains his proper position in society. While the films of the Nazi period aimed at integrating the protagonists into the *Volksgemeinschaft*, the 1950s show individual initiative to be the way of reaching the goal – family life in a detached house. Still, the basic structure – finding an identity in accord with socially accepted power relations and values – and the basic traits of the Rühmann characters remain the same.

Rühmann's films thus reveal strong continuities in their narratives as well as in the characters and the mentality they represent, but with a shift in the ideological framework from hierarchical power structures and the Nazi community to the imperatives of economic performance (*Leistungsgesellschaft*). The ideal of the nuclear family, the corresponding male gender role, the primacy of the private sphere as the place of self-realisation and above all conformity to the social status quo remain largely invariant.

The attraction of the little man

The double character of Rühmann's image as the 'little man', but also as a model figure and male lead, may help explain why he could succeed equally well in the last years of the Weimar Republic, under Nazism and afterwards. Rühmann's image and roles invoke identification and projection simultaneously. The meek little man is close to the audience, but he is also a winner who uses his wits to overcome ostensibly more powerful opponents and thus can embody wish-fulfilment fantasies. Rühmann's image has consistently been described in terms of dichotomies like 'snotty but with a lot of gentleness – the unheroic, nice hero',[23] or 'roguish and clever, but at the same time shy and shaken by fate'.[24]

In contrast with more heroic German male stars of the 1930s and 40s, Rühmann presented a surprisingly advanced, and at the same time thoroughly petit bourgeois, version of individuality consistent with the modern, consumerist lifestyle that was a consistent element of German ideology from the 1920s through Nazism and the post-war period.

Looked at critically, the Rühmann character is an opportunist, seeking his place in the status quo, including that of Nazism, but the audience could also view him as comically rebellious and as the opposite of the official heroes. In the post-war period he was rarely associated with Nazism and even managed to gain an image as having represented a 'notorious civilian' and non-conformist.[25]

However, this view systematically ignores the latent element of authoritarianism underneath the harmless surface of the Rühmann characters. This emerges in their dealings with subordinates (or women) or when they are able to gain some power. The authoritarian side may, however, also have contributed to their appeal. Participation in power was part of what made National Socialism attractive, especially to the middle classes and ambitious technocrats. Rühmann implied that the meek petit bourgeois could learn to assert himself, succeed and 'be someone', while retaining his old identity and values. Karsten Witte suggested that Rühmann's character as the eternally juvenile star, playing infantilised characters such as in *Die*

Feuerzangenbowle, also expressed a regressive fantasy of flight back to childhood and its denial of responsibility. This reflected not only the war situation, which robbed many people of their youth, but also the authoritarian Nazi system, which allowed its subjects to deny their own political responsibility.[26] The denial of responsibility continued in the post-war period, and the 'little man' pushed about by authority figures and powers beyond his control, but retaining his identity and integrity, was certainly an attractive figure. Thus, it is no coincidence that even a serious attempt to deal with the 'Third Reich' in a film like *Mein Schulfreund* casts Rühmann as the helpless victim of authoritarian structures. The rhetorical strategy of designating the 'ordinary people' as victims of Hitler, the Nazis, the war, or fate, long functioned as a way to avoid assuming guilt or responsibility for having gone along with or even supported the Nazi system.

Rühmann's image and roles were ambivalent. While his role as *aufsässiger Untertan* (rebellious subject) has often been used to exonerate him in the post-war period,[27] it seems more likely that his films had a predominately affirmative function in the Nazi era. They conform to everyday ideology in National Socialism, much of which was not specific to, but compatible with or supportive of, the Nazi system. As studies of everyday life have shown, the system depended not only on terror and control, but to a large degree on the impression of spheres of private life free of politics.

Rühmann – as a specifically German, non-exportable star – also raises the issue of the determining factors for a national cinema and a national mentality or sensibility. Klaus Kreimeier has suggested that the 'Third Reich' did not really produce a 'Nazi cinema' so much as the conditions under which specifically German films, stars and genres developed.[28] Rühmann's career may well support this thesis, particularly considering his long-term and nationally specific success. Above all, it points to larger questions of the continuity of stars, films and motifs from Weimar to the 1950s and beyond. Long-term developments in mentalities, forms of feeling, subjectivity and collective identity (as part of a specifically German process of modernisation) are involved. Although Rühmann's star image and its meaning are not identical in the differing contexts of National Socialism and the 'Economic Miracle' of the 1950s, they do show a high degree of consistency. What the star Rühmann makes visible are particular adaptations and negotiations of petit bourgeois subjectivity in the course of German history since 1930.

Notes

1 See Sabine Hake, 'Heinz Rühmann und die Inszenierung des "kleinen Mannes"', *montage/av*, 7 January 1998, pp. 33–56, for a discussion of Rühmann's physiognomy and acting style.

2 Joachim Kaiser, 'Ein deutscher wie Gott ihn träumt', *Süddeutsche Zeitung*, 7 March 1992.

3 Cf. ibid.; Boleslaw Barlog, 'Der Meister der leisen Töne', *Die Welt*, 17 April 1982.

4 In 1934, a film – *Heinz im Mond* (*Heinz on the Moon*) – used his name for the title character to capitalise on his growing popularity.

5 Cf. Anon., 'Neue Filme ja und nein: Mein Schulfreund', *Die andere Zeitung*, 11 November 1960; Else Goelz, 'Mann mit Herz', *Stuttgarter Zeitung*, 7 March 1962.

6 Joachim Kaiser, 'Rühmann und die Kunst', *Bunte*, no. 42, December 1994, pp. 56 and 60.

7 Anon., 'Er gab uns das Lachen und dahinter die Tränen', *Die Aktuelle*, no. 41, 7 October 1994. In German, the last sentence also means: 'We were lucky to have him.'

8 R. Kramer-Benner, 'Heinz Rühmann: Er schlief mit einem Lächeln ein', *Das Neue*, no. 41 (8 October 1994), p. 3.

9 See Andrea Winkler-Mayerhöfer, *Starkult als Propagandamittel. Studien zum Unterhaltungsfilm im Dritten Reich* (Munich: Olschläger, 1992), pp. 144–6, for a discussion of star publicity for Rühmann.

10 Käthe Brinker, *Heinz Rühmann. Hertha Feiler. Er und Sie* (Berlin: Wilhelm Gründler, undated [1941]).

11 Hake, op.cit.

12 Cf. Karsten Witte, 'Wie faschistisch ist die "Feuerzangenbowle"? Bemerkungen zur Filmkomödie im "Dritten Reich"', *Kirche und Film*, 29 July 1976, pp. 1–4; Stephen Lowry, 'Politik und Unterhaltung – Zum Beispiel "Die Feuerzangenbowle"', in Louis Bosshart and Wolfgang Hoffmann-Riem (eds.), *Medienlust und Mediennutz. Unterhaltung als öffentliche Kommunikation* (Munich: Olschläger, 1994), pp. 447–57.

13 See Stephen Lowry, 'Die Umwege der Ideologie. Überlegungen zur NS-Unterhaltung an Hand eines Rühmann-Films', *medium*, July–September 1990, pp. 27–30, for a more complete discussion of this film.

14 Fritz Aeckerle, 'Heinz Rühmann – Der Weg eines Humoristen' (orig. 1941), in Matthias Peipp and Bernhard Springer (eds.), *Ich bin ein Anhänger der Stille. Ein Gespräch mit Heinz Rühmann* (Munich: belleville, 1994), pp. 113–14.

15 Joachim Kaiser, 'Heinz Rühmann oder der schlendernde Deutsche', *Süddeutsche Zeitung*, 6 March 1982.

16 Thanks to Irmbert Schenk for this observation.

17 Cf. Hake, op.cit. pp. 48–53.

18 This was the subtitle of a 1997 conference on Weimar and Third Reich cinema, sponsored by the BFI, the University of Warwick and the London Goethe Institute (cf. Patrice Petro, 'Nazi Cinema at the Intersection of the Classical and the Popular', *New German Critique*, 74, Spring–Summer 1998, pp. 41–55). For various 'new takes' on Nazi cinema see: Klaus Kreimeier, *Die Ufa-Story. Geschichte eines Filmkonzerns* (Munich and Vienna: Hanser, 1992); Stephen Lowry, *Pathos und Politik. Ideologie in Spielfilmen des Nationalsozialismus* (Tübingen: Max Niemeyer, 1991); Eric Rentschler, *The Ministry of Illusion: Nazi Cinema and its Afterlife* (Cambridge, MA, and London: Harvard University Press, 1996); Linda Schulte-Sasse, *Entertaining the Third Reich: Illusions of Wholeness in Nazi Cinema* (Durham and London: Duke University Press, 1996); Karsten Witte, *Lachende Erben, Toller Tag: Filmkomödie im Dritten Reich* (Berlin: Vorwerk 8, 1995) and special issues of *New German Critique*, 74, Spring–Summer 1998 and *montage/av* (3 February 1994).

19 Exceptions are Johannes von Moltke's study of the *Heimat* discourse in his 'Trapped in America. The Americanization of the *Trapp-Familie*, or "Papa's Kino" revisited', *German Studies Review*, vol. 19, no. 3, October 1996, pp. 455–78, as well as his article in this volume; Irmbert Schenk's '"Derealisierung" oder "aufregende Modernisierung"? Film und Kino der 50er Jahre in der Bundesrepublik', in Irmbert Schenk (ed.), *Erlebnisort Kino* (Marburg: Schüren, 2000), pp. 112–29; and Heide Fehrenbach's study, *Cinema in Democratizing Germany* (Chapel Hill: University of North Carolina Press, 1995).

20 Cf. Kaspar Maase, *BRAVO Amerika. Erkundungen zur Jugendkultur der Bundesrepublik in den fünfziger Jahren* (Hamburg: Junius, 1992).

21 Cf. Moltke, in this volume.

22 *Illustrierte Film-Bühne* (nr. 1961).

23 *Morgenpost*, Berlin 1932, quoted in Gregor Ball and Eberhard Spiess, *Heinz Rühmann und seine Filme* (Munich: Goldmann, 1982), p. 37.

24 Hans-Jochen Kaffsack, 'Mehr als ein populärer Filmkomiker. Zum 85. Geburtstag Heinz Rühmanns', *Frankfurter Rundschau*, 7 March 1987.

25 H. H., 'Heinz im Glück', *Neue Zürcher Zeitung*, 4 March 1972; Günther Rühle, 'Landschaft mit drei Größen. Johannes Heesters, Zarah Leander und Heinz Rühmann. Rückblick aus bestimmtem Anlaß', *Frankfurter Allgemeine Zeitung*, 16 March 1977; Michael Schwarze, 'Kleiner Mann ganz groß. Heinz Rühmann, der deutschen liebster Kinoheld, wird achtzig Jahre', *Frankfurter Allgemeine Zeitung*, 6 March 1982; Joachim Kaiser, 'Ein deutscher wie Gott ihn träumt', *Süddeutsche Zeitung*, 7 March 1992.

26 Witte, 'Wie faschistisch …', pp. 1–4.

27 Siegfried Diehl, 'Exzesse des Untertreibens', *Die neue Ärztliche*, 6 March 1987.

28 Klaus Kreimeier, 'Von Henny Porten zu Zarah Leander. Filmgenres und Genrefilm in der Weimarer Republik und im Nationalsozialismus', *montage/av*, 3 February 1994, pp. 41–53.

8

Armin Mueller-Stahl – From East Germany to the West Coast

Claudia Fellmer

Since the 1980s, Armin Mueller-Stahl has become one of the internationally most recognised German film and television actors. In order to understand the changing parameters of acting and stardom in Germany as well as in international cinema, Mueller-Stahl provides an interesting case study. His career not only spans several decades, but also encompasses different cultural contexts, from the state-regulated film industry of the former GDR (where he was perceived as a 'star') via New German Cinema to Hollywood and international arthouse productions (*Shine*, 1996), where he found his niche as a sought-after character actor.

Mueller-Stahl began his career in East Germany in the 1950s, where the emphasis was on 'public' art, subsidised by the state. The mass media were meant to educate and 'enlighten' the public on the ideals of a socialist life supposedly determined 'by the people for the people'. Although the degree of interference from the SED (Socialist Unity Party, the governing party of East Germany) and its cultural officials varied at certain periods (see Horst Claus in this volume), all artistic production was state controlled. Mueller-Stahl advanced quickly in the East German cinema and theatre landscape, even though his performances frequently offered subversive readings. In 1976, in an unprecedented move, state authorities reaffirmed their control in the events following the so-called 'Biermann affair'. Wolf Biermann, a critical East German songwriter, had been expatriated while performing at a concert in West Germany. Hundreds of East German artists signed a manifesto requesting the government to reconsider this decision. This led to unofficial blacklistings,

which resulted in many artists leaving the country. In the wake of this, Mueller-Stahl emigrated to West Germany in 1980, where he continued his career in television and cinema, working with renowned *auteurs* of the New German Cinema such as Rainer Werner Fassbinder, Alexander Kluge and Volker Schlöndorff. Since 1986, Mueller-Stahl's career has taken him from Europe to Hollywood and beyond. Interestingly, a large number of his screen roles have been Eastern European (Poles, Russians, Hungarians).

The aim of this chapter is to investigate Mueller-Stahl's career and the following questions: how have historically and culturally specific discourses on stardom and acting affected Mueller-Stahl's public image and screen persona? How do different audiences relate to the notion of stardom? What particular social significance did stars have in the GDR? For each of the three main stages in Mueller-Stahl's career a short discussion on stardom in its specific context will be given and one film will serve as a paradigmatic example.

'Audience darling' in East Germany

Within German discourses on film and theatre, stardom has been a highly ambivalent concept. Knut Hickethier has pointed out how a discourse about actors, virtuosos and stars was mobilised from the early twentieth century to distinguish 'professional' European artists from those succumbing to the 'commercial' system of Hollywood.[1] Notions of naturally talented character actors in Europe were set against artificially 'produced' ones from

Hollywood. As suggested by Erica Carter in this book, this opposition continued to dominate discourse on stardom throughout the Nazi era and beyond. Nonetheless, the German film industry (including during the Nazi period) did at various points attempt to foster an indigenous star system.

For about a decade after the end of the Second World War, in an attempt to fashion East German cinema in the mould of Italian neo-realism (see Horst Claus in this volume), stardom did not play a significant part in film-making. This changed in the mid-1950s, when the print media began to discuss notions of stardom and whether stars were needed at all in socialist Germany.[2] This discourse relied once again on the opposition of 'sincere, professional character acting' vs 'artificial, profit-oriented acting'. This opposition was explicitly linked to ideological and cultural differences, in that East German and other socialist actors were favoured over Hollywood, but even more decidedly over West German actors.

An important part of the discourse was a general disapproval of the term 'star' itself. Instead, popular artists were called *Publikumsliebling* (audience darling), interestingly a term which does not connote professional ability. It did, however, foster notions of egalitarianism, accessibility and a 'down-to-earth' character, which were important in the relationship between actors and audience in socialist cinema. One of the key features of stardom suggested by Edgar Morin, Alexander Walker and Richard Dyer is the fluctuation between ordinariness and extra-ordinariness in a given star image.[3] Edgar Morin's conception of the 'de-divinisation' of stars offers a valuable tool in thinking about stardom in socialist cinema. When stars move from representing ideal to typical ways of behaving, these changes do not lead to them losing their special status. Rather, the exceptional combines with the ordinary so that the average becomes the ideal.[4] Morin's underlying suggestion is that 'more average' stars are potentially more acceptable because of their greater accessibility as a role model. This was, of course, vital for the educational function of socialist cinema, where the effectiveness of role models was considered essential.

Morin's conceptions apply to the on-screen images of stars, although these – as demonstrated by Richard Dyer among others – always have to be negotiated with the star's off-screen persona. Off-screen ordinariness in the Hollywood sense is often seen to involve the process of social mobility (the industry's implicit promise that anyone can become a star). In the context of East Germany, where the ideological emphasis was on celebrating the working class and overall 'equality', the notion of a star's social mobility was inflected in a different way: in fact there was more of an emphasis on their social 'immobility'. While press reports acknowledged actors' professional success, they equally stressed their place in a society of equals: they had small flats with few luxuries, an average amount of clothes, acting was depicted as 'hard work' and, most important of all, they were described as being in touch with the needs of their fellow workers.

East German star discourse clearly pursued a cultivation of the ordinary in the sense that the myth of a working-class background and of remaining within such a background were reinforced. To create a relationship between actors and their working-class audiences, actors would frequently be used in public events, such as visits to manual workers. Such personal appearances were intended to provide audience feedback, to use 'star' popularity as an incentive to watch more films, but also to prevent actors from losing touch with 'real' people.[5] It is important to note that such personal appearances often gave rise to open critical discussions, thus compensating for the non-existent arena of free public debate elsewhere.[6]

By the early 1960s, a national star system organised around the so-called *Publikumsliebling* was beginning to become entrenched in GDR cinema. This was partly coincidental and partly the result of a conscious effort. First, DEFA encouraged a move towards popular genres, and the print media began to organise polls on the most popular cinema (and later also television) actresses, actors and films for each year.[7] Paradoxically, another important event defined the new *Zeitgeist* in East German cinema: the building of the Berlin Wall in 1961. A newly emerging generation of film-makers welcomed this as a means of eliminating the constant, direct struggle with the West, as they 'felt that they would enjoy a greater degree of autonomy than hitherto'.[8] Attention was shifting towards internal matters; conceptions of the self and affirmation of national pride were emphasised. No doubt audiences had their favourite performers before the 1960s, but the 'synergetic' effects of a new generation of films and film-makers, a particular *Zeitgeist* and increased press coverage gave immense support to the rise of a national star system.

Anti-fascists with a flaw

Although Mueller-Stahl had been performing in cinema, television and theatre since 1953, he only received wider attention when he became part of the emerging national star system. His breakthrough came in 1960 with Frank Beyer's *Fünf Patronenhülsen* (*Five Cartridges*), in all likelihood helped by his physical features and mannerisms: blue eyes, an inscrutable gaze, sensual lips and the low pitch and timbre of his voice. In terms of content, several of Mueller-Stahl's films in the early 1960s – *Fünf Patronenhülsen*, *Königskinder* (*Star-Crossed Lovers*, 1962) and *Nackt unter Wölfen* (*Naked Among Wolves*, 1963) – focused on the anti-fascist past. Anti-fascist resistance was a key theme in East Germany, as it served as the primary source for its self-definition and, as in many other European countries, was the 'basis of post-war claims to political and moral legit-imacy'.[9] The topic was particularly suitable to generate a distinction from West Germany, which was seen not to have broken with the Nazi past. As Cora Stephan puts it,

> The state ideology of antifascist resistance … exonerated East Germans from guilt [for] Nazi crimes since, according to the [anti-fascist] myth, their country was free of malefactors, the high-level Nazis having fled west at the end of the war. Since the roots of fascism had been eradicated in the GDR, where antifascists had won out and established a state committed to peace, there was nothing to apologize for. This sense of distance from the Nazi perpetrators and of moral superiority [over] the Federal Republic permitted some in the post-war generation of East Germans to develop a sense of national pride rare among their West German counterparts.[10]

Although there had been far less active resistance among Germans than the East German narratives suggested, the positive depiction of the East German past was based on foregrounding political persecution and *active* resistance.[11] In this respect, Mueller-Stahl's depictions of anti-fascist resistance fighters offered their audiences an embodiment of the ideals and myths of a socialist German society. Assigned the traits of a popular action hero (an individual-ist fighter, who is courageous, fast-thinking and successful), Mueller-Stahl's persona provided a successful synthesis between an anti-fascist role model and a screen type based on established generic conventions. What Mueller-Stahl achieved was to advertise the East German social system as attractive,[12] establishing the promise of 'achievability' through individual traits in his screen characters. Yet at the same time, the heroes he portrayed retained some ambi-guity. Mueller-Stahl's own term for these figures is 'broken heroes'; and his performance in *Fünf Patronenhülsen* is a paradigmatic example.[13]

Set during the Spanish Civil War, the film centres on five men fighting for the International Brigades. The more physical stress the five experience, the closer the camera gets, with an effect diametrically opposite to the glamoris-ing close-ups of classical Hollywood cinema. These close-

Mueller-Stahl in his breakthrough *Fünf Patronenhülsen* (1960)

ups function on several layers: the 'close' depiction of suf-fering creates a high potential for empathy among the audi-ence. Empathy merges with identification, as the 'close' depiction of perseverance provides potentially effective role models. Simultaneously, the close-ups 'introduce' the faces of five aspiring actors to their audiences, establishing their role model function on-screen.

In the figure of Pierre, played by Mueller-Stahl, the conventional, purely positive representation of an anti-fas-cist is 'broken' and rendered imperfect by the character's weakness. Overcome by thirst, Pierre carelessly, and against the warnings of his comrades, approaches a well and is shot dead. This outcome is anticipated in shot (Pierre alone)/reverse shots (the other four men) which indicate the separation of Pierre from the group. The figure of Pierre thus functions on two different levels for the spec-tator. First, Pierre as anti-fascist provides identification with a normative figure. Second, he offers identification through 'sameness', as the 'ordinary' audience is invited to identify with the imperfection and true-to-lifeness of the ideal.

Mueller-Stahl's ambiguous socialist heroes contributed to his ambivalent star status, as his on-screen image was never fixed at either end of the dichotomies of good and evil. This was underlined by the performance style he developed during his East German career: understated and restrained acting, small gestures and fixed gazes instead of verbal expression. Such gestures were open to different interpretations and ambiguity. Mueller-Stahl's figures embodied diversity, functioning as socialist role models and simultaneously as the very subversion of them. His subversive roles encouraged more explicit audience affinity with the beginning of social disillusionment in East

Germany in the mid-1970s, in productions such as: the East German 'James Bond' television serial *Das unsichtbare Visier* (The Invisible Visor, 1972–6); *Nelken in Aspik* (Carnations in Aspic, 1976); a comedy about the malfunctioning socialist production system; or *Geschlossene Gesellschaft* (*Private Party*, 1978), an allegory about the stagnation of GDR society, and Mueller-Stahl's last production in East Germany.

'Stars' in New German Cinema

When New German Cinema aspired to break away from the West German commercial film industry, this also influenced audiences' and critics' perceptions of film. By reflecting the social context of the late 1960s, 'cinema became a place where one expected not entertainment, but information, not distraction but instruction. … This activated the audience, restored to them an identity as social beings, rather than merely as consumers.'[14]

This changing perception also implied a new angle on stardom. Whereas off-screen discussion of stars abated, star discourse became internalised in films. This internalisation became apparent through four major strands: the rejection of established stars through the use of lay actors (notably in Werner Herzog's films): the creation of new stars, such as Hanna Schygulla: the revival of West German stars from the 1950s, such as Brigitte Mira or Karlheinz Böhm (most notably in Fassbinder's films): and the involvement of acclaimed theatre actors such as Bruno Ganz.

Film-makers alluded to conceptions of stardom in their films in particular through *mise-en-scène*, make-up and lighting. According to Thomas Elsaesser, strategies such as these had the effect of embedding unknown actors in a *mise-en-scène* which treated them as 'stars' long before talent or reputation legitimated them as such.[15] The use of these devices was theatrical, indicating a self-conscious mode of presentation. Elsaesser argues that the recognition of new 'stars' derived in part from a renewed mobilisation of the traditional domestic star discourse; their recognition was enhanced by the fact that they came from extremely well-known theatre companies and were presented as 'character' actors.[16]

In addition, New German Cinema took on 'the dimension of a star system' because the actors, through appearing in different films by different directors, or in different roles under the same director, 'helped establish an intertextuality sufficiently stable to give the impression of a coherent fictional universe, although sufficiently variable to inhibit typecasting'.[17] Elsaesser defines this phenomenon using the term 'high-visibility character actors', that is actors who

appeared in many productions with varying degrees of role importance. It was precisely this function that was fulfilled by Mueller-Stahl, whose performance in films such as Rainer Werner Fassbinder's *Lola* (1981) and *Die Sehnsucht der Veronika Voss* (*Veronika Voss*, 1982), Herbert Achternbusch's *Rita Ritter* (1984) and Alexander Kluge's *Der Angriff der Gegenwart auf die übrige Zeit* (The Assault of the Present on the Rest of Time, 1985) confirmed his 'high-visibility' status. In all these roles Mueller-Stahl enacted complex figures, such as the blind film director in *Der Angriff der Gegenwart auf die übrige Zeit* who transfers images inside his head onto film. It is significant that three of these figures, the former film producer Max Rehbein in *Veronika Voss*, the *auteur* director Cloos in *Rita Ritter* and the blind director of *Der Angriff der Gegenwart auf die übrige Zeit*, directly allude, through their professional involvement in film, to the self-referentiality of New German Cinema.

With respect to New German Cinema's internalised star discourse, Fassbinder's *Die Sehnsucht der Veronika Voss* is particularly significant. Set in 1950s Munich, this melodrama about the half-forgotten Ufastar Veronika Voss (based on the real Ufastar Sybille Schmitz) takes up the figure of the film star and uses Nazi cinema as its reference point, a cinematic self-referentiality which is further heightened by the formulae of melodrama and visual tropes of aestheticisation.[18] The film provides a second form of self-referentiality through the casting of Cornelia Froboess, a former star of 1950s cinema. Audiences would have remembered Froboess as a highly popular teenage singer and actress alongside Peter Kraus in musical films. Yet by casting her as a soft-spoken woman now in her early forties, Fassbinder dims and diverts her direct recognition by the audience.

Armin Mueller-Stahl plays Veronika's ex-husband Max Rehbein. In contrast to Froboess, the film does not mobilise his former film star status in East Germany as a reference point, as it would not have been recognised by the majority of West German audiences. Upon his arrival in the West, Mueller-Stahl was introduced as 'one of the best-known actors of the GDR', yet television producers cast him for his 'unknown face', confirming the fact that he was little known in West Germany. In the climate of the Cold War, the predominantly anti-fascist and 'anti-imperialist' themes of his films in the 1960s did not attract West German distributors or exhibitors. Equally, Mueller-Stahl's 1970s productions, which criticised the socialist system, such as *Die Flucht* (*The Escape*, 1977) or *Geschlossene Gesellschaft*, were never considered for export by the GDR authorities. Consequently, it was Mueller-Stahl's theatrical background and the perception of him not as a star but as a character actor which was to become his point of reference in *Veronika Voss*.

As with Froboess, this is expressed in a self-referential twist. According to the traditional assumption that theatrical star performance needs to be overstated in terms of gestures and vocal delivery, in order to be perceived by the whole audience, including those at the very back of the theatre, one might expect a direct reflection of a 'theatrical' performance from Mueller-Stahl in *Veronika Voss*. Yet the way he enacts the figure of Max Rehbein is pure restraint and understatement and as such suggests an inverted reference to theatrical acting. The underacting of the whole body – Mueller-Stahl's movements and gestures are minimal – is matched by his restrained facial expressions. Nevertheless, it is precisely these suppressed facial movements which articulate the fictional character's disillusionment and tenderness, hidden behind a seemingly disinterested surface. Max Rehbein is a complex figure whose role is typical of those traditionally assigned to supporting character actors in theatre and film. At the same time, he also emerges as but a mere part of the whole ensemble. In contrast to Rosel Zech/Veronika Voss, who is given priority within the ensemble, the performance of Mueller-Stahl/Max Rehbein is privileged in neither narrative nor lighting. The assertion of the actor within the ensemble *in toto*, itself an important strand in the discourse on stardom in Nazi cinema (one of the film-historical reference points for *Veronika Voss*), suggests the proximity of the film medium to theatre. Mueller-Stahl is marked as a character actor who achieves the portrayal of in-depth character without the aid of overtly foregrounded performance. As such, Mueller-Stahl's part in the internalised discourse on stardom in *Veronika Voss* is to represent the character actor in the triangular constellation next to Froboess (old star) and Zech (newly created star).

Hollywood – an international career

The suggestion of deep emotions behind a restrained façade was to remain a recurring feature of Mueller-Stahl's characters in many of his West German film and television productions. But Mueller-Stahl's breakthrough beyond domestic film-making in the mid-1980s was grounded in the international attention both Istvan Szábo's *Oberst Redl* (*Colonel Redl*, 1984) and Agnieszka Holland's *Bittere Ernte* (*Angry Harvest*, 1985) received when they were nominated for the Academy Award of Best Foreign Language Film. The actor's high-visibility status, gained through appearing in films directed by Fassbinder, Achternbusch and Kluge, had attracted the attention of other European directors. For his

performance in *Bittere Ernte*, Mueller-Stahl won the Best Actor award in Montreal in 1985. These nominations and awards opened doors in North America, and Mueller-Stahl's career became more international in the process.

When Mueller-Stahl's career in Hollywood began in the mid-1980s, he was 'exotic' in at least two respects. On the one hand, his psychologically focused roles stood in sharp contrast to the conception of character typical of Hollywood's blockbuster stars of the time. On the other hand, his exoticism was marked as 'Eastern Europeanness', which his roles have retained ever since. In his American and international productions, he has portrayed Soviets, Hungarians, Poles, Russians, East Germans and Jewish characters. In doing so, he has portrayed characters from nations and religions which tend to carry associations with victimisation, rather than 'German aggression'. As Mueller-Stahl's accent has remained recognisably German, this victimisation gives a strange twist to more conventional notions of 'Germanness'.

Films where he was cast in a leading role – as in *Music Box* (1989), *Avalon* (1990), or *The House of Spirits* (1993) – always received critical acclaim, but were never blockbusters in the US, while his recent parts in more commercially oriented productions (e.g. *The Peacemaker*, 1997; *The X-Files*, 1998; *The Game*, 1998; *Mission to Mars*, 2000) have often been mere cameo appearances. Indeed, Mueller-Stahl is not part of Hollywood star discourse and he himself denies being a star:

> in the States a star is a person who makes audiences go to the cinema, which is what I am not. I am a character actor who is in a film, [and] my efforts have always been concerned with my understanding of art, [which is] to explore the limits of my capabilities ...[19]

This statement clearly echoes the traditional German distinction between actor and star I referred to earlier. Despite the new flexibility of his career, Mueller-Stahl appears to have internalised the division between professional acting and stardom.

In Mueller-Stahl's 'homeland', however, a conflicting discourse has evolved around him since his move to Hollywood. The popular press refers to him as a star but at the same time often relativises this definition by mobilising the traditional differentiation between artistic character and artificial glamour actor. Although there is not much difference between the East and West German star discourse, as both sides foreground Mueller-Stahl's status as character actor, the East German press tends to emphasise his international star status. After his first success in

America in the early 1990s, an East German newspaper reported that 'his rise would not be stopped. Armin Mueller-Stahl, reprimanded, honoured, exiled – [is] now a Hollywood star.' He was further described as, 'our only Hollywood star' and 'one of the few German actors [who is an] international top star'.[20] Although Mueller-Stahl's US productions were rarely great box-office successes in Germany, this press coverage articulates belief in the 'Hollywood myth'. Hollywood still serves as a symbol for fame and success, thus an actress/actor only needs to work there to be considered 'internationally famous' by the popular press in Germany. At the same time, the press coverage also articulates national pride in Mueller-Stahl's achievement of moving from 'ordinary' domestic to internationally acclaimed actor.

The particular monopolisation of Mueller-Stahl's stardom by the East German press, which is especially eager to stress his GDR background, reveals a very specific sense of national pride. Thus, the insistence on, and affirmation of, the actor's origins needs to be seen in the context of a wider social process of reconstructing self-confidence and identity among East Germans after unification. Moreover, this monopolisation reveals a sense of subtle but continuing rivalry and competitiveness between East and West Germany.[21]

Mueller-Stahl's victimised oppressors

Hollywood film-maker Costa-Gavras said he chose Mueller-Stahl for the male leading role in *Music Box* because of his professionalism and because he was not a well-known star who was already typecast.[22] Costa-Gavras wanted to avoid the audience expectations and predictability that an established star would have brought to the film, and indeed the film seems to validate Mueller-Stahl's statement about the division between character actor and star; for example, the film's (Hollywood) star, Jessica Lange, receives considerably more close-ups than Mueller-Stahl.

The actor's character in *Music Box* introduced traits which would resurface in his part in the Australian *Shine*. More than any other films, these two dealt with conceptions of victim and oppressor, and with different approaches to memory and dealing with the past. Crucially, both films relied on Mueller-Stahl's ability to convey ambiguities. *Music Box* revolves around Mike Laszlo, a Hungarian who emigrated to the United States at the end of the Second World War, and is now accused of war crimes. His daughter Ann (Lange), convinced of his innocence, defends him in court, but gradually realises that her father is not the person he appears to be. In the beginning, when the audience is led to believe that Mike Laszlo is the victim of some false accusation, he is framed as part of the community: long shots and deep focus indicate his integration. Gradually, however, this integration is reversed in a series of court scenes, where the camera moves into medium shot and medium close-up, singling Laszlo out and separating him from the community, represented by the courtroom audience. The discovery of the 'real' Laszlo, and of his guilt, is mainly conveyed non-verbally; in court, he does not say much, but his restrained facial expression, the subtle twitches shown in close-up, begin to reveal a hidden, dark side.

Mueller-Stahl in *Music Box* (1989)

As portrayed by Mueller-Stahl, Mike Laszlo does not conform to conventional film clichés of an evil Nazi criminal. He is depicted as an everyman suffering under his own past, a figure enriched with multiple layers of politeness and pride, shyness and smugness, giving the audience the opportunity to form its own judgment.[23] The former oppressor has become a victim of his own past, unable to allow this past to become part of his memory. The film and Mueller-Stahl's casting also convey a fractured sense of Germanness and national identity, namely in its use of a German actor to portray a non-German Nazi collaborator in a Hollywood production.[24]

Mueller-Stahl's career, in sum, has traversed three different production and national contexts. Star discourse in the context of his first career aimed at constructing specifically socialist and East German notions of stardom. In opposition to the ideological values of wealth and individualism represented by stars in consumer economies, the values of 'non-luxury' and integration into the socialist community were foregrounded, suggesting a cultivation of the ordinary. At the same time, star debates were embedded in traditional German-European discourses on stardom, which place professional character actors above those imagined as artificially created for mere box-office profits. The on-screen images of Mueller-Stahl were, however, often subtly ambiguous, tending to subvert officially proclaimed, clean-cut ideals of the socialist hero.

In the New German Cinema of the 1970s and 80s, Mueller-Stahl participated in what can be referred to as an internalised star discourse. The self-referentiality of his films in West Germany fractured notions of stardom and put them into question. Mueller-Stahl's involvement with New German Cinema (often in cameo appearances) was that of a high-visibility actor, not as a star.

In international productions, Mueller-Stahl has performed in a number of leading and supporting roles. While he has been celebrated as a star in the German press, he has not achieved traditional American film stardom. Far more attention has been devoted to the on-screen characters he has portrayed, rather than his off-screen persona, reinforcing the traditional distinction between character actor and star. Two of his highly acclaimed performances, *Music Box* and *Shine*, can be seen as paradigmatic for other ambiguous film characters that followed. These roles challenge assumptions about good and evil, oppressor and victim. Through the diversity of his roles, many of which are Eastern European and Jewish, he has dismantled notions of 'Germanness'. But his roles also seem to be pointing up a more general characteristic of stars with transnational careers. Located in different 'homes' and production studios over the world, these star personae dismantle the stable category of nationality. The identity of Mueller-Stahl's persona has become transnational because he is neither entirely German nor US-American. His film roles have contributed to this unstable identity – many of his characters are immigrants and as such symbolise a fluctuation between a rootedness in the 'homeland' culture and an (often self-conscious) adjustment to the culture of their host nation. With figures such as Mueller-Stahl, the concept of national identity itself becomes questionable.

Notes

1 Knut Hickethier, 'Theatervirtuosinnen und Leinwandmimen. Zum Entstehen des deutschen Stars im deutschen Film', in *Die Modellierung des deutschen Kinofilms. Zur Geschichte des Kinoprogramms zwischen Kurzfilm und Langfilm (1905/06–1918). Mediengeschichte des deutschen Films*, vol. 2 (Munich, 1998), pp. 333f.

2 *Neues Leben*, 9, 1955, p. 8; 'Haben wir keine Stars?', *Filmspiegel*, 25, 1964.

3 Richard Dyer, *Stars* (London: BFI, 1979), pp. 25f.

4 Ibid., p. 25.

5 The GDR had *Patenschaften* ('god-parenthoods') between actresses/actors and teams of workers.

6 Stefan Wolle, *Die heile Welt der Diktatur. Alltag und Herrschaft in der DDR 1971–1989* (Bonn: Bundeszentrale für politische Bildung, 1999), pp. 135f.

7 Annual polls on film stars appeared in *Neues Leben* between 1960 and 1982 (excluding the post-Biermann phase 1977–80).

8 Seán Allan, 'DEFA: An Historical Overview', in Seán Allan and John Sandford (eds.), *DEFA: East German Cinema, 1946–1992* (New York and Oxford: Berghahn, 1999), p. 11.

9 Sarah Farmer, 'Symbols that Face Two Ways: Commemorating the Victims of Nazism and Stalinism at Buchenwald and Sachsenhausen', *Representations*, 49, 1995, p. 98.

10 Cora Stephan, 'Die DDR, das "bessere Deutschland". Ein historisches Gutachten', *Kursbuch 3*, February 1993; translation quoted from Farmer, op. cit., pp. 102–04.

11 Herfried Münkler, 'Antifaschismus und antifaschistischer Widerstand als politischer Gründungsmythos der DDR', in *Aus Politik und Zeitgeschichte*, vol. 45, 1988, p. 21; and Peter Monteath, 'Narratives of Fascism in the GDR: Buchenwald and the "Myth of Antifascism" ', *The European Legacy*, vol. 4, no. 1, 1999, p. 102.

12 Harry Blunk, *Die DDR in ihren Spielfilmen* (Munich: Profil, 1984), p. 124.

13 Translated from 'Aus den Gesprächen der Herausgeber mit Armin Mueller-Stahl', in Harry Blunk and Dirk Jungnickel (eds.), *Filmland DDR: Ein Reader zur Geschichte, Funktion und Wirkung der DEFA* (Cologne: Wissenschaft und Politik, 1990), p. 65.

14 Thomas Elsaesser, *New German Cinema: A History* (London: BFI and Macmillan, 1989), pp. 155f.

15 Ibid., p. 285.

16 Ibid., p. 286.

17 Ibid.

18 Thomas Elsaesser, *Fassbinder's Germany: History – Identity – Subject* (Amsterdam: Amsterdam University Press, 1996), pp. 116 and 170.

19 Translated from 'Herunter vom Schmollthron der Geschichte' [interview with Mueller-Stahl], *Der Morgen* (Berlin), 25 December 1990.

20 *Die Union* (Dresden), 15 January 1991; *Der Tagesspiegel* (Berlin), 6 September 1991; *Neues Deutschland* (Berlin), 20 February 1992.

21 Anon., 'Einst DDR-Mime, jetzt Weltstar', in *Sächsische Zeitung* (Dresden), 26 February 1992; 'Armin Mueller-Stahl: Der Meister der leisen Töne wird 70', in *Märkische Oderzeitung*, 16/17 January 2000.

22 Gabriele Michel, *Armin Mueller-Stahl. Die Biographie* (Munich: List, 2000), pp. 190f.

23 'A Star Was Born', in *Premiere* (US film magazine, no publication date given), quoted in Michel, op. cit., p. 193.

24 By raising the issue of the victimised oppressor, Mueller-Stahl's role in *Music Box* was to become paradigmatic for other ambiguous characters, such as Adolf Hitler in Mueller-Stahl's own film *Conversation with the Beast* (1996), and most importantly in *Shine*. For a different kind of victimisation and Germanness, Jim Jarmusch's *Night on Earth* (1991) is noteworthy, where Mueller-Stahl features in the New York episode as an East German ex-clown émigré.

9

German Stars of the 1990s

Malte Hagener

German cinema from the mid-1960s to the mid-1980s was characterised by the *Autorenfilm*, the *auteurist* cinema of Rainer Werner Fassbinder, Werner Herzog, or Wim Wenders – to name only the famous directorial triumvirate. One of the founding assumptions of the *Autorenfilm* was that the film represented the director's unique vision. As a consequence, there was little room for actors to become stars, since the director-author of the film often occupied that role. Although well-known actors were identified with the New German Cinema, they often functioned and were widely perceived as the filmic alter ego of the director, such as Rüdiger Vogler for Wenders or Hannelore Hoger for Alexander Kluge. Fassbinder is an exception in this respect: his desire to create 'German Hollywood films' made him realise his need for stars, primarily actresses, and most importantly Hanna Schygulla.[1] Herzog's work with Klaus Kinski can be seen as another special case, as Kinski was already an established international actor before he appeared in Herzog's films. Herzog's documentary on their collaboration, *Geliebter Feind (Beloved Enemy*, 1998), is a monument to his most important actor and Herzog's acknowledgment of Kinski's star status. In fact, the film could be interpreted as a somewhat late and grudging concession that stars were lacking in the New German Cinema.

Most poignantly bracketed by the dates of the Oberhausen manifesto (28 February 1962) and Fassbinder's death (10 June 1982) the twenty-year period in which the New German Cinema enjoyed an international (critical) reputation is, however, in some respects only a passing intermezzo, since, arguably, 'German cinema has, for most of its existence, been a star-and-genre cinema'.[2] Any film industry creates and reinforces elements, including successful stars or proven genre formulae, which

guarantee some degree of stability and predictability in economic terms. Logically, industry leaders are rather conservative in their strategies (as long as the audience keeps watching films), while critics are more likely to find fault with predictable formules, repeated structures and typecast actors. In this vein – but with an added note of regret for the demise of the New German Cinema – Eric Rentschler has labelled the German cinema of the 1990s a superficial 'cinema of consensus'[3] and likened it to the allegedly shallow cinema of the Adenauer years against which the Young German Cinema revolted. Certainly, the emergence of young film stars in the 1990s is not a novelty in German cinema, but should rather be regarded as a return to a situation typical of any commercial film industry. The resurgence of stars in German cinema can thus best be understood in light of broader economic changes from the mid-1980s onwards.

In the second half of the 1980s and in the 90s, film production shifted towards a more commercial orientation. This change of focus has often been associated with a comedy boom, even though comedy represented only a small percentage of total production and its supposed 'boom' was only evident in terms of box-office return for a handful of years in the mid-1990s.[4] It remains to be seen whether German cinema will find a regular basis (in terms of funding, production, distribution and audience) for a domestic market share much above 10 per cent. The situation in 1998 (8.1 per cent), 1999 (13.1 per cent) and 2000 (12.5 per cent), following a brief peak in 1996 (15.3 per cent) and 1997 (16.7 per cent), was cause neither for euphoria nor pessimism. But no matter what the future brings, one fundamental change has already taken place: the preference of film funding boards, TV stations, film schools, cultural journalists and practically everybody professionally engaged with German cinema has shifted towards a mode of production which aspires to be commercially successful. In other words, the institutions which provide money and set the tone for any activity related to film are increasingly fond of US-script manuals,[5] genre films and stars. With the same verve with which Wenders' vision was discussed in the 1970s, producers and film journalists nowadays talk about plot points and box-office return, cash flow and star images.

Using Til Schweiger as my main case study, I evaluate below the situation of German stars in the 1990s.[6] As *the* top German film star of the decade, Schweiger remained consistently popular throughout the 1990s.[7] He was an emblematic figurehead as well as an exception, thus deserving special treatment here. He also provides the springboard for a discussion below of the relation between the 1990s and the 50s that seeks not to unveil the 90s as a period of a conservative film culture, but to make visible changes and continuities across both periods.[8]

Makin' up: TV, film industry and marketing

Inseparably intertwined, yet still distinguishable, TV and cinema share the same pool of actors and technicians, scripts and ideas, newcomers and established names. Accordingly, Til Schweiger began his career in 1989 as a heartthrob in the popular weekly TV soap *Lindenstrasse* (*Lime Street*), one of the longest running TV series in Germany, whose social democratic slant renders it something of a German equivalent of the British *EastEnders*. Schweiger here played Jo, a soldier who questions his military duties and falls in love with his mother-in-law. Schweiger's characteristic mix of macho toughness, boyish good looks, a reliable yet mildly rebellious personality and a lurking sense of irony or parody can already be seen in his first TV role. Even though he only appeared sporadically in the series, audience responses to Schweiger were remarkably positive.[9]

Before his role in *Lindenstrasse* Schweiger attended a private acting school in Cologne and performed in the theatre in Bonn for some years. There is still a persistent bias in Germany towards ranking theatre work more highly than film or TV. A 'proper' (i.e. traditional and theatrical) acting education is almost indispensable for an actor to become recognised critically and therefore be offered more serious roles. Yet stage actors are normally regionally confined to fixed-site theatres and companies; they only become widely recognised when they achieve success on

national TV. The effects of this normative career path are quite diverse. Katja Riemann, Schweiger's female equivalent in terms of popularity and box-office power for some years in the mid-1990s, had her first TV role in Peter Beauvais' quality-TV historical drama *Sommer in Lesmona* (1986). She made her cinema debut only after four years of TV and theatre in *Ein Mann für jede Tonart* (*A Man in Major and Minor Key*, Peter Timm, 1992). Heike Makatsch, on the other hand, began her career as a presenter on VIVA (a German music TV channel) before becoming an overnight sensation in *Männerpension* (*Jailbirds*, Detlef Buck). Other VIVA-presenters such as Ill-Young Kim (*St Pauli Nacht* [*St Pauli Night*, Sönke Wortmann, 1998]) or Tyron Ricketts (*Kanak Attack*, Lars Becker, 1999) have also recently made forays into acting for cinema films. Yet despite such successful direct crossovers from TV to film, distinctions in status between television and theatre are difficult to shake off. Makatsch, for example, sustains her VIVA 'girlie' image precisely to compensate for her lack of a traditional theatrical acting education – though she stresses in numerous interviews that she has taken acting lessons.

The importance of a theatrical background is evident in German performance style: German films which are praised domestically are often considered stilted and even histrionic in their acting when released abroad, largely as a result of most actors' traditional German theatrical education. Actors such as Moritz Bleibtreu or Benno Fürmann, who had their breakthrough in the second half of the 1990s, have responded by taking acting lessons at the Actors' Workshop in New York, and thus introduced a different performance style into German films. It was Schweiger, however, who led the way in this respect, since his popularity results in part from his imitation of a US-acting style which is physical rather than verbally oriented. Judged by traditional German theatrical standards, his pronunciation is poor, more mumbling than declamation; his physical presence, by contrast, is relaxed to the point of negligence.

One reason for the increasing influence of TV on film production is the post-1983 liberalisation of the TV market, which led a substantial number of private TV stations to turn to self-produced programmes. As the cost of US films and series – the initial staple of Germany's new generation of private German TV channels – continued to rise, it became a reasonable alternative for stations to produce their own shows and films. TV movies in particular now often rival films made for cinema release in their production values, star power and audience response. Recent examples of big-budget popular TV-movies include *Adrenalin* (Dominique Othenin-Girard, 1996), featuring

Til Schweiger as an action hero, and *Jack's Baby* (Jan-Josef Liefers, 1998) starring Veronika Ferres as a career woman, a role that breaks with her previous typecasting as a dumb blonde. The two-part *Der Tunnel* (*The Tunnel*, Roland Suso Richter, 2000), with Heino Ferch, reinforced that actor's tough-guy image: centring on a 1962 escape from East Berlin, the programme was produced on a budget of DM13 million – higher than the budget of most domestic cinema productions.

For stars, TV work performs a triple function: it allows greater stability, in terms of regular income and work; it offers a greater range of roles, allowing actors to develop their image in more diverse and differentiated ways; and it secures greater audience visibility (by contrast, of the sixty to eighty films produced for the cinema each year, a substantial number never get regular distribution and are therefore not seen by the general public, or outside the festival circuit).

The factor connecting stability, diversity and visibility is continuity, which is a necessary condition of stardom (even if continuity manifests itself as change).[10] Whereas continuity could be guaranteed by cinema alone in the 1950s, it is nowadays only possible if actors combine film and TV assignments. Herein lies an important distinction from the 1950s to the 90s, as TV constructs a different relation between audience and film text from the cinema. Thus a star image may change from one medium to the other: Götz George, for example, is famous on TV as the tough and unconventional macho cop Schimanski, while in cinema productions he has played villains such as the serial killer Haarmann in *Der Totmacher* (*The Deadmaker*, Romuald Karmakar, 1995) or the Nazi doctor Josef Mengele in *Nichts als die Wahrheit* (*Nothing but the Truth*, Roland Suso Richter, 1999). The same holds true for Katja Riemann, who has mainly been seen in comedies on the screen 'with only occasional forays into thriller . . . and drama . . ., genres she has so far kept very much reserved for her stage and TV roles'.[11] It is often cinema, then, that allows stars to work against type and to take on 'different' characters which shift their image in new directions.

Although the combination of TV and cinema sustains German stars, no German star *system* exists, in the sense of a vertically integrated and stable studio structure in which publicity departments nurture and build stars. Historically, star systems have evolved in the context of relatively stable markets, where a constant demand for star vehicles has led to a constant supply of star films. This equilibrium is usually maintained by a few big companies controlling the market for production, distribution and exhibition, preferably in a vertically integrated industry. In Germany, both

industry and star system are, by contrast, dependent on a steady flow of money from government funding agencies and TV stations. Despite some (slightly) more successful interludes, the German film industry seems suspended eternally in a precarious state which threatens with every big production to tip over into either triumph or devastation. The significant variations in market shares for German films over the last thirty years have rendered unachievable that stability that would allow a fully-fledged star system to develop. A number of key changes in the 1990s have certainly allowed a handful of German actors to become stars, but a veritable star system would require greater stability.

A further key difference between German and 'classical' star systems (dominated by large production companies) is that in Germany actors, agencies and production companies only react after an actor becomes popular; the few attempts at 'making a star' in the Hollywood sense have met with minimal success, as my example below of newcomers Nina Hoss and Lea Mornar will show. 1994 saw the repeal of a law banning private persons and enterprises from working as agents for actors.[12] With the breaking of the state monopoly, agencies were for the first time permitted to act as go-betweens in film casting. The market place was quickly filled with new companies, the current leader being Players, which has under contract the majority of Germany's young talent, including Til Schweiger, Jürgen Vogel, Jan Josef Liefers, Meret Becker and Corinna Harfouch. Agents are important elements in the creation and maintenance of star images as they are basically responsible for all communication to the public: arranging press reports and interviews, selecting photographs, dealing with fan enquiries, helping in the choice of roles, giving a career a new direction, etc. Since the off-screen appearance of stars is of equal importance to the screen image, the agent's role is crucial and possibly indispensable for the evolution of a star system, but it is too early at the time of writing to estimate how significant the role of agencies will be in the creation of a German star system – not least because of what Mechthild Holter, director of the agency Players, has identified as a major problem for a German star system, namely a deep-seated suspicion regarding stardom. In Germany, claims Holter, being ambitious is synonymous with 'being a sophisticated actor of high standards who achieves high goals, rather than longing feverishly for the pretence of fast, empty fame as an end in itself'.[13] The belief, in other words, remains widespread that a star is a shallow individual chasing after (transitory) fame, while a 'true' actor is a soul-searching artist longing for (eternal) truth – a perception traceable to nineteenth-century ideals of artists and their public roles (see Erica Carter in this volume).

Knockin' on heaven's door: success at home and abroad

Stars, of course, are only one factor in the planning and creation of economically successful films. Genre is equally important to sustain economic predictability. In 1990s comedy, a whole sub-genre revolved around questions of gender roles, sexual orientation and the singles syndrome. The urban dwellers in these films were around thirty, successful in their jobs and upwardly mobile, lived in large and stylish lofts, and were – mostly – unhappy with their single lifestyle. Cinema led a public discourse on gender stereotypes and roles, on single women who wanted to keep their independence, and on single men with children who had forgotten the mechanisms and rules of dating. Not coincidentally, off-screen images of stars also dealt with issues of gender and sexuality: Schweiger constantly stressed his

image as a family man, while Katja Riemann's motherhood was an important topic in her star publicity.[14]

Sexuality and gender, relationships and lifestyle were, then, the main topics of the German comedies of the 1990s, and their stars should be understood in that context. The film that propelled Schweiger and Riemann to stardom, for example, was *Der bewegte Mann* (*Maybe, Maybe Not / The Most Desired Man*, 1994), directed by Sönke Wortmann, the figurehead of the 1990s commercial revival, with Schweiger and Riemann as the dream couple of German comedy. Domestically the film was hugely successful, drawing more than six million spectators. Schweiger and Riemann were stars in the making at that time, not yet firmly established but both already known to the audience from TV and relatively successful cinema films: Schweiger from *Manta Manta* (Wolfgang Büld, 1991), Riemann from the sleeper *Abgeschminkt* (*Makin' Up*, Katja von Garnier, 1992).

In *Der bewegte Mann*, Schweiger plays the gigolo Axel, who moves in with the gay Norbert (Joachim Król) when his girlfriend Doro (Riemann) throws him out after

Katja Riemann in *Abgeschminkt* (1992)

another of his many affairs. Axel is desired by everybody: by the sensitive Norbert, by his gay friends and by all the women in the film. Yet Axel does very little to generate such reactions; in fact he is – especially in his effect on men – completely unaware of them. He shows Norbert nude photographs of himself, falls asleep on his sofa and undresses in front of him. His 'natural' or 'buddy' behaviour is responsible for the sexual uproar he creates. Unlike the clichéd homosexuals (with the exception of Norbert) in the film, he neither acts effeminately nor is he overtly masculine. Even his conscious attempts at seduction happen more or less accidentally, always as an apparently 'natural' reaction to the behaviour of women who make the first move. Axel negotiates two extreme poles of masculinity as portrayed in the film: the men's discussion group on the one hand, which features married men discussing whether it is misogynous even to think the word 'tits', and the gay community on the other. However, the film never offers these polar opposites as real possibilities, since all the characters, barring Axel, Doro and Norbert, are treated as caricatures.

Axel's attractiveness, desirability and naturalness perfectly fitted Schweiger's off-screen persona, but with one important twist. In interviews Schweiger stresses his role as a family man, and emphasises that he reserves time for his wife and children.[15] Press coverage of his private life concentrated from the beginning on him and his wife Dana, and later on their (to date three) children. This double strategy of appearing at the same time monogamous (in his off-screen persona) and promiscuous (in his roles) is the key to Schweiger's success. The audience perceives Schweiger as sexually desirable and virile, yet faithful to his wife. This image of masculinity seems an attractive offer to many audience segments (male as well as female), and is reinforced by Schweiger's naturalness off-screen, as well as

on-screen in an acting style which is untheatrical and sits well with his image as a man who is not acting at all: this is just the way he is.

Riemann, 'a refurbished Doris Day',[16] portrays the nice girl in *Der bewegte Mann*, 'emancipated, . . . but whose emancipation does not hurt anyone and ends when she can subordinate herself to a strong and protecting arm'.[17] In her off-screen persona, Riemann has emphasised her personality as independent and modern – character traits she also exhibits in *Ein Mann für jede Tonart*, *Abgeschminkt* and *Stadtgespräch* (*Talk of the Town*, 1995). But Riemann's roles in these films always have her end up with a man, thus reinforcing traditional notions of gender roles. Her attempts to change her image from comedy star to 'serious actress' have resulted in a series of flops – a fact that again reflects the German unease with stardom. Riemann's promotion of her new image earned her a reputation as 'difficult', both with directors and journalists. While Schweiger came across as natural, easygoing and uncomplicated, Riemann, who tried to establish an image that contradicted her roles, was increasingly perceived as problematic. A star image where screen roles and private roles diverge too much is, as Riemann's example shows, hard to sustain.

Both Schweiger and Riemann were typecast by *Der bewegte Mann*, and both have followed different paths in the late 1990s with regard to their respective images. Their films fared increasingly poorly with audiences, to the point where 'a relationship comedy with Katja Riemann' became a shorthand warning against specific releases.[18] Schweiger turned to directing with the US-style crime comedy *Der Eisbär* (*The Polar Bear*, 1998), and chose roles that consolidated his 'nice-boy' image. He lives partly in California and is openly toying with the idea of a Hollywood career. Indeed, he has played small parts in US productions such as *The Replacement Killers* (Antoine Fuqua, 1998), *Judas Kiss* (Sebastian Gutierrez, 1998), and *S.L.C. Punk* (James Merendino, 1998), as well as producing the comedy thriller *Jetzt oder nie – Zeit ist Geld* (*Now or Never – Time is Money*, Lars Püschel, 2000). His future roles at the time of writing include the boxer Max Schmeling in a German-American co-production about the historical fight between Schmeling and Joe Louis; an important role in Renny Harlin's racing film *Driven* (2001); and a major character (alongside Nick Nolte, Jeremy Davies and Dermot Mulroney) in Alan Rudolph's *Investigating Sex* (2001).

Katja Riemann, similarly, has sought to diversify her roles since the 1990s. In the stylish thriller *Long Hello and Short Goodbye* (Rainer Kaufmann, 1998) she plays a darker and more enigmatic character than heretofore. She has also

Til Schweiger in *Der bewegte Mann* (1994)

attempted to shed her 'nice-girl' image by posing for erotic photographs, publishing two children's books and releasing her first CD. She has returned to the theatre and increasingly withdrew from film and television in the late 1990s.[19] Thus both Schweiger and Riemann have consciously worked against typecasting; yet they remain widely perceived as repeatedly playing the same roles. Roles which fail to fit earlier versions of their star image have been largely ignored, and it remains to be seen how far they will succeed in developing star images that transcend the 1990s comedy genre.

The Big Bagarozy: Bernd Eichinger, the 1950s and the 90s

Bernd Eichinger has rightly been characterised as one of the key players in the German cinema of the last twenty years; and it is certainly plausible to see him as Germany's only contemporary starmaker. Eichinger, possibly the only German producer with something of a global vision, not only produces for Germany, but for European markets and beyond; he has even been called 'a latter-day Erich Pommer'.[20] After graduating in the early 1970s from film school in Munich, he became a media personality whose populist mission to create quality best-seller adaptations with international casts and high production values placed him in some respects closer to David O. Selznick than to an Erich Pommer. According to industry folklore, it was Eichinger who discovered Schweiger on TV; and certainly, Schweiger still holds up Eichinger as his professional model.[21] Eichinger cast Schweiger in the comedy *Manta Manta*, thus significantly developing his tough guy-soft core image. Schweiger also had a supporting role in Eichinger's directorial debut, *Das Mädchen Rosemarie* (*A Girl Called Rosemarie*, 1996) and in Eichinger's debut for the cinema, *Der grosse Bagarozy* (*The Big Bagarozy*, 1999).

In his star-studded remake of Rolf Thiele's 1958 *succès de scandale Das Mädchen Rosemarie*, Eichinger deliberately refused to cast an established actress in the title role, but instead chose the newcomer Nina Hoss, still in acting school at the time. The film's considerable promotion concentrated on the 'star is born' aspect of Hoss, in a conscious attempt at a 'star launch' that demonstrated a new professionalism in terms of PR for the German cinema. A similar star launch was attempted for the model Lea Mornar in Detlef Buck's *Liebe deine Nächste* (*Love Thy Neighbour*, 1998); yet despite massive publicity, neither actress succeeded as a star, thus reinforcing the fact that 'instant stars' are not the rule in Germany.

The 1990s have, by contrast, rediscovered films and stars from the 1950s, a period the film-makers of the New German Cinema once attacked and denounced as 'Papas Kino' (Daddy's Cinema). Eichinger's conscious homage to 1950s cinema paralleled Chancellor Kohl's modelling of himself after 1950s Chancellor Adenauer, as well as reflecting a broader renewal of cultural interest in the 1950s in Germany. Georg Seeßlen has characterised Eichinger as

> a signal for the reconciliation of the old and the new German film. . . . He stands at the beginning of a new German . . . producer's cinema which directors such as [Wolfgang] Petersen and Uli Edel use as a springboard to Hollywood, and in which the restoration of old German cinema traditions is cunningly and tenaciously pursued.[22]

Traces of this reconciliation of the 1950s with the 90s can be found in several of Eichinger's films: in *Knockin' on Heaven's Door* (1996) Til Schweiger's mother is played by Cornelia Froboess, who, with Peter Kraus, formed one of the most popular film couples of the *Wirtschaftswunder* (economic miracle). In *Das Superweib* (*The Superwoman*, Sönke Wortmann, 1995), Joachim Król's mother is played by Lieselotte Pulver, well-known as a girl-next-door in German 1950s cinema, successful in domestic light comedies but also in international productions.[23]

Despite such parallels, there are differences. Schweiger's private persona as a domestically oriented 'new man' certainly distinguishes him from 1950s male stars. It should also be remembered that German cinema's break with a domestic tradition of commercially successful stars and genres was especially radical. As Thomas Jahn, director of *Knockin' on Heaven's Door*, puts it: 'Grandpa's cinema was not dead, the Oberhausen manifesto killed it. 1960s Germany was on its way to becoming a filmic world power. . . . [W]e had everything in Germany, with the Edgar Wallace films we had the right ideas. . . . We have to take up where we left off in 1968.'[24] Jahn's Oedipal reaction against the New German Cinema is meant as much as a polemic against the parental generation as that generation's Oberhausen manifesto was a polemic against the German cinema of the 1950s. How seriously his and other recent celebrations of 'Daddy's Cinema' are to be taken remains, at this point, an open question.

Short, sharp, shock: audience segments, target groups and hybridity

Since the 1990s, the German film market has become increasingly diversified and fragmented; and the same holds true for stars. A German 'Sissi', a Romy Schneider for the 1990s, is hardly imaginable nowadays. Instead, what is emphasised in star images from the 1990s is stars' knowledge of stock value and share certificates, their ownership of companies and shares. It may be that this capitalist imaginary is a hallmark of the late twentieth century, a time when popular heroes are no longer rebels with or without a cause, but cleverly investing dealers, picture-book celebrities who have learned how to accumulate and invest money, and how to titillate the interest of the popular press. Again, Til Schweiger's case is emblematic here. In 1996, Schweiger founded Mr Brown Entertainment, named, in conscious homage to Quentin Tarantino, after one of the characters in *Reservoir Dogs* (1992). Tarantino not only provides the model for Schweiger's acting style; his influence is also discernible in Schweiger's directorial debut *Der Eisbär*, and in his diversification into acting, directing, writing and producing. Jürgen Vogel, similarly, runs a production company, Schwarzweiss Filmproduktion; and Peter Lohmeyer, who co-founded the agency Die Agenten, claims:

> I have founded the agency because I want to establish a circle of people around me with whom I like to work. In a wider sense this also means directors and authors. . . . I like the fact that actors like Jürgen Vogel and Til Schweiger have become more active, that they have risked giving form to the wishes they have.[25]

These stars and others like them, then, are conscious of their economic power, and actively work on modelling their image by venturing into production – possibly the only way to remain popular in an ever-changing industry situation without firm studio structures.

Finally, one important feature of German stars in the 1990s should be noted – they were almost exclusively of German extraction. An exception is Jasmin Tabatabai, an Iranian who is not only a popular actress but also a well-known musician with her own band, Even Cowgirls Get the Blues. Given the success and popularity of non-German personalities in music and sport, or as TV presenters, one wonders why similar developments in German cinema have been much slower. Indeed, Germany's principal cur-

rent 'ethnic star' is the ethnic German, Moritz Bleibtreu, who plays a Turkish gang leader in Peter Timm's *Einfach nur Liebe* (*Simply Love*, 1993), a witless Arab gangster in Thomas Jahn's *Knockin' on Heaven's Door*, and in the German-Russian co-production *Luna Papa* (Bakhtiar Khudojnazarov, 1999), the handicapped Nasreddin, whom a war injury has transformed into something of a idiot savant.

As German society becomes more diversified, pluralistic and multi-ethnic, German cinema and its stars will necessarily pursue a similar path. A 2001 exhibition on contemporary German stars at the Filmmuseum Berlin, 'Starometer', included not only photographs of Til Schweiger and Moritz Bleibtreu, Franka Potente (of *Lola rennt* [*Run, Lola, Run*, 1998] fame) and Christiane Paul, but also Minh-Khai Phan-Thi and Jale Arikan, Mehmet Kurtulus and Erdal Yildiz. While the New German Cinema rummaged through history and took on the job of working through the repressed past of Germany, the 2001 exhibition is perhaps the sign of a hope that a new German cinema will not only be a superficial 'cinema of consensus', but will take on the job of becoming a critical and keen observer of past, present and future German realities, contradictions and developments.

Notes

1 See the chapter on Hanna Schygulla in Stephen Lowry and Helmut Korte, *Der Filmstar* (Stuttgart and Weimar: Metzler, 2000), pp. 218–43.

2 Joseph Garncarz and Michael Wedel: 'Star System', in Thomas Elsaesser and Michael Wedel (eds.), *The BFI Companion to German Cinema* (London: BFI, 1999), p. 226. A similar argument on the popular tradition of the German film can be found in Jan-Christopher Horak, 'Die Tradition des deutschen Films', in Heike Amend and Michael Bütow (eds.), *Der bewegte Film: Aufbruch zu neuen deutschen Erfolgen* (Berlin: Vistas, 1997), pp. 13–24.

3 Eric Rentschler: 'From New German Cinema to the Post-Wall Cinema of Consensus', in Mette Hjort and Scott MacKenzie (eds.), *Cinema and Nation* (London and New York: Routledge, 2000), pp. 260–77.

4 For exact numbers see Carsten Pfaff: 'Deutsche Kinofilme in Zahlen', in Amend and Bütow (eds.), *Der bewegte Film*, pp. 65–74; also the annually updated yearbooks published by the Spitzenorganisation der Deutschen Filmwirtschaft (Spio), Wiesbaden, and by the EU-institution Media Salles, Milan, or the trade magazine *Blackbox*.

5 Since 1990 at least a dozen translations of US script manuals have been published in German, and the same number

of handbooks have been written for the German market, copying the US models of Linda Seger, Robert McKee, Christopher Vogler or Syd Field.

6   For a recent overview of the literature on stars see Stephen Lowry, 'Stars und Images. Theoretische Perspektiven auf Filmstars', in *montage/av*, 6 February 1997, pp. 10–35. On stars in general see the indispensable work by Richard Dyer, especially *Heavenly Bodies. Film Stars and Society* (New York: St Martin's Press, 1986) and *Stars*, 2nd edn (London: BFI, 1998). Also see Christine Gledhill (ed.), *Stardom. Industry of Desire* (London and New York: Routledge, 1991); and Jeremy G. Butler (ed.), *Star Texts. Image and Performance in Film and Television* (Detroit MI: Wayne State University Press, 1991).

7   Judging by popular biographies Schweiger is clearly Germany's top star: cf. Katharina Blum, *Til Schweiger* (Munich: Heyne, 1997); Annette Kilzer, *Til Schweiger. Vom Bewegten Mann zum Großen Bagarozy* (Hamburg and Vienna: Europa-Verlag, 2001). For biographies of female stars, see e.g. Katharina Blum, *Katja Riemann. Mit Charme und Power* (Munich: Heyne, 1998); and Rolf Thissen, *Veronica Ferres. Facetten eines Stars* (Munich: Heyne, 1999). An affirmative overview of German stars is Heiko R. Blum and Katharina Blum's *Gesichter des deutschen Films*, 2nd edn (Munich: Heyne, 1999).

8   At the time of writing, the Filmmuseum Berlin is holding an exhibition on German film stars, titled 'Starometer' ('starometer', linguistically a blending of 'star' and 'barometer', i.e. a ranking of film stars, an invention of 1950s fan magazines), with a special focus on the 'comparison of actors and actresses from the 50s and the 90s' (press release).

9   For Schweiger's career see the popular star biographies Blum, *Til Schweiger*; Kilzer, *Til Schweiger*; the chapter in Blum and Blum, *Gesichter*, pp. 130–40; and Tim Gallwitz's entry on 'Til Schweiger', in Hans-Michael Bock (ed.), *CineGraph: Lexikon zum deutschsprachigen Film* (Munich: edition text+kritik, 1984ff. [here inst. 31, 15 April 1999]).

10 See Werner Faulstich, Helmut Korte, Stephen Lowry and Ricarda Strobel, ' "Kontinuität" – zur Imagefundierung des Film- und Fernsehstars', in Faulstich and Korte (eds.), *Der Star. Geschichte – Rezeption – Bedeutung* (Munich: Fink, 1997), pp. 11–28.

11 Michael Wedel: 'Katja Riemann', in Elsaesser and Wedel (eds.), *BFI Companion*, p. 205.

12 The so-called 'Aufhebung des staatlichen Arbeitsvermittlungsmonopols'. See Lowry and Korte, *Der Filmstar*, pp. 262f.

13 Mechthild Holter: 'Über deutsche Stars', in Amend and Bütow (eds.), *Der bewegte Film*, p. 77.

14 Besides *Der bewegte Mann*, many films, such as *Stadtgespräch* (*Talk of the Town*, 1995) and *Echte Kerle* (Rolf Silber, 1996), dealt in a comic way with gay characters in particular. Male–female relationships were dramatised for comic effect in many forms, from teenage sex comedy, as in Marc Rothemund's *Das merkwürdige Verhalten geschlechtsreifer Grossstädter zur Paarungszeit* (1998) or *Harte Jungs* (2000), through films aimed at an 'adult' audience in *Frauen sind was Wunderbares* (Sherry Hormann, 1993) and *Frau Rettich, die Czerny und mich* (Markus Imboden, 1997), to Doris Dörrie's more intricate mosaics on private life in Germany in *Keiner liebt mich* (1994) and *Bin ich schön?* (1998). Indeed, it was Dörrie who provided the blueprint for the commercial recovery of the German cinema when she directed her surprise hit *Männer* (*Men*, 1985).

15 Quoted in Blum, *Schweiger*, p. 11.

16 Rentschler, 'From New German Cinema to the Post-Wall Cinema of Consensus', p. 273.

17 Malte Hagener, 'Katja Riemann', in Bock (ed.), *CineGraph: Lexikon zum deutschsprachigen Film*, inst. 31, 15 April 1999.

18 One review of a German comedy read: 'Nothing positive? Oh yes, Katja Riemann is *not* in it.' Anon., '2 Männer, 2 Frauen = 4 Probleme', *die tageszeitung*, 5 March 1998, p. 25.

19 See Nils Klawitter, 'Komödiantin der Wirrungen', on Riemann's withdrawal from film and her return to the theatre, which Klawitter attributes to hostile media reactions. *Süddeutsche Zeitung*, 27 February 2001, p. 16.

20 Thomas Elsaesser, 'Introduction: German Cinema in the 1990s', in Elsaesser and Wedel (eds.), *BFI Companion*, p. 4.

21 Newspaper clippings, no source cited, Starometer exhibition (24 August–9 December 2001, Filmmuseum Berlin).

22 Georg Seeßlen, 'Neo-Adenauer-Stil', *die tageszeitung*, 12 June 1997, p. 15.

23 In films by Jacques Becker (*Les aventures d'Arsene Lupin*, 1957), Douglas Sirk (*A Time to Love and a Time to Die*, 1957/8), Billy Wilder (*One, Two, Three*, 1961) and others.

24 Thomas Jahn, *Onscreen. Regisseure, Schauspieler und ihre Filme in Interviews* (Bochum: Paragon, 1999), p. 131.

25 Blum and Blum, *Gesichter*, p. 103.

PART THREE

INSTITUTIONS AND CULTURAL CONTEXTS

Introduction

Tim Bergfelder

The socio-economic analysis of any national cinema operating under a capitalist system needs to account for the contexts of film production, distribution, exhibition and audience constituencies, and to consider how nationally as well as historically specific factors affect cinema's performance in these areas. Such factors conventionally include the development of industrial strategies, from the initial stages of technological invention, patenting and individual enterprise, to increasing horizontal and vertical corporate integration; the constraints imposed by the wider national and global economy (including inflation, exchange rates, trade agreements, etc.); more targeted forms of state support and protection (e.g. funding mechanisms, preferential taxation rates, import quota regulations) and state interference (e.g. film censorship); and finally, the social demographics and cultural infrastructure of the industry's target market, which provides the supply-and-demand dynamic that determines both the industry's product and its modes of distribution and exhibition.

In the case of German cinema, such an analysis gets complicated, not least because the German film industry has not developed exclusively according to the logic of capitalism, but at times under, and in collusion with, authoritarian political regimes (the Third Reich and the GDR, in particular) which explicitly prioritised ideological objectives over, and sometimes at the expense of, purely economic ones. Of course, Germany does not hold a monopoly on such state interference, nor are film industries in capitalist democracies in general immune to ideological pressures, witness, for example, Hollywood's Production Code or the McCarthy witchhunts during the Cold War. Even under a conventional market economy, political pressures in Germany often conspired against the consolidation of the indigenous film industry; witness, for example, the Allies' dismantling of industrial infrastructures after the Second World War, which paved the way for the dominance of American distribution companies in the West German

market (see Bock and Töteberg's contribution in this section); or the state interventions, informed by Cold War imperatives, in West German film production and distribution during the 1950s, which frequently overruled economic considerations (see Loiperdinger's essay in this section). In a very different way, the government support for the New German Cinema in the 1970s also helped promote what Thomas Elsaesser famously called a national media 'ecology' rather than a film economy.[1]

As in previous sections, the aim of the following contributions on industrial developments and their relation to both audiences and state involvement is to elaborate on the cultural specificity of their chosen case histories, while allowing for international comparisons, similarities and convergences to emerge. As outlined in our general introduction, a substantial proportion of groundbreaking research in German film history over the last ten years has focused on the early years of German cinema from 1895 to 1918. This return to previously unexplored and often misrepresented origins has been triggered by an interest in the emergence and development of cinema as both a modern industry and a social institution. This dual emphasis is equally evident in the two contributions on Wilhelmine cinema by Frank Kessler and Eva Warth, and Joseph Garncarz in this section, though there are also some interesting differences in approach.

For Garncarz, the key to an understanding of how film in Germany became a national mass medium are the early period's exhibition practices, and in particular the circulation the medium achieved through pre-existing forms of entertainment such as variety theatres and travelling shows, which gradually gave way to the medium-specific fixed site of the cinema. Drawing extensively on archival sources, Garncarz maps a materialist history of early German film which is similar in approach and methodology to the pioneering studies of US scholars on the beginnings of American film production and exhibition.[2] Such a comparison is strengthened by the fact that, at least in the broadest sense, German film exhibition appears to have developed in similar ways to the American context, out of pre-cinematic entertainments, via small and basic fixed sites (the nickelodeon in the US, *Ladenkinos* in Germany) into the later picture palaces. However, as Garncarz stresses, a national distinctiveness can be charted both through the particular programming the various exhibition practices adopted, and through their relative importance vis-à-vis each other.

While covering in part the same period as Garncarz, Frank Kessler and Eva Warth's contribution extends the historical focus up to the First World War, with occasional previews of later developments. Their contribution marks a shift in emphasis from the material contexts of exhibition towards a focus on the conventionalisation of filmic narratives and audience experiences. Kessler and Warth chart a development from the internationalism of the early period, when the German market was dominated by French and American films, to a gradual attempt to create a national cinema in the 1910s, the characteristics of which were determined by bourgeois conceptions of art and concomitant modes of reception, and which found its ultimate expression in the *Autorenfilm*. This process, Kessler and Warth argue, had fundamental implications for audiences. Thus, while Garncarz stratifies the early film spectators of variety theatres and travelling shows primarily according to categories of class and differences between urban and regional audiences, for the post-1908 period Kessler and Warth propose that 'gender emerges as a far more productive category'. Drawing on the work of feminist historians Heide Schlüpmann and Miriam Hansen,[3] they conclude that German cinema's gradual institutionalisation served to regulate and ultimately displace female audiences, as well as the aesthetic norms of early cinema.

On an industrial level, this institutionalisation process culminates in the founding in 1917 of Ufa, German cinema's most celebrated film company, associated in the popular imagination with its monumentalist productions, its internationally sought-after technicians and filmmakers, and its star system. Moreover, Ufa spans both German cinema's 'golden age' of the 1920s and its darkest hour under Nazism, which simultaneously granted the company national monopoly status, and brought it under the exclusive control of Joseph Goebbels' propaganda ministry. Hans-Michael Bock and Michael Töteberg's historical survey documents the conflicting demands of Ufa's economic strategies, artistic aspirations, and the ideological pressures of the state and right-wing lobbies, which determined the company's operations from its beginnings.

Unlike the major Hollywood studios with which Ufa has often been compared, the company was not the brainchild of a single producer or entrepreneur, but the result of tactical mergers, facilitated by the German military and major banks. Over the next two and a half decades of its corporate existence Ufa was hardly as consistently successful or dominant as has often been assumed. As Bock and Töteberg point out, the Ufa legend has often occluded the existence of other important companies of the 1920s and 30s, a misconception that has begun to be corrected through recent research into Ufa's competitors.[4] Nevertheless, Ufa did achieve a remarkable degree of vertical and horizontal integration, as well as technological sophistication, which rivalled at least any European film company at the time, and have never been repeated in German cinema since.

Ufa's legacy affected the development of the two parallel national film industries after 1945 in different ways. In the West, the Ufa trademark and the company's various, if fragmented, assets became the subject of protracted legal wranglings, providing Ufa with a ghostly afterlife that has persisted to the present day. What followed in the wake of Ufa's demise in West Germany was an overall fragmented industrial network of individual entrepreneurs, which included such colourful personalities as Artur 'Atze' Brauner, who, despite having been persecuted as a Jew by the Nazis, remained so dazzled by his youthful memory of Weimar cinema, that he set out to recreate and remake its classics for the 1950s.[5] More powerful, however, were distributors such as the female tycoon Ilse Kubaschewski, who provided 1950s audiences with a steady supply of *Heimatfilme*, and Walfried Barthel of Constantin who targeted an increasingly younger audience with thrillers and Westerns.[6]

In the East meanwhile, one of Ufa's greatest former assets, the studio complex at Babelsberg near Berlin, became the centre of a newly nationalised film industry, DEFA, which monopolistically represented East German cinema until its demise in 1992 after German reunification. As Horst Claus' contribution in this section outlines, like Ufa, from which it inherited many internal structures and hierarchies of organisation as well as aesthetic principles, DEFA charted a precarious course between the artistic aspirations of its workforce and persistent state control and interference, which manifested itself in shifting ideological directives, continuous vetting procedures and occasional bans. Although financial considerations mattered far less in the GDR than in a market economy, DEFA was neither isolationist, nor did it ignore the demands of its target audience, which after all could not be completely sheltered from the influence of western cinema and media. Thus, DEFA upheld an active exchange with other East European cinemas, and, more tentatively, pursued co-productions with the West, while adopting certain western styles (e.g. Italian neo-realism) and creating its own brand of popular genres.

Germany's forms of political governance during the twentieth century, from autocratic monarchy to Weimar's parliamentary democracy, followed by fascist dictatorship, communist one-party rule and the Federal Republic, have thus consistently maintained a significant, if qualitatively and quantitatively variable, state involvement in the national cinema. While this holds true for most national cinemas in the broadest sense, it is notable that the relationship between film and state in Germany has often deliberately differentiated itself from the economic liberalism that has characterised the American film industry. As Martin Loiperdinger emphasises in his contribution, there is a remarkable continuity across different political systems in Germany in the way state involvement in national cinema has been defined and regulated, and in the institutions and personnel assigned to this task. Loiperdinger thus charts the mechanisms of state control across the main historical caesura, focusing on censorship regulations, as well as on the double-edged sword of state support in terms of funding. Importantly, Loiperdinger locates the relationship between cinema and state within wider national discourses and concerns, ranging from the so-called moral hygiene argument, child protection and national prestige, to the regulation of anti-social behaviour. Loiperdinger documents how calls for film control and censorship have frequently originated not only in a perception of cinema's supposedly harmful effects on audiences, but also with a variety of pressure groups and lobbies, from the early 'film reformers' to nationalist organisations and print media, and Germany's two main churches, whose objectives then became enshrined in state legislation and in the composition of control boards. However, while the protagonists and institutions of this historical narrative are nationally specific, the concomitant discourses are not necessarily; note, for example, the remarkable similarity in conceptualisation between early German 'effect' theories and recent debates in the US and Britain about 'copy-cat' crimes.

Notes

1 Thomas Elsaesser, *New German Cinema: A History* (London: BFI and Macmillan, 1989), p. 3.

2 For references, see note 5 in Garncarz' contribution in this section.

3 Miriam Hansen, 'Early Cinema – Whose Public Sphere?', in Thomas Elsaesser, *Early Cinema. Space, Frame, Narrative* (London: BFI, 1990), pp. 228–46; Heide Schlüpmann, *Die Unheimlichkeit des Blicks: Das Drama des frühen deutschen Kinos* (Basel and Frankfurt am Main: Stroemfeld/Roter Stern, 1990).

4 In recent years, the annual *CineGraph* symposia in Hamburg have, for example, focused on companies such as Deutsche Universal, Nero, and Tobis. See also Petra Putz, *Waterloo in Geiselgasteig. Die Geschichte des Filmkonzerns Emelka (1919–1933) im Antagonismus zwischen Bayern und dem Reich* (Trier: Wissenschaftlicher Verlag Trier, 1996); and for an investigation of German–American relations, Thomas Saunders, *Hollywood in Berlin: American Cinema and Weimar Germany* (Berkeley: University of California Press, 1994).

5 Claudia Dillmann-Kühn, *Artur Brauner und die CCC: Filmgeschäft, Produktionsalltag, Studiogeschichte 1946–1990* (Frankfurt am Main: Deutsches Filmmuseum, 1990).

6 Manfred Barthel, *So war es wirklich: Der deutsche Nachkriegsfilm* (Munich: Herbig, 1986).

10

The Origins of Film Exhibition in Germany

Joseph Garncarz

The history of film in Germany before 1907 is an area on which, unfortunately, little research has so far been done.[1] There exist only case studies on specific local film shows or single film producers.[2] Because film history has largely been conceived of as *cinema* history, the importance of other exhibition practices has been underestimated. No attempt has been made to give an account of the emergence of cinema as a cultural institution out of other media and forms of exhibition.[3] By contrast, the following contribution attempts to outline the development of film as a new medium in Germany before 1907. The study foregrounds the interaction of different media, and is based on systematic research on hitherto unused primary sources. The central question posed is that of how it was possible for film to develop a distinct cultural identity and become a mass medium during this period. The answer lies in the history of exhibition practices, since exhibition played a central role in the success of the new medium with audiences and thus was a crucial factor in determining production and distribution. Such established sectors of the national entertainment business as the variety theatre and the travelling show made use of the new medium and shaped its cultural form. Film presentations in variety theatres and travelling shows became the two most important film exhibition forms in Germany during this early period. The primary sources of the greatest value are thus the trade journals of these two entertainment sectors, *Der Artist* and *Der Komet*, which served as forums for communication among variety artists and travelling showmen.[4] Due to their differing cultural traditions, these two film exhibition practices developed their own film forms and programming patterns and defined how and with what purpose films were to be shown. By the time the cinema boom set in during 1905/06, variety and travelling shows had already given

film a cultural identity of its own, providing models that could be adapted for the new form of exhibition. The cultural institution of cinema was thus not built from nothing, but resulted from a complex combination of cultural forms developed earlier by variety artists and travelling showmen.[5]

Film exhibition in variety shows

Variety was the most popular form of theatre in Germany at the end of the nineteenth century.[6] These shows, which presented a colourful mixture of different acts, did not aspire to educate their audiences; they wanted to provide diversion and raise the spirits. Here, uninhibited laughter was the mark of a successful night. Serving food and drink was common in variety theatres, which were also known as *Rauchtheater* ('smoking theatres'), because in contrast to legitimate theatres, smoking was permitted during performances.

There were two types of variety theatre at the end of the nineteenth century in Germany: the local or 'folk' theatre (*Tingel-Tangel* was its colloquial, somewhat derogatory designation) and the international variety theatre.[7] The folk variety theatres presented programmes with local artists, while their international counterparts presented international stars in programmes that were shown in similar form in the most prestigious variety theatres across Europe. The international stars of the variety stage travelled constantly all over Europe, just as did later the showmen with their cinematographs. In folk variety theatres the show itself was of secondary interest, and was often even presented free of charge, since its sole purpose was to further beer consumption, which provided the main income source. In international variety theatres, by contrast, the show was the main event, and refreshments only an additional service; thus admission charges were always made. Folk variety theatre patrons were mainly lower class; international variety theatre audiences came mainly from the middle and even upper classes.

As can be gathered from the contemporary trade press, films were shown in international variety theatres, but not in folk variety. Variety show film presentations spread rapidly in Germany. The first film show in a German variety theatre, which was also the first ever public film exhibition in Germany, was presented by the Skladanowsky brothers in the Wintergarten, a high-class variety theatre in Berlin, on 1 November 1895. By 1897, 10 per cent of Germany's international variety theatres were regularly showing films; by 1898 25 per cent; by 1900 40 per cent; and between 1906 and 1910, 60 per cent.

Moreover, most international variety theatres that included films in their programmes were to be found in larger cities; the larger the city, the greater the number of variety theatres showing films. The centres of variety show culture in Germany were Berlin, Hamburg, Munich, Leipzig, Dresden and Cologne. During this period, cities were growing more rapidly than the general population: in the nineteenth century, Germany's total population increased from 20 to 60 million, while Berlin's population, for example, increased from 150,000 to 1.5 million -- and city audiences especially longed for diversion.

Audiences for international variety theatres, and consequently, for films, were thus urban as well as middle and upper class – class in this case being defined more by money than education, since the well educated usually preferred the legitimate theatre. A contemporary newspaper description of the Hamburg Hansa-Theater's audience reads, for example: '[T]he Hansa-Theater has an exclusive audience, which not only attends the season premiere but also the nightly gala-premieres, and which eagerly awaits new endeavours and attractions.'[8] At the turn of the century, international variety shows were mainly reserved for the wealthy; the less wealthy, such as clerical workers and civil servants, could afford only standing room tickets, and these only occasionally.

Variety theatres presented loosely structured programmes comprising diverse acts by different artists. The artists did not perform behind a 'fourth wall', but interacted with spectators and encouraged lively audience response. On average, programmes included around a dozen acts, each around twelve minutes long. The acts were dramaturgically independent of each other, so spectators missed nothing if they chose to eat and drink or even talk to their companions during a performance. However, the order of acts was not arbitrary: contrasts and climaxes structured the programme. The show was divided into two parts, with a break in the middle. A first climax was presented before the break; another climax of greater impact, usually an act with a star, was presented second-to-last. Acts of similar character were not programmed in immediate succession. The last act was the chaser, which meant that audiences often began to leave while it was still in progress. (Films changed this habit for a while, a point discussed further below.)

When films were shown in variety theatres, they were made to conform to the existing programme structure. A film presentation became only one act among others of the traditional kind. The films were usually very short, less than two minutes before 1902, and no more than six minutes between 1903 and 1907. Several films were shown in direct succession; the entire set of films, at around twelve minutes, was as long as every other act in the show. The structure of the film segment followed the same principles as the show as a whole: the order of films was chosen to provide contrasts and build-up towards climaxes.

Before 1901, anyone wishing to present a film show in a variety theatre bought their own projectors and films, offered their services to variety impresarios in the manner of all other variety artists, and worked under the same terms as other acts. Around 1902, however, the producers of projectors and films reacted against the decline in prices that this practice had engendered: they rented projectors and films to theatre owners directly, often as a package, thus eliminating competition from middlemen. Some film firms became closely connected as a result to specific theatres; between 1902 and 1907, Oskar Messter, for example, regularly provided equipment and films to the Apollo-Theater in Berlin, the Apollo-Theater in Düsseldorf and the Munich Blumensäle.

Since technical inventions had always been a popular spectacle in variety shows, it was only logical that audiences would show an interest in films. Variety shows were based on the traditional arts as well as the latest innovations; ventriloquists, equilibrists, masters of mnemonics, singers and comedians vied for attention along with all kinds of gadgets:

> Whenever major inventions and achievements in art, science, engineering, technology or sports appear, [variety] artists contribute to the popularisation of these novelties. It should for example be remembered that the invention of liquid oxygen was presented to the public for the first time on a variety stage, as were the production of synthetic gemstones and navigable balloons.[9]

The first film show by the Skladanowsky brothers, advertised as 'a full variety programme in 15 minutes',[10] presented only filmed variety acts; its attraction thus could not have been its content, but the technical innovation necessary to produce it.

The mere reproduction of variety acts on film was unlikely, however, to hold the audience's interest once the novelty value of the filmic apparatus had diminished. Thus, as early as 1896, film content began to change. It became clear that film had a unique potential to create the illusion for the audience that they were actually taking part in the represented event.

> When we see images recorded in Henley-on-Thames, it is almost impossible to imagine that they are an illusion conjured up by man's hands and intelligence. It is as if we were living right in the middle of the scene; we are not sitting in a theatre, but instead our mind shares the fresh impressions of the pleasant hustle and bustle along the Thames.[11]

Thus, though variety programmes did present fictional, narrative films, so-called *optische Berichterstattung* ('visual reports') became the staple of the show around 1900. Non-fictional films made particular use of the fact that 'there is no better means [than film] of participating in events that one did not witness in person.'[12] Unlike fiction films, which sought primarily to entertain, the main purpose of these visual reports, which were the predecessors of the later cinema newsreels, was to visualise events considered culturally relevant by producers and audiences. As one commentator wrote in 1901, 'any educated person who feels the need to read a good newspaper will feel the same need to have the events reported in that paper parade past him in moving pictures.'[13] Films, however, had to be transported physically from their place of production to their place of reception; unlike news, which could be transmitted by telegraph, the new medium could never be as up-to-date as the traditional newspaper. The visual reports, therefore, did not provide new information, but visualised events that were already known. The favourite national items of the period were the military and Kaiser Wilhelm II. The most popular international items were the Boxer uprising (1900–01) and the Russo-Japanese War (1904–05). 'As these [war] images in particular will universally demonstrate, the true significance of the visual reports is their superior ability to represent in perfect clarity the events reported in the daily papers. Here we see embodied what reports of several columns' length convey.'[14] As the last film of the visual reports section, it was common practice to present some comic relief – usually a

fictional, narrative film; this practice was also transferred to the presentation of newsreels in cinemas.

Many strategies were developed to heighten the illusion of actual participation in events represented in the visual reports. In contemporary understanding, the use of fictional material and narrative techniques did not stand in opposition to claims of documentary truth, but were only different means to the same end. Theatre newsletters and printed programmes handed out to audiences show that no deception was ever intended, since the material's origin was always clearly explained. Many films showed events not artificially created for the camera, for example a statesman's funeral or the unveiling of a monument. However, for events on remote continents, when images could not be produced quickly enough, any visually similar documentary material would be used (for example, military exercises could represent an army preparing for a battle). Only when no documentary material of similar nature was available were events staged for the camera. Even films that appear to us today to be pure fiction were sometimes accepted as visualisations of events of which the audience had no personal experience; thus for example *The Great Train Robbery* (1904), which was based on a play, was described as a 'very realistic portrayal of a hold-up on an American train'.[15]

No other act proved as successful as film in German variety theatres at the beginning of the twentieth century. At first, films were used as the last number, a hugely unpopular spot with artists, since audiences were in the habit of leaving before it was over. An article in *Der Komet* from 1900 comments:

> It used to be difficult even for the most prestigious variety theatres to obtain a good closing number, because no

H.I.M. the German Emperor – Arrival at Port Victoria (1902), filmed by the Deutsche Mutoskop- und Biograph-Gesellschaft mbH, by special appointment of the Kaiser

artist wanted to appear last, with audiences always rushing off even before the last act had begun. Then 'living pictures' appeared, and became an attraction of the first order.[16]

Thus it was due to the popularity of films, especially visual reports, that the status of the last act of the variety show changed from chaser to climax. In a 1905 edition of the *Artistische Nachrichten*, a newspaper from the Hamburg Hansa-Theater, one commentator observes, 'for a great portion of the audience, the visual reports are the main event; unlike any other closing number, they succeed in keeping the audience in their seats until the very end.'[17]

Film exhibition in travelling shows

Variety shows were only accessible to urban audiences, but travelling shows brought film to almost every region in Germany. Thus, travelling shows were even more crucial in shaping film's development into a new mass medium. Many showmen who had hitherto entertained their audiences with diverse other attractions turned to exhibiting films at the end of the nineteenth century. David Lindner, for example, had travelled with a carousel and Robert Melich had run a speciality theatre before presenting cinematographs. In contrast to variety shows, where films were only one feature in a varied schedule, travelling shows presented only films; they did not offer refreshments or allow smoking, and developed sales strategies, programme patterns and film forms that were quite distinct from those of the variety theatres.

Travelling shows exhibiting films spread more and more rapidly. The first shows of this kind can be traced to 1896, at a point when film itself had only just appeared. By 1900 only 100 locations had been visited by travelling film shows, by 1902 about 200, by 1903 about 300, by 1905 about 400, and between 1906 and 1910, a peak of 500 locations was reached. By 1907, around 500 travelling film exhibitors shared the German market.

Most of the travelling shows were family businesses: David Lindner, for example, worked with his two sons, David and Gustav. The size of these businesses varied considerably.[18] Some companies owned several travelling shows, and thus controlled a greater market share. Heinrich Hirdt, for example, operated six shows in 1908.[19] Smaller companies, Geister for instance, usually worked in regions closer to home, whereas larger companies travelled farther across the country. Geister took his show only to Aachen, Düsseldorf and Bonn, but Hirdt travelled across the entire south and southwest of Germany.

Travelling shows concentrated less on larger cities, where variety theatres already regularly presented films. Instead, they primarily visited small towns, especially those with a population of less than 20,000. Because the railway was well developed by this time, the travelling shows could travel even to very small places. By 1907, about 1,300 different towns had been visited by travelling shows; thus – statistically speaking – every German town with more than 5,000 inhabitants had seen a travelling show at least once.

Travelling shows usually did not appear in isolation, but at festivals, markets and trade fairs, all of which offered a wide range of amusements, including carousels, swings, shooting galleries and beer stands.[20] This context explains why travelling shows, unlike variety theatres, did not offer refreshments: there was always an ample supply of food and drink at other stands (smoking was prohibited for safety reasons). At the end of the nineteenth century, festivals, markets and trade fairs were popular forms of entertainment for the general public. They usually lasted two or three days, sometimes up to two weeks. Some of the festivals were rooted in religious traditions, such as the *Kirchweihfest* ('church consecration festival'), also known by such diverse regional names as *Kirmes, Kirbe, Kilbe* or *Dult*. Then as now, markets were places for buying and selling goods, but during this period they also offered entertainment for the locals. Trade fairs, which primarily provided information and introduced new products to representatives of a particular trade, sometimes also became public spectacles. Because they took place frequently and had such wide appeal, festivals and markets were especially suitable contexts for travelling showmen to exploit the public's need for diversion.

In contrast to the international variety theatres, the travelling show patrons did not belong to the middle and upper classes, but to a much broader social spectrum. However, contrary to the claims of traditional film historiography, the film audience of the early period was not mainly the proletariat; in fact, the proletariat was not well represented at all, since industrial regions, for example, the Ruhr, were rarely visited by travelling shows. That travelling shows aimed for the broadest possible audience can be demonstrated by their pricing policies. A gradation of ticket prices was introduced shortly after the turn of the century. Wilhelm Schmitz, for example, charged 75 Pfg. for first-class seats, 50 Pfg. for second and 30 Pfg. for third.[21] The seating was differentiated by its position in relation to the screen – the seats farthest away from the screen were the most expensive – as well as by comfort.

Only during the early years did travelling shows use small wooden booths with simple benches. From 1902 on, many reports refer to the travelling shows' so-called 'palaces on wheels'.[22] These mobile constructions could accommodate up to 600 or 700 patrons, had comfortable and luxurious furnishings and splendidly decorated façades:

> Herr Ludwig Ohr's cinematographic palace, built this winter [1904–05] and just now opened, is the sensation of Pirmasens. It truly deserves to be called a palace; anything more splendid and magnificent can hardly be imagined. The façade is monumental . . . It is 13 metres high in the middle, decorated with rich gilding, mirrors and ornaments as well as several larger-than-life-sized statues, and every line is faultless. At night, the whole edifice is flooded with dazzling lights. 16 carbon-arc units and as many as 800 incandescent bulbs, arranged most tastefully, create an immense sea of light. . . . A giant concert organ was also greatly admired . . . and one was at a loss as to what to admire more: the marvellous music or the splendid façade. . . . The interior is equal to the exterior, and one is most pleasantly surprised by the elegant furnishings and the convenient positioning of seats as well as entrances and exits; the best seats are arranged in ascending order and covered with red silk plush, just like the seats of a modern urban legitimate theatre.[23]

At the Munich *Oktoberfest*, film palaces such as these were usually the most eye-catching attraction. Even in daylight, a film show's 'palace on wheels' was the most impressive sight on the festival grounds, and at night, its striking illumination signalled its status. Munich's city council obviously recognised the film shows' value for the city's image; they chose only the most prestigious shows and reserved the best festival site locations for them.[24] At

A travelling film show's 'palace on wheels'. *Leilichs Cinematrograf* at the *Oktoberfest* in Munich, 1904

the end of a season (the onset of winter), many larger companies sold their mobile film palaces in order to buy newer, larger and yet more luxurious models at the beginning of the next season (usually in March). This trend reflected growing competition in the travelling show business; as the number of travelling shows rose, it became more common for more than one show to open simultaneously in the same location.

While in variety shows films were only one part of the programme, travelling shows usually presented only films. Their programmes were fifteen to twenty minutes long; allowing time for patrons to enter and leave the show, two such shows per hour could be presented. A travelling show's film programme was usually longer than the typical film segment in a variety show, which meant that travelling shows either used more films or longer ones – most commonly the latter. Variety shows would sometimes show short versions of longer titles (for example, *Voyage dans la lune* [1902] and *The Great Train Robbery*). Around 1906–07, however, the average length of travelling show film programmes doubled; this was undoubtedly a reaction to cinemas, which appeared at this time showing longer programmes.

Variety shows could offer their patrons a varied programme by presenting a diversity of acts; they thus had no need to diversify the range of film types on offer during the film segment of the show. Instead, the film type that represented the clearest contrast to the rest of the show became the most important part of the film segment, namely visual reports (see above). Travelling shows, however, relied solely on films, and thus aimed for the greatest possible diversity of film material. This produced a quite different programme structure from that of the film segments in variety shows. At first, travelling show programmes typically consisted of eight to twelve films; this number decreased somewhat over the course of several years, as the average length of the films increased (until 1906–07, the total length of the programme stayed the same). The programmes were mixtures of comedies, dramas, nature scenes and actualities, and included fiction as well as non-fiction films; the only dramaturgical principle was to provide as much diversity as possible. In 1906–07, however, the share of fiction films increased, undoubtedly also in connection with the cinema boom of those years.

For variety theatres, renting films was more practical than buying them, but this was not the case for travelling showmen. First, it would have been a logistical problem to guarantee the delivery of films to constantly changing locations. Second, since travelling showmen had different audiences in each new location, they did not need to change their programme as often as variety theatres to keep their patrons interested. It was therefore more economical to buy than to rent films, since the same films could be used as many times as their life permitted, often over a number of years. If travelling showmen did decide to stay longer in one location, or to visit the same locations more often, they also had to build a larger stock of films. Heinrich Hirdt, for example, was able to change his programme several times daily only because, by 1904, he had accumulated over 1,000 films.[25]

A number of contemporary reports testify to the great success of the new film medium at festivals, markets and trade fairs: 'The success of the new cinematograph [Ludwig Ohr's] was ... enormous, since despite appalling weather, the queues were always long and the new films enthusiastically applauded.'[26] Another report reads: 'The most popular attraction was ... Herr Hirdt's large and splendid cinematograph. The local audience attended in such great numbers that it was almost dangerous to try to get a seat.'[27] That these examples represent a general trend can be substantiated by the year-on-year increase in the numbers of locations visited by travelling showmen, as well as the increasing amounts of money invested in 'palaces on wheels'. Neither would have been possible economically had audiences not responded so favourably to film presentations.

From variety theatres and travelling shows to cinemas

As shown above, before the cinema boom, variety shows and travelling shows in particular had already made film well known and popular throughout Germany. These two exhibition forms had divided the market between them, with variety shows catering to the middle and upper social classes in larger cities and travelling shows serving all social classes in smaller towns. In neither case, however, was filmed entertainment a cheap amusement form; it had a definite prestige value, as is evident from the architectural design of exhibition sites as well as admission prices. Variety and travelling shows both developed characteristic distribution methods, programming patterns and film forms, each uniquely adapted to the shows' different contexts.

Around 1905, however, film presentations in variety and travelling shows were joined by a third form of film exhibition, namely cinemas. 'Something new and highly significant has appeared: competition from cinemas! It is commonly agreed that no other technical invention besides film has had and still has such enormous mass appeal.'[28] The cinema boom was tremendous. In 1905 there were only forty cinemas in Germany, but by 1906 there were 200, by 1908 over 1,000, by 1910 almost 2,000, and by 1912 more than 3,000. The first cinemas emerged in large urban centres, but they quickly spread to remaining metropolitan areas, as well as to medium-sized and smaller towns.

The driving forces behind the cinema boom were neither the variety theatre impresarios nor the travelling showmen, but tradesmen and street salesmen. With the emergence of large new department stores offering low-priced wares, small independent shops all but disappeared, and street salesmen too went out of business.

> On the founding of these *kinematographische Geschäfte* ['cinematographic shops', i.e. cinemas] I was able to observe that many [street-]salesmen have turned to this business because it is highly profitable, because they are known to be good businessmen, and because there is currently [1906] little money to be earned in consumer goods. Many salesmen are investing savings of several thousand German marks in these shops, and will doubtless reap great benefits.[29]

The early German 'cinematographic theatres' were known as *Ladenkinos* ('shop cinemas', similar to US nickelodeons), because of their status as hastily transformed urban shops, usually comprising one single, long and narrow room. They became a form of *Unterhaltungskneipe* ('entertainment pub'), where patrons could drink, smoke and enjoy entertainment.[30] The film programme was around one hour in length, and contained fiction as well as non-fiction films. Admission prices were lower than for travelling shows and variety: 'The *Kientopp* [also *Kintopp*, a colloquial term for cinema] costs 10 Pfg., less than the cheapest *Tingel-Tangel*.'[31] The low admission prices for the *Ladenkinos* indicate that the composition of the film audience changed during the cinema boom. The first comprehensive study of film audiences in Germany, *Zur Soziologie des Kino* (*On the Sociology of Cinema*) by Emilie Altenloh, shows that around 1912 in Mannheim, a medium-sized industrial city, the cinema audience comprised mainly blue-collar and lower-status white-collar workers.[32]

Yet the cinema did not appear from nowhere, but was based on an innovative combination of cultural forms developed earlier by variety artists and travelling showmen. The *Ladenkinos*' fixed location, their distribution method (renting instead of buying films) and the practice of offering refreshments and allowing smoking were inherited from variety shows. The economic importance of smoking and concessions can be demonstrated by the fact that in Berlin in 1912, the number of cinemas decreased by 25 per cent after smoking in cinemas was banned and selling refreshments was no longer permitted for newly opened cinemas, or when a cinema changed its owner. The variety shows' popular visual reports became the forerunners of cinema newsreels, a non-fiction format that provided film audiences over many decades with images of current events. As shown above, in contrast to variety shows, where films were only one feature among many, travelling shows presented only films. Thus, the varied nature of the cinema's fiction programme, containing humorous as well as dramatic presentations, originated primarily in travelling shows, the main purpose of which was to entertain – also the cinema's declared function.

Contrary to commonly held assumptions, the new cinemas did not immediately supplant variety and travelling shows. At first, all three exhibition forms equally enjoyed a boom phase in Germany. Between 1906 and 1910, enthusiasm for film swept the country and was shared by all social classes. But by 1911, cinemas had sprung up across the length and breadth of Germany, and film presentations in variety and travelling shows began to decline. Around 1900, film had established the closing number of the variety programme as the show's climax , but by the end of the second decade of the century, the closing number had again become the chaser: 'When the audience realises that it will no longer be subjected to the tedium of cinematographic presentations, it will give up its habit of leaving the show helter-skelter before the end.'[33] But not only did film presentations disappear from the variety stage; variety shows themselves declined for a number of reasons, including competition from cinemas (other reasons included the unpopular strategy of showing forms adapted from the legitimate theatre, such as operettas, instead of the regular variety programme comprising various short numbers, as well as the disappearance of variety artists following call-up to the First World War).

Since they were not fixed in one place, travelling shows were able to sustain themselves for a while in small towns that did not yet have cinemas. But it did not take long for cinemas to conquer even this last retreat. Appended to a 1914 letter from Peter Lindner to the Munich city council was the following note:

> [T]hat the travelling shows are faring less well than a few years ago is probably due to the fact that the urban population is over-saturated with cinemas, and film shows on the [Oktoberfest] festival site are only attended by visitors from out of town. For the townspeople,

cinematographic presentations are no longer a novelty. On days when there are no out-of-town visitors, the travelling shows do little business.[34]

Owners of variety theatres and travelling shows had no choice but to react to this trend. Consequently, 'one variety theatre after another was converted for film';[35] owners either sold their theatres or changed profession. Some travelling showmen gave up showing films; Leilich, for example, appeared at the 1910 Munich *Oktoberfest* with an animal act instead of a cinematograph. Others gave up travelling shows altogether and opened their own cinemas. However, these were no longer the simple 'entertainment pubs' described above; like the 'palaces on wheels', they resembled modern, urban legitimate theatres.

> On November 15 [1913], Herr Heinrich Ohr [possibly a relative of Ludwig Ohr], a showman well known and respected among colleagues, opened a magnificent and splendid cinema at the Landauertor in Pirmasens. The night before witnessed a gala to which the town authorities, as well as individuals with a particular interest in cinema, were invited. There was general surprise at the grand scale and the solid, classically designed furnishings of this new cinema.[36]

In contrast to the *Ladenkinos*, this new kind of cinema was prestigious enough to attract middle- and upper-class patrons and thus competed even with international variety theatres.

The success of cinemas, which would have been impossible without the pioneering efforts of variety artists and travelling showmen, finally led to the disappearance of film presentations in variety and travelling shows, and even contributed to the decline of these entertainment forms as such. The two film exhibition forms that had dominated the early period had become so marginal by the 1920s that they have almost disappeared from memory. Even in academic studies of German film history, this early period, though it is of central importance for the development of the cultural identity of film as a mass medium, has largely been neglected.

Translation by Annemone Ligensa

Notes

1   I would like to thank the students who looked through many contemporary sources relevant for this article in connection with their MA theses, for which I acted as adviser: Ralph Alexowitz, Alexandra Kling, Anne Kosten, Erik

Krämer, Marcus Maassen, Tanja Schmitt, Christine Specht and Martin Wolf.

2 See e.g. Martin Loiperdinger, *Film & Schokolade: Stollwercks Geschäfte mit lebenden Bildern* (Frankfurt-am-Main and Basel: Stroemfeld/Roter Stern, 1999); Bruno Fischli, 'Das Goldene Zeitalter der Kölner Kinematographie (1896–1918)', in Bruno Fischli (ed.), *Vom Sehen im Dunkeln: Kinogeschichten einer Stadt* (Cologne: Prometh, 1990), pp. 7–38; Paul Hofmann, 'Auf der Suche nach den Anfängen der Kinematographie im rheinisch-westfälischen Industriegebiet', in Lisa Kosok and Mathilde Jamin (eds.), *Viel Vergnügen: Öffentliche Lustbarkeiten im Ruhrgebiet der Jahrhundertwende* (Essen: Ruhrlandmuseum, 1992), pp. 218–57; Corinna Müller, 'Anfänge der Filmgeschichte: Produktion, Foren und Rezeption', in Harro Segeberg (ed.), *Die Mobilisierung des Sehens: Zur Vor- und Frühgeschichte des Films in Literatur und Film* (Munich: Fink, 1996), pp. 295–325.

3 The first trade journals devoted specifically to film, *Kinematograph* and *Lichtbildbühne*, which served the communication needs of producers, distributors and exhibitors, appear in the context of the German cinema boom around 1907. Because these journals have been researched in detail, our knowledge of German film history after 1907 is well documented; see Corinna Müller, *Frühe deutsche Kinematographie: formale, wirtschaftliche und kulturelle Entwicklungen 1907–1912* (Stuttgart and Weimar: Metzler, 1994).

4 *Der Artist: Fachblatt für Unterhaltungsmusik und Artistik* (Düsseldorf: Droste, 1883–1995); *Der Komet: Fachblatt für Reisegewerbe und Markthandel; offizielles Organ des deutschen Schaustellerbundes e.V.* (Pirmasens: Der Komet, 1884–1943). Unfortunately, due to restrictions of space, I am only able to note sources for direct quotations. A fuller presentation of sources will be found in my forthcoming book.

5 It would be interesting to compare my study of early German film history with studies of US film by Richard Abel (*The Red Rooster Scare: Making Cinema American, 1900–1901* [Berkeley: University of California Press, 1999]), Robert C. Allen (*Vaudeville and Film, 1895–1915: A Study in Media Interaction* [New York: Arno Press, 1980]) and Charles Musser (*The Emergence of Cinema: The American Screen to 1907* [Berkeley: University of California Press, 1990]). However, space neither permits a detailed comparison of the development in the two countries nor of the different methodologies of the studies. A few notes must therefore suffice. According to the studies mentioned, the family vaudeville shows were of central importance in the USA; in Germany, by contrast, the international variety shows were most important. Concerning the travelling shows, which were crucial in Germany, the question arises whether they were insignificant in the US, or whether their role has simply not come into view because the trade journals of this entertainment sector have not been consulted.

6 Wolfgang Jansen, *Das Varieté: die glanzvolle Geschichte einer unterhaltenden Kunst* (Berlin: Hentrich, 1990).

7 Eberhard Buchner, *Varieté und Tingeltangel in Berlin*, 6th edn (Berlin: Seemann, 1905).

8 *Artistische Nachrichten*, 27 (September 1897), p. 1.

9 *Der Artist*, 1501 (16 November 1913), cover page.

10 Ibid., 569 (5 January 1896), Bioscop, Gebrüder Skladanowsky (advertisement).

11 *Artistische Nachrichten*, 63 (December 1901), p. 5

12 Ibid., 53 (October 1900), p. 5

13 Ibid., 60 (September 1901): p. 5.

14 Ibid., 89 (November 1904), p. 5.

15 Ibid., 102 (March 1906), p. 3. On contemporary reactions to the film in the USA, see Charles Musser, 'The Travel Genre in 1903–04: Moving Toward Fictional Narrative', *Iris*, vol. 2, no. 1 (1984), pp. 47–59.

16 *Der Komet*, 803 (11 August 1900), p. 5.

17 *Artistische Nachrichten*, 107 (November 1905), p. 5.

18 *Der Komet*, 1550 (5 December 1914), cover page.

19 Oktoberfest-Repetitorium Akte 136, 1908–10 (Stadtarchiv München).

20 On festivals, markets and trade fairs: Leander Petzoldt, *Volkstümliche Feste: Ein Führer zu Volksfesten, Märkten und Messen in Deutschland* (Munich: Beck, 1983).

21 Oktoberfest-Repetitorium Akte 105, 1901 (Stadtarchiv München).

22 *Der Komet*, 1125 (13 October 1906), p. 7.

23 Ibid., 1042 (11 March 1905), p. 11.

24 Oktoberfest-Repetitorium Akte 106, 1901–10 (Stadtarchiv München).

25 Oktoberfest-Repetitorium Akte 117, 1904 (Stadtarchiv München).

26 *Der Komet*, 1042 (11 March 1905), p. 11.

27 Ibid., 789 (5 May 1900), p. 6.

28 *Der Artist*, 1874 (17 February 1921), cover page.

29 *Der deutsche Händler und Hausierer*, 13 (30 December 1906), p. 6.

30 Hans Schliepmann, *Lichtspieltheater: eine Sammlung ausgeführter Kinohäuser in Groß-Berlin* (Berlin: Wasmuth, 1914), p. 8.

31 Hanns Heinz Ewers, 'Der Kientopp', *Der Morgen*, vol. 1, no. 18.

32 Emilie Altenloh, *Zur Soziologie des Kino: die Kino-Unternehmung und die sozialen Schichten ihrer Besucher* (Jena: Diederichs, 1914). A translation of the Introduction

and Part II of Altenloh's study appears in *Screen*, vol. 42, no. 3, Autumn 2001, pp. 249–93.

33 *Der Artist*, 1948 (20 July 1922), unpaginated.
34 Oktoberfest-Repetitorium Akte 169, 1914 (Stadtarchiv München).

35 *Der Artist*, 1583 (13 June 1915), cover page.
36 *Der Komet*, 1497 (29 November 1913), p. 14.

11

Early Cinema and its Audiences

Frank Kessler and Eva Warth

In our contribution we want to sketch out some characteristics of early moving picture shows and their audiences as well as the implications of the institutionalisation process for cinema exhibition and reception. We concentrate on the period prior to the First World War, during which a German film market largely dominated by foreign companies is gradually transformed by efforts to establish a more unified, nationally specific form of cinema. This tendency towards a nationalisation of German cinema becomes particularly obvious during the War when foreign competitors, especially French and American, are excluded from the market. It culminates in Weimar cinema when German productions succeed in holding a key share not only in the domestic, but also the international market, where they are perceived as genuinely German films. We argue, however, that the gradual development towards a more or less stabilised institution with an emergent national specificity was based on the destruction and instrumentalisation of early cinema's aesthetic and social qualities, and of its public.

Early period: 1894–1908

The first presentations of animated photography in Germany took place at a broad range of different sites and on (or in) a variety of machines. The first viewers of moving pictures were, moreover, anything but cinema audiences. In November 1894, a Berlin lecture hall became the venue for a display of Ottmar Anschütz's *Projektions-schnellseher* (Projecting Electrotachyscope), a device showing a series of images mounted on two large disks. The Italian Exhibition in Hamburg in May 1895 offered visitors the opportunity to drop a coin into Anschütz's *Schnellseher-Automaten*; while in Hamburg, they could

also go to the *Gänsemarkt Kinetoscope* parlour to put money into Edison's peeping box and view short scenes on celluloid film. Patrons of the *Wintergarten*, a variety theatre in Berlin, applauded the Skladanowsky brothers' *Bioskop*, which premiered on 1 November 1895, while visitors to the 1896 *Gewerbeausstellung* in Berlin admired the *Cinématographe Lumière*, brought to Germany by Ludwig Stollwerck, a Cologne chocolate manufacturer. A few days earlier, the *Cinématographe* had been exhibited in the *Panoptikum* at Friedrichstrasse 65a.[1]

Thus already, a decade before the emergence of the first storefront theatres (*Ladenkinos*), moving pictures were shown at many different locations and attracted mass audiences. This diversity of exhibition sites continued for several years. As Joseph Garncarz has shown,[2] variety theatres, together with travelling shows, were the major venues for moving picture shows before 1907, and the composition of film audiences in terms of class and gender was congruent with the patronage of these sites. It is only with the emergence of sedentary film theatres and the establishment of a regulated market that one can begin to talk about cinema audiences proper.

The shift from moving picture shows to cinema shows was closely linked to the medium's gradual institutionalisation. By the end of the First World War, cinema had become one of the leading mass entertainment forms. The national film industry was not only highly organised, but – thanks to government policy during the war, culminating in the foundation of Ufa – also relatively integrated. However, the previous two decades of film history in Germany (and anywhere else, for that matter) show that cinematography was anything but a unified field or practice. In particular, the phenomenon of stardom differs fundamentally in the early period from its later form. Strictly speaking, film stars only start to emerge in the early 1910s, and are closely linked in Germany to a new distribution system, the so-called *Monopolfilm*, a system granting local or regional exclusivity to exhibitors.[3] In earlier years, a number of phenomena seem to have functioned in ways similar to the star system, but not identical with it. During the so-called novelty period before 1897 the machine itself was the main interest.[4] Early reports emphasised the qualities of the representation instead of dwelling upon the meaningful aspects of the represented as such. Crispness of image, richness of detail and the lifelike quality of movement were the main attractions. The famous anecdote of spectators fleeing in panic from the train entering a station at the first public screening of Lumière's *Cinématographe* has in fact been shown to be a myth; yet it did derive more or less directly from a journalistic discourse on the new moving images that emphasised their lifelike quality and authenticity.[5]

Quite rapidly, however, an important shift occurred. To retain audiences, films themselves had to become an attraction through the subject matter they depicted. The German Lumière films are a case in point, since they offer a rich sample of subjects satisfying the visual curiosity of spectators in different ways. Lumière's street scenes not only presented the spectacle of continuous movement running across the screen; in some cases they may also have allowed audiences to see an image of themselves, or at least places they were familiar with. On the other hand, *Danse tyrolienne* (Lumière catalogue no. 31), filmed by Constant Girel, a Lumière cameraman working in Cologne in 1896, gave a filmic rendition of a popular folklore entertainment. Another type of film, or rather *vue*, which showed public affairs such as parades, the inauguration of monuments or official visits of state, had an additional value as a recording of news events. Living pictures of important politicians and heads of state were of particular interest to audiences. All these films offered the attraction of both the medium and the depicted: the lifelike rendering of political events, continuous movement in front of the camera or the movement of the camera itself, the familiar spectacle of the everyday as well as images of the exotic. It was this broad spectrum which brought viewers back again and again to watch the display of animated photographs.

In variety theatres, audiences were similarly addressed through a foregrounding of content. To differentiate film screenings from the rest of the programme, exhibitors highlighted the documentary qualities of moving pictures. Presented as *Optische Berichterstattung* (visual reports of actual events from all over the world), films were described as providing a different kind of entertainment from the

staple variety fare. At the same time, and perhaps paradoxically, it was within non-fiction film that something like a film star phenomenon first occurred, helping to build a large and faithful audience for moving pictures, since 'screen personalities' turned out to be one of the major factors for cinema's success and, consequently, for its institutionalisation. In fiction films it was not until 1910 that actresses' and actors' names became known to the wider public and could be used as a marketing strategy. In non-fiction films, however, important personalities appearing on the screen were always identified.

Given the decidedly nationalistic atmosphere in imperial Germany, it is hardly surprising that audiences were especially keen on images showing the Kaiser and his family. In contrast to other monarchs, Wilhelm II took an active interest in appearing in films, an attitude which the film industry in Germany gratefully acknowledged by producing a massive volume, *Der Kaiser im Film* (*The Kaiser on Film*), on the occasion of his silver jubilee. Even foreign companies contributed to this publication, in which the Emperor was presented as 'one of the most active friends and supporters of film art' and 'the most interesting personality at whom the lens of a cinematograph has ever been aimed'.[6] Surprising as it may seem, even French companies joined in and paid their tribute to the Kaiser. Thus for example the 1913 Pathé production *S. M. Kaiser Wilhelm II. bei der Hirschjagd in Bückeburg* (*Kaiser Wilhelm II Hunting Deer in Bückeburg*) opens with a title gratefully acknowledging the privilege granted by the monarch in authorising the shooting of this film.[7]

Already in 1898, Oskar Messter had used the Kaiser's image to promote his films. His sales catalogue from that year featured several films related to Wilhelm II. The comment on catalogue no. 38, *Seine Majestät Kaiser Wilhelm II.*

Kaiser Wilhelm II hunting deer

in Stettin, advertised the film by emphasising that, 'his Majesty can be clearly recognised'. Even when the Kaiser himself did not appear on-screen, his sheer presence at any given event could be turned into a promotional argument. Thus in Messter's catalogue no. 36, *Stapellauf vom Kreuzer 'Wilhelm der Grosse'*, the launching of a battleship on 4 May 1897, the catalogue entry stressed that the event took place 'in the presence of His Majesty Kaiser Wilhelm II'. This fact alone, apparently, was enough to give additional value to the film. An even more interesting case is no. 37, *Vergnügungsdampfer auf der Oder (Pleasure Cruise Ships on the Oder)*. Here the catalogue insists that the steamship *Neptun*, which makes a brief appearance at the end of the film, is carrying the Kaiser. Again, the virtual and fleeting presence of the Kaiser seems to have constituted the main attraction of the film, at least in the catalogue's advertising strategy.[8]

With the emergence of permanent and sedentary exhibition sites devoted more or less exclusively to films, the situation changed profoundly. Increasing demand brought about a regulated market with efficient distribution systems and, of course, an increasingly standardised mode of production, with narrative fiction becoming more and more the industry's dominant product. Until way into the First World War, audiences in Germany saw mainly foreign films, especially from France and America.[9] This was not necessarily always obvious to spectators, since, for example, many French comic actors appeared on German screens under a different, often explicitly German, name: thus Calino became Piefke, Gaumont's child star Bébé was renamed Fritzchen, Rigadin dubbed Moritz and Gavroche turned into Nunne, a Berlin counterpart to an originally Parisian character.

Audiences came at this point, then, to be addressed as national, or at least as entities defined by language and culture, in films of foreign origin produced for an international market. The importance of nationality and a national cinema increased, moreover, in the years before the War. In an attempt to conform to bourgeois cultural norms and thus demonstrate cinema's respectability, the *Autorenfilm* (films based on works by famous contemporary authors or written by them directly for the screen) mobilised national literary and cultural traditions. Hence, most famously perhaps, *Der Student von Prag The (Student of Prague*, Stellan Rye), whose concern with the *doppelgänger* clearly echoes romantic cultural tradition. On the other hand, foreign films adapted to the German cultural context began to be perceived as problematic, as the following quote illustrates:

When a typically Gallic buffoon and his wife in her typically French outfit are called Herr and Frau Lehmann all the time, then this may not qualify as an offence against the honour of the German nation, but it certainly shows a lack of good taste . . . and demonstrates [cinema's] continued status as a parvenu.[10]

From around 1907–08, debates on the cultural, legal, social and moral status of cinema became increasingly intense, and expressed growing concerns about the status of this emerging form of mass entertainment. They also explain, *ex negativo*, the importance of films about the Kaiser for the industry: as non-fictional images of the highest representative of the nation, who not only authorised these films, but in so doing showed his benevolent attitude towards the cinematograph, they were literally beyond reproach. Dignified by their subject matter, they were the acme of respectability, and at the same time were a first step towards addressing the viewers as a national audience. They were, moreover, both immensely popular and financially successful.

Towards institutionalisation: 1908–14

In the opening chapter of Emilie Altenloh's landmark study *Zur Soziologie des Kino* (1914),[11] a social science doctoral dissertation supervised by Alfred Weber which not only represents the beginning of film sociology in Germany but also of empirical mass media audience research, Altenloh reflects on the profound changes that had begun to reshape German cinema since 1908. Although she concludes that 'cinema has not yet found its definite form',[12] the transformations which occurred between 1908 and 1914, the year her study was published, were consolidated during the War and relegated the cinematic forms developed during the early period to a marginal role. These transformations involved all aspects of cinema as a social, cultural and economic practice. While small investors were not completely replaced in the area of production, the tendency towards monopolisation of production, the industry's increasing entanglement with state intervention, which reached a peak during the War, and the foundation of Ufa, formed the basis for the emergence of a German national cinema during and after the war years. The ensuing rationalisation and standardisation of the production process was in line with an increasing orientation towards bourgeois cultural and aesthetic standards. The formal and thematic heterogeneity of the short film programme was replaced by the integrated multi-reel picture, which reflected the modes of perception and contemplation associated with bourgeois forms of art. However, it was in the area of exhibition that these transformations converged. Next to the small store-front cinemas, larger, more comfortable establishments modelled after regular theatres began appearing in urban centres which addressed a mainly middle-class clientele. These were characterised by steep ticket prices, full orchestras, cloakrooms and ushers in uniform. Movie-going became a planned event offering experiences and pleasures going beyond traditional forms of filmic entertainment and the social spaces associated with it.

Until recently, these transformations have usually been characterised as a shift from early cinema as a predominantly proletarian form of entertainment to a medium geared towards a middle-class audience. As Miriam Hansen and Martin Loiperdinger, among others, have pointed out however, this particular myth of origin must be seen as a discursive construction within leftist media theory enabling cinema to be regarded as a 'good object', i.e. as an emancipatory tool of the working class appropriated and destroyed by the bourgeoisie.[13] But, as Hansen demonstrates, this connection between early cinema and the lower classes also informed contemporary German assessments of the new medium. In contrast to American discourses, which embraced cinema as a genuinely democratic and – thus specifically American – cultural practice, in imperial Germany this egalitarian appeal and integrative potential was perceived as a threat to a social structure which, despite the changes brought about by industrialisation and modernisation, was still rooted in hierarchical class structures.

It was precisely cinema's democratic ability to integrate members of different classes in the new social formation of consumer society that made the new social space of the emerging cinemas an area calling for control. It is therefore significant that public debates about cinema's social function were initiated by the film reform movement at the very moment cinema was acquiring a fixed space. Sedentary film theatres were perceived as a public 'grey area' in need of regulation and control. Next to issues of moral, physical and social hygiene, which were considered particularly important because of the large attendance of women and children, the issues raised by the reform movement concentrated on the films themselves. Focusing on the medium's social and collective function, the movement emphasised its educational potential. The standard fare of melodramatic narratives was linked to the lower classes and thus rejected as morally dangerous, geared only towards private pleasures, in contrast to programmes including newsreels and nature films, which were seen as fit

for public display. Censorship and taxation strongly reinforced this notion of cinema as popular education, and a class-based dichotomy of private and public spheres which linked lower classes and melodrama to the private, upper classes and educational films to the public sphere.[14] The rhetorical force of this characterisation of early German cinema as a decidedly working-class institution which is instrumentalised in these different historical and political discourses, be it pejoratively or in celebratory mode, is revealed when reading these accounts against Emilie Altenloh's empirical investigation of cinema as a new social space. Her study is a unique source on spectator stratification, and Altenloh's findings, based on 2,400 questionnaires answered by movie-goers in the industrial town of Mannheim in 1912, clearly indicate that early cinema audiences were a much more complex phenomenon than contemporary reformist or later film historiographic discourses were prepared to see them as being.

The study's detailed breakdown of categories – differentiations based on class, age, sex and profession – allows an audience to emerge which does not lend itself to preconceived notions. Preferences, habits, pleasures and meanings do not stay within clearly demarcated class confinements but cut across and transcend borders to form unexpected alliances, demonstrating that class affiliation may not always be the most decisive social category determining the meaning cinema acquires for its audiences. The most striking insight of Altenloh's pioneering study is, however, the fact that contrary to the above-mentioned discourses, adult male workers (metal-workers in her case) are far from constituting the majority of movie audiences. Contextualising movie patronage with other forms of cultural practices at the disposal of her informants, Altenloh argues that the participation of these workers in social-democratic political culture, with its emphasis on middle-class education values, accounts for an alignment with the reform movement's rejection of a popular cinema lacking a didactic purpose. On the other hand, the categories of age and profession deconstruct the concept of a unified working class to reveal that it is the male adolescent worker holding a menial job in the service industries who holds the record in attendance rates, closely followed by female adolescents, women and children. The popularity of cinema was, however, not restricted to working-class women who saw it as 'a form of entertainment of the utmost importance':[15] upper-class women and female white-collar workers shared this appreciation of the movie theatre. Although the meaning of going to the movies may differ for these women – a place to relax after an afternoon of shopping for the upper-class woman, a place to avoid the dreariness of domestic life for the working-class woman and girl – their attendance confirms the importance of cinema as a new public sphere open to females of different ages and class.

The conclusions of Altenloh's study therefore lead, as Martin Loiperdinger points out, 'to a hypothesis that contradicts conventional wisdom: the most significant feature of the cinema-going public before World War I was not its proletarian origins (however significant a proportion this represented) but its class and gender diversity'.[16] This is confirmed by close examinations of the social topography of movie theatres. While, as in Dieter Prokop's study,[17] the proletarian-public thesis relied on the density of movie theatres in working-class areas and statistics on greater inhabitants-per-theatre ratios in industrial cities, recent investigations of local cinema cultures reveal, as Loiperdinger points out, that theatres were established mainly at central traffic points, catering to a casual, not locally specific audience, and that statistics controlling for theatre size significantly alter the population/theatre ratio, contradicting Prokop's previous findings.[18]

The early cinema audience is thus characterised by social diversity and anonymity which, as Loiperdinger observes, provides the basis of film's status as a mass medium: 'It is precisely this social and cultural heterogeneity that turned the big-city casual audience into the modern masses and the cinematograph into a modern mass medium – despite the status limitations of the domineering Wilhelmine aristocracy and the siege mentality of class consciousness among working class movement.'[19] As recent studies – above all Heide Schlüpmann's influential *Unheimlichkeit des Blicks. Das Drama des frühen deutschen Kinos (The Uncanny Gaze. The Drama of Early German Cinema)*[20] and Miriam Hansen's work[21] – demonstrate, gender emerges as a far more productive category in the assessment of early movie audiences than class, in terms of discourses as well as practices. Thus gender plays a crucial role in the sexual subtext of the reformists' discursive construction of cinema entertainment, in which sexual fears, particularly in the metonymic link between cinema and prostitution, are projected onto the proletarian 'other'.[22] While female movie patronage was the subject of heated discussions at the end of the first decade, the film industry tended to embrace women as customers and cater to their special needs and interests. In contrast to the diversity Altenloh makes out among male spectators, the responses of her female informants prove surprisingly homogeneous despite class differences. What unites these women is an addiction to film, with shared preferences for specific formal and plot characteristics: the filmic synergy of image and music, the importance of aesthetic rather than

factual-informative aspects in natural spectacles (*Naturaufnahmen*) and the choice of romances and social drama with female protagonists played by Asta Nielsen and Henny Porten, who represented the new generation of film stars. In films dealing specifically with women's issues, these two actresses represented opposite constructions of femininity. Henny Porten was promoted as a genuinely German counterpart to Asta Nielsen, a Danish actress with international acclaim: while the somewhat plump and dowdy Porten often starred in melodramatic stories of sacrifice and renunciation, the agile and expressive Nielsen portrayed a broad range of strong female characters, specifically in social dramas.[23]

While Altenloh accounts for cinema's appeal in general with social processes associated with capitalist development, such as alienation, fragmentation, isolation and the emergence of a new public sphere, Heide Schlüpmann characterises the specific meaning cinema acquired for its female audiences as a 'secret conspiracy' between cinematography and women's emancipation in Wilhelmine society: a conspiracy traceable in German fiction films from 1909–15. If German cinema before the First World

Asta Nielsen

War provided a counter-public sphere for its audiences, it mainly spoke to those excluded from the dominant bourgeois public sphere: workers in menial jobs and women across class divisions. The tenth anniversary issue of the periodical *Kinematograph*, published in 1916, is thus dedicated to women and gratefully acknowledges 'the invaluable cooperation and the unflagging interest of women in movie theatres'.[24] The opening article not only honours the contribution of women's work in film production, but attributes such thematic and stylistic developments in film as technical experiments (*féeries* and trick films) and sophisticated plots to the demands of cinema's powerful female clientele.

Yet, as Heide Schlüpmann demonstrates in her astute analysis of the transformations of German cinema from the pre-war to the Weimar years, this public recognition of the importance of women as movie theatre audiences coincided with a reorganisation of German cinema that undermined and ultimately destroyed this intrinsic link between film and its female audiences.[25] While early cinema had provided a new public sphere for women that addressed their physical, psychological and social needs, the rationalisation of the production process, the formal and stylistic unification of the big picture and the behavioural constraints theatre owners were encouraged to impose on their audiences all worked to reclaim this territory and recuperate cinema as a patriarchal practice.

In the area of production, the rationalisation and integration demanded by the large and prestigious productions which were now *en vogue* resulted in the growing importance of the director as the guarantor of stylistic unity. This restructuring not only marginalised the cameramen and actresses previously held as creative authorities in early film production, but the resulting new film style relying on a logic of causality and coherence was designed to erase the improvisation, ruptures, diversity and multiple perspectives characteristic of short film programmes. The new film's affinity to bourgeois cultural traditions also engendered a new generation of stars such as Albert Bassermann. He was the first performer to bring his enormous prestige as a stage actor to the screen (as, for example, in *Der Andere* [*The Other*, 1913]), thereby transcending the cultural gap which until then had clearly set off the high-culture sphere of legitimate theatre from cinema with its popular culture connotations. The efforts to eliminate early cinema's 'messiness' by increasingly adopting bourgeois cultural values were not restricted to production and representation but were implemented by a programme geared towards the 'education of the audience'[26] and the regulation of the exhibition sphere. Trade papers provided theatre owners

with detailed instructions on how to discipline audience behaviour. If audience comments, laughing, whispering and physical commotion had been an integral part of the early cinema experience as an interactive social event, these manifestations were now sanctioned as unruly behaviour. Although this campaign for audience 'education' did not explicitly mention women, there is no doubt, as Heide Schlüpmann demonstrates in her close analysis of instructional texts in trade papers, that the disciplining of women and their film experience was one of the main targets. Whereas early cinema had provided a public sphere in which women were encouraged to respond sensually and physically, the model of reception now reduced film experience to a more passive form of perception and involvement. Thus the director's task of repressing women's experiential depth was complemented by the theatre owner's measures to curb the expression of experience. The implementation of a mode of reception modelled on traditional bourgeois art audiences interpellated the spectator as a bourgeois and decidedly male subject. The reality of the audience's experiences, desires and fantasies was replaced by an adaptation to the modes of perception based on the abstract forms of space and time, rational logic and reason implemented by the new film style.

This displacement of real female audiences by an ideal audience inscribed in the film must be seen as a gradual and uneven process in which traditional cinema practices associated with early cinema coexisted alongside these new developments. As the work of Franz Hofer illustrates, narrative forms centred on the female protagonist and explicitly addressing the experiential realm of its female audiences still persisted during the War but were eventually marginalised in Weimar cinema.[27] The patriarchal implications of the burgeoning German national cinema are also highlighted by Asta Nielsen's career: while in her pre-war features she was celebrated as the uncontested artistic centre of her films, supported by director and cameraman alike, her authority was later replaced by that of her post-war directors such as Ernst Lubitsch in *Rausch* (1919) or G. W. Pabst in *Die freudlose Gasse* (*Joyless Street*, 1925).

Contrary to those film historiographic narratives in which Weimar cinema is celebrated as the culmination of German cinema's first period, the close analysis of early cinema's audiences sheds a different light on the development of a German national cinema, which in this context must be seen as the gradual extinction of early cinema's aesthetics and its public. As Schlüpmann demonstrates, it is women who are most affected by the drastic reformation of cinema and its audiences. For a brief moment, female spectatorship once more became a publicly debated topic at the beginning of the War when the meaning of cinema for women became a controversial issue between the film industry and the state's interventions sanctioning female movie attendance by cuts in state subsidies for soldiers' wives. Although the trade papers' allegiance oscillated between the voyeurism and curiosity of cinema's female clientele and the power claims of the state, it settled for a patronising attitude, defending the importance of cinema for women as a cultural need. This concession to female audiences is relativised, however, when periodicals like the *Kinematograph* simultaneously hasten to state in no uncertain terms that this cultural need can only be met by 'higher culture' as exemplified in the new big picture productions, which alone were considered capable of yielding the kind of bourgeois cultural experience now advocated as the cinema's ideal.

Notes

1 See the chronology of cinema 1889–96 established by Deac Rossell in *Film History*, vol. 7, no. 2, Summer 1995. For closer analyses of the exhibition of moving images in Germany see Deac Rossell, *Faszination der Bewegung. Ottomar Anschütz zwischen Photographie und Kino* (Basel and Frankfurt am Main: Stroemfeld/Roter Stern, 2001); Martin Loiperdinger, *Film & Schokolade: Stollwercks Geschäfte mit lebenden Bildern* (Basel and Frankfurt-am-Main: Stroemfeld/Roter Stern, 1999).

2 See Joseph Garncarz, 'Die Entstehung des Kinos aus dem Varieté: ein Plädoyer für ein erweitertes Konzept der Intermedialität', in Jörg Helbig (ed.), *Intermedialität: Theorie und Praxis eines interdisziplinären Forschungsgebiets* (Berlin: Erich Schmidt, 1998), pp. 244–56 and also his contribution to this volume.

3 For the economic aspects of early German film history see Corinna Müller's important study *Frühe deutsche Kinematographie. Formale, wirtschaftliche und kulturelle Entwicklungen 1907–1912* (Stuttgart and Weimar: Metzler, 1994).

4 For the concept of 'novelty period' see Charles Musser, *The Emergence of Cinema. The American Screen to 1907* (New York: Scribner's, 1990).

5 For critical analyses of the 'train myth' see Martin Loiperdinger, 'Lumières *Ankunft des Zugs*. Gründungsmythos eines neuen Mediums', in *KINtop. Jahrbuch zur Erforschung des frühen Films*, 5, 1996, pp. 37–70 and Stephen Bottomore, 'The Panicking Audience? Early Cinema and the "Train Effect"', *Historical Journal of Film, Radio and Television*, vol. 19, no. 2, 1999, pp. 177–216.

6 Paul Kleebinder, *Der deutsche Kaiser im Film* (Berlin: Paul Kleebinder, 1912), quoted in Martin Loiperdinger, 'The Kaiser's Cinema: An Archaeology of Attitudes and Audiences', in Thomas Elsaesser (ed.), *A Second Life: German Cinema's First Decades* (Amsterdam: Amsterdam University Press, 1996), p. 48.

7 This general fascination with films about the Kaiser is the reason why Martin Loiperdinger apostrophises Wilhelm II and his family as 'the first German film stars'. Cf. ibid., p. 47.

8 See *Special-Katalog No. 32 über Projections- und Aufnahme-Apparate für lebende Photographie, Films, Grammophons, Nebelbilder-Apparate, Scheinwerfer etc. der Fabrik für optisch-mechanische Präcisions-Instrumente von Ed. Messter* (Berlin, 1898), reprinted in *KINtop-Schriften*, vol. 3 (Basel and Frankfurt am Main: Stroemfeld/Roter Stern, 1995), pp. 74–5.

9 For the importance of French productions on the German market see Frank Kessler and Sabine Lenk, 'The French Connection: Franco-German Film Relations before World War I', in Elsaesser, *A Second Life*, pp. 62–71.

10 Willy Rath, 'Emporkömmling Kino' [1912/13], in Jörg Schweinitz, *Prolog vor dem Film: Nachdenken über ein neues Medium 1909–1914* (Leipzig: Reclam, 1992), p. 79.

11 Emilie Altenloh, *Zur Soziologie des Kino: Die Kino-Unternehmung und die sozialen Schichten ihrer Besucher* (Jena: Diederichs, 1914). An English translation of parts of Emilie Altenloh's work was published as 'A Sociology of the Cinema: The Audience', trans. by Kathleen Cross. *Screen*, vol. 42, no. 3, Autumn 2001, pp. 249–93.

12 Altenloh, *Zur Soziologie des Kino*, p. 1.

13 See Loiperdinger, 'The Kaiser's Cinema', p. 48, and Miriam Hansen, 'Early Cinema – Whose Public Sphere?', in Thomas Elsaesser, *Early Cinema. Space, Frame, Narrative* (London: BFI, 1990), pp. 228–46.

14 The repressive nature of taxation is highlighted by the fact that in contrast to melodramatic features, educational and nature films were tax-free. See Altenloh, *Zur Soziologie des Kino*, p. 43.

15 Ibid., p. 78.

16 Loiperdinger, 'The Kaiser's Cinema', p. 44.

17 Dieter Prokop, *Soziologie des Films*, rev. edn (Frankfurt am Main: Fischer, 1982).

18 Loiperdinger, 'The Kaiser's Cinema', p. 44.

19 Ibid.

20 Basel and Frankfurt-am-Main: Stroemfeld/Roter Stern, 1990.

21 Hansen, 'Early Cinema – Whose Public Sphere'., pp. 228–46.

22 Ibid., p. 238.

23 For an extensive comparative study of female address in
    German melodramas and social dramas see Heide
    Schlüpmann, *Die Unheimlichkeit des Blicks*. See also Heide
    Schlüpmann, 'Asta Nielsen and Female Narration: The
    Early Films', in Elsaesser, *A Second Life*, pp. 118–22.

24 Quoted in Heide Schlüpmann, ' "Die Erziehung des
    Publikums"– auch eine Vorgeschichte des Weimarer Kinos',
    in *Kintop. Jahrbuch zur Erforschung des frühen Films*, 5,
    1996, p. 142.

25 Ibid.

26 See R. Gennecher's article 'Die Erziehung des Publikums',
    Kinematograph, October 1915, quoted by Schlüpmann in
    ' "Die Erziehung des Publikums" '.

27 On Hofer see Heide Schlüpmann, 'The Sinister Gaze: Three
    Films by Franz Hofer from 1913', in Paolo Cherchi Usai
    and Lorenzo Codelli (eds.), *Before Caligari: German
    Cinema 1895–1920* (Pordenone: Biblioteca dell'Immagine,
    1990), pp. 452–73; Michael Wedel, 'Melodrama and
    Narrative Space: Franz Hofer's *Heideröslein*', in Elsaesser, *A
    Second Life*, pp. 123–31; Yuri Tsivian, 'Two "Stylists" of the
    Teens: Franz Hofer and Yevgenii Bauer', in Elsaesser, *A
    Second Life*, pp. 264–76; Elena Dagrada, 'The Voyeur at
    Wilhelm's Court: Franz Hofer', in Elsaesser, *A Second Life*,
    pp. 277–84; Uli Jung and Stephanie Roll, 'Women Enjoying
    Being Women: Some Observations on the Occasion of a
    Retrospective of Franz Hofer's Extant Films in
    Saarbrücken', in *Kintop. Jahrbuch zur Erforschung des
    frühen Films*, 8, 1999, pp. 159–68.

12

A History of Ufa

Hans-Michael Bock and Michael Töteberg

In terms of reputation and market position, Ufa represents the quintessential German national film corporation. With close ties to the state, the Deutsche Bank and conservative backers, Ufa dominated the German film industry between 1917 and 1945, acquiring a degree of power and influence never equalled since.

The corporation itself was brought into being not as a result of market influences, but through an act of political determination. Its foundation represented a decisive shift towards modernisation, with the consolidation of economic resources engendering a corporation at once shaped by conservative ideology, and by the most up-to-date management style. Unlike the Hollywood majors, Ufa was headed not by a tycoon, but by a joint-stock company board whose members were level-headed businessmen who recognised the need to ally themselves to creative talents, and allowed production teams to work in relative independence. Prior to 1917, production companies had been (and many indeed still continued to be) family-run enterprises organised around an individual star or entrepreneurial personality. Ufa, by contrast, established a German studio system in which directors, cinematographers and art directors aimed at creating a unified aesthetic standard, or 'Ufa style'. The strategies underpinning the corporation's business policy extended to the promotion of stars, who were tied to the company by long-term contracts (though they could, when their popularity waned, be hired out – for a fee – to other companies).

Ufa charted a similar course to many corporations, signing up creative talent from elsewhere and lavishing generous budgets on projects with no certainty of either artistic or economic success. Figures such as Fritz Lang or F. W. Murnau made their best films not with Ufa, but for smaller independents either before or after their involve-

Bird's-eye view of the Ufa complex in Neubabelsberg

ment with the corporation. Ufa's penchant for monumentalism sometimes caused logistical difficulties; yet its marketing, sales and distribution practices always remained innovative. Long before such terms had been coined, Ufa practised modern marketing, cross-media promotion campaigns and product placement, developed new ideas for merchandising and tie-ins, and consistently prioritised a corporate identity.

The Ufa legend frequently obscures the existence of other companies and independents whose films continued to be made alongside Babelsberg's colossal productions. In the popular imagination, however, classic German film art and Ufa are practically synonymous. Within its own promotional writings, as well as through the establishment of the Ufa-*Lehrschau* (a kind of company museum) and other similar activities, the corporation ensured that the Ufa trademark stood for more than the films it produced, distributed or released through its cinemas.

Since its demise, film historians have kept the Ufa myth alive; there is no other German production company about which such numerous and detailed studies have been published.[1] The situation with regard to primary sources is likewise unique. Holdings at the Federal Archive (*Bundesarchiv*) include balance sheets, company files, minutes of board meetings, and countless other materials: nothing even remotely comparable is preserved of other companies.

Genesis in the First World War

In 1917, the First World War entered its third year with a virtual impasse on the battlefront. Such decisive developments as did occur were taking place back in Germany. Since late August 1916, when Paul von Hindenburg and Erich Ludendorff took charge of the military, these two generals had become essentially the key power-holders in the German Reich. While the ruling classes continued to foster illusions of Germany as a great world power, shortages of basic supplies in the major industrial cities fuelled rising dissent among the starving masses. Social tensions at home were exacerbated by developments abroad: the February Revolution in Russia was followed by the US declaration of war on Germany on 6 April 1917, prompted by Germany's unrestricted U-boat warfare.

It was against this backdrop that the military – for whom cinema had hitherto been largely an object of distrust – discovered film as a means for overseas, and above all domestic, propaganda. General Ludendorff ordered the consolidation of all official press and film activities within the so-called *Militärische Stelle* (Military Board), under the leadership of Lieutenant Hans von Haeften. The Board's most important department was the *Bild- und Film-Amt* (Photograph and Film Office, or BUFA), which spent over 18 million marks in the space of its first year, mostly on military documentaries. Von Haeften's much-envied rival was the successful *Deutsche Lichtbild-Gesellschaft* (German Photoplay Co., or DLG). Founded by various industrial and financial bodies in 1916 with a mission to publicise German industry and tourism at home and abroad, the DLG was the brainchild of Ludwig Klitzsch, a young publishing manager and confidant of Alfred Hugenberg, who in turn represented the steel and armaments manufacturer Krupp on the DLG's administrative board. Von Haeften saw his plans for centralised film production under state control threatened by competition from the DLG, and set about forging a rival alliance. Reluctant to join forces with the DLG, despite its proven track record in cinema, the military preferred to co-operate with Dr Emil Georg Stauß

who, as director of the Deutsche Bank, had connections to a cartel of fairly liberal-minded chief executives of electrical, petroleum and chemical companies, all of whom were opposed – both politically and economically – to the reactionary Hugenberg group. On 4 July 1917, Ludendorff signed a memorandum calling for a united German film industry that could exert an ordered and effective influence on the broad masses from a unified position and in the state's interest.

On 18 December 1917, Universum Film AG (Ufa) acquired registered company status, with a starting capital of 25 million marks. Apart from the Deutsche Bank, Ufa's capital came principally from the electrical concerns AEG and Bosch, the shipping giants Hapag and Norddeutscher Lloyd, and the gramophone company Carl Lindström. The government took on – secretly – a share of 8 million marks (which passed to the Deutsche Bank in 1921). Ludendorff's propaganda specialist Major Grau was enlisted into Ufa's board of directors to further ensure government influence.

Field Marshall Hindenburg welcomed the newly founded Ufa as an enterprise of tremendous national, political, economic and cultural significance; and indeed, Ufa's foundation created at a stroke the largest film company in Europe. Yet the corporation was no creation *ex nihilo*, but rather the product of Ufa's integration of firms already operating in different areas of the film industry. Ufa's acquisitions included the Danish Nordisk Film's subsidiary Nordische Film GmbH and its production arm Oliver-Film GmbH; the assets of film pioneer Oskar Messter in their entirety, including his large glass-house studio at Tempelhof; Paul Davidson's Projektions-AG Union (PAGU), which brought with it an established cinema chain and a second glass-house at Tempelhof; and numerous smaller companies.

Defeat in the First World War ended both the monarchy and the military's propaganda dreams. Yet Ufa's various subsidiaries – who had apparently laid speculative plans for peacetime from the corporation's very moment of inception – continued production unabated, operating under the established names and producing lines defined primarily by successful stars and directors: thus Ernst Lubitsch directed PAGU comedies starring Ossi Oswalda; the period's greatest star, Henny Porten, continued her work for the Messter team; and producer-director Joe May (whose company was temporarily under Ufa ownership) impressed audiences with his three-hour spectacle *Veritas Vincit* (1919).

Ufa's hefty financial resources, meanwhile, allowed it to develop its artistic reputation in new directions. Alongside his successful comedies, Lubitsch, for instance, also directed a series of high-budget historical films. *Madame Dubarry* (*Passion*, 1919), with Pola Negri and Emil Jannings, was fêted across Europe and America alike, prompting President Friedrich Ebert to visit the set of Lubitsch's *Anna Boleyn* (*Deception*) at Tempelhof in the autumn of 1920, thereby acknowledging the director, and film in general, as a major foreign currency earner for Germany.

Erich Pommer and the classical German silent film

Ufa's market dominance did not go unchallenged. In 1921, the *Europäische Film-Allianz* (European Film Alliance, or EFA) was founded with American financial backing, and attracted several of Ufa's key players. Both Joe May and Ernst Lubitsch now worked for EFA production subsidiaries bearing their name. Lubitsch's group was managed by Paul Davidson, the founder of PAGU and, until recently, head of production at Ufa.

At the same time, significant mergers took place within a general framework of film industry consolidation. The amalgamation of two of Ufa's leading competitors into Decla-Bioscop AG in March 1920 was followed by a further marriage of the Titans. Behind the back of Erich Pommer – who, as founder and director of Decla, remained one of the German film industry's leading figures – Ufa head Emil Stauß secretly bought up Decla-Bioscop shares. By November 1921, the buy-out was complete, with the celebrated Decla-Bioscop name retained by Ufa as a trademark. In the process Ufa gained possession not merely of its main competitor, but also of Decla's vast studio lot. Deutsche Bioscop had built its first glass-house in Neubabelsberg, halfway between Berlin and Potsdam, in the winter of 1911–12, and had gradually transformed the site into one of Europe's largest studios through the addition of new buildings and massive exterior sets. Ufa's acquisition of Decla-Bioscop also brought new creative capacity into the company, in particular in the shape of the company's charismatic producer Erich Pommer. Pommer saw himself not simply as an executive, but as a 'creative producer' who, in the early 1920s, had gathered around himself the film-makers who were to provide the cornerstone of German silent cinema's reputation, including directors Fritz Lang, Ludwig Berger and E. A. Dupont, scriptwriter Thea von Harbou, set designer Rochus Gliese and cinematographer Carl Hoffmann. Pommer laid particular emphasis on fostering teamwork among directors and writers, set designers and cameramen, while at the same time ensuring that they retained a large degree of

artistic independence from the company. In 1924, he instituted what was arguably the most fruitful collaboration in German silent film: that of director F. W. Murnau, scriptwriter Carl Mayer, cameraman Karl Freund, and set designers Robert Herlth and Walter Röhrig. The team's first collective effort – *Der letzte Mann* (*The Last Laugh*, 1924) starring Emil Jannings – also proved their greatest. Pommer's directive for the film had been to 'invent something new, even if it's crazy!' Foremost among the team's 'crazy' innovations was the so-called 'unchained camera' (*entfesselte Kamera*) that Freund employed consistently as a narrational device in the film. *The Last Laugh* proved a major hit in the US, and elicited the standard response; both Murnau and Jannings were bankrolled by Hollywood, and their 1926 adaptation of *Faust* constituted a joint farewell to Ufa.[2]

Corporate expansion

Another international success for Ufa was *Varieté* (*Variety*, 1925), directed by E. A. Dupont and again featuring Karl Freund's 'unchained camera' and Jannings in the lead role. Ufa's earnings on the film were threefold: as producer, distributor and exhibitor. The corporation's power and omnipresence stemmed from a vertical structure which secured market dominance in both distribution and exhibition. Thus it was not only classic titles by Lubitsch, Lang and Murnau that appeared under the Ufa logo, but also run-of-the-mill comedies, mediocre imports and movies licensed from minor German independents.

A good example of the latter was *Fridericus Rex* (1922), a reactionary historical feature that glorified the Prussian monarch Frederick the Great and was unmistakably anti-republican in tone (see also Martin Loiperdinger in this volume). Director Arzén von Cserépy had produced the film independently, but Ufa picked it up for distribution and, when it proved a success, secured a production deal with Cserépy-Film. A sequel was rushed out, followed by third and fourth parts, as well as numerous subsequent Frederick the Great cash-ins, invariably starring Otto Gebühr as the eponymous hero. Thus a production into which Ufa had no input nonetheless became associated with the Ufa name in the public mind.

Between 1917 and 1922, Ufa's exhibition capacity expanded massively. In 1917, Ufa's acquisition of PAGU's Union-Theater (UT) chain secured the corporation a network of forty cinemas across Germany. Half a decade later, the company's exhibition circuit had doubled in size. Prestigious first-run cinemas newly under Ufa control in Berlin included the *Ufa-Palast am Zoo*, the *Gloria-Palast* and the elegant *Marmorhaus*; but there were Ufa cinemas throughout the Reich, in the cities and provinces alike. Although it would be mistaken to describe Ufa as a monopoly in the exhibition sector, since its movie theatres made up scarcely 10 per cent of all cinemas, the largest and best-appointed movie palaces in any location always sported the Ufa company crest. Indeed Ufa had a presence wherever German films were shown. Ufa distribution offices and subsidiaries were established in France (under the *Alliance Cinématographique Européenne*, or ACE), Holland, Italy, Poland, Sweden, Austria and Hungary, as well as New York. Throughout the world, then, German film became synonymous with Ufa.

In Germany, furthermore, the *Ufa-Handelsgesellschaft* (Ufa Trading Co.) supplied cinemas with projectors and associated equipment, and offered special cine-film projectors for educational use. The corporation had a division specialising in advertising and industrial film production, as well as its own Berlin-based labs, the *Aktiengesellschaft für Filmfabrikation* (Film Fabrication Co., or Afifa). Associated rights to films were exploited by Ufa's publishing house and magazines, as well as by its music publishers, Ufaton and Wiener Bohème. The company's newsreel, the *Ufa-Wochenschau*, was both politically and financially significant: it became the market leader with a weekly distribution of a hundred copies. Ufa, in other words, was equipped to furnish cinema owners with a complete film package including one significant element: the short film, which might take the form of the so-called *Kulturfilm*.

The culture film (*Kulturfilm*)

The production of the *Kulturfilm*, a particularly German variant of the documentary film, had commenced in 1918, during the final months of the War, and by spring 1919, the *Kulturfilm* catalogue already boasted some eighty-seven titles. In the beginning, many Ufa productions were conceived specifically as instructional films for medical personnel. At that time film's status as art remained disputed, but its scientific applications were readily accepted. Rare diseases and complex procedures could be documented on celluloid, and within five years the Medical Film Archive of Ufa's *Kulturabteilung* comprised 135 titles – a number that would systematically grow in subsequent years. This branch of Ufa was also commercially successful, selling films to universities in Germany and overseas for instructional purposes.

It took greater publicity to establish *Kulturfilme* for mass educational purposes. Ufa went so far as to screen a selection of educational films before the National Assembly in Weimar, and political support was finally secured when tax breaks were agreed for exhibitors who included *Kulturfilme* with an official seal of approval (*Prädikat*) in cinema programmes. From this point on, educational and popular scientific instructional works played regularly alongside the main feature in cinemas. Wildlife and nature films, as well as travelogues predominated here (see Marie-Hélène Gutberlet in this volume). The first film of the type was *Der Hirschkäfer* (*The Stag Beetle*, 1921); but three years later, Ufa chanced its hand with a more audacious venture: the production of feature-length *Kulturfilme*.

The risk paid off; for such titles as *Wein, Weib, Gesang* (*Wine, Women, Song*, 1924), a study of viniculture and wine-making, or *Des Menschen Freund* (*Man's Best Friend*, 1924), on dog breeding and training, had crowds flocking to cinemas. The most popular *Kulturfilm*, however, was *Wege zu Kraft und Schönheit* (*Ways to Strength and Beauty*, 1925), a film that promoted modern body culture, and was produced in multiple versions for different overseas markets. *Wege* extolled the harmony of body and mind with scenes recalling the cultural ideal of classical antiquity (though in 1943, Nicholas Kaufmann, who, along with director Wilhelm Prager had been responsible for the film, revealed that the production's ulterior political motives had been to encourage physical training as preparation for a desired German rearmament).

Into crisis with *Metropolis*

In the mid-1920s, it looked as if Ufa had successfully survived the inflationary period. Then, seemingly overnight, the company was reporting losses running to tens of millions of marks. The corporation was in trouble and, without powerful financial backers, was no longer able to pay its 5,000 employees.

The Ufa copying factory, Tempelhof (Berlin)

Help came from America. A deal in December 1925 securing a $4 million loan was signed with Paramount and Metro-Goldwyn-Mayer, and Ufa was saved from bankruptcy. The corporation agreed to a joint distribution arm for the three studios, known as Parufamet, which was to release sixty films a year in Germany, twenty productions from each studio. At the same time, Ufa was obliged under state quota regulations to produce forty German pictures for every forty American titles imported. The company also agreed to dedicate at least 75 per cent of the available screen time in Ufa cinemas to Parufamet releases. In exchange, its American partners agreed to show Ufa productions in the United States – with the proviso that each and every title could be rejected at any time. The result was that few films from Neubabelsberg ever made it onto American screens. Thus rather than securing a new overseas market, Ufa diminished its own chances in a domestic market which it had thrown open to competitors. The conditions of the Parufamet deal were so unfavourable for Ufa that they drew the company deeper into crisis.

Yet this debilitating deal was not the cause of Ufa's astronomical debts (the precise magnitude of which has only recently come to light), but rather a consequence of them. Ufa's desire to compete with Hollywood had produced years of financial mismanagement. No expense was spared when eminent directors sought to realise their artistic visions at the Babelsberg studios. Murnau's *Faust* proved suitably prestigious for Ufa, but was – as the company had indeed anticipated – a box-office loss-maker. Even *Der letzte Mann* grossed only half its production costs. Careful budgeting clearly did not feature high on Ufa's agenda.

The corporation's frivolous monumentalism can best be demonstrated by Fritz Lang's *Metropolis* – a gargantuan production undertaken at the height of Ufa's financial malaise. Originally budgeted at 1.5 million marks, it finally came in at 6 million, following 310 days and sixty nights of shooting, as well as the use of some 620,000 metres of negative stock and 1.3 million metres of positive film. Ufa propaganda had declared that *Metropolis* should be 'a film of titanic dimensions'.

The Hugenberg takeover

Metropolis' producer, Erich Pommer, found himself under fire and was sacked even before shooting ended (only to resurface at Paramount in Hollywood a few months later). The film's final balance sheet exposed a financial fiasco: *Metropolis* flopped in America, and the German market recouped just one-seventh of the production costs. The dilapidated concern had no means of absorbing such losses, and executive Ferdinand Bausback – appointed by the Deutsche Bank – introduced the usual array of unsuccessful measures to regenerate the company. Those measures involved in particular the selling-off of valuable real estate, including Ufa's head offices on Potsdamer Platz.

The dream factory stood on the brink of ruin. The state had promised aid, but an assistance package from the Trade Ministry was repeatedly delayed. It was at this point that Alfred Hugenberg interceded. An influential press baron with political ambitions, Hugenberg had taken control of the Scherl publishing house in 1916, and steered its newspapers on a right-wing course. Excluded from the process of Ufa's foundation in 1917, he now explained that it was his wish to preserve Ufa for the nation: otherwise, he observed, it might be swallowed up by the bourgeois-liberal Ullstein or Mosse publishing houses, or even worse – a veritable vision of hell on earth for the nationalist Hugenberg – by the Americans.

Hugenberg's negotiations for Ufa revealed his takeover as no hazardous gamble. Hugenberg forced the Deutsche Bank to write off debts of 6 million marks, and to transfer its preferential shares to his name, along with its twelve votes on the executive board. Other substantial share allocations were acquired by the Otto Wolf corporation and IG-Farben, which, as a major manufacturer of Agfa film stock, had a vested interest in Ufa. Although Hugenberg owned less than 50 per cent of the company's stock, he managed to secure the majority vote, and Ufa's economic management now passed entirely into his hands. Hugenberg became president of the board, and von Stauß his deputy. Ludwig Klitzsch, newly advanced to director general of Scherl publishing, now assumed the same position at Ufa.

It took Klitzsch less than two years to restore Ufa to its flagship position in the German film industry. Klitzsch put an end to the corporation's financial mismanagement and streamlined its broad operational base. Unprofitable subsidiaries were shut down, personnel laid off, and a system of financial controls introduced for the first time to oversee costly studio work. Klitzsch even managed to secure a relaxation of the Parufamet deal. The screen time allocated to Paramount and MGM productions in Ufa cinemas was reduced by one-third, and an agreement reached to annul the Parufamet contract after four years (against immediate repayment of the $4 million loan by Ufa).

Klitzsch also brought Erich Pommer back from Hollywood; yet a new rift soon developed. Pommer's first production – Joe May's *Heimkehr* (*Homecoming*, 1928) – led the new Ufa board to accuse him of 'Bolshevist tendencies'. However ludicrous, this accusation was telling of the company's distrust of Pommer, whose presence at the board's production conferences, it was stressed, was henceforth no longer welcome.

The Hugenberg takeover signified a drastic rightward shift for Ufa, with decisions on films now frequently shaped by the board's ideological position rather than economic sense. The Ufa sound studios, for instance, refused to dub into German Universal's 1930 anti-war picture *All Quiet on the Western Front*, and the film was boycotted by all Ufa cinemas.

The coming of sound

Following the Hugenberg takeover, one of the first measures adopted by the new Ufa directorship was the shelving of all 'talking film' experiments, which the company had pursued for some years. In 1922, the Tri-Ergon sound on film process had been successfully demonstrated before a Berlin audience. It was not until 1925, however, that Ufa signed a licensing deal with the now Zurich-based *Tri-Ergon AG*, and established an Ufa-Tri-Ergon sound film department. A twenty-minute fairy-tale adaptation – *Das Mädchen mit den Schwefelhölzchen* (*The Little Match Girl*) – was rushed into production, and premiered on 20 December 1925. The screening proved a technical disaster, and Ufa's initial experiment with sound a resounding failure.

In the US, Warner Bros. released *The Jazz Singer* in October 1927. In Germany, meanwhile, where some fifteen competing systems existed, considerable uncertainty still surrounded the issue of sound. In autumn 1927, Ufa's licensing rights for the Tri-Ergon process expired. A lengthy patent dispute was finally resolved on 13 March 1929, when a deal was struck by the two largest sound film companies. The *Tonbild-Syndikat AG* (Sound Pictures Syndicate, or

Tobis), financed by Swiss and Dutch backers, was to deal with the production of films and recording equipment, while *Klangfilm GmbH* (Sound Film Co.) would be responsible for projectors and sound reproduction equipment in cinemas. It was to this cartel that Ufa affiliated itself. The corporation's existing Neubabelsberg studios were initially unsuitable for sound film production, and the Ufa board under Ernst Hugo Correll decided to add a new studio complex, the *Tonkreuz* comprising four windowless soundstages arranged in the form of a cross around a central courtyard. Shooting began here on 29 September 1929, with half of all productions that year already scheduled as talkies.

Ufa's first all-talking feature, *Melodie des Herzens* (*Melody of the Heart*) starring Dita Parlo and Willy Fritsch, premiered on 16 December 1929. The film was produced – with foreign distribution in mind – in multiple language versions. *Melodie des Herzens* was an Erich Pommer production, and it was his division at Ufa that was initially responsible for the majority of the corporation's sound film output. Unlike other film-makers, Pommer committed himself to the new technology from the start, and sought to establish a scriptwriting section specifically for talkies.

The first peak of Ufa sound film production was *Der Blaue Engel* (*The Blue Angel*). The movie's star, Emil Jannings, had been the first ever recipient of Hollywood's Academy Award for Best Actor in 1927, but had returned to Berlin following the introduction of sound. The director, hired out from Paramount by Pommer, was Josef von Sternberg, and the female lead Marlene Dietrich, cast after a lengthy talent search. Although Dietrich received just one-tenth of Jannings' fee, *Der Blaue Engel* became *her* film in the public imagination. Ufa, however, found itself unable to retain Dietrich, and she sailed for Hollywood the day after the premiere.

One film that epitomises Ufa's early talking pictures was *Liebeswalzer* (*The Love Waltz*, 1930) starring Lilian Harvey and Willy Fritsch. Director Wilhelm (later in the US William) Thiele established with *Liebeswalzer* a form of film operetta, which, in its integration of musical numbers and narrative, pre-empted an important element of subsequent Hollywood musicals. Thiele successfully reproduced the same formula in *Die Drei von der Tankstelle* (*The Three from the Filling Station*). This film once again demonstrated Erich Pommer's success in gathering a team of youthful talent, including Thiele, the brothers Kurt and Robert Siodmak, scriptwriters Billie Wilder and Robert Liebmann, as well as composers Werner Richard Heymann and Friedrich Hollaender.

All of these, of course, soon found themselves forced to pursue careers in Hollywood. Thus the enduring nostalgic

Tonkreuz – the four new Ufa soundstages

symbol of this period – and for many, of Ufa productions as a whole – remains a song by Lilian Harvey from the film operetta *Der Kongress tanzt* (*Congress Dances*, 1931) directed by 1920s revue king Erik Charell: '*Das gibt's nur einmal, das kommt nicht wieder*' ('It happens just once, and never again').

The New Era

On 30 January 1933, President von Hindenburg appointed Adolf Hitler Chancellor. The National Socialists' accession to power dealt a deathblow to German republicanism; yet it did not constitute a radical departure for Ufa or the German film industry. With the exception of a few minor independent producers who were in any case regarded as industry outsiders, Weimar film culture had contained few progressive or pro-republican tendencies. Ufa figured squarely among those Weimar media organisations which more or less consciously helped lay the ideological foundations for the Third Reich. Ufa's nationalism, admittedly, was not synonymous with Nazism. Hugenberg, as leader of the *Deutschnationale Volkspartei* (German National Popular Party), served in Hitler's first cabinet as Minister for Trade, but resigned after just a few months once his political impotence became evident. Moreover, Hugenberg was no anti-Semite, and nor were most members of the Ufa board, several of whom – including Erich Pommer – were themselves Jews. However, Hitler's seizure of power and installation of Joseph Goebbels as Propaganda Minister and 'patron of the German film' brought increased pressure to bear on Ufa to distance itself from Jews in its workforce, despite the fact that many of their names were synonymous with the company's greatest hits. As early as March 1933, the board determined to dissolve the contracts of Jewish employees, including Pommer and Charell.

The title of the patriotic U-boat drama *Morgenrot* (*Dawn*), directed for Ufa by the Austrian Gustav Ucicky, came to symbolise the arrival of what the Nazi regime termed the New Era. Hitler demonstratively attended the film's Berlin premiere at the *Ufa-Palast am Zoo* together with Hugenberg on 2 April 1933. The film's tale of German U-boat men's noble struggle and heroic death during the First World War was as ambiguous as Ufa's own position at the time. Bombastic lines such as, 'We Germans may not know how to live, but we know how to die' competed with scenes whose pacifist undertones called the very notion of heroic death into question, and paid tribute to enemy fatalities. Nazi censors later deleted these scenes.

Ufa soon found itself discouraged, moreover, from producing open propaganda for the NSDAP and its subordi-

nate organisations. The Nazis recognised that such blatant propaganda as Ucicky's *Hitlerjunge Quex* (*Hitler Youth Quex*, 1933) could prove counter-productive, and sought instead to disseminate National Socialist ideology through tendentious portraits of great historical Führer-figures, as well as through non-fiction genres, in particular the Ufa weekly newsreel.

The Ufa output continued, meanwhile, to be dominated by lavish entertainment films. The director Reinhold Schünzel, although classed as a 'half-Jew', was given a special work permit by Goebbels to produce apparently frivolous comedies such as *Viktor und Viktoria* (*Viktor and Viktoria*, 1933) and *Amphitryon*, 1935, both shot simultaneously in French-language versions and internationally acclaimed. Similar success was enjoyed by newcomer Detlef Sierck (Douglas Sirk), whose Zarah Leander vehicles *Zu neuen Ufern* (*To New Shores*, 1937) and *La Habanera* (1937) represented his first successful attempts at film melodrama. Forced into emigration in 1937–8, Sierck and Schünzel were just two representatives of the vast artistic exodus suffered by the German film industry in the 1930s under the Nazis' policy of racist and socio-political exclusion (see Peter Krämer in this volume).

Gleichschaltung (co-ordination) and nationalisation

In 1933, there were forty-nine film companies in Germany. By 1939, just fifteen remained, of which four – Ufa, Terra, Tobis and Bavaria – accounted for three-quarters of all production. Further moves towards centralisation and nationalisation in the industry were at first covert, then quite open. In 1937, Goebbels had appointed Max Winkler 'state representative for the German film industry', with a brief including the buying-up of shares and shareholder interests in remaining independents. Winkler had been a faithful servant of successive governments since 1920, and after 1937, began to work as a behind-the-scenes spin doctor, influencing press opinion and building up the *Cautio Treuhand GmbH* (Cautio Trust Company) as a cover for gradual nationalisation (see Julian Petley in this volume).

It was Hugenberg, first, who had to relinquish power. Powerless to resist the enforced sale of his controlling holding of Ufa shares, he was reasonably satisfactorily remunerated, receiving just over 21 million marks, a sum corresponding broadly to the 1927 purchase price. Winkler also acquired the Deutsche Bank's shares at 67 per cent of their market value, and spent the next several years buying up smaller holdings in the corporation. By March 1939, the state – via Cautio – controlled exactly 99.25 per cent of Ufa's ordinary share capital. The new owners maintained an outer semblance of continuity, retaining Klitzsch as chief executive, and later appointing him chairman of the board. Yet the corporation's change of ownership had immediate consequences, not least in the form of an internal communication to the press prohibiting criticism of Ufa productions.

After a similar 'rationalisation' of ownership of Germany's remaining film companies, the state was able to establish a super-corporation in 1941, with *Ufa-Film GmbH* (known as UFI) as its parent organisation. On a purely superficial level, this course of events seemed reminiscent of Ufa's original foundation, with the state uniting a fragmented national film industry in times of war, and shaping its existing components into a powerful corporation. However, as Goebbels himself conceded in a communication to the *Reichsfilmkammer* (Reich Film Chamber), UFI was in fact in no sense comparable to the old Ufa. The similarity of the two acronyms stemmed directly from Hitler, who had not wanted to abandon Ufa's internationally renowned trademark. But UFI, owned outright by Cautio, was no more than a holding company. Film technology, distribution and exhibition remained the province of *Universum Film AG* (Ufa), while production was handled separately by *Ufa-Filmkunst GmbH* (Ufa Film Art Co.) which, along with Terra, Tobis and Bavaria, was directly subordinate to UFI. Thus, while the processes of manufacture, distribution and public screening were consolidated (facilitating a more streamlined – and cost-effective – deployment of studios and equipment), production companies continued to enjoy a certain independence, since it was deemed necessary to protect creative projects from the bureaucracy of a mammoth organisation.

In theory, then, creative competition in Third Reich cinema was apparently sustained at the level of film production, while the state simultaneously retained complete political control over all film activities. In practice, however, it was almost impossible for different production companies to maintain distinct profiles. Hate films were a staple of every studio: the anti-Semitic *Jud Süß* (*Jew Süss*) was a Terra production, the militaristic *Kameraden* (*Comrades*, 1941) a Bavaria film, while the euthanasia picture *Ich klage an* (*I Accuse*, 1941) was made by Tobis. Since all such titles were certificated as films 'of national political value', they premiered, moreover, under the Ufa banner and at the company's most prestigious movie palaces. They also shared a single distributor – the *Deutsche Vertriebsgesellschaft* (German Distribution Co., or DVG), a subsidiary of UFI – and the cinema programme remained uniformly determined by the Propaganda Ministry.

One director in particular at Ufa-Filmkunst turned out an endless succession of Nazi propaganda pictures: Karl Ritter, a card-carrying NSDAP member since the 1920s.[3] Yet his output is not representative; indeed propaganda films remained in the minority after war broke out, when comedies, melodramas and revue films predominated on German screens, featuring stars such as Marika Rökk tripping the light fantastic in *Kora Terry* (1940), or Willy Birgel 'horse-riding for Germany' in the film of the same title, *… reitet für Deutschland* (1941). In a diary entry for 8 February 1942, Goebbels noted that 'for the state today, entertainment too is of political significance, perhaps even crucial for the war'. A fortnight later, he added: 'Keeping our people in high spirits is an equally important part of the war effort.'

Filming to the end – in colour

Otto Kriegk wrote in 1943: 'The substantial liberation of the German market from American influence has made it possible to undertake the separate development of a German colour film process independent of foreign patents.'[4] Yet Ufa's prolonged – and initially unsuccessful – experiments with colour were at first largely concealed from the public eye. The documentary *Bunte Tierwelt* (*The Colourful World of Animals*) was shot and released in the two-colour Ufacolor process as early as 1931. But ten years passed before Agfa and Ufa set up a colour film laboratory at Babelsberg, where they developed Agfacolor, a subtractive three-colour process that was again first showcased in a *Kulturfilm*, *Bunte Kriechtierwelt* (*The Colourful World of Reptiles*, 1941). The first Agfacolor feature film – Ufa's musical comedy *Frauen sind doch bessere Diplomaten* (*Women Make Better Diplomats*, 1941) – revealed substantial technical shortcomings, and, according to director Veit Harlan, left Goebbels ranting over its unnatural colour reproduction. Harlan later went on to create *Die goldene Stadt* (*The Golden City*, 1942), an Agfacolor feature truly deserving of the international release and recognition it subsequently received.

Colour was of course the only option when it came to producing a prestige work, *Münchhausen*, to mark Ufa's twenty-fifth anniversary in 1942. The intention here was to demonstrate that German cinema remained robust, despite the War, and all technical tricks in the dream factory's arsenal were marshalled to that end. *Münchhausen*'s narrative proved an exceptionally rich source, and the resulting 1943 adaptation was a lavish extravaganza, a magical work sporting not only a wealth of fantastic effects, but also a first-rate cast headed by Hans Albers as the mendacious baron. The script was furnished by writer Erich Kästner, whose publication ban was lifted specifically for this production.

Ufa's silver jubilee was celebrated with great pomp and circumstance. The entire workforce – or Gefolgschaft (retinue) in the Nazi vernacular – was called to assemble for a company address at Babelsberg's *Ufastadt*, or 'Ufa city', as the studio lot was now known. Following a speech by Goebbels, chief executive Klitzsch took the platform and offered a retrospective of the corporation's history, culminating in the words: '1933 witnessed the fruitful alliance of this momentous epoch with cinema. Film was rightly seized upon in that moment to serve as a hitherto unused, yet most effective weapon in the National Socialist struggle for the German people's soul.'[5]

Ufa continued to serve the Nazi struggle until the enemy was at its very gate. Long after theatres had closed their doors, those cinemas which survived the bombing raids stayed open to the bitter end. While all about was reduced to rubble, shooting continued both at Ufa's Tempelhof studio and at Babelsberg, which remained largely unscathed by air attacks. Veit Harlan's *Kolberg*, premiered on 30 January 1945 in the so-called 'Atlantic fortress' of La Rochelle, represented the very worst of Nazi cinema's appeals to bulldog courage. At a press conference before the beginning of shooting, Harlan expounded: 'I want to make the cinemagoers of today aware of their ancestors' heroism, and to tell them, "this is the stuff you are made of and descended from, the source of an inherited strength that you too can now draw upon for victory." '[6] Harlan's propaganda film, whose 8.5 million mark production costs rendered it Ufa's most expensive film ever, received every conceivable accolade from the state. *Kolberg* was to be Ufa's final call to die for Hitler's Germany.

UFI, DEFA and Bertelsmann

On 24 April 1945, Red Army units occupied the Ufa city in Babelsberg, and Ufa's most significant lot became part of the Soviet zone. Soon after, under agreements between the Allies, all former Reich-controlled companies – including UFI and Ufa – were confiscated and claimed as reparations. It was at this point that the Red Army apparently transported cameras and equipment to the Soviet Union, along with most of the *Reichsfilmarchive*'s print collection. The studio buildings themselves remained intact, and housed British and French troops during the Potsdam Conference.

On 17 May 1946, members of the *Filmaktiv* (Film Work Team) – who had already produced a number of documentaries and newsreels – were licensed by the Soviet military administration to operate as *Deutsche Film AG*. As at the foundation of Ufa in 1917, the company's foundation was marked by the coining of an acronym – DEFA, a name obviously modelled on 'Ufa', as was DEFA's centralised structure, which it consciously adopted from Ufa, alongside the company's studio lots (the latter after 1947).

The Allies in the western zones, meanwhile, pursued a strategy of decartelisation with respect to UFI, in an attempt to prevent the re-emergence of a powerful indigenous cinema industry. Their actions were guided not merely by political, but also economic motives: the Hollywood lobby was keen to secure the German market for its films, and has indeed occupied a dominant position in Germany ever since.

September 1949 saw the American and British military governments enact the so-called 'Lex UFI', in accordance with which all former Reich film assets were to be administered by trustees prior to their planned sell-off, while use of the Ufa name was prohibited outright. This restrictive regulation was partly lifted in 1953, when a new law was passed allowing potential buyers to undertake a limited purchase of film studio buildings, technical operations such as printing laboratories, or cinemas. It subsequently emerged that the West German government was planning to set up a new Ufa corporation: in April 1956, a bank consortium – again headed by the Deutsche Bank – paid 12.5 million marks for *Ufa-Theater AG* (the cinema chain), along with *Universum-Film AG* including the Afifa laboratory and Tempelhof studios. Arno Hauke, hitherto general trustee for UFI assets in the British zone, was appointed chairman of both companies.

Hauke's attempts to build up a new Ufa production company floundered, however, after just a handful of promising productions – including for example Georg Tressler's *Das Totenschiff* (*Ship of the Dead*, 1959) – as a result both of disreputable management and, above all, the generally miserable state of the German film industry. *Universum-Film AG*, including all its films and associated rights, as well as the Ufa cinema chain, again came onto the market, and were purchased in January 1964 by the Gütersloh-based Bertelsmann corporation which, at this time, was known mainly for its book club, publishing and (on the Ariola label) record company operations. Bertelsmann's interest lay primarily in acquiring the rights to Ufa's back catalogue of songs and music; there was never any intention to produce films, and the company planned to dispose of numerous Ufa assets forthwith. When the

Canadian Seven Arts showed an interest in purchasing the rights to around 3,000 features and *Kulturfilme*, however, the German film industry responded with a government-backed initiative aimed at preventing any sell-out to a foreign party: the *Friedrich-Wilhelm-Murnau-Stiftung* was founded, and in 1966 secured – at a cost of 14 million marks – the rights to all films made by production companies under the UFI umbrella. It continues to maintain these rights today. Ufa's movie theatres, meanwhile, were bought in 1972 by cinema entrepreneur Heinz Riech, who converted most of them into multiplexes.

When Bertelsmann sold its Ufa assets, it reserved the right to continue using the Ufa name and the company's diamond-shaped crest for its own purposes. Now a multinational corporation, Bertelsmann uses the Ufa name predominantly in television, radio and licensing. Thus the tradition-laden Ufa brand is today associated principally with the television holding company CLT-Ufa (which includes the commercial TV channel RTL), the Ufa video company (whose range includes few classical Ufa titles), and a production company responsible for such daily television soaps as *Gute Zeiten, schlechte Zeiten* (*Good Times, Bad Times*, since 1992) and even the occasional film for television or cinema.

Translated by Robert J. Kiss

Notes

1   Key sources include Hans-Michael Bock and Michael Töteberg (eds.), *Das Ufa-Buch: Kunst und Krisen, Stars und Regisseure, Wirtschaft und Politik* (Frankfurt am Main: Zweitausendeins, 1992); Jan-Christopher Horak, 'Ufa', in Hans-Michael Bock and Wolfgang Jacobsen (eds.), *Recherche: Film. Quellen und Methoden der Filmforschung*

(Munich: edition text+kritik, 1997), pp. 186–91; Wolfgang Jacobsen (ed.), *Babelsberg. Das Filmstudio*, 3rd edn, (Berlin: Argon, 1994); Klaus Kreimeier, *Die Ufa-Story: Geschichte eines Filmkonzerns* (Munich and Vienna: Hanser, 1992). (English trans., *The Ufa Story* [New York: Harcourt Brace, 1996]); Otto Kriegk, *Der deutsche Film im Spiegel der Ufa: 25 Jahre Kampf und Vollendung* (Berlin: Ufa-Buchverlag, 1943) (a Nazi history of Ufa); Rainer Rother (ed.), *Die Ufa 1917–1945. Das deutsche Bilderimperium* (Berlin: Deutsches Historisches Museum, 1992 [boxed set of twenty-two magazines]); Hans Traub (ed.), *Die Ufa. Ein Beitrag zur Entwicklungsgeschichte des deutschen Filmschaffens* (Berlin: Ufa-Buchverlag, 1943. (Ufa in its own words); William Uricchio, 'An Image Empire Remembered: Ufa between Memory and History', *Historical Journal of Film, Radio and Television*, vol. 13, no. 2, 1933, pp. 229–35 (an introduction to the most important publications edited for the 75th anniversary of Ufa, 1992).

2   For a more detailed account, see Wolfgang Jacobsen, *Erich Pommer. Ein Produzent macht Filmgeschichte* (Berlin: Argon, 1989); and Ursula Hardt, *From Caligari to California: Eric Pommer's Life in the International Film Wars* (Providence, RI, and Oxford: Berghahn, 1996).

3   Ritter's film titles from this period include *Verräter* (*The Traitor*, 1936), *Patrioten* (*Patriots*, 1937), *Pour le mérite* (1938), *Legion Kondor* (*Condor Legion*, 1939), *Kadetten* (*Cadets*, 1941), *Über alles in der Welt* (*Above All in the World*, 1941), *Stukas* (1941), and *G. P. U.* (*The Red Terror*, 1942).

4   Kriegk, *Der deutsche Film im Spiegel der Ufa*, p. 276.

5   *Der Film*, 6 March 1943.

6   *Film-Kurier*, 21 December 1943.

13

DEFA – State, Studio, Style, Identity

Horst Claus

For many, the key event of the thirty-ninth Berlin Film Festival in February 1990 was the screening of the so-called *Verbots* – or *Regalfilme* – films made in the former German Democratic Republic in 1965, which had been forbidden, withdrawn, or shelved before the end of production, and, as a consequence, had acquired an almost mythical status. Spectators not familiar with GDR cinema must have been disappointed. From a western perspective, there is nothing spectacular or controversial about them. Nevertheless, their very existence is remarkable. Production in East Germany's state-owned DEFA (Deutsche Film AG – the country's one and only film producer, distributor and exhibitor) was heavily influenced by shifts and changes in GDR politics. Though most directors and screenwriters believed in and were committed to socialism it was difficult for them to criticise or address negative aspects of GDR society. Walking a tightrope of trying to square personal beliefs with audience expectations for entertainment and the Socialist Unity Party's (SED) demands for the advancement of socialist ideals, critical film-makers developed a system of filmic narration which tacitly communicated their stance. Its codes were understood by spectators at home and contributed to certain films becoming East German box-office hits. Western distributors hoping to cash in on successes such as *Die Legende von Paul und Paula* (*The Legend of Paul and Paula*, Heiner Carow, 1973), however, were disappointed. Their audiences did not realise that the form and content of the romantic love story that this film tells flouted the official guidelines and expectations of socialist art.

Since unification, the impression of fundamental differences between East and West German film culture has been reinforced by books recording and analysing DEFA as a self-contained and closed chapter in the history of German film. Prompted by the desire to preserve a significant component of twentieth-century German culture, these valuable undertakings tend to explain the company's films and policies as products of political influences and pressures exerted by the state, and – where applicable – film-makers' attempts to resist them. As DEFA was expected to contribute significantly to the creation of an East German identity (which defined itself as different from that of West Germany), and as its period of existence (1946–93) almost coincided with that of the GDR (1949–90), the approach seems legitimate. But it risks neglecting the interrelationship between East German film-making and German cinema history as a whole – including that of West Germany. This introduction to DEFA tries to avoid the problem by pointing at some links and parallels with other European art cinemas (specifically Italian neo-realism), and with West German popular cinema. At the same time, it will draw on selected pictures from different periods which were aimed at and focus on the younger generation, and explore the extent to which these films reflect a specifically East German identity.

Practice and theory of film production

East German film-makers usually worked under more favourable conditions than their West German colleagues. At the time of the fall of the Berlin Wall, DEFA employed almost 2,500 people and produced approximately fifteen to eighteen feature and thirty to thirty-five television films per year. The studio was well-equipped, if (by western standards) technologically old-fashioned. Like all employees from construction hand to studio head, directors received regular monthly pay-cheques. Their rigorous professional training normally consisted of studies at film academies in Moscow (Konrad Wolf, Helmut Dziuba, Iris Gasner), Prague (Frank Beyer), or the GDR's own 'Hochschule für Film und Fernsehen' (HFF) in Potsdam-Babelsberg (Roland Gräf, Evelyn Schmidt, Rainer Simon, Lothar Warneke, Herrmann Zschoche), followed by a period as assistant to established directors. Before progressing to their first feature, they usually directed a documentary or a children's film. Though the GDR depended on a large and steady stream of foreign imports to maintain its cinema programmes (of which approximately one-third came from the West), directors did not have to worry about competition from abroad. With DEFA's distribution arm, Progress, as the country's sole distributor, they could always be sure of a space for home-grown product as long as it did not fall foul of the political climate of the time.

GDR directors occupied an important place within their country's social structure. But social prestige, job security and favourable working conditions came at a price. Even after a subject had been given initial approval, it took an average of two-and-a-half to three years for the picture to be realised.[1] Topic and story development lay in the hands of a central *Lektorat* and groups of *Dramaturgen*. The former – a kind of scouting and record-keeping office – usually did not directly influence a topic's artistic aspects, but carefully documented its progress. Looking for and nurturing new talents, the *Dramaturg*'s job originated from that of the literary adviser in the German theatre. Within DEFA, persons holding this position significantly affected the creative aspects of film production. Operating in groups of five or six, the *Dramaturgen* were attached to individual production units, the most important of which were Babelsberg, Roter Kreis, Berlin, and Johannisthal. As mediators between state authorities, screenwriter and director, they assembled a film's creative personnel, and supervised the development of its plot, characters and structure. Point of departure was the long-term party political plan for the development of socialist art. Whether a film would pass the many stages of approval by individuals and committees and would be realised more often than not depended on a *Dramaturg*'s personality, critical judgment, persuasive powers and, last but not least, courage. Most were members of the Socialist Unity Party, and some apparently collaborated with the GDR's secret police. DEFA's working atmosphere has been characterised as that of a big family nurturing and taking care of their own. From the early 1980s onwards, however, newcomers felt increasingly isolated and neglected since the *Dramaturgen* tended to rely on well-established teams of directors and screenwriters.[2]

Film, as all the arts in socialist countries, had the specific function of contributing towards the development, improvement and advance of socialism and the socialist state. Artists were expected to reflect and influence actively the social conditions of their country, and in the process were faced with the difficulty of having to reconcile contradictions between everyday and ideal socialism. This task was all the more difficult as DEFA's production programme and policies were heavily influenced by issues external to film production. Depending on whether the GDR was going through a period of entrenchment or liberalism, film form and content wavered between the artistic concepts of socialist realism and critical realism (both of which were hotly debated at film as well as party political conferences). Officially artists had to work within the constraints of socialist realism which regards film as a propaganda tool and rejects experiments in film form. Based on a set pattern of plots and characters it insists on easily understandable, uncomplicated, straightforward storylines, on types rather than characters, and on positive, forward-looking protagonists who achieve self-realisation through work within a collective. Socialist realism presents a world in which the ideals of socialism have become a reality. Critical realism, by contrast, shows the world as it is. Inspired by the films of Italian directors, the approach may be described as an East German variant of neo-realism. It observes rather than leads, offers a realistic depiction of controversial issues and opens them up for debate. There is space for formal experiments which enhance and deepen the understanding of that reality. While the SED's party apparatus and politically motivated theoreticians insisted on orthodox socialist realism, creative film-makers tended to favour critical realism.[3]

Ufa traditions and influences of neo-realism

Between its founding and demise, DEFA produced 700 feature films covering all genres. More than 130 of these were children's pictures ranging from fairy-tales to imaginative adventures set in a contemporary environment. The figure attests to the importance the state attributed to those whom it expected to be the beneficiaries and carriers of the banner of socialism. It is all the more impressive as in addition to these children's films, DEFA made a large number of films which address social issues and/or concerns relevant to teenagers and people between twenty and thirty. According to the GDR's constitution, youth (embracing everybody up to the age of twenty-five or, in the case of deputies or parliamentarians, thirty) enjoyed the state's special support and protection. Young people were organised in the state youth organisation FDJ (*Freie Deutsche Jugend* – Free German Youth), active membership of which was advisable if a young person wanted to get on in life. As the interests of state, society and youth were considered to be identical in their pursuit of socialist ideals, conflicts between the generations were deemed to be non-existent.[4] Prompted by the adults' desire to keep control rather than understand and engage in dialogues with the young, fantasies of peaceful coexistence can thus be found in DEFA from its earliest days on.

The company's first feature for and about young people, *Irgendwo in Berlin* (*Somewhere in Berlin*, 1946), focused on twelve- to fourteen-year-olds (i.e. a generation raised under the influence of the Hitler Youth which had experienced – but not fought in – the Second World War). It was made after DEFA's founding in the Soviet zone of a Germany still under Allied control, and directed by Gerhard Lamprecht three years before political developments led to the founding of two German states.

Lamprecht had previously been responsible for Ufa's *Emil und die Detektive* (*Emil and the Detectives*, 1931), one of the rare pre-war films aimed specifically at child audiences, but approaching their subject from an adult perspective. Like its predecessor, *Irgendwo in Berlin* is set in the present and revolves around stolen money (with the thief being played in both films by Fritz Rasp). However, while in *Emil und die Detektive* the theft is central to the plot, here it is mainly a dramaturgical device to add action to a film which (a) aims to highlight the negative influences of war and corruption on children, and (b) emphasises the energy and optimism with which the younger generation is supposed to resist them. The young protagonist (and counterpart to Emil) is Gustav, who, like Emil, has an idealised, trusting relationship with his mother. When his father, a disillusioned prisoner of war, returns home without hope or perspectives for the future, Gustav and his friends actively encourage him to make a new start by rebuilding the bombed-out garages which, before the war, provided for the family's livelihood. In one scene the father, in a burst of anger, destroys his son's favourite toy tank; in another the boy's closest friend

Irgendwo in Berlin (1946)

Willi tries to demonstrate his courage by climbing up the last remaining wall of a bombed-out building while a demented ex-soldier suffering from shell-shock salutes and hails him as a hero. The negative effects of false hero-worship become apparent when Willi is killed by falling off the wall. His final utterance, 'Why?', underlines the senselessness of his death. The film's message is loud and clear: this is a generation of new Germans who are learning from their mistakes and deliberately turn their backs on the past. Though they never express it in words, these children reject Nazi teaching and Nazi ideology, and simultaneously rediscover human and humanist values. Uncritical obedience to a military-style youth organisation and leadership, as reflected in a sequence in which they imitate war games and shoot at each other with firework rockets, is replaced by an optimistic, forward-looking attitude demonstrating initiative and a voluntary commitment to build a new Germany.

However, for attentive viewers familiar with Ufa film practices, Lamprecht's ideals and good intentions are undermined by his adherence to pre-1945 filmic conventions. The carefully composed shots of the dying boy's face in a diffuse bright light,[5] accompanied by soft, heavenly music, do not relate the gruesome, bloody consequences of a senseless act of 'heroism'. Instead, they signal a peaceful, semi-religious transition into a supposedly better world. Though DEFA deliberately pursued a policy of breaking with the past and offering a genuine alternative to pre-1945 productions, *Irgendwo in Berlin* suggests that, in the Russian-controlled zone as elsewhere, there was no *Stunde Null* (zero hour).

These filmic traditions become clearer when *Irgendwo in Berlin* is compared with Roberto Rossellini's *Deutschland im Jahre Null* (*Germany Year Zero*, 1948). Shot on location a year later with the support of DEFA, the Italian director's film also relates the life and experiences of a boy in post-war Berlin. Having chosen a child as protagonist to 'accentuate the contrast between the mentality of a generation born and brought up in a certain political climate, and that of the older generation . . .',[6] Rossellini almost imperceptibly conveys his humanist-Christian position (the film ends on an image evoking a *mater dolorosa*) that 'a small ethical flame still burned' within the boy and that 'he killed himself to escape his sense of moral disquiet'.[7] But he does not bombard the spectator with the message. Instead, he expects it to emerge from what he presents on the screen. As he is not interested in the story, Rossellini – in contrast to Lamprecht – disregards the conventional shooting and editing techniques of mainstream narrative cinema, avoids aesthetically 'perfectly balanced'

images, and observes his main character rather than intrudes on his life. His film has an episodic structure and does not attempt to capture or 'tie in' the spectator. The approach has been summed up by the French critic André Bazin in a metaphor linking the elements in a Rossellini film to stones in a brook. By use of imagination a person wanting to get across can turn them into a bridge. Once they have fulfilled their task, they revert to being just large stones.[8]

For GDR cultural functionaries and theoreticians the idea of spectators arriving at their own conclusions was anathema. Afraid neo-realism's variant, critical realism might lead to unfavourable conclusions about socialist society, they rejected it for contemporary films set in their own country, and deliberately torpedoed the work of progressive film-makers who took their inspiration from the Italians.

Struggle for critical realism

One of the most successful pictures inspired by neorealism is *Eine Berliner Romanze* (*A Berlin Romance*, 1956), the second of three so-called Berlin Films by a team consisting of director Gerhard Klein and scriptwriter Wolfgang Kohlhaase. Set in the divided (but not yet separated) city of Berlin, it focuses on the generation born during the Second World War. It relates the development of the relationship between Uschi, an East German trainee sales girl with aspirations for a modelling career, and Hans, a West Berlin unemployed youth, who does not dare tell her that he is not participating in the growing wealth of the glitzy and tempting world of western capitalism. The film is unspectacular and does not rely on action or suspense. Initially Uschi displays outright hostility towards Hans, but gradually changes her attitude, and firmly stands by him when his personal circumstances become desperate. In the end, he chooses to move to East Berlin where he will have the opportunity to train as a motor mechanic. Unlike Lamprecht, Klein avoids looking at his protagonists from an adult perspective. Hans and Uschi are not used to convey messages, moral or otherwise. They are human beings who argue with each other. Their more or less legitimate grievances with their parents can be traced back to their respective social environments, to pressures on (mainly) overworked mothers, and to the cramped living conditions most teenagers grew up in during the 1950s.

Though Klein and Kohlhaase repeatedly referred to Rossellini's work as their model, *Berliner Romanze* does not strictly follow his example, but deliberately and carefully reconstructs rather than observes everyday reality. Scenes depicting the back yards of Berlin's tenement houses and working life are rooted in traditions of socialist film-making from the 1920s and early 30s. The film clearly refers to Slatan Dudow's *Kuhle Wampe (Whither Germany?, 1932)* when, in a desperate attempt to find work, Hans races from one employer to the next only to be told there is none to be had. Neither he nor Uschi can be identified as having a specifically East or West German identity. They are simply young Germans living in a city divided not by national boundaries, but by competing economic systems. Their decision to settle in East Berlin has to be seen as the film-makers' concession to the GDR's aim to forge an East German identity. With implied severe criticism of the 'other Germany' an artificial voice-over commentary declares in the film's final moments that in East Berlin, Uschi and Hans 'will find their place, right amongst us; *here* they will have employment, will fight [for a better future], and find love'.

Counting Klein and Kohlhaase among their most promising newcomers, DEFA administrators and/or state officials were, however, possibly also concerned that Uschi's decision to remain in East Berlin is not brought about by socialist arguments or party activists, but by practical, at times harsh advice from her hardworking mother, a domi-nating, determined woman with a strong sense of tra-ditional family values. Young people also fully identified with *Berliner Romanze*, its milieu and characters. Their enthusiastic reaction drowned those voices from the estab-lishment which criticised the film for its unbiased rep-resentation of the two Berlins. Pressured into a follow-up by the overwhelming response, Klein and Kohlhaase created another box-office hit, *Berlin – Ecke Schönhauser (Berlin – Schönhauser Corner*, 1957), which draws a sym-pathetic portrait of rebellious, young East Berliners whose personal circumstances did not necessarily promote the benefits of life in a socialist state. At the 'Second Film Conference' in July 1958, cultural functionaries singled the film out as further proof of the unsuitability of critical real-ism for the cinematic rendition of everyday life in the GDR, and used it as an excuse to reverse liberal trends.[9] Concern about critical films also put an end to a period of relaxation which followed the building of the Berlin Wall in August 1961. Using potentially negative effects on young people as pretext, and reprimanding DEFA for not adhering to the principles of socialist realism, the Eleventh Congress of the SED's Central Committee, in December 1965, initiated the withdrawal of twelve films.[10] All except one were set in the present, most featured sceptical, bored or disillusioned young GDR citizens (among them students, young metal-workers, a drop-out pupil and a newly qualified teacher).

They examined the relationship between the generations and looked critically at the myth and reality of values prop-agated by GDR socialism. In the process, they reflected the younger generation's desire to find their own way of life – and, through it, their own identity.

The most original and subtle portrayal of the feelings and attitudes of those who grew up in a socialist society without having had to fight for it was made by documentary film-maker Jürgen Böttcher in his first and only feature, *Jahrgang '45 (Born in '45*, 1965/90). Like *Berliner Romanze*, it is set in Berlin. Looking at the lives of motor mechanic Al and chil-dren's nurse Li whose marriage of two years has gone stale, Böttcher observes his (fictional) characters and their environment in a documentary fashion. His film opens on the day before Al's file for divorce is to be heard, chronicles the deepening rift between the couple when the application is rejected, and ends with both partners gradually rebuilding their relationship. Tension also exists between Al, his mother, and his grandfather, both of which latter are convinced of the values of socialism, and do not understand Al's sudden aimlessness. Compared with their own experiences of pre-1933 economic hardship and war, his life appears to them full of milk and honey. The film neither contains blunt pol-itical statements nor does it criticise either position. Instead it searches for an understanding of the situation, and seems to reveal the rift between the generations and their different attitudes to life in a socialist state almost by accident. Al's comments on his reality relate to more than his relationship with Li; he rejects both material wealth and social comforts, and contemplates his personal situation in following vein:

> You sit in a room, both of you, each expecting something new and incredibly important from the other. . . . [Our generation] is down-to-earth, matter-of-fact, realistic and so on. Perhaps much more so than past generations. And there are reasons for it. It is precisely for these reasons that I cannot help but have this shitty feeling that sitting within my four walls I am missing out on something extraordinary and exciting.

But, as Li observes, his malaise is self-imposed:

> You [Al] always only know what you don't want, but never what you want. . . . You think you can impress others with your relaxed attitude and indifference. But you are just pretending. You are really weak, because you yourself don't know where to turn.

This attempt to present a balanced picture and point at weaknesses and deficiencies within GDR society –

especially the rift between the generations – was unacceptable to the East German authorities. Branded 'glorification
of the abnormal',[11] the film was banned at the editing stage.
When Böttcher tried to finish it twenty-five years later, it
proved impossible to restore the original soundtrack. His
solution – a low-key, at times seemingly accidental rendition of sounds and voices – reinforces rather than detracts
from the film's unobtrusive visual narration. It also documents the state's resistance to attempts by those born after
1945 to find and assert an identity rooted in post-war
rather than pre-war experiences. Compared with similar
projects by Böttcher's contemporaries in the Federal
Republic, *Jahrgang '45* is arguably the most sensitive observation of the psychological state of mind of the first post-
war generation and points to common ground between
young Germans in East and West.

Retreat into popular subjects

Similarities and parallels are also evident in audience tastes.
Desperate to halt the decline in cinema attendance figures
caused by the rapid spread of television and changing patterns in leisure-time activities since the second half of the
1950s, DEFA took up popular trends which emerged in the
Federal Republic during the early 60s. The most important
of these were the Karl-May-Filme, a specifically West
German variant of the Western, which drew their inspiration from adventure stories by one of the most popular
and widely read German authors of the late nineteenth and
early twentieth century, Karl May (1842–1912).[12] Starting
with *Der Schatz im Silbersee* (*The Treasure of Silverlake*,
Harald Reinl, 1962) most of them are set in the American
West and unite Germanic heroes and noble savages in a
fight against red and white villains. The East German
answer to the genre was the *Indianerfilm* (Red Indian film),
the first of which, *Die Söhne der großen Bärin* (*The Sons of
Great Bear*, Josef Mach), opened in February 1966. In contrast to the Karl May model, which emphasised action and
never entirely abandoned the romantic and imperialist
sentiments of the Wilhelminian era, DEFA situated its
characters and plots in carefully recreated historical
moments from the conquest of the West. Focusing on the
struggle of the American Indian against white supremacy,
the company successfully infused popular entertainment
with propaganda and identified western capitalism and
imperialism as the main sources of human suffering.
Particularly popular with young East Germans, the
Indianerfilme topped DEFA's list of box-office hits for
almost a decade and – with an overall total of fourteen features – became the company's most popular genre.

Ideologically and financially, the *Indianerfilm* appeared
at just the right time, since the politicians' bans and repri-
mands of December 1965 forced DEFA into a period of
insecurity and retreat. As the Central Committee in its rep-
rimand of the film industry had not even spared DEFA
founder member Kurt Maetzig, one of the most respected,
influential and socially committed directors of the first
generation of GDR film-makers, the studio subsequently
shunned critical or controversial approaches to contemporary issues. Directors turned to 'safe' subjects drawn
from literature and history, to comedies such as DEFA's all-
time comedy hit *Der Mann, der nach der Oma kam* (*The
Man Who Came After Grandma*, Roland Oehme, 1972) and
the occasional musical, such as the teenager-romp *Heisser
Sommer* (*Hot Summer*, Joachim Hasler) which – with its
strong references to the dance sequences of *West Side Story*
– packed in audiences during the summer of 1968.

Towards a self-critical cinema

Ironically it was not until Erich Honecker, one of the most
vociferous critics of the industry in 1965, was elected
Party Secretary in 1971 and subsequently became Head of
State, that a new period of cultural relaxation set in. In
1973, *Die Legende von Paul und Paula*, the poetic rendition of a tragicomic love story between a career-oriented,
married employee with the Ministry of Foreign Trade and
an unmarried mother of two caused a stir within the cultural establishment. Rooted firmly in everyday experiences of life in East Germany, the film not only
emphasised the importance of *personal* happiness, but its
imaginative use of dream sequences also presented a
refreshing contrast to the dreary aesthetics of orthodox
socialist realism (which normally rejects dreams or legends as subjects of artistic creation). Though politicians
intervened once again and slowed down the film's aspirations towards liberalism, they were unable to prevent *Paul
und Paula* becoming a cult film. Its full significance for
cinema developments in the GDR still needs to be inves-
tigated, but there can be no doubt that *Paul und Paula*
eased the emergence during the 1970s of a number of pictures which – building on the experience of productions
in the critical realist mode – focused on personal relations
in crisis and prioritised individual happiness over the collective good. At the end of the decade, this development
culminated in *Solo Sunny* (1979), directed by Konrad
Wolf, President of the GDR's Academy of Arts and his
country's foremost film-maker.

The son of a well-known dramatist who, in 1933, had
been forced into exile for his communist beliefs, Wolf

Solo Sunny (1979)

had been raised in Moscow with Russian as his first language, and, in 1945, had returned to Germany as a member of the Red Army. Throughout his life he was torn between his German roots and Russian upbringing. Acutely aware of the problems and complexities associated with the construction of identity, his film (scripted and co-directed by Wolfgang Kohlhaase) portrays Sunny, a young pop singer, as she tries to find herself and assert her individuality within society. In contrast to the films discussed so far, *Solo Sunny* makes no direct references to history or politics. Unlike *Irgendwo in Berlin*, *Berliner Romanze*, or *Jahrgang '45*, it is not concerned with encouraging a new beginning after National Socialism, propagating an alternative to western capitalism, or questioning the relevance of traditional socialist values for contemporary society by pointing at the generation gap. Never having known her parents, twenty-seven-year-old Sunny signals a generation which has no clearly identifiable roots and must find its own directions in life. She has no difficulties with the older generation or the system she lives in, but objects to the attitudes around her, to the general lack of sympathy for and understanding of individual needs and aspirations. She wants people to accept her as she is. She spends a long time studying her face in mirrors trying to discover herself. As implied by the title, the film raises questions about the extent to which society is prepared to allow an individual to go 'solo'. Konrad Wolf's answer was clear when he stated that socialist society depended on characters like Sunny:

> The real conditions under which socialism has to develop and assert itself demand a considerable amount of staying power. This is not to say that one should piously wait and avoid the issue by concentrating on things which have to

be done today. We must encourage such people and developments, we must encourage them – and us.[13]

Weeks of controversial discussions about *Solo Sunny* in the GDR press reflect the topicality of the issue at the time. Young East Germans reacted with enthusiasm and extensively modelled themselves on Sunny's appearance and lifestyle. Their response suggests that the policy of making an individual place his or her identity second to that of the group had failed, that those born and raised in the GDR wholeheartedly embraced the idea of individualism and aspired to take charge of their own lives. Furthermore, the film's positive reception in the Federal Republic (where *Solo Sunny* had the biggest launch of an East German film ever) indicates that, far from being fundamentally different, young Germans in East and West were united in what they expected to get out of life.

A delay of several months between the completion of *Solo Sunny* and its release into GDR cinemas has led to speculations about behind-the-scenes arguments and claims that its production was only possible because of Wolf's position and artistic reputation. The film-makers have always denied this. Even if there were difficulties, there is no reason not to accept the director's assurance that his film signalled changes within his country's social and political climate.[14] Though releases were often severely restricted and almost always accompanied by controversy, the 1980s witnessed further pictures about subjects which previously had been taboo. *Das Fahrrad* (*The Bicycle*, Evelyn Schmidt, 1982), for example, focuses on a female worker's everyday experiences, and does not at all conform to the socialist ideal of emotionally well-balanced, level-headed women enjoying total equality and the same opportunities as men. *Märkische Forschungen* (*Research in the Brandenburg Marches*, Roland Gräf, 1982) highlights the practices of an academic who suppresses evidence contradicting established socialist thinking for fear of losing his professional standing. *Insel der Schwäne* (*Island of Swans*, Hermann Zschoche, 1983) documents the dreary reality of children's lives in East Berlin's satellite towns. Symbolically, the night of the fall of the Berlin Wall saw the opening of *Coming Out* (Heiner Carow), which addresses a previously unmentionable key aspect in debates about questions of identity – the coming out of a homosexual teacher.

Studying DEFA

For almost fifty years, GDR film historians have carefully documented DEFA's production output.[15] Debates about theoretical issues and practical problems have been

recorded in internal discussion papers, the company's publication series *Aus Theorie und Praxis des Films*, and the
HFF's *Beiträge zur Film- und Fernsehwissenschaft*. Insight
into audience (and official) reaction can be gained from
the popular biweekly *Filmspiegel*, audience studies[16] and an
extensive collection of reviews in the HFF.[17] Except for the
immediate post-war output, western interest in DEFA
began during the first half of the 1980s when the films were
studied as a window on GDR society. A decade later, as previously unattainable documents became available, attention shifted to selected periods of the company's history, its
interrelationship with GDR politics, and to films as historical documents for the study of a state no longer in existence. With the dawn of the millennium, the perspective
widened and scholars began to study DEFA no longer as an
isolated subject, but as part of German film and/or cultural
history.[18] Within Germany, significant collections of
DEFA-documents and/or films may be found in the
Bundesarchiv and the *Bundesarchiv-Filmarchiv* in Berlin,
the *Filmmuseum*, Potsdam, the Library of the *Hochschule
für Film und Fernsehen* in Potsdam-Babelsberg, and the
Library of the University of Oldenburg.[19] Particular
interest has come from scholars in English-speaking countries, where conferences have been held at centres specialising in DEFA studies, such as the University of Reading in
the United Kingdom and the University of Massachusetts,
Amherst, USA (which is also operating a distribution
centre of DEFA films and materials). As the majority of
book-length studies so far have been written by insiders or
film scholars of the former GDR, this widening of perspective can only be welcomed.

Though the interrelationship between film and state in
the former GDR will continue to be of interest as further
documents from the GDR's various ministries become
accessible, the main focus will have to continue to move
away from analysing GDR cinema as a closed chapter.
DEFA was more than a sideline in German cinema history.
The appeal throughout the united Germany of script
authors such as Ulrich Plenzdorf or Jurek Becker and the
general popularity of GDR-trained stars such as Manfred
Krug, Katharina Thalbach, Armin Mueller-Stahl, or
Corinna Harfouch can hardly be explained by some of
them having once been used as pawns in the political war
of propaganda between East and West.

Notes

1 For a detailed study of the decision-making process cf. Kurt
Werthmann, 'Einige Grundprobleme der Leitung und
Planung des Kinospielfilmschaffens der DDR und deren

Vervollkommnung zur weiteren Entwicklung der liter-
arisch- und künstlerisch schöpferischen Tätigkeit und
ihrer Effektivität', unpublished dissertation, Humboldt-
Universität, Berlin, 1975.

2 Cf. Sibylle Schönemann, 'Stoff-Entwicklung im DEFA-Studio
für Spielfilme', in Harry Blunk and Dirk Jungnickel (eds.),
Filmland DDR (Cologne: Wissenschaft und Politik, 1990), pp.
71–81. For the reaction of the younger generation to the
DEFA establishment cf. *DEFA NOVA – Nach wie vor? Versuch
einer Spurensicherung, Kinemathek*, no. 82, December 1993.

3 Cf. for example Alexander Abusch's speech 'Aktuelle
Probleme und Aufgaben unserer sozialistischen Filmkunst'
(in *Deutsche Filmkunst*, September 1958, pp. 261–70) and
Wolfgang Kohlhaase's reaction 'Das Neue in neuen For-
men gestalten' (in *Deutsche Filmkunst*, October 1958,
pp. 298–300).

4 Remark by Siegfried Lorenz during a 1974 debate on the
Law Relating to Young People, quoted in *Junge Welt*, vol. 18,
no. 26B, p. 4, in Bundesministerium für innerdeutsche
Beziehungen (ed.), *DDR Handbuch* (Cologne: Wissenschaft und Politik, 1975), p. 441.

5 Cameraman Werner Krien had previously worked on,
among others, Arthur Maria Rabenalt's ... *reitet für
Deutschland*, a patriotic picture advancing Nazi ideology,
and *Über alles in der Welt*, a film about the *Luftwaffe* by one
of the leading propagandists of the Third Reich, Karl Ritter,
which enthusiastically embraces the idea of war and the
supposedly pending Nazi conquest of Europe.

6 Roberto Rossellini, 'Germany Year Zero', in Adriano Aprà
(ed.), *Roberto Rossellini – My Method* (New York: Marsilio,
1987), p. 21.

7 Roberto Rossellini, 'Ten Years of Cinema', ibid., p. 65.

8 André Bazin, 'In Defence of Rossellini', in André Bazin,
What is Cinema?, vol. 2 (Los Angeles, Berkeley and
London: University of California Press, 1977), p. 99.

9 Cf. 'Für die Entwicklung der sozialistischen Filmkunst in
der DDR. Empfehlungen der Kommission für Fragen der
Kultur beim Politbüro des ZK der SED', in *Deutsche
Filmkunst*, September 1958, pp. 257–9.

10 Cf. reports on and reprints of speeches given to the
Eleventh Congress in the party daily *Neues Deutschland*, 14
–19 December 1965.

11 'Die Heroisierung des Abseitigen', in *Jahrgang '45*, information leaflet *20. internationales forum des jungen films*, no.
21 (Berlin, 1990).

12 For ideological reasons, May's works were ignored in the
GDR.

13 Wolfgang Kohlhaase, Konrad Wolf and Klaus
Wischnewski, 'Was heißt denn "happy end" . . .', in *Film
und Fernsehen*, January 1980, p. 15.

14 'Es ist etwas im Gange in der DDR', interview with Konrad Wolf, in *Der Spiegel*, 7 April 1980.

15 For an analysis of GDR approaches to cinema history cf. Dorothea Becker, *Zwischen Ideologie und Autonomie: die DDR-Forschungüber die deutsche Filmgeschichte* (Münster: LIT, 1999).

16 Lothar Bisky and Dieter Wiedemann, *Der Spielfilm – Rezeption und Wirkung. Kultursoziologische Analysen* (Berlin: Henschel, 1985).

17 For bibliographical source materials cf. Seán Allan and John Sandord (eds.), *DEFA. East German Cinema, 1946–1992* (New York and Oxford: Berghahn, 1999), pp. 309–19; Horst Claus, 'DEFA', in Hans-Michael Bock and Wolfgang Jacobsen (eds.), *Recherche: Film* (Munich: edition text+kritik, 1997), pp. 216–23; and Lydia Wiehring von Wendrin and Kirsten Lehmann (eds.), *Auswahlbibliographie – 50 Jahre DEFA* (Babelsberg: Hochschule für Film und Fernsehen 'Konrad Wolf', 1996). Online: www.bibl.hff-potsdam.de/defa50

Websites containing extensive bibliographical references, information, and links: Hochschule für Film und Fernsehen (Library): www.bibl.hff-potsdam.de
Icestorm (GDR-films with English subtitles): www.defa-expert@icestorm-video.com
University of Massachusetts, Amherst (DEFA-Collection): www.umass.edu/defa/
University of Oldenburg (DEFA-Collection): www.defa@uni-oldenburg.de

18 Hans Joachim Meurer, *Cinema and National Identity in a Divided Germany 1979–1989* (Lewiston, Queenston and Lampeter: Edwin Mellen, 2000).

19 For Oldenburg University's holdings of DEFA films cf. Günther Willen, *DEFA-Filme: Ein Bestandsverzeichnis* (Oldenburg: Universität Oldenburg, 1998). Online (including a selection of DEFA film posters): www.defa@uni-oldenburg.de

14

State Legislation, Censorship and Funding

Martin Loiperdinger

Like all economic activities in modern societies, the production and commercial exploitation of films are subject to legal regulation by the state. In terms of industrial law, trade and safety regulations, patenting, concessions and taxation, cinema is scarcely distinguishable from other branches of the information and entertainment industry. In one central respect, however, the authorities afford cinema special attention, and that is by placing strict conditions on film exhibition. While theatre and press censorship were abolished in Germany following the dissolution of the monarchy in 1918, the new Weimar democracy introduced uniform film censorship measures which for the first time applied throughout the Reich. Film legislation in Germany aims primarily at controlling film exhibition – either directly through censorship, or by way of subsidies, including tax relief for screenings or the provision of funding and guarantees to help finance production. The rejection or acceptance of a funding application is often decisive in determining whether or not a film is made; thus state subsidy constitutes a highly effective means of indirect censorship. When the state itself holds the monopoly over production – as was the case with DEFA in East Germany – state subsidy *per se* is indeed synonymous with explicit, direct censorship.

Direct film censorship

Film censorship is generally thought of in terms of films being banned or having cuts imposed prior to release. The standard case, however, is not for films to be banned, but rather approved for public exhibition with the proviso that production companies apply for permission prior to putting them into distribution. Thus the state initially imposes a ban on all films, thereby assuming a fundamentally nega-

tive stance towards cinema. A film can be passed for release with or without conditions: certain sections of the public may be excluded from screenings (i.e. through ratings prohibiting either younger children or minors from attendance), or specific scenes may have to be cut from release prints.

In Wilhelmine Germany, there was no universally applicable film legislation. Uniform censorship was introduced in 1920 through the *Reichslichtspielgesetz* (Reich Motion Picture Act); only after the Second World War was the film industry in West Germany permitted to take censorship into its own hands. Until the early 1970s, there were few changes to the basic criteria of film censorship: indeed, a pronounced continuity extends from imperial Germany, across the Weimar Republic and Third Reich, and on into the Federal Republic. The situation in the German Democratic Republic, meanwhile, where the state itself had a monopoly over film production, was fundamentally different.

Imperial Germany

Prior to 1920, Prussian State Law was used as a basis for censoring so-called 'living pictures'. Local police were responsible for the 'upholding of public peace, safety and order', and travelling showmen and owners of motion picture theatres had to submit film programmes to them for approval. Decisions on individual titles could differ substantially between localities, but a first step towards uniform state censorship was taken in 1906 when police ordinances were issued by various German states in response to several films, which depicted the case of the real-life fugitive murderer Rudolf Henning, and which were seen to ridicule the police. On 5 May 1906, the Berlin police commissioner introduced preventive censorship to curtail the dissemination of such 'offensive' works: from now on, films required an 'exhibition certificate' for public screenings. A decree by the Prussian Interior Minister in 1910 went on to centralise censorship by allowing films passed in Berlin to be shown throughout Prussia. Official lists were published citing all titles which were either completely or partially banned in Berlin, or to which children or under-fourteens were prohibited access.

From 1907, heated debates raged over the boundaries of acceptability in film: groups comprising teachers, judges and clergy (the *Kinoreformer* or 'cinema reformers') mobilised against the 'scourge of cinema' and demanded that the authorities implement rigorous measures against cinematic 'trash and filth'. In principle, police censorship supported these groups' theories of influence and emulation, which maintained that cinematic representations of violence and eroticism could 'incite' audiences – in particular children and young people – to criminal or morally reprehensible acts. Depictions of sex and crime became subject to stringent control, with images of death, murder, adultery and pre-marital sex forbidden outright. As a result, numerous films were rendered incomprehensible by the removal of key scenes; the film industry saw its economic interests under attack, while audiences felt cheated of promised sensations.

During the First World War, responsibility for censoring films passed to the military administration. Significantly, the War allowed the state to discover cinema's 'positive' aspects, including its usefulness for entertainment and propaganda both among the troops and on the home front. Through the founding of the *Bild- und Film-Amt* (Photograph and Film Office, known as BUFA) in early 1917, the German Reich itself became a producer and distributor of films; and when Ufa was founded on 18 December 1917 (see Hans-Michael Bock and Michael Töteberg in this volume), the Reich itself secretly took a 7 million mark share – a move towards state funding that decisively altered the cinematic landscape, and this not merely in Germany.

Weimar Republic

In its proclamation 'To the German People!' on 12 November 1918, the Council of People's Representatives explicitly outlawed censorship.[1] However, local and regional film censorship continued to be practised widely by way of police ordinances and direct intervention, and was aimed especially at so-called *Aufklärungsfilme* and *Sittenfilme* (sexual enlightenment and sexual morality

films). Even politically engaged works such as Richard Oswald's anti-Paragraph 175 film *Anders als die Andern* (*Different from the Others* 1919) could fall foul of such measures (see Robert J. Kiss in this volume), and it was not long until state-sanctioned censorship was introduced.

THE *REICHSLICHTSPIELGESETZ* (REICH MOTION PICTURE ACT)

The draft version of the Weimar Constitution stated expressly: 'Censorship – and in particular pre-censorship of theatrical performances and motion picture shows – will not take place.'[2] However, the finalised text of paragraph 118 read: 'Censorship will not take place, but motion pictures may be made subject by law to special regulations.' The conservative parties were by this time already drawing up the *Reichslichtspielgesetz*, which was subsequently passed in the National Assembly despite opposition from the *Unabhängige Sozialdemokratische Partei Deutschlands* (the forerunner to the German Communist Party). Reich President Friedrich Ebert of the Social Democrats approved the act on 12 May 1920.

The *Reichslichtspielgesetz* imposed a ban in principle on all films, requiring them to be examined by a state censorship board prior to being passed for release. Paragraph 1.1 stipulated: 'Motion pictures (films) may only be exhibited publicly, or put into circulation for the purposes of exhibition either domestically or overseas, if passed by official certification boards.'

Films were submitted by production companies to certification boards in Berlin and Munich, while a head certification office in Berlin dealt with appeals against the lower boards' rulings. All three offices fell under the jurisdiction of the Interior Minister, who appointed their chairpersons. Consultation with welfare organisations and other similar bodies helped decide the composition of the boards' panels of examiners, with the result that many cinema reformers now had a direct influence on censorship matters.

Films passed for public screening were issued with a so-called 'exhibition certificate' listing title and cast, as well as the text of inter-titles, the length in metres, and the number of reels. Where cuts had been ordered, these were also briefly described.[3] Alongside the films themselves, all pictorial publicity materials – posters and lobby-cards – had to be submitted to the boards for approval. In the case of banned films, the grounds for rejection generally corresponded to the 'moral hygiene' arguments of Wilhelmine cinema reformers. Free speech was also substantially restricted in films that questioned the political leadership and its organs, or public morality. Indeed, paragraph 1 of the *Reichslichtspielgesetz* protected not only the organs of state authority, including the army, navy, police, judiciary, civil service and members of public service professions such as teachers, doctors and lawyers, but also the legally enshrined relations of private individuals, and in particular the institution of marriage. Nationalism, or 'legitimate feeling for the fatherland', also enjoyed legal protection under a passage within the motion picture act referring to the 'undermining of Germany's reputation and standing'. Films depicting social conflicts were especially susceptible to threats of a ban on these grounds.

The *Reichslichtspielgesetz* firmly protected the existing state order and institutions, and afforded censors on the certification boards sweeping discretionary powers. Indeed, film certification constituted political censorship since, strictly speaking, it was not the films submitted that were examined, but rather their presumed influence and 'effects' on audiences. Under the guise of the Act's stipulation to prevent the 'undermining of public safety and order', film censors thus practised a 'censorship of influences', deciding *ex ante* on the capacity of a given film to elicit audience reactions that might endanger the state.

POLITICAL DETERMINANTS ON WEIMAR FILM CENSORSHIP

With the *Reichslichtspielgesetz*, the Interior Ministry had gained, then, a flexible instrument for 'repelling' supposed 'threats to the state' from German screens – threats that were consistently located in the leftist political camp, while the certification boards remained blind to threats from the right. Arguments over Ufa's *Fridericus Rex* series during the crisis years of 1922 and 1923 make abundantly clear that reactionary films were not the target of the *Reichslichtspielgesetz*. The working-class press assessed the cinematic exaltations of the Prussian monarch Frederick the Great as 'anti-republican provocation'; the argument swiftly spilled out onto the streets, with pamphlets condemning '*Fridericus Drecks*' ('Frederick Trash'), demonstrations, and boycotts against Ufa cinemas prompting police intervention. When the Hessen Interior Minister called for the films' exhibition certificates to be revoked within his state on the grounds that they constituted a 'threat to public safety and order', the head certification office rejected his appeal on the grounds that this threat was 'not permanent'.

By contrast, the 'threat to public safety and order' ostensibly represented by pacifist and socialist films was consistently interpreted as a permanent condition that at once threatened the state and needed to be forestalled through censorial intervention. A textbook example is *Battleship Potemkin* (1925) which, following massive public debate

after its initial ban in Germany, ultimately gained release only in a toothless version cut by over a hundred metres.[4] The first version submitted by the German distributor Prometheus-Film had already been toned down; thus the 1905 mutiny was no longer compared expressly to the Bolsheviks' October Revolution, as in Eisenstein's original cut, but instead described in intertitles as a one-off event. This version was banned by the Berlin certification board on 24 March 1926 on the grounds that it was 'capable of permanently endangering public order and safety'. The head certification office lifted this ban on 10 April 1926, dismissing objections from the Defence Ministry, which demanded that an outright ban be upheld 'in the interests of military discipline'. Nevertheless, a number of cuts were demanded: all depictions of violence by the mutinying sailors against their officers were excised, along with several shots from the celebrated Odessa steps sequence, 'since the excessive violence contained herein is likely to have a brutalising effect'. Before the day was out, Defence Minister von Seeckt had already lodged a protest against the film's release and forbidden all soldiers from seeing *Potemkin*. While the daily press engaged in tendentious discussions of the film, the police had nothing extraordinary to report about its Berlin screenings, other than overcrowded auditoria and expressions of approval or condemnation by various audience members.

The state government of Württemberg, which described Eisenstein's film as 'a treacherous and dangerous lunge at the state's throat', petitioned, however, for its exhibition certificate to be revoked; Bavaria, Hessen, Thuringia and Mecklenburg-Schwerin swiftly followed suit. On 12 July 1926, the head certification office banned *Potemkin*. Further appeals were no longer possible, and the only remaining option for Prometheus-Film was to submit a yet shorter print for examination, this time cut by an additional hundred metres. This version was granted a certificate in late July, thereby quelling the various calls for an outright ban, although minors were prohibited from attendance.

All this underlines not only the defeat of *Potemkin*'s labour movement supporters at the hands of ministerial bureaucracy and military administration, but also the directly political nature of Weimar film censorship. Numerous German documentaries and features produced after 1928 by small production companies with links to the labour movement charted a similar course to *Potemkin*. The most famous is Bertolt Brecht and Slatan Dudow's *Kuhle Wampe* (*Whither Germany?*, 1932) which, following an outright ban and an unsuccessful appeal, was finally passed for adult audiences only after the submission of a drastically 'sanitised' version.[5] However, even such sanitised versions could not be certain of release throughout the Reich. Since 'public safety and order' ultimately fell under the jurisdiction of local police, individual state governments could still suppress films approved by the official censors. The Munich state government, for example, was frequently dissatisfied with the Berlin censor's decisions, and its appeals to the head certification office did not always meet with success. Consequently, it installed a kind of parallel censor, using the police to withhold various films passed for the Reich as a whole from Bavarian audiences. Screenings of *Battleship Potemkin* were indeed banned in several Bavarian towns on the strength of police ordinances.[6]

During the world economic crisis, the censors' rulings reflected nationalist public opinion: thus paragraph 1 of the *Reichslichtspielgesetz*, with its reference to the possible 'undermining of Germany's reputation and standing', was increasingly invoked. Even the Oscar-winning *All Quiet on the Western Front*, based on Erich Maria Remarque's novel, was not safe, since the Defence Ministry regarded it as a threat to the German army's reputation. The German press attested pacifist tendencies even to the film's abridged German release, which the distributor had taken the precaution of trimming from 140 to eighty-five minutes. Less than three months earlier, on 14 September 1930, the NSDAP had emerged as the second strongest party in the Reichstag elections. While the Berlin premiere of *All Quiet on the Western Front* at the Mozartsaal on Nollendorfplatz passed off without incident on 4 December 1930, the following night saw SA men in the auditorium throwing stink bombs, and setting loose white mice, to stop the screening. The next few evenings saw SA men again occupying the Mozartsaal, and the film was withdrawn. After petitions from several state governments, the head certification office banned *All Quiet* on 11 December 1930. The film's producer, Carl Laemmle of Universal Pictures, had to agree to a yet more abridged version, which was approved on 2 September 1931 on the stringent condition that, in order not to undermine 'Germany's reputation and standing', only the version passed by the Berlin censor be distributed *anywhere in the world*.

The banning of *All Quiet* was symptomatic of the political collusion between the NSDAP and conservative elites. Goebbels, by arranging for massive SA disruptions at screenings, was able to contrive a 'spontaneous' sense of indignation to which ministerial officials could in turn respond by stating that the Remarque adaptation was 'felt by the broadest sections of the populace involved in the war – regardless of political allegiance – to be an act of derision'.[7] Thus, the 'voice of the people' – in the shape of the SA – served as incontrovertible evidence that Germany's reputation was being undermined.

National Socialism

Hitler's appointment as Chancellor on 30 January 1933 had immediate and far-reaching consequences for the German film industry. For years, the National Socialists had attributed Germany's 'degeneration' in large part to the ostensibly corrupting decadence of Weimar cultural life, with vitriol aimed in particular at 'the film-Jews of Berlin'. Jewish and left-wing film artists now lived in fear of persecution, and fled the country.

As Minister for Popular Enlightenment and Propaganda, Joseph Goebbels ascended to the role of 'patron of German film' and set about 'Aryanising' the industry. In this context, he made use of a 'Law on the Exhibition of Foreign Motion Pictures' originally introduced on 15 July 1930 as a quota regulation, which established criteria to distinguish between 'German' and 'foreign' films and thereby limited imports. On 28 June 1933, Goebbels passed a decree stipulating that, for a film to qualify as 'German', *all* those involved in its production needed to be 'German' too: holding a German passport was no longer sufficient, since 'in accordance with this decree, "German" refers to whoever is of German descent and nationality'.[8] The racist criterion of 'German descent' allowed the National Socialists to 'single out' all those Germans whom they counted as Jewish; the participation of a single 'non-Aryan' was now enough for a work produced in Germany to be labelled 'a foreign picture'.

The ability of Jewish film personnel to find work was conclusively ended by paragraph 3 of the 'Law on the Foundation of an Interim Film Chamber', introduced on 14 July 1933. Membership of the Film Chamber was compulsory in order to gain employment in the industry, and those deemed 'not to possess the necessary dependability for film work'[9] were no longer hired. Those without documentation proving 'Aryan' descent, or without loyalty to the regime, stood no chance.

CONTINUITY IN FILM CENSORSHIP

Film censorship under National Socialism was marked by its continuity from Weimar. The most senior Weimar censors had already proved their worth, and stayed in office. The revised *Lichtspielgesetz* (Motion Picture Act), which came into force in 1934, introduced no fundamental changes; numerous regulations were adopted wholesale from a 1929 parliamentary proposal. The section concerning the 'undermining of Germany's reputation and standing' was extended to apply to foreign films, insofar as these addressed German issues, even in their original version, which effectively gave German censorship boards the authority to actively intervene in other national industries. This presumptive step officially enshrined what the Weimar authorities had already successfully achieved in the case of *All Quiet on the Western Front.*

The addition of 'violation of artistic feeling' to the act's rubric was noteworthy, since this added the political censorship of 'taste' to the duties of film assessors. The new ruling powers thus distinguished themselves from their republican forerunners by defining their relationship to film not merely negatively through preventive action against perceived threats, but also by claiming the right actively to shape and (re-)configure films through reference to the new state doctrine of National Socialism. (On the resultant promotion of films through a system of predicates [*Prädikate*], see Julian Petley in this volume.)

The most important revision in the 1934 *Lichtspielgesetz*, however, involved the introduction of pre-censorship by the Reich Dramaturgical Office, to whom all film scripts now had to be submitted for assessment. In conjunction with the newly founded *Filmkreditbank*, which granted funding only against confirmation of script approval, this regulation constituted a massive act of state intervention into film production – though it also corresponded to the demands of film financers who had for years supported pre-censorship akin to the American Hays Code on the grounds that it reduced the risk of bans for completed productions.

The German censors of *All Quiet on the Western Front* at work. Left, Dr Seeger, head of the certification office. Photo taken by Erich Salomon in 1930. (Courtesy Bildarchiv Preussischer Kulturbesitz.)

However, as the institutions of law and order became eroded through the establishment of a state dictatorship[10] based around the 'Führer's will', so too the *Lichtspielgesetz* grew increasingly irrelevant, especially as the state itself became ever more active in film production. By 1939, most of the German film industry was nationalised, and the supreme censor was the Führer himself. When, in 1935, he personally approved Leni Riefenstahl's Nuremberg rally film, *Triumph des Willens* (*Triumph of the Will*) – in which he, of course, was the star – this was still an exception to the rule.[11] Yet by the outbreak of the war, he had begun to play a massive role in film censorship, frequently inspecting the weekly newsreels (the *Deutsche Wochenschau*) and indeed involving himself in their production. A single disparaging remark by Hitler during one of his almost nightly private screenings usually sufficed to prompt a ban. At the same time, films were safeguarded by the pre-censorship of scripts; thus scarcely two dozen *German* productions were banned during the entire twelve years of National Socialist rule.[12]

German Democratic Republic (GDR)

The Soviet military administration in the Russian-occupied zone had fewer reservations regarding the resumption of German film production than did the Occupying Military Government in the US zone. The founding of DEFA, and the premiere of the first German post-war production – Wolfgang Staudte's *Die Mörder sind unter uns* (*The Murderers are Among Us*) – on 15 October 1946, represented a triumphant new start for the film industry in East Germany. Over the next three years, DEFA produced further anti-fascist films, which found similar audience favour.

DEFA's film plans were of course subject to scrutiny and censorship by the occupying Soviet forces. Representatives of the USSR's state distribution company Sovexport – overseen by the Cinema Ministry in Moscow – examined scripts and cast-lists, issued filming permits and inspected completed works. After the founding of the GDR, film censorship was initially carried out by the DEFA Commission within the ruling SED's politburo.

DEFA held the monopoly over film production in the GDR, and was finally nationalised in 1953. DEFA studios' production timetables were scrutinised, decisions reached about the feasibility of individual scripts, and finished productions thoroughly scrutinised. While such limitations on artistic freedom are also the rule for privately financed film-making under capitalism, where they stem from a desire to maximise profits, in the case of DEFA creative censorship became synonymous with state intervention. The 'really existing socialism' of the GDR was steadfastly committed to ideologically irreproachable and artistically polished feature films that could bolster political conviction among Cold War audiences. State supervision of state film production aimed at keeping in check DEFA production heads and film artists – even those staunchly loyal to the state – and ensuring that they in no way undermined the GDR's central anti-fascist and socialist tenets. The SED's censorship bodies thus displayed an institutionalised distrust towards film production. DEFA's intention was to unite cinematic art with political directives – especially since artistic interpretations of the SED's current party line by DEFA's directors and production heads often ran contrary to the actual thinking of those in power. Film censorship in the GDR ensued from this constant tension between film-makers and the Party, and was shaped more or less directly by the SED's Cold War manoeuvring in regard to domestic policy towards West Germany and the Soviet Union.

From 1949 to 1952, the SED committed feature production at DEFA to the Soviet doctrine of 'socialist realism', an aesthetic rejection of western 'formalism' and 'critical realism' (see Horst Claus in this volume). Meetings of the DEFA Commission at this time were attended by Soviet advisers. In 1951, the resultant power struggle between film-makers and the Party crystallised around *Das Beil von Wandsbek* (*The Meat Cleaver of Wandsbek*), the debut film of DEFA's artistic director Falk Harnack. Based on Arnold Zweig's 1947 novel, the film centred on the historical figure of a Hamburg butcher who beheaded four resistance fighters, sentenced to death by the Nazis. The butcher was boycotted by his customers, and in the end committed suicide. The film was withdrawn after six weeks on the grounds of 'political shortcomings': for the executioner of anti-fascist resistance fighters was presented here in an ambiguous light, as both instrument and victim of National Socialism.[13]

Similar 'bureaucratic hindrances' – the continual interference of the state in production – led to many film projects never reaching completion, or coming to the screen only after lengthy delays. By 1952, in contrast to the pre-GDR days of DEFA, East German films met only limited success. In September 1952, the SED's politburo organised a film conference to discuss the artistic difficulty of transferring socialist realism to films featuring convincing positive heroes. The Party, berating the absence of 'any successful deployment of working class representatives as

heroes in [DEFA] films',[14] rushed a two-part colour film biography of the pre-war communist leader *Ernst Thälmann* (1952) into production, and, in late 1952, set up the State Committee for Cinematic Affairs as a general authority overseeing all film and cinema matters. After the workers' uprising of 17 June 1953, the granting of yet greater artistic freedoms was discussed and, in an attempt to win back audiences for DEFA productions, it was agreed that more entertainment films be made. From January 1954, the various studios and divisions of DEFA fell under the newly founded Culture Ministry, presided over by the writer Johannes R. Becher. The resultant thaw in cultural policy gave rise to a series of 'local studies' influenced by Italian neo-realism and depicting everyday life in a divided Berlin. However, following the suppression of the Hungarian uprising in 1956, as well as the shattering of the East German government's hopes for reunification as a result of Konrad Adenauer's policy of western integration, the SED leadership returned to a more restrictive line, including in cultural policy. The so-called 'revisionism' proclaimed by the SED leadership at the 1958 Film Conference singled out in particular two 'Berlin films', Wolfgang Kohlhaase's *Eine Berliner Romanze* (*A Berlin Romance*) and Gerhard Klein's *Berlin – Ecke Schönhauser* (*Berlin – Schönhauser Corner*).

The Party's new watchword was 'that naturalism and critical realism are wholly unsuited for depicting socialist reality',[15] and the next year saw *Sonnensucher* (*Sun Seekers*, 1959) – a socially critical work about uranium mining in the GDR by the highly regarded director Konrad Wolf – withdrawn at the last minute before its scheduled premiere.

Following the erection of the Berlin Wall in 1961, the socialist state gained an increased sense of self-assurance and, from 1963, it extended DEFA's aesthetic freedoms. Some film-makers seized on this new liberalism to produce critical works questioning contemporary realities in the GDR; but the situation was dramatically reversed once again in 1965, when the XIth Plenum of the SED Central Committee arranged for the immediate vaulting of some twelve recently shot DEFA features. Foremost among these were Kurt Maetzig's *Das Kaninchen bin ich* (*I Am the Rabbit*), whose depiction of a judge's opportunism questioned key principles of 'Party loyalty'; and Frank Beyer's *Spur der Steine* (*Traces of Stones*), in which a team of anarchic roofers on a major construction site was shown to triumph over incompetent Party bureaucracy. None of these so-called '*Rabbit*' films was to be shown in East Germany until 1990. DEFA itself never really recovered from this drastic censorial intervention, and showed few signs of revival right up until its post-unification dissolution.

Federal Republic of Germany

Immediately after the Third Reich's capitulation, the Anglo-American occupying forces prohibited all publishing activities – including the production, distribution and exhibition of films. At the same time, the US military government confiscated all circulating prints of German films. From autumn 1945, however, around 200 features produced under National Socialism were gradually released as reruns to supply cinemas in bombed-out German cities. A further 300 titles remained subject to an outright ban. In all, more than half of the features made during the Third Reich were ultimately deemed suitable for re-release, albeit after the removal of all scenes featuring Nazi uniforms and swastikas. There was no standardised censorship in the three western zones prior to the foundation of the Federal Republic, and a film banned in the American zone could well be approved in the British and French zones, or vice versa.

The Federal Republic's constitution (*Grundgesetz*) stipulated that 'censorship will not take place'. In practice this meant very little, and 'general laws' were employed as a means of curtailing cinema's freedom: not only were the police and public prosecutors able to take action against films, but the Bonn government too implemented measures to ensure that the free democratic order could under no circumstances be challenged on-screen.

THE INTERMINISTERIAL COMMITTEE AND THE IMPOUNDAGE ACT

In order for films to be accorded permission for cinema release, at least one copy had to be available for inspection within the borders of the Federal Republic. Foreign films in general and, in the Cold War climate that prevailed until the early 1970s, GDR and Eastern bloc productions in particular thus became subject to a form of politicised import control.[16] The so-called 'Interministerial Committee', a non-statutory body established in 1954 at the behest of the *Amt für Verfassungsschutz* (Office for the Defence of the Constitution), was charged with deciding for or against the import of individual titles from Eastern bloc nations. The existence of this body was only made public in 1957 in response to a question in parliament. Trade and Industry Minister Erhard justified the Committee's mode of political censorship by analogy with the Federal Constitutional Court's outlawing of the German Communist Party in 1956. Politically motivated import controls subsequently gained a legal basis through the introduction in 1961 of the Impoundage Act, which explicitly outlawed the import of films 'that might function as propaganda against the free

democratic order or the spirit of international understanding'.[17] The upholding of such bans fell to the Federal Office for Commercial Affairs in Frankfurt am Main; it is estimated that the Interministerial Committee impounded around 130 films in total, including most notoriously Jiří Krejčík's Czechoslovak production *Vyssi Princip* (*Higher Principle*, 1960). The film showed the SS unleashing terror on the civilian population after the 1942 assassination of Reinhard Heydrich in Prague – a representation of Nazi violence which the Interministerial Committee perceived in 1963 as 'a threat to Germany's reputation and standing'.

CENSORSHIP THROUGH SUBVENTIONS AND FUNDING

The demise of the Third Reich certainly did not signal the end of direct state intervention in film production. Through the awarding or withholding of subventions during the early 1950s, local and national government could exercise control over more than half of all West German films even before they entered production. This represented a successful attempt on the state's part to become an active film producer, and thus to bypass the effects of the break-up of Ufa – the nationalised pride and joy of the National Socialist period. An Interministerial Subventions Committee was set up to process all applications from the film industry during the first wave of awards between 1950 and 1953. This Committee in turn enlisted the services of the *Deutsche Revisions- und Treuhand AG* (German Trade and Audit Co.) – the same body that had managed the film industry's finances for the *Reichskreditgesellschaft* (Reich Credit Institution) between 1933 and 1937, and whose former head, Dr Robert Liebig, continued to take a leading role. An additional six-member panel inspected scripts from a dramatic, economic and *political* standpoint: numerous of the examination criteria employed would later be adopted by the FSK (see below). Neither the grounds for a proposal's rejection nor the titles of successful applications were made public, but during this first wave of subventions some forty-four applications were rejected, while eighty-two films received subsidies amounting to 30 per cent of their projected production costs. The various ministries involved exerted a huge influence on the content, casting and form of subsidised productions, although there were some conflicts of interest between the Trade and Industry Ministry, which considered films primarily in terms of their commercial potential, and the Interior Ministry, which was more concerned with upholding the constitution. The latter aim led the ministry to object in particular to the involvement of film artists who had previously worked for DEFA, since this was regarded as undermining state values: thus, the sure-fire box-office draw of Marika Rökk – the Third Reich's most popular revue film star – and her director-husband Georg Jacoby for *Die Czardasfürstin* (*The Csardas Princess*, 1951) was initially rejected on the basis of the couple's prior participation in DEFA's *Kind der Donau* (*Marika*, 1950).

The financial aid packages offered by the state in more recent years have likewise functioned unambiguously as a vehicle of censorship. The Film Funding Act of 1967 contains a 'controlling clause' stipulating that all state funding is liable to repayment if the completed film offends moral or religious sensibilities, or contravenes the constitution or any other law. Here, then, political pressure compounds the commercial imperatives within a free market economy; the result is an absolute dearth of critical film-making. The various instances in which the 'controlling clause' has been invoked include one spectacular example in 1983, when, following the change from liberal to conservative government, Herbert Achternbusch's *Das Gespenst* (*The Ghost*) was rejected by the FSK. The conservative Interior Minister Zimmermann reneged on payment of 70,000 marks previously promised to the film's producers on the grounds of the film's alleged blasphemous content.

THE FSK (*FREIWILLIGE SELBSTKONTROLLE DER FILMWIRTSCHAFT*/VOLUNTARY SELF-REGULATORY BODY OF THE FILM INDUSTRY)

As Film Officer for the American Military Government, former Ufa production head Erich Pommer had as early as 1946 proposed a voluntary self-regulatory body taking as its model the American Production Code of 1930/34. Since individual states of the Federal Republic retained independence in matters of cultural and educational policy, holders of film exhibition licences feared a decentralisation of censorship and petitioned state culture ministries for the establishment of a central agency for film certification. Following an agreement between the various culture ministries and the German film industry's administrative body SPIO, the FSK came into being on 15 July 1949. It was to remain West German cinema's most potent censor until the early 1970s.

Despite its name, this body was clearly neither 'self'-regulatory nor 'voluntary'; producers, distributors and cinema owners were prohibited from any dealings with films not previously approved by the FSK. Anyone trying to circumvent FSK approval faced action from their local SPIO branch association, could be boycotted by other industry members, and ultimately driven to financial ruin. In the face of such rigour, state censorship became effec-

tively superfluous.[18] The FSK, moreover, was hardly independent of state control. Its internal organisation bore unmistakable similarities to the Weimar certification boards; its examination panels comprised equal numbers of industry officials and public servants, including federal and state government representatives, church leaders and members of the Federal Youth Ring. The blueprint for the FSK's examination criteria was indeed the 1920 *Reichslichtspielgesetz*, though in a form adapted to contemporary political concerns such as the Allies' victory over National Socialism and the Cold War.

The exact nature of FSK censorship rulings is difficult to assess, since absolute secrecy surrounded all decisions: neither the number of titles which the FSK objected to, nor the grounds for objection, were ever made public. Insofar as any pattern can be discerned from the handful of leaked cases, FSK practice seems to have corresponded to the political directives of the Cold War. Following West Germany's decision to rearm in 1956, the majority of war films no longer gave cause for complaint – although the FSK appeared remarkably sensitive about representations of Germany's National Socialist past. Its 1963 ruling on Vittorio de Sica's Jean-Paul Sartre adaptation *I sequestrati di Altona* (*The Condemned of Altona*, 1962) provoked a particular furore. Of the four sections of dialogue objected to, the first ran as follows: 'Do you think I respect the things father stood for? Or that I admire Flick, Krupp and father? Every time I see a Mercedes-Benz, I smell the stench of the gas ovens.' The FSK ordered the names Flick, Krupp and Mercedes-Benz to be removed, since 'leading German companies cannot be associated with crimes whose instigators and perpetrators should be sought . . . in quite different quarters'. It was also commented 'that these lines are wholly indistinguishable from the jargonistic rabble-rousing of the Eastern zone'. Another section of excised dialogue was: 'We've got weapons and butter. And soldiers. And tomorrow the bomb.' The FSK asserted that 'these lines in principle ironise and indirectly reject the current existence of the Federal Army'.[19]

In Hollywood productions, representations of the Nazi past were more inconspicuously 'retouched' through alterations in the German-language version. Warner Bros., for example, altered its post-war German release of Michael Curtiz's *Casablanca* (1942) by erasing Conrad Veidt's SS Major Strasser character entirely, while transforming the figure of Paul Henreid's resistance fighter into a scientist.[20]

The FSK's decisions in respect of 'public morality' seem to have been less stringent – and certainly insufficient to satisfy church demands. The passing without cuts of *Die Sünderin* (*The Sinner*) – featuring a naked Hildegard Knef

Erased: Conrad Veidt in *Casablanca* (1942)

started to play an important role again in television's ratings wars. Many films originally passed for over-sixteens or over-eighteens only could not be broadcast during prime time; thus they commanded smaller audience shares and lower advertising revenues for broadcasters. These films were now resubmitted in efforts to secure a lower age certification. Thus the main duty of the FSK today is to decide on children's access to representations of violence and sexuality. Film censorship in Germany today, then, continues to address the very same concerns that preoccupied the first police censors during the Wilhelmine period.

Translated by Robert J. Kiss

Notes

1 'An das deutsche Volk!', *Reichs-Gesetzblatt*, 153 (1918), p. 1303.

2 §32.2 of the draft constitution of 17 February 1919.

3 The full text of the *Reichslichtspielgesetz* is reprinted in Klaus-Jürgen Maiwald, *Filmzensur im NS-Staat* (Dortmund: Peter Nowotny, 1983), pp. 248–53.

4 On the censoring of *Battleship Potemkin* in Germany, cf. Sergej M. Eisenstein and Eduard Tissé, 'Der Weg des *Potemkin* durch die deutsche Zensur' [1926], in Hans-Joachim Schlegel (ed.), *Sergej M. Eisenstein: Schriften 2, Panzerkreuzer Potemkin* (Munich: Hanser, 1973), pp. 200–07; Gertraude Kühn, Karl Tümmler and Walter Wimmer (eds.), *Film und revolutionäre Arbeiterbewegung in Deutschland 1918–1932* (Berlin [GDR]: Henschelverlag, 1978), vol. 2, pp. 323–69 (including quotations from the censor's report); and Ernst Seeger, *Reichslichtspielgesetz: Kommentar*, 2nd rev. edn (Berlin: Carl Heymann), p. 29.

5 On the censorship of *Kuhle Wampe*, cf. Wolfgang Gersch and Werner Hecht (eds.), *Bertolt Brecht – Kuhle Wampe: Protokoll des Films und Materialien*, 2nd edn (Frankfurt-am-Main: suhrkamp, 1973), pp. 62–6; and Kühn *et al.*, op. cit., vol. 2, pp. 130–85.

6 Cf. Stefan Fisch, 'Der Weg des Films "Panzerkreuzer Potemkin" (1925) in das Kino der zwanziger Jahre – ein Konflikt von verfassungsmäßiger Reichszensur und landesrechtlicher Polizeigewalt', *Speyerer Arbeitshefte*, 108, Hochschule für Verwaltungswissenschaften, Speyer, 1997.

7 Seeger, op. cit., p. 68.

8 Cited in Wolfgang Becker, *Film und Herrschaft: Organisationsprinzipien und Organisationsstrukturen der nationalsozialistischen Filmpropaganda* (Berlin: Volker Spiess, 1973), p. 70.

9 Cited in ibid., p. 49.

10 See Ernst Fraenkel, *The Dual State* (New York: Oxford University Press, 1941).

– in 1951 prompted the resignations of the two church representatives on the FSK board, while outraged Catholics threw stink bombs and provoked the police into issuing local exhibition bans. A similar response greeted Ingmar Bergman's *Tystnaden* (*The Silence*, 1964), the film which initiated the foundation of a 'Clean Screens Campaign' by Catholic protesters. In the end, however, such boycotts generally succeeded only in providing the films with additional publicity. From the late 1960s, moreover, the FSK's powers began to wane in the face of shifting moral attitudes and more liberal policies towards the East. In 1972, the officially appointed members of the FSK board announced that their role would henceforth no longer involve passing films for adult audiences; instead, they would restrict their activities to the protection of minors. New laws – including paragraphs 131 and 184 of the *Grundgesetz*, with their references to the 'glorification of violence' and 'dissemination of pornography' – still afforded police and public prosecutors opportunities for action against films, and 1976 witnessed the seizure of both Pier Paolo Pasolini's *Salò o le 120 giornate di Sodoma* (*Salo, or the 120 Days of Sodom*, 1975) and Nagisa Oshima's *Ai No Corrida* (*The Realm of the Senses*, 1976) following tirades in the conservative press.

With the opening-up of television to both state- and privately funded broadcasters, FSK decisions, whose significance had been in decline since the 1960s, suddenly

11 At the time, Leni Riefenstahl expressed pride at Adolf Hitler having personally approved *Triumph des Willens* without a single objection, just four days prior to its premiere. Cf. Martin Loiperdinger, *Rituale der Mobilmachung. Der Parteitagsfilm 'Triumph des Willens' von Leni Riefenstahl* (Opladen: Leske + Budrich, 1987), p. 161.

12 Cf. Kraft Wetzel and Peter A. Hagemann, *Zensur: Verbotene deutsche Filme 1933–1945* (Berlin: Volker Spiess, 1978).

13 Cf. Thomas Heimann, *DEFA-Künstler und SED-Kulturpolitik* (Berlin: Vistas, 1994), pp. 123–6.

14 Cited in Wolfgang Gersch, 'Film in der DDR: Die verlorene Alternative', in Wolfgang Jacobsen, Anton Kaes and Hans-Helmut Prinzler (eds.), *Geschichte des deutschen Films* (Stuttgart and Weimar: Metzler, 1993), p. 332.

15 *Deutsche Filmkunst*, 9 (1958), cited in ibid., p. 334.

16 For a detailed discussion, cf. Werner Wohland, *Informationsfreiheit und politische Filmkontrolle: Ein Beitrag zur Konkretisierung von Art. 5 Grundgesetz* (Munich, PhD thesis, 1967), pp. 153–89.

17 Cited in ibid., p. 154.

18 Reinhold E. Thiel, 'Die geheime Filmzensur', *Das Argument*, 27 (November 1963), pp. 14–20, reprinted in von Bredow *et al.*, op. cit., pp. 327–33.

19 Cited in Lothar Hack, 'Filmzensur in der Bundesrepublik', *Frankfurter Hefte*, vol. 19, no. 10 (1964), pp. 706–07.

20 Cf. Joseph Garncarz, *Filmfassungen: Eine Theorie signifikanter Filmvariation* (Frankfurt am Main: Peter Lang, 1992).

PART FOUR

CULTURAL POLITICS

Introduction

Tim Bergfelder and Erica Carter

In our introduction to the previous section, we emphasised continuities in the dominant economic structures in German cinema. The contributions in this section are concerned with film-makers, periods and movements whose cinematic and political interventions were conceived in explicit antagonism to the mainstream film industry of their time. Their motivations were, of course, politically and historically distinct. Thus on the one hand, both the independent film-makers of the Weimar period, and those of the New German Cinema, opposed the mainstream industry's capitalist mode of operation, as well as its perceived complicity in the construction and dissemination of hegemonic and repressive national and social discourses. During the Nazi period, by contrast, as Julian Petley documents below, the commercial industry was absorbed, via the Propaganda Ministry, into the political structures of the Nazi state, there to be functionalised as a primary ideological instrument of a repressive and ultimately genocidal regime.

It is worth remembering, however, that in the early years of the Third Reich at least, industry leaders, film practitioners and party ideologues alike often deployed verbal and visual rhetorics directly pillaged from the leftist Weimar film movements that are the subject of Marc Silberman's contribution below. Uncanny echoes of Weimar revolutionary socialism resound, for instance, through Propaganda Minister Joseph Goebbels' early promises to liberate German cinema from commercial constraint, or to place a rejuvenated German film in the service of higher political goals. To an extent, of course, Goebbels reveals himself here merely as an early practitioner of that now familiar mode of political image manipulation that dresses authoritarian politics in the borrowed clothes of grass-roots movements for social change. But – uncomfortable as this may be politically – discernible continuities and correspondences run through the history of cinematic movements in Germany that have placed culture in the service of political projects of both Right and Left.

The first common thread in accounts below of Weimar and Nazi cinema, as well as the New German Cinema and feminist film, is a shared wariness in relation to the avant-garde and experimental traditions in German film. Unlike a number of other national avant-garde or independent cinemas, the socio-political re-purposing of a mass medium has often taken precedence in Germany over innovations and experiments in cinematic technique, narration, or style. As Marc Silberman documents, many of the Weimar period's politically most radical films employed classical techniques of filmic narration, or relied on realist documentary conventions. Thus it is that Weimar modernists like director and theoretician Hans Richter, an early exponent of Dada who collaborated with Eisenstein in the late 1920s, were not embraced by contemporary leftist film movements, and the experimental and formalist tradition that Richter represents has not found a place in the post-1970s historiography of 'political' film. Thus it is too that, at the other end of the political spectrum, Nazi cinema avoided experiments in film style, and, despite Goebbels' proclaimed admiration for Soviet montage, as well as such prominent exceptions as Leni Riefenstahl's work, relied for the realisation of its ideological aims on strictly conventional principles of narrative film.

Within alternative cinemas, indeed, the priority attributed to content over form has on occasion even led to the ostracising of film-makers perceived as overtly 'formalist' (see, for example, Ulrike Sieglohr's contribution on Ulrike Ottinger). What has thus frequently united otherwise diametrically opposed conceptions of a self-defined 'political cinema' in Germany is a suspicion towards filmic form and style, which betrays a profound unease and often contradictory engagement with the realm of the image *per se*, particularly when compared with the cultural resonances of, and importance accorded to, the written and spoken word and aural experiences. In this respect, alternative and independent cinema movements in Germany have often simultaneously, and seemingly paradoxically, been at the forefront of progressive socio-cultural politics, and at the same time functioned as guardians to the heritage and memory of a literary-based national culture (a tendency which differentiates them from more iconoclastic movements such as, for example, the early *nouvelle vague* in France in the late 1950s and early 60s).

It is therefore no surprise that German alternative or independent cinema has been constructed from early on, with few exceptions (e.g. see Silberman's references to the film co-operatives of the 1920s, and the 'workers' film' of the 1970s), around the unifying voice of the individual *auteur*-director, whose function, authority and status hark back to that of the literary author. It is this foregrounding of cinema's literary heritage that in part explains the status of Bertolt Brecht as one of the few exceptions to the rule that situated avant-garde practice on the margins of the Weimar film-cultural Left. Certainly, both Brecht's reputation as a prominent playwright and drama theorist, and the collective production mode he espoused, locate him within a leftist tradition that often aims to reinscribe a writerly as well as artisanal dimension in the filmic storytelling process. However, in the context of German culture, as Thomas Elsaesser has argued, the recourse to the individual author has also served a second function, particularly for independent and politically engaged cinema movements, in that it connects to the nineteenth-century romantic conceptions of the author as political dissident, social visionary and moral authority, and therefore legitimate commentator on the national culture, state and politics.

As Ian Garwood points out in his contribution, the German notion of the *Autorenfilm*, which dates back to the 1910s, thus differs from, as much as it shares common elements with, the better known concept of an *auteur* cinema, with which it has often been conflated. Unlike the early *nouvelle vague's* rethinking of popular canons and their appropriation for modern film-making, in German discourses about the respective merits and values of popular culture vs bourgeois ideals of high art, the *Autorenfilm* has in most cases squarely sided with the latter. As Garwood's article documents, the idea of the *Autorenfilm* was after all originally set up during the Wilhelmine period in antagonism to what was denounced as trash cinema (*Schundfilm*), and as an incentive to 'respectable' artists from the legitimate stage and literature to lend their prestige to the medium. The *Autorenfilm* of the New German Cinema in the 1970s

functioned in a similar context, again conceived in antagonism to prevailing cinematic norms and institutions, and grounding both its aesthetics and its public prestige in a close relationship between film and literature, or more generally high culture (e.g. Wenders' and Peter Handke's collaborations, Schlöndorff's literary adaptations, Werner Herzog's and Werner Schroeter's connection to opera, Fassbinder's and Hans-Jürgen Syberberg's crossovers between theatre and film).

There have been exceptions to this bourgeois and anti-popular bias; witness, for example, Fassbinder's appropriation of generic formulae from gangster film to melodrama, and his critical as well as personal engagement with popular traditions (e.g. his collaborations with actors from 1950s German cinema, or his idolisation of Douglas Sirk). Witness too Wim Wenders' homages to American thrillers, road movies and Westerns. However, Wenders' work, and in particular his *Der Himmel über Berlin* (*Wings of Desire*, 1987), also highlights some ultimately irreconcilable contradictions the *Autorenfilm*. One of the central tenets of the New German Cinema was its claim that cinematic technique provided no stumbling block for genial amateurs (provided, of course, that they were grounded in, and motivated by, the appropriate political stance) to enter and use the medium as a means of aesthetic self-expression and cultural comment. This promotion and celebration of autodidacticism, which became part of the personal mythology of film-makers such as Fassbinder and particularly Herzog, not only functioned as a snub against the institutionalised training and professionalism of commercial film-making, but it also matched the movement's DIY ethos of a pre-industrial form of cultural production. Twenty years after his first film, however, Wenders' *Wings of Desire* has understandably little left of such untutored immediacy. Although, as Garwood's analysis of the film documents, the director still pursues his ideal of an artisanal form of film-making through a number of aesthetic strategies, *Wings of Desire*, like Fassbinder's and Schlöndorff's later films, is indistinguishable, at least in its professional approach to cinematography, editing and *mise-en-scène*, from the film-making process the New German Cinema once aimed to unhinge. The few *Autoren* to have emerged since the 1990s, on the other hand, have either completely rejected the principles of the *Autorenfilm* proper (e.g. such popular directors as Sönke Wortmann, or Detlef Buck), or have, as the case of Tom Tykwer illustrates, at least a much more cautious relationship to overt and transparent cultural politics, and a far greater grounding in the technologies and styles of a fundamentally altered media landscape.

This leads us to a third nexus around which the politics and film culture have regularly converged, and that is the representation in German cinema of the national past. It was of course in the Nazi period that representations of a glorious past were most notoriously harnessed to serve (especially inglorious) political ends. Historians of Third Reich cinema have regularly noted the important role of historical narrative in cementing what Linda Schulte-Sasse has termed the 'illusions of wholeness' underpinning Nazi discourses of nation.[1] The first efforts to disentangle German film from the Third Reich's dense repertoire of historical genre and narrative conventions were made during the cultural-political interregnum of 1945–9, when such 'rubble film' (*Trümmerfilm*) directors as Wolfgang Staudte, Helmut Käutner and Kurt Maetzig drew on the modernist film languages Nazism had so reviled (German Expressionism in Staudte's case, surrealism in Helmut Käutner's whimsical *Der Apfel ist ab* [*The Apple Has Fallen*, 1948]) to explore post-fascist models for German historical representation in film.

In classical histories of German cinema's development after the Second World War, the rubble film is often seen as the last gasp of an anti-fascist cinema that gave way in the 1950s and 60s to the far more conservative modes of popular genre film. Elsewhere in this book, we have of course questioned the critical orthodoxy that associates popular film indissolubly with political reaction. It is certainly the case, however, that despite what Tim Bergfelder and Johannes von Moltke identify in Part One as the modernising and internationalist impulses discernible in aspects of 1950s and 60s West German genre films, they remained culturally conservative in respect of what von Moltke terms the 'underlying sense of continuity' that pervaded such genres as the post-war *Heimatfilm* and the historical biopic. Analogous continuities were evident in DEFA's reconstructions of the recent past, where narratives of anti-fascist resistance often paradoxically replicated the heroic-realist narrative and genre conventions of Third Reich historical film. No surprise, then, that it was around a resistance to those conventions that post-war cinema's most celebrated oppositional movements, the 'Young' and the 'New' German Cinema, initially coalesced. As both Thomas Elsaesser and Ian Garwood remind us below, the New German Cinema in particular was characterised by what Elsaesser has elsewhere termed a 'brooding obsession with Germany's unresolved and irredeemable past as a nation'.[2] What unites the oeuvre of such directors as Rainer Werner Fassbinder, Alexander Kluge, Hans-Jürgen Syberberg, Helma Sanders-Brahms, Margarethe von Trotta and Edgar Reitz is not at all their common chal-

lenge to mainstream cinematic conventions (their work is stylistically disparate in the extreme), but rather their common address to Germany's troubled national past, and thus their contribution to broader cultural processes of so-called *Vergangenheitsbewältigung* (coming to terms with the past).

Within post-1970s film-historical discourses which, as we saw in the general introduction to this book, have traditionally validated activist traditions of political and ethical engagement in German film, it is, then, above all the New German Cinema directors' dogged commitment to historical critique that is the source of their works' canonical status. The contributions on New German Cinema below, however, shed a somewhat critical light on some at least of the founding assumptions in a post-1970s historiography that so positively values the revisionist historical project of New German film. Despite (or perhaps because of) its preoccupation with a working through of the national trauma of German fascism, post-1970s film, it has been suggested, may have become paradoxically complicit in the reconstruction of a cultural exclusionary national identity. This is not to claim that the New German Cinema simply reproduced the cinematic models of its conservative or right-wing nationalist predecessors. As in the Weimar case discussed by Silberman below, the cultural-political project of the New German Cinema included a focus on creating the institutional structures and networks – independent production companies, collectively run distributors, new funding structures, national and international festivals and fringe events at Hof, Berlin and elsewhere – that might establish post-Oberhausen film as a political catalyst within a revitalised democratic public sphere. At the level of textual practice, however, it is in particular films that attempt a critical address to the national past, including such seminal examples of the post-war *Autorenfilm* as Fassbinder's *BRD-Trilogie* (FRG Trilogy, 1979–82),[3] Edgar Reitz' epic of everyday life in his native Hunsrück, *Heimat* (1984), the collectively produced *Deutschland im Herbst* (*Germany in Autumn*, 1978), or Helma Sanders-Brahms' autobiographical *Deutschland, bleiche Mutter* (*Germany, Pale Mother*, 1979), that are critiqued, not only for an over-investment in issues of personal identity and the (German) self, but more seriously, for the way in which that obsession begins to reproduce rightist culture's characteristic disavowal of difference. Anton Kaes puts the case succinctly when he describes the New German Cinema's mode of *Vergangenheitsbewältigung* as one in which fascism's victims, inmates of the death camps for instance, can be hidden by a search in which Germans become the victims of history.[4]

Thomas Elsaesser's case study below focuses not so much on New German film's occlusion of fascism's victims, but on what he insists is the spectacular *presence* of filmic representations that obsessively re-enact the experience of a failure to inscribe an image of Jewish identity into post-war West German film. Elsaesser uses Freud's concept of parapraxis (*Fehlleistung*) – slips of the tongue or *faux pas* that belie a barely repressed anxiety or trauma – to describe not only such spectacularly misconceived public gestures of remembrance as President Reagan's trip to an SS cemetery at Bitburg in 1985, but also cinematic representations of the German past that performatively re-enact post-war cinema's failure to bring the Jewish experience in particular into filmic representation. Elsaesser's examples include the 'blindless egotism' of Werner Herzog's actorly alter egos, Klaus Kinski and Bruno S., whose megalomania, he claims, enacts an ironic critique of the New German Cinema's hyperinflated introspection. In Herzog's work, in other words, the impossibility of the New German Cinema's desire to bring the excluded 'others' of fascist history into representation is, suggests Elsaesser, established as a focus of more distanced (and possibly critical) contemplation through the hero figure's hyperbolic overinflation.

Elsaesser's argument sheds interesting light on other films that display with equal insistence their own failure to symbolise the death camp experience within their revisionist narratives of the fascist past. Especially in films criticised in their own time for their 'repression' of the Holocaust, such features as tumbledown buildings with high chimneys (this in *Deutschland, bleiche Mutter*), or, in the case of *Heimat*, a prison camp, appear fleetingly in shot, only to be equally pointedly 'forgotten' as the film returns to its central narrative concerns.

What is at issue here, Elsaesser quite contentiously claims, is an insistent 'presence-in-absence' of the Jewish experience: a presence which, he further suggests, provides a useful block to closed constructions of Germanness, and in that sense sustains an openness to cultural difference in some corners at least of the New German Cinema (his example is Kluge's work). At this point in the early twenty-first century, Elsaesser implies (and he is echoed in this by Deniz Göktürk later in this volume), such an engagement with difference remains a minority pursuit in contemporary German film. Both Ian Garwood and Ulrike Sieglohr, finally, are perhaps more optimistic. Sieglohr sees in the avant-garde practice of Ulrike Ottinger a celebration of diversity that usefully transcends what she dubs the 'political correctness' of 1970s and 80s feminist film. Garwood, meanwhile, reads Tom Tykwer's *Lola rennt* (*Run, Lola, Run*, 1998) as attempting a similar engagement with 'otherness' when it embraces the global image cultures of computer and video games, virtual reality and digital recording. The New German Cinema *auteurs'* contemporary successors, Garwood suggests, may be involved in a cultural politics pitched no longer at the level of historical narrative, but at an embracing of history-in-the-making in contemporary media represenations. Time (as Tykwer himself might say) will tell.

Notes

1   Linda Schulte-Sasse, *Entertaining the Third Reich: Illusions of Wholeness in Nazi Cinema* (Durham and London: Duke University Press, 1996).

2   Thomas Elsaesser, *New German Cinema: A History* (London: BFI and Macmillan, 1989), p. 239.

3   The trilogy comprises *Die Ehe der Maria Braun* (*The Marriage of Maria Braun*, 1979); *Lola* (1981); and *Die Sehnsucht der Veronika Voss* (*Veronika Voss*, 1982).

4   Anton Kaes, *From Hitler to Heimat: The Return of History as Film* (Cambridge, MA: Harvard University Press, 1989), pp. 127ff.

15

Political Cinema as Oppositional Practice: Weimar and Beyond

Marc Silberman

What is meant by political cinema? Situated at the intersection of art, ideology and entertainment, all films are political in their content or in their omissions. In this broad sense popular genres engage political values because their conventions shift over time in response to changing social realities. Similarly, even the most innocuous escapist fantasies convey (conservative) political messages by reinforcing values of the status quo. From this perspective all films may be seen as refracting lenses that reveal more or less clearly the needs, desires and fears of a society. A more narrow definition regards only films about political processes or topical social issues to be political. This functional definition limits the domain to films produced or distributed by oppositional groups with the intention of bringing about political change. In the extreme case this definition could be further restricted to agitational and propaganda films that deliberately attempt to influence an audience through manipulation of myths, symbols and emotions. A third definition sets off political film-making from a consumerist mode of entertainment. For this kind of cinema intellectual argument is the hallmark of a formal, aesthetic practice that insists on educating the viewer, on teaching not what, but how to think. These and other possible definitions are never entirely distinct. Moreover, a film-maker's intentions may not always conform to the effects on the viewer when considering politics in and of the cinema. Hence, when looking at political films, it is necessary to account for their oppositional practices as well as the audience they engage.

During the 1920s Germany saw the rise of the earliest and most sustained efforts at an alternative, oppositional political cinema. The existence of two well-organised working-class parties – the German Social Democratic Party (*Sozialdemokratische Partei Deutschlands*, SPD) and the German Communist Party (*Kommunistische Partei Deutschlands*, KPD) – as well as the strong cultural ties between the young Soviet Union and newly republican Germany created the framework for an unprecedented surge of politically motivated activity in all areas of the cinema: production, distribution, exhibition and reception. Here the seed was planted for what became by the 1930s a European and international movement of radical, left-wing cinema and in the post-war era the touchstone for self-consciously political film-making. Usually sparked by workers' organisations or national communist parties that recognised the potential of film for mobilising the masses politically, these groups were, however, not alone in exploring and exploiting the power of moving images for partisan ends. In Germany, for example, both the commercial movie industry and the Nazis were also competing for the popular audience with political 'message' films and working-class oriented entertainment.

As economic and political conditions of the working class deteriorated in Germany after the First World War, the Left began to develop ideas for an alternative cinema. Faced with the escapist fare of the commercial movies, government censorship and problems of distribution, both the SPD and the KPD produced first short documentaries on the plight of the workers and later their own entertainment features inspired by the revolutionary films imported from the Soviet Union. The Left avant-garde, most prominently Bertolt Brecht and Walter Benjamin, recognised in the course of the 1920s that the cinema was not simply a new technology, but was rather revolutionising all previous ideas about art and representation.[1] The discovery of new visual techniques for expressing emotions in the Weimar cinema (e.g. chiaroscuro lighting, distorting camera angles and set design, the 'unchained' camera) and the development of montage editing pioneered by Soviet directors like Sergei Eisenstein and Dziga Vertov dissolved the traditional, 'common-sense' relation between art and reality as one of reflection and explanation. The perception of reality that had been centred in the individual subject contemplating the work of art shifted to the mechanical function of a technical, optical apparatus with various perspectives and means of reproduction at its disposal. In short, the cinema demonstrated that everyday consciousness is not natural but constructed and that the real does not exist as such but is constituted by aesthetic practices.

Weimar modernism emerged when these kinds of philosophical concerns dovetailed with the experience of war's mass destruction and its resulting traumas. Not only in the cinema but also in painting, theatre and literature artists were seeking and finding aesthetic strategies for the ontological and epistemological shifts in how they were making sense of the world around them. But the cinema more than any other cultural practice radicalised these questions. Caught between American models of consumerist entertainment and traditional European notions of art, functionalised for competing ideological agendas, subject to rapid innovations in technology, the cinema offered the most precise idea of how all perceptual co-ordinates were under attack around the issues of sight and sound.

This, then, is the context for examining the oppositional cinema of the Weimar Republic. The consolidation after the war of the commercial movie industry with the founding of Ufa as a vertical monopoly and attention to the Russian Revolution, including Lenin's prominent statements in 1919 and 1922 defining the cinema as the most important of the arts, provoked the organised workers' movement in Germany to evaluate its options. In the early years of the Republic both the SPD and the KPD considered political art to be an extension of mass organising, and movies – a mass medium in the hands of big business – were not seen as art but as an opiate. Furthermore, a narrowly operative concept of political art excluded formal experimentation that might have led to innovative 'proletarian aesthetics'. Hence, although both left-wing parties acknowledged the potential of moving images for propaganda and information, they did not explore that potential. The SPD and labour unions produced a small number of

documentaries beginning in 1919, and there were isolated attempts at establishing local film clubs and production companies in the early 1920s, but lack of capital and halting support condemned them to failure.[2] The KPD initially assumed a position of resigned patience: as long as the capitalist bourgeoisie and state censors controlled the movie industry, there would be no revolutionary, proletarian cinema. The ownership of the means of production would have to change for the cinema to become a tool in the class struggle.

The most remarkable contributor to political film-making in the Weimar Republic was Willi Münzenberg. Head of the Communist Youth International, he was commissioned by Lenin in 1921 to establish an organisation that could help funnel charitable aid to the Soviet Union in order to offset the disastrous harvest and resulting famine. Under Münzenberg's leadership, a sponsoring committee including Albert Einstein, Bernard Shaw and George Grosz announced the founding of the Workers' International Relief (WIR; in German *Internationale Arbeiterhilfe*, or IAH) with headquarters in Berlin. For fundraising purposes WIR distributed Soviet documentaries showing the impact of the famine as well as Soviet achievements. At the same time it supplied the nationalised but impoverished Soviet movie industry with raw film stock and equipment (covering up to 80 per cent of its needs in 1922–3, for example). The positive response to the documentaries emboldened Münzenberg to have WIR produce documentaries about its own relief work in the Soviet Union as well as on the misery of German workers subject to hyperinflation. To facilitate this expansion from distribution to production, WIR put up 50 per cent of the capital for a production company called Mezhrabpom-Russ, which produced narrative and agitational films specifically for use in Germany.[3] When the German government introduced import regulations in 1925 that required one domestically produced film for every foreign feature screened, the co-operation fostered by the WIR-Mezhrabpom alliance allowed Münzenberg to make German-Soviet features with mixed casts and teams. Counted as domestic features, these co-productions in turn allowed him to distribute Soviet films in Germany under the new protectionist import regulations. To this end he established in 1925–6 the Prometheus distribution company in Germany which promoted WIR's co-productions, Soviet films and documentaries about the KPD and other mass organisations.

Münzenberg's initiatives were aimed at modernising agitation and propaganda instruments as weapons of class enlightenment for the proletariat.[4] Inspired by the agitational trains and open-air theatres in the post-revolutionary Soviet Union, he sought to adapt such forms to Germany as a way to democratise the cinema and its social function.[5] He was not, however, seeking new art forms but rather new practical forms of mass education and political training. The turning point came in 1925. With the stabilisation of the German economy it became clear to the KPD that a political revolution was not imminent, and therefore it acknowledged the need to focus more attention on cultural work and propaganda rather than direct political intervention. Taking a cue from Soviet initiatives, the Party recognised that harnessing the power of moving images could also serve the emancipation of exploited workers in Germany. This view of the potential of revolutionary cinema was confirmed with the distribution by the new Prometheus company of *Battleship Potemkin*, Eisenstein's second film and the beginning of a wave of popular Russian films in German cinemas.

Three factors coalesced here. First, faced with discriminatory censorship when it first opened in Berlin in January 1926, Eisenstein's film finally passed in July with serious cuts after a major press campaign to defend films against political censorship (see Martin Loiperdinger in this volume). This became the first in a series of contentious film censorship cases during the Weimar Republic, marking the beginning of serious and politicised film criticism among liberal and left-wing intellectuals in Germany.[6] Second, Eisenstein's innovative use of montage editing modelled a new film language for the contemporary audience. It demonstrated that the cinema's value for leftist propaganda purposes was not only to be found in the treatment of political themes but also in the potential to transform spectatorship from mere passive consumption into an intellectually challenging response by means of its powerful formal, visual rhetoric. Hence, the very attendance at a screening of Eisenstein's film was perceived not only as an artistic but also as a political event, signalling both in content and form a new, politicised film art. Finally, this film proved that there was an alternative to the commercial movie industry, a kind of narrative that could be both a box-office success and a dramatic rendering of class conflict from a working-class perspective.[7]

The perspective and representation of the masses became major concerns of politicised intellectuals in the 1920s, and Münzenberg's rhetoric and practice vis-à-vis the cinema as mass medium are related to the larger context of urbanisation, massification, and the crisis of the autonomous subject that characterises Weimar modernism. Contrary to the commercial cinema, left-wing political cinema was concerned not with the loss of individuality but with the gain of collective freedom and power, represented as the heroic quality of the masses. Historical pageants like Ernst Lubitsch's *Madame Dubarry* (*Passion*, 1919), a rendering of the French Revolution in which the powerful choreography of the masses in scenes of revolutionary violence shows them at the mercy of their emotions, were seen by leftist critics as typical bourgeois distortions of the downtrodden. Similarly, Fritz Lang's dystopian fantasy of modern workers in *Metropolis* (1925/6) represents revolution as a collective act but in the form of hysterical loss of control. Socially critical films like F. W. Murnau's *Der letzte Mann* (*The Last Laugh*, 1924) and G. W. Pabst's *Die freudlose Gasse* (*The Joyless Street*, 1925) featured the ragged proletariat and the tenement architecture of the class system, but left-wing commentators criticised them for their depoliticised individualism. For the KPD these were just examples of how the commercial movie industry was able to market even pessimism and discontent with personal narratives of class retribution and social harmony. Based on this understanding of the dominant media manipulating emotions and conspiring against the working class, Prometheus – with KPD support – began to devise its own strategies for oppositional films.

While the distribution of Soviet features remained the cornerstone of Prometheus' earnings, Münzenberg's conviction that the cinema was potentially more significant for developing class consciousness than either the press or educational efforts justified for him a major financial investment in 'proletarian-revolutionary' entertainment films. Yet Prometheus' feature-length productions, announced with great fanfare in 1927, were slow in coming and neither particularly proletarian nor revolutionary. Perhaps the growing threat of politically motivated censorship was too great a risk for the investment; possibly the Soviet practice of using kitsch films to lure the public into the cinema for the agitation presented in newsreels and documentaries framing the main feature made more sense; or conceivably the producers were unable to imagine entertaining ways to articulate working-class problems without disavowing their own political convictions. Finally, however, in the autumn of 1929 Prometheus released two films that combined demands for attractive entertainment and a proletarian message.

Leo Mittler's *Jenseits der Strasse* (*Harbour Drift*) reworked the popular 'street film' genre with a mixture of documentary city-life footage and a sentimental, star-crossed love story involving a prostitute, an old beggar and a young unemployed man. The visual appeal of authentic working-class locations and everyday topicality frames the implicit critique of a harsh economic system that disallows compassion as a response to social misery. Yet, like competing commercial features, the proletarian experience was not portrayed as a site of contradiction and struggle, as the Left's political programme proclaimed, but rather as an oppressive existence to be tolerated.[8] Piel Jutzi's *Mutter Krausens Fahrt ins Glück* (*Mother Krause's Journey into Happiness*, (1929) went further.

A melodrama set in a lumpenproletariat family, the narrative follows parallel stories of the family members when faced with eviction for non-payment of rent: the hardworking mother commits suicide in despair over her poverty, the unemployed son becomes involved in a burglary, and the daughter toys with the idea of prostitution. Countering the tragic spiral is the daughter's discovery of new meaning in her life by sharing her lover's political commitment to the workers' movement. The final sequence with its triumphant images of the heroine being swept away in a street demonstration marked this feature as the first fiction film from Germany that pointed directly

to class struggle as an alternative to political resignation. At the same time, the young woman's spontaneous 'coming to class consciousness' under the authority of her male companion revealed a voluntarism characteristic of the KPD's cultural policy in general. While both films resort, then, to conventional narrative and visual structures aimed at awakening empathy in the spectator through pathos and victimisation, they do point to fundamental defects in the capitalist system.

The second strategy Münzenberg implemented for oppositional cinema extended WIR's positive results with Soviet documentaries by having Prometheus distribute and produce documentaries that could accompany commercial features in the cinemas or be used by workers' organisations for agitational purposes. These included shorts such as *Quer durch Sowjetrussland* (*Straight through Soviet Russia*, 1927), the documentation of a German workers' delegation to the Soviet Union, and *Das Dokument von*

Mutter Krausens Fahrt ins Glück (1929)

Shanghai (*The Shanghai Document*, 1928), covering the exploitation and revolt of workers in China, as well as the feature-length semi-documentary *Hunger in Waldenburg* (1929). Naturally these films were subject to serious interventions on the part of censors, but often they could be screened without cuts in closed events sponsored by labour unions, political groups, schools and clubs. In 1927 WIR founded *Weltfilm*, a centralised agency responsible for the non-commercial distribution of agitational films to these organisations. *Weltfilm* held as well the monopoly on the international distribution of all Soviet films for non-commercial screenings. In 1929 it began producing its own newsreels and documentaries, and with a new technology patented in the Soviet Union it expanded in 1931 to distributing films in 16mm copies, which increased rentals because of the reduced costs for projection equipment.[9]

In retrospect, then, 1929 marked a high-point in left-wing cinema of the Weimar Republic. Both the SPD and the KPD were supporting commercial film releases with proletarian content, both had developed extensive distribution networks, and both had rallied sympathetic public attention and intellectual support for alternative films.[10] Yet 1929 also witnessed significant developments that exacerbated the weaknesses of an independent Left cinema: the introduction of the sound film, the onset of the international market crash and the fatal polarisation of German society. For the commercial movie industry the novelty of sound was a blessing in disguise, a new technology that despite its high investment costs promised to increase flagging audience attendance. Independents, however, could not afford patents and new equipment. The world-wide depression only complicated these tendencies. Major studios produced more escapist fare for a public with less discretionary income. Prometheus cut back production and went bankrupt finally in late 1931. The SPD ceased film production entirely, and the KPD abandoned its support of feature-length entertainment films in favour of agitational and informational shorts. Other left-wing support shrunk as well because the growing rifts in German politics affected working-class cultural agencies, which were devoting reduced resources to battle each other. Moreover, the growing popularity of the Nazis among workers and low-level employees was eroding the potential audience for left-wing recruitment.

The last years of the Weimar Republic did nevertheless witness ongoing activity in the political cinema. Independent film productions like Pabst's *Westfront 1918* (*Western Front*, 1930), *Kameradschaft* (*Comradeship*, 1930) and *Dreigroschenoper* (*The Threepenny Opera*, 1931), Victor Trivas's *Niemandsland* (*No Man's Land*, 1930) and Leontine

Sagan's *Mädchen in Uniform* (*Girls in Uniform*) were high-quality features with anti-war, anti-national, anti-capitalistic and anti-authoritarian messages.[11] In addition, Prometheus continued through 1931 to distribute Soviet productions, while *Weltfilm* expanded its distribution list as an internationally networked agency, released its own documentaries and short 'reportages', and even began a monthly workers' newsreel in 1930 (*Monatsschau*). Following its model for proletarian writers and theatre associations, the KPD shifted its focus to 'proletarian film criticism', i.e., training workers to articulate their own class perspective about films in KPD journals or newspapers and to organise boycotts of right-wing entertainment features. All these efforts, however, fell short of Münzenberg's original goal of developing proletarian, revolutionary films. None of the workers' organisations or parties provided the kind of leadership that would have been necessary to make the cinema into a progressive social force rather than representing social forces in the cinema.

Kuhle Wampe (*Whither Germany?*), produced in 1931–2 under KPD protection by a collective including the Bulgarian-born director Slatan Dudow and Bertolt Brecht with the participation of many prominent leftist artists, is especially noteworthy because it was the last explicitly left-wing film to be released before the Nazis came to power and one that sought an innovative form for political agitation. While the stock characters, the themes of impoverishment and housing shortages, and even the closure focusing on the utopian solidarity of the younger generation at a workers' sports festival resemble previous proletarian melodramas, it is unlike other oppositional films in its visual aesthetics and open structure that drew formally on avant-garde Soviet montage principles. Like Brecht's interventionist aesthetics in the theatre, *Kuhle Wampe* incorporates

Kuhle Wampe (1932)

formal strategies of disruption and fragmentation aimed at a cognitive process of viewer reception. Narrative interruptions (expository titles, printed inserts, songs, choruses), the contrast of sound and image (commentary, voice-off, autonomous music), documentary footage (shots of Berlin streets and architecture, intercut newspaper headlines) and disruptive editing (unusual camera angles spliced together, sudden extreme close-ups, direct address to the camera) produce the film's visual quality and polemical effects.

Cited in film histories as the high-point of proletarian, revolutionary cinema in the Weimar Republic, *Kuhle Wampe*'s impact as a model for left-wing political film-making was in fact negligible. Prometheus' first sound production (a contributing factor to the company's bankruptcy), it revealed symptomatic deficits and illusions on the part of the Left at this time of social crisis. The conditions under which it was conceived and produced – with an eye to censorship problems and to its precarious financial backing – necessitated compromises at every level of its realisation. This meant, for example, that its agitational message of solidarity was camouflaged behind the relatively harmless allegory of mass sports races, concealing the serious splits in the German Left with the appeal of energetic, youthful participants. Furthermore, after a successful but short-lived run of one year, *Kuhle Wampe* was among the first films forbidden by the Nazis, who interrupted not only its distribution but also the very working-class struggle which was its subject. Meanwhile, during the Third Reich the Soviet montage of attractions found an enthusiastic admirer in the propaganda minister and film enthusiast, Joseph Goebbels, who appreciated how the metaphorisation of dialectical movement through rhythmic editing of images could be adapted for the ecstasy and pathos of Nazi documentary films and newsreels as well, for example, those of Walter Ruttmann and Leni Riefenstahl.

While the politics of restoration in West Germany left practically no room for an oppositional, non-commercial cinema during the 1950s, East Germany's state movie industry (DEFA) integrated the analytical montage tradition of the left-wing Weimar cinema into socialist-realist norms. Personal continuity yielded feature films in the Weimar proletarian tradition such as Slatan Dudow's *Stärker als die Nacht* (*Stronger Than the Night*, 1954) and topical documentaries about the construction of socialism in the GDR. The latter, however, adopted an affirmative, testimonial mode rather than a socially critical one, and by the mid-1950s accomplished documentarists like Andrew and Annelie Thorndike and later Joachim Hellwig and Walter Heynowski had shifted their agitational polemics to

historical or international subjects: documentaries about the Nazi past, exposés about former Nazis in the West German government and investigative reports about hotspots around the world (the Vietnam War, the putsch in Chile etc.). A younger generation of documentarists (e.g. Jürgen Böttcher, Karl Gass, Kurt Tetzlaff) emerged in the 1960s and 70s and once again turned their attention to everyday life in the GDR, adapting new technologies of hand-held cameras and synchronous sound for studied portraits of workers in their private and work spheres. Even more distinctive were the ongoing documentaries that followed in a longitudinal approach the development of an entire school class (Winfried Junge's series on children in Golzow) or an industrial workers' team (Volker Koepp's series on workers in Wittstock). Eschewing polemical agitation and interventionist aesthetics, these 'quiet' films were political for the GDR viewers who could recognise the pregnant silences or the gaps that opened up between images and spoken words.

Not until the late 1960s and 70s did the Federal Republic witness a rebirth of political film-making. Seeking a new approach to the medium as a progressive alternative to the commercialised 'culture industry' in the West as well as to the socialist-realist orthodoxy in the East, independent directors – often with state subsidies or public television funding – turned to anti-Hollywood aesthetics and non-narrative structures as strategies for a politicised mode of cinematic spectatorship. Denying both entertainment and enjoyment as values, they grounded their political film-making sociologically and didactically like their forerunners in the 1920s. Unlike Weimar oppositional cinema, however, this cinema did not define itself primarily by working-class characters or proletarian themes. Thus, although contemporary 'workers' films' (e.g. by Christian Ziewer) did hark back to Weimar's proletarian melodramas, for others like Alexander Kluge, Helke Sander or Jutta Brückner the 'politics' did not reside in an explicit class perspective but rather in the aesthetics of distanciation that aimed to make visible everyday social relations as oppressive and intolerable. Their films explored human interaction through realistic details, stills, distancing intertitles, voice-over commentaries and documentary footage. In general the New German Cinema directors, whose films rarely reached a broader domestic public and arguably sought to address only niche audiences nationally and internationally, were less interested in revolutionary politics or mass political education than in allegories about social alienation and outsiders.

Documentary productions were limited almost exclusively to the television feature format with the attendant broadcasting time constraints. Among the most uncompromising documentarists were Klaus Wildenhahn and Eberhard Fechner who, for instance, examined the everyday life of workers and artists, reconstructed the history of the middle class, or documented trials against those responsible for the Holocaust. Their model of 'participatory observation', an approach that sought to avoid the false dichotomy between observation and intervention, also characterised much of the oppositional film-making around identity-oriented movements in post-1960s West Germany. Early work by feminists like Helga Reidemeister (on mothering), Christine Perincioli (on domestic violence), Elfi Mikesch (on senior women) and Jeannine Meerapfel (on Turkish women) or by gay director Rosa von Praunheim formulated its social critique through social reportage about individual private lives.

Today it has become clear that the very nature of politics and political cinema are being transformed. Television, video, computers and the internet have triggered a restructuring process of the entire communications domain. At the same time, the politics of any particular film seem less and less to be related to the (political) intentions of the filmmaker or the (political) effect on the viewer. Competing discursive practices – emancipatory, repressive, reactionary – may coexist and interact with each other and be governed by structural rather than political conventions. Indeed, films are only one factor in political socialisation, which is a cumulative process shared by family, friends, school, workplace and other cultural activities, all of which teach, reinforce and challenge ideas about society. In retrospect, then, the political cinema of the Weimar Republic reveals the Left's isolation and the limitations of the semi-autonomous cultural space constructed by left-wing intellectuals at a time when new technologies were establishing the very phenomenon of mass culture. Notwithstanding a few exceptions, it never reached the mass base it sought to address and it never realised the ambitious goals of creating alternative proletarian films. Looking back, however, helps us understand how people in a specific time and place thought about politics and how films rearranged (real) problems in order to articulate the constraints and opportunities for solving them.

Notes

1 See Bertolt Brecht, 'The Threepenny Lawsuit', in Marc Silberman (ed. and trans.), *Bertolt Brecht on Film and Radio* (London: Methuen, 2000), pp. 147–99; and Walter Benjamin, 'The Work of Art in the Age of Mechanical Reproduction', in Hannah Arendt (ed.), *Illuminations*, trans. by Harry Zohn (New York: Schocken, 1969), pp. 217–51.

2 With financial support from the labour union confederation and the SPD, Martin Berger produced the first 'proletarian' feature film from Germany in 1924, *Die Schmiede* (*The Forge*), which contrasts the impact of a spontaneous work stoppage and a union-organised strike for the eighthour workday. On Berger, see Gerd Meier, 'Ein unbekannter Regisseur: Martin Berger', in Uli Jung and Walter Schatzberg (eds.), *Filmkultur zur Zeit der Weimarer Republik* (Munich: Saur, 1992), pp. 90–119.

3 Mezhrabpom-Russ was founded on 1 August 1924, as a co-operative endeavour of the Russ film artists' collective and WIR. Mezhrabpom is the Russian short form of *Mezhdunarodnaia Rabochaia Pomoshch* or International Workers' Aid.

4 For details on Münzenberg, see Rolf Surmann, *Die Münzenberg-Legende: zur Publizistik der revolutionären Arbeiterbewegung 1921–1933* (Cologne: Prometh, 1982). For a sometimes unreliable presentation in English, see Babette Gross, *Willi Münzenberg: A Political Biography* (Lansing: Michigan State University Press, 1974), a translation of the original West German edition of 1967. Münzenberg himself authored one of the most interesting contributions to the discussion of political cinema in the Weimar Republic: *Erobert den Film! Winke aus der Praxis für die Praxis proletarischer Filmpropaganda* (Berlin: Neuer Deutscher Verlag, 1925).

5 On Soviet 'agit-trains' and their agitational films (*agitka*), see Richard Taylor, *Film Propaganda: Soviet Russia and Nazi Germany*, 2nd edn (London and New York: Tauris, 1998), pp. 29–34. On agitprop theatre in Germany, see John Willett, *Art and Politics in the Weimar Period: The New Sobriety 1917–1933* (New York: Pantheon, 1978), pp. 150 and 156.

6 The most prominent censorship controversies involved Lewis Milestone's Hollywood adaptation of Remarque's novel *All Quiet on the Western Front* in 1930 and the Dudow/Brecht collaboration on *Kuhle Wampe* in 1932.

7 On the commercial success of *Battleship Potemkin*, see Surmann, *Die Münzenberg-Legende,* pp. 116f. Revolutionary Soviet films were not especially popular in the Soviet Union itself. The early Bolshevist government needed the entertainment tax revenue from cinema tickets and therefore encouraged the production of kitsch and the import of Hollywood films in order to keep the cinemas full. See Willett, *Art and Politics in the Weimar Period* p. 70. This may explain as well why Prometheus' own first independent productions in 1926 were fairly conventional – an adaptation of a Chekhov story, a light comedy and a romance.

8 Examples include Werner Hochbaum's *Brüder* (*Brothers*, 1929) and Marie Harder's *Lohnbuchhalter Kremke* (*Bookkeeper Kremke*, 1930) – both supported by unions and the SPD – as well as Carl Junghans' *So ist das Leben* (*That's Life*, 1930) and Hans Tintner's *Cyankali* (*Cyanide*, 1930). Harder was the director of the SPD's film office (*Film- und Lichtbilddienst*), established in 1925 and, like the WIR's *Weltfilm* (see below), at first specialised in non-commercial distribution of shorts and documentaries to support SPD election campaigns and rallies. Harder was the only woman associated directly with the Left who produced a film during the Weimar Republic.

9 While high production costs and censorship were serious hindrances, distribution was the bane of political cinema in the Weimar Republic, as it would be later for the New German Cinema of the 1960s and 70s. Münzenberg estimated that Prometheus had access only to about 8 per cent of the cinemas in Germany, since the majority were owned or controlled by American and German production companies interested in screening their own features. Often Prometheus' films had to be scheduled on 'slow' days such as Sunday mornings, or workers' organisations rented cinemas or other communal halls for special screenings. Consequently, WIR and *Weltfilm* experimented with new techniques such as open-air events and regional tours with their own projection equipment, sometimes in conjunction with agitprop groups, workers' choirs and/or speeches by prominent left-wing journalists or politicians.

10 The SPD's *Film- und Lichtbilddienst* and the KPD's *Rote Hilfe* were party-affiliated audience organisations, but the most influential one was the *Volksfilmverband* (People's Film Organisation, VFV), founded in January 1928 as a non-partisan, progressive membership association with many prominent artists and intellectuals on its governing board. Through members-only screenings, discussion forums and its journal *Film and Volk* the association aimed to educate the general audience and pressure the movie industry for higher-quality entertainment, but under pressure from the KPD in 1929 the VFV surrendered its neutrality and joined the centralised KPD umbrella organisation *Interessengemeinschaft für Arbeiterkultur* (Co-ordinated Interest Group for Workers' Culture, IfA).

11 Pabst's adaptation of the musical *Die Dreigroschenoper* in fact led to a famous court case in 1930 in which the author and composer, Bertolt Brecht and Kurt Weill, tried to enforce an injunction against its distribution on the grounds that it breached their copyright protection by not reflecting the original play's anti-capitalist message. For Brecht's lengthy essay on the trial and its implications published in 1932, see 'The Threepenny Lawsuit' (note 1).

16

Film Policy in the Third Reich

Julian Petley

In March 1933, Hitler announced in the ideological mouthpiece of the National Socialist Party (NSDAP), the *Völkischer Beobachter*

> a systematic campaign to restore the nation's moral and material health. The whole educational system, theatre, film, literature, the press and broadcasting – all of these will be used as a means to this end. They will be harnessed to help preserve the eternal values that are part of the integral nature of our people.[1]

As a fundamentally anti-democratic party, the NSDAP were clearly not afraid of ruling by overtly authoritarian means, but they also understood the crucial importance of winning the battle for hearts and minds. As Propaganda Minister Joseph Goebbels put it at the 1934 Nuremberg Rally: 'it may be a good thing to possess power that rests on arms. But it is better and more gratifying to win and hold the heart of the people'.[2]

To this end, one of the new regime's first and most significant acts was to establish the Reich Ministry for Popular Enlightenment and Propaganda (RMVP), with Goebbels at its head, charged with 'the spiritual direction of the nation'. The RMVP contained a Chamber of Culture (RKK), whose task was 'furthering German culture and regulating economic and social aspects of cultural affairs'. The RKK was in turn divided into separate chambers, including a Chamber of Film (RFK), each of which was responsible for one of the arts. The RMVP also had its own Film Department. At the same time, the NSDAP maintained its own Central Propaganda Office, which was responsible for 'spreading National Socialist ideology and the achievements of the Party leadership', and this contained a Central Film Office. Many of the key posts in the Party's Propaganda Office and

in the RMVP were held by the same people, all of whom were ultimately responsible to Goebbels.

One of the main functions of such bodies, early in the regime's history, was to facilitate the expulsion of the Jews and other *entartete Kunstler* ('degenerate artists') from the cultural sphere, since only those who were members of the appropriate chambers were allowed to work in the arts at all. Trade unions were, of course, banned, and the main film industry union, the *Dach-Organisation der Filmschaffenden Deutschlands* (DACHO), was absorbed initially into the *Nationalsozialistische Betriebszellen-organisation* (NSBO), which was in turn absorbed by the *Deutsche Arbeitsfront* (DAF), the only permitted 'trade union'. All of these measures are particularly vivid examples of how the National Socialist principle of *Gleichschaltung* (co-ordination) was put into operation. This denotes the process whereby all German institutions were synchronised to conform with National Socialism; as Klaus Fischer points out:

> *Gleichschaltung* proceeded along two related paths: synchronisation of all government institutions and mass mobilisation of all citizens for the National Socialist cause. The first approach involved the eradication of all political opponents and parties and the second the creation of mass organisations for mass control.[3]

Change and continuity in German film policy 1927–36

Before examining the manifestations of *Gleichschaltung* specifically within the film industry, however, we need to understand the extent to which National Socialist film policy was, at least in part, a response to problems which had their origins in the Weimar era, and, in particular, in the crisis which hit the German film industry in 1926–7. By then, the effects of the wider economic crisis, coupled with rising production costs and increasing number of US imports, were threatening the existence of even German's largest film company, Ufa. It was at this point that the media magnate and head of the highly conservative German National People's Party (DNVP), Alfred Hugenberg, acquired the majority holding in Ufa, buying out the American interests in the company, which were such an affront to nationalist sentiments, in the process. Hugenberg appointed as Ufa's managing director one of his chief lieutenants, Ludwig Klitzsch, and he set about restructuring it along the lines of a Hollywood studio. The company was divided into four sections covering administration, production, distribution and exports; some of Ufa's subsidiaries were hived off, and others absorbed into the company. The central producer system was introduced, with production being divided up between different heads of production, thereby achieving both greater central control and greater division of labour. Klitzsch also introduced stricter shooting schedules, tighter budgets and greater accountability.[4]

The major restructuring of Ufa thus dates from 1927, not 1933, which requires us to put its later reorganisation into the context of not simply National Socialist film policy but also of the 'modernisation' of Weimar cinema with the coming of sound and the development of the company, with its diverse, vertically integrated media interests, into one of the world's first multi-media empires. On the other hand, however, this should also alert us to the clear ideological continuities between many of Ufa's Weimar and Third Reich productions. Siegfried Kracauer's readings of the former may strike one now as decidedly problematic in certain respects, but in broad terms it would surely be hard not to detect a distinct rightward lurch post-Hugenberg. Nor is this simply a matter of enjoying the benefits of hindsight, given the wealth of contemporaneous complaint about these films' politics in the Left and liberal press. Typical is this example from Willi Münzenberg, the founder of Prometheus-Film, arguing in *Film und Volk* that: 'Hugenberg's film activity is a hundred times more dangerous than his newspapers. Very few workers read the Hugenberg papers, but millions of workers see the nationalistic and counterrevolutionary films from Hugenberg's poison laboratory.'[5]

Following his installation as managing director of Ufa, Klitzsch was also appointed president of the *Spitzenorganisation der Deutschen Filmindustrie* (SPIO) in 1927. This body was founded in 1923 as an umbrella for the industry's six largest professional organisations; however, it soon came to be dominated by the major production and distribution interests, and by Ufa in particular. In 1932, with the industry in trouble again due to the ongoing problems of rising production costs and increasing foreign imports, now coupled with falling audience figures as well, many smaller production and distribution companies were going to the wall and even the majors were feeling the heat. At this point SPIO came up with a master plan for the film industry. This called for the creation of a ministry of film, and for SPIO itself to be turned into an administrative body with considerably enhanced powers. Production equipment would be made available only to those approved by SPIO. Over-production would be cut back, and the industry rationalised (in other words, subjected to further concentration). Production costs would be reduced by cutting stars' salaries and patent and licence fees. A special bank for the film industry would be established as a form of trust company which would administer and safeguard conventional banks' investments and loans. In return, the bank would have to approve the entire production schedule of any film with which it was involved. Distribution would have to be guaranteed before any production could start, and the distributor would have to be a member of the SPIO-originated *Verleih-Treuhand GmbH*. Thus SPIO would effectively regulate the entire production and distribution process. Much of the blame for the poor state of the industry was laid at the door of the exhibitors, who were accused of igniting a damaging price-cutting war and so eating into the returns to distributors and producers. SPIO consequently argued that films should be distributed and exhibited only by those who agreed with its programming, ticketing and returns policies. Thus SPIO would regulate the exhibition sector too.

The important point to grasp here, however, is that the way in which the new regime would set about reforming the film industry would owe a great deal to the SPIO plan. In June 1933 there took place the first meeting of the SPIO-*Kommission*, which brought together representatives of industry and government to discuss the reorganisation of the entire industry. This examined the problems outlined above and came to the same conclusions – hardly surprisingly, as the commission was simply an expanded version of the old SPIO board. Its president was Ludwig Klitzsch, and other key members were Dr Fritz Scheuermann of the Filmkreditbank (see below), Arnold Raether of the RMVP and Dr Botho Mulert of the Ministry of Economic Affairs. One of its first acts was to order all firms to join SPIO if they wished to continue working in the industry.

The Chamber of Film was provisionally set up in July 1933 and permanently established in September. Its president was Fritz Scheuermann who, like Walter Funk (the Secretary of State at the Propaganda Ministry), was one of the key link men between big business and the National Socialist government, and who had also been a member of the SPIO-*Kommission*. Its vice-president was Arnold Raether, who was also deputy head of the Film Department of the RMVP and head of the Film Office of the Propaganda Office of the NSDAP. The advisory council was selected by Goebbels and consisted of members of the propaganda and finance ministries, as well as of various major banks. There was also an administrative council composed of representatives of the various sections of the industry – in effect the various constituent parts of SPIO. One of its earliest measures was to put an end to ticket price cutting and to set minimum ticket prices. In short, it is difficult to avoid the conclusion that the roots of the Chamber of Film lay deeply in SPIO. As Wolfgang Becker puts it:

> The former interest groups had now become administrative departments in the RFK, i.e. organisational sections without independent legal status. The dissolution of legally independent bodies and the establishment of administrative departments brought the internal organisational structure of the RFK in line with the principles of public administration.[6]

As has already been pointed out, one of the central recommendations of the 1932 SPIO plan was the creation of a special bank for the film industry. Precisely such a bank, the Filmkreditbank (FKB), was founded in 1933 and incorporated within the Chamber of Film. The man most responsible for its inception was the above-mentioned Walter Funk, who was to become Minister of Economic Affairs in 1938 and president of the Reichsbank in 1939. The FKB is a particularly important institution from our point of view since its *modus operandi* clearly demonstrates the extent to which the most powerful of the old guard of the Weimar film industry were involved in its reorganisation under the new order, the Propaganda Ministry's desire to maintain the industry's capitalist structure, and the complex intertwining of economic profitability and ideological efficacy within that structure. Hugenberg was also made Minister of Economics in the new government. And in his first address to the film industry in March 1933 Goebbels assured it that: 'We have no intention of obstructing production . . . Neither do we wish to hamper private enterprise: on the contrary, this will receive a great impetus

through the national movement as a result of the sure foundation which these days have created for a new Germany.'[7]

Apart from Funk, those involved in the setting up of the bank were the Reichskreditgesellschaft, Ufa, the Deutsche Bank, the Dresdner Bank and the Commerzbank. Operating as it did within the Chamber of Film, the bank may have been effectively state owned but it was the conventional banks which remained the real source of loans to the film industry (as, indeed, to all the other major industries in the Third Reich), loans which were simply channelled through the FKB. In the economic sphere its role was therefore not to limit the role of the conventional banks but to safeguard their investments. However, it also functioned as much more than just a bank, playing a key ideological function in that it refused to finance films or firms of which the government did not approve; furthermore, when a potential film project's creditworthiness was being judged at the pre-production stage, the bank, which possessed a *dramaturgisches Büro*, could demand any changes which it deemed necessary. And since it was charged with encouraging films that showed the way towards 'a truly German art', its aesthetic decisions, within the context of the National Socialist *Kulturkampf*, were hardly likely to be ideologically uncontaminated. Furthermore, whatever the original intentions of the *Filmkreditpolitik* may have been, its actual lending policies favoured the big four film companies – Ufa, Tobis, Bavaria and Terra – and so only encouraged the greater concentration of the industry. As Becker puts it:

> The coming together of finance capital, giant concerns and political power groups in the realm of film finance encouraged the capitalist trend towards economic monopoly and concentration, which was in line with the Nazis' political centralism . . . The economic (and to some extent also political) interests of the bankers and film industrialists were identical with the programme of the Nazi film clique.[8]

Thus through the Chamber of Film a degree of entrepreneurial independence was maintained while at the same time introducing an element of state control both over the market and the industry's products. However, the RFK could do little to ameliorate the industry's essentially *structural* problems (rising production costs, over-supply of films in a market with limited capacity, declining exports and so on) because it was dominated by precisely those powerful industrial interests most responsible for the industry's problems. Meanwhile Goebbels was not prepared to alienate an industry turning out such useful ideological products, and his Propaganda Ministry's demands for high-quality, prestigious, 'artistic' movies (see below) served only to increase production costs.

The centralisation of the film industry 1936–45

As small- and medium-sized companies continued to go to the wall and even the majors faced difficulties, the idea of a centrally organised film industry was raised by Walter Funk in a letter to the Finance Ministry at the end of 1936. Outright nationalisation would not only have presented the National Socialists with major ideological problems – although it would have delighted 'radicals' such as Alfred Rosenberg – but it would also have placed huge burdens on the Finance Ministry. The solution was to turn to Dr Max Winkler and his *Cautio-Treuhandgesellschaft*, a trust company through which the government had discreetly channelled vast funds in order to enable it to buy an 'invisible empire' of newspapers on their behalf.

Thus Winkler, who in 1937 was appointed Reich Delegate to the German Film Industry, was asked to buy majority holdings in all of the major film firms with funds supplied by government. Between 1936 and 1939 these firms were changed from public to private limited liability companies, and Winkler, who himself kept a low profile but whose representatives occupied key positions in these *staatsmittelbar* (state funded) firms, administered their finances both as a majority shareholder and as a government trustee through *Cautio*. Thus the film companies were directly answerable to *Cautio*, which was in turn answerable to the Propaganda Ministry, for which it held the shares in trust. In turn, the Propaganda Ministry was to some extent answerable to the Finance Ministry, which had originally supplied the funds for the whole operation.

Wolfgang Becker estimates that this *Verreichlichungsprozess* cost the government 64,886,900 marks. However, it was well worth the expense in that Winkler's 'rationalisation' of the industry made it more profitable and thus, ultimately, *less* dependent on state aid while remaining firmly under National Socialist supervision. His principal aim was to moderate the competition between the majors, introducing a degree of co-operation and co-ordination which would help to stabilise the market and, in particular, halt the inflation of production costs which had so bedevilled the industry. In this he was largely successful.

By 1941, however, more changes were required. Germany's various annexations and invasions had increased both audience numbers and production capacity, and the war meant that more people were going to the cinema than ever, partly to see the newsreels, partly because they had more money but less on which to spend it, and partly for morale-boosting reasons. At the same time, however, the war was also taking its toll: production costs were rising faster again, increasingly strict censorship meant that productions had to be altered or abandoned, the RMVP was commissioning increasingly elaborate films, and production targets were not being met. Winkler decided that what was now required was the centralisation of the administrative and financial structure of the *staatsmittelbar* firms and the absorption of the remaining privately owned production and distribution companies. Winkler proposed a holding company which would control all future investment in the industry and oversee the distribution of profits. The *staatsmittelbar* firms would retain their own names (thus shielding from public gaze the full extent of the monopolisation process which had taken place) but would now be *staatseigen* (state owned) and function only as production companies. Allocation of studio space would be centrally organised. In 1941 the *Deutsche Filmtheater GmbH* was set up to facilitate the buying up of existing cinemas and the building of new ones, so that more monies from the exhibition sector would flow back into the industry. In 1942 Winkler formed the *Deutsche Filmvertriebs GmbH*, a centralised, non-profit-making distribution organisation to which all the *staatsmittelbar* companies had to belong. The trust itself – *Ufa Film GmbH* (Ufi) – was set up the same month, with its capital stock (the amalgamation of all the assets of the old *staatsmittelbar* firms) held by *Cautio*. The non-production side of the old *Ufa* became a holding company for a number of subsidiary companies, the most important of which was the above-mentioned distribution organisation, the others including companies involved in short film distribution, newsreel production, publicity material, copyright, film printing and so on. *Cautio's* functions were now largely taken over by Ufi, but all positions in the giant combine were filled under the supervision of Winkler and Goebbels.

Overall artistic control of film production was now placed in the hands of a new body within Ufi, the *Reichsfilmintendanz*. This was headed by Dr Fritz Hippler, an NSDAP stalwart since 1927 and the man responsible for *Der Ewige Jude* (1940). In line with the principles of *Gleichschaltung*, however, he still retained his position as head of the Film Department of the RMVP, which continued to look after directly political matters such as newsreel organisation, predicates, censorship and so on. The

Filmkreditbank was taken over by *Cautio* and functioned as Ufi's house bank.

The vast *staatseigen* trust showed a healthy profit in its first two years, and was independent of state aid although effectively state owned. It was the fourth largest industry in the Reich, the strongest film industry in Europe, many of its films were massively popular, and it paid healthy tax revenues to the Finance Ministry. The intensifying war obviously caused increasingly serious problems, but it's hard to avoid the conclusion that National Socialist film policy was extremely successful in its own terms. As we shall see below, Goebbels fully understood that only a strong, economically sound film industry could function as a truly effective ideological state apparatus. Furthermore, his insistence, against the clamour of the National Socialist 'radicals', on maintaining as far as possible the capitalist *modus operandi* of the industry, clearly appealed strongly to its leaders. These worked with the new regime because its plans, which they had been instrumental in drawing up in the first place, looked like offering a solution to the industry's recurring crises from which they would benefit in that they would only further strengthen their firms' and their own personal economic positions.

Sticks and carrots

Let us now turn to National Socialist film policy towards the actual content of the films produced during this period, examining first of all formal censorship procedures in the Third Reich. A new cinema law, the *Lichtspielgesetz*, was passed in 1934 (see also Martin Loiperdinger in this volume). This replaced the previous law of 1920, but, like the development of Ufa, Third Reich film censorship needs to be seen as a continuation of a process with its roots deep in the politics of Weimar. Thus, for example, the 1920 law established a censorship office (*Filmprüfstelle*) which was empowered to ban any film which threatened to 'endanger public order or security, to harm religious sensibilities, to brutalise or deprave, or to endanger German prestige or Germany's relations with foreign states', to which an emergency decree of 1931 added any film that might 'endanger the essential interests of the state'. The 1934 law simply decreed that, along with religious sensibilities: 'National Socialist, moral and artistic' ones must be protected too. Up until 1934 there were two censorship offices, one in Berlin and one in Munich. Each had a chair, who examined films with the aid of four assessors drawn from the teaching and legal professions and from the industry itself. The new law combined these offices in Berlin and incorporated them into the Film Department of the Propaganda

Ministry. It also did away with the majority voting system and vested all effective power in the chairman, who was a Ministry official. A new system of pre-production censorship was instituted, whereby all screenplays (as well as all completed films) were to be submitted to the *Reichsfilmdramaturg*, who also worked in the Film Department of the Propaganda Ministry and had the power to intervene in the affairs of the censorship office. The first *Dramaturg* was Willi Krause, formerly a journalist on Goebbels' paper *Der Angriff*. Naturally, in line with the *Führerprinzip*, Goebbels had the right to overrule any decisions taken by the censorship office or the *Dramaturg*. In the event, there was little film censorship of anything other than a fairly trivial (and, during the war, increasingly paranoid) kind, for the simple reason that National Socialist film policy ensured that no seriously problematic films were ever made in Germany in the first place.[9]

In many ways more significant than its additions to the censorship system was the Third Reich's development of a system of positive incentives to produce films deemed worthwhile by the authorities. This was the *Prädikat* (predicate) system, whose origins, again, predate the Third Reich. Predicates were special honours, carrying tax relief, which were given to films judged to be particularly worthwhile by the Chamber for Film Evaluation of the Central Institute for Education and Training. During the Weimar period, predicates could be awarded to films on the grounds that they were either instructional, popularly improving, culturally valuable, or artistic. The 1934 Film Law decreed that predicates would in future be awarded by the RMVP *Prüfstelle*, and the system became more overtly politicised. Predicates available during all or part of the 1933–45 period were: especially valuable, politically valuable, politically especially valuable, artistically valuable, artistically especially valuable, politically and artistically especially valuable, valuable for youth, nationally valuable, film of the nation, and commendable. The highest distinction (politically and artistically especially valuable) meant that the film was entirely exempt from entertainment tax, while the film of the nation and valuable for youth predicates carried no actual tax relief but greatly enhanced a film's status and made it more likely to be selected for showing in schools and Nazi youth organisations. After 1938 no exhibitor was allowed to refuse to show a politically valuable film if offered one. The predicate system not only carried tax advantages but, like the elaborate publicity which accompanied the release of predicated films, it also helped to establish certain audience expectations.

Propaganda and ideology

Hitler and Goebbels fundamentally disagreed about the most effective forms of film propaganda. Above all, Hitler believed in directness; as he put it: 'I want to use the film fully and completely as a medium of propaganda, but in such a way that every viewer knows that today he's going to see a political film'.[10] Goebbels, however, in a speech marking the inauguration of the Chamber of Culture, stated that: 'what we want is more than a dramatisation of the Party's programme' and that there was 'no particular value in having our stormtroopers march about on stage or screen. Their place is on the street ... The National Socialist government has never issued an order for stormtrooper films to be made. On the contrary, it would regard an excess of them as dangerous.'[11]

However, Goebbels' most revealing (though rarely cited) remarks on propaganda and on the cultural role of National Socialist ideology are contained in a speech made to the Chamber of Film in 1937:

> In general one doesn't bother to talk much about those things that are necessary to life, since their very necessity makes them a matter of course. For example, we don't bother to talk about the air which we breathe in and out, although we couldn't live two minutes without air. For us air is a matter of course and we regard talking about it as superfluous: it is there, it surrounds us, it is an element of our lives. National Socialism, which concerns basic attitudes and the spiritual and holy character of the Nation, is akin to the air's function concerning the human respiratory organs. We breathe it in and we breathe it out. We live in its atmosphere. We see how it is gradually materialising in every sphere, in every circumstance, question and person. An art which tries to ignore this will not be understood by the people. There is no sphere which can shut itself off from this commonly shared atmosphere ... I do not in the least want an art which proves its National Socialist character merely by the display of National Socialist emblems and symbols but, rather, an art which expresses its attitude through its National Socialist character and through raising National Socialist problems. These problems will penetrate the hearts of the German and other peoples more effectively the less ostentatiously they are handled. Overall, it is a fundamental characteristic of efficacy that it never appears as intended. At the moment that propaganda is recognised as such, it becomes ineffective. However, the moment that propaganda, message, bent or attitude as such stay in the background and appear to people only as storyline, action

> or side-effect then they will become effective in every respect ... I don't want art for the sake of a message but to insert the message into the greater overall design.[12]

The most obvious point to be drawn from these remarks is that Goebbels clearly realised that *covert* was far more effective than *overt* propaganda. From a contemporary perspective, one might say that Goebbels was arguing for the primacy of ideology over politics in the cinema. And certainly, his parallel between National Socialism and the air that we breathe reveals an understanding of the workings of ideology at an everyday, taken-for-granted, unacknowledged level that irresistibly recalls Gramsci's analyses of the ideological dimensions of 'common sense'. Indeed, it's sometimes hard to avoid the conclusion that Goebbels understood the ideological dimension of the movies rather better than did the early historians of Third Reich cinema, with their overly narrow focus on politics and propaganda.

Reactionary modernism

Recent historians of Third Reich cinema have taken Goebbels' emphasis on covert propaganda as the starting point for an argument that National Socialist film policy's greatest achievement was not the creation of the ruthless and sinister propaganda machine of popular imagining – what Eric Rentschler refers to as the 'Teutonic Horror Picture Show' – but of a highly successful, modern, commercial cinema producing movies that ideologically underpinned the Third Reich in ways more subtle than has generally been suggested. In this, it could be seen as an excellent example of the 'reactionary modernism' delineated by Jeffrey Herf, or of what Goebbels himself called '*stählernde Romantik*' ('steely romanticism'). As the latter put it:

> We live in an era of technology. The racing tempo of our century affects all areas of our life. There is scarcely an endeavour that can escape its powerful influence. Therefore, the danger unquestionably arises that modern technology will make men soulless. National Socialism never rejected or struggled against technology. Rather, one of its main tasks was to consciously affirm it, to fill it inwardly with soul, to discipline it and to place it in the service of our people and their cultural level.[13]

Undoubtedly the really striking aspect of most German cinema from this era, on first acquaintance at least, is not how 'other' it is but just how closely it resembles contemporaneous Hollywood, with its stars, studios, genres, formulae, 'classical' narrative structures and so on. It's a world

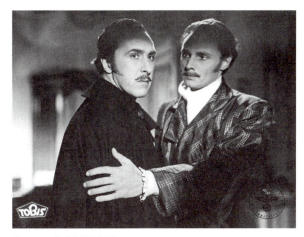

Romanze in Moll (1943)

Everyday fascism

What this requires, clearly, is that analyses of Third Reich movies are firmly grounded in an understanding of National Socialist ideology, not forgetting its contradictions (which are contained in its very name) and concentrating in particular on how this ideology manifested itself in the most mundane, taken-for-granted aspects of daily life in the Third Reich – 'everyday fascism', if you will. Such analyses need, crucially, to take into account the fact that these films have much in common with their Hollywood contemporaries – especially in formal terms – and the equally important fact that they contain much that is unique to them. Thus both Hollywood and Third Reich movies offer their viewers a whole range of imaginary seductions, but although the ways in which this is done may be strikingly similar, the seductions themselves differ in certain important respects, informed as they are by different social, political, cultural and ideological realities. However, having once isolated the particular 'social fantasies' which animate Third Reich movies, fantasies which typically attempt to reinforce a particular *kind* of imaginary collective identity and sense of social harmony, it is important to avoid an oversimplified, homogenised, cari-

of historical period pieces, biopics, frothy musicals, tear-jerking melodramas, and a rather hand-me-down Romanticism, all adding up to what Rentschler aptly calls a 'kitschy hyper-*gemütlichkeit*'.[14] As Linda Schulte-Sasse puts it: 'The fact that the first five minutes of any Nazi feature film generally tells us where our emotional alignment belongs (even if today, with our twenty-twenty hindsight, we may refuse to co-operate) should tell us we're in familiar territory.'[15] Rentschler himself reinforces this crucial point, albeit from a very different standpoint, when he notes that, 'in many respects, these images from the past are very close to us, closer than we might imagine, closer than some people might like'.[16]

This is not of course to deny that the Third Reich produced overtly 'political' and propagandist films such as *Hitlerjunge Quex* (1935), *Jud Süß* (1940) and the like. However, this approach does succeed in moving beyond the limiting notion that the only ideological function of the vast majority of apparently 'non-political' films made in the Third Reich was, in Erwin Leiser's words, to 'distract the audience from reality and lull them to sleep, generally by means of the battery of clichés manufactured in the arsenal of Nazi propaganda', sound in the comfortable belief that 'the old, cosy idyll still prevailed'.[17] Rather, as Rentschler argues, in order to grasp

> how Nazi films captivated spectators and promulgated
> political meanings, one must comprehend the way in
> which films interacted with and resonated within larger
> social constellations. Ideology more often than not came
> sugar-coated, in gripping, engaging and pleasant packages
> of entertainment which co-existed with other emanations
> of everyday culture.[18]

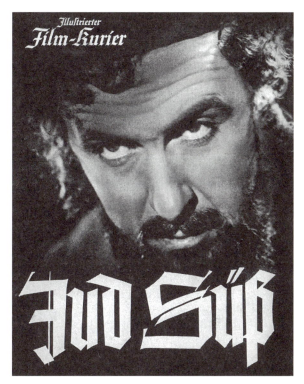

Jud Süß (Courtesy Harmssen Collection, University of Warwick)

caturial image of National Socialism becoming what Schulte-Sasse calls 'another kind of social fantasy, a convenient Other against which we can find our own, untroubled identity'.[19]

Rather more problematic, however, is Schulte-Sasse's argument that Third Reich films reveal the contradictions within National Socialist ideology on occasion; this they certainly do, but she then goes on to suggest of these films that: 'not only are they riddled with the same ruptures and internal subversions that beleaguer virtually all narrative texts, but that the popular success many enjoyed may be tied precisely to those ruptures, which compromise – if not necessarily contradict – their "Nazi message" '.[20] The problem is, however, that Schulte-Sasse fails to adduce much evidence, other than her own textual analyses, for such a suggestion, drawing neither on the weekly SD (*Sicherheitsdienst der SS*) reports which, from 1940 onwards, recorded public reactions to the more prestigious films, nor on works such as Detlev Peukert's *Inside Nazi Germany: Conformity, Opposition and Racism in Everyday Life* and Hans Dieter Schäfer's *Das gespaltene bewusstsein: uber deutsche Kultur und Lebenswirklichkeit 1933–1945* (*The Divided Consciousness: German Culture and the Reality of Life 1933–1945*) which explore the gaps between 'official' culture and various forms of everyday popular culture in the Third Reich. This is not, of course, to object to Schulte-Sasse's textual analyses *per se*, nor to textual analysis in principle, nor to its application to Third Reich movies. If it is accepted that the majority of these films are less 'other' than was once generally supposed, then clearly they are as amenable as any other 'classical' narrative films to textual analysis. Furthermore, if one accepts that National Socialist ideology has significant elements in common with other forms of bourgeois ideology, then Third Reich films are open to similar kinds of ideological critique as other forms of dominant cinema. As Thomas Elsaesser has argued, German films produced between 1927 and 1939 can be regarded as a form of propaganda for the modern lifestyle (albeit a modernity conceived largely in reactionary terms), which is one reason for their continuing popularity: 'After all, we still share the same aspirations towards the good life, embodied in lifestyles and consumption, and our sense of history, tradition, the nation and cultural identity is still shaped by the technological media (re-)constructing their human interest value and personal significance.'[21]

Whilst fully agreeing with Elsaesser, Rentschler and others who have come increasingly to take this kind of approach to Third Reich cinema, it is, however, important to stress the elements in National Socialist cinema which do indeed make it 'other': in particular, the role played by both state and party in the film industry, the elements of specifically National Socialist ideology contained in the films which it produced, and, of course, the viewing context itself, which, to put it mildly, was hardly conducive to 'deviant' readings of films. This last factor, I would argue, does give rise to a certain uneasiness about Schulte-Sasse's textually based approach. Furthermore it is an approach which, unfortunately, offers – entirely unwittingly no doubt – intellectual ammunition both to political naifs such as David Stewart Hull, whose *Film in the Third Reich* paints a bizarre picture of the Third Reich film industry as a hotbed of political subversion, as well as, more seriously, to those who need no encouragement to argue that the National Socialist state was perhaps not so brutally oppressive after all. On the contrary, however, the real lesson of Nazi film policy is just how easily entertainment, spectacle and diversion lent themselves to the most abhorrent political and ideological ends, and just how willing were apparently 'unpolitical' bureaucrats and businessmen in the entertainment industries to facilitate and profit from this process. As Rentschler puts it: 'Nazi media culture demonstrated just how potent and destructive the powers of fascination and fantasy can be, especially when systematically appropriated by a modern state and strategically implemented by modern technology.'[22] Today, it is no longer states which wield such formidable powers but the vast global media conglomerates of Berlusconi, Murdoch and their ilk, none of whom has hesitated for a moment to utilise their media for their own political and ideological purposes when it suits them. The politics themselves may be different (although not *that* different in the case of some of Berlusconi's allies), but the media – and, in a broad sense, some of their messages – are the same, except now vastly augmented by the resources of television and the information superhighway.

Notes

1 Eric Rentschler, *The Ministry of Illusion: Nazi Cinema and its Afterlife* (Cambridge, MA: Harvard University Press, 1996), p. 227.

2 Quoted in David Welch, *Propaganda and German Cinema 1933–1945* (Oxford: Oxford University Press, 1983), p. 20.

3 Klaus P. Fischer, *Nazi Germany: A New History* (New York: Continuum, 1996), p. 278.

4 For a detailed discussion of the 1927 reorganisation of Ufa see Klaus Kreimeier, *The Ufa Story: A History of Germany's Greatest Film Company, 1918–1945* (Berkeley: University of California Press, 1999) and Jürgen Spiker, *Film und Kapital:*

der Weg der deutschen Filmwirtschaft zum nationalsozialistischen Einheitskonzern (Berlin: Volker Spiess, 1975), pp. 42–6.

5 Quoted in Kreimeier, op. cit., p. 166.

6 Wolfgang Becker, *Film und Herrschaft: Organisationsprinzipien und Organisationsstrukturen der nationalsozialistischen Filmpropaganda* (Berlin: Volker Spiess, 1973), p. 104. Non-German speakers can find a summary of Becker and Spiker's main points in Julian Petley, *Capital and Culture: German Cinema 1933–45* (London: British Film Institute, 1979), pp. 29–94.

7 Quoted in Gerd Albrecht, *Der Film im Dritten Reich* (Karlsruhe: DOKU-Verlag, 1979), pp. 30–31.

8 Becker, op. cit., p. 41. The construction of Ufi is described in detail on pp. 35–42, in Kreimeier, op. cit., and in Spiker, op. cit., pp. 98–102.

9 For a detailed discussion of film censorship in both Weimar and the Third Reich see Becker, op. cit., pp. 72–96, and Klaus-Jürgen Maiwald, *Filmzensur im NS-Staat* (Dortmund: Peter Nowotny, 1983). Films censored during the Third Reich are the subject of Kraft Wetzel, *Zensur: verbotene deutsche Filme 1933–1945* (Berlin: Volker Spiess, 1978).

10 Quoted in Richard Taylor, *Film Propaganda: Soviet Russia and Nazi Germany*, 2nd edn (London: I. B. Tauris, 1998), p. 148.

11 Quoted in Erwin Leiser, *Nazi Cinema* (London: Secker and Warburg, 1975), pp. 34–5.

12 Gerd Albrecht, *Nationalsozialistsche Filmpolitik: eine soziologische Untersuchung uber die Spielfilme des Dritten Reiches* (Stuttgart: Enke, 1969), pp. 456–7.

13 Quoted in Jeffrey Herf, *Reactionary Modernism: Technology, Culture and Politics in Weimar and the Third Reich* (Cambridge: Cambridge University Press, 1984), p. 196.

14 Rentschler, op. cit., p. 2.

15 Linda Schulte-Sasse, *Entertaining the Third Reich: Illusions of Wholeness in Nazi Cinema* (Durham and London: Duke University Press, 1996), p. 232.

16 Rentschler, op. cit., p. 7.

17 Leiser, op. cit., p. 12.

18 Rentschler, op. cit., p. 217.

19 Schulte-Sasse, op. cit., p. 11.

20 Ibid., p. 4.

21 Thomas Elsaesser, *Weimar Cinema and After: Germany's Historical Imaginary* (London and New York: British Film Institute, 2000), pp. 408–09.

22 Rentschler, op. cit., p. 222.

17

New German Cinema and History: The Case of Alexander Kluge

Thomas Elsaesser

Irreconcilable memories: the New German Cinema's return to history

Asked why American rock music and movies had been his 'life savers' during the 1960s Wim Wenders once replied: 'Twenty years of political amnesia had left a hole: we covered it with chewing gum and Polaroids.'[1] When international audiences applauded H.-J. Syberberg's *Hitler – ein film aus Deutschland* (*Our Hitler*, 1977), R. W. Fassbinder's *Die Ehe der Maria Braun* (*The Marriage of Maria Braun*, 1979), Helma Sanders-Brahms' *Deutschland, bleiche Mutter* (*Germany, Pale Mother*, 1979), Volker Schlöndorff's *Die Blechtrommel* (*The Tin Drum*, 1980) and Edgar Reitz' *Heimat* (1984), the New German Cinema appeared not only to have overcome amnesia, but to have its identity firmly located in an obsession with the recent past. During the 1970s, many national cinemas explored their country's history in order to rewrite it as spectacle: France, Italy, Britain, Australia all had their filmic *mode rétro* or heritage movie moment. But none had quite as horrific a past to examine, narrativise or otherwise to 'master'. In several of the above examples, the genre of the family melodrama became the favoured mode, while the more historically probing accounts remained the territory of others: throughout the 1960s and 70s, film-makers such as Alain Resnais, Marcel Ophuls, Claude Lanzmann and Edgardo Cozarinsky arguably looked more deeply into Germany's 'heart of darkness' than German directors themselves.

But the New German Cinema's turn to the past comprised several different facets. Besides the feature films, there were lesser-known but no less searching and self-searching reconstructions: political chronicles, collage films about Hitler's *Autobahns* or about the steel industry; films that let Nazi propaganda shorts speak about pocket money and pollution, and films that let ex-Nazis and anti-Nazis speak about the Spanish Civil War. The documentary mode metamorphosed into the so-called 'essay film', setting out to be political about the personal, and personal about politics. Neither straightforwardly fictional, nor autobiographical or documentary, these essay films often had a distanced, discursive stance, arguing private feelings and emotional limit situations. Such, for instance, was the case of Alexander Kluge, notably in two essay films that secured his international standing: *Die Patriotin* (*The Patriot*, 1979) and *Die Macht der Gefühle* (*The Power of Feelings*, 1983).

Of the many non-fiction films made during those decades, few reached the attention of an international public, but bore witness to the doubts which the first post-war generation had about West Germany's too easily restored normality. Thus they addressed themselves primarily to domestic (television) audiences. But with the anti-authoritarian student movement of the late 1960s and urban terrorism of the mid-1970s as two of its historical pressure points, the New German Cinema even here retained an international political perspective and a radicalised subjectivity. Yet one feature was remarkable, not least for going unremarked for a very long time: the absence of the Holocaust in either the feature films or the essay films.

The Holocaust in West German cinema: absence as presence

Today, it is a cliché to say that if one looks for traces of the Holocaust in West German films of the immediate post-war period, one is likely to be disappointed. But the fact that the same is almost as true of the so-called 'New German Cinema' of the 1970s and 80s is something of a surprise. While in the internationally known films mentioned above, the home front during the Second World War became a major topic, the plight of the Jews, their persecution and annihilation is rarely mentioned. Nor did the post-war diaspora and the difficult Jewish-German dialogue, sometimes known as the 'negative symbiosis' after Auschwitz, receive much attention.[2] The few occasions where Jewish characters do appear, their representations have invariably given offence. One thinks of R. W. Fassbinder's controversial play *Der Müll, die Stadt, und der Tod* (*Garbage, The City and Death*, made in 1975 into the film *Schatten der Engel* [*Shadows of Angels*] by Daniel Schmid), Hans-Jürgen Syberberg's resentful remarks about West Germany after the War having too readily accepted the Jewish émigré version of post-war culture, the Charles Aznavour figure in *The Tin Drum*, or Edgar Reitz' *Heimat*, where the deportations and the camps are conspicuous by their absence. What could be more natural, if not inevitable, than to conclude from this that a pervasive disavowal was in place, and that in the face of the unimaginable at such proximity, repression and invisibility had set in? One is even inclined to fear that the most gifted generation of film-makers in Germany since the 1920s has been guilty of complicity, or at the very least, has sinned by omission.[3]

There are two things that concern me about this, apart from the fact that, as with all received wisdom, there is a grain of truth in it. First, I am worried by how perfectly legible this absence now is from the vantage point of the ubiquity of the Holocaust in the media since the 1990s. What is it that in turn is now barely being seen, what is overlooked in the perhaps excessive looking during the 1990s? And second, I also wonder whether the absence of the German-Jewish dialogue need always be read across the paradigm of repression and amnesia, of denial and disavowal. In both cases, it is probably the seeming security of our own position of knowledge from hindsight that makes me uncomfortable. But it is also the way in which, more generally, presence and representation are equated, and given a positive valuation in an opposition that makes absence the negative term.

For what would the presence of say, credible, positive or sympathetic Jewish characters in these films have signified?

It seems fairly obvious that a depiction by a German film-maker of the Holocaust from the perspective of the victims, or a version of the Jewish experience in Germany after the War would have been at once too much and too little. Too much, in that it would have easily given the illusion of normality: the good Jew, the positive identification figure is a trap that Fassbinder for instance, always wanted to expose, and one that Henryk Broder once satirised in his imaginary German who says: 'If I take the trouble to be philosemitic, the least I can expect is that the Jews know to behave themselves.' Crucially, a fictional story of a specific Jewish character, embedded in post-war German everyday reality, invariably serves in some sense as a token delegate, a fetish: the burden of representation this Jew would have to carry would in several senses be 'monstrous'. But such positive or even monstrous representations would also be too little, because they might afford the viewer a good conscience at too small a price. The cinema's dilemma, as the discussion around *Schindler's List* (1993) has proven, is its temptation to show, to bring to life, to animate – but it runs the risk of bringing back to life too much, and therefore, to betray to representation and immediacy what owes its place in time and its commemorative presence precisely to the signifiers of a distance that is irrecoverable.

An example of the *mise-en-scène* of an outright denial can be found in Alexander Kluge's first film *Abschied von Gestern* (*Yesterday Girl*, 1966), where the heroine Anita G. appears before a judge for shoplifting. After going through her personal data and noting that her parents had been deported to Theresienstadt and their property confiscated, the judge provocatively asks whether Anita claims that what happened to her parents in 1938 had any bearing on the case for which she was before him. 'No,' replies Anita, 'nothing whatsoever.' This unsettlingly matter-of-fact scene makes denial visible, but it does so from the knowledge position of superior irony. The judge, framed from the back with a thickset neck and a rasping voice, becomes the epitome of the arrogant German, sitting in judgment over others when it is he who probably deserves to be tried. But the exchange also makes clear that merely to feature a character who says s/he is Jewish does not represent the presence of the Holocaust in German post-war society. And how could it, given that we are concerned with something whose significance at least in part resides in its absence: an absence determined by physical absence and material destruction, but also by an absence in the thoughts and emotions of the West Germans that are the films' protagonists?

In other words, the absence of Jews in the films of the New German Cinema in the first instance confirms – and in this sense, truthfully records – the fact that their absence in the public and private life of West Germany in the 1960s and 70s was not missed. Invisibility was the order of the day even for the small Jewish communities who made Germany their home after 1945. They kept themselves doubly invisible: invisible to the Germans, for fear of arousing hostility and in order to allow more efficient negotiations behind the scenes with the federal authorities about compensation and reparation. But they made themselves invisible also because of the disapproval they knew themselves exposed to in Israel and the US diaspora, for continuing to live in Germany, the land of the murderers.

Why was mourning work for these murdered Jews in the immediate post-war period such an impossible task for Germans, why did it appear to encounter such obduracy? The reply sometimes given refers to the affective deadlock of the so-called 'ordinary Germans', who, it is said, could not mourn someone else's dead, if they were not allowed to mourn their own dead. One cannot share the grief of the other, if one cannot grieve for oneself. These and related issues were at the core of the acrimonious exchanges also known as the 'historians' debate' about two kinds of catastrophe, about two kinds of victims – 'theirs' and 'ours': the dead of the firestorms and the expulsions from the East, and the dead of the camps and of forced labour.[4] Some of the contributions not only seemed to measure and set up as equivalent what was uniquely incommensurable, they also set off 'Germans' against 'Jews', thus depriving German Jews of their citizenship twice over.

The problem faced by the directors of the New German Cinema – assuming they put it to themselves – was therefore: how to show what is not there, especially if its not-being-there is not missed? But even then, the question of representing German–Jewish relations in the New German Cinema is imperfectly put, if it does not factor in the insisted-upon, frequently demanded, and never adequately shown repentance expected by the world of the German people. This inadequacy, which is not a measurable quantity, but the locus of several kinds of impossibility, points to one of the paradoxes with which I began, namely the all-too perfect legibility of this absence today. The deadlock can, in my view, only be opened up, if absence and presence are not constructed antithetically, but if the possibility of presence is recognised within absence: in this case of remembering and forgetting, it is only *within* absence that can one begin to look for signs of presence, not against it. In other words, how can the cinema show this missing as missing, how can it 'perform' this double missing, and come to terms with it?

Presence as parapraxis

As I indicated, it is generally assumed that most attempts in Germany at 'mourning work' have failed (this is the famous 'inability to mourn', as described in Alexander and Margarete Mitscherlich's *Die Unfähigkeit zu trauern*).[5] My working hypothesis will be a different one: first, I shall introduce a distinction between different kinds of mourning work, and second I shall argue that nowhere is the absence of the consequences of the Holocaust more present than in the New German Cinema of the 1970s. Yet the figures of such presence-in-absence do not function according to the repression/disavowal mode, nor do they conform to the standard model of 'mourning work', that of mourning work as 'working through' of loss, the de-cathecting of the internalised love object, and a letting go. Instead, one may have to imagine a multi-stage process, with one crucial step being situated somewhere between the 'acting out' of melancholia and the 'working through' of mourning.[6] This step I am calling 'presence as parapraxis'.

By parapraxis I am referring to Freud's *Fehlleistung*, usually translated in English as parapraxis. The German term is more precise, not least because *Fehl-* can mean both failure and missing, and *Leistung* refers specifically to the performative aspect which interests me, as well as to the concept of 'work', as in mourning work. As we shall see, 'work' is also the concept of choice in Alexander Kluge, the film-maker I am here especially concerned with. I define parapraxis for my purposes therefore not as the 'slip of the tongue', or the lapse in attention, but as a kind of effort, a kind of persistence, usually one with unexpected or unwanted results, including typical reversals or displacements in time and space. For instance, one feature of parapraxis I shall highlight is the way in which it often seems to figure 'the right thing at the wrong place, the wrong thing at the right time'. Such an example of parapraxis might be the final scenes of R. W. Fassbinder's *The Marriage of Maria Braun*, when the heroine places a rose on a hat stand, and a handbag in the flower-vase.

This shift of terms from 'working through' to 'parapraxis' would not discard the idea of mourning work. On the contrary, it would clarify and expand the term, making it productive where it at first sight might appear to have failed most spectacularly, namely the communication between Germans and Jews since 1945. *Fehlleistung* would thus quite literally be 'performed failure', which I see in contrast to 'failed performance' (about which more below). Mourning work in Freud, it will be recalled, does not consist merely of 'working through': according to his essay 'Mourning and Melancholia' it encompasses three stages –

'remembering, repetition and working through'. My hypothesis would be that the films of the New German Cinema implicitly take the first two stages to be as necessary and indispensable to mourning work as the third, which means that as historians and analysts we need to attend to them, too, as well as to their textual effects and figurative presences. With regard to the Holocaust, we may – collectively and culturally – even after fifty years or so, be only at the stage of 'remembering', or possibly at the stage of 'repetition', which suggests that the very omnipresence of the Holocaust as media-event in the 1990s and beyond partakes in mourning work, but in a way that makes compulsive iteration symptomatic for its in-completion.

In order to find a somewhat more direct way into these regimes of repetition of the New German Cinema, I would like to illustrate briefly the distinction 'parapraxis as mourning work' ('performed failure') and 'mourning work as parapraxis' ('failed performance'). By the latter I mean the often spectacularly failed, officially prescribed acts of public mourning in West Germany, usually resulting in a kind of repetitive ubiquity of mishaps and *faux pas*. In particular, I am referring to the many incidents and occasions in the public life of the old and the new Federal Republic during the last fifty years when something went badly wrong with Germany's ability to either commemorate or celebrate. It stretches from the *faux pas* of a German diplomat at a Russian Embassy reception in 1955 who angered his hosts when he refused to toast the liberation of Germany by the victorious Red Army in 1945 (as a patriot he saw it as a 'defeat'), to the novelist Martin Walser, who as recently as 1998 and as publicly as in his acceptance speech for the Frankfurt Book Fair Peace Prize, meant to pay his respects to the memory of the Jews when he spoke of Auschwitz as the 'moral stick' that the world was still beating Germany with, prompting a violent and despairing attack from Ignaz Bubis, the then Head of the Council of Jews in Germany.[7] In between lies a seemingly unending catalogue of such public embarrassments and scandals, of which the Kohl–Reagan visit to the Bitburg military cemetery in 1985 and the November 1988 speech by the President of the Bundesrat, Philip Jenninger, commemorating the so-called *Kristallnacht* in 1938 are among the most notorious examples.

The New German Cinema, on the other hand, I would argue, gave in the 1970s many examples of the opposite, 'performed failure', where figurative tropes such as catachresis or zeugma, stylistic peculiarities such as repetition or abrupt montage, as well as rhetorical strategies of reversal and irony all point to a 'politics of performative misalignments' whose effect is an ongoing return and repetition

around something which, perhaps only now and certainly only with hindsight, can be read and deciphered differently: as a 'mourning work-in-progress'. Among the parapraxes as mourning work one would, for instance, count some of the works of R. W. Fassbinder and Werner Herzog, including:

- R. W. Fassbinder's already mentioned *Der Müll, die Stadt und der Tod*. This is, although a play, the most extreme attempt at an identification with the perpetrators, staging a mimicry of the anti-Semite that was destined to be 'misunderstood'. Here it is noteworthy that it was the play that caused the scandal, while the film (Daniel Schmid's *Schatten der Engel*) did not. Fassbinder, it seems, used the public sphere of theatre for his spectacular parapraxis, while his filmic mourning work or requiem on the same theme, but in much more muted tones was the film 'about' the suicide of his former lover, Armin Meyer:
- *In einem Jahr von 13 Monden* (*In a Year with 13 Moons*, 1978). There, Fassbinder tries to transpose German-Jewish relations after Auschwitz into the terms of the melodramatic temporality 'if only', coupled with a science-fiction temporality of 'what-if'. Their mutual non-alignment results in the most extreme form of loss of body-image, gender identity and subjectivity, with the hero no longer able to symbolise either, in language of body, the relation between self and other.[8]
- Parapraxis as mourning work in Werner Herzog: across his alter egos Klaus Kinski und Bruno S. and their respective polarities, in films such as *Aguirre, der Zorn Gottes* (*Aguirre, Wrath of God*, 1972), *Fitzcarraldo* (1982), *Wozyeck* (1978), *Jeder für sich und Gott gegen alle* (*The Mystery of Kaspar Hauser*, 1974) and *Stroszek* (1977), Herzog has given us a fairly consistent meditation about two extremes of a human (but also typically German) habitus. The ten films that Herzog made with or about these two actors are studies of boundless egoism and immoderation, of self-abandon and extremes of non-violence. The films are about a peculiar communication within non-communication, they are a reflection about victims that do not feel as victims, about perpetrators who are their own worst enemies. One could speak of Herzog's mourning work as taking place in the mode of inversion. The humility and remorse demanded of the Germans make themselves known in Herzog only across the repetition of the gesture of hybris and excess, as a consequence of which if not remorse, then a special kind of insight may perhaps follow. Often in Herzog, a conscience, overwhelmed by an awareness of punishment, invents for itself a crime that justifies the acting out of guilt and self-reproach as its after-effect.

Alexander Kluge's building sites of history

How does mourning work present itself in the films of Alexander Kluge, the director who has often been called the father of the New German Cinema? One has to step back and look at this most enigmatic director in a broader context to come to an answer. He made a remarkable start in the late 1960s with *Abschied von Gestern* and *Artisten in der Zirkuskuppel: Ratlos* (*Artists Under the Big Top: Perplexed*, 1967). But after his role in the omnibus film *Deutschland im Herbst* (*Germany in Autumn*, 1978) and the two films already mentioned – *The Patriot* and *The Power of Feelings* – Kluge the film-maker was presumed to have disappeared behind the activist in film-politics and the professorial author of sociological treatises. In the mid-1980s, by appearing to abandon the cinema in favour of television, Kluge furthermore seemed to have become a sort of 'traitor' to the *Autorenfilm* and a double agent for the new commercialised media-landscape.

One could, however, say that in vacating the space of making films, he opened up a space of reflection on how to look differently at the cinema's role in and for (German) history. He has recently published his collected stories, reconfirming his strong voice as the foremost chronicler of Germany during the second half of the twentieth century. More controversially perhaps, my argument will be that Kluge's work – in its entirety, his stories and treatises included – can be seen as an exemplary case of mourning work, and as a probably unique way of 'figuring' the Holocaust in post-war Germany, not by representing it, but by bringing into focus what stopped it from being represented. It was in part due to the incomplete mourning work of Germany for itself, not begun in earnest until the belatedly opened debate – eventually named by Jürgen Habermas – of how Germany would find a new 'patriotic' relation to its history, and how especially the (unified) nation could come to acknowledge the disasters of two world wars, while still looking ahead to its role in (unified) Europe.

In Kluge's work, the figure of Anita G. from *Abschied von Gestern* has remained unique. Kluge was never again to use such heavy and direct irony as he did in 1965. Something else took over, though I do not think his critics have always understood what this was. For instance, the absence of Jewish protagonists in Kluge has not gone unnoticed. The critic Jörg Drews, after a lengthy stay in the USA, asked in 1985: 'what does it mean, incidentally, that in [Kluge's film] *The Patriot* the murder of the Jews appears to be entirely excluded from Gabi Teichert's excavations of German history – a fact noted with great amazement by my American students?'[9]

Yet if one starts from the premise that in Kluge's work too, the Holocaust is present, though in the mode of *Fehlleistung*, 'performed failure', then Drews' question does begin to find a possible answer. Indeed, it opens up such a wide field of reference that it becomes difficult to know where to begin. If one adds one of Kluge's books, a certain logic begins to emerge. *Geschichte und Eigensinn* (co-written with Oskar Negt, 1981) presents itself at first sight as an extended historical meditation on human productivity and human labour power, a kind of third volume to Karl Marx's *Das Kapital*.[10] But it makes even more sense to see this vast tome that chronicles 2,000 years of Germanic history in the context of the paradigm of parapraxis, of what in the world of work and human labour constantly misfires, goes awry and misses its intended goal or target. This central thematic in Kluge revolves around the concepts of 'history' (*Geschichte*) as deferred action (*Nachträglichkeit*) and of subjectivity as 'obstinacy' or 'obduracy' (*Eigensinn*).

Emblematic for instance – and altogether paradigmatic for Kluge's view of subjectivity and deferred action – is an episode in *The Power of Feelings*. It is introduced by Kluge in voice-over saying: 'saved thanks to someone else's fault' ('*gerettet durch fremde Schuld*'). In the scene a woman, slumped unconscious in her car in a car park, is raped by a commercial traveller who happens to park his car next to hers. However, by raping her, he actually and accidentally saves her from death, because – abandoned by her lover – she had swallowed an overdose of sleeping pills and was intending to commit suicide. What might this strange scene signify? Its anecdotal-episodic appearance in the film – we never see either the woman or her rapist again – is altogether typical for the apparently frivolous-farcical nature of many of the unconnected incidents littering Kluge's films. Yet supposing we consider it under the heading of *Fehlleistung*, and turn this bizarre fictional/narrative construction by 180 degrees, as it were. In so doing, we arrive at an intriguingly different, 'alternative' situation. Instead of 'rescued through someone else's guilty act', we get the inverse possibility, namely of someone incurring guilt and making himself guilty, by *not* rescuing someone in mortal danger. Held against the background of the presence-in-absence of the German response to the Holocaust, the reference of the scene then becomes clearer: it would be to the guilt (-feelings) of those not having come to the Jews' rescue during the years of confiscation, expulsion and deportation. This 'guilt by omission' is one of the central aspects of the relation between German Jews and 'ordinary' Germans during the Third Reich. But the purpose of the reversal of the historical situation as (para)practised by Kluge would go further than merely alluding to this fact. It would allow for a 'virtual' or utopian dimension, nurturing the insanely forlorn hope that in the non-existent, forever deferred and therefore always present trial of the German people regarding its responsibility for the Holocaust, the victim – as in the case of the raped woman – might testify on behalf of the guilty party, by claiming not to have seen/noticed/been aware of having been raped. In other words, the 'dialogue' or communication tentatively initiated in this scene expresses the hope that the Jews might one day absolve the Germans by yet another sort of 'uneven exchange',[11] but at what price: murder becomes attempted suicide, the Jewish people become 'feminised', and genocide becomes a sort of 'consenting rape'. As if to underline the transgressively absurd nature of this proposition, Kluge's voice-over – commenting on a no less improbable hostage-taking and kidnap –

asserts: 'what is an even stronger bond than a marriage? – an act of murder, if all know about the fact that each of the others is implicated.' This, too, sounds familiar: such bonding in mutual guilt has often been cited as an explanation for the homophobic-homoerotic blood-brotherhood that kept the Nazi leadership together and beholden to the Führer.

If this construction sounds a little far-fetched, one might consider another scene in *The Power of Feelings*, in which Kluge gives a kind of meta-commentary on his own method in yet another trial scene. A housewife is accused of having grievously wounded her husband with a shotgun. The judges are trying to establish what her motive was and whether she acted in self-defence, which she denies. Then, one of the judges laboriously twists and turns the imagined firearm, in the hope of understanding how it was possible for the heroine to shoot her husband when, according to her, she only wanted to produce a loud enough bang to shut him up. Here the physical gestures of aligning weapon and target, and not succeeding in doing

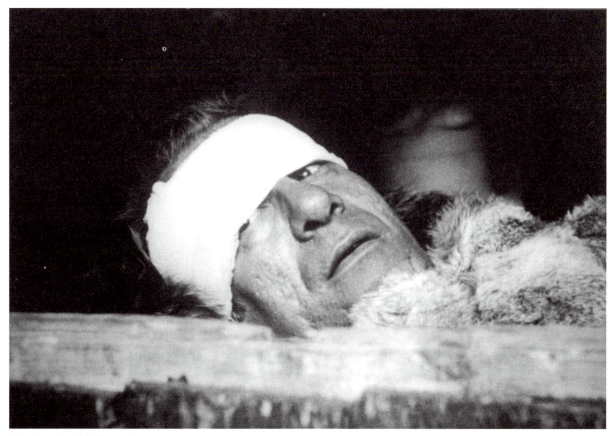

Die Macht der Gefühle (1983)

so, are like a graphic illustration of the kinds of cognitive twists and misalignments which constitute Kluge's argumentative method.

Am I merely reading this into the films? Yes and no: yes, of course, in that, the unspoken and the not-seen, which I claim was typical for the New German Cinema, makes such a 'presence-in-absence and absence as parapraxis' only legible when held against a double frame of reference. One frame of reference is the contemporary, universalised Holocaust discourse, which gives us the illusion of being able to formulate the question of representation 'objectively', from a presumed position of knowledge. The second one emerges from the blocked dialogue or 'negative symbiosis' between Germans and Jews *after* Auschwitz, where, across the official discourse of 'mastering the past' a mandate confronts a demand, with each rendering the other at once 'impossible' and 'inaccessible'. It is this deadlock, I argue, that produces *Fehlleistungen* both in politics and in the films. So: no, I'm not making this up, since the two public spheres – cinema and politics – relate to each other mirror-fashion: to the instances of 'failed performances' of public life, the reflexivity of the films responds with 'performed failures'. The New German Cinema thus becomes the 'allegorical' mode of West German political discourse, figuring both *Fehl* and *Leistung*. Loss becomes (hit-and-) miss, miss is mis-, and mis- or para- becomes the necessary task of the filmmaker: to work on the images and representations, to work on the different non-synchronicities and temporalities, to work on the discourses of guilt and responsibility, on the moments of omission and commission. In short, such work is indeed that form of mourning work, where 'acting out' must precede 'working through', leaving its traces in the form of compulsive repetitions, conceptual catachreses, cognitive re-alignments and tragi-grotesque reversals.

In *The Patriot*, where some of these complex filiations of historical montage-effects ('the violence of contexts' as Kluge calls them) are worked out in greatest detail, it is the knee joint of a dead German soldier – the body part standing for the whole – that is made to voice a demand for recording and reclaiming these energies, in scenes whose pathos would be unbearable if the conceit, and Kluge's manner of handling it, was not so whimsical.[12]

Yet the whimsicality is also a purposively performed parapraxis, in the form of mimicry and dissemblance. For it is not impossible to see what sort of displacements, gaps and reversals have taken place around this *pars-pro-toto* of the German knee. One would only have to substitute for the knee of Soldier Wieland a solitary shoe, a pair of

Die Patriotin (1979)

glasses, a comb or a gold tooth, to get a sense of what this passage would be like if it was these part-objects, so familiar from the archive footage of the camps, that had suddenly decided they no longer wanted to be silent. It would be both monstrous and unbearable. But, then, if one takes a closer look at the pictures that Kluge uses in this sequence from *The Patriot*, one is struck by an uncanny recognition: are these not the 'right images', but in the 'wrong' place? Do these prisoners of war who are looking at us, not belong to the images we have become used to seeing from the camps or from the rounding up of ghetto inhabitants, rather than from the trek of hungry Germans, marched here into Soviet camps after the defeat at Stalingrad? And why does the scene start with a deceptively idyllic picture of the Wartburg, the home of Martin Luther, one of pre-Hitler Germany's most notorious and vociferous anti-Semites, if not to name something the more insistently by *not* naming it? The same shock of recognition in misprision overcame me when coming across the images near the opening of another of Kluge's films, *In Gefahr und grösster Not bringt der Mittelweg den Tod* (*The Middle of the Road Is a Very Dead End*, 1972), set in Frankfurt during the student movement and the housing riots (events which were to haunt the German foreign minister Joschka Fischer in 2001). Among the high-rises of 'Mainhattan', the camera focuses on some municipal workers digging up a street. But do these workers silently pushing their shovels not look like forced foreign labour, once again facing the camera with the wordless hostility of those having to bear the indignity of being classified, registered, objectified by the gaze of a camera? It was only then that I remembered the sentence that serves as the motto at the very beginning of the film: 'Inge Maier looked on: she had the feeling she was watching the wrong movie.'

Trauma, scar and wound: let it bleed

What memories do these images evoke, what feelings might they stir in an audience, what rebus pictures have to be deciphered in Kluge's work? To give an example from *The Power of Feelings*: at one point Kluge enigmatically announces: '*Die Narbe arbeitet nicht wie die Wunde*' ('a scar does not work like a wound').[13] This is followed by a scene where the heroine interviews a British airforce officer about the RAF bombing raids. But instead of offering a political rationale or apologies for the firestorms of Dresden, Hamburg, Magdeburg or Halberstadt, the officer uses an oddly clinical simile about the conditions under which a wound can heal without leaving a scar. The officer speaks of the firestorm as a necessary wound, tearing open the scar tissue of a grown city in order to make it bleed, because only fresh blood can clean a wound and commence the healing process. Strangely incongruous and inappropriate to the terrible damage inflicted on Germany's venerable cities and its civilian population, this metaphor nonetheless gains in plausibility if applied to the 'scarred' (the word Kluge's officer uses is 'scabby') relationship of Germans to their own historical conscience, but also to the sensitivities between Germans and Jews after 1945, scarred and rendered scabby by the misunderstandings, mistakes and tactlessness which have kept the 'skin' (i.e. contact and context of the 'failed' encounters) at once oversensitive and overexposed.

Let it bleed: narrating the German disaster from such a perspective thus serves also another end. By making history bleed, Kluge wants to bring the past back to life, but neither as spectacle nor even as documentary simulacrum. Kluge revives feelings Germans once had about themselves that have become tabooed, which he does with extracts from such films as Fritz Lang's *The Nibelungen* (1924), Rudolf Foster's famous lines 'a German knows how to die' from *Morgenrot* (1933), or by playing snatches of once popular songs ('*Schwör' mir nicht, du bist für immer mein, keine Liebe kann für ewig sein . . .*'/'Don't swear you will be mine forever, no love can last eternally'), while showing smudged, grainy photographs torn out of newspapers in somebody's secret scrapbook.[14]

Is Kluge, then, a revanchist, a conservative nationalist masquerading as a concerned liberal and even left-winger? Certainly, in his rumination about memory and history, about the singular event and the repetition-effects of trauma, the dead he thinks he needs to mourn are not the victims of the Holocaust: they are the (West-)Germans, as they see themselves and their history. The 2,000 years of futility itemised in *Geschichte und Eigensinn* are the back-

projection to a traumatic core that Kluge identifies as the years 1943 to 1947, the period of the retreat and exodus, military and civilian, from the East, following the collapse. The Germans Kluge and Negt are thinking of may have been 'willing executioners' or they may have been victims, they may have been victims who thought themselves heroes, they may have thought themselves victims but were actually criminals, or they may not have thought of themselves in any of these categories, but simply tried to survive. In all events, one's first impression is that the authors' *Trauerarbeit* concentrates on those publicly forgotten dead, and those who perished in – or survived – the aerial bombing raids, the refugee treks heading west, fleeing or expelled, ahead of the victorious Soviet troops.[15] Given the impasse between unacceptable anti-Semitism and self-censoring silence, Kluge seems to say, a way must be found of also mourning this history, but it will have to take a very special form if it is ever to become part of a dialogue, opening up a space of communication. Under these circumstances, parapraxis becomes the only form of authenticity, the only kind of speech act of troubled souls.[16]

But there is another twist, which reverses the image of the revanchist. I have argued that Kluge's mourning work – as indeed the logic of his entire oeuvre – is located at the stage of 'repeating', moving, as Freud might have said 'on the path of imitation'. This, too, has not escaped the critics, and again, it has been noted disapprovingly. Drews has gone so far as to call Kluge a ventriloquist, someone who speaks only through others, not merely creating 'personas', but 'impersonating' them as a ventriloquist uses his dummy.[17] And it is true: one never knows when Kluge is serious, and when – in his deadpan way – he merely feigns seriousness. But the fact that he so often appears in a disguise that denies that it is disguise seems more likely to be proof of his belief in the authentic than the contrary, since the very nature of his task presumes that the only way towards proper mourning is through the mimicry of necessary failure. What earlier I called the uncanny aspect of Kluge is his ability to simulate the tabooed, and put himself in its place. Where he differs from Fassbinder in *Der Müll, Die Stadt und der Tod*, or from Jenninger's misguided attempt to speak on behalf of both Germans and Jews, is in his strategy of disavowing the disavowal, in order to reveal the possibility of reversal, and thus of coming to some form of exchange. Kluge mourns for his Germans, paradoxically by exposing them to ridicule, and even more paradoxically, by punishing them: after being shown as hopelessly naive, his protagonists mostly perish, often in humiliating and always pointless circumstances. The strategy hints at the therapeutic purpose of the reversal of roles:

the characters he describes so vividly, whose biographies he supplies – factory workers, farm-hands, smallholders, shopkeepers, bureaucrats, accountants – were these not precisely those Germans of whom the majority not only did *not* perish, but actually prospered both during the War and since? Were they not among the tens of thousands who after 1945 were never brought to account, never had to confront their part in history and catastrophe? Kluge concentrates in his stories and films on the biographies of the petit bourgeois, most of whom could have been Nazis, and probably were Nazi sympathisers: among the many lives he recounts, there are, for instance, no Jewish biographies. Those who actually died in their millions, and who were left alone in the absurdity and meaninglessness towards which their lives were moving, it would seem, have lent their fate to Kluge's Germans, wearing the futility and incomprehension of their Jewish compatriots' death like a disguise, a mask, another form of mimicry. Yet more uneven exchanges are being enacted, a mortgage is taken out on the future, in which 'ventriloquist' irony and the cold gaze of the satirist's discourse become a kind of camouflage for the (yet to be voiced) 'authentic' response to both kinds of death. Across the battle of Stalingrad and the firestorm of Halberstadt, he seems to want to approach Auschwitz, about which no German can presume to speak 'authentically'. In this situation, does it make sense to try and separate the 'good' dead from the 'wrong' dead? If redemption is ever to come to Germany for its crimes against humanity, Kluge seems to imply, it can only come when it comes to all.

In this light, Kluge's move from film-making to film politics and to television journalism also takes on another meaning: it becomes the politics of experience and memory, in direct relation to the cinema's ambiguous role as both 'too cold' (Stalingrad) and 'too hot' (Halberstadt) for history, since this history can never be simply 'relived' just as it is never 'dead'. As the constantly renewed experience of loss, the cinema's power of feeling is necessarily melancholic. But if this melancholy derives in Kluge from the knowledge that in mourning the 'wrong' Germans, he mourns himself, then his marathon perseverance comes from an equally certain knowledge that as a 'wrong' German, he is not alone. My sense is that Kluge's memory and mourning work has once more become important, not to say topical, because it is like a template for the way West and East Germans may not even have begun to do *Trauerarbeit* for each other. In 1995 Kluge published the conversations he had had on his TV programmes with Heiner Müller, the East German playwright. *Ich schulde der Welt einen Toten* (*I Owe the World One of the Dead*) was

the title.[18] It is a sentence that not only East and West Germans can heed. Elsewhere in the world, too, in the aftermath of civil wars or ethnic cleansing, such melancholy and mimicry as Kluge's may have to prepare the mourning work for the twenty-first century. With his parapractical discourse Kluge may have found a 'learning process' that is open to the future, precisely to the degree that its repetitions are programmatic, and its absences the result of too much presence fighting for a space in which all manners of non-presence can be made to signify. We recall the heroine's thought from *In Gefahr und grösster Not*: '*sie hatte das Gefühl, sie sei in den falschen Film geraten*' (she felt she was sitting in the wrong movie). To have persisted with so much *Eigensinn* in making 'the wrong movie' for the past thirty-five years: this is surely Kluge's greatest contribution to the mourning work of post-war Germany, for it is in his artfully constructed and yet nevertheless deeply disturbing *Fehlleistungen* that the outlines of a possible dialogue designate themselves, however negatively its lines of communication may have to be inferred, and however deferred or delayed its redemptive presence may still remain.

Notes

1 The line originally is from Velvet Underground ('her life was saved by rock'n'roll'). See L. M. Kit Carson, 'Dejeuner Diary', *Film Comment*, June 1984.

2 Dan Diner, 'Negative Symbiose – Deutsche und Juden nach Auschwitz', *Babylon*, 1 (1986), pp. 9–20.

3 See M. Hansen *et al.*, 'Dossier on *Heimat*', *New German Critique*, 36 (Autumn 1985), pp. 4–16.

4 Jürgen Habermas, *The New Conservatism: Cultural Criticism and the Historians' Debate* (Cambridge, MA: MIT Press, 1989); A. Hillgruber, *Zweierlei Untergang: Die Zerschlagung des Deutschen Reiches und das Ende des europäischen Judentums* (Berlin: Siedler, 1986).

5 Alexander and Margarete Mitscherlich, *The Inability to Mourn* (London: Tavistock, 1975).

6 Dominick LaCapra, *History and Memory after Auschwitz* (Ithaca, NY: Cornell University Press, 1998).

7 References to the Martin Walser–Ignaz Bubis controversy are from *Die Zeit*, September 1999.

8 This argument can be found in my chapter 'Beyond Schuld and Schulden', in *Fassbinder's Germany: History–Identity–Subject* (Amsterdam: Amsterdam University Press, 1996), pp. 197–216.

9 Jörg Drews, 'Leseprozesse mit tödlichem Ausgang', *text+kritik, Heft 85: Alexander Kluge*, 85–6 (Munich: edition text+kritik, 1985), p. 31.

10 In its size, binding, lettering and colour-scheme, the edition of *Geschichte und Eigensinn* mimics the (East-) German edition of the MEGA, the *Marx-Engels Gesamtausgabe*, widely acquired (but rarely read) by students in the early 1970s.

11 See my discussion of 'uneven exchange' in *Fassbinder's Germany*, pp. 253–6.

12 The conceit of the knee goes back to a famous nonsense poem by Christian Morgenstern, 'Ein Knie geht um die Welt'.

13 *Geschichte und Eigensinn*, p. 125.

14 In an interview with Gary Indiana, Kluge speaks of his slots on television as responding to the need for a microscope and a telescope within general programming. *Village Voice*, 25 October 1988.

15 For a commentary on Syberberg's 'anti-Semitism', see Eric L. Santner, 'The Trouble with Hitler', *New German Critique*, no. 57, Summer 1992, pp. 5–24. The repatriates from the East made an appearance in the so-called *Historikerstreit*, when Andreas Hillgruber, in his essay *Zweierlei Untergang*, polemically demanded equal attention for them as victims as was given to the victims of the Holocaust. See Saul Friedlander (ed.), *Probing the Limits of Representation* (Cambridge, MA: Harvard University Press, 1992).

16 The relation between *Nachträglichkeit* and disavowal is specified by Kluge in a footnote, *Geschichte und Eigensinn*, p. 501.

17 Jörg Drews, 'Leseprozesse mit paradoxem Ausgang', in *text+kritik, Heft* 85: *Alexander Kluge* (Munich: edition text+kritik, 1985), p. 23. Similarly, Werner Barg complained that Kluge, in his television interviews, misuses his interviewee merely to make them say what he wants and needs them to say. Werner Barg, 'Ein Dokumentarist des Protests', in Manfred Hattendorf (ed.), *Perspektiven des Dokumentarfilms* (Munich: diskurs film, 1995), p. 126.

18 Alexander Kluge/Heiner Müller, *Ich schulde der Welt einen Toten* (Hamburg: Rotbuch, 1995). Their television dialogue over several years constitutes one of the most interesting and intriguing records of a nation's 'talking cure' that ever was conducted in the public media

18

Women Film-Makers, the Avant-Garde and the Case of Ulrike Ottinger

Ulrike Sieglohr

Introduction

Unlike other feminist film histories which acclaim the contributions made by female pioneers to the national film industry, German feminist film history has revealing lacunae concerning the fascist period, constructing either a post-fascist matriarchal legacy from the mid-1960s – as if May Spils, Ula Stöckl and Erika Runge were the pioneers for post-war West German women directors – or else returning to pre-fascist 'pioneers'. Controversial figures such as the scriptwriter Thea von Harbou and the documentary film-maker Leni Riefenstahl, even though more powerful in the 1930s than almost any other women in the international film industry – tainted as they were by their fascist connections – were best ignored.[1] Characteristically, the post-war generation of women film-makers in West Germany preferred to perceive themselves in terms of their film practice as a 'motherless generation' (as did their male counterparts in New German Cinema). Thus while Anglo-American feminist film criticism proudly excavated a forgotten female film history (including contributors such as Dorothy Arzner, Ida Lupino, Wendy Toye and Muriel Box), for German feminist film historians this pursuit of legitimate 'role models' was more ideologically selective, but perhaps as a consequence also led to broadening the quest beyond directorial assignments. This was, for instance, the case with pre-fascist Asta Nielsen, the star of many silent films, who by 1913 had *auteur*ist control of her own films and an entitlement to a third of the profit.[2] In this context Leontine Sagan should also be mentioned, even though she only made one film in Germany, *Mädchen in Uniform*

(*Girls in Uniform*, 1931), since her film is still internationally acclaimed as a milestone in lesbian film-making.

Moreover, until German reunification in 1989, West German film histories remained largely ignorant about developments in the GDR in general and specifically about women film-makers' involvment in the state-owned DEFA. Despite women's constitutional legal equality, from the late 1970s only a few women like Iris Gusner, Evelyn Schmidt and Helke Misselwitz directed feature films, and women's contribution was mostly in the field of children's films and documentaries which depicted the realities of women's experiences under state-controlled socialism.[3]

Frauenfilm and the Other cinema

This very brief introduction provides a broader frame for understanding the key concerns of this chapter, namely the institutional promotion – albeit limited – of a women's cinema movement, the *Frauenfilm*, as part of the state- and television-subsidised but male-dominated New German Cinema.[4] In the wake of the 1968 student rebellion and with the emergence of the women's movement, new institutional frameworks emerged that helped women film-makers by providing funding. From the mid-1970s in particular, the experimental *Das kleine Fernsehspiel* – a television drama department of the national station, *Zweites Deutsches Fernsehen* – offered opportunities to many first-time film-makers, including women. Nonetheless, in general women had to compete with already established male *auteurs* such as Rainer Werner Fassbinder, Werner Herzog and Wim Wenders, and to campaign intensively to receive funding and media access. Recognising the need for an infrastructure to combat this gender inequality, Helke Sander and Claudia von Alemann organised, in 1973, the first International Women's Film Seminar and in 1974 the feminist film journal *frauen und film* was founded. The journal became an important forum for discussing ideas and organising practical issues, such as distribution, exhibition, film festivals and the Association of Women Film Workers (1979).[5]

During the 1970s many women film-makers had a political commitment to the Left and were actively engaged in the women's movement. Therefore, their concern was initially less with formal experimentation than with didactic socialist/feminist agitation and information. Crucially, many feminist film-makers developed their aesthetics through practice, rather than through prior theoretical engagement with dominant cinema.[6] West German feminist film-makers, the 'cine-feminists' as they became known, tended to engage with the indigenous art cinema's mode of address (i.e. ambling narratives that lingered on details and seemingly unimportant events, stressed mood rather than actions, and conveyed an overall sense of ambiguity). While some women worked in the tradition of an *auteur* cinema in the general sense of self-expression, for most authorship came into play pragmatically in the more specific sense of the New German Cinema, which was organised around the concept of *Autorenfilm*. Unlike films made under the classical studio system, the *Autorenfilm* involved the author/film-maker in all stages of a film's production. This artisanal approach to film-making was often determined by chronic underfunding rather than by aesthetic/ideological considerations. But it was thanks to this financial-practical configuration that aspects of formal experimentation – often dismissed as amateurish – informed much of the work of New German Cinema in general, and specifically *Frauenfilm*.

Sander tirelessly argued that it was not enough to attack the ruling patriarchal ideology, but to confront it concretely at the workplace, namely the arts industry. In that confrontation she recognised the inevitability of 'amateurish' outcomes but argued nonetheless for women's right to self-representation – to 'seeing their bodies with their own eyes'. Her polemic captures the spirit of the time: '[W]omen's most authentic act today – in all areas including the arts – consists not in standardizing and harmonizing the means [patriarchal conventions of expression], but rather in destroying them. . . .[7] Sander's comments are typical of this early period in the sense that political activism rather than *auteur*ist self-expression is seen to be the motivating force for many women film-makers.

Margarethe von Trotta, like Fassbinder, uses melodrama as a powerful device for an engaged political cinema, as for instance in *Die bleierne Zeit* (*The German Sisters*, 1981).[8] A number of films engaged also with historical processes from a feminist perspective: Jutta Brückner's semi-autobiographical film *Hungerjahre – in einem reichen Land* (*Years of Hunger*, 1979) depicts growing up in the repressive Adenauer era, and Helma Sanders-Brahms' internationally acclaimed but nationally controversial autobiographical film, *Deutschland, bleiche Mutter* (*Germany, Pale Mother*, 1929) indicts patriarchy for the rise of fascism and the atrocities of war. While most women film-makers worked within the margins of the subsidised New German Cinema, for a very few, including Birgit Hein and Dore O., the co-op-based avant-garde Other Cinema became the enabling framework. It had its separate infrastructure, organising alternative distribution, screenings and film shows through its own venues. Crucially, here film-makers had to exist largely without government subsidies, and they had a greater affinity with the international experimental cinema (in terms of organisational structure and aesthetic preoccupations) than with the contemporaneous New German Cinema. Whereas the latter, despite formal inventiveness, had a basically narrative orientation, the Other Cinema tended to investigate the specificity of the medium, with narrative playing only a minor role.[9] These film-makers, many from a fine art background, examined the structural possibilities of filmic parameters such as static camera, flickering effects, superimpositions, slow and speedy camerawork, repetition and loops. Birgit Hein identifies some of the key ideas and strategies as follows: '[T]he main thing was that we wanted to work with film as with painting: not to tell stories, not to represent reality, but to show rhythm, movement and light.'[10]

Despite its ideological and formal radicalism, however, the Other Cinema was another mostly male enclave, which gave prominence to such figures as Lutz Mommartz, Werner Nekes, Adolf Winkelman and Klaus Wyborny, while perceiving its participating women as minor players and supportive wives. The Other Cinema's commitment to experimentation and to breaking with conventional forms of cinema did not really challenge a privileged male perspective. To put it bluntly, its approach – albeit formally innovative – remained in the tradition of historical avant-garde movements which had promoted radical politics and sexual freedom – as long as they did not erode patriarchal power. It is revealing that the two foremost experimental women film-makers worked closely with their husbands: Dore O. set up a group in Hamburg with Werner Nekes and they collaborated on a number of films before she made her own structuralist and poetic films, starting with *Alaska* (1968); Birgit Hein switched from abstract painting to film-making because it enabled collaboration with her husband, Wilhelm. In 1968 the two co-founded X-SCREEN (a forum for propagating and showing innovative films) in Cologne, and for over two decades they continued jointly making films and staging multi-media events. Though frustrated with the label of film-maker's wife (she established herself independently as an art historian and critic of experimental film[11]), Hein rejected notions of a specific female aesthetic, and argued in 1984 that even a film like *Love Stinks* (1982), despite its focus on female sexuality, remains very much a joint project with her husband.[12]

Thus importantly, even though the Other Cinema's co-op infrastructure promised equal opportunities, more women film-makers flourished within the government-funded New German Cinema. Certainly in the 1980s, a new generation of women turned towards experimentation, but this was with different concerns and different strategies from those of the Other Cinema. With hindsight the rigorous formal aspect of structuralist film-making, the prevalent tendency of the Other Cinema, did not seem an appropriate expressive mode for feminist film-makers who wanted counter-images and counter-strategies for representing themselves – body and psyche.

It is important to realise that the strategies developed by New German Cinema 'cine-feminists' contributed to the general development of a feminist aesthetic polemics concerned with challenging male-defined notions of femininity and liberating women from prescriptive models. Sander's work can be seen as exemplary in the way it developed from didactic shorts towards feature-length films with intricate image tracks matched with increasingly complex soundtracks. An early example of this tendency is Sander's *Die allseitig reduzierte Persönlichkeit – Redupers* (*The All-round Reduced Personality*, 1977). This film, like her subsequent films, mixes fiction and documentary non-narrative montage sequences, the soundtrack constructs a female non-authoritative voice-over commenting sympathetically and sometimes ironically while shifting from first person to collective voice mode of address, which, alongside music passages, conveys a troubled female subjectivity. Similarly Brückner, whose earlier work had also been characterised by attention to realistic details – including stills and documentary footage – turned towards performance art. *Ein Blick – und die Liebe bricht aus* (*One Glance – and Love Breaks Out*, 1986) is a compulsive and stylised re-enactment of women's enslavement to passionate love. She foregrounds non-verbal strategies (music, sound effects,

pitch, rhythm, colour and choreographed gestures), and thus for Brückner spectacle and music rather than narrative become strategies for a feminist cinema. As she noted in 1982: 'The goal: recuperating the means to reconstruct symbolically . . . I mean recuperating our capacity to look. This has nothing to do with a specific style. There is no one feminist style . . . I am talking new departures.'[13]

Ulrike Ottinger's films – a case study

The films of Ottinger don't quite fit the expectations engendered by labels such as 'women' and 'avant-garde' film-maker, not least because her 1970s anti-realist films had hostile receptions from women when they were first shown, and similarly figureheads of the contemporary German avant-garde dismissed her work as too narrative-bound. Moreover, Ottinger's film-making trajectory from post-modernist surface to ethnographic authenticity, from surrealist fantasy to documentary realism constitutes a reversal of the more typical *Frauenfilm* development from documentary realism towards spectacular narrative fantasies. However, because of this lack of an easy fit into either 'women's' or 'avant-garde' cinema, Ottinger's early films are particularly significant in the way in which they straddle the two, sometimes antagonistic, areas. It is precisely her problematic status which makes her a useful figure through which to highlight some of the broader relationships between these groups and also vis-à-vis the male representatives of New German Cinema. Ottinger, as a case study, clarifies retrospectively what was at stake for some 'cine-feminists' in their turning away from didactic realism towards an engagement with formal experimentation. Her rejection of realist conventions initially alienated many women. In other words, her experimental approach to representing female subjectivity was at the expense of accessibility, and her exclusive appeal to minority audiences was at odds with feminist egalitarian principles. Yet Ottinger's work, while out of synch with dominant trends in the 1970s, foreshadows contemporary developments; indeed she can now be seen – and this is a final reason for her inclusion as a case study here – as a figure who created continuities with the post-modernist/feminist present.

Although Ottinger's films were produced within the institutional framework of the New German Cinema, her most obvious allegiances were neither with its privileged and established male *auteurs*, nor with the dominant feminist ideology of contemporary women film-makers, but with the more experimental margin of underground cinema. Ottinger's work, with its stylised theatricality, its promotion of excessive artifice, its playful sound/music strategies, its appropriation of camp parody – albeit for lesbian spectators – had initially more in common with the films by gay film-makers Werner Schroeter[14] and Rosa von Praunheim than with those of other women film-makers (excepting Elfi Mikesch).[15] Significantly Ottinger's training in fine art,[16] conjoined with a lesbian aesthetic-erotic sensibility, enabled her to develop an idiosyncratic non-patriarchal aesthetic quite a few years before formal challenges had become a central issue among feminist film-makers. In this sense her work, like that of Valie Export and Hein is shaped by specific historical avant-garde movements, but originates in a homosexual subjectivity – hence her affinity with Schroeter and von Praunheim – rather than with feminist counter-cinema. Though Ottinger's work is concerned with an exploration of image/sound relation, in opposition to narrative drive, it is not experimental in the structuralist mode of the Other Cinema; rather her style of associative visual-musical collage is inspired by earlier avant-garde movements, in particular surrealism.[17]

A detailed discussion of *Bildnis einer Trinkerin* (*Ticket of No Return*, 1979) as an exemplary film may illustrate to what extent Ottinger's experimental tropes are derivative of the historical avant-garde movements and other *auteurs*,[18] and also clarify how her approach linked the developing experimental tendency, especially in relation to sound, to that of the 'cine-feminists' for non-patriarchal ends. But first I want to refer briefly to the films which established Ottinger's reputation as an idiosyncratic experimental film-maker.

Having made a documentary, *Berlinfieber – Wolf Vostell* (*Berlin Fever*, 1973), and two short fiction films, *Laokoon & Söhne* (*Laokoon & Sons*, 1972–4) and *Die Betörung der blauen Matrosen* (*The Seduction of the Drunken Sailors*, 1975), she made her first feature *Madame X – eine absolute Herrscherin* (*Madame X – An Absolute Ruler*, 1977–8), which was a television co-production and shown in independent cinemas. Ottinger described the film as '[a] comedy about the women's movement'.[19] It is a parodic reworking of the pirate film genre: a group of women sail off on the Chinese junk 'Orlando' to find adventures, but having broken with a male-dominated society, they only reproduce among themselves the same destructive rituals of domination and submission.[20] The film, which has since become a lesbian cult film,[21] exemplifies Ottinger's efforts to renegotiate the image of woman as a figure of visual pleasure for the female spectator, but also to eroticise her

image for the lesbian spectator. She claimed in the early 1980s that *Madame X* 'was really misunderstood at the time'.[22] Nonetheless 'outspoken rejection and aggression' seemed to be matched by 'speechless fascination'.[23] Monika Treut, another lesbian film-maker, defended the film (four years after its release) on the basis of aspects which have since been appreciated for contributing towards an erotic aesthetic for women. She noted that *Madame X* does not represent female power, or its absence, but merely simulates reality by employing and parodying the signs and symbols of power.[24]

Ottinger's next feature films, *Bildnis einer Trinkerin*, *Freak Orlando* (1981), and *Dorian Gray im Spiegel der Boulevardpresse* (*Dorian Gray in the Mirror of the Popular Press*, 1983–4), feature the kind of visual tropes (camp exaggeration, artifice and parody) and sound strategies which became her authorial signature, and they continue to show a preoccupation with female identity as a construct, i.e. femininity as an explicitly artificial figure. As such they are further contributions to an experimental women's cinema. *Freak Orlando*, based on Virginia Woolf's novel and featuring Werner Schroeter's muse Magdalena

Madame X (1978)

Montezuma, relates the mythology of the social/sexual outcast through the ages.[25] *Dorian Gray in the Mirror of the Popular Press* engages with the themes of power, narcissism and identity. The film features a female drag figure, Dorian Gray (played by the model Veruschka von Lehndorff), and a female media tycoon, Dr Marbuse (Delphine Seyrig), and is a feminist/lesbian reworking of Fritz Lang and Oscar Wilde, imbricating German film history with gay history.[26]

What should also be noted is Ottinger's shift towards a documentary mode. In *China – Die Künste – Der Alltag* (*China – The Arts – The Everyday*, 1985–7), Ottinger's recurring theme of exoticism in her own culture is extended to engage with the 'real' exotica of Chinese art and society. As a westerner she approached the subject of a 'foreign' culture, by keeping the camera at a respectful distance, refraining from the use of penetrating zooms.[27] She let the images and sounds speak for themselves without imposing a commentary. In opposition to her controversial fiction films, this documentary was unanimously acclaimed by the critics. A further aesthetic renegotiation occurs in *Johanna d'Arc of Mongolia* (1988). Whereas the first part is highly stylised and reminiscent of early cinema, the interior of the Trans-Siberian/Trans-Mongolian Express compartments function like a stage and the scenic view is provided on painted backdrops, the second part is shot on location and the emphasis is on real time.[28] This is thus a feature film that straddles fiction and documentary, and sets in opposition western and oriental culture.

Ottinger's most recent films are also documentaries: *Countdown* (1990) observes Berlin in the final ten days before German reunification. *Taiga* (1991–2) is in three parts, an eight-hour-long ethnographic epic about the nomadic tribes of Mongolia. It is an extremely slow film with long takes/shots and few notable edits, thereby giving an impression of real time, of people being governed by seasonal changes. No narrator provides a commentary; instead the camera is positioned at some oblique vantage point 'watching people as they live their lives'.[29] *Exil Shanghai* (1997) – in two parts and over four hours long – chronicles the nineteenth-century Sephardim and then the Second World War European Jewish immigration to the city. The film mixes interviews, archival footage and contemporary scenes. 'Ottinger searches the present-day metropolis for synagogues, schools and saloons, the last traces of a Jewish expatriate culture.'[30] Thus the last two films, like *China*, continue to make strange a western outlook on distant locations and 'foreign' cultures. Although the documentaries appear to be the opposite of the earlier

fantasy films, they share with them a pursuit of 'authentic' modes of living. Moreover, films such as *Bildnis* and *Johanna d'Arc of Mongolia* also include documentary-style sequences, and as Brenda Longfellow comments about *Johanna d'Arc of Mongolia*:

> Ottinger's interest in the cultural Otherness of Mongolia is preceded, in her other features, by the recurring ironic representation of orientalism. The Chinese cook and Mao Mao, the South Pacific native in *Madame X*; or Hollywood, the faithful Chinese servant in *Dorian Gray*, are culled from the cultural stereotypes of western popular culture . . .[31]

Ottinger's awareness of the imaginary exotic has always underpinned her fantasies, but whereas in earlier films, as for example in *Madame X*, this is rendered as an explicit artifice and lesbian masquerade,[32] in the documentaries such as *China* and *Taiga* the camera observes, recording what is there for an ethnographer rather than appropriating and aestheticising 'orientalism' for a lesbian imaginary.

Bildnis einer Trinkerin

HOSTILE RECEPTION AND FORMAL PLEASURES

Bildnis einer Trinkerin is not, as the German title, 'Portrait of a Woman Drinker', suggests, a social problem film, but an often humorous surrealist fantasy of two women drinkers embarking on an unending binge in the city of Berlin. 'She' is young and beautiful, wealthy and never speaks. Her companion is Lutze, a well-known vagrant, who keeps all her belongings in a supermarket cart. Three women scientists, called 'Social Questions', 'Accurate Statistics' and 'Common Sense', arrive at the same time as the lady drinker, but for a conference on alcoholism. Dressed in hounds-tooth costumes, they accompany the drinkers and provide a running commentary on alcoholism. Emphasising surface and artifice, paradoxically, the film aims to represent female desire, but instead of psychologically fleshed out characters, we are confronted with the self-consciously artificial figure of 'She' and the allegorical three fates. The only 'realistic' figure is the bag lady and drinking companion, Lutze, who is depicted in documentary fashion.[33]

Bildnis explicitly foregrounds voyeurism and exhibitionism, parodying the conventions of woman as spectacle, and these controversial strategies engendered a violent debate among feminists. Interestingly, while the feminist journal *Courage*[34] appreciated the film, *frauen und film* reviewed *Bildnis* from an essentialist perspective, and was thus dismissive.[35] Ilse Lenz, for example, started her review in *frauen und film* by asserting that she liked some images and that this was not a polemic against Ottinger 'but I want to attack the image which this film has received as a women's or feminist film. I expect at the very least from a "feminist film" that women are not despised nor objectified, and that the person is given some autonomy, movement and development'.[36] Lenz took issue with the beauty of the central protagonist which reminded her of 'sexist advertisements'. She found it, she said, superficial, distancing and boring.

Helen Fehervary's comments were more ambiguous: 'I had an ambivalent reaction when watching Ottinger's films: I was exceedingly bored by all the familiar conventions regarding female beauty; yet at the same time the aesthetics fascinated, even seduced me. As a female viewer I have to account for both these reactions.'[37]

FEMINIST SOUND INTERVENTIONS

This divided reception would seem to indicate that *Bildnis* was not, as Lenz had suggested, antithetical to feminism, but that it in fact arose from differing reactions to an emerging tendency in feminist film. This tendency centres broadly around non-realist uses of the modes of representation and Ottinger's use of sound is one particularly striking example of it.[38] In her films sound becomes multi-layered, frequently associative and extra-diegetic, while also at times magnifying noises. A disjunctive sound/image relationship creates a tension productive of meaning which would be impossible in classical synchronised editing. To give a humorous example, when in *Madame X*, the leather-clad pirate queen is seduced by another woman, the images are synchronised to the sound of a lion roaring and then purring like a pussy-cat.

In *Bildnis* while Ottinger, in a manner reminiscent of the avant-garde Schroeter, employs music to underscore the highly stylised tableaux, she also includes unusual and heightened noises. In *Bildnis* sound compensates for the heroine's silence, and becomes the key device for conveying in complex ways an embattled female subjectivity. The multi-layered soundtrack includes extra-diegetic noises, or exaggerated sounds, such as the clicking of high heels on the pavement and the noise of breaking glass. Post-synchronisation allows for distorting sounds; thus in spite of synchronisation with the image, sound editing is not so much motivated by verisimilitude as by association. For instance, one scene involving the gun-slinging movie star Eddie Constantine contains the transformation of a shrieking voice into the whistling noise of a bullet. It seems that the silent drinker conveys her subjectivity to us through Ottinger's mediation of the aural. In the aural we register the obsession with intoxication, and its effect of ever-increasing isolation is signified by the suppression of diegetic sounds, and by snatches of drunken, meaningless conversation. Thus muffled and exaggerated sounds can be understood on one level as the effect of 'She's' permanent intoxication, while the associative quality of the sound is also an expression of her subjectivity.

RENEGOTIATING AESTHETICISM/VISUAL PLEASURE

While these experimental devices have been appreciated by some cinephile critics, those episodes which promote a heightened sense of aestheticism through fantastic costumes and use of stylish props have enraged some feminist critics, like Lenz. In many scenes in *Bildnis* the protagonist, played by the statuesque and beautiful Tabea Blumenschein, is purely staged for visual pleasure, and not for narrative purpose, nor for psychological insights. Aestheticism is foregrounded in the manner in which the heroine's decline and alienation is projected onto the surface, with colour/tones changing from vibrant red to an icy metallic blue. Similarly Berlin becomes like a glass cage with gleaming surfaces incessantly reflecting her own image. In other instances too aesthetic sensibilities dictate the *mise-en-scène*, for example when 'She' is depicted slowly ascending in a glass tower, or drinking the nectar of an exotic flower.[39]

Fehervary asserts that in Ottinger's films '[w]e find so much that is characteristic of the male avant-garde: the fetishisation of beauty and the female body; the directorial concept projected onto the "star"; images of sado-masochism.'[40] While Fehervary is not formally wrong, since the beautiful heroine is erotically objectified, ideologically Ottinger's striking visual strategies are motivated to engender a new aesthetic for women and lesbians. She develops a formal system of polarities for representing the female figure(s) through framing and camera distance, alternating between isolating close shot framing and her movement through the static frame (from close-up to extreme long shots of the heroine). The rigorous formal play of cinematic signifiers is a familiar strategy from experimental film-making, as is Ottinger's manipulation of sound, in particular with its associative potential and its juxtaposition with images. Yet here, they serve a different purpose, which is to subvert patriarchal mainstream conventions.

* * *

Bildnis einer Trinkerin (1979)

In the contemporary context of post-modernist debates, Ottinger's aesthetics have become familiar enough strategies. It is therefore perhaps not surprising that although her films were initially vilified by feminist reviewers, they were subsequently acclaimed by feminist scholars who recognised them as an exemplary contribution to a non-patriarchal woman's cinema. Her insistence on mythologising and aestheticising women's experience has retrospectively been validated by many critics as a more fruitful approach than a didactic feminism which focused on subject matter. Angela Hans Scheirl and Ursula Pürrer's (with Dietmar Schipeck) surrealist approach and 'cyberdyke' style in *Rote Ohren fetzen durch Asche* (*Flaming Ears*, 1991)[41] recall the amateurish lesbian aesthetic of *Madame X*. Most of all her former defender, Monika Treut, with her anti-moralistic, provocative and formally inventive films, has taken on the legacy of Ottinger, and like her she refuses political correctness and moves between features and documentaries.[42] Her film *Jungfrauenmachine* (*Virgin Machine*, 1988), although stylistically very different

from Ottinger's films, mixes fiction and documentary approaches and renegotiates visual pleasure for female and lesbian spectators.

The critical debates engendered by Ottinger's work in the 1980s and the early 90s include contributions by many of the most notable feminist film theorists who were exploring aesthetics other than those of the social real. Ottinger's films have been productive for illustrating some of the key feminist film theories, such as psychoanalytical concepts (fetishism, masquerade and narcissism);[43] post-modernism;[44] genre and gender (from a lesbian perspective);[45] and ethnographic and documentary issues.[46] Some of Ottinger's original pre-occupations with femininity as a playful, artificial rather than essential identity reverberate in contemporary feminist philosophical writings,[47] and even find a reflection in those recent scientific developments in medicine and computer technology which enable a radical reassignment of gender beyond the wildest dreams of 1970s gender utopias.

Conclusion

By the early 1980s New German Cinema, and therefore the *Frauenfilm*, no longer had institutional, or ideological support. Instead state subsidies and international co-productions gave rise to a much more populist, genre-orientated cinema. If there is any role model for contemporary women film-makers it is Doris Dörrie, whose post-feminist comedies in the 1980s showed a new tendency towards popular cinema. *Männer* (*Men*, 1985) was one of the most successful German films of the 1980s and an international hit. The popularity of *Men*, both with audiences and the critics, was a kind of reaction to the perceived doom and gloom of the former New German Cinema and *Frauenfilm*. *Men*, with its witty cynicism – which proposes that changing identity is just a change of clothes – was the antithesis of that earlier politicised and feminist film-making. Dörrie is not a feminist film-maker, indeed she is at pains to reject the label as marginalising her achievements with men.[48] Her role models were not fellow German feminist film-makers, Margarethe von Trotta, Helke Sander, Helma Sanders-Brahms – or any other female director – but Cassavetes and Scorsese, i.e. New American Cinema rather than New German Cinema.[49]

Among the 'cine-feminists' few remain active. The majority of women film-makers have only produced intermittent, low-budget films and thus remained marginal, and although in the 1980s von Trotta and Sanders-Brahms' were acclaimed, they were so as international *auteurs* rather than as part of a women's cinema. The diverse manner in which the enormous upheavals of the re-unification of Germany in 1990 were addressed by the 'cine-feminists' is revealing. As already mentioned, Ottinger documented this in *Countdown*, Sander made a complex historical documentary, *Befreier und Befreite* (*Liberators Take Liberties*, 1990),[50] while others made art films such as Sanders-Brahms' *Apfelbäume* (*Apple Trees*, 1991) and von Trotta's *Das Versprechen* (*The Promise*, 1994) – love stories set against the fall of the Berlin Wall.

Nowadays young women film-makers – mostly graduating from film school – would like to perceive themselves on equal terms with their male peers in a categorically commercially oriented German film industry. Indeed, arguably, they have now the same opportunities, although Katja von Garnier's acclaimed graduation film, the comedy *Abgeschminkt* (*Makin' Up*, 1993)[51] and her subsequent MTV-style trashy musical *Bandits* (1996), seem not to have led to a successful film career for the director but only for her star, Katja Riemann. Among the new generation, male directors such as Dominik Graf, Tom Tykwer and Sönke

Wortmann have managed to establish themselves while few women directors get to make films regularly; indeed, there appear to be fewer now than there were in the 1970s. If one takes the programmes of the German Film Festival (initiated by the Export Union of German Films) and the London Film Festival as indicators for recent trends and successes then a few women directors are still getting promoted. Among them are acclaimed features such as Caroline Link's *Jenseits der Stille* (*Beyond Silence*, 1998) and her *Pünktchen und Anton* (*Annaluise and Anton*, 1999), Vanessa Jopp's *Vergiss Amerika* (*Forget America*, 2000), Maren-Kea Freese's *Zoe* (1999) and Dörrie's comedy *Erleuchtung Garantiert* (*Enlightenment Guaranteed*, 1999). While in the new millennium some 'signs of life' seem to be re-emerging for a non-genre and independent cinema (see for example the films of Angela Schanelec, especially *Mein langsames Leben* [*My Slow Life*, 2001]) moving away from the relentlessly commercial impulse towards more personal storytelling, in the 1990s post-feminist film-making resembled more pre-feminist film-making. No special case, merely commercial viability counts, and ironically the most prominent young female figure of 1990s German cinema was a woman in front of the camera rather than one behind it (Katja Riemann rather than Katja von Garnier).

Notes

Thanks to Tim Bergfelder, Erica Carter, Jim Cook and Martin Shingler for their generous and detailed comments; also to Margaret Deriaz for keeping me up-to-date.

1 Von Harbou (who wrote all scripts for Fritz Lang's German films) joined the Nazi Party and had a thriving solo career scripting and supervising propaganda films. Riefenstahl, a close friend of Hitler, became most famous for directing *Triumph des Willens* (*Triumph of the Will*, 1935, a documentary about the 1934 Nuremberg Party Convention.

   Interestingly, Riefenstahl was celebrated in the 1970s in retrospectives at a number of international women's film festivals, though for obvious reasons this was not the case in Germany.

2 Heidi Schlüpmann, 'Ein Feministischer Blick: Dunkler Kontinent der frühen Jahre', in Wolfgang Jacobsen, Anton Kaes and Hans-Helmut Prinzler (eds.), *Geschichte des deutschen Films* (Stuttgart and Weimar: Metzler, 1993), p. 467.

3 See Margrit Frölich, 'Behind the Curtains of a State-Owned Film Industry: Women Filmmakers at the DEFA', in Ingeborg Majer O'Sickey and Ingeborg von Zadow (eds.) *Triangulated Visions: Women in Recent German Cinema* (Albany: State University of New York Press, 1998), pp. 43–63.

4 This emerged in response to an elaborate state funding system introduced in 1964 (television screenings were usually part of the deal).

5 For a history of this journal see Miriam Hansen, 'Messages in a Bottle?', *Screen*, vol. 28, no. 4, Autumn 1987, pp. 30–39; or Hansen, '*Frauen und Film* and Feminist Film Culture in West Germany', and also Ramona Curry, '*Frauen und Film*: Then and Now', both in Sandra Frieden *et al.* (eds.), *Gender and German Cinema*, vol. II (Providence, RI, and Oxford: Berg, 1993), pp. 293–308.

6 This is in contrast to the Anglo-American context where the thrust of feminist critiques was to analyse 'ruptures' in the text, as a basis for developing new oppositional strategies, and to envisage a feminist counter-cinema based on visual 'unpleasure'. See Laura Mulvey, 'Visual Pleasure and Narrative Cinema', *Screen*, vol. 16, no. 3, Autumn 1975; and Claire Johnston, 'Women's Cinema as Counter Cinema', in Claire Johnston (ed.), *Notes on Women's Cinema* (London: BFI, 1973).

7 Helke Sander, 'Feminism and Film' (1977), in Eric Rentschler (ed.), *West German Filmmakers on Film: Visions and Voices* (New York and London: Holmes & Meier, 1988), p. 81.

8 This approach is already evident in her first solo feature, *Das zweite Erwachen der Christa Klages* (*The Second Awakening of Christa Klage*s, 1978), a contemporary tale about a morally justified bank robbery.

9 Birgit Hein, *Film im Untergrund* (Munich: Ullstein, 1971), p. 132. See also Dietrich Kuhlbrodt, 'Querblicke: Vom Anderen Kino zum jüngsten deutschen Film', in Hoffmann and Schobert (eds.), *Abschied von Gestern: Bundesdeutscher Film der sechziger und siebzieger Jahre* (Frankfurt-am-Main: Deutsches Filmmuseum, 1991), pp. 100–05. Kuhlbrodt also provides a brief historical account.

10 Birgit Hein, 'Some Notes about our Film Work' (1980), in Rentschler (ed.), *West German Filmmakers*, p. 83.

11 Hein, *Film im Untergrund*.

12 Bo Meyerle *et al.*, 'Ein Interview mit Birgit Hein', *frauen und film* (Avantgarde und Experiment), no. 37, October 1984, pp. 95–102.

13 Jutta Brückner, 'Recognizing Collective Gestures', interview with Marc Silberman, *Jump Cut*, no. 27, 1982, p. 46.

14 She rejects, however, the frequently made comment that Schroeter influenced her work.

15 Elfi Mikesch, better known as a cinematographer, should also be mentioned as one of the few contemporary film-makers who shared a similar sensibility. Her films include documentaries, experimental shorts, stylised sexual fantasy scenarios and fiction films. See for e.g. the documentaries – *Was sollen wir denn machen ohne den Tod* (*What Would We do Without Death*, 1980) and the recent *Verrückt Bleiben, Verliebt Bleiben* (*Mind the Gap*, 1997); and the feature (directed and scripted with Monika Treut) – *Verführung: Die grausame Frau* (*Seduction. the Cruel Woman*, 1985).

16 Ottinger worked as a fine art painter, learned engraving techniques with Johnny Friedländer, created photomontages, and ran an art gallery and a film club before making her first film in 1972–4.

17 Ottinger proclaimed: 'I find myself rather isolated in the German film scene, particularly among my women colleagues, because my films come out of the tradition of fantasy and surrealist filmmaking.' Marc Silberman, 'Interview with Ulrike Ottinger – Surreal Images', *Jump Cut*, no. 29, February 1984, p. 56.

18 Some scenes are pastiches from other film-makers, such as one scene with a dwarf which is reminiscent of Herzog's films, and the absurd staging of acrobats, which recalls Fellini.

19 Grisham, 'An Interview with Ulrike Ottinger', p. 30.

20 See Patricia White, 'Madame X of the China Seas', *Screen*, vol. 28, no. 4, Autumn 1987, pp. 80–95; and Sabine Hake, ' "Gold, Love, Adventure": The Postmodern Piracy of Madame X', *Discourse*, vol. 11, no. 1, Autumn–Winter 1988–9.

21 Andrea Weiss, 'Women's "Art" Cinema and its Lesbian Potential', in Andrea Weiss, *Vampires and Violets* (London: Penguin Books, 1992), pp. 128–36; Judith Mayne, 'Mistresses of Discrepancy', in Judith Mayne, *The Woman at the Keyhole: Feminism and Women's Cinema* (Bloomington and Indianapolis: Indiana University Press, 1990), pp. 136–53.

22 Erica Carter, 'Interview with Ulrike Ottinger', *Screen Education*, no. 41, Spring 1982, p. 36. Cillie Rentmeister's negative review took the film to task for its lack of realism, and she would seem to have represented a dominant view among feminists. (Cillie Rentmeister, 'Frauen, Körper, Kunst: Mikrophysik der patriarchalichen Macht', *Ästhetik und Kommunikation*, no. 37, 1979, p. 65, cited in Monika Treut, 'Ein Nachtrag zu Ulrike Ottinger's Film Madame X', *frauen und film*, no. 28, June 1981, p. 17.

23 Treut, 'Ein Nachtrag', p. 15.

24 Ibid., p. 17.

25 See Mary Russo, '*Freak Orlando*: A Genealogy of the Female Grotesque', in Mary Russo, *The Female Grotesque* (New York and London: Routledge, 1995).

26 See Alice A. Kuzniar, 'Allegory, Androgyny, Anamorphosis: Ulrike Ottinger's *Dorian Gray*', in *The Queer German Cinema* (Stanford, CA: Stanford University Press, 2001), pp. 139–56; and Roswitha Mueller, 'The Mirror and the Vamp', *New German Critique*, no. 34, 1984, pp. 176–93.

27 See also Annette Kuhn, 'Encounter between Two Cultures – Discussion with Ulrike Ottinger', *Screen*, vol. 28, no. 4, Autumn 1987, pp. 74–9; and Janet Bergstrom, 'The Theatre of Everyday Life: Ulrike Ottinger's China: The Arts, Everyday Life', *Camera Obscura*, no. 18, September 1988.

28 See Julia Knight, 'Observing Rituals: Ulrike Ottinger's Johanna d'Arc of Mongolia', in Majer O'Sickey and von Zadow eds., *Triangulated Visions*, pp. 103–15.

29 Roger Ebert, 'Taiga', reviewed 24 February 1995, accessed 7 March 2000 on http://www.suntimes.com/ebert-reviews/1995/02/967209.html

30 Accessed 7 March 2000 on http://www.news.cornell.edu. Chronicles/1.28.99/cinema.html

31 Brenda Longfellow, 'Lesbian Phantasy and the Other Woman in Ottinger's Johanna d'Arc of Mongolia', *Screen*, vol. 34, no. 2, Summer 1993, p. 99.

32 See also White, 'Madame X of the China Seas'.

33 See also Miriam Hansen, 'Visual Pleasure, Fetishism and the Problem of Feminine/Feminist Discourse: Ulrike Ottinger's Ticket of No Return', *New German Critique*, no. 31, Winter 1984, pp. 95–108; and Kaja Silverman, 'Narcissism: The Impossible Love', in Majer O'Sickey and von Zadow (eds.), *Triangulated Visions*, pp. 139–52; and *Threshold of the Visible World* (New York and London: Routledge, 1996), chapter 2.

34 Gesine Stempel, 'Interview mit Ulrike Ottinger', *Courage*, no. 3, 1979 (available in English at the BFI on Microfiche).

35 Hansen, 'Visual Pleasure', p. 98.

36 Ilse Lenz, 'die öde wildnis einer schmnkerin: zu "bildnis einer trinkerin" ' [sic], *Frauen und Film*, no. 22, December 1979, p. 28, my translation. See also in the same issue: Claudia Lenssen, Mit glasigem blick: zu "bildnis einer trinkerin" ' [sic], pp. 23–5; and Karin Reschke, 'frau ottingers (kunst)gewerbe: zu "bildnis einer trinkerin" ' [sic], p. 29.

37 Interview with Claudia Lenssen, Helen Fehervary, Judith Mayne, 'From Hitler to Hepburn: A Discussion of Women's Film Production and Reception', *New German Critique*, nos. 24–5, Autumn/Winter 1981–2, p. 184.

38 Experimental sound mixing was already evident in such films as Valie Export's *Unsichtbare Gegner* (*Invisible Adversaries*, 1976); in von Aleman's, *Die Reise nach Lyon* (*Blind Spot*, 1980) – which literally and aurally traces the footsteps of the nineteenth-century writer Flora Tristan; in Sander's *Liebe is der Anfang alles Schreckens* (*Love is the Beginning of All Terrors*, 1984).

39 Fetishistic scopophilia, Mulvey argues, stops the narrative flow and allows for erotic contemplation of woman as icon (Mulvey, 'Visual Pleasure', p. 11). 'She' is frequently trapped behind glass, seemingly caught in ornamental claustrophobic stairwells. It is as if her own beauty and beauty in general enforces her isolation. However, as Hansen notes, Ottinger attempts to disentangle visual pleasure from the inherent voyeurism of patriarchal cinema. Hansen, 'Visual Pleasure', p. 103.

40 Lenssen, *et al.*, 'From Hitler to Hepburn', p. 184.

41 See Kuzniar, 'Experimental Visions: Bryntup, Müller, Schillinger, Scheirl, and Pürrer', in *The Queer German Cinema*, pp. 224–35.

42 Treut's films have frequently angered the lesbian community. Rejecting the exclusiveness of lesbian politics, its political correctness and its promotion of positive images, she wants to make films that are accessible and pleasurable for all through their use of humour.

43 See Hansen, 'Visual Pleasure'; and Silverman, 'Narcissism'.

44 See Hake, 'Gold, Love, Adventure'; White, 'Madame X of the China Seas'; and Mueller, 'The Mirror and the Vamp'.

45 See Mayne, 'Mistresses of Discrepancy'; Longfellow, 'Lesbian Phantasy', pp. 94–106; and Weiss, 'Women's "Art" Cinema'.

46 See Kuhn, 'Encounter between Two Cultures'; and Knight, 'Observing Rituals'.

47 I am thinking particularly of Judith Butler, *Gender Trouble: Feminism and the Subversion of Identity* (New York and London: Routledge, 1990); and Donna Haraway, 'A Cyborg Manifesto', in Donna Haraway (ed.), *Simians, Cyborgs and Women* (London: Free Association Books, 1991), pp. 127–48.

48 *Spiegel*, no. 7, 1986.

49 Although Dörrie is probably the commercially most successful German female director in the contemporary scene, like her predecessors, the New German film-makers, she diversifies into other areas: writing novels and staging, in Berlin 2001, Mozart's 'Cosi Fan Tutte'.

50 A controversial documentary about the mass rapes of German women in spring 1945 when the Red Army advanced on Berlin. It includes contemporary interviews, but is based on formerly secret archive material in East Berlin which only became accessible after re-unification.

51 Released by the international distributor Buena Vista.

19

The *Autorenfilm* in Contemporary German Cinema

Ian Garwood

'*Auteur* theory' became a fundamental part of the vocabulary of Anglo-American film criticism through film critic Andrew Sarris' mis-translation of the phrase *politique des auteurs*, coined by the French film journal *Cahiers du Cinéma*.[1] Conceived as a strategic intervention on behalf of the hitherto culturally denigrated Hollywood director, the polemic (*politique*) was attributed the weight of 'theory' in Sarris' loose re-formulation of the original French phrase. Thus, what began as a partisan call for Hollywood to be taken seriously as art became burdened with the implication that it had developed into a full-blown theory. As such, the term '*auteur* theory' became a hostage to fortune when romantic notions of the individual creative artist were deconstructed in the 1970s. Against the intimidating theoretical arsenal, drawn from structuralism, post-structuralism and psychoanalysis, deployed by film studies academics, the claims of *auteur*ism to the status of theory seemed flimsy indeed.

The mis-translation of *politique des auteurs* to *auteur theory* obscured the term's origins as a polemical intervention which occurred at a specific historical moment and within a particular cultural situation. There is a similar danger inherent in the temptation to regard the *Autorenfilm* as the German equivalent of an *auteur* cinema. Despite the linguistic similarities between the two terms, such a translation would risk diluting the specificity of a term that precedes '*auteur*' theory' by some fifty years, and that has signified different values in different periods of German film history. This essay considers the role of the *Autorenfilm* in two specific contexts: the celebrated New German Cinema of the 1970s, and contemporary post-

Wall cinema. While these phases of German film history are routinely set in opposition to each other, I will argue that there are significant continuities between them, with certain contemporary German films sharing key characteristics, albeit in mutated form, with the critically lauded *Autorenfilme* of the 1970s.

The origins of the *Autorenfilm*

The concept of the *Autorenfilm* first appeared in Wilhelmine film culture, as German cinema attempted to legitimise itself alongside other more established arts, in particular the theatre. The significant authors of films such as *Der Andere*, *Der Student von Prag* and *Das Fremde Mädchen* (1913) were writers and actors contracted from the theatre to add prestige to the productions, in a manner intended to differentiate the *Autorenfilm* from the *Schundfilm* (trash film).[2] As such, the early use of the term *Autorenfilm* contained an emphasis on the literary and theatrical (rather than purely cinematic).

The theatrical remained important to certain evaluations of authorship in Weimar cinema, as evidenced in Lotte Eisner's seminal book on film and theatrical expressionism, *The Haunted Screen*.[3] However, three other framing contexts orient discussion of the *Autorenfilm* in different directions. First, *From Caligari to Hitler*,[4] Siegfried Kracauer's highly influential post-Second World War account of Weimar cinema, brought film criticism into the realm of social psychology, reducing the importance of the individual author in favour of an account of the films as symptoms of the nation's inevitable slide towards Nazism.

Second, renowned Weimar film-makers such as Fritz Lang, G. W. Pabst and F. W. Murnau built reputations as film authors which lay as much in their stylistic differences from another film-making mode, Hollywood, as they did to any literary or theatrical legacy. Finally, the difference of Weimar cinema from Hollywood was also inscribed in the production process promoted by Ufa, Germany's main film studio (see Bock and Töteberg in this volume): Thomas Elsaesser has pointed to the artisanal ethos that characterised the studio's production practices, as opposed to Hollywood's factory-line process. By the 1920s, the American film industry had moved towards a mode of production characterised by a broad division of labour under the supervision of a central producer. By contrast, Ufa's Head of Production, Erich Pommer, established a working practice which allowed the director a comparatively high degree of autonomy and control, at least for the studio's prestige productions (*Großfilme*).[5]

The *Autorenfilm* in New German Cinema and contemporary cinema

This brief characterisation of its origins points to key qualities in the *Autorenfilm* that were re-activated by the New German Cinema of the 1970s, at the points of production and reception: namely, the propensity of the *Autorenfilm* to be read as nationally representative, in terms of both its distinctive aesthetics as well as its application to themes of national import; its adoption of a mode of production that valued individual craftsmanship (the 'artisanal') over the factory-line process of the mainstream film industry; and its construction of a dialogue between film and 'higher' art forms such as literature and theatre.

Wim Wenders is one of the film-makers most prominently associated with the New German Cinema of the 1970s. After making a number of movies now firmly established as part of the canon of New German film (e.g. *Alice in den Städten* [*Alice in the Cities*, 1974], *Im Lauf der Zeit* [*Kings of the Road*, 1976] and *Der Amerikanische Freund* [*The American Friend*, 1977]), Wenders relocated to America to direct the troubled production *Hammett* (1982) and the more successful *Paris, Texas* (1984).

Der Himmel über Berlin (*Wings of Desire*, 1987), Wenders' 'return' to German film-making, charts the angel Damiel's (Bruno Ganz) passage to Earth, and his pursuit of trapeze artist Marion (Solveig Dommartin), with whom he has fallen in love. This journey, filmed in black and white and colour, takes place against the backdrop of a divided Berlin, the 'scarred' features of which are returned to insistently by the film (e.g. the Wall and a derelict and deserted Potsdamer Platz).

The self-styling of the film as a type of 'homecoming' for Wenders makes itself felt both through its use of a recognisably German geographical setting as well as its remobilisation of the qualities associated with the German *Autorenfilm*: an engagement with nationally specific themes; the adoption of an 'artisanal' aesthetic; and an involvement of the filmic with 'higher', or more established, art forms, in this case the written word and a tradition of oral storytelling.

If New German Cinema represents a film movement where notions of the *Autorenfilm* seem particularly influential, the opposite has been seen to be the case with regard to contemporary post-Wall German cinema. The post-Wall 'cinema of consensus', as Eric Rentschler has named it, appears, at least according to its critics, to share little with the New German Cinema: politically complacent rather than politically engaged; genre-based rather than the work of individual 'authors'; and indebted to the 'low' cultural form of television (through its persistent use of a shared genre, the domestic comedy), rather than the high arts.[6]

One of the major commercial successes of post-Wall cinema has been Tom Tykwer's *Lola rennt* (*Run, Lola, Run*), a film which replays the quest of its titular heroine (played by Franka Potente) to bail out her boyfriend Manni, 1998 (Moritz Bleibtreu) from a life-threatening situation three times, until a satisfactory conclusion is reached. In what follows, *Lola rennt* is set beside *Der Himmel über Berlin* to demonstrate how *both* works may lay claim to the status of *Autorenfilme*. Before this claim can be made, however, it is necessary to outline the critical orthodoxies which typecast New German Cinema and post-Wall cinema as polar opposites.

THE *AUTORENFILM* AS NATIONALLY REPRESENTATIVE

The support New German Cinema received from the West German state during the 1970s was partly due to a perceived need to rehabilitate German culture. Along with other cultural and political initiatives, a number of film-makers in the 1970s took up the project of *Vergangenheitsbewältigung*, a confrontation with the legacy of the Third Reich that had been seen to have been forgotten in the years of the *Wirtschaftswunder* (economic miracle) during the 1950s. In an article which valorises the provocative political engagement of New German Cinema over the post-Wall 'cinema of consensus', Eric Rentschler claims: '[New German Cinema] militated against collective forgetting, taking leave of a problematic national past by constantly problematising that past's presence'.[7] Landmark German films of the 1970s, such as Fassbinder's FRG-Trilogy (*Die Ehe der Maria Braun* [*The Marriage of Maria Braun*, 1979], *Lola*, (1981), *Die Sehnsucht der Veronika Voss* [*Veronika Voss*, 1982]), Margarethe von Trotta's *Die Bleierne Zeit* (*The German Sisters*, 1981) and Hans-Jürgen Syberberg's *Hitler – Ein Film aus Deutschland* (*Our Hitler*, 1977), all staged a provocative confrontation with their nation's troubled past. *Der Himmel über Berlin* follows in this tradition with its representation of a Berlin divided in the present, through the Wall, and haunted by its past, in the inserts of archive war footage which punctuate the film.

Against this explicit confrontation with the root causes and consequences of Germany's disastrous encounter with fascism, contemporary cinema, exemplified, according to both Thomas Elsaesser and Eric Rentschler, by the 'yuppie' lifestyle comedy, seems complacent indeed.[8] Rather than forcing a dialogue between present and past, the contemporary German film is accused of simply responding 'to the rhythms of the *Zeitgeist*'.[9] *Lola rennt* could be held to be paradigmatic in this regard, with its action focused insistently on the present, as the same narrative situation is replayed three times.

THE *AUTORENFILM* AS AN 'ARTISANAL' PRODUCTION

As Thomas Elsaesser has observed, practical, ideological and commercial imperatives ensured that the state-subsidised cinema of the Federal Republic in the 1970s favoured projects headed by a discernible, single author. This emphasis on the personal expression of the individual film-maker, according to Elsaesser, made its mark on the films themselves through the demonstration of an artisanal aesthetic, a sense that the objects that arrived in the cinema were the result of an act of individual craftsmanship.[10] This artisanal mode of production differentiated New German Cinema from mainstream film-making practices, and linked the 1970s *Autorenfilm* with that of the Weimar Republic.

In post-Wall German cinema, by contrast, the emphasis has shifted from an artisanal mode of production to a film-making process more overtly driven by market forces: there have been changes in film funding (from the complex system of state subsidies available in the 1970s to the mixture of private backing, regional [rather than state] funding and television finance that predominates today); a transformation in the status of cinema as a cultural institution (now competing against a plethora of audio-visual media accessed in the home); and a shift in the audiences the films seek to attract (from the 'lost' domestic audience, troubled by its nation's past, that was hailed by New German Cinema, to the 'distracted' young audience who see cinema as just one of many 'leisure-time diversions').[11]

THE *AUTORENFILM* AND HIGH CULTURE

The third distinction which seems to cement New German Cinema's relationship with the *Autorenfilm*, while distancing post-Wall cinema from it, is the alliance of each with high art. The major film-makers of New German Cinema exhibited a particularly intimate relationship to other art forms. For example, a Brechtian influence is apparent in the films of Rainer Werner Fassbinder, who in fact wrote and produced a number of stage productions of his own. Werner Herzog not only made a film about a visionary who wanted to build an opera house in the middle of the Amazonian rainforest (*Fitzcarraldo*, 1982), but has also directed operas himself. Wim Wenders worked on a number of occasions with the Austrian playwright and author Peter Handke, a collaboration that was resumed for *Der Himmel über Berlin*.

Contemporary cinema, by contrast, is characterised, in dominant accounts, by its debt to popular culture and television genres such as the sit-com. *Lola rennt* may be prefaced by a quotation from T. S. Eliot, but this is followed immediately by a less erudite piece of sporting 'philosophy' from German football coach, Sepp Herberger ('*Nach dem Spiel ist vor dem Spiel*' ['After the game is before the game']). The only further explicit literary reference in the film is the incongruous appearance of a copy of John Milton's *Paradise Lost* in the phone box from which Lola's boyfriend calls to ask her to find the money that will save his life.

New German Cinema, therefore, may appear to draw on those periods of film history where notions of authorship (the artisanal aesthetic), the value attributed to art cinema, and the connections between film and high culture were at their strongest (the Wilhelmine and Weimar cinemas). Contemporary German cinema seems, by contrast, to share its values with the cinema of the *Wirtschaftswunder*, where domestically produced films operated within the conventions of a commercial star and genre cinema. However, there are continuities, as well as dissonances, between New German Cinema and post-Wall cinema. Throughout the course of New German Cinema, there was a self-conscious support of the notion of the *Autorenfilm* as a central tenet of the film-making and film-going experience. While this may no longer hold true for many contemporary German film-makers, *Lola rennt* nevertheless aligns itself with the *Autorenfilm* of the New German Cinema in at least three ways: through its artisanal notion of authorship; its self-styling as a type of art cinema that rejects a linear narrative structure; and in its attention to particular themes that marked the films of New German Cinema (namely, the search for a 'usable' story and the relationship of the present to the past).

However, while there are points of comparison, fundamental differences remain between the *Autorenfilm* of New German Cinema (and in particular Wim Wenders' *Der Himmel über Berlin*) and that represented by *Lola rennt*: differences that reside in the level of trust each film-maker has in the ability of its film's images to construct a 'usable' story, and in the extent to which the stories they construct can be viewed as nationally representative.

Der Himmel über Berlin and the New German Cinema

Wim Wenders' *Der Himmel über Berlin* was released at a time usually seen to reside outside the periodisation of New German Cinema (conventionally the late 1960s to the early 80s). However, Wenders' strong association with the New German Cinema of the 1970s, together with his 'exile' in Hollywood during the 80s, ensured that *Der Himmel über Berlin*, his first 'German' fiction film since *Der Amerikanische Freund*, was received as an *Autorenfilm*, marking the director's return both geographically and in his choice of themes.

The film aligns itself with the dominant storytelling mode of the New German *Autorenfilm* in a number of ways. Elsaesser cites Wenders' *Der Amerikanische Freund*, which features a frame-maker as its protagonist, as the chief example of an artisanal approach,[12] and this emphasis on craftsmanship is equally evident in *Der Himmel über Berlin*. Peter Handke and Wenders wrote the script for *Der Himmel über Berlin* while film-making was taking place, albeit from a general scenario. The self-conscious conflation of the writing and filming process attests to Wenders' determination to escape the normal workings of the industrial process. The decision to film much of the narrative in black and white continues his long-established practice of 'colour-coding' his films, whereby 'completed' scripts are filmed in colour (*Der Angst des Tormanns vorm Elfmeter*, 1971, and *Der Amerikanische Freund*), whereas films whose scripts are improvised during shooting are filmed in black and white (*Alice in den Städten* and *Im Lauf der Zeit*).[13] Wenders thus uses colour-coding to 'scar' each film with a reminder of the particular process that has gone into its crafting. Seen in this context, the shift from black and white to colour in *Der Himmel über Berlin* denotes a develop-ment from the 'improvised' interior monologues that populate much of the first part of the film to the more structured and 'scripted' narrative that dominates its latter stages.

The shift from black and white to colour also corresponds to the transformation of the film's protagonist, the angel Damiel, whose desire to fall from the heavens (an ethereal but colourless realm) and join the flow of everyday 'real' life (a colourful world) is eventually granted. This quest of its narrative's protagonist 'to enter the history of the world' is another factor that locates *Der Himmel über Berlin* within the *Autorenfilm* mode of New German Cinema. Read in the light of the project of a nation coming to terms with its past (*Vergangenheitsbewältigung*), the inability of many New German films to tell a straight story could be seen to represent its viewers' difficulties in constructing a usable narrative through which they could understand their country's traumatic recent past. In *Der Himmel über Berlin*, Damiel is also searching for a 'usable' story: one in which he will be able to differentiate between past, present and future, and between observing and feeling, in a way that his omniscient yet non-sensuous existence as an angel forbids him from doing.

Usable stories: memory work vs memory play

Lola rennt is at first glance a film whose aesthetic qualities and narrative concerns are entirely distinct from the *Autorenfilm* of the New German Cinema, as exemplified by *Der Himmel über Berlin*. Tykwer's film possesses a number of the 'negative' qualities attributed to contemporary German cinema, which is seen to present

> characters whose primary sense of person and place is rarely an overt function of their national identity or directly impacted by Germany's difficult past. Instead [it] offers tableaux of mobile young professionals, who play with possibility and flirt with difference, living in the present and worrying about their future, juggling careers, relationships and lifestyles.[14]

Lola rennt's demonstration of these attributes is at times hyperbolic, centring as it does on 'mobile' youth (Lola's mobility is the chief focus of the narrative), who 'play with possibility and flirt with difference' (Lola replays the narrative scenario three times until she gets it right), and who live in the present and worry about their future: the pressure on Lola to get the money to Manni in twenty minutes motivates an intensity of experiencing the present and an acute fear for the immediate future. In addition, the two sequences of Manni and Lola discussing their relationship in bed suggests that the main scenario being played and replayed is actually a metaphor for their romantic anxieties.

Lola rennt's sense of constant movement, its refusal to settle upon one version of narrative events, its use of a plethora of visual styles (film, 'low-quality' digital camera, high-quality digital effects, photomontage and animation), and its persistent trance-techno soundtrack could be seen as a triumph of style over substance – the 'high quality, low affect' that Rentschler attributes to contemporary German film's 'world of show and simulation'.[15] However, it is also possible to view the film's restlessness in settling on one version of its narrative as evidence that it shares one of the key concerns of the New German *Autorenfilm*: the search for a usable story.

New German Cinema's specificity has often been located in its self-conscious attempt to use film as a type of 'memory work', with the specific aim of coming to terms with the legacy of Nazism. Films by the major authors of the 1970s and 80s share a status as 'art cinema' through their adoption of a non-linear storytelling mode and their self-stylisation of the film-maker as 'artisan'. In all these aspects, however, there are correspondences between *Lola rennt* and *Der Himmel über Berlin*. Both films problematise the relationship between present and past, a relationship that must be constructed to allow for the possibility of memory. There can be no meaningful memory of experience if there is no coherent past constructed in which those experiences were meant to have taken place. There is, admittedly, a difference between the two films' handling of memory. *Der Himmel über Berlin*

problematises memory on the level of narrative representation, featuring a protagonist whose chief desire is to create a personalised set of memories for himself, and to liberate himself from the position of simply observing the memory process being enacted around him. Before Damiel falls to earth, the viewer is allowed to hear what Damiel hears: individuals working through their memories (often involving family trauma) in their interior monologues. The viewer also observes Berlin from the angels' perspective, becoming privy to the sights of the memories that Berlin as a city has accumulated, which angels view simultaneously rather than laid out in a chronological time-line. On a number of occasions the past of Berlin comes to the surface of the present through the angels' point of view, in the form of archive footage of Berlin during and after the War.

In contrast to this explicit marking of memory, the narrative of *Lola rennt* appears to locate itself resolutely in an urgent present, as Lola races against the clock to find the money that will save her boyfriend. When the film does digress from Lola's immediate pursuit of the money, it is only to accelerate briefly into the future, with photomontages that chart possible developments in the lives of characters she encounters. If one of the major projects of New German Cinema was to encourage its viewers to come to terms with the nation's traumatic past, *Lola rennt* appears to involve a determined, self-contained 'coming to terms with the present'.

However, memory is still important to the operation of the narrative. By replaying the same basic situation and returning to many of the same locations, the viewer is encouraged to relate Lola's progression at any point with the corresponding point in the episodes that have preceded it. Thus the process of remembering becomes a game, as the viewer's recollection of the previous episodes is rewarded through the identification of similarities between different scenes, while new narrative elements are added in each replayed episode.

The memories brought to recollection by the narrative of *Lola rennt*, therefore, are entirely self-contained ones. Damiel's search for his own set of memories in *Der Himmel über Berlin*, by contrast, involves his observation of a number of nationally specific (rather than merely narrative-specific) memories. The interior monologues and images of Berlin's past provided by viewing Berlin from the angels' viewpoint serve to delay the introduction of a single narrative. *Lola rennt*, on the other hand, explicitly references the past (i.e. the opening ten minutes of the film) only to speed the film to its central narrative situation.

Manni (Moritz Bleibtreu) and Lola (Franka Potente) in *Lola rennt* (1998)

This interest in memory only in relation to the immediate narrative situation (in terms of both the games the viewer plays in comparing one episode to a previous one and in the accelerated flashbacks that begin the film) apparently supports the view of post-Wall cinema as essentially apolitical, in comparison to New German Cinema's eagerness to confront the past. In place of the 'memory work', encouraged by *Der Himmel über Berlin*, which offers the viewer a number of 'national' memories with which to engage, *Lola rennt*'s narrative repetitions invite its audience to engage on a seemingly more superficial level of 'memory play'.

The status of the image in *Der Himmel über Berlin* and *Lola rennt*

If both *Der Himmel über Berlin* and *Lola rennt* are involved in the search for a narrative, then the strategies they adopt to this end are quite distinct. In *Der Himmel über Berlin* the process of working towards a usable story is enacted both by Damiel, as he resolves to insert himself into the history of the world (rather than merely observing it), and encouraged in the viewer, as (s)he is confronted by the fragmented interior monologues of the first half of the film, which only slowly give way to a more coherent narrative involving Damiel's search for Marion, the woman with whom he has fallen in love.

Der Himmel über Berlin inches tentatively towards its story, discovering it amid a number of other stories, revealed as much through the written and spoken word as the image: the film begins with the act of writing and ends with the voice-over of the old storyteller whose musings punctuate the film. *Lola rennt*, on the other hand, arrives at its central narrative premise very quickly, but then proceeds to rework it over and over again. *Lola rennt* approaches its narrative confidently, constructing and deconstructing it through an array of different visual strategies, and a deeply layered soundtrack that is both propulsive, driving Lola forward on her quest, and responsive, adding aural elements as the course of events changes from episode to episode.

Thus, while both films describe a quest for a 'usable' narrative, there is a fundamental difference in attitude towards the audio-visual material employed to 'find' their stories. *Der Himmel über Berlin* suggests that the photographic image no longer has the ability to present experience 'authentically', representing a number of other storytelling modes (the written word, the monologue, the oral storyteller) which may be more suitable to construct

Daniel (Bruno Ganz) and Marion (Solveig Dommartin) in *Himmel über Berlin* (1987)

the 'epic of peace' which the old storyteller argues for while looking at photos of wartime devastation in the library. *Lola rennt*, on the other hand, attempts a seamless fusion of the various visual modes it uses in the telling of its story, effecting integration between differently textured visual material, and between soundtrack and image, that contrasts completely with the fragmentation evident in *Der Himmel über Berlin*.

Statements from both directors point to the roots of this discrepancy in style: Wenders distrusts the photographic image, while Tykwer aims to master it. Tykwer claims that the idea for *Lola rennt* stemmed from a single image that returned time and again to his mind: 'For *Lola rennt* it was the image of this running woman, for me a primal image of the cinema, because it combines motion with emotion.'[16] *Lola rennt* constructs its narrative primarily around the image of a running woman, marshalling its disparate visual discourses and its layered soundtrack around Lola's moving body with a confidence in contemporary audio-visual media that *Der Himmel über Berlin* lacks. Wenders, by contrast, displays a loss of faith in the ability of the filmed image to be truly emotionally expressive, a distrust which he associates with both his own problematic experiences making movies in America and with a more widespread 'abuse' of the image for commercial purposes. As Wenders explained, in a lecture given after his return 'home':

Images have distanced themselves more and more from reality and have hardly anything to do with it anymore. If you think back ten or twenty years, the rate of the expansion and inflation of images will make your head spin ... Let me return to what brought me 'home': that is, language, the German language. Even if the world of images is out of joint, and even if progress and technology foster the proliferation of images so that they are out of control and will get even more out of control in the future, there still exists another culture, a counterculture that has not changed and that will not change: the realm of storytelling, reading and writing, the word.[17]

Whereas Tykwer is confident enough in the power of the cinematic to build his narrative upon a single 'originary' image of a running woman, bestowing upon it an audio-visual density by the complex layering of different images and sounds, Wenders sees such a proliferation of the image as a threat, which he believes to be particularly potent in the face of Germany's past:

> It is a particular catastrophe in Germany, a country that is highly susceptible to images and already almost totally engulfed in foreign images. Too many images cause a loss of reality – and this country that has had great difficulty securing an identity for itself needs, above all, to be grounded in reality.[18]

Here, Wenders locates his anxiety about the proliferation and abuse of the photographic image in a nationally specific context, whereas Tykwer's use of different types of image in *Lola rennt* is non-geographically specific, minimising its use of landmark Berlin locations,[19] and mimicking, through its narrative repetitions, the storytelling mode of the computer game. Tykwer revels in the possibilities of combining different types of image, a practice not dissimilar to that most internationally mass-marketable of audio-visual phenomena, the music video.

A comparison of two pivotal narrative moments in both films demonstrates the propensity for *Der Himmel über Berlin* to resist an immersion in the visual and to retain the markings of the nationally specific, while *Lola rennt* layers its images and soundtrack together in a textured and sensuous matrix, which 'de-realises' the narrative from a recognisable geographical location. Both films initiate their quest narratives (Damiel's for Marion, Lola's for money) by having their protagonists descend to 'ground level': Damiel in the moment by the Berlin Wall when he breaks through the ethereal realm of the angels to the human realm of 'real' experience, and Lola as she runs down the stairwell of her apartment block and hits the streets in her search for the money.

The moment in *Der Himmel über Berlin* is figured by the sudden introduction of colour during a close-up of Damiel as he stands by the Wall explaining his resolve to 'fall' to Earth to his fellow angel Cassiel. The transition makes narrative sense, in that the earthly (and Damiel's desire for it) is represented in colour throughout the film, with the angelic perspective in black and white. Yet, seen from Cassiel's point of view, the moment of Damiel's descent marks a disruption of the heavenly perspective, rather than the seamless flow from Heaven to Earth as Damiel experiences it. After Cassiel assures Damiel that his dream to enter the earthly realm 'will never happen', the camera moves towards Cassiel. This is followed by a close-up of Damiel, now suddenly in colour, the camera moving across his face in the opposite direction to the previous shot. A return to the close-up of Cassiel, the camera still moving across him, shows him looking perturbed and glancing to his left where Damiel has left a trail of footprints behind him (thus demonstrating his earthly presence). This moment, then, enacts the shock Cassiel feels as he sees his declaration (Damiel will never become human) contradicted before his very eyes. There is a deliberate effort not to offer the viewer the more sensually 'satisfying' experience of seeing colour seep into Damiel's life (as occurs earlier in Marion's trailer when her image blossoms from black and white to colour under Damiel's desiring gaze).

In addition, at this pivotal point in Damiel's narrative, which essays his desire for sensuous experience, the viewer is not allowed to forget that there are other politically informed and nationally specific stories taking place alongside Damiel's personal narrative. Not only does his descent take place by the politically charged totem of the Berlin Wall; there is also a pan away from Damiel as he collapses into Cassiel's arms to the border police whose presence had already been signalled earlier in the scene.

By contrast, the moment Lola puts the phone down on Manni, and runs down the stairs and out of the house to begin her quest in *Lola rennt*, is presented through a range of disparate audio-visual materials that, nonetheless, congregate together around Lola's leap into dynamic action. The stylised nature of the images serves to abstract Lola's quest from the realistic environment of a post-Wall Berlin. In the two minutes it takes for Lola to put the phone down on Manni, flick through her memory banks to decide who she will try to get the money from (she settles on her father) and run downstairs, four different modes of representation interweave: film, television, animation and still photographs. Fluidity between the different modes is emphasised, rather than the separation that is maintained in *Der Himmel über Berlin*. Apart from the speed with which one mode is exchanged for another, there are a number of moments when different forms are mixed together: a cartoon casino croupier, who will crop up as a human figure later on, asserts himself in a live action frame, and actually pulls across a new image to overlay the previous one; the passport photos, which represent the people Lola thinks of as she raids her memory banks, alternate so rapidly with the image of Lola that the two images merge; finally, the animated sequence which shows Lola running down the stairs actually enters in a television within the film frame. Lola herself becomes a figure who can move between screens, both big and small, and who can migrate effortlessly between live action and animation.

The *Autorenfilm* in post-Wall cinema: the digital artisan

The slipping of *Lola rennt* into animation is indicative of its disinterest in Berlin as a 'real' politically charged landscape, and contrasts strongly with *Der Himmel über Berlin*'s insistent return to the Wall and insertion of documentary footage which reminds the viewer of the city's scarred history. The lack of concern *Lola rennt* shows in nationally specific issues does mark its difference from the *Autorenfilm* of the New German Cinema. In other respects, though, its mode of production and address *does* suggest continuities. Tykwer may be using the tools of an international, mass-marketed audio-visual language (the computer game, the music video, dance music), but the production of his movies nevertheless adheres to the 'artisanal' principles of much New German Cinema. Tykwer makes his films for his own production company, X-Filme: his first four feature films (*Die Tödliche Maria* [*Deadly Maria*, 1994], *Winterschläfer* [*Wintersleepers*, 1997], *Lola rennt* and *Der Krieger und die Kaiserin* [*The Princess and the Warrior*, 2000]) were all self-scripted, are often populated by the same actors, and feature music co-composed by him.[20]

Der Himmel über Berlin bears the traces of an 'author' whose enthusiasm for the photographic image has given way to scepticism. The film begins with the written word, and closes with the return to Damiel writing in his diary, and a coda which features a voice-over from the old storyteller, urging the audience to reconnect with an older tradition of oral storytelling. As such, *Der Himmel über Berlin* asserts a connection with both the literary and the 'theatrical' (with its connotations of 'live' oral performance) that associates it with the earliest conception of the *Autorenfilm* in the Wilhelmine period. *Lola rennt*'s claims as an *Autorenfilm* have a much more contemporary base, resid-

ing in the extent to which Tykwer retains a personal imprint on material that maps out the changed audio-visual landscape in which German cinema, as a national institution, now operates. Whereas Wenders' distrust of the image is exacerbated through its exploitation in 'computers, video games, virtual reality, and . . . digital recording',[21] Tykwer embraces the possibilities of combining all these new technologies, while retaining a sense of personal expression and creative control.

There is an unwillingness in *Lola rennt*, or any of Tykwer's films to date, to engage with the political or multicultural realities of post-Wall Germany. Despite this lack of specific national references, however, *Lola rennt* attempts to find a storytelling mode that explores the possibilities of incorporating into narrative cinema new media forms: forms that *are* an integral part of Germany's contemporary audio-visual culture. A key aim of the *Autorenfilm* in the New German Cinema was to reconnect with a lost domestic audience. In a contemporary context, *Lola rennt* could be seen to be searching for an appropriate way to address its chosen constituency: an audience literate in the forms of global multi-media. Viewed from this perspective, *Der Himmel über Berlin*'s retreat into the literary and theatrical could be seen as a form of evasion.[22] *Lola rennt*, by contrast, strives to integrate into its narrative those media forms that have complicated cinema's status as the primary audio-visual medium through which a national audience is offered an image of itself.

Notes

1 See Edward Buscombe, 'Ideas of Authorship', in John Caughie (ed.), *Theories of Authorship* (London: Routledge, 1981), pp. 22–35.

2 Joseph Garncarz and Michael Wedel, 'Autorenfilm', in Thomas Elsaesser and Michael Wedel (eds.), *The BFI Companion to German Cinema* (London: BFI, 1999), pp. 31–3.

3 Lotte Eisner, *The Haunted Screen: Expressionism in the German Cinema and the Influence of Max Reinhardt* (London: Thames and Hudson, 1969).

4 Siegfried Kracauer, *From Caligari to Hitler: A Psychological History of the German Film* (Princeton, NJ: Princeton University Press, 1947).

5 Thomas Elsaesser, *Weimar Cinema and After: Germany's Historical Imaginary* (London and New York: Routledge, 2000), pp. 117–21.

6 It should be noted that the New German Cinema was also indebted to television, in terms of its provision of finance and programming slots dedicated to the showcasing of

domestically produced films. However, the aesthetics of New German Cinema have generally been evaluated in relation to art cinema conventions, rather than televisual ones.

7 Eric Rentschler, 'From New German Cinema to the Post-Wall Cinema of Consensus', in Mette Hjort and Scott Mackenzie (eds.), *Cinema and Nation* (London: Routledge, 2000), pp. 260–78.

8 Thomas Elsaesser, 'Introduction: German Cinema in the 1990s', in Elsaesser and Wedel (eds.), *The BFI Companion to German Cinema*, pp. 3–16; Eric Rentschler, op.cit. pp. 262–3.

9 Eric Rentschler, op.cit. p. 270.

10 Thomas Elsaesser, *New German Cinema: A History* (London: BFI and Macmillan, 1989), pp. 101–03.

11 Eric Rentschler, op.cit. p. 268.

12 Thomas Elsaesser, *New German Cinema*, p. 103.

13 Wim Wenders, 'Impossible Stories', in Roger F. Cook and Gerd Gemünden (eds.), *The Cinema of Wim Wenders: Image, Narrative and the Postmodern Condition* (Detroit: Wayne University Press, 1997), pp. 33–41.

14 Eric Rentschler, op.cit., p. 272.

15 Ibid., p. 270.

16 Tom Tykwer, 'Generalschlüssel fürs Kino', in Michael Töteberg (ed.), *Szenenwechsel: Momentaufnahmen des Jungen Deutschen Films* (Hamburg: Rowohlt, 1999), pp. 17–35.

17 Wenders, 'Talking about Germany', pp. 51–60.

18 Ibid., pp. 58–9.

19 Recognisable Berlin locations *are* featured in *Lola rennt* (e.g. the Oberbaumbrücke, Friedrichstraße, the Gendarmenmarkt). However, their historical significance is not dwelt upon as in *Der Himmel über Berlin*. Instead, each location is organised as a kind of visual support for the representation of Lola's constantly moving body.

20 Twyker's fifth film, *Heaven* (2002), abandons an overtly home-grown, 'artisanal' approach, in favour of an international cast and co-production with the US major-independent Miramax. However, different affinities with the *Autorenfilm* of the New German Cinema become apparent: by basing itself on a script written by the acclaimed Polish auteur Krzysztof Kieślowski, the film aligns itself with a particular type of internationally marketable introspective European art cinema, of which New German Cinema was a key brand.

21 Wenders, 'Talking about Germany', p. 58.

22 Subsequent films by Wim Wenders have been noticeably more 'internationalist' in their geographical settings and themes than the nationally specific focus of *Der Himmel über Berlin*. However, these films remain marked by an anxiety that the status of the image has been fatally compromised by its exploitation within mainstream media industries (see, for example, *Bis ans Ende der Welt* [*Until the End of the World*, 1991] and *The End of Violence* [1997]).

PART FIVE

TRANSNATIONAL CONNECTIONS

Introduction

Deniz Göktürk

Migrants are no anomaly in German cinema. Film history is populated with immigrants and émigrés who – voluntarily or forcibly, for economic or political reasons – laboured far from their birthplace in other countries. Asta Nielsen, one of the first international stars of the silent era, came to Berlin from Denmark with her director Urban Gad and played an errant foreigner in *Der fremde Vogel* (*The Strange Bird*, 1911). Pola Negri arrived from Poland, dazzled the audience in fiery, exotic roles, and was soon called to Hollywood, just as her successful director Ernst Lubitsch was in 1922. On the other hand, Louise Brooks, the unforgettable Lulu with the black page-boy haircut, came from Hollywood to Berlin. The English-born 'blonde dream' Lilian Harvey sang and danced in musical comedies of the early sound era – often acting in all three German, French and English versions of the same film. Lya de Putti came from Hungary and made her breakthrough as the seductive temptress in *Variété* (1925) before continuing her career as a European femme-fatale in Hollywood, a role which was taken over in 1930 by Germany's 'prodigal daughter' Marlene Dietrich (see Erica Carter's contribution in this volume). Friedrich Wilhelm Murnau's films centred around travel, transition and transgression, whether he was filming in Slovakia and on the shores of the Baltic (*Nosferatu*), in a German village built at the Fox Studios (*Sunrise*, 1927) or in Tahiti (*Tabu*, 1931).

In 1933, more of Weimar's film directors followed, such as Fritz Lang, Billy Wilder, Robert Siodmak, and some two thousand of their associates in the film industry. Most of these film workers were Jewish and had been forced to emigrate from Nazi Germany. They found refuge in Hollywood – often with detours through France or England, for example the actors Peter Lorre and Conrad Veidt, and the producer Erich Pommer. The émigré actors from Germany frequently tended to be typecast as demonic or funny Nazis. Meanwhile, the 'Aryanised' cinema of National Socialism did not do altogether without foreign players.

Lewis Brody was cast as an 'exotic' by the Reich's Chamber of Film and was allowed to play the 'colonial nigger' in tropical dramas. The German revue film would be unthinkable without the Cairo-born, Budapest-raised Marika Rökk or the Latina Rosita Serrano and no one could voice the longing for home more movingly than the Swedish Ufa-star Zarah Leander.

After 1945, international actors and directors arrived to work in the German film industry. Roberto Rossellini directed neo-realistic dramas about guilt and responsibility against the rubbles of Germany in the year zero. Many émigrés returned. Billy Wilder produced US American comedies in Berlin, such as *A Foreign Affair* (1948), starring Marlene Dietrich, and *One, Two, Three* with Liselotte Pulver who herself came from Switzerland. Bill Ramsay and Chris Howland, who had been soldiers in the US military occupation forces, stayed in Germany and were typecast as British or American in the cinema of the 1950s and 1960s. The Italian singer and actress Caterina Valente, along with Freddy Quinn, lured German cinema audiences of the 1950s to an imaginary Scala and to the sunsets of Capri. The French Pierre Brice as Winnetou and the American Lex Barker as Old Shatterhand were, together with Terrence Hill (Mario Girotti) and Bud Spencer (Carlo Pedersoli), trademarks of the Euro-Western and figured among the most popular actors of the 1960s. Hugo Fregonese, a director of European co-productions of 'Karl May' and 'Dr Mabuse' films, came from Argentina.[1] Ivan Desny, the son of Russian émigrés and born in Peking, was known to German television audiences as the gentleman-gangster and appeared with customs investigator Kressin in several 'Tatort'-episodes on WDR in the early 1970s. Later he reappeared as a distinguished stranger in Fassbinder films such as *The Marriage of Maria Braun* (1979). He had lived in France and had acted since the 1950s in many French, British, German, Italian and even a few American films.

Given so much 'foreign blood', it is difficult to define the boundaries around 'pure' German cinema. The large number of travelling actors and directors suggests that international collaboration has been an integral element of film production all along, and calls for a rethinking of national canons constructed in film historiography. If we add aspects of international co-production, distribution and reception, the picture gets even more complicated. As Andrew Higson has pointed out in his conceptual discussion of 'national cinema', assumptions of coherence, unity and cultural specificity form part of a mythologising process, which, in the European context, is often intertwined with a prescriptive and defensive rhetoric, privileging quality art cinema over the commercial success of Hollywood.[2] Indeed, the national is a primary category when it comes to writing academic analysis, to packaging publications and book series on national cinemas, and to organising conferences or programming film series. Audiences, however, often tend to be less concerned with national bonding than with entertainment. From the angle of consumption, rather than production, all films shown and watched in a particular country, including foreign imports, would have to be regarded as part of that national culture, as they shape the experience of audiences. Rather than prescriptively positing 'national cinema' as a coherent body of films which can be read allegorically as projections of an 'imagined community' (based on ethno-nationalist definitions of culture), Higson suggests that we read 'histories of national cinema … as histories of crisis and conflict, of resistance and negotiation'.[3]

In his argument about 'imagined communities', Benedict Anderson points out the key role of print media such as newspapers, novels, maps and the census in creating a sense of boundedness between people who have never been in personal contact, but are connected as subjects in one nation state or colonial empire.[4] This view of modernity is still a poignant argument in times of global audiovisual transmission and mass migration. However, communities in our mediated world often connect across national boundaries and proliferate into a multitude of disconnected networks. As we are beginning to think about cultural production and reception in transnational terms, the notion of a unified national public sphere is increasingly complicated and fragmented into parallel spheres where deterritorialised producers as well as viewers engage in 'dispersed and diverse forms of transnational allegiance and affiliation', and where many different experiences of modernity occur at the intersections of the global and the local.[5]

An investigation of cultural contacts – both past and present – on a global scale suggests a reframing of cinema history with a focus on exchanges, collaborations and cross-cultural representations rather than on national coherence and closure. Meanwhile, different kinds of encounters occupy very different locations in the geography of cultural memory. The following section on 'transnational connections' was conceived as an attempt to connect histories which have hitherto been perceived as unrelated. The exile of film-makers from Nazi Germany and the much longer-lasting Hollywood connection of travelling stars, directors and other personnel, at first sight, appear to have little in common with other scenarios of travel such as colonial and ethnographic visions of Africa or pictures of the post-1960s labour migration from Turkey. However, each of these axes of travel and cinematic imagination raises questions of representation, incorporation and authenticity in different locations and thereby complicates narratives of national cinema.

Exile studies, for example, have tended to separate and privilege the narrative of refugees from Nazi Germany after 1933 as incompatible with other kinds of relocations.[6] Recent work, however, has highlighted continuities and similarities as well as differences in the various stories of emigration and participation of expatriate Germans in Hollywood, starting with those who emigrated in the 1920s from Weimar Germany, coming from a strong film industry to seek better prospects in the world's film capital. Thomas Elsaesser concludes that the German presence in Hollywood cannot be explained either solely in economic or in purely political terms, but rather as 'uneven exchanges' of 'mutually sustained imaginaries of otherness'.[7] Sabine Hake's case studies on Ernst Lubitsch and Fritz Lang in the following chapter analyse the production of 'simulacra of authenticity' by these directors in relation to both Europe and America. Even if we identify waves of emigration and patterns of employment, each and every biography still remains different, and indeed the meandering careers of G. W. Pabst, Edgar Ulmer, Curtis Bernhardt, E. A. Dupont and many others suggest that exile was in fact often a 'two-way traffic' rather than a one-way journey.[8]

Rather than essentialising and homogenising the experience of exile as loss and trauma, more productive approaches engage in an analysis of cliché images of America and of Europe. Operettas about Viennese decadence, film noir, or anti-Nazi films can be read not just as testimonies of linear influence, but also as interventions in the context of US culture at their specific historical moment.[9] The dynamics of assimilation and differentiation are explored further by Peter Krämer in chapter 21, also with regard to German film-makers who have worked in Hollywood in recent years. Krämer traces correlations between the input of Germans in the American film industry and the box-office success of Hollywood films in Germany. He concludes that before the 1970s, European-themed films made by expatriate European directors were more likely to succeed on the German market. Since the 1970s, when German audiences began to show a clear preference for the Hollywood product and American subject films became dominant at the German box-office, no longer depending on enactments of familiar settings and European themes, directors such as Roland Emmerich and Wolfgang Petersen have built successful careers by fully assimilating themselves into the American mainstream.

Today, in a world where almost twenty-two million people live in exile as refugees, and many more have relocated for economic reasons, home and belonging have become contested categories on a global scale. In the context of questions regarding the politics of place and mobility, the exile of German film-makers needs to be reframed in relation to questions raised by post-colonial and migration studies.[10] Hamid Naficy's work on exilic and diasporic film-making since the 1960s as 'an accented cinema', in particular, opens up a range of stylistic and thematic correspondences. His discussion of the use of cinematic spaces which centres around common tropes of exile such as claustrophobia, imprisonment, imagined home-lands, borders and border crossings, journeys and symbolic locations and objects of itinerancy such as trains, buses, airports, hotels, suitcases, as well as the questions he raises about the performance of identities, pose an enriching challenge for future work on earlier configurations of exile.[11]

This challenge is to be extended further to include other kinds of travel and itinerant identities which – for different reasons – are not commonly associated with the canon of artistic innovation in the field of film studies. Documentary (and at times also dramatic) films about non-western locations have tended to be studied in the context of ethnography, but have, if at all, occupied a marginal place in film studies in the context of third cinema studies. Marie-Hélène Gutberlet's chapter on cinematic representations of Africa opens up a continuum between colonial imaginations (which in the German context outlived the existence of colonies by several decades), documentary, television and feature films – indeed she concludes that 'only in film did Germany succeed in annexing Africa'. In a similar vein, a conference on 'Triviale Tropen' (Trivial Tropics) organised by CineGraph in 1996, which took place at the ethnographic museum in Hamburg, unearthed interesting connections between ethnographic expeditions, often accompanied by a documentary film team, as well as the display of foreign cultures in museums and on fairgrounds, and adventure films set in exotic locations, often assembled in the studio with artifacts borrowed from ethnographic museums.[12] For future research, the opulent construction of a fantasy India in German cinema, in the absence of colonial involvement, would be equally interesting to explore. Franz Osten's East-bound transnational career and involvement in the Indian film industry, for example, producing among other films *Shiraz* (1928) and *A Throw of Dice* (1929), which are considered classics of silent Indian cinema, Joe May's and Fritz Lang's exotic adventure films set in an imaginary India as well as appearances of diasporic Indians and Pakistanis in recent multi-cultural films such as *Drachenfutter* (1987) or *Ich Chef, Du Turnschuh* (1998) would all have to be included in this analysis.

This, finally, raises the question of how strangers in the nation are represented. Around 9 per cent (7.5 million) of Germany's resident population today is 'foreign' (although not necessarily foreign born). The concentration in certain cities is considerably higher (17.4 per cent in West Berlin). An account of German cinema today has to take into account the presence of migrants and their descendants who live multi-lingual, at times multi-local, lives and their various forms of participation and incorporation in the national media. Deniz Göktürk's chapter focuses on Turkish–German exchanges in cinema, rethinking the history of these exchanges in a global context of transnational migration. She argues that the mass immigration of labourers from Southern European countries from the 1960s has commonly been depicted along the conventions of a social-realist genre which developed in a sub-national ghetto of parochial paternalism and miserabilism, largely oblivious of other kinds of traffic in and out of German cinema and culture. In comparison to various travelling performers named earlier who were embraced as an enrichment to German cinema, the new migrants tended to be dutifully represented as victims and problems on the margins of society. Only recently, film-makers of an immigrant background have begun to challenge these representations and introduce more playful stagings of contact, conflict and mutual mimicry. Göktürk suggests unfixing the common trope of immigrant identities based on ethno-nationalist definitions of cultural heritage, and reframing these enactments of difference in a broader consideration of strategies of acting and performance, masquerade and camouflage in the force-field between assimilation and differentiation.

More work along these lines remains to be done, focusing on various forms of border traffic, on transnational careers of travelling writers, directors, actors and technicians, on the marketing politics of ethnicity and otherness, and on hybridity and heteroglossia not only at the margins, but at the core of national cultural production. The contributions in this section form part of this work in progress.

Notes

1 For a study of European co-productions see Tim Bergfelder, *International Adventures: Popular German Cinema in the 1960s* (Berghahn, 2003, forthcoming).

2 Andrew Higson, 'The Concept of National Cinema', in *Screen*, vol. 30, no. 4, Autumn 1989, pp. 36–46. Reprinted in Alan Williams (ed.), *Film and Nationalism* (New Brunswick and London: Rutgers University Press, 2002), pp. 52–67.

3 Ibid., p. 54.

4 Benedict Anderson, *Imagined Communities: Reflections on the Origin and Spread of Nationalism* (London and New York: Verso, 1983).

5 Arjun Appadurai, 'Disjuncture and Difference in the Global Cultural Economy', in *Modernity at Large: Cultural Dimensions of Globalization* (Minneapolis and London: University of Minnesota Press, 1996).

6 Jan-Christopher Horak, 'German Exile Cinema, 1933–1950', in *Film History*, vol. 8, no. 4, 1996, pp. 373–89.

7 Thomas Elsaesser, *Weimar Cinema and After: Germany's Historical Imaginary* (London and New York: Routledge, 2000), p. 368 and p. 429.

8 Ibid., p. 367.

9 Cf. Anton Kaes, "A Stranger in the House: Fritz Lang' *Fury* and the Cinema of Exile" forthcoming in *New German Critique* (2003).

10 Hamid Naficy (ed.), *Home, Exile, Homeland: Film, Media, and the Politics of Place* (New York and London: Routledge, 1999). This volume contains a chapter by Thomas Elsaesser on 'Ethnicity, Authenticity, and Exile: A Counterfeit Trade? German Filmmakers and Hollywood': pp. 97–123.

11 Hamid Naficy, *An Accented Cinema: Exilic and Diasporic Filmmaking* (Princeton, NJ, and Oxford: Princeton University Press, 2001).

12 Jörg Schöning, *Triviale Tropen: Exotische Reise- und Abenteuerfilme aus Deutschland 1919–1939* (Munich: edition text+kritik, 1997).

20

Transatlantic Careers: Ernst Lubitsch and Fritz Lang

Sabine Hake

Film authorship, film history and national cinema

German film history has been sustained by the double equation of Weimar cinema with art cinema as the prevailing aesthetic model and with authorship as the predominant filmic practice. The overdetermined status of Weimar cinema – as the utopian dream of a progressive mass culture and the prefiguration of a fascist media dictatorship – has profoundly influenced the critical reception of its most famous directors and their changing association with aesthetic sensibilities identifiable in the broadest sense as 'German'. The films of Ernst Lubitsch and Fritz Lang have played a key role in these patterns of explanation, most crucially through their changing identification with the signatures of the national on domestic and international markets. Both directors took advantage of the discourses of the national and made their contribution to classical cinema through internationally recognisable forms and styles.

The significance of such a highly mobile definition of the national can be seen in the transatlantic careers that brought Lubitsch and Lang from Berlin to Hollywood and situated their films productively between 'Europe' and 'America'. Sustained by the resultant traffic in images and imaginations, their German and American films shed light on the function of the national as an instrument of product differentiation and cultural ambition and, under certain circumstances, as a conduit for new aesthetic and critical sensibilities. The processes of cultural adaptation and transformation that, over the course of five decades,

informed their directorial styles, from generic preferences and thematic concerns to various aspects of camerawork, editing and *mise-en-scène*, took place in an international market-place defined by increasing economic competition between European and US-American production and distribution companies, and by the not always unproblematic enlistment of the national as a category of difference in visual and narrative strategies. In these transatlantic constellations, both directors continuously redefined the meaning of the national as a marker of difference: through their self-stylisation as celebrities (e.g. the jovial Lubitsch with his cigar, the stern Lang with his monocle); through the use of stereotypes and clichés; and through references to high culture in their approach to production design and *mise-en-scène*.

Hollywood has always used the perceived ethnicity or nationality of its stars and directors to create public personalities or screen personas and classify different attitudes and mentalities. Early German cinema, too, made extensive use of ethnic and national stereotypes, a tendency that culminated in its ambivalent relationship to 'America' as the embodiment of modern mass culture and a new multi-ethnic, transnational society. The particular contribution of Lubitsch and Lang during these formative years lay in their acute awareness of the national as a category of difference – in other words, a shifting signifier – and of its alternatively critical and affirmative functions under changing conditions of production and reception. Not surprisingly, both directors found their directorial style in genres that simultaneously acknowledged and denied the burdens of identity: ethnic comedy in the case of Lubitsch and the urban thriller in the case of Lang. Within the confines of these genres, both also found the formula of accommodation most suited to their professional and artistic ambition: Lubitsch through a play with stereotypes and Lang through crises of subjectivity.

Lubitsch and Lang developed their filmic styles in a national and international context and through changing definitions of authorship in these contexts. Both directors made their first films within the structures of economic co-operation and artistic exchange that, by the mid-1920s, found expression in the project of Film Europe and its various attempts to redefine the national, within a self-consciously European framework of reference. Lang and Lubitsch appropriated diverse elements from literature, theatre, operetta, architecture and design and, through camerawork, editing and *mise-en-scène*, transformed them into uniquely filmic effects. Furthermore, both relied heavily on the established national iconographies that contributed to the rise of cinema to a middle-class diversion and modern art form.

Sustained by this circulation of images, texts, and discourses, Lubitsch and Lang played an important role in German–American film relations during the Weimar years. The international success of the innovative expressionist films and the big-budget costume dramas that were Ufa's greatest export articles sparked widespread fears among Hollywood studio heads about a 'German invasion'. The lucrative offers subsequently extended to Lubitsch, Murnau and many others brought a first wave of film professionals to Hollywood. They participated in the internationalisation of cinema as a visual language and popular diversion. This process gave rise to an imagination of the national that, in contrast to the national imagination, required mobility and adaptability from both the producers and the images themselves. But in the same way that both directors contributed actively to the international reputation of the German art film during the silent period, they found themselves enlisted in the very different discourses of the national that emerged during the transition from silent to sound film.

In German film histories, the wave of economic migration during the 1920s and the wave of political emigration after 1933 have been treated very differently. The 1920s are usually examined as part of the international film trade and the laws of circulation that turned famous actors and directors into marketable commodities. By contrast, exile cinema has been described as the 'other' of Nazi cinema, with refugees maintaining the image of a better Germany during the Third Reich (e.g. through their participation in anti-Nazi films) and offering critical perspec-tives on American culture and society (e.g. through their contribution to film noir). My own comparative approach to the German–American careers of Lubitsch and Lang suggests that both transatlantic journeys involved similar problems of cultural adaptation but produced very different aesthetic solutions.

While the distinction between economic migration and political exile is undoubtedly important on the level of the individual biographies of such figures as Lubitsch and Lang, the early reception of German directors in Hollywood rarely extended to political arguments, and that despite widespread anti-German sentiments after the First World War and strong isolationist tendencies until the late 1930s. The association of Lubitsch and Lang with European culture became more politicised during the Second World War and established a pattern of reception that, in the case of Lang, continued throughout the 1950s. While his lack of commercial success in the 1940s can be attributed in part to wartime patriotism, the director's re-emergence in the 1950s can only be understood in the context of post-war illusionism and a greater openness among audiences towards dissenting voices and darker perspectives.

Since their canonisation as film *auteurs* in the 1970s, Lubitsch and Lang have been closely identified with art cinema and its transnational effects: Lubitsch through his humorous reflections on rituals of desire, and Lang through his cynical reflections on power and destiny. Despite their similarly high standing during the 1910s and 20s, both directors have come to occupy very different places in national film histories and more text-oriented author-based studies. The early Lubitsch is usually described as an astute observer of human behaviour who exposes social and sexual hypocrisies through comic or ironic effects that simultaneously challenge convention and affirm the status quo.[1] Inviting often contradictory readings, the early Lang, by contrast, is either seen as a precise diagnostician of Weimar society or hailed as an innovative artist with a unique filmic vision.[2] Nowadays critics evoke the name of Lubitsch when they bemoan the underdeveloped tradition of filmic irony and the equally rare moments of erotic sophistication in German cinema. Yet they turn to Lang and his social dystopias, technological utopias and modern mythologies when examining this nation's troubled history.

Both directors have also inspired very different readings in the context of classical cinema and, more specifically, the rise of the sound film during the early 1930s. In terms of professional reputation, the American Lubitsch became the model immigrant who adapted quickly to the studio system and its functionalisation of his otherness; hence his collaboration with major studios and leading stars even after repeated commercial failures.[3] Known for his authoritarian demeanour, Lang, on the other hand, struggled in the dream factory and remained an outsider even during the years of greatest success.[4] As for their artistic reputation, both directors are identified with very different aesthetic and ideological projects. The late Lubitsch stands for the kind of liberal humanism associated with continental Europe and its traditional social and cultural elites.[5] By contrast, the late Lang has been enlisted in more theoretical reflections on the dialectics of mass culture and modernity and its articulation through new structures of domination as well as new forms of visual pleasure.[6] Identified with nostalgia and sentimentality, Lubitsch has come to represent a model of cultural assimilation that, in its instrumentalisation of stereotypes and clichés, offers very little to today's debates about transnational cinemas. By contrast, Lang has allowed scholars to contemplate forms of cultural transfer and exchange that suggest the possibility of aesthetic opposition within dominant culture. This difference in the functionalisation of difference accounts for the relative lack of scholarly interest in Lubitsch and the renewed interest in Lang especially over the last two years.[7]

The discourse of Germanness represented an important organising principle behind Lubitsch's and Lang's heavy reliance on the markers of the national in a transnational context. The constituent elements of this discourse include individual biographies as well as cultural representations, aesthetic preferences as well as filmic conventions, critical intentions as well as socio-psychological functions. In such an expanded definition of film authorship, Lubitsch stands for the principle of self-commodification, and for an underlying belief in role-playing as a necessary element in all social relations. His early slapstick comedies demonstrate his close familiarity with the dreams of social advancement and material gain that sustained the Wilhelmine empire, including in the (Jewish) milieu of small shop owners and businessmen. Yet his romantic comedies and costume dramas already present the complications of gender and sexuality within a model of individualism seemingly unaffected by social pressures and constraints. For that reason, Lubitsch has been most attractive to traditional genre criticism. With very different intentions, Lang displaces the crisis of identity into aesthetic constellations but, in so doing, also critically reconstructs its constituent elements. This tension makes his work available to modernist and post-modernist readings. Lang's orientalist fantasies and medieval epics bear

witness to a remarkable ability to forge the most diverse elements of Wilhelmine aesthetics into convincing simulacra of authenticity. Yet his urban thrillers enlist the same visual strategies in an analysis of Weimar modernity that, through their formal qualities, comments critically on the political situation in the late 1920s and early 30s.

During their formative years in Germany, both directors resisted the trend towards seamless narratives by developing filmic styles and techniques that became identified with the project of Weimar art cinema.[8] Once in Hollywood, Lubitsch lost interest in the social and political consequences of sexual transgressions and concentrated instead on private arrangements that could be realised only under the safe conditions provided by money and privilege. In contrast, Lang after 1933 turned the perceptiveness of the foreigner into a critical tool for studying the most advanced manifestations of mass culture and modernity through moments of failure and breakdown in the social contract. Making productive use of their status as exiles and émigrés, both directors fell back on the class-based categories – an arriviste mentality in the case of Lubitsch and cultural elitism in the case of Lang – that had already informed their German films and processed these categories of distinction through the discourses of the national that defined the work of many foreign-born directors in Hollywood in aesthetic terms. Ironically, it was Lubitsch, the Berlin-born Jew, who became identified with a Central European sensibility mapped onto the imaginary topography of Vienna, Paris and Budapest and its highly codified rituals of erotic and cultural sophistication. On the other hand, it was the Viennese-born Lang who personified the typical Prussian with all the negative connotations of authority, discipline and reserve. Fully committed to a Hollywood fantasy of the Old World, Lubitsch ended up recreating 'Europe' in the conventional terms established by operetta and boulevard theatre. Lang, on the other hand, used the attributes that contributed to his reputation as a very 'Germanic' director to become a detached observer of contemporary American life. This double displacement in the relationship between nation and narration – Lubitsch's American(ised) vision of Europe and Lang's European(ised) vision of America – continues to inform the critical reception of their films and still accounts for their different position in histories of German cinema and studies on film authorship.

Ernst Lubitsch: inventing Europe through American eyes

The German films of Ernst Lubitsch are inextricably linked to the transition from the early cinema of visual spectacle to the classical cinema of narrative integration. This transition brought greater attention to ethnicity in the representation of social milieus and established a system of differences that became central to his own work and career. Born on 29 January 1882, Lubitsch started out by playing bit parts in Max Reinhardt productions at the famous Deutsches Theater in Berlin. His first screen appearances as an apprentice in the PAGU films *Die Firma heiratet* (*The Firm Marries*, 1914) and *Der Stolz der Firma* (*The Pride of the Firm*, 1914) established the main elements of his comic style: its focus on the world of small shop owners and businessmen, on social ambition and material wealth, most centrally on sexual desire and other physical pleasures. Moving to three-reelers after his first directorial effort, *Schuhpalast Pinkus* (*Shoe Salon Pinkus*), Lubitsch continued to work in the tradition of ethnic comedy, including through extensive references to German–Jewish life. Soon he integrated the slapstick elements into a uniquely filmic approach to comedy that combined the performative excess of the early one- and two-reelers with a greater emphasis on the filmic articulation of irony and wit. Lubitsch completed the transition from acting to directing in two popular genres, romantic comedies and costume dramas. During this formative period, he entered into productive working relationships with PAGU director and later Ufa producer Paul Davidson, screenwriter Hanns Kräly, cinematographer Theodor Sparkuhl, set designer Kurt Richter, costume designer Ali Hubert, and rising stars Pola Negri, Henny Porten and Emil Jannings.

Wenn vier dasselbe tun (*When Four Do the Same*, 1917) is an example of a film that took key elements of ethnic comedy (e.g. the experience of exclusion) and applied them to more general human concerns, such as the fleeting nature of desire, the importance of appearances and conventions, and the liberating effect of detachment and self-irony. Once freed of the markers of social and ethnic specificity, Lubitsch could apply his visual commentaries to the most diverse places and times and test the transgressive potential of desire in comic as well as dramatic registers. Such provocative openness in Lubitsch's play with identities coincided with a growing conventionality of means. For that reason, even the films he made after 1919 remained under the influence of a Wilhelmine culture of excess inspired by art nouveau and expressionism, as well

as various forms of exoticism and historicism. More problematically, these debts extended to the ideological legacies of the empire, including the belief in social hierarchies and the resistance to social change. Treating cinema as the quintessential mixed medium, Lubitsch adapted Shakespeare plays, Viennese operettas and Hungarian drawing-room comedies, but infused their familiar structures with contemporary references to sexual liberation, mass consumption, technological progress and modern entertainment culture.

Lubitsch's post-war comedies continued in this provocatively un-German spirit of unabashed hedonism. Increasingly, his critical commentaries were achieved through such filmic means as point-of-view shots, shot/counter-shots and parallel editing. Through the calculated use of doors, windows and mirrors, the director celebrated the power of the gaze but also identified psychological obstacles to the fulfilment of desire, for instance through the ongoing triangulation of looks among characters, spectator and narrator. These formal strategies aligned Lubitsch's directorial style with new sensibilities that promoted more tolerant views on individual behaviour, while at the same time confirming the existing social structures as the most effective compromise between public and private life. Accordingly, *Die Austernprinzessin* (*The Oyster Princess*) presents a mocking commentary on Americanism that extends from typical anti-American stereotypes (e.g. the rich oyster king and his spoiled daughter) to new principles of industrial production such as Fordism and Taylorism. *Die Puppe* (*The Doll*, 1919) translates the demonic of German romanticism into the register of the wondrous, with the automaton no longer a figure of self-alienation but of instant wish fulfilment American-style. Similarly, *Die Bergkatze* (*The Mountain Cat*, 1921) offers a high-spirited female alternative to the crisis of male subjectivity depicted in *Das Cabinet des Dr Caligari* (*The Cabinet of Dr Caligari*) and other expressionist classics. Even the rural setting of *Kohlhiesels Töchter* (1920), a taming-of-the-shrew-story with Porten in a double role, allowed the director to promote his fundamentally urban philosophy of pleasure and self-gratification. The early comedies approach the question of sexual difference through an effective mixture of fairy-tale, slapstick, parody, farce and irony. All of these elements come together in strong-willed, independent-minded screen heroines who – part vamp, part flapper – embody the utopian promise of an all-pervasive eroticism.[9]

Like his comedies, Lubitsch's costume dramas achieved their humorous effects on the intimate scale of the cham-

Die Austernprinzessin (1919)

ber play but projected the more dramatic consequences of male passions and female deceptions onto world historical events. Conceived as an alternative to monumental Italian epics, Lubitsch's costume dramas paid special attention to the relationship between history and narrative and its heightened articulation through the tension between public and private life. The inevitable complications of power and desire are played out with fatal consequences in *Madame Dubarry* and *Anna Boleyn*, two Ufa films famous for their convincing large-scale reconstruction of pre-revolutionary Paris and Tudor London. Some contemporary critics rejected these big-budget productions because of their cynical attitude towards social progress and political change. Nonetheless, the popular success of these costume dramas suggests that their unabashed illusionism also fulfilled important socio-psychological functions. The films acknowledge the reality of individual desire and show the obstacles to its fulfilment in contemporary life. Whereas their emphasis on material goods and physical pleasures implies a critique of humanist idealism, their almost mechanical approach to plot structure and character development suggests an almost materialist anti-psychologism.

Both qualities endow the director's German films with a refreshingly contemporary quality, regardless of their actual subjects or settings. What made Lubitsch so important for Ufa marketing strategies, and what brought him an offer from Hollywood, was precisely this remarkable ability to combine artistic quality with popular appeal and to make big-budget films that were innovative and conventional, provocative and conciliatory at the same time.

Identified with such elusive qualities, Lubitsch became one of the first to use the camera as an instrument of authorial commentary as well as narrative continuity. Maintaining a sense of distance through his famous sense of irony, he expressed a fundamental scepticism about human nature but also showed a deep understanding for individual weaknesses. Lubitsch made international stars out of Jannings and Negri, but he could hardly be called an actor's director, not even in his work with major Hollywood stars. Indifferent to psychological nuances and complexities, he relied primarily on the objects of everyday life in mediating between internal and external reality and producing the ironic perspectives that became known as the 'Lubitsch touch'.[10] Whether in historical, contemporary or fantastic settings, with melodramatic, satirical or farcical overtones, Lubitsch always returned to the elusive dynamics between appearance and reality as the driving force behind all human relationships. He confirmed the power of the image, and of surface phenomena, through provocative insights into the voyeuristic and exhibitionistic tendencies that sustained the rituals of society and the attractions of cinema. Reaching the high-point of his German career during the transition towards classical narrative cinema, Lubitsch remained indifferent towards cherished notions such as love, honesty and truth. His preoccupation with sexual temptation explains the characterisation of his costume dramas as 'history from the key-hole perspective'. Yet his debunking of romantic love was predicated on a cynical view of gender roles, social structures and historical processes that implied a basic agreement with the status quo. In that sense, Lubitsch remained profoundly conservative, but in an open-minded fashion that, from the American perspective, seemed refreshingly Old World.

Following an invitation from Mary Pickford, Lubitsch left for the United States in 1922. He was the first among several European film professionals enlisted by the majors to build an arthouse audience on domestic markets and consolidate their position on foreign markets, among other things by exploiting the national origins of some of their leading stars and directors. For Warner Bros. Lubitsch directed a number of drawing-room comedies in the style of *The Marriage Circle* (1924) that applied the intimate choreography of the comedy of manners to the screen. Following in the Central European tradition, these comedies promoted a more enlightened approach to sexual matters through their refusal of moral judgment (e.g. on issues such as adultery) and, even more important, through their enlistment of the spectator's complicity through visual and verbal innuendoes. In his contribution to the fun mentality of 'the roaring 20s', Lubitsch resisted a tragic view of love and passion but also presented the rituals of seduction with a deep scepticism about the liberating effect of sexual freedom on social relations. Nonetheless, the move from Berlin to Hollywood resulted in a fundamental realignment within the European–American opposition. Now the 'Americanised' protagonists who once infused Lubitsch's early Germany comedies with an air of openness and possibility gave way to 'Europeanised' characters who advocated a tacit acceptance of hypocrisy as a necessary part of everyday life.

Informed by such patterns of adaptation, Lubitsch's deceptive play with national stereotypes – namely as a performance of identity – ended up promoting old-fashioned notions of gender and class as stabilising elements in middle-class society. This quality became more pronounced with the further codification of visual and narrative strategies in the early sound film. Lubitsch joined Paramount and, beginning with *The Love Parade* (1929), directed several successful film operettas with Jeanette McDonald and Maurice Chevalier that confirmed his identification with the kind of continental sophistication only achieved within the confines of illusionism. During the 1930s, the director specialised in sophisticated comedies like *Trouble in Paradise* (1932), whose attractive protagonists, spectacular art deco settings, and above all, verbal banter and spirited repartee expressed his enduring belief in the primacy of form over content. Again Paris and London functioned as imaginary locations in a transatlantic traffic in national physiognomies and topographies freed of all social or political relevance. Directing the leading female stars of the 1930s, Marlene Dietrich in *Angel* and Greta Garbo in *Ninotchka*, Lubitsch continued to make highly stylised comedies about temptation, deception, consumption and other favourite games of the European leisure class. Not surprisingly, his contribution to the anti-Nazi genre, *To Be or Not to Be*, was attacked for its inappropriate use of humour in the representation of the Polish resistance.

Later comedies like *The Shop Around the Corner* that focused on the problems of the 'little people' only ended up recycling generic formulas (in this case, inspired by Jewish clothing manufacture) but without any specificity of social or ethnic milieu. As before, a vaguely Central European setting came to stand in for the director's suppressed German–Jewish identity. Like earlier attempts to address more serious themes (e.g. in the 1932 anti-war drama *The Man I Killed)*, the search for greater authenticity ended up in sentimentality and kitsch.

After Lubitsch's death on 30 November 1947, his distinctive mixture of sexual innuendo and visual wit was developed further by fellow German émigré Billy Wilder, and it served as an important source of inspiration for Mitchell Leisen, George Cukor and Preston Sturges. Nonetheless, Lubitsch's particular blend of ironisation and stylisation became increasingly irrelevant after the Second World War and the historical traumas of nationalism, racism and anti-Semitism. As a consequence, the transnational effects that made possible his transatlantic career during the 1920s and 30s have come to be seen in a very different light: namely as a reminder of a different time and its very liberating, but also limited, views on identity as a game of appearances.

Fritz Lang: the dissecting gaze on American life

Despite countless studies about his life and work, the films of Fritz Lang continue to resist critical assessments that rely only on categories of filmic style or artistic quality. While covering a range of characters, settings and periods, his films are always structured around the same psychological or epistemological crises. Unlike Lubitsch, whose strategies of assimilation in Berlin and Hollywood reveal him as someone fixated on difference, Lang conveys an understanding of cinema and modernity that, precisely in its tendency towards abstraction, seems uniquely German in its philosophical underpinnings and therefore inextricably linked to Weimar culture and its social and political dilemmas. Whereas Lubitsch's conventionality is most apparent where he mocks conventions, Lang's resistance to classical narrative seems most pronounced whenever he works within established genres. His configurations of vision, knowledge and power grew out of the disillusionment of post-war society and developed further through the cold pragmatism associated with New Objectivity. His alienated consciousness functions as a productive force that illuminates modernity's levelling of social and ethnic differences and its crisis of subjectivity in relation to two momentous historical events, the collapse of the Wilhelmine empire and the rise of National Socialism.

Lang was born on 5 December 1890 in Vienna, studied art and architecture, and served in the First World War. He made his first contacts with the film business through Joe May by writing scripts for his popular Joe Deebs series. In 1918 Lang moved to Berlin, the centre of the European film industry, and began to work for Erich Pommer's Decla-Bioscop. His first directorial efforts, *Halbblut* (*Half Blood*, 1919) and the two-part *Spinnen* (*Spiders*, 1919–20), profited from the sensationalism and exoticism of early cinema. Beginning with May's *Das Indische Grabmal* (*The Indian Tomb*), Lang repeatedly worked with Thea von Harbou, a successful writer and his second wife. Their collaboration trained his talent for forging incompatible thematic and stylistic elements into uniquely modern constellations. Harbou has sometimes functioned as a repository of the more problematic tendencies separating Lang, the cosmopolitan modernist, from his 'Germanic' interest in history and mythology.[11] Like Lubitsch, Lang developed his trademark style with the help of skilled professionals who included, apart from Harbou and Pommer, cinematographers Carl Hoffmann and Fritz Arno Wagner and set designers Otto Hunte and Erich Kettelhut. But unlike Lubitsch, Lang always insisted on his own vision of cinema and never adapted to popular tastes.

Nonetheless, the director's association with the powerful Ufa concern has been used to interpret his social fantasies as a reflection of problems in the Weimar Republic. Among others, Kracauer has interpreted Lang's fixation on power relations as a manifestation of pre-fascist tendencies, and dismissed his heavy reliance on set design as a symptom of social paralysis.[12] The case of Lang suggests that a combination of two factors, the particular mode of production at Ufa and the creative vision of its most famous director, provided the conditions for the transnational movements that began with filmic references to 'Germany' and 'America' in the context of Weimar Americanism and that culminated in two transatlantic moves between Hollywood and Berlin. Whereas Lubitsch exploited his European heritage in very American ways (i.e. by turning his immigrant status into a marketable commodity), Lang resisted these discourses of identity by cultivating a German aura on the level of aesthetic preferences and philosophical beliefs.

During his Weimar years, Lang appropriated diverse traditions and discourses for a vision of modernity that was defined less through certain themes and motifs than through a specific core problematic concerned with the question of power. By moving beyond the customary division between modernity and myth, he conjured up contemporary scenarios of fear, ambition and desire that thematised the disappearance of all distinctions between image and reality. Eclectic in his choice of source material but consistent in his emphasis on stylisation as a filmic effect, Lang worked primarily in two genres, monumental epics and urban thrillers. Both addressed a number of shared concerns: the helplessness of the individual in the face of power; the ubiquity of chaos and violence; the fascination with death and destruction; and, most importantly, the inescapable forces of fate and destiny. From the historical episodes in *Der müde Tod* (*Destiny*) and the monumental two-part *Die Nibelungen* (*The Nibelungs*) to the social dystopia of *Metropolis* and the technological fantasy of *Frau im Mond* (*Woman on the Moon*, 1929), architecture provided the director with a framework for staging the movements of the individual and the masses and showing their dependence on visual and spatial relations.

Like no other German film, *Metropolis* has served to demonstrate the alignment of Weimar cinema with the modern imagination and of the Langian style with a transnational, transhistorical modernity.[13] This overdetermined function is particularly obvious in comparison

Metropolis (1926)

with *Die Nibelungen*, the national epic that brings into relief the more problematic aspects of Lang's heavy reliance on a national iconography and mythology.[14] The static quality of *Metropolis*' *mise-en-scène* attests to Lang's pessimistic views about human nature and its openness to change. At the same time, the film's eclecticism of forms and styles can be read as a compelling model of mass culture and modernity that combines German myths and legends with the most advanced expression of Americanism and, in so doing, dissolves traditional differences into the more fluid constellations established by vision and visuality. Moving beyond the false alternatives of realism vs illusionism, Lang reproduces the modern experience through close attention to visual relations as the foundation of knowledge in a world increasingly dominated by anonymous power structures.

Lang's thrillers and detective films address similar concerns about the limits of individual agency, but in more contemporary settings. Their reflections on the dangers of urban life confirm the author's growing emphasis on vision as both an instrument in, and a form of resistance to, the process of modernisation. The anti-humanism that in his monumental films joins forces with new populist mythologies turns in his urban thrillers into an instrument of critical analysis and social commentary. Lang stages the alienation of modern man through filmic ciphers that, as secondhand images, are always already mediated by other systems of representation; hence his preference for trivial literature and elaborate architectural metaphors.[15] Thus his Mabuse series explores the pathologies of post-war society, from the perspective of hyperinflation in the two-part *Dr Mabuse, der Spieler* (*Dr Mabuse, the Gambler*), to media tyranny in the banned sequel, *Das Testament des Dr Mabuse* (*The Testament of Dr Mabuse*). Through the figure of the

madman/master criminal, the series demonstrates the corrupting influence of modern mass media on established forms of authority, as represented by the state and its representatives.

Lang's diagnosis of a breakdown in systems of representation also extends to the kind of visual and narrative authority thematised in his sustained reflections on the crisis of the real in modernity. *Spione* (*Spies*, 1928) explores modernity's inevitable crisis of legitimisation through a close look at global capitalism and its corrosive effect on urban life. The haunting story of the child murderer in *M*, Lang's first sound film and a continuation of his visual experiments in the auditory realm, directly addresses the problem of individual and collective action.[16] On the one hand, these films capture the social dilemmas of Weimar society by establishing a thematic link between the traumas of the past (e.g. the war experience) and the problems of the present (e.g. the rise of political violence). On the other, the director's highly symbolic *mise-en-scène* and object symbolism give rise to a filmic language of fear and paranoia that receives its abstract qualities from the problems of modernity and modernisation prevalent during the Weimar Republic.

If Lang's cynicism before 1933 can be linked to the ideology of New Objectivity, his growing pessimism after 1933 must be seen as an expression of the difficulties of exile and the changing relevance of his modernism under the economic and aesthetic terms dictated by the Hollywood studio system. Leaving Berlin after the Nazi takeover, Lang arrived in the United States via Paris in 1934 to embark on a moderately successful career as a director respected by his colleagues and valued for his critical views on American culture and society. He started out with social realist dramas like *Fury* (1936) and *You Only Live Once* (1937) that showed the mechanisms of mob rule against the backdrop of the Depression and used the failures of the criminal justice system to examine the mass psychology of racism and, by extension, fascism. Similar considerations informed the director's use of individual transgressions as a heuristic device in studying the modern condition. Thus during the 1940s, Lang directed a number of melodramas about lonely city dwellers that, like *The Woman in the Window* (1944) and *Scarlet Street* (1945), problematise the growing separation of public and private life in an increasingly anonymous mass society. His observations on the possibilities of individual resistance even extended to world political events, including in a difficult collaboration with Bertolt Brecht on the anti-Nazi film *Hangmen Also Die* (1943).

Returning to the sensationalist combination of sex,

crime and the big city from the German period, Lang during the 1950s developed an increasingly sceptical approach to the blessings of modernity. This most un-American preoccupation with the limits of freedom and choice informed his contribution to film noir and inspired his detached observations on the rituals of power and violence in such classics as *The Blue Gardenia* (1953), *The Big Heat* (1953) and *While the City Sleeps* (1956). In these suspenseful stories of murder, fear and revenge, Lang finally adapted his German modernism to the American way of life and modified its more problematic aspects (e.g. its fatalism) in light of the greater resourcefulness of post-war individualism. Unfortunately, this turn to more realist styles occurred at a time when the collapse of the studio system made it increasingly difficult for the director to work under the conditions most suited to his self-understanding as a film artist.

Partly because of such developments, Lang returned to West Germany in the late 1950s to direct sequels to *Das Indische Grabmal* and the *Mabuse* series for Artur Brauner's CCC. While successful at the box-office, these films failed to attract much critical attention. The sensibility of the returning exile – Weimar sensationalism channelled through Hollywood conventions – seemed out of place in the atmosphere of pragmatism that defined the society of the Economic Miracle. It was, however, precisely this modern consciousness that would make him interesting to later generations of film-makers who challenged the conventions of classical narrative. Revered by a new generation of critics, including those associated with the French nouvelle vague, Lang thematised his position between old and new definitions of film authorship when he appeared one last time as an ageing director in Jean-Luc Godard's *Le mépris* (Contempt, 1963) before he died after a long illness in Beverly Hills on 2 August 1976. The ongoing engagement with his work confirms the productive tension between historical specificity and formal abstraction in his films and accounts, among other things, for the enduring significance of his vision of a transnational cinema. Together with Lubitsch, who responded to the challenges of the transnational by creating an artificial world organised around fixed but empty markers of identity, Lang, with his very modernist approach to film as both a leveller and a preserver of identities, established a model of film authorship that continues to elude traditional definitions of national cinema.

Notes

1 Cf. Hans-Helmut Prinzler and Enno Patalas (eds.), *Lubitsch* (Munich: C. J. Bucher, 1984); Herta-Elisabeth Renk, *Ernst Lubitsch* (Reinbek: Rowohlt, 1992); Herbert Spaich, *Ernst Lubitsch und seine Filme* (Munich: Heyne, 1992).

2 Cf. Peter W. Jansen and Wolfram Schütte (eds.), *Fritz Lang* (Munich: Hanser, 1976); Lotte Eisner, *Fritz Lang*, trans. Gertrud Mander (New York: Oxford University Press, 1977); Frederick W. Ott, *The Films of Fritz Lang* (Secaucus, NJ: Citadel, 1979); Rolf Aurich, Wolfgang Jacobsen and Cornelius Schnauber (eds.), *Fritz Lang* (Berlin: Filmmuseum, 2001).

3 Cf. Scott Eyman, *Ernst Lubitsch: Laughter in Paradise* (Baltimore, MD: Johns Hopkins University Press, 2000).

4 Cf. Patrick McGilligan, *Fritz Lang: The Nature of the Beast: A Biography* (New York: St Martin's Press, 1997).

5 Cf. Leland A. Poague, *The Cinema of Ernst Lubitsch* (South Brunswick, NJ: A. S. Barnes, 1978); William Paul, *Ernst Lubitsch's American Comedy* (New York: Columbia University Press, 1983).

6 Cf. Stephen Jenkins (ed.), *Fritz Lang: The Image and the Look* (London: BFI, 1981); Reynold Humphries, *Fritz Lang: Genre and Representation in his American Films* (Baltimore, MD: Johns Hopkins University Press, 1989).

7 Cf. Tom Gunning, *The Films of Fritz Lang: Modernity, Crime and Desire* (London: BFI, 2000).

8 Cf. Thomas Elsaesser, *Weimar Cinema and After: Germany's Historical Imaginary* (London and New York: Routledge, 2000), pp. 143–222.

9 Cf. Sabine Hake, *Passions and Deceptions: The Early Films of Ernst Lubitsch* (Princeton, NJ: Princeton University Press, 1992).

10 Cf. Hermann G. Weinberg, *The Lubitsch Touch*, 3rd edn (New York: Dover, 1977).

11 Cf. Reinhold Keiner, *Thea von Harbou und der deutsche Film bis 1933* (Hildesheim: Olms, 1991).

12 Cf. Siegfried Kracauer, *From Caligari to Hitler: A Psychological History of the German Film* (Princeton, NJ: Princeton University Press, 1947), pp. 162–4.

13 Cf. Fritz Gehler and Ullrich Kasten, *Fritz Lang: Die Stimme von Metropolis* (Berlin: Henschel, 1990); Michael Minden and Holger Bachmann (eds.), *Fritz Lang's 'Metropolis': Cinematic Views of Technology and Fear* (Rochester, NY: Camden House, 2000); Thomas Elsaesser, *Metropolis* (London: BFI, 2000).

14 Cf. Sabine Hake, 'Architectural Hi/stories: Fritz Lang and *The Nibelungs*', *Wide Angle*, vol. 12, no. 3, 1990; Angelika Breitmoser-Bock, *Film, Filmbild, Schlüsselbild: zu einer*

kunstwissenschaftlichen Methodik der Filmanalyse am Beispiel von Fritz Langs 'Siegfried' (Deutschland, 1924) (Munich: Schaudig, Bauer, Ledig, 1992); David J. Levin, *Richard Wagner, Fritz Lang, and 'The Nibelungen': The Dramaturgy of Disavowal* (Princeton, NJ: Princeton University Press, 1998).

15 Cf. Fritz Lang, *Die Spinnen*, afterw. Cornelius Schnauber (Munich: Virgilio Iafrate, 1987); Gunter Scholdt (ed.), *Norbert Jacques Fritz Lang Dr Mabuse: Roman/Film/Dokumente* (St Ingbert: W. J. Röhrig, 1987).

16 Cf. Anton Kaes, *M* (London: BFI, 2000).

21

Hollywood in Germany/Germany in Hollywood

Peter Krämer

It is well known that, from their beginnings in the early decades of the twentieth century, the major Hollywood studios have had a strong presence in the German market, and German-speaking immigrants in turn have had a strong presence in the American film industry. What is less well known is that despite their strong presence in Germany, Hollywood films have not always been successful at the German box-office. At the same time, the enormous success of Germans (as well as Austrians) in Hollywood from the 1920s to the 60s and again since the 80s has not been fully appreciated. In this chapter, I want to investigate the changing fortunes of Germans (and Austrians) in Hollywood and of Hollywood films in Germany, presenting some of the reasons for these changing fortunes, and asking what, if any, connections have existed between the success of German speakers in Hollywood and the popularity of Hollywood films in Germany.

Germans and Austrians in Hollywood before the 1970s

Any systematic account of German speakers in Hollywood is confronted with a bewildering variety of people. There are those born in the US to German-speaking parents (some of whom were American citizens), and immigrants from Europe. Among immigrants, there are further distinctions between those from Germany (Imperial Germany, the Weimar Republic or Nazi Germany) or Austria (the Habsburg Empire or the Austrian Republic), and German speakers from elsewhere in Europe (especially Russia); between those whose first language was German and those who acquired it as a second or third language (especially non-German subjects of the Habsburg Empire,

such as Hungarians, and also immigrants to Germany or Austria from all over Europe).[1] The initial task, then, is to delimit the group under investigation. While many writers have adopted a broad definition,[2] the following survey focuses on people born in Germany or the German-speaking parts of the Habsburg Empire.[3] Furthermore, it only deals with a select group of outstandingly successful directors, stars, producers and crafts personnel, whereby success is measured in terms of box-office rankings and recognition by the Academy of Motion Picture Arts and Sciences. This small sample will establish a baseline for gauging the overall success of German speakers in Hollywood.

The reign of German- and Austrian-born directors at the American box-office started in the silent period. A listing of the most popular forty-one films (those estimated to have sold the most tickets) for the years 1922–7 includes Erich von Stroheim's *Foolish Wives* (1922) and *The Merry Widow* (1925) as well as Ernst Lubitsch's American debut *Rosita* (1923).[4] Another list based on box-office rentals for the years 1914–31 ranks Lubitsch's German production *Madame Dubarry* (1919; distributed in the US under the title *Passion*) among the top sixty-seven films of the period.[5] When *Variety* and other trade papers introduced annual charts of the top grossing movies in the 1930s, they included several Lubitsch films: *The Love Parade* (1929), *The Smiling Lieutenant* (1930), *One Hour With You* (1932) and *Ninotchka* (1939).[6] Other top hits were directed by Josef von Sternberg (*Morocco*, and *Shanghai Express* [1932], William Dieterle (*The Story of Louis Pasteur* [1936], *Juarez* [1939], *The Hunchback of Notre Dame* [1939] and *A Midsummer Night's Dream* [1935, co-directed by Max Reinhardt]) and William Wyler (*These Three* [1936] and *Dodsworth* [1936]). Three of these films made it onto the list of the sixty-seven top grossing movies of the years

1932–40, as did Dieterle's *The Life of Emile Zola* (1937) and Wyler's *Dead End* (1937).[7]

These listings indicate a high level of success, considering the fact that throughout the 1920s and 30s every year between 500 and 1,000 films were released in the US, of which 300 to 500 came from the major studios.[8] During this period, then, directors born in Germany and Austria were consistently involved in the production of top hits.[9] It is noticeable that in the 1920s and early 30s most of their big hits had German, Austrian or 'Ruritanian' (that is imaginary Central European) settings. Throughout the 1930s, this narrow focus was replaced by a wider range of films, most of which did, however, continue to feature foreign (mostly but not exclusively European) settings and/or characters (several of them famous historical personalities), and continued to be based mostly on European source material (novels, plays, biographies).

The main exceptions to the above trend are William Wyler's American-themed *Dodsworth*, *These Three* and *Dead End* (all based on American plays). Indeed, Wyler's ability to produce hits with both American and European subject matter was to become characteristic of German- and Austrian-born directors from the 1940s onwards.[10] Wyler himself was by far the most successful of this group and, arguably, the most successful of *all* Hollywood directors. Wyler's numerous hits covered an impressive range of genres: serious drama and romantic comedy, crime and Western, musical and biblical epic. In addition to appearing in the end-of-year charts, some of Wyler's films became massive breakaway hits: *The Best Years of Our Lives* (1946) was the top grossing movie of the 1940s, and *Ben Hur* (1959) the top grossing movie of the 1950s. *Mrs Miniver* (1942) also made it into the top twenty of the 1940s, while *Funny Girl* (1968) was in the top ten of the 1960s.[11]

Fred Zinnemann and Billy Wilder had similarly impressive strings of hits from the 1940s to the 60s, although only one of their movies (*From Here to Eternity*, 1953) made it into the top ten of the decade of its release. Other successful directors included Otto Preminger and Henry Koster, whose biggest hit was *The Robe* (1953), the fourth highest grossing film of the 1950s. Broadening the scope of the investigation beyond directors reveals another major hitmaker in independent producer Sam Spiegel, who was responsible for a string of successes in the 1950s and 60s, among them *The Bridge on the River Kwai* (1957), the sixth highest grossing film of the 1950s. Finally, there were a number of box-office hits starring German- and Austrian-born actors, including Marlene Dietrich, Paul Muni, Luise Rainer, Paul Henreid and Hedy Lamarr, whose biggest hit *Samson and Delilah* (1949) was the third highest

grossing film of the 1940s. While, from the 1940s to the 60s, Hollywood's Germans and Austrians succeeded across a range of genres, films with European and/or biblical subject matter continued to have a prominent place in their output.

In addition to turning out hit movies on a regular basis, German- and Austrian-born personnel were regarded very highly by the Academy of Motion Picture Arts and Sciences.[12] At its very first Awards ceremony, Josef von Sternberg's *The Last Command* was nominated for Best Picture of 1927/8, Emil Jannings won the Best Actor award for *The Last Command* (1928) and *The Way of All Flesh* (1927), and Friedrich Wilhelm Murnau's American debut *Sunrise* (1927) won a special Oscar for 'Artistic Quality of Production'. A conservative estimate[13] of the Academy Award successes of German- and Austrian-born personnel suggests that before 1970 they won seven Best Director Oscars from thirty-six nominations (Wyler again being the most successful),[14] six Best Picture Oscars (an award given to a film's producer) from sixteen nominations, three Irving G. Thalberg Memorial Awards, five Best Actor/Actress Oscars from twelve nominations, one Best Supporting Actor/Actress Oscar from five nominations, seven Oscars for Best Script or Best Original Story from twenty-four nominations, three Best Cinematography Oscars from ten nominations, nine Oscars for Best Score or Best Song, and nine Oscars for Interior Decoration/Art Direction.

Clearly, the elite group of Hollywood's Germans and Austrians, whose success with the Academy and at the box-office I have surveyed, was central to the operations of the American film industry. Indeed, no other countries – with the exception of Britain and Canada – could claim an equally impressive group of Hollywood personnel as their own. Yet, of course, this group constituted only a fraction of the German and Austrian community in Hollywood, which numbered hundreds of people, ranging from bit players to seminal filmmakers such as Fritz Lang and Douglas Sirk. While the diverse achievements of this much larger group were rarely recognised by the Academy or by American cinema-goers, their overall contributions to American cinema probably equalled those of the elite group. So why were there so many Germans and Austrians in Hollywood, and what were the specific circumstances that allowed many of them to join the top ranks of the Hollywood establishment?

Hollywood, German immigration and Weimar cinema

When German- and Austrian-born film-makers, actors, writers and craftsmen first rose to prominence in the American film industry in the 1920s, Hollywood had already established itself as the international film capital.[15] As such, Hollywood was an attractive destination for European film personnel (such as Lubitsch, Jannings and Murnau) aiming to further their career.[16] Hollywood provided greater resources and rewards than any other national film industry, and also access to the world's biggest national market as well as efficient international distribution and thus provided film-makers with, potentially, the largest possible audience. German and Austrian film personnel arriving in great numbers in Hollywood in the 1920s encountered a movie colony filled with earlier immigrants from Germany and the Habsburg Empire, and also those immigrants' descendants. Some among the earlier generation had migrated to the US specifically to work in the film industry,[17] but most of them had had no such intention. Instead they belonged to the vast wave of German and Austrian immigration into the US that began in the nineteenth and continued through the early twentieth century.[18] Arrivals from Germany outnumbered those from any other country, and by 1900 these immigrants and their descendants made up over 10 per cent of the US population, forming the second largest ethnic group, after the English, in the country.

There is ample evidence that the huge number of German-Americans made significant contributions to American cultural forms and industries: witness, for example, the popularity of operetta on the legitimate stage and of 'Dutch' (misspelling of 'deutsch') comedians in vaudeville, as well as the dominance of German-American performers, composers and conductors in classical music in the US. Furthermore, many leading theatrical entrepreneurs in turn-of-the-century America were first or second generation immigrants from Germany and Austria, including the Frohmans, the Hammersteins and the Shuberts. The major Hollywood studios emerging in the 1910s had their origins in the theatrical enterprises (nickelodeons and variety theatres) of their founders, and throughout the 1910s they collaborated closely with established theatrical producers. It is no surprise, then, that German-Americans played as important a role in the American film industry as they had in the theatre industry. Hollywood's founding fathers included German-born Carl Laemmle (Universal) as well as William Fox

who was born to a German-speaking family in the Hungarian part of the Habsburg Empire (also the birth place of Hungarian-speaking Adolph Zukor). Other Hollywood moguls such as Harry Cohn (Columbia) and Marcus Loew (MGM) were the children of German and Austrian immigrants.

From the 1910s onwards, the moguls consolidated their position by filling many key positions with people to whom they were related (hence the sayings 'Carl Laemmle has a big family' and 'The son-in-law also rises'), or who at least belonged to the same immigrant group. Examples include leading executives such as Irving Thalberg and Walter Wanger who were children of German immigrants. Similarly, right from the start many of Hollywood's leading composers, cinematographers, writers, etc. were second generation German and Austrian immigrants. The moguls also employed many recent arrivals in the US such as Erich von Stroheim and Josef von Sternberg, who had emigrated before the First World War, and William Wyler, who was brought over by Carl Laemmle (a cousin of his mother) in the early 1920s. This also applied to immigrants from other parts of Europe, who had lived in Germany (such as Russian-born Lewis Milestone). Furthermore, Laemmle, Fox, Cohn and Loew developed connections on the basis of their Jewish background, which they shared with many Germans, Austrians and Eastern Europeans working in Hollywood, and also with those movie moguls who had come from various parts of the Russian Empire (such as Louis B. Mayer, Sam Goldwyn, the Schencks and the Warner brothers), and, more generally, with the massive turn-of-the-century influx of Jewish immigrants from Eastern Europe, who constituted a key audience for early film exhibition.[19]

The moguls' Central and Eastern European networks, both within Hollywood and outside of it, helped attract and accommodate career-oriented immigrants of the 1920s, including some of the top directors, writers, actors, cinematographers, etc. of Weimar and Austrian cinema, many of whom had come to work in Berlin or Vienna from abroad (such as the Hungarian Michael Curtiz); again many of these were Jewish. Hollywood's ability and willingness to help such immigrants was even more in evidence in relation to the political refugees of the 1930s. After the National Socialists took power in Germany in 1933, over a thousand mostly, but by no means exclusively, Jewish film workers fled the country, many eventually ending up in the US.[20]

Thus, beginning in the 1920s, there was a steady supply of qualified film personnel from Germany and Austria, many of whom had personal or professional ties with

Erich von Stroheim

German-American members of the Hollywood establishment. The careers of the new arrivals were helped by the specific demand for German and Austrian personnel in the American film industry, where they were deemed particularly suited to two important genres: the war film and the film operetta. From the mid-1910s onwards, most American war films – with the exception of relatively small groups of Civil War, Korean and Vietnam movies – focused on international conflicts (the First and Second World Wars) in which Germany was the enemy.[21] This opened up tremendous employment opportunities for German- and Austrian-born personnel: Erich von Stroheim, for example, acted as a military adviser and played German officers in war films of the late 1910s, while anti-Nazi films of the late 1930s and early 40s employed numerous refugees.[22] Fred Zinnemann managed the transition from B-movies to A-features with two war-related films set in Germany, *The Seventh Cross* (1944) and *The Search* (1948) (the latter film was actually shot in Germany and Switzerland).[23]

The second important genre for German- and Austrian-born personnel was the film operetta. Tremendously popular on the American stage,[24] operettas were successfully adapted to the silent screen, most notably in one of Erich von Stroheim's big hits of the 1920s, *The Merry Widow*. More generally, there was a demand for films

with operetta-like settings and concerns. These included films such as Stroheim's other big hit of the 1920s, *Foolish Wives*, which portrayed the exploits of the European leisure class, in particular the aristocracy of the Russian, German and Austrian empires. Again, German- and Austrian-born personnel were assumed to have a special affinity with the historical settings and cultural traditions these films drew on. It is, therefore, no coincidence that the majority of Lubitsch's films (including most of his big hits) of the 1920s and especially the early sound period belonged to this genre.[25] The film operetta also provided Billy Wilder with his first opportunities to make an impact in Hollywood. One German film scripted by Wilder, *Ihre Hoheit befiehlt* (1931), was remade in 1933 as *Adorable*, and the following year his second Hollywood script was made into the European-themed musical comedy *Music in the Air*. Even in the 1940s, one of his two major hits was the Viennese operetta *The Emperor Waltz* (1948).

Cutting across these two as well as many other genres, there was an underlying trend in Hollywood film-making which favoured European personnel, including many Germans and Austrians: the big-budget prestige film.[26] In addition to being expensive, prestige films were based on well-known source material (novels, plays, folklore, myth or history) and they were typically made by the industry's top personnel; they were often given a special release, in particular as so-called roadshows (a very limited release in selected movie theatres for prolonged runs at increased ticket prices). From the first full-length feature films of the early 1910s to the historical epics and super-expensive musicals of the 60s, prestige films included many of Hollywood's biggest hits and multiple Academy Award winners. Although some of the most famous prestige pictures such as *The Birth of a Nation* (1915) and *Gone With the Wind* (1939) dealt with specifically American themes, on the whole they were heavily biased towards European and/or biblical subject matter. Many of the greatest successes of German and Austrian film-makers arose out of this production trend, ranging from Stroheim's super-productions and Dieterle's biopics to the biblical epics made by Koster and Wyler.

From the late 1910s onwards, then, the popularity of film operettas and war films created a demand for German and Austrian personnel in Hollywood, and prestige pictures provided them with excellent opportunities for breaking through into Hollywood's top ranks.[27] Their career chances were further improved by the commercial clout, artistic prestige and technical innovations of Weimar cinema in the 1920s. German films such as *Madame Dubarry* and *Das Cabinet des Dr Caligari* had high profile and commercially successful releases in the United States,[28] and the German film industry dominated its domestic market as well as exporting successfully into Northern, Eastern and Central Europe.[29] For most of the decade, directors and craftsmen at Ufa enjoyed considerable freedom to experiment and established an international reputation as filmic innovators (see Bock and Töteberg's contribution in this volume).[30] This made them attractive to Hollywood studios, which hoped to harness technical and stylistic innovations to their regular production system, or to associate themselves with the critical reputation of German film-makers, thus increasing their cultural, if not their economic capital.[31] Finally, with their strong orientation towards foreign markets, Hollywood studios hoped that the employment of top personnel from Germany might weaken the Weimar film industry, while the cultural sensibilities of this personnel might in turn make their Hollywood films more accessible to Central and Eastern European audiences, especially in Germany itself. This, then, raises the question how successful Hollywood films made by German- and Austrian-born personnel were in Germany.

Hollywood in Germany before the 1970s [32]

Between the 1920s and the early 70s, Hollywood had few box-office hits in Germany, although across this period it provided about half of all films released in the German market.[33] In fact, many of the films (such as the James Bond films or David Lean epics) which would generally be regarded as Hollywood productions or co-productions were officially registered as British films for their German release. Since many undoubtedly British productions (such as *The Third Man*) in turn had significant American input, it makes sense to deal with American and British films together. For the years for which reliable box-office statistics are available, 1925–32 and 1950–71, there were on average only two American or British productions in the annual top ten; the other top ten hits were mostly German and Austrian films or, especially in the 1960s, continental European imports. These figures force us to revise the received notion of Hollywood's early dominance of the German market, and suggest instead that until the 1970s, German audiences by and large preferred domestic films and films from other European countries to American imports. In fact, this is not so surprising if one assumes that initially most people will prefer that which is close and familiar to that which is somewhat distant and strange.

Did the presence of German- and Austrian-born personnel in Hollywood make their films more familiar to, and successful with, German audiences? Among the few Hollywood successes in Germany, there were indeed several made by German and Austrian directors, most notably *The* number eight list of 1928/9 *Last Command* (number eight hit of 1928/9 season), *Atlantic* (E. A. Dupont; 7, 1929/30), *From Here to Eternity* (2, 1953/4), *Battle Hymn* (Sirk; 7, 1956/7), *The Nun's Story* (4, 1959/60), *Ben Hur* (2, 1960/61) and *Irma la Douce* (2, 1963/4); there also were the Sam Spiegel productions *On the Waterfront* (10, 1954/5) and *The Bridge on the River Kwai* (1, 1957/8). Hungarian and Russian immigrants with strong German/Austrian connections were also successful with *Noah's Ark* (Michael Curtiz; 4, 1929/30) and *All Quiet on the Western Front* (Lewis Milestone; 6, 1931/2). Furthermore, quite a few of the American and British hits featured German and Austrian actors, mostly in supporting roles. Examples include *The Third Man* (5, 1950/51), *The Longest Day* (6, 1962/3; co-directed by Bernard Wicki), several Bond films (which were consistently listed in the German top ten from 1963 onwards) and *Those Magnificent Men in Their Flying Machines* (2, 1965/6; with Gert Fröbe of Goldfinger fame). There were also two American/British hits with German stars: *The Last Command* and *The One That Got Away* (starring Hardy Krüger; 2, 1957/8).

While this is quite an impressive track record in the light of the low incidence of American/British hits in Germany, the specific contributions of German- and Austrian-born personnel do not appear to have been the single decisive factor. In fact, the majority of Hollywood hits in Germany had no significant German/Austrian input. However, most of them had European (or Mediterranean) settings in common. Thus, in the silent and early sound era, biblical epics and Russian-themed films dominated. These included *Ben-Hur* (4, 1926/7 and 1, 1927/8) as well as *The Volga Boatman* (3, 1926/7 and 6, 1927/8), *Love* (5, 1928/9) and *The Last Command*. Further examples in the 1950s and 60s included *The Ten Commandments* (7, 1957/8), *Salomon and Sheba* (9, 1959/60) and *Ben Hur* (2, 1960/61) as well as *Taras Bulba* (9, 1962/3) and *Doctor Zhivago* (1, 1966/7).

Another key genre across both periods is the war film. The success of *Noah's Ark* (4, 1929/30) and *All Quiet on the Western Front* was followed by a string of post-Second World War hits, set both in the European and Pacific theatres of war: *From Here to Eternity* (2, 1953/4), *Battle Hymn*, *The Bridge on the River Kwai*, *The One That Got Away*, *The Battle of the River Plate* (5, 1957/8), *The Naked and the Dead* (6, 1959/60), *The Longest Day* and *The Battle of Britain* (9, 1969/70). Closely related are films dealing with specific aspects of European history: post-war devastation in *The Third Man*, the German occupation of Belgium towards the end of *The Nun's Story*, Napoleon in *Conquest* (made in 1937; 8, 1950/51), and the Egyptian and Roman empires in *Cleopatra* (7, 1963/4).

What all of these films, which make up about two-thirds of American and British hits in Germany up to 1971, have in common, then, is their thematic focus on important aspects of European culture and history (especially the two world wars), which are highly familiar and pertinent to German audiences. It is also important to note that many of these hits were big-budget prestige productions. A closely related group of hits consists of international adventure films, such as *Into the Net* (5, 1925/6), *Those Magnificent Men in Their Flying Machines*, *The Brides of Fu Man Chu* (7, 1966/7) and Bond films. Hollywood or British films made by, or with, Austrian/German personnel only had a chance to be hits in Germany if they fitted into these successful categories, and they were likely to fail if they did not.

In addition to British and American imports which dealt with German or European themes or international adventure, there were other film types which succeeded despite, or indeed because of, their distance from mainstream German culture. These were films dealing with rebellious youth and/or starring icons of youth rebellion (*On the Waterfront*, *Rebel Without a Cause*, [9, 1955/6], *Giant*, [4, 1956/7], *Rock Around the Clock*, [6, 1956/7], *Help!*, [8, 1965/6] and *Easy Rider*, 3, [1969/70]) and romantic comedies or dramas, usually – but not always – focusing on women struggling to meet the conflicting demands of their careers and their private lives. The latter include *Bathing Beauty* (6, 1950/51), *Rebecca* (1940; 9, 1951/2), *The Rose Tattoo* (8, 1955/6), *Irma la Douce*, several Doris Day vehicles – *Lover Come Back* (4, 1961/2), *That Touch of Mink* (10, 1962/3) and *Move Over, Darling* (6, 1963/4) – and *Love Story* (2, 1970/71).[34]

These films mirrored gender and generational developments in German society. Indeed, broad cultural changes in Germany from the 1950s to the 60s, driven especially by younger generations who came to constitute the bulk of the cinema audience, appear to be the main reason for the much greater success of Hollywood films in the German market from the 1970s onwards.[35] In the 1950s and especially in the 60s, young people increasingly shunned the values and cultural forms of their parent culture (including the German popular cinema), partly because it was seen to have been compromised severely by fascism. Many of them embraced Anglo-American popular culture instead, most notably Hollywood movies.

Hollywood and Germany since the 1970s

How has the picture of Hollywood–German relations changed since the early 1970s? In the 1970s, Hollywood still had to share the top ten with a significant number of German productions (especially in the early part of the decade) and continental European imports (throughout the decade), yet the range of genres with which Hollywood succeeded in Germany was already expanding, and began to include children's films, sex films, gangster, horror, science fiction and disaster movies. In the early 1980s, Hollywood largely took over the top ten, with an average eight films per year, complemented by, on average, one German production and one British or continental European import. As suggested above, the changing outlook of young cinema-goers was the main force behind this development. Once the dominance of Hollywood films was established, it became self-reinforcing. Since the 1970s, new generations of cinema-goers have grown up almost exclusively with Hollywood films, and choose Hollywood films as the most likely available source of a familiar cinema-going experience.

The German box-office top ten, then, have come to look increasingly like the American charts. There are differences such as the extraordinary success of animated features in Germany since the 1970s. However, with few exceptions (such as the success of *Amadeus*, [8, 1985], and *Schindler's List*, [3, 1994]), these differences had little to do with specifically European subject matter. It is possible, though, that the German or Austrian nationality of certain stars and film-makers, which was highlighted in the publicity surrounding their films, contributed to their early success in Germany. Thus, Arnold Schwarzenegger had a top ten hit in Germany with *Conan, the Barbarian* (4, 1982) long before he had one in the US. The same applies to Roland Emmerich (*Stargate*, 5, 1995).[36]

This brings us back to the fate of the Germans and Austrians in Hollywood. By the 1970s, many of Hollywood's German- and Austrian-born veterans had died or gone into retirement. Almost all of them had arrived in the US before the Second World War, and their long and successful careers in Hollywood contrasted sharply with the American careers of those Germans and Austrians who participated in Hollywood's international co-productions and/or went to Hollywood itself in the two decades after the war. Despite the nominations of actors such as Curt Jürgens, Horst Buchholz, Elke Sommer and Senta Berger as 'Stars of Tomorrow' by American exhibitors

The Perfect Storm (2000)

(in the years 1959, 1961, 1964 and 1965 respectively),[37] their Hollywood careers were limited. Bernard Wicki, similarly, could never match the success of *The Longest Day*, which he had co-directed. Thus, in the 1970s very few Germans or Austrians worked at the top level in Hollywood.[38]

At the same time, the critical success of the so-called New German Cinema in the United States, which culminated in the Academy Award for Best Foreign Language Film for Volker Schlöndorff's *Die Blechtrommel* (*The Tin Drum*) in 1979, seems to have prepared the ground for a new and eventually hugely successful German 'invasion'.[39] Beginning in the late 1970s and gaining momentum since the 1980s, a large number of German and Austrian actors (from Nastassja Kinski and Jürgen Prochnow to Til Schweiger and Franka Potente), directors (from Wim Wenders and Schlöndorff to Uli Edel), producers (most notably, Bernd Eichinger), cinematographers (from Michael Ballhaus to Dietrich Lohmann) and composers (from Giorgio Moroder to Hans Zimmer) have worked in, and often moved temporarily or permanently to, Hollywood.[40] As in the 1920s, they have been attracted by Hollywood's far superior resources, audience reach and financial rewards.

Also comparable to the 1920s is the process through which critical prestige and export hits combine to stimulate interest in German and Austrian personnel on the part of the Hollywood establishment.[41] While, on the whole, the critically celebrated New German films were commercially insignificant, both in Germany and the US, there were important exceptions. *Die Blechtrommel*, for example, the fourth highest grossing film in Germany in 1979, was also widely seen in the US. Two years later, *Das Boot* (*The Boat*), a big-budget war movie by former TV director Wolfgang Petersen, became a huge hit, not only in Germany where it was the sixth highest grossing film of 1981, but also in the US, where it became the highest grossing German film ever and the fifth highest grossing foreign-language film of all time.[42] Wenders' *Der Himmel über Berlin* (*Wings of Desire*, 1987) and Tom Tykwer's *Lola rennt* (*Run, Lola, Run*, 1998) also were major foreign-language hits in the US, and the latter in particular is closely tied to the latest wave of migration from Germany to Hollywood.

Unlike the 1920s, most German- and Austrian-born film personnel who have worked in Hollywood since the 1970s have not enjoyed the benefits of networks of German-Americans in the Hollywood establishment (although a rudimentary new German-language community did eventually emerge). By and large, they also were not identified with films that draw on their specifically German or European cultural background. Actors, cinematographers and composers were initially more successful than directors, participating in major box-office hits and gaining Academy recognition, with Oscar nominations for, among others, Klaus Maria Brandauer and Ballhaus, and a win for Giorgio Moroder. In the 1990s, there were further nominations, for example, for actor Armin Mueller-Stahl and a win for composer Hans Zimmer (who has also received several nominations since he started working in Hollywood in the late 1980s).[43] It was also in the 1990s that directors finally caught up with the success of other German film personnel, albeit only in commercial, not in critical terms. Most notably, after a few years in Hollywood Petersen and Emmerich established themselves as A-list directors with a string of massive hits – *In the Line of Fire* (no. 8 in the US in 1993), *Independence Day* (the no. 1 hit in the US and, indeed, world-wide in 1996), *Air Force One* (4, 1997) and *Godzilla* (8, 1998).[44] This remarkable series culminated in the parallel release in summer 2000 of two blockbusters by Petersen and Emmerich: *The Patriot* and *The Perfect Storm*, respectively the sixteenth and fourth highest grossing movie of the year in the US.

Conclusion

From the beginning of the twentieth century numerous Germans and Austrians have found work in the American film industry. While Hollywood's Germans and Austrians were only a tiny fraction of the millions of immigrants and refugees from Germany and Austria arriving in the US before the 1940s, they included many of the most successful and best known of all German-Americans. Like other immigrants, their lives and work were shaped by the twin forces of assimilation (into the American mainstream) and differentiation (the maintenance of a separate group identity). Whether they were moguls or studio employees, Hollywood's German and Austrian immigrants were most successful when they managed to blend into the society and culture they encountered, while also making use of resources (such as contacts, cultural capital and preconceptions on the part of the host society) which only they had access to. Among other things, it was the ubiquity of symphonic film scores, the popularity of operetta and of films about the two world wars, as well as the centrality of European-themed prestige productions to Hollywood's operations into the 1960s, which gave Germans and

Austrians excellent opportunities for drawing on their specific cultural background.

Before the 1970s, European-themed films also proved to be more likely than other Hollywood products (independently of the participation of Germans and Austrians in their production) to succeed in a German market largely dominated by domestic product and, in the 1960s, by films from other European countries. However, in the 1970s the German cinema audience not only turned increasingly towards Hollywood product, but also favoured specifically American subject matter over Hollywood's European-themed output. The most immediate cause of this dramatic change was the increasing alienation of post-war youth, growing up in the 1950s and 60s and constituting the bulk of the cinema audience, from traditional German culture. By the 1980s, Hollywood dominated the German box-office charts, and many German film-makers as well as other film personnel looked again to Hollywood for career opportunities. The most successful of the new migrants were those who fully assimilated themselves into the American mainstream, directors like Petersen and Emmerich, for example, who had already specialised in action, fantasy and science fiction in Germany and continued in this vein in Hollywood.

Notes

1 Stephan Thernstrom (ed.), *Harvard Encyclopedia of American Ethnic Groups* (Cambridge, MA: Belknap, 1980), pp. 164–71, 405–30.

2 See, for example, Ronny Loewy (ed.), *Von Babelsberg nach Hollywood: Filmemigranten aus Nazideutschland* (Frankfurt-am-Main: Deutsches Filmmuseum, 1987); Christian Cargnelli and Michael Omasta (eds.), *Aufbruch ins Ungewisse: Österreichische Filmschaffende in der Emigration vor 1945* (Vienna: Wespennest, 1993); Helmut G. Asper, '*Etwas Besseres als den Tod . . .*': *Filmexil in Hollywood* (Marburg: Schüren, 2002); and Heiko R. Blum, *Meine zweite Heimat Hollywood: Deutschsprachige Filmkünstler in den USA* (Berlin: Henschel, 2001). The last two books include extensive bibliographical information on the topic.

3 I have determined birth places with the help of the Internet Moviedatabase and various other sources. Of course, birth places do not necessarily tell us very much, because people may have grown up somewhere else, and because it is not always easy to determine whether a particular birth place is located in a German-speaking part of the Habsburg Empire. In fact, I have included the offspring of some German-speaking families (such as the Galician-born Billy

Wilder) who lived in areas of the Habsburg Empire that were predominantly non-German, although there is not always agreement in the literature about which families were German and which were not. Finally, it has to be noted that my selection does not take into account the circumstances under which people went to the US (as children or adults, as film workers or people in other lines of work).

4 Richard Koszarski, *An Evening's Entertainment: The Age of the Silent Feature Picture, 1915–1928* (New York: Scribner's, 1990), p. 33. This list was compiled by James Mark Purcell who aimed to adjust figures for box-office rentals to varying ticket prices and combine them 'with such other data as exhibitors' reports appearing in the trade papers'.

5 Joel Finler, *The Hollywood Story* (London: Octopus, 1988), p. 276. This list is 'derived from the *Motion Picture Almanac* and information provided by the individual companies'. Ibid., p. 278.

6 These 1930s lists have been reprinted in Cobbett Steinberg, *Film Facts* (New York: Facts on File, 1980), pp. 18–19; and Tino Balio, *Grand Design: Hollywood as a Modern Business Enterprise, 1930–1939* (New York: Scribner's, 1993), pp. 405–06. The lists are of varying lengths (between five and forty films) and most of them present the entries in alphabetical order.

7 Finler, op. cit., p. 276.

8 Ibid., p. 280. In the mid-1940s there is a drop in the output of the majors and from then until the late 1960s the annual output is between 140 and 320 films.

9 They also received top salaries. In the mid-1920s, for example, Ernst Lubitsch was probably the highest paid director in Hollywood. See Koszarski, op. cit., pp. 212–13.

10 Hit lists for the period 1940–70 can be found in Thomas Schatz, *Boom and Bust: American Cinema in the 1940s* (New York: Scribner's, 1997), pp. 465–8, and Steinberg, op. cit., pp. 19–28. Here the hits are ranked by revenue rather than being presented in alphabetical order.

11 Finler, op. cit., pp. 276–7.

12 The following information on the Academy Awards is taken from Steinberg, op. cit., pp. 197–257. While Steinberg provides a list of winners in all categories, he lists nominations only in the major categories and not, for example, for music, art direction and editing. The prominence of Germans and Austrians in some of these categories would be even more obvious, if nominations were taken into account. Max Steiner, for example, received twenty-two music nominations, and Hans Julius Salter six. See Blum, op. cit., pp. 253 and 264.

13 It is difficult to determine who among the hundreds of people nominated for Academy Awards was born in Germany or Austria. I have only included those people in my count about whom I could be sure. Therefore, some of the figures below may seriously underestimate the prominence of German- and Austrian-born personnel, especially where producers are concerned.

14 Wyler also had three nominations for producing. According to his biographer, Wyler's films 'won thirty-eight Academy Awards on one hundred and twenty-seven nominations (half in best picture, director and actor categories). There are record numbers, roughly twice what any other director's pictures have earned.' Jan Herman, *A Talent for Trouble: The Life of Hollywood's Most Acclaimed Director – William Wyler* (New York: Da Capo, 1997), p. 474.

15 See, for example, Kristin Thompson, *Exporting Entertainment: America in the World Film Market, 1907–1934* (London: BFI, 1985).

16 The careers of these and other directors as well as other European film personnel are discussed, for example, in John Baxter, *The Hollywood Exiles* (London: MacDonald and Jane's, 1976) and Graham Petrie, *Hollywood Destinies: European Directors in America, 1922–1931* (London: Routledge and Kegan Paul, 1985).

17 Several of these are listed in Hanns-Georg Rodek, 'Europäische Filmemigration in die USA vor 1920', *Kintop*, no. 10 (2001), pp. 151–91.

18 On German and Austrian immigration see Thernstrom, op. cit., pp. 164–71, 405–30; Roger Daniels, *Coming to America: A History of Immigration and Ethnicity in American Life* (New York: Harper Perennial, 1990); and Frank Trommler and Joseph McVeigh (eds.), *America and the Germans: An Assessment of a Three-Hundred-Year History*, 2 vols (Philadelphia: University of Pennsylvania Press, 1985).

19 See Thernstrom, op. cit., pp. 571–98; and Neal Gabler, *An Empire of Their Own: How the Jews Invented Hollywood* (London: W. H. Allen, 1989). A discussion of the widespread perception of Hollywood as a 'Jewish invention' can be found in Steven Carr, *Hollywood and Anti-Semitism: A Cultural History up to World War II* (Cambridge: Cambridge University Press, 2001).

20 See, for example, Asper, op. cit.; Jan-Christopher Horak, 'Exilfilm, 1933–1945', in Wolfgang Jacobson, Anton Kaes and Hans-Helmut Prinzler (eds.), *Geschichte des deutschen Films* (Stuttgart and Weimar: Metzler, 1993), pp. 101–18; and John Russell Taylor, *Strangers in Paradise: The Hollywood Emigrés, 1933–1950* (London: Faber and Faber, 1983).

21 On war-related films see, for example, Craig W. Campbell, *Reel America and World War I* (Jefferson, NC: McFarland, 1985), Andrew Kelly, *Cinema and the Great War* (London:

Routledge, 1997) and Jeanine Basinger, *The World War II Combat Film: Anatomy of a Genre* (New York: Columbia University Press, 1986).

22 On anti-Nazi films see Horak, op. cit., and Michael E. Birdwell, *Celluloid Soldiers: The Warner Bros. Campaign Against Nazism* (New York: New York University Press, 1999).

23 Billy Wilder's second film as a director was *Five Graves to Cairo* (1943), which featured Erich von Stroheim as Field Marshal Erwin Rommel.

24 See Gerald Bordman, *American Operetta: From* H.M.S. *Pinafore to Sweeney Todd* (New York: Oxford University Press, 1981).

25 On the importance of operetta in Weimar cinema and in the output of Austrian and German film-makers in Hollywood, see Thomas Elsaesser, *Weimar Cinema and After: Germany's Historical Imaginary* (London and New York: Routledge, 2000), pp. 330–82. On American film operettas, see Rick Altman, *The American Film Musical* (Bloomington: Indiana University Press, 1987).

26 Balio, op. cit., pp. 179–211; Steve Neale, 'Hollywood Blockbusters: Historical Dimensions', in Julian Stringer (ed.), *Movie Blockbusters* (London: Routledge, forthcoming); Sheldon Hall, 'Tall Revenue Features: The Genealogy of the Modern Blockbuster', in Steve Neale (ed.), *Genre and Contemporary Hollywood* (London: BFI, forthcoming).

27 Additionally, Austrian- and German-born composers were in particular demand because of their intimate familiarity with the classical idioms that dominated film music.

28 See David B. Pratt, ' "O, Lubitsch, Where Wert Thou?": *Passion*, the German Invasion and the Emergence of the Name "Lubitsch" ', *Wide Angle*, vol. 13, no. 1 (January 1991), pp. 35–70; Kristin Thompson, 'Dr Caligari at the Folies Bergères', in Mike Budd (ed.), *The Cabinet of Dr Caligari: Texts, Contexts, Histories* (New Brunswick, NJ: Rutgers University Press, 1990), pp. 139–49.

29 On the German film industry's dominance of the domestic market, see Joseph Garncarz, 'Hollywood in Germany: The Role of American Films in Germany, 1925–1990', in David W. Ellwood and Rob Kroes (eds.), *Hollywood in Europe: Experiences of a Cultural Hegemony* (Amsterdam: VU University Press, 1994), pp. 122–35; and Garncarz, *Populäres Kino in Deutschand: Internationalisierung einer Filmkultur, 1925–1990*, unpublished post-doctoral dissertation (*Habilitationsschrift*), University of Cologne, 1996. On exports see Thomas Elsaesser and Michael Wedel (eds.), *The BFI Companion to German Cinema* (London: BFI, 1999), pp. 82–4.

30 See, for example, Kristin Thompson, 'Early Alternatives to the Hollywood Mode of Production: Implications for Europe's Avantgarde', *Wide Angle*, vol. 5, no. 4 (December 1993), pp. 386–404. On Ufa, see Elsaesser, op. cit., pp. 106–42; and Ursula Hardt, *From Caligari to California: Erich Pommer's Life in the International Film Wars* (Oxford: Berghahn, 1996).

31 See, for example, case studies of Murnau's move to Hollywood in Petrie, op. cit., pp. 26–61; and Robert C. Allen and Douglas Gomery, *Film History: Theory and Practice* (New York: Alfred Knopf, 1985), pp. 91–104.

32 The following section is heavily indebted to the writings of, and my conversations with, Joseph Garncarz. See his 'Hollywood in Germany' and *Populäres Kino in Deutschland*. This section is primarily concerned with the relative success of American films at the German box-office, or in other words with the demand of German audiences for particular Hollywood imports. Annual top ten lists up to 1990 are reproduced in Garncarz, 'Hollywood in Germany'. For the hit lists since 1990 see the charts published annually in *Film-Jahrbuch* and in one of the January issues of *Filmecho/Filmwoche*. There is also a substantial literature on the supply of American films in the German market (most notably, Thompson, *Exporting Entertainment*), on political measures to stem Hollywood imports (see again Thompson) and on the reception of, and debates about, American films in Germany. Examples of this literature include Deniz Göktürk, *Künstler, Cowboys, Ingenieure . . . Kultur- und mediengeschichtliche Studien zu deutschen Amerika-Texten 1912–1920* (Munich: Wilhelm Fink, 1998); Thomas Saunders, *Hollywood in Berlin: American Cinema and Weimar Germany* (Berkeley: University of California Press, 1994); and Markus Spieker, *Hollywood unterm Hakenkreuz: Der amerikanische Spielfilm im Dritten Reich* (Trier: Wissenschaftlicher Verlag, 1999).

33 Germany here refers only to West Germany for the years 1949 to 1990.

34 There were also a small number of circus films and revisionist Westerns.

35 See Garncarz, 'Hollywood in Germany' and *Populäres Kino in Deutschland*. Garncarz has also argued that generational change in the film industry, associated closely with the so-called New German Cinema of the late 1960s and 70s, and a fundamental shift of public funding policies from commercial to 'art' cinema, contributed to the success of American films. See Garncarz, 'Drei Generationen: Wandlungen in der Institution Kino in der Bundesrepublik Deutschland', in Elmar Buck (ed.), *Frauen und Männer* (Cologne: Theaterwissenschaftliche Sammlung der Universität zu Köln, 1999), pp. 138–53.

36 It is even possible that the partly German background of Sandra Bullock (her mother is German and she partly grew up in Germany and still speaks the language) was a factor in the enormous German success of her first star vehicles *While You Were Sleeping* (2, 1995) and *The Net* (27, 1995).

37 Steinberg, op. cit., pp. 63–4.

38 There are two curious exceptions at executive level. Austrian-born entrepreneur Charles Bluhdorn, who was chairman of Gulf and Western, took control of Paramount in 1966, and Austrian-born Eric Pleskow became a top executive at United Artists, serving as the company's president for much of the 1970s.

39 Thomas Elsaesser, *New German Cinema: A History* (London: BFI and Macmillan, 1989), pp. 290–303. Two years after *Die Blechtrommel*, the Hungarian–German co-production *Mephisto* won the award for Best Foreign Language Film.

40 See Blum, op. cit.

41 Austrian cinema may have gained more recognition after Wolfgang Glück's *38 – Heim ins Reich* (1985) was nominated for Best Foreign Language Film.

42 The editors of *Variety*, *The Variety Almanac 2000* (London: Boxtree, 2000), p. 67.

43 Most of this information is from Blum, op. cit.

44 US box-office charts are taken from *Variety*, which publishes them annually in one of its January issues.

22

In the Wilds of the German Imaginary: African Vistas

Marie-Hélène Gutberlet

Africa's filmic 'discovery' and cinematic 'invention' are as old as cinema itself. Directly after the cinematograph's invention, European cameramen set off to tour the world. The cinematic curios they brought back from Africa included street scenes, views of markets, ports and railway stations, oases and waterfalls, deserts and rainforests, as well as wildlife and other inhabitants of the 'dark continent'. Africa was tropical film setting and anthropological research field in one; early cinema in particular combined in its visions of Africa rapt dream and documented image from afar. Since the early period, and although African cinema (that is, film-making by African directors) has provided a counter-perspective since the 1950s, the West has continued to hold sway over filmic visions of Africa. In western productions, the nature of a continent which today comprises over fifty nations has been repeatedly explored in both its real and imagined manifestations. The hundred years of western film practice in Africa have, however, aroused no substantial film-historical interest, though they have been the focus of ideological critique. It is, moreover, impossible to offer a comprehensive overview of German visions of Africa across a century of cinema history. The mass of pertinent titles would be too disparate to fit within standard classifications, and would bear only a loose connection to scientific and academic topoi. This geographically extraterritorial and therefore marginal phenomenon within German film history can, however, be usefully approached from three perspectives:

1. The most obvious approach relates to the shared history of Germany and Africa. The first section below looks at

the traces of that history in selected films in an attempt to illustrate the particularity of the German–African connection both during and after the German colonial period (1884–1918).

2. Representations of Africa in German film encompass the most disparate forms, genres and formats. It is however noteworthy that only a fraction of this mass of films – made up primarily of documentaries – is known at all. The second section of this article thus examines film production (and, briefly, reception) across a broad spectrum since the 1920s.

3. Finally, it is conspicuous that since the 1960s – when documentary film migrated into television – only a handful of cinema releases relevant to this article have occurred. Significantly, these address German contemporary history of the post-war period and the years since reunification in 1989, with just a few German productions gradually coming to address the German–African connection.

History: German–African encounters

The particularity of the relationship between Germany and Africa lies in the connection between film history and colonial history. The territorial division and appropriation of Africa by western powers was first secured at the Berlin Conference of 1884–5. Until the 1960s, Britain retained protectorates (Namibia until 1990), France held onto overseas territories, and Belgium kept its diamond mines, while Portugal retained colonies into the 1970s. Germany, though, lost its protectorates – the 'model colony' of Togo, as well as Cameroon, German South West Africa (now Namibia) and German East Africa (comprising modern-day Tanzania, Burundi, Rwanda and northern Mozambique) – to the Allies in 1918.

The brevity of this colonial era is no reason, however, to assume the non-existence of a filmic relationship. On the contrary, countless novels, expeditions and films attest a persistence of colonialist thinking and exploratory impulses in German film that find their heyday in the 1920s and 30s. Films centring on colonial possessions for the German economy, such as *Die Weltgeschichte als Kolonialgeschichte* (*World History as Colonial History*, 1926), *Das koloniale Bilderbuch* (*The Colonial Picture-Book*, 1938/9), *Deutsches Land in Afrika* (*German Land in Africa*, 1939) and *Auf deutschen Farmen in Deutsch-Südwestafrika* (*On German Farms in German South West Africa*, 1941) all relate to Germany's former possession of African soil, but refocus attention rhetorically towards German settlers in Africa who await the status of 'normalisation' vis-à-vis the re-establishment of lands settled by Germans as German

Afrique, Je te plumerai, 1992

colonial territory. Under the Third Reich, this recouping of German colonies, though in fact only a marginal concern within Nazi efforts to promote Germany to the level of world power, became the explicit focus of such titles as the historical biopic *Carl Peters*, shot at Berlin's UFA studios during the wartime winter of 1940–41. Set in 1884, the film traces the story of the German envoy Carl Peters (played by Hans Albers), who travels to East Africa to secure protectorates for the German Empire. Peters arrives just a few days in advance of his British and French rivals – caricatured as snobbish gentlemen and dandified aristocrats – and promises the 'natives'[1] his assistance in countering the fanatical greed of the Belgians, French and British. The film skilfully combines territorial interest in the lost colonies with exotic entertainment, while defaming not only other nations with colonial interests, but also German social democrats and Jews who aspire to renounce colonial expansionism.

The German quest for power and increased territory in the Third Reich led to inconceivable atrocities: yet only on the cinema screen did Germany succeed in annexing Africa. After 1945 therefore, and in contrast to other colonial empires, Germany's longing for colonies was neither subjected to radical revision nor faced with the anti-colonial movements that emerged elsewhere after the Second World War. Unlike France, Belgium, Portugal and Britain, Germany was neither at war with its (albeit imaginary) colonies as they struggled for independence, nor was it confronted with waves of immigrants and returning colonial émigrés once independence had been declared. Germany remained untouched by these decisive historical shifts. What distinguished post-war Germany, then, was actually the absence of migration ensuing from colonial possession – and thus of any imperative to enter into a collective public debate that questioned Germany's relationship with Africa. What has remained in its place is an inhibited and therefore strongly romanticised longing.[2]

The work of Hans Schomburgk, who began shooting films in Africa during the 1910s, exemplifies this attachment marked by longing. Schomburgk undertook his first film-making expedition to Liberia in 1912–13, followed by an expedition to Togo in 1913–14 on which he was accompanied by the British cameraman James Hodgson and the actress Meg Gehrts. During the Togo expedition, he produced anthropological, wildlife and feature films, though these were confiscated in England at the outbreak of the First World War and have since disappeared without trace.[3] Schomburgk undertook a second trip to Liberia in 1922 together with Paul Lieberenz[4] and Eugen Risch. The release of his *Mensch und Tier im Urwald* (*Man and Beast in the*

Jungle) took place in 1924; it was reissued (in 1948) with a soundtrack added under the title *Frauen, Masken und Dämonen* (*Women, Masks and Demons*). In the 1930s, Schomburgk shot in Southern Africa, gained employment as a constable in South Africa, and directed *Die Wildnis stirbt* (*The Wilderness is Dying*, 1936/8). In 1940, he published his memoirs under the title *Ich such' in Afrika das letzte Paradies* (*In Africa, I Seek the Last Paradise*). Later interned on account of his non-Aryan extraction, he joined the resistance under Canaris in 1941, and returned to North Africa in 1942, before filming his final trip through Africa in 1956, at the age of seventy-six, in *Mein Abschied von Afrika* (*My Farewell to Africa*, 1958).

Both *Die Wildnis stirbt* and *Mein Abschied von Afrika* are travelogues in which the animal kingdom – also comprising 'natives' within Schomburgk's conception – plays a major part. Strictly speaking, Schomburgk's films constitute amateur movies extolling his vision of Africa. The earlier work, *Die Wildnis stirbt*, draws together material from various sources, with Schomburgk's commentary linking sequences from feature films and newsreels as well as scenes shot by himself. The rhetoric of technological progress and the physical savagery of 'natives' coalesce here with that of the nature-lover. Thus, at the sight of a caravan of bearers, Schomburgk intones in voice-over: 'They can cover thirty kilometres a day, yet the car, as we see, can manage a hundred.' A car stuck in the mud appears on the screen. This ironic commentary is followed by a longer passage showing wild animals – ostriches, giraffes, a leopard, apes, marabous, lions, vultures circling in the air, and finally a panorama over which the sun is setting. The journey continues: Schomburgk's plane flies over Egypt and the Sudan, until we reach the Congo and encounter elephants. 'I have shot sixty-three elephants,' he explains. The animal kingdom, he enthuses incessantly, is 'the real Africa ... '. And, over the film's concluding aerial shots: 'The wilderness is dying. An alien culture has conquered Africa. May it bring joy and prosperity to the land.' The wilderness both of 'natives' and animals is at risk. Conserving it in pictures for future generations demands technological penetration (by car, aeroplane, hunting rifle, camera) – even if this technology should ultimately prove to be the undoing of animals and 'natives' alike.

In *Mein Abschied von Afrika*, Schomburgk expounds similarly: 'While sixty years ago the blacks still lived primitively, today they are much more advanced. . . . They no longer want their old world, they want to live and work like whites, and are happy when their work is praised.' Schomburgk, always wary of his fellow man, does not go to some South African factory to illustrate these words, but to

a workshop for the blind producing basketwork articles. Later, there follow asphalted roads, advertising hoardings, an 'especially black' missionary, a hairdressing salon. Nannies hold white children in their arms. Just as, at the beginning of *Mein Abschied von Afrika*, Schomburgk reaffirms his love for this continent, its people and animals, and for 'the mysteries . . . of Europe's dark sister', so in the end he also finds it easy to bid farewell to all this, 'secure in the knowledge that the black children of this continent are no longer alone – they have teachers who show them the right path'. Images of 'eternal Africa' – Kilimanjaro, wildlife, the final elephant that Schomburgk 'bags with the camera' – are bookended with dance sequences performed by the 'Dombak tribe': 'Africa's drums still resound in my ears whenever I think back. These drums which have echoed through the Dark Continent since primeval times.'[5] Finally, Schomburgk bids farewell 'to our lower brothers and sisters', the animals.

Footage: Africa in German film

The equation of man and beast in Schomburgk's 'dark continent' is by no means exceptional. Like animals, African peoples have persistently been seen to be without history, land or culture, and to act instinctively. Like Schomburgk fifty years earlier, film-making tourists today still claim to be 'experts' on an Africa that suffers a presumed historical, economic and cultural deficit. Consequently, it is seen as an adequate representational style even for contemporary films, whether amateur or professional, to simply depict an African wilderness, and to embellish such images with anecdotes.[6] Without questioning our own involvement in the instrumentalisation processes inherent in technological progress, Africa is seen as an undisturbed nature reserve or as an anthropological *terra nulla* of humanity. Yet at the same time, this eternally enduring and much-desired Africa is perceived to be threatened by extinction from western influence. Schomburgk's films, for instance, plead for conservation: but this is a conservation that involves a partitioning off of that 'real' Africa which is unable to withstand increasing – yet desired – processes of modernisation. Within the western technological model, the antithesis between the picturesque that is worthy of conservation, and development that needs to be supported, finds a common denominator in the rhetoric of infantilisation. *Mein Abschied von Afrika* at once demands protection for 'our' animals and 'our' blacks'; they both need our help and instruction. Schomburgk's films are testaments to a fascination with 'nature' and a romantic attachment to it. Thus, the very fascination that contributes to nature's obliteration also leads to film-making. The noble goal of documenting a disappearing world is, then, supported by a quite different motive – that of preserving nature in artificial enclaves, such as zoological gardens, safari parks and films.

The objective of conserving a vanishing reality for future generations also underpins ethnographic films that aim to record precisely and authentically how genuine African societies, traditions and customs function. In Germany, ethnographic films have been produced primarily under the direction of the documentary film project of the Göttingen-based *Institut für den Wissenschaftlichen Film* (IWF, or 'Institute for Scientific Film'), founded in 1956. Films of international origin produced since the 1920s are also collected here. The IWF's African collection comprises over 450 titles, catalogued according to nations, directors, production companies and ethnic groups, as well as keywords.[7] Founded as a central repository of documentary material for all the Federal states, the IWF enjoys something of a monopoly over ethnographic films in Germany. Its strict conditions of hire preclude public screenings, and thus impede awareness of an ethnographic film history, which has elsewhere become associated with names such as John Grierson, MacDougall or Jean Rouch.[8] The forty-eight shorts catalogued at the IWF under 'Ivory Coast', for example, were all shot by H. Himmelheber in 1963 and 1968, and released a few years later by the IWF. They include such titles as *Baule (Westafrika, Elfenbeinküste) – Herstellen von Rindenbaststoff* (*Baule (West Africa, Ivory Coast) – Making Bark-Fibre Cloth*, 1966, IWF #E 886) or *Baule (Westafrika, Elfenbeinküste) – Sänger mit zwei Harfen, begleitet von Rassel und Glocke* (*Baule (West Africa, Ivory Coast) – Singer with Two Harps accompanied by a Rattle and Gongs*, 1970, IWF #E 1571). The latter is described in a style typical of the IWF catalogue: 'In the village of Afotobo, the itinerant singer Yao sings proverbs and stories with a symbolic moral while playing two harps which he rests on his knees, accompanied by a musician with two rattles and two further musicians with percussion instruments (hollow gongs).'[9] The interest in the Baule focuses on their craftsmanship, rituals, music and masked dances. The Baule films follow a classical pattern for ethnographic films, juxtaposing every image with a specification or vernacular description that effectively neutralises the visual image and subsumes it within a framework of general comparisons. Yet on account of the genre's scientific designation, the style and construction of ethnographic films have seldom been objects of research in German film history. What is more, precisely because they arise from scientific rather than filmic interest, these films

remain unknown to the broader public; many still languish in archival collections to which access is restricted.[10] The problem is especially acute in relation to early cinema. It was not until the 1990s that film archives began restoring nitrate film material systematically, in the process of which films produced in Africa were also 'rediscovered'. Within the framework of the Lumière Project, some 200 such films from the *Cinémathèque Royale de Belgique* (Brussels) and the *Nederlands Filmmuseum* (Amsterdam) have been identified and restored. The legacy of African films in Germany, by contrast, has yet to become the object of such concerted efforts at restoration. Moreover, even publications accompanying the Lumière Project have continued to employ standard ethnographic classifications, such as: 'General interest; Agriculture and other economic activities; Films about Natives' way of life; expeditions and trips through the Dark Continent.'[11] This seems especially paradoxical, since early cinema precisely both predates the division of films into genres and so-called 'scientific' works, and readily acknowledges and exposes its own filmic practices, thus undermining the very notion of film's capacity for 'scientific' observation.

There are however certain films that break with the ethnographic conventions of observing, documenting and collecting objects and events perceived as threatened with extinction. The avoidance of the increasing conventionalisation that affects documentary and feature films alike is most obvious in amateur movies, which both depart from filmic and generic conventions, and manage to escape traditional constructions of an exotic screen-Africa by frankly acknowledging and representing the adventure of being in Africa and filming there. Two sequences from *An den heiligen Wassern des Nils* (*Along the Holy Waters of the Nile*, 1928) are of interest in this regard. After an inter-title reading 'Sons of the Desert', we see riders galloping on horseback and camels through a barren valley, against a background of pyramids. After subsequent shots of banana plants and blossoms, we see various members of the expedition – including a certain Dr Mertens, and women sporting wide-brimmed hats – seated in a row, with desert all about them. They watch the riders' antics, obviously staged as a spectacle for their pleasure. The image of reality offered here is unintentionally complex: the two scenes are inconsistent in their approach to the real and thus expose the film as a combined record of documentary and fictional happenings.

Another amateur movie, *Durch Afrika im Automobil* (*Through Africa by Automobile*, 1929), illustrates further breaks with conventional representational modes. As the title indicates, the film deals with the traversing of Africa by car: the car is the star and Africa the backdrop through which it is driven. Everything else is incidental. Yet it is the incidental moments which render visible that world through which the car fleetingly passes, as well as the encounter with land and people. Passers-by may give the car a push, youths may help change tyres, or stand about and watch the car, its drivers, the movie camera. At one point, the drivers *cum* actors, Prince Ferdinand von Liechtenstein and Ladislaus Eduard von Almàsy,[12] with Rudi Mayer at the camera, save a village from an attacking lion; there follow images of the landscape, scenes depicting motor sport, and a big game hunt. A variety of genres – travelogue, documentary, comedy and drama – are swiftly juggled from scene to scene. The colonialist attitude towards 'natives' that predominates in professional productions from this period is equally evident here, in the same casual manner that animals are shot and cars driven. The drivers pose alongside villagers, hunting trophies and British regiments; their ubiquitous presence holds the whole stylistic blend together as a form of travel diary.

It is the amateur's receptivity to a wide range of conventional modes of filmic representation which on the one hand distances these films from professional cinematic modes, and which on the other – quite unintentionally and contradictorily – proves more revealing than the distanced descriptive style of the anthropological or ethnographic. The documentary style of observation does prevail, however, within another genre, the so-called *Kulturfilm* (cultural film), a specifically German genre with its origins in the silent period.[13] In contrast to ethnographic films, these are rooted not purely in scientific interest, but in the desire for an accessible medium in which to inform audiences on particular forms of life and production, flora and fauna. *Kulturfilme* constituted an independent component of cinema programmes until the 1960s, and were then introduced into classrooms and adult education by the various *Landesbildstellen* (regional audio-visual services) founded in the post-war period. Characteristic of these films is their essayistic style, as well as their recourse to a cultural and historical schema marked by technological and civilising concerns: a schema that measures and evaluates the various other forms of life and labour the films uncover against 'our' level of an alleged development. The West German productions *Nichts als ein Obdach – Wohnformen in Tunesien* (*Nothing but a Roof over one's Head – Forms of Dwelling in Tunisia*, 1959) and *Nomaden heute* (*Nomads Today*, 1964) are typical of the genre. The former takes a superbly photographed look at different forms of Tunisian habitation, ranging from simple palm branch or stone shelters

through to clay structures and impressive multi-storey cave dwellings. The voice-over tells of the contingency of these various forms on local building materials, while simultaneously assuring us of their primitiveness. The film makes significant omissions: we learn nothing of the advantages of these 'traditional' dwellings, nor is the 'modern' metropolitan architecture of Tunis or Sousse offered up for comparison.

Nomaden heute, made five years later, has a more complex rhetorical structure. Nomadic life is portrayed as an autonomous form whose continued existence is endangered by the increased technologisation of transportation networks. The film is neither enslaved to some romanticised vision of a desert filled with camels and tents, nor does it blindly affirm or reject technological progress. Rather, it treads a middle way by considering the lives of nomads – shown adopting sedentary lifestyles as they take on work as day labourers in order to make ends meet – from the viewpoint of their everyday struggle for existence.

One sub-group of the *Kulturfilm* is the wildlife film. Its immense popularity derives from its capacity to offer audiences the chance to go on safari without danger, either safely ensconced in the cinema auditorium or in front of the television set at home. One of the best-known German film and television classics of the genre is Bernhard Grzimek's *Serengeti darf nicht sterben* (*Serengeti Shall not Die*, 1959). Grzimek's wildlife and naturalist programmes – akin to Jacques-Yves Cousteau's *Le monde sans soleil* (1964) or David Attenborough's productions for the BBC – captivated German television audiences with their depictions of Africa's animal kingdom from the 1960s through to the 80s (Grzimek died in 1987). More than any other German film-maker, he succeeded in presenting Africa as a living biosphere, and his name is associated with an unspectacular, restrained and informative style of commentary that would come to establish itself as standard during this period.

On the one hand, wildlife films promote innovations in film technology (lenses, portable cameras, etc.), and on the other, they construct an animal kingdom shaped by changes in time and space. The filming of animals in the wild positions them within 'narratives of the natural':[14] outside of specific narrative structures they are meaningless. Some examples from the 1920s and 30s serve to illustrate this point. In *Afrikanische Dickhäuter* (*Animal Pachyderms*, 1930) – a production of the *Reichsstelle für den Unterrichtsfilm* (Reich Educational Film Bureau) – rhinos charge at the camera, then stop abruptly and disappear in a cloud of dust. The inference here is that wild animals are both stubborn – and, of course, dangerous. Within the context of the wildlife film, the 'Negro' is constructed in similar terms. In the photograph collection *Film-Photos wie noch nie* (*Film-Photos as Never Before*), published in 1929, it is maintained that:

> Earlier, film saw the Negro merely as an object to be photographed, much like cats and dogs or wild animals. Today, however, we know that he too is a human being, hot blooded and full of life. Negro films will always be most effective if one lets the Negro roam freely in front of the camera without trying to teach him specific movements, which would go against his race and his temperament.[15]

What is explicit in the above quote becomes implicit in the 1930 production of the *Reichsstelle für den Unterrichtsfilm* in Berlin, *Deutsche Kamerun-Bananen* (*German Cameroonian Bananas*), a silent film designed to be accompanied by live commentary at screenings. We discover here that the Hamburg-based *Afrikanische Frucht-Kompagnie* (African Fruit Trading Company) imports up to 60,000 heads of bananas per shipload. Countless black workers are put to work on a plantation cutting down banana plants which are then transported to warehouses, hung up to ripen and dry, then packed ready for shipping. In the film, a white supervisor strolls with his arms crossed along a group of tables, looking for the best fruits. Wooden crates and banana plants are loaded aboard the cargo-ship *Pionier*. In the next shot, we are already at the port in Hamburg, where the bananas are being lifted out of the ship's hold. The film's final shot is of a goods wagon bearing the inscription '*Kamerun-Bananen*'.

Deutsche Kamerun-Bananen is by no means suited for use in biology lessons: it is concerned neither with soil condition, nor with tools and techniques. Even the consistency of the fruits is irrelevant. This is no educational film seeking to explain processes of growth and production through graphs and diagrams. Instead, the impression is given of Cameroon as one gigantic German plantation, all of whose bananas, warehouses and docks are the property of the *Afrikanische Frucht-Kompagnie*. Cameroonian factory workers belong as much to the plantation's inventory as do its water pumps and drying ovens. The film fails to mention that Germany had to cede Cameroon to France and Britain in 1917. Yet at the same time – quite incidentally – it manages to effect the re-establishment of Cameroon as German territory. Only the presence of the white supervisor openly exposes this connection, as he assumes the function of reference to and substitute for an otherwise invisible instance of colonial authority, which ensures productivity and upholds the colonial project to civilise and discipline.

This rhetoric is characteristic of many *Kulturfilme* of the period, including *Pygmäen, ein Zwergvolk Inner-Afrikas* (*Pygmies, a Dwarf People of Central Africa*, ca. 1930), *Bei den Buschnegern in Südwest* (*Among the Bush Negroes in Southwest Africa*, 1930), *West-Afrika* (*West Africa*, 1935) and *Das Riff – ein Kulturbild aus Spanisch-Marokko* (*The Reef – a Cultural Picture from Spanish Morocco*, 1935). All these titles display a penchant for territorial annexation that is symptomatic of the 1930s, a penchant that gives way in the post-war period to the cautious fascination for Africa that Grzimek's wildlife films, for example, display. Grzimek uses the simplest of means to break with earlier rhetoric. By positioning himself in front of the camera as a reporter, and by alluding in his commentary to the film-making process, he became the visible mediator of the wilderness's reality, and liberated it thus from its timeless and supposedly neutral construction. In this way, he altered not only the image of Africa – and its wilderness – but also the entire medium.

The shift in documentary film-making during the 1960s from cinema to television marked a significant change in the German imaginary of Africa. Films that would not have stood a chance as cinema releases benefited from these changing conditions. A particularly fine example is the work of Bernd Mosblech, who started as a cameraman with WDR in 1963, before moving to NBC's Nairobi office in 1966. Mosblech later maintained his attachment to Africa through long-term projects as cameraman, scriptwriter, producer and director. He shot *The Last Warrior* in Kenya between 1992 and 1996, featuring Masai he had befriended and who had already appeared in his documentary *Ich bin die tolle Katja* (*I Am the Crazy Katja*, 1991). Mosblech brings no preconceived theses with him to Africa. Rather, he allows events to develop on location in a way that goes far beyond Grzimek's initial circumventions of conventional television formats. *White Kings in Africa*, shot in southern Ghana in 1998, is one example. The film begins with the annual meeting of the elected Ghanaian and European chiefs under the chairmanship of the Paramount Chief. The film takes an unexpected turn when Mosblech's soundman and friend Csaba Klcsar is elected to the post of chief of development by the local population, and takes up the position. Since the staging in this and other Mosblech films is made quite evident, they depart radically from the documentary style of simple observation of a supposedly authentic reality, and approach a concept of Africa as a reality which Mosblech and his crew share with the indigenous population, and to which all visibly and audibly belong.

Evidence of the erosion of difference

The above discussion reveals a transition: what began as a desire to conquer Africa and to save its disappearing environment in film has gradually given way to an erosion of the essential division between 'here' and 'there', timeless and historied, 'traditional' and 'modern' Africa. Classical conventions and genres are likewise in dissolution today. Nevertheless, the predominant constructions of Africa in German films and advertising, as well as religious and political discourse, still represent it primarily as a continent of famine, civil war, killer disease, strange rites and nature in need of conservation. There is, moreover, no 'black' cinema in Germany. Two recent documentaries, *Black in the Western World* (1992), directed by Wanjiru Kinyanjui, a Kenyan graduate of the *Deutsche Film- und Fernseh-Bildungsakademie* (German Film and Television Academy), and *Dreckfresser* (*Shit Eaters*, 2000) by the Nigerian Branwen Okpako, stand out as exceptions to this general rule. The relative success in Germany of film imports from the US that ride the wave of the hip-hop vogue – *Do the Right Thing* (1989), *Boyz n the Hood* (1990) or *Menace II Society* (1992) – or the early reggae and soul cult musicals *The Harder they Come* (1972) and *Car Wash* (1976) are the nearest that Germany gets to a 'black' cinema.

In contrast to such pop-cultural engagements, from the 1960s to the 80s, Germany's connections to Africa were above all politically determined: there was solidarity with the political prisoners on Robben Island, apartheid bananas were boycotted, and African students joined German universities. The latter in turn influenced the German image of Africa. Independent productions, such as Malte Rauch's films from the early 1980s, correspond to this critical engagement and the goal of consciousness-raising. During the Cold War, this political engagement was characterised by different forms of social acceptance in the two Germanys. In the GDR, international solidarity shaped official policy, while the Federal Republic primarily pursued a programme of economic development. Two films – the East German *Kommando 52* (*Commando 52*, 1965) and the West German *Hungerjahre in einem reichen Land* (*Hunger Years*, 1979) – show just how different attitudes towards Africa were during the Cold War (insofar, that is, as Africa was dealt with in film at all).

The documentary *Kommando 52* shows German legionnaires in the Congo (subsequently Zaire, now the Democratic Republic of Congo). In front of the camera, German mercenaries murder supporters of Patrice Lumumba's party, the MNC (*Mouvement National Congolais*).[16] Piles of corpses recall images of the Holocaust. Yet the film's condemnation of unimaginable brutality does not lead to solidarity with the Africans, but rather to an affirmation of the GDR as the 'right' side in the Cold War. The end credits conclude with the words: 'We are ashamed, as Germans, at the crimes committed by Germans which this film exposes.' The film thus uses the Congolese civil war as a pretext to enable the GDR to appear superior within the inter-German Cold War, and to liberate itself from its share of responsibility for Germany's fascist past.

The unmastered National Socialist past surfaces similarly in Jutta Brückner's *Hungerjahre*, an autobiographical feature film narrative of a post-war family in which familial stuffiness, restricting speechlessness, bitterness, disgust and shame prevail. The film-maker's own experiences are used here to explore the narrative of a young woman growing up. Her first sexual experience, with a 'black' in a lake, resembles a dream of liberated desire whence the forces of Germanness, family and speechlessness have been exiled: for a single moment, the promise of mutual acceptance between the socially disempowered (the white girl and the black man) is realised. Made in 1979, the film recalls the lost awakening and fleeting dream of the 1960s, stifled beneath the weight of German self-absorption. Germany thus continues to be dominated by an enduring 'national autism', as it works through its National Socialist past, and focuses on suspect mothers, fathers, grandparents, neighbours, and their cinema. Africa, accordingly, finds scant representation in New German Cinema. Werner Herzog's sorry and belated effort *Cobra Verde* (*Slave Coast*, 1988, based on Bruce Chatwin's novel *The Viceroy of Ouidah*), shot in Columbia and Ghana, is an exception that in the end only proves the rule. Klaus Kinski here plays the slave trader Cobra Verde (Francisco Manoel da Silva) and, as in his role in *Aguirre, der Zorn Gottes* (*Aguirre, the Wrath of God*), exudes the allure of what Rüdiger Schaper has termed 'a seemingly invincible member of the master race'. Yet Herzog's approach to blacks and their culture – or what he considers black culture to be – remains literally superficial. As Schaper stresses, locating Herzog's predilection for crowd scenes in the realm of Leni Riefenstahl's *Olympia* films, 'The images on the screen as it teems with black bodies are stolen ones, film sequences brought home like trophies from the Third World.'[17] Films released in the same year as *Cobra Verde* included Uwe Schrader's *Sierra Leone* (1987) and Jan Schütte's *Drachenfutter* (*Dragon Food*, 1987), featuring anti-heroes – in *Sierra Leone*, a construction worker who can no longer find his way in Germany after years of working overseas, and in

Drachenfutter, two asylum seekers who want to open a pub in Hamburg, but instead fall victim to unfeeling bureaucracy and are expelled from the country – and addressing the question of what it means to be 'foreign' in Germany. Praised for their cinematic artistry, both films flopped at the box-office, overshadowed in appeal by the monumental hit *Cobra Verde* and the American television series *Roots* (1988), which enjoyed tremendous popularity in West Germany, with its central character, the runaway slave Kunta Kinte, becoming the very byword for 'black'.

Only in the 1990s, following German reunification, did a handful of documentary film-makers risk direct explorations of the relationship to Africa. *Wir hatten eine Dora in Südwest* (*We Had a Dora in Southwest Africa*, 1991) by Tink Diaz offers an insight, tinged by shattered romance, into marriage policy among German-Namibian settlers from the 1890s on, when, to counter the threat of 'mongrelisation' ('*Verkafferung*'), and in accordance with Aryan racial doctrine, spirited young German women were instructed in agriculture and armaments, and thus prepared for mar-

riage with settlers who might otherwise fall into 'wild' marriages with African women. Christoph Schuch's *Namibia – Rückkehr in ein neues Land* (*Namibia – Return to a New Nation*, 1997) follows three young people who grew up as children of Namibian guest workers in the GDR, then returned to Namibia following independence in 1990. Martin Baer's *Befreien Sie Afrika* (*Free Africa!*, 1998) explores the myth of Africa within German military policy, combining excerpts from feature films, news reports, cartoons, advertisements, music videos and computer games dating from the Second World War through to the present day with interviews with war veterans, legionnaires and officers discussing their dreams of Africa. A further exception is Christoph Schlingensief's *Die Spalte* (1996), an ironic look at the military, shot in Zimbabwe. The film's international title, *United Trash*, sums up Schlingensief's rationale and his blatant disregard both for issues pertaining to the Nazi past, and for political correctness. The film pursues the implications of the UN deployment in Africa, which has brought German troops once again to

Befreien Sie Afrika (1998)

foreign soil. German soldiers fire a human-powered V2-rocket at the White House, with Udo Kier and film critic Dietrich Kuhlbrodt playing a pair of perverse, Prussianesque generals who surround themselves with dancing 'natives' in short straw skirts. The film's 'trash' aesthetic met with widespread incomprehension, and was indeed responsible for a brief suspension of diplomatic relations between Germany and Zimbabwe.

In this contribution, I have attempted to sketch the representation of Africa in German film, primarily though not exclusively in documentaries. These of course are just as subject as are feature films to constructions of a fantasy Africa. The unabated production of African fantasies in scientific and cultural film-making was, I have suggested, to a certain extent encouraged by the loss of German colonies in 1918, which stemmed public contact with African realities. The extended post-war reception of American images of Africa in films from *Casablanca* (1942) and *The African Queen* (1951), to *Out of Africa* (1985) or *I Dreamed of Africa* (2000) has also influenced German imaginaries, and still needs to be properly researched. In the final analysis German productions scarcely differ from other European and American works in their locating of Africa, as the films discussed here attest, 'at the bottom of the pile' or 'on the very margins' of the world's cultures. While globalisation draws African realities ever closer, imaginary constructions change but slowly.

Translated by Robert J. Kiss

Notes

1 There is little research on the 'black' extras in Ufa's exotic productions, where they lived or what became of them. Cf. Katharina Oguntoye, *Eine afro-deutsche Geschichte. Zur Lebenssituation von Afrikanern und Afro-Deutschen in Deutschland von 1884 bis 1950* (Berlin: Hoho-Verlag Christine Hoffmann, 1997).

2 Interest in African film-makers since the 1970s is indebted to this sense of longing. As alternative public spaces, African film festivals – including Touki Bouki (Hanover), Jenseits von Europa (Cologne), Cinema Afrika (Berlin) and Africa Alive (Frankfurt-am-Main) – assume an important role. On the connection of these to German film development and support programmes, cf. Deutsche Stiftung für internationale Entwicklung (ed.), *Cinema and Culture in Africa* (Berlin: DSE, 1989), pp. 51–4.

3 During the Togo expedition, alongside ethnographic films, the features *The White Goddess of the Wangora* (a remake of which appeared in 1921 under the title *Weisse*

unter Kannibalen [*White Woman among the Cannibals*], employing 600m of original material from the 1913/14 Togo expedition along with new sequences shot in Rüdersdorf and on the North Sea coast), *Odd Man Out*, *The Law of the Sadu Mountain* and *The Heroes of Paratau* were produced, all of which caused a furore when shown in London in June 1914. Cf. Meg Gehrts, *Weiße Göttin der Wangora* (Wuppertal: Peter Hammer, 1999 [orig. *A Camera Actress in the Wilds of Togoland*, 1915]), p. 258.

4 During the Third Reich, Lieberenz became the foremost producer of colonial films, including *Die deutsche Frauenschule Rendsburg* (*The German Women's School at Rendsburg*, 1937), excerpted in *Wir hatten eine Dora in Südwest* (*We had a Dora in Southwest Africa*, 1991).

5 The staging of an 'Africa through which drums echo' is yet more striking in *Die Wildnis stirbt*, which includes unattributed footage in which a naked woman – a black Venus – dances in the moonlight.

6 Cf. Gerlinde Waz, 'Auf der Suche nach dem letzten Paradies. Der Afrikaforscher und Regisseur Hans Schomburgk', in Jörg Schöning (ed.), *Triviale Tropen: Exotische Reise- und Abenteuerfilme aus Deutschland 1919–1930* (Munich: edition text+kritik, 1997), pp. 95–109.

7 Cf. *Institut für den Wissenschaftlichen Film, Verzeichnis Ethnologie: Afrika* (Göttingen: IWF, 1986).

8 In the 1960s, ethnographic film-making in the USA, France and Britain underwent far-reaching changes stemming from *direct cinema* and *cinéma vérité*. These changes led to a reorientation of ethnology, ethnography and anthropology. Films produced within this context were released in West Germany, but despite their call for critical engagement with images of Africa, exerted no discernible influence on German ethnographic film.

9 Ibid., p. 39.

10 For example, within the holdings of the *Deutsches Institut für Filmkunde* (Wiesbaden) or the *Bundesarchiv-Filmarchiv* (Berlin).

11 Cf. '*The Lumière Project'. European Film Archives at the Crossroads* (Lisbon: Projecto Lumière 1996), p. 78.

12 The story of the Hungarian Almàsy's life as a cartographer with the Royal Geographical Society commissioned to map the Sahara, and as a double agent, became well-known through the Anglo-American film *The English Patient* (1996, based on Michael Ondaatje's novel of the same name).

13 Cf. for example Klaus Kreimeier, *The Ufa-Story: A History of Germany's Greatest Film Company 1918–1945* (New York: Hill and Wang, 1996).

14 Valentin Yves Mudimbe, *The Idea of Africa* (Bloomington and London: Indiana University Press, 1994), p. 168.

15 *Film-Photos wie noch nie* (Cologne, facsimile reprint, 1978), p. 59, pertaining to Phoebus-Film's *Das schwarze Geschlecht*, Ufa's *Wege zu Kraft und Schönheit* and Marc Allégret's *Voyage au Congo*.

16 *Kommando 52* offers no explanation of the complex political situation in the Congo following independence in 1960; presumably, German mercenaries were hired by President Chiombé in order to eliminate his political opponents.

Chiombé advocated the partitioning of Katanga province from the rest of Congolese territory, whereas Lumumba and his MNC party stood for the upholding of national unity. Lumumba conceived of his path to independence as a 'positive neutrality' towards East and West alike. He was murdered in mysterious circumstances on 17 January 1961.

17 *Tip-Filmjahrbuch – Daten, Berichte, Kritiken*, 4 (1988), p. 70.

23

Beyond Paternalism:
Turkish German Traffic in Cinema[1]

Deniz Göktürk

This chapter proposes a new, transnational perspective on Turkish German encounters in cinema, and, more generally, on the status of minority cultures in multi-cultural Germany. The Turkish–German axis is not the first route that comes to mind if one starts to rethink German cinema in a global perspective. The cinema of migration as a social-realist genre, which established itself in Germany following the mass immigration of labourers from Southern European countries from the 1960s, has developed largely apart from the canon of national cinema and oblivious of other kinds of traffic in and out of German film-making. Instead, it has set out to represent these migrants as victims on the margins of society. Countless documentaries and didactic films deal with the 'problem of foreigners'.[2] Only recently, films have begun to challenge the parameters of a paternalist discourse and started exploring more playful and less miserabilist scenarios of contact and mutual mimicry.

For a long time, the Turkish 'guest worker' in Germany has tended to be evoked as what John Berger first termed the 'seventh man', a mythic mute figure – unable to communicate and integrate.[3] Surprisingly, the figure of the mute Turk was resurrected by Homi Bhabha as an emblem of displacement and incompatibility, which stands somewhat at odds with his theoretical explorations of hybridity and liminality.[4] Bhabha and other post-colonial critics have generated an understanding of the status of border-crossers and migrant populations as a productive provocation of the concept of a pure national culture. The presence of foreigners is here acknowledged as a challenge to imagine new narratives of the nation from its margins.

Traditional concepts of culture assume a locally rooted, self-contained system of shared practices, rituals and beliefs. The mobility of migrants stands in critical contrast to any such closed system and opens up what Bhabha terms a 'third space' of transnational translation.[5] Constructions and appropriations which arise in definitions of culture on the basis of national or ethnic membership are thus destabilised in favour of scenarios which allow for mobile citizens. Meanwhile, the national still remains a primary category in framing, describing and labelling culture, for example in film programmes and book series on national cinemas. Migrants (at least from some parts of the world) are often perceived as odd deviations from the national norm, as archaic figures outside modernity, even by critics who are otherwise concerned with unpacking the myth of unified national cultures.

It is, moreover, not only the myth of the homogeneous 'host nation' that needs to be reconsidered, but also that of the culture-of-origin. In fact, the 'seventh man' is as much a reality in Turkey, where a large part of the national population has migrated to cities. Their lifestyles and expectations deviate from those of the western-oriented urban elites, which leads not infrequently to conflicts on buses, in parks and other public spaces. Thus in Turkish cinema we encounter emigrants as well as interior migrants from country to the city. Their training in civilised behaviour and resistance to the temptations of urban decadence forms a prominent theme – both in melodramas and comedies.[6]

Why is it, then, that Turks in German cinema have been cast for decades in one-dimensional roles which allow for little change and development? Is a new trend towards mutual mirroring and border-crossing emerging? Under the sign of 'integration', attention has certainly been turned since the 1960s towards the different mores of foreign cultures. The assumption of clearly defined, homogeneous cultural identities has led to a rhetoric about minorities which is sustained by ethnographic interest and social engagement, while promoting integration. The paternalist treatment of 'Ausländer' by institutions of the welfare state led to 'clientelism' and to an 'ethnicisation' of minorities which were no longer perceived in terms of their social roles, but as 'representatives of their national culture of descent'.[7] Impulses and models for a politically engaged rhetoric about minorities were appropriated from the US civil rights movements, and have produced well-meaning projects encouraging multi-culturalism that, however, often result in the construction of binary opposition between 'Turkish culture' and 'German culture'. The postulate of cultural difference, though it purports to be liberating, has obstructed the perception of the cross-cultural exchanges that in fact already exist, and often hindered dialogue instead of facilitating it.

In this context, cultural production by new migrants has faced difficulty in delivering a successful critique, since it is not seen to fulfil the separatist criteria of multiculturalism. Of what nationality, for example, is a film which is set in Hamburg and German-produced, but in which Turkish actors speak Turkish and German and enact Turkish milieus? Is it to be attributed to German or Turkish cinema? Does it make a statement about German culture, Turkish culture, or both? Does it make any difference if the director is a Turk living in Germany who works under the same production conditions as his/her German colleagues? Is classification easier or more difficult in this case?

In an era of mass migration and increasing global mobility of people and media, questions about the status of transnational cultural productions by travellers, emigrants and the exiled, have achieved a new explosiveness. Film critics, concomitantly, have begun to call for a new genre category which explodes the boundaries of 'original' national cultures as well as filmic boundaries, and is variously described as 'independent transnational cinema',[8] 'postcolonial hybrid films'[9] or simply as 'world cinema'[10] – a descriptor which, in contrast to older separatist categories such as 'third cinema'[11] or 'sub-state cinema',[12] stresses the universality of mobility and diversity. These categories foster a new cultural imagination, in which migrants begin to grow beyond sub-national niches and enter into transnational networks. As one German critic of the Turkish–German film Berlin in Berlin (1993) put it, 'min-

ority cinema has become appealing to the mainstream'. Peitz goes on to compare this film to other successful cinematic treatments of migrant experience as Gurinder Chadha's Bhaji on the Beach (1993), Jan Schütte's German-Polish co-production Goodbye America (1993), Wayne Wang's The Joy Luck Club (1993), and Ang Lee's The Wedding Banquet (1993).[13] Such a comparison was indeed pioneering in terms of re-contextualising minority perspectives in German cinema in a broader international horizon.

Minority cinema in the prison of subsidy

For many years, however, migrants only appeared in German cinema as prisoners of a patronising culture of compassion. The New German Cinema of rebellious auteurs who declared 'Papa's Cinema' dead in the 1960s and confronted the nation with the mirror of its past came into being at a time when popular cinema in Europe was in decline. Hollywood continued to secure for itself greater shares in the market, while television was simultaneously establishing itself as a mass medium. The rise of the New German Cinema was facilitated by public subsidy of film, as well as television co-productions, and the reputations of certain star directors at international festivals.[14]

The New German Cinema's combination of social mission and public subsidy opened a space for the portrayal of the experiences of outsiders, primarily those of women, but gradually also of ethnic minorities, as a topic of feature film productions. Among the authors of the New German film, Fassbinder stood out for his interest in minorities which did not rely on exclusionary empathy. In Katzelmacher (1969), a satire on the restrictions, boredom and hostilities of petit bourgeois life, he directed himself in the role of a 'Greek from Greece'. The working title for Angst essen Seele auf (Fear Eats the Soul, 1973) was 'All Turks are named Ali' – all North Africans as well, one might add, since no Turks appear in the film. This deconstructivist melodrama about the impossible love between an old woman (Brigitte Mira) and a beautiful young Arab (played by Fassbinder's lover Ben Hedi El-Saalem) was unusual in its representation of a man as object of desire and exotic projection.

The contrast to other New German Cinema productions is telling. Film subsidy on the federal and regional level, as well as opportunities for co-production with public television facilitate the production of many 'migrant films' and create a fertile soil for film projects which search for a new rhetoric of ethnic difference and minority cultures. In particular *Das kleine Fernsehspiel'* (Television Short Feature) at the public broadcasting channel ZDF has a mission to promote experimental film-making and support young *auteurs*. The criteria for selection and funding, however, have often been conditioned by a limited focus on the problems of integration. Conscientious issue-films created, a 'cinema of duty', as it was called in the British context.[15] Foreigners were condescendingly shown their cultural place, and film-makers saw themselves as tied to sorrowful stories about being lost 'between two cultures'. One example is *Shirins Hochzeit* (*Shirin's Wedding*, 1975), in which the feminist director Helma Sanders tells the sad story of Shirin (Ayten Erten), who leaves her poverty-stricken village in Anatolia to search for her fiancé Mahmut (played by the poet Aras Ören) in Cologne. Shirin ends up on the street and is finally killed by a pimp – at which point Helma Sanders' elegiac voice-over delivers a commentary on Shirin that incorporates her 'otherness' into the universality of women's suffering.[16]

It was, moreover, not only indigenous German directors whose screenplays and films reproduced clichés about the 'foreign' culture and its archaic manners and conventions. Immigrant authors and directors living in Germany were constrained by the same funding criteria, and for a long time, only screenplays depicting the repression of backward, rural people attracted monies. Subsidy schemes fostered a ghetto culture which went to great lengths to propagate integration, but seldom achieved popularity.

Until well into the 1980s, then, minority films in Germany often followed Sanders' model in telling stories of Turkish women repressed by patriarchal fathers, brothers and husbands, of their exclusion from public spaces, or of imprisonment in closed spaces. Tevfik Başer's *Vierzig Quadratmeter Deutschland* (*40 Square Meters of Germany*, 1986) is one such film, a 'chamber play' in the truest sense of the word, about a woman imprisoned by her husband in a Hamburg apartment. The film begins with the arrival of the newly wed couple, loaded with provisions, from Turkey. The woman (played by jazz singer Özay Fecht) wears village clothing and appears awkward in the apartment. In the morning she tries to turn on the electric stove with matches. Turna begins cheerfully to unpack and clean up, but her mood darkens when she notices that her husband Dursun has locked her in the apartment, claiming that he intends to protect her from the deleterious influence of the German environment. For months, she stays restricted to '40 square meters of Germany'. The camera captures her imprisonment in claustrophobic frames, either in front of

the mirror cutting her braids or looking out of the window onto a grey courtyard. The daily monotony is interrupted only by subjective flashbacks and memories of Turna's home. When Dursun dies of a heart attack in the shower at the end, and Turna steps out into the foreign world, it is uncertain whether life will improve or worsen for her, since the credits begin before she crosses the threshold into the street.

40 Square Metres of Germany was nominated for the Federal Film Prize in 1987 and received awards for Özay Fecht's performance as well as Claus Bantzer's musical score. This national recognition, however, only served paradoxically to further cement 'immigrant culture' in its sub-national status. The film sparked off a series of joyless representations of migrants as victims shut out of German society and unable to communicate with their native culture. Turkish women particularly were represented as double victims, imprisoned by their husbands and barred from contact with the outer world. Thus, for instance, in Başer's second film, *Abschied vom falschen Paradies* (*Farewell to a False Paradise*, 1988), the director continued his exploration of the captivity of women in closed spaces, albeit under reversed conditions. The plot centres on a German prison, which appears paradoxically as a refuge. A fragile young woman, Elif (Zuhal Olcay, known from challenging roles in theatre and film productions in Turkey), slashes her wrists just before her release. Her story is then told in flashback. Sentenced to six years in jail for killing her husband, she has experienced her imprisonment as a liberation, learning fluent German and thus achieving integration into German society, or rather into a community of women. But this emancipation takes place all too smoothly. The women's solidarity which Elif experiences in prison is set against flashbacks of the women's community in her home village. Thus the prison, which often serves as a symbolic space for Turkish film-makers in Europe, is positively reinscribed.

Hamid Naficy sees in the configuration of claustrophobic spaces a characteristic iconography of transnational cinema, a restrictive spatial demarcation which Başer's women figures escape by retreating into their subjectivity, memories and imagination.[17] His films have been acclaimed by feminist criticism for surveying 'the cultural no man's land in which Turkish women in German exile live – exploited and disregarded both by their own compatriots and by Germans'.[18] It is worth noting, however, that the stories of suffering which these films narrate have been taken at face value by feminist critics and generalised to represent the 'experience of the Turkish woman'. From 'third world cinema', it seems, one expects factual stories about social outrages; fantasy, fiction, or ironic distance are reserved for western mainstream or art cinema. Thus Başer's third film, *Lebewohl, Fremde* (*Farewell, Stranger*, 1993), a German-Turkish love story with individualised characters set on the North Sea island of Langeness, met with scant success. It appears that Başer's name has become so closely associated with the representation of migrant misery that no space remains for him to explore other subjects.

Similar discursive structures in the representation of Turkish immigrants were adopted by the director Hark Bohm, who was considered since *Nordsee ist Mordsee* (1975) as the personified social consciousness of the New German Cinema. Among the German films of the 1980s which dealt with migrants' experiences, Bohm's *Yasemin* (1988) was certainly the greatest popular success. The film is still shown today at 'Turkish film events', and has been circulated abroad, via the Goethe-Institut, as far afield as Thailand and India. The director's moral credentials were established when he acted in such films as Fassbinder's *The Marriage of Maria Braun*, where he played opposite the returned émigré Oswald (Ivan Desny) in a key dialogue emphasising the merits of those who remained at home in Germany. In *Yasemin*, Bohm's political engagement focused on the problems of Turks in Hamburg. This 'Romeo and Juliet' story centres on a romance between the lively seventeen-year-old student Yasemin (Ayşe Romey), and Jan (played by Uwe Bohm, the director's son), who pursues her initially because of a bet, but then really falls in love with her. Yasemin is shown leading the prototypical double life prescribed for Turkish girls of her time: 'Germany in daytime, Turkey by night.'[19] Her double identity is reflected in the linguistic mix of family talk, as well as in scenes from her life at home. When she comes home to her father's greengrocery, she lets down her shortened skirt, pulls a sweater over a sleeveless summer dress, and becomes a conscientious Turkish daughter who helps in the store and must be accompanied on the street by her cousin Dursun. The situation seems about to change when, with the help of the mother (played by the writer Emine Sevgi Özdamar), the father is finally convinced of Yasemin's plans for university. However, the benevolent atmosphere changes radically when Yasemin's sister cannot produce a bloodstained sheet after her wedding night to prove her pre-marital virginity. His honour impugned, the loving father is suddenly transformed into a brutal patriarch who disowns his oldest daughter and locks up Yasemin, only to tear her out of bed in the middle of the night and ship her off to Turkey.

The film has been multiply cited as an empathetic milestone in German–Turkish understanding. In reality, it reconfirms long-held stereotypes according to which German society is considered enlightened and civilised, while the Turkish patriarchy is bound to archaic rituals and traditional beliefs. Within this model (which was also commonplace in 1980s German policies towards migrant minorities), integration can only be realised through a radical break between the so-called first and second migrant generations. Thus the playful engagements with both worlds which Yasemin begins to practise so charmingly in school, in her judo club, in the grocery store, at the market, or while dancing at her sister's wedding, are retracted at the end and declared impossible. The popularity of the film is thus founded upon an assumption that Turkish women – especially the young and beautiful – can only be liberated by saving them from their repressive men. The end of the film follows this logic: Yasemin 'does the right thing' – she threatens suicide, the father lets her go, she leaves the Turkish men behind, jumps on the back of Jan's motorcycle and rides off with him into the dark.

Hark Bohm has not only been rightfully critiqued for his 'longing for harmony' and his tendency to depict 'a good cliché'.[20] His film also reinforced a broader tendency to package stories of Turks in Germany in terms of gender relations. The liberation of the poor Turkish woman from captivity, repression, dependence, or prostitution is a popular fantasy, in which empathy with the victims of a violent 'other' culture primarily serves the purpose of self-confirmation. Nor is this fantasy confined to German film-makers. The films of Hark Bohm and Tevfik Başer developed out of the same funding and production conditions and are ideologically quite close. Both define the Turkish woman as a victim of relationships. The films of both feed from the same arsenal of popular assumptions, images and stories and finally confirm the superiority of German culture. The cultural production of ethnic minorities is all too easily understood as an authentic expression of the experiences of the entire group. In reality, however, the rhetoric of authors, directors and artists of foreign origin is no more authentic than that of their German counterparts; they may simply be quite astute at satisfying the expectations of the German public.

Humour and mutual mimicry

One of the few films in which Turkish–German encounters are humorously staged is Şerif Gören's *Polizei (Police)*, a Turkish production from 1988, the same year as *Yasemin* and *Farewell to a False Paradise*. The main protagonist of this comedy set around Kottbusser Tor in Berlin-Kreuzberg is the kind, naive street sweeper Ali Ekber (played by the popular comedian Kemal Sunal). A love of acting drives Ali to join a community theatre whose director is German, but speaks Turkish – one of many cultural mutations in this film. Ali gets a small role as a police officer, and likes the uniform so much that he continues to wear it on the street and act as an officer, which leads to confusion. His countrymen finally pay respect to him and keep him in good spirits with petty bribes.

Polizei is an adaptation of *Der Hauptmann von Köpenick* (*The Major of Koepenick*, 1931), Carl Zuckmayer's tragic comic, biting satire on high-handed bureaucrats and military officers in Wilhelmine Germany. Zuckmayer's play, which revolves around the arduous process of obtaining a passport, had already been filmed several times: in 1931 and in 1941 by Richard Oswald and in 1956 by Helmut Käutner with Heinz Rühmann in the starring role. In Gören's hands, the play is appropriated and transformed; into the German police uniform slips without ado a Turkish street sweeper. Ironic role-play throughout opens perspectives which reach beyond the social realism of migrant films of previous years and carnivalistically subvert clear categorisations of ethnic and cultural identity.

A further exception to the rule that excludes migrant cinema from humoristic treatment is *Berlin in Berlin*, a Turkish–German co-production and genre-mix of thriller, melodrama and comedy set in post-Wall Berlin. *Berlin in Berlin* is notable for the racy style of the Istanbul-based director and commercial film-maker Sinan Çetin, as well as for its transcendence of dutiful recitations on 'foreigner culture'. Centring on a German photographer who finds himself a captive guest in the home of an extended Turkish family in Berlin-Kreuzberg, the film explores the bizarre symbiosis that ensues between the 'foreigner' and the family. Their enforced union produces a reversal of the ethnographic, voyeuristic gaze. Now it is Turks who observe the German like an animal at the zoo; the camera lingers on him in close-up, ironically reconfiguring the claustrophobic situation of captivity that Naficy describes as characteristic of exile films. The reversal of the asylum situation and the enforced symbiosis of the German foreigner with extended Turkish family creates the potential for mutual humoristic mimicry, and thus transcends the conscientious productions of the 1980s. The film does not shy away from boldly teasing out familiar clichés, rituals and values about honour, hospitality and family revenge. But it also glistens with moments of playful irony (though it could perhaps afford this distanced perspective only because it was produced primarily outside of the German funding structures).[21]

More recently, however, immigrant film-makers working within the German production context have also started to attack critical expectations of minority German cinema in comedic fashion. *Ich Chef, Du Turnschuh* (*Me Boss, You Sneaker*, 1998), a production facilitated by ZDF, is Hussi Kutlucan's second film. The Berlin-based actor directs himself in the lead role of the Armenian refugee Dudie. This anarchistic comedy is notable for scenes in which ethnicity is staged as masquerade and role-play. The film opens with the arrival of a busload of Indians, while simultaneously another group is driven out of the home to be deported back to Turkey, to the accompaniment of South Indian pop music. The debate over territorial rights that ensues, as old immigrants make room for new arrivals, is a recurrent focus of the film. The protagonist, Dudie, finds work, for instance, on a central Berlin construction site populated by illegal workers of various origins and skin colours, who are treated with hostility by already 'naturalised' Turkish 'guest workers'. Dialogue, music and images satirise such social-realist journalistic exposés on exploitative labour conditions as Günther Wallraff's *Ganz unten* (1985). Through humour and irreverence, received conventions of representation are overturned and current debates around old and new immigrants, asylum, citizenship, national unity and identity ironically infiltrated. The film indicates parallels between traditions of 'ethnic roleplay' and of the 'anarchistic comedy' as it has been discussed in relation to US cinema in the early days of sound, for example the Marx brothers' *Monkey Business* (1931).[22] This non-commercial anarchistic comedy was shown at various festivals, and televised on the late programme on 27 July 1998 at 10.45pm (in a series titled *Gefühlsecht. Junge deutsche Filme* [*True Emotions. Young German Films*]), and again on 3 October 2000 – *Tag der deutschen Einheit* (German Unity Day, a public holiday), a nationally significant date – at prime time 8.15pm on 3sat (as part of a series titled *Jung, deutsch und türkisch. Die zweite und dritten Einwanderergeneration*). In 2000, the film received the Grimme Prize, awarded by the Institute of Journalism in Cologne. It was also nominated for a European Television Award in Amsterdam.

Me Boss, You Sneaker targets the kind of mixed urban audience also addressed by the Berlin radio station MultiKulti. Whether the film appeals more broadly to a Turkish immigrant family audience is rather questionable, since the preference of that group is often for satellite television from the homeland. The diaspora cinema does not always correspond to the taste of the diaspora audience, while the mainstream German audience still seems to expect migrant cinema to present coherently narrated family drama. *Me Boss, You Sneaker* does show, however, that a film about migrants in Germany can also be a film about Germany. The new immigrants have settled down, they have established themselves in German cities and on German screens and feel at home enough to poke fun at German authorities. The final deportation of the protagonist Dudie appears particularly ironic as a German child in Turkish disguise is deported with him. Films like *Me Boss, You Sneaker* suggest the possibility that the ghost of the mute Turkish guest worker is finally being driven out. Migrants have become operative – behind and in front of the camera – as self-confident subjects and know how to assert themselves rhetorically.

Lola und Bilidikid (1998)

New German Cinema – by young Turks

Since the autumn of 1998, a breakthrough in Turkish–German film production has been discernible. A new generation of film-makers and actors are gradually making their mark, mainly in Hamburg and Berlin. At the February 1999 Berlin Film Festival, and in a context in which national debates on citizenship and the possibility of 'dual passports' were at their peak, a series of transnational films shown under the rubric 'New German Cinema' were celebrated by critics as a ghetto renaissance. The Festival's 'Forum of Young Film' showed a new film by Thomas Arslan, *Dealer*, a production from ZDF's '*Das kleine Fernsehspiel*', with Tamer Yiğit in the starring role. *Dealer* sets its minimalistic views of life in Berlin-Kreuzberg, where the director himself has lived for some years, against a background of concrete tower block apartments, green park meadows and *pointilliste* traffic lights. Encounters in private or public spaces are enacted with a restraint that seems to typify the stagnation in this district of the city which appears to be lightyears away from the sparkling architecture of the reunified capital.

Lola und Bilidikid, a drama from the Berlin transvestite milieu, caused a further sensation as the opening film of the 'Panorama' section of the 1999 festival. The director Kutluğ Ataman, who studied at UCLA and lived in London for several years, staged his characters in urban spaces, on streets, in parks, nightclubs, public toilets, decaying factory grounds and against sites of national significance such as the Olympic stadium or the Victory Column. In Kreuzberg, in front of a façade designed by the artist Ayşe Erkmen, the camera lingers for a long moment on a poster which reads 'Diaspora'. Lola (Gandi Mukli) dazzles as a belly dancer in a transvestite trio, *Die Gastarbeiterinnen* (The Guest Workers). Her friend Bilidikid (Erdal Yıldız) is a tough guy in a leather jacket, who dreams of happiness in Turkey – until, that is, Lola is found dead in the river Spree. The film develops from this point as a thriller in which, after various disguise and chase sequences, Lola's adolescent brother Murat (Baki Davrak) finally realises that Lola was not killed by neo-Nazis as had been assumed, but by her elder brother Osman, a macho-man who seeks to hide his own homosexual inclinations. The film ends with Murat and his mother on the street, having deserted the hypocritical patriarch Osman. The mother's appropriation of public space as she tears off her headscarf is echoed by Lola's transvestite associates, as they romp about in the Tiergarten under the shadow of the Victory Column.

The German figures in *Lola and Bilidikid* are partially caricatured, and the analysis of family relationships and Turkish machismo at times falls back into melodrama and ethnic stereotyping. However, the film does succeed in capturing the fluidity of biologically understood gender identities, and reminds the viewer that such binary oppositions as masculine/feminine or German/Turkish are built on unsteady ground. The fact that the film ran in German cinemas for many weeks following the festival, and that world distribution rights have been acquired by the New York firm Good Machine International, which also distributes Ang Lee's Taiwanese–American gay family comedy *The Wedding Banquet*, may perhaps be a sign that Turkish–German film production has crossed the threshold of paternalist sub-national culture and broken through into transnational spheres in which global diasporas are attracting increasing interest.

Regional film promotion in Hamburg has also produced a recent flourishing of Turkish–German film. *Kurz und schmerzlos* (*Short Sharp Shock*, 1998), a debut film by Fatih Akin set and produced in Hamburg, was nominated for the Federal Film Prize and, though it failed to achieve its expected box-office success, was honoured at international film festivals. The film deals with three friends from the Hamburg gangster milieu: Gabriel, the Turk (Mehmet Kurtuluş), Costa, the Greek (Adam Bousdoukos) and Bobby, the Serb (Aleksandar Jovanovic). This constellation of three angry young men from diverse origins is reminiscent of the controversial French film *La Haine* (1995), in which the focus is not on a singular ethnic group, but rather on marginal social positions and their media portrayal. In *Kurz und Schmerzlos*, the gangster film aesthetic à la Martin Scorsese's *Mean Streets* is transported into the streets of Hamburg. The film is one of a growing number of Hamburg productions that focus on young men on the social margins. Two examples are *Aprilkinder* (*April Children,* 1998), a tri-lingual melodrama by Hamburg-based director Yüksel Yavuz, and *Kanak Attack!,* another gangster film set in Hamburg and directed by Lars Becker.

Unlike the increasingly diverse repertoire of representations of young Turkish men in Germany, however, rhetoric on Turkish women often remains trapped in binary models that imagine migrants as victims 'between the cultures'. *Yara* (*The Scar*, 1998) by Yılmaz Arslan, a German–Turkish–Swiss co-production with promotion by Eurimages, could very well be a sequel to *Yasemin*. The fragile young Hülya (Yelda Renaud) is taken against her will to relatives in Turkey, runs away, and ends up in a psychiatric institution. Her mother (played by Özay Fecht, the imprisoned housewife from *40 Quadratmeter Deutschland*) had left the family, married again in Turkey, and wants nothing to do with her daughter. At the end, the distraught Hülya finds herself back in Germany, with no idea any more where she belongs. The attempt to stage her subjective visions brings forth dubious images more reminiscent of posed glamour photos than the daydreams of a confused teenager.

Thomas Arslan's most recent film *Der schöne Tag* (*A Fine Day*, 2000), the last one in his Kreuzberg trilogy, is an exception to the rule of dreariness that apparently governs depictions of Turkish women. The film follows a day in the life of a young Berlin actress, Deniz Turhan (Serpil Turhan), whom we see leaving her sleeping boyfriend in the morning. She makes eye-contact with a stranger at an underground station, performs in a casting agency and works in a dubbing studio, lending her voice to Amanda Langlet in a discussion about love in Eric Rohmer's *Conte d'été* (*Summer's Tale*, 1996). Turhan's subdued acting style, coupled with the film's focus on her daily life, allows the viewer to witness the life of a confident young female urbanite, without foregrounding her Turkishness. In the discussion following the film's premiere at the 2000 Berlin

Film Festival, however, *Der schöne Tag* was critiqued for its perceived failure to engage in established ways with the social problems of Turkish women. The critics, it seems, have not yet noticed that women, and especially young women of migrant background, are making a mark in contemporary Germany, among other things, as film directors experimenting with new forms of representation.

On the road – crossing borders

Ayşe Polat, another Hamburg resident, has thus for instance enjoyed international success with a series of dream-like fantastic miniature films about exile situations, including *Fremdennacht* (1991), *Ein Fest für Beyhan* (1994) and *Gräfin Sophia Hatun* (1997). Funded by ZDF's 'Das kleine Fernsehspiel', Polat has now completed her first feature *Die Auslandstournee* (*Tour Abroad*, 1999), a road movie pairing Şenay, a young orphan girl (Özlem Blume), and Zeki, a transvestite singer (Hilmi Sözer), in search of her mother. Their journey from Germany, via Paris and (in scenes reminiscent of Wim Wenders' *Alice in the Cities*) Wuppertal, then on to Stuttgart and finally Istanbul, ultimately develops into a journey into the past. The story unfolds as a triangular relationship between the singer Zeki, the belly dancer Çiçek and Şenay's deceased father Mahmut, a former *karagöz* (shadow play) performer; all three of them had left Turkey on a 'tour abroad'. When the mother Çiçek (Özay Fecht) is finally found, she is not interested in her daughter; thus in the end, Zeki and Şenay find themselves back on the road to Germany, but armed this time with a sense of having formed a utopian community as a defence against a hostile world. The history of migration is thus revisited through the lens of travelling performers and homeless children.

Another recent example of migrant cinema hitting the road is Fatih Akın's *Im Juli* (*In July*, 2000). This pleasurable road movie follows schoolteacher Daniel (Moritz Bleibtreu, from *Run, Lola, Run*) on a transformative journey from Hamburg across the Balkans to Istanbul. The journey is initiated by a brief encounter with charming Melek (Idil Üner) who mentions plans to meet Isa (Mehmet Kurtuluş) under the Bosporus Bridge at high noon on the following Friday. Meanwhile, Juli (Christiane Paul) has chosen to follow Daniel and introduces him to unknown pleasures such as smoking his first joint and singing 'Blue Moon', while they are travelling down the Danube as stowaways, before Daniel is thrown off the barge and has to continue on his own. Performances of border-crossing are at the core of this film, including a self-ironic cameo appearance of director Fatih Akın who stages himself as a corrupt custom's officer, who will not let Daniel pass: 'No passport, no Romania!' At this moment, an unexpected reunion with Juli takes place and a mock wedding ceremony is performed right on the border which ensure Daniel's right of passage. The shots of this scene at the toll bar are modelled closely on the popular Turkish border comedy *Propaganda* (1999) by Sinan Çetin, underscoring the absurdity of border control. They open up a horizon of cinematic reference points which reaches beyond German cinema, producing fusions in acting styles, and projecting a new southbound 'axial' geography where being equals travelling – not only for migrants from Turkey, but also for their friends from Germany. Incidentally, the film was co-produced by a Turkish tourism company: Argos Filmcilik Turizm, and the video release is preceded by a commercial for Öger Tours. Whether this example of cinema promoting tourism and vice versa will set a new trend and open up new possibilities of funding beyond the paternalism of public funding schemes and broadcasting channels remains to be seen.

Mobility and migration have moved to the focal point of world-wide discussions and are understood as a challenge to territorially and puristically defined national cultures. In cinema too, migrants are gradually liberating themselves from the prison of a sub-national paternalism, forging transnational alliances and evading ethnic attribution and identification through ironic role-play. *Im Juli* reminds us of the liberating pleasures of cinema, of its potential in projecting fantasies of travel, transgressing the boundaries of realist representation and performing national identities with self-conscious irony. Perhaps the German discussion about multi-culturalism and minority cultures is gradually growing beyond its provinciality towards a stage of mutual reflection. Certainly, more and more film-makers, producers and critics are learning to portray processes of cultural blending with occasional humour. In this era of globalisation, as international financing and co-productions become the norm, films are opening new perspectives beyond the ghettos of a culture of subsidy. To broaden the horizon further, we need to remember that cinema as a modern medium has been shaped by migration and mobility and has offered a home to many searchers and travellers.

Im Juli (2000)

Notes

1 An earlier version of this paper was published as: 'Migration und Kino – Subnationale Mitleidskultur oder transnationale Rollenspiele?', in Carmine Chiellino (ed.), *Interkulturelle Literatur in Deutschland. Ein Handbuch* (Stuttgart and Weimar: Metzler, 2000), pp. 329–47. Thanks to David Gramling for helping with the translation.

2 Gerhard Schoenberner and Ursula Seifried, 'Ausländer unter uns. Ein Filmkatalog', in *Deutsch lernen. Zeitschrift für den Sprachunterricht mit ausländischen Arbeitnehmern*, vol. 2/3, 1983, pp. 1–273.

3 John Berger and Jean Mohr, *A Seventh Man* (Harmondsworth: Penguin, 1985).

4 Homi Bhabha, 'DissemiNation: Time, Narrative, and the Margins of the Modern Nation', in Homi Bhabha (ed.), *Nation and Narration* (London and New York: Routledge, 1990). See pp. 291–322, esp. pp. 315–17.

5 Homi Bhabha, *The Location of Culture* (London and New York: Routledge, 1994).

6 Oğuz Makal, *Sinemada Yedinci Adam. Türk Sinemasında İç ve Dış Göç Olayı* (*The Seventh Man in Cinema. Migration Within and Abroad in Turkish Cinema*) (Izmir: Ege Yayıncılık, 1994). For examples from Turkish cinema cf. 'Turkish Cinema', *Encyclopedia of Middle Eastern and North African Film*, Deniz Göktürk and Nezih Erdogan, ed. by Oliver Leaman (London: Routledge, 2001); pp. 533–73.

7 Frank-Olaf Radtke, 'The Formation of Ethnic Minorities and the Transformation of Social Into Ethnic Conflicts in a So-Called Multi-Cultural Society: The Case of Germany', in John Rex and Beatrice Drury (eds.), *Ethnic Mobilisation in a Multi-Cultural Europe* (Aldershot: Avebury, 1994), pp. 30–37.

8 Hamid Naficy, 'Phobic Spaces and Liminal Panics: Independent Transnational Film Genre', in Rob Wilson and Wimal Dissanayake (eds.), *Global/Local: Cultural Productions and the Transnational Imaginary* (Durham and London: Duke University Press, 1996), pp. 119–44.

9 Ella Shohat and Robert Stam, *Unthinking Eurocentrism: Multiculturalism and the Media* (London and New York: Routledge, 1994), p. 42.

10 Martin Roberts, '*Baraka*: World Cinema and the Global Culture Industry', *Cinema Journal*, vol. 37, no. 3 (Spring 1998), pp. 62–82.

11 Jim Pines and Paul Willemen, *Questions of Third Cinema* (London: BFI, 1989).

12 Stephen Crofts, 'Concepts of National Cinema', in John Hill and Pamela Church Gibson (eds.), *Oxford Guide to Film Studies* (New York: Oxford University Press, 1998), pp. 385–94.

13 Christiane Peitz, 'Überall ist es besser, wo wir nicht sind', in *Die Tageszeitung*, 13 May 1994.

14 Thomas Elsaesser, *New German Cinema: A History* (London: BFI and Macmillan, 1989).

15 Sarita Malik, 'Beyond "The Cinema of Duty"? The Pleasures of Hybridity: Black British Film of the 1980s and 1990s', in Andrew Higson (ed.), *Dissolving Views: Key Writings on British Cinema* (London: Cassell, 1996), pp. 202–15.

16 Annette Brauerhoch, 'Die Heimat des Geschlechts – oder mit der fremden Geschichte die eigene erzählen: zu Shirins Hochzeit von Helma Sanders-Brahms', in Ernst Karpf, Doron Kiesel and Karsten Visarius (eds.), '*Getürkte Bilder': Zur Inszenierung von Fremden im Film* (Marburg: Schüren, 1995), pp. 109–15.

17 Naficy (1996).

18 Heike Kühn, 'Mein Türke ist Gemüsehändler: zur Einverleibung des Fremden in deutschsprachigen Filmen', in Karpf *et al.* (eds.), (1995), pp. 41–62.

19 Krista Tebbe (Kunstamt Kreuzberg) (ed.), *Morgens Deutschland – Abends Türkei* (Berlin: Fröhlich & Kaufmann, 1981).

20 Kühn (1995).

21 Deniz Göktürk, 'Turkish Delight – German Fright: Migrant Identities in Transnational Cinema', in Deniz Derman, Karen Ross and Nevena Dakovic (eds.), *Mediated Identities* (Istanbul: Bilgi University Press, 2001), pp. 131–49.

22 Deniz Göktürk, 'Strangers in Disguise: Role Play beyond Identity Politics in Anarchic Film Comedy', in Ulla Haselstein, Berndt Ostendorf and Peter Schneck (eds.), *Iconographies of Power. Poetics and Politics of the Image* (Heidelberg: Carl Winter, 2002 [forthcoming]).

Select Bibliography and Resources

The bibliography and resources section below is organised in four parts. **Part I** covers print, online and CD-Rom sources for general and reference works on German-language cinema. **Part II** offers a range of resources for further research in the fields covered in parts one, two and five of this book (genre, stars and transnational connections). **Part III** provides a bibliographical overview of German-language cinema from 1895 to the present day, organised under classical period headings from Wilhemine cinema to film post-1990. **Part IV** lists UK and US addresses for film, video and DVD sources.

References are confined largely to full-length works, though some space is given to single articles deemed to be of special significance in the field. Most works cited are in German and/or English, with exceptions, again, for works of particular significance. Studies of single films or personalities (directors, actors/actresses etc.) have largely been omitted, except where the work sheds light on larger issues. Where a single work spans more than one section, it may occasionally be referenced more than once (although for space reasons, such repetitions are kept to a minimum).

Part I: German-language cinema, general and reference

REFERENCE WORKS: GERMANY, AUSTRIA, SWITZERLAND

(I) Print sources

Encyclopedias, handbooks and dictionaries

Arnau, Frank (ed.), *Universal Filmlexikon* (Berlin: Universal-Filmlexikon GmbH, 1933).

Austrian Film Commission, *Austrian Film* (Vienna: PVS, 1986ff).

Elsaesser, Thomas and Wedel, Michael (eds.), *The BFI Companion to German Cinema* (London: British Film Institute, 1999).

Fischer Film Almanach (Frankfurt am Main: Fischer, 1980ff).

Gesek, Ludwig (ed.), *Kleines Lexikon des österreichischen Films* (Vienna: Österreichische Gesellschaft für Filmwissenschaft, 1959).

Jason, Alexander, *Der Film in Ziffern und Zahlen: die Statistik der Lichtspielhäuser in Deutschland 1895–1925* (Berlin: Deutsches Druck- und Verlagshaus, 1925).

Jason, Alexander, *Handbuch der Filmwirtschaft*, 3 vols (Berlin: Verlag für Presse, Wirtschaft und Politik, 1930–32).

Kirschner, Jürgen, *Fischer Handbuch. Theater, Film, Funk und Fernsehen* (Frankfurt am Main: Fischer, 1997).

Prinzler, Hans-Helmut, *Chronik des deutschen Films 1895–1994* (Stuttgart and Weimar: Metzler, 1995).

Read, Paula K. and Bartsch, Anja, *FilmTalk. Film Dictionary German–English, English–German* (Hamburg: Verlag für Medienliteratur, 1993).

Straschek, Günter Peter, *Handbuch wider das Kino* (Frankfurt am Main: suhrkamp, 1975).

Vincendeau, Ginette (ed.), *Encyclopedia of European Cinema* (London: Cassell/British Film Institute, 1995).

Wolffsohn, Karl (ed.), *Jahrbuch der Filmindustrie. 5 Bände* (Berlin: Lichtbildbühne 1923–33).

Film reference

Bauer, Alfred (ed.), *Deutscher Spielfilm-Almanach 1929–1950*, 2nd edn (Munich: Winterberg, 1976).

Bauer, Alfred (ed.), *Deutscher Spielfilm-Almanach 1946–1955* (Berlin: Winterberg, 1981).

Birett, Herbert, *Verzeichnis in Deutschland gelaufener Filme: Entscheidungen der Filmzensur 1911–1920* (Munich, New York, London and Paris: Saur, 1980).

Birett, Herbert, *Das Filmangebot in Deutschland 1895–1911* (Munich: Winterberg, 1991).

Dahlke, Günther and Karl, Günter (eds.), *Deutsche Spielfilme von den Anfängen bis 1933: Ein Filmführer* (Berlin [GDR]: Henschelverlag, 1988).

Findbücher zu Beständen des Bundesarchivs (Koblenz and Berlin: Bundesarchiv-Filmarchiv, 1971ff).

Fritz, Walter, *Die österreichischen Spielfilme der Stummfilmzeit (1907–1930)* (Vienna: Österreichische Gesellschaft für Filmwissenschaft, 1967).

Fritz, Walter, *Die österreichischen Spielfilme der Tonfilmzeit (1929–1938) mit dem Anhang, Die Spielfilmproduktion in den Jahren der Annexion (1938–1944)* (Vienna: Österreichische Gesellschaft für Filmwissenschaft, 1968).

Fritz, Walter, *Dokumentarfilme aus Österreich 1909–1914* (Vienna: Österreichische Gesellschaft für Filmwissenschaft, 1980).

Gerull, Brigitte (ed.), *DEFA-Dokumentarfilme 1946–1992* (Berlin: Hochschule für Film und Fernsehen 'Konrad Wolf', 1996).

Habel, Frank-Burkhard, *Das große Lexikon der DEFA-Spielfilme: die vollständige Dokumentation der DEFA-Spielfilme von 1946 bis 1993* (Berlin: Schwarzkopf & Schwarzkopf, 2000).

Helt, Richard C. and Helt, Marie E., *West German Cinema since 1945: A Reference Handbook* (Metuchen, NJ: Scarecrow, 1987).

Helt, Richard and Helt, Marie E., *West German Cinema 1985–1990: A Reference Handbook* (Metuchen, NJ: Scarecrow, 1992).

Hohnstock, Manfred and Bettermann, Alfons (eds.), *Deutscher Filmpreis 1951–1980* (Bonn: Bundesminister des Innern, 1980).

Holba, Herbert, *Katalog der Illustrierten Film-Bühne Kino-Programme* (Vienna and Ulm: Action/Knorr, 1978).

Klaus, Ulrich J., *Deutsche Tonfilme: Filmlexikon der abendfüllenden und deutschsprachigen Tonfilme nach ihren deutschen Uraufführungen 1929–1937*, 8 vols (Berlin and Berchtesgarten: Klaus, 1988–97).

Knorr, Günther, *Deutsche Kurz-Spielfilme, 1929–1940* (Ulm: Günther Knorr, 1977).

Kramer, Thomas (ed.), *Reclams Lexikon des deutschen Films (Deutschland, Österreich, Schweiz)* (Stuttgart: Reclam, 1995).

Lamprecht, Gerhard, *Deutsche Stummfilme 1903–1931*, 9 vols and index (Berlin: Deutsche Kinemathek, 1967–70).

Mertens, Eberhard (ed.), *Filmprogramme* (Hildesheim: Olms, 1977ff).

Michl, H. A., *Filmspiegel: Liste der in den Jahren, 49–54 in Österreich gezeigten abendfüllenden Spiel- u. Kulturfilme* (Graz: Landesjugendreferat Steiermark, 1955).

Mühsam, Kurt and Jacobsohn, Egon, *Lexikon des Films* (Berlin: Licht-Bild-Bühne, 1926).

Petzke, Ingo (ed.), *Das Experimentalfilm-Handbuch* (Frankfurt am Main: Deutsches Filmmuseum, 1989).

Schieber, Elke (ed.), *Die Sammlungen des Filmmuseums Potsdam: Bestandsübersicht* (Potsdam: Filmmuseum, 2001).

Schulz, Günter (ed.), *DEFA-Spielfilme 1946–1964: Filmografie* (Berlin [GDR]: Staatliches Filmarchiv, 1989).

Smith, David Calvert, *The German Filmography 1895–1949* (Jefferson, NC: McFarland, forthcoming).

Trebbin, Frank, *Die Angst sitzt neben Dir: Psychothriller, Horror- und SF-Filme*, 6 vols (Berlin: Frank Trebbin, 1991–6).

Wedel, Michael (ed.), *German Cinema, 1895–1917: A Checklist of Extant Films in International Archives* (Amsterdam: University of Amsterdam, 1995).

Willen, Günther, *DEFA-Filme: Ein Bestandsverzeichnis* (Oldenburg: Universität Oldenburg, 1998).

Personalities

Almanach der deutschen Filmschaffenden (Berlin: Hesse, 1943).

Beyer, Friedemann, *Die Gesichter der Ufa: Starportraits einer Epoche* (Munich: Heyne, 1992).

Blum, Heiko R. and Blum, Katharina, *Gesichter des deutschen Films*, 2nd edn (Munich: Heyne, 1999).

Bock, Hans-Michael (ed.), *CineGraph: Lexikon zum deutschsprachigen Film* (Munich: edition text+kritik, 1984ff).

Bucher, Felix, *Screen Series: Germany. An Illustrated Guide to the Work of over 400 Directors, Players, Technicians, and other Leading Film Figures in the German Cinema, with an Index to over 6,000 Films* (New York and London: A. S. Barnes/Tantivy Press, 1970).

Glenzdorf, Johann C., *Glenzdorfs Internationales Filmlexikon: Biographisches Handbuch für das gesamte Filmwesen*, 3 vols (Bad Münder: Glenzdorfs Internationales Filmlexikon, 1961).

Habel, Franz-Burhard and Wachter, Volker, *Lexikon der DDR-Stars: Schauspieler aus Film und Fernsehen* (Berlin: Schwarzkopf & Schwarzkopf, 1999).

Heinzlmeier, Adolf and Schulz, Berndt, *Lexikon der deutschen Film- und TV-Stars* (Berlin: Lexicon, 2000).

Holba, Herbert, Knorr, Günter and Spiegel, Peter, *Reclams deutsches Filmlexikon: Filmkünstler aus Deutschland, Österreich und der Schweiz* (Stuttgart: Reclam, 1995).

Huber, Herbert J. (ed.), *Langen Müller's Schauspieler-Lexikon der Gegenwart* (Munich and Vienna: Langen Müller, 1986).

Kaltenbach, Christiane (ed.), *FrauenFilmHandbuch* (Berlin: Verband der Filmarbeiterinnen, 1983).

Klaue, Wolfgang, Mückenberger, Christiane and Reichow, Joachim (eds.), *Film A–Z. Regisseure, Kameraleute,*

Autoren, Komponisten, Szenographen, Sachbegriffe (Berlin [GDR]: Henschel Verlag, 1984).

Krautz, Alfred (ed.), *International Directory of Cinematographers, Set- and Costume Designers in Film: Volume 1, German Democratic Republic (1946–1978) and Poland (from the Beginnings to 1978)* (Munich, New York, London and Paris: Saur, 1981).

Krautz, Alfred (ed.), *International Directory of Cinematographers, Set- and Costume Designers in Film: Volume 4, Germany (from the Beginnings to 1945)* (Munich, New York, London and Paris: Saur, 1984).

Reinert, Charles (ed.), *Wir vom Film. 1300 Kurzbiographien aus aller Welt mit rund 1000 Filmtiteln* (Freiburg: Herder, 1964).

Seydel, Renate (ed.), *Schauspieler: Theater, Film, Fernsehen* 3rd edn (Berlin [GDR]: Henschelverlag, 1976).

Sobek, Daniela, *Lexikon lesbischer Frauen im Film* (Munich: Belleville, 2000).

Bibliographies

Herlinghaus, Hermann *et al.* (eds.), *Film- und Fernsehliteratur der DDR. Eine annotierte Bibliographie. 1946–1982, Vols. 1 & 2* (Berlin [GDR]: Hochschule für Film und Fernsehen der DDR, 1984); *Vol. 3. Ergänzungsband. 1946–1983* (Berlin [GDR]: Hochschule für Film und Fernsehen der DDR, 1984); *Vols. 4 & 5. Diplom- und Abschlussarbeiten der Hochschule für Film und Fernsehen der DDR* (Berlin [GDR]: Hochschule für Film und Fernsehen der DDR, 1984).

Prodolliet, Ernst, *Die Filmpresse in der Schweiz: Bibliographie und Texte* (Freiburg: Institut für Journalistik und Kommunikationswissenschaften, 1975).

Schmidt, Margarete and Krautz, Alfred (eds.), *Bibliografie zur Geschichte der sozialistischen Film- und Fernsehkunst* (Potsdam [GDR]: Hochschule für Film und Fernsehen der DDR, 1972).

Traub, Hans and Lavies, Hanns Wilhelm (eds.), *Das deutsche Filmschrifttum: eine Bibliographie der Bücher und Zeitschriften über das Filmwesen* (Leipzig: Hiersemann, 1940).

Wulff, Hans Jürgen, Möller, Karl-Dietmar and Horak, Jan-Christopher (eds.), *Bibliographie der Filmbibliographien/Bibliography of Film Bibliographies* (Munich, New York, London, Oxford and Paris: Saur, 1987).

(II) Journals, yearbooks and newsletters

Apropos: Film Jahrbuch der DEFA-Stiftung (Berlin: Das neue.

Augen-Blick (Marburg: Marburger Hefte zur Medienwissenschaft).

Aus Theorie und Praxis (Potsdam-Babelsberg: Betriebsakademie des VEB DEFA Studio für Spielfilme).

Beiträge zur Film-und Fernschwissenschaft. Eine Schriftenreihe der Hochschule für Film und Fernsehen 'Konrad Wolf' (Berlin, Vistas).

diskurs film (Munich: Münchener Beiträge zur Filmphilologie).

epd-film (Frankfurt am Main: Evangelischer Pressedienst).

Film und Fernsehen (Potsdam-Babelsberg: Filmverband Brandenburg).

Film und Kritik (Frankfurt am Main: Stroemfeld/Roter Stern).

Filmblatt (Berlin: Cinegraph Babelsberg/Berlin-Brandenburgisches Zentrum für Filmforschung).

Filmexil (Berlin: Stiftung Deutsche Kinemathek/edition text+kritik).

Filmgeschichte (Berlin: Filmmuseum Berlin).

frauen und film (Frankfurt am Main: Stroemfeld/Roter Stern).

Kinemathek (Berlin: Freunde der deutschen Kinemathek).

Kintop Jahrbuch zur Erforschung des frühen Films (Frankfurt am Main: Stroemfeld/Roter Stern).

montage/av. Zeitschrift für Theorie und Geschichte audiovisueller Kommunikation (Berlin: montage/av).

New German Critique. An Interdisciplinary Journal of German Studies (Ithaca, NY: Cornell University Press).

UFITA. Archiv für Urheber – Film-, Funk- und Theaterrecht (Bern: UFITA).

(III) CD-Roms

Deutsches Institut für Filmkunde (ed.), *Die deutschen Filme: Deutsche Filmographie 1895–1998. Die Top-100* (Frankfurt am Main: Deutsches Institut für Filmkunde, 1999).

Dewald, Madeleine and Lammert, Oliver, *Vom Hirschkäfer zum Hakenkreuz: der Kulturfilm als Wegbereiter des nationalsozialistischen Propagandafilms: eine filmhistorische CD-Rom* (Hamburg: film und gestaltung, 1996).

F.A.Z.-Filmkritik '93–97. Streifzüge durch die Kinolandschaft mit der F.A.Z. von 1993–1997 (Frankfurt am Main: F.A.Z., 1998).

Goble, Alan, *International Film Index on CD-Rom* (East Grinstead: Bowker-Saur, 1996).

International Federation of Film Archives (FIAF) (ed.), *International Film Archive CD-Rom* (Brussels: FIAF, biannual).

Österreichische Nationalbibliothek (ed.), *Filmplakate aus der Österreichischen Nationalbibliothek (1910–1955): Film Posters* (Munich: Saur, 1998).

(IV) Internet resources

Film schools, selected universities and independent research centres

http://www.cinegraph.de – Cinegraph (Hamburg): data on history of German-speaking film, Cinegraph events, and links to online version of *Cinegraph-Lexikon*.

http://www.hff-potsdam.de – Hochschule für Film und Fernsehen (Film and Television School), Potsdam.

http://www.defa@uni-oldenburg.de – comprehensive data on DEFA film.

http://www.deutsches-filminstitut.de – Deutsches Filminstitut: Frankfurt-based film research institute, formerly Deutsches Institut für Filmkunde.

http://www.nananet.de/gfs/gfs.htm – Gesellschaft für Filmstudien: Hanover-based independent film research centre.

http://www.umass.edu/defa/ – DEFA Film Library, University of Massachusetts, Amherst. Archive and Study Centre devoted to DEFA film, and post-1990 films related to former GDR.

http://www.uni-frankfurt.de/fb10/tfm – Institut für Theater-, Film- und Medienwissenschaft, Johann-Wolfgang-Goethe-Universität, Frankfurt am Main.

http://www.uni-koeln.de/phil-fak/thefife/home/ – Institut für Theater-, Film- und Fernsehwissenschaft, University of Cologne: excellent links to German film studies sources.

http://www.univie.ac.at/Theaterwissenschaft – Institut für Theater-, Film- und Medienwissenschaft, University of Vienna.

http://www.warwick.ac.uk/fac/arts/German/resources/culture.html#film – comprehensive links to German-language sources on film.

http://www.film/uniz.ch – link to Seminar für Filmwissenschaft, University of Zurich.

http://www.lib.berkeley.edu/MRC/Germanfilm.html – Media Resources Centre, UC Berkeley.

http://www.lib.berkeley.edu/MRC/Germanfilmbib.html – selected bibliography of materials in the UC library.

http://www.lib.berkeley.edu/MRC/germanfilmresources.html – German cinema on DVD and video: resources for collection development and scholarship (includes further links to video and DVD vendors etc.).

Museums and archives

http://www.bundesarchiv.de – Bundesarchiv (National Archive), with links to film holdings.

http://www.cinematheque.ch – Swiss National Film Archive.

http://www.defa-stiftung.de – DEFA-Stiftung (DEFA-Foundation: archive of DEFA feature films).

http://www.deutsche-wochenschau.de – commercial newsreel archive with comprehensive holdings from the years 1945–77.

http://www.deutsches-filmmuseum.de – Deutsches Filmmuseum (German Film Museum), Frankfurt am Main.

http://www.filmmuseum-berlin.de – Berlin Film Museum (formerly Deutsche Kinemathek): links to film archive and other collections, including Marlene Dietrich Collection, Berlin.

http://www.filmmuseum-potsdam.de – Potsdam Film Museum (extensive DEFA holdings).

http://www.murnau-stiftung.de – Friedrich-Wilhelm-Murnau-Stiftung, Wiesbaden: comprehensive archival holdings for period before 1945, and 1956–62.

http://www.stadtmuseum-online.de/filmmu.htm – Munich Film Museum.

Bibliographies and databases

http://www.bibl.hff-potsdam.de/misc.cdrom/index.html – annotated index of selected CD-Roms relevant to the study of German and Austrian cinema.

http://www.bsz-bw.de/wwwroot/text/fabioFILM.html#Film – film page of Bibliotheksservice-Zentrum (Library Service Centre), Baden-Württemberg. Links to specialist bibliographies and film databases online.

http://www.unibw-muenchen.dc/campus/Film/wwwfilmbi.html – database for Wilhelmine and Weimar cinema, including extensive bibliography 1940–80.

Magazines and journals

http://www.celluloid.at – online edition of Austrian film magazine, *celluloid*, with reviews of current Austrian releases.

http://epd.de/film – online edition of Germany's foremost film monthly: includes current film reviews.

http://www.filmgeschichte.de – English- and German-language magazine site on early film, focusing on early horror, the fantastic and the adventure film.

http://www.filmrezension.de – online review magazine for current releases.

http://www.german-cinema.de – film review site (1954–present) of German Cinema Inc. (Export-Union des Deutschen Films GmbH).

http://www.kinoweb.de – reviews site for post-1996 releases.

http://www.swissfilms.ch – Schweizerisches Filmzentrum (Swiss Film Centre) site: reviews etc. of current Swiss cinema.

http://www.unitrier.de/~kintop – *Kintop*: Yearbook of Early Cinema Research.

Contemporary German-language film
http://www.bellnet.com/suchen/medien/kino.htm – links to ca. 300 current film sites.

FILM THEORY AND CRITICISM

Arnheim, Rudolf, *Film als Kunst. Mit einem Vorwort zur Neuausgabe* (Munich: Hanser, 1974 [orig. 1932], in translation as *Film as Art* [London: Faber and Faber, 1933]).

Balázs, Béla, *Der sichtbare Mensch oder die Kultur des Films* (Vienna and Leipzig: Deutsch-österreichischer Verlag, 1924).

Balázs, Béla, *Der Geist des Films* (Halle and Saale: Knapp, 1930).

Balázs, Béla, *Der Film. Werden und Wesen einer neuen Kunst* (Vienna: Globus, 1947, in translation as *Theory of the Film. Character and Growth of a New Art* [New York: Dover, 1955]).

Diederichs, Helmut H., *Anfänge deutscher Filmkritik* (Stuttgart: Fischer & Wiedleroither, 1986).

Greve, Ludwig, Pehle, Margot and Westhoff, Heidi (eds.), *Hätte ich das Kino! Die Schriftsteller und der Stummfilm* (Munich: Kösel, 1976).

Groll, Günter, *Film – Die unentdeckte Kunst* (Munich: C. H. Beck, 1937).

Güttinger, Fritz (ed.), *Der Stummfilm im Zitat der Zeit* (Frankfurt am Main: Deutsches Filmmuseum, 1984).

Güttinger, Fritz (ed.), *Kein Tag ohne Kino: Schriftsteller über den Stummfilm* (Frankfurt am Main: Deutsches Filmmuseum, 1984).

Hake, Sabine, *The Cinema's Third Machine: Writing on Film in Germany, 1907–1933* (Lincoln, NE, and London: University of Nebraska Press, 1993).

Heller, Heinz-B., *Literarische Intelligenz und Film: zu Veränderungen der ästhetischen Theorie und Praxis unter dem Eindruck des Films 1910–1930 in Deutschland* (Tübingen: Max Niemeyer, 1985).

Hetze, Stefanie, *Happy-End für wen? Kino und lesbische Frauen* (Frankfurt and Dülmen: tende, 1986).

Iros, Ernst, *Wesen und Dramaturgie des Films* (Zürich: Niehans, 1957).

Kaes, Anton (ed.), *Kino-Debatte: Literatur und Film 1909–1929* (Tübingen: Max Niemeyer, 1978).

Kaes, Anton, 'Literary Intellectuals and the Cinema. Charting a Controversy (1909–1929)', in *New German Critique*, 40, Winter 1987, pp. 7–33.

Koch, Gertrud, *Was ich erbeute sind Bilder. Zum Diskurs der Geschlechter im Film* (Frankfurt am Main: Stroemfeld/Roter Stern, 1989).

Kracauer, Siegfried, *From Caligari to Hitler: A Psychological History of the German Film* (Princeton: Princeton University Press, 1947).

Kracauer, Siegfried, *Theory of Film. The Redemption of Physical Reality* (New York: Oxford University Press, 1960, in translation as *Theorie des Films. Die Errettung der äusseren Wirklichkeit* [Frankfurt am Main: suhrkamp, 1964]).

Kracauer, Siegfried, *Das Ornament der Masse. Essays 1920–31*, Karsten Witte (ed.) (Frankfurt am Main: suhrkamp, 1977, in translation as *The Mass Ornament: Weimar Essays* [Cambridge, MA, and London: Harvard University Press, 1995]).

Kracauer, Siegfried, *Kino. Essays, Studien, Glossen zum Film*, Karsten Witte (ed.) (Frankfurt am Main: suhrkamp, 1977).

Kracauer, Siegfried, *Aufsätze (1915–1926, 1927–1931, 1932–1965)*, Inka Mülder-Bach (ed.), 3 vols (Frankfurt am Main: suhrkamp, 1990).

Müller, Gottfried, *Dramaturgie des Theaters, des Hörspiels und des Films* (Würzburg: Konrad Triltsch, 1954 [orig. 1941]).

New German Critique, 40, Winter 1987. Special issue on Weimar Film Theory.

Paech, Joachim, *Literatur und Film* (Stuttgart: Metzler, 1988).

Paech, Joachim, 'Aktuelle deutsche Filmtheorie', in *Internationales Archiv für Sozialgeschichte der deutschen Literatur*, vol. 18, no. 2 (1993), pp. 194–204.

Richter, Hans, *Filmgegner von heute – Filmfreunde von morgen* (Frankfurt am Main: Fischer, 1968 [orig. 1929]).

Richter, Hans, *Der Kampf um den Film. Für einen gesellschaftlich verantwortlichen Film* (Munich: Hanser, 1976 [orig. 1939], in translation as *The Struggle for the Film: Towards a Socially Responsible Cinema* [Aldershot: Wildwood House, 1986]).

Riecke, Christiane, *Feministische Filmtheorie in der Bundesrepublik Deutschland* (New York: Peter Lang, 1998).

Schenk, Irmbert (ed.), *Filmkritik. Bestandsaufnahmen und Perspektiven* (Marburg: Schüren, 1998).

Schlüpmann, Heide, *Abendröthe der Subjektphilosophie. Eine Ästhetik des Kinos* (Frankfurt am Main and Basel: Stroemfeld, 1998).

Schlüpmann, Heide, 'Die Wiederkehr des Verdrängten. Überlegungen zu einer Philosophie der Filmgeschichte aus feministischer Perspektive', *frauen und film*, 56/57, pp. 41–58.

GERMAN FILM HISTORY: APPROACHES

Bock, Hans-Michael and Jacobsen, Wolfgang (eds.), *Recherche: Film. Quellen und Methoden der Filmforschung* (Munich: edition text+kritik, 1997).

Elsaesser, Thomas, 'The New Film History', in *Sight and Sound*, vol. 55, no. 4, Autumn 1986, pp. 246–51.

Hickethier, Knut (ed.), *Filmgeschichte schreiben. Ansätze, Entwürfe und Methoden* (Berlin: Edition Sigma, 1989).

Kaes, Anton, 'German Cultural History and the Study of Film: Ten Theses and a Postscript', in *New German Critique*, 65, Spring–Summer 1995, pp. 47–58.

Schlüpmann, Heide, 'Die Wiederkehr des Verdrängten. Überlegungen zu einer Philosophie der Filmgeschichte aus feministischer in Perspektive', *frauen und film*, 56/57.

GENERAL HISTORIES

(I) Germany

National

Agde, Günter, *Flimmernde Versprechen: Geschichte des deutschen Werbefilms im Kino seit 1897* (Berlin: Das neue Berlin, 1998).

Albrecht, Gerd (ed.), *Die großen Filmerfolge: Vom Blauen Engel bis Otto, der Film. Die erfolgreichsten Filme vom Beginn des Tonfilms bis heute* (Ebersberg: Edition achteinhalb, 1985).

Alter, Nora, *Projecting History: Non-Fiction German Cinema, 1967–2000* (Ann Arbor: University of Michigan Press, forthcoming).

Bandmann, Christa and Hembus, Joe, *Klassiker des deutschen Tonfilms 1930–1960* (Munich: Goldmann, 1980).

Barkhausen, Hans, *Filmpropaganda für Deutschland im Ersten und Zweiten Weltkrieg* (Hildesheim, Zurich and New York: Olms, 1992).

Berghan, Daniela and Bance, Alan (eds.), *Millenial Essays on Film and Other German Studies* (Oxford: Peter Lang, 2002).

Bock, Hans-Michael and Töteberg, Michael (eds.), *Das Ufa-Buch: Kunst und Krisen, Stars und Regisseure, Wirtschaft und Politik* (Frankfurt am Main: Zweitausendeins, 1992).

Borgelt, Hans, *Die Ufa – ein Traum: Hundert Jahre deutscher Film. Ereignisse und Erlebnisse* (Berlin: edition q, 1993).

Bredow, Wilfried von and Zurek, Rolf (eds.), *Film und Gesellschaft in Deutschland: Dokumente und Materialien* (Hamburg: Hoffman & Campe, 1975).

Buache, Freddy, *Le cinéma allemand, 1918–1933* (Renens: Hatier, 1984).

Buchka, Peter, *Deutsche Augenblicke: eine Bilderfolge zu einer Typologie des Films* (Munich: Schriftenreihe des Filmmuseums im Münchner Stadtmuseum, 1995).

Cziffra, Geza von, *Es war eine rauschende Ballnacht: eine Sittengeschichte des deutschen Films* (Munich and Berlin: Herbig, 1985).

Faulstich, Werner and Korte, Helmut (eds.), *Fischer Filmgeschichte*, 5 vols (Frankfurt am Main: Fischer, 1994–5).

Fraenkel, Heinrich, *Unsterblicher Film: die große Chronik von der Laterna Magica bis zum Tonfilm* (Munich: Kindler, 1956).

Frieden, Sandra, McCormick, Richard W., Peterson, Vibeke and Vogelsang, Laurie M. (eds.), *Gender and German Cinema*, 2 vols (Providence, RI, and Oxford: Berg, 1993).

Geiss, Axel (ed.), *Filmstadt Babelsberg: zur Geschichte des Studios und seiner Filme* (Berlin: Nicolai, 1994).

Ginsberg, Terri and Thompson, Kirsten Moanna, *Perspectives on German Cinema* (London, Mexico City, New Delhi, Singapore, Sydney and Toronto: G. K. Hall, 1996).

Gregor, Ulrich and Patalas, Enno, *Geschichte des Films* (Gütersloh: Mohn, 1960).

Hake, Sabine, *German National Cinema* (London and New York: Routledge, 2002).

Hattendorf, Manfred, *Perspektiven des Dokumentarfilms* (Munich: diskurs film, 1995).

Hein, Birgit, *Film im Untergrund* (Munich: Ullstein, 1971).

Jacobsen, Wolfgang (ed.), *Babelsberg: Das Filmstudio*, 3rd edn (Berlin: Argon, 1994).

Jacobsen, Wolfgang, Kaes, Anton and Prinzler, Hans-Helmut (eds.), *Geschichte des deutschen Films* (Stuttgart and Weimar: Metzler, 1993).

Jung, Uli (ed.), *Der deutsche Film: Aspekte seiner Geschichte von den Anfängen bis zur Gegenwart* (Trier: Wissenschaftlicher Verlag, 1993).

Kalbus, Oskar, *Vom Werden deutscher Filmkunst*, 2 vols (Altona-Bahrenfeld: Cigaretten-Bilderdienst, 1935).

Kinter, Jürgen, *Arbeiterbewegung und Film (1895–1933)* (Hamburg: Medienpädagogik-Zentrum, 1985).

Kreimeier, Klaus, *The Ufa Story: A History of Germany's Greatest Film Company, 1918–1945* (New York: Hill and Wang, 1996 [orig. in German as *Die Ufa-Story: Geschichte eines Filmkonzerns*, 1992]).

Kriegk, Otto, *Der deutsche Film im Spiegel der Ufa: 25 Jahre Kampf und Vollendung* (Berlin: Ufa-Buchverlag, 1943).

Kuzniar, Alice A., *The Queer German Cinema* (Stanford, CA: Stanford University Press, 2000).

Ledig, Elfriede (ed.), *Der Stummfilm: Konstruktion und Rekonstruktion* (Munich: Verlegergemeinschaft Schaudig, 1988).

Loewy, Ronny, *Das jiddische Kino* (Frankfurt am Main: Deutsches Filmmuseum, 1982).

Manvell, Roger, *Masterworks of the German Cinema* (London: Lorrimer, 1973).

Manvell, Roger and Fraenkel, Heinrich, *The German Cinema* (London: J. M. Dent, 1971).

Marquardt, Axel and Rathsack, Heinz, *Preußen im Film* (Reinbek-bei-Hamburg: Rowohlt, 1981).

McCarthy, Margaret and Halle, Randall (eds.), *Light Motives: German Popular Film in Perspective* (Detroit: Wayne State University Press, forthcoming).

Meurer, Hans Joachim, *Cinema and National Identity in a Divided Germany, 1979–1989* (Lewiston, NY: Edwin Mellen, 2000).

Moldenhauer, Gebhard and Zimmermann, Peter, *Der geteilte Himmel: Arbeit, Alltag und Geschichte im ost- und westdeutschen Film* (Constance: UVK Medien, 2000).

Moreck, Curt, *Sittengeschichte des Kinos* (Dresden: Paul Aretz, 1926).

Murray, Bruce and Wickham, Christopher (eds.), *Framing the Past: The Historiography of German Cinema and Television* (Carbondale: University of Southern Illinois Press, 1992).

Ott, Frederick W., *The Great German Films: From Before World War One to the Present* (Secaucus, NY: Citadel, 1986).

Rentschler, Eric (ed.), *German Film and Literature: Adaptations and Transformations* (New York and London: Methuen, 1986).

Riess, Curt, *Das gab's nur einmal: die große Zeit des deutschen Films*, 3 vols (Frankfurt am Main: Ullstein, 1985).

Rother, Rainer (ed.), *Die Ufa 1917–1945: das deutsche Bilderimperium*, boxed set of twenty-two magazines (Berlin: Deutsches Historisches Museum, 1992).

Schaudig, Michael (ed.), *Positionen deutscher Filmgeschichte: 100 Jahre Kinematographie – Strukturen, Diskurse, Kontexte* (Munich: diskurs film, 1996).

Schenk, Irmbert, *Dschungel Grossstadt. Kino und Modernisierung* (Marburg: Schüren, 1999).

Schenk, Irmbert, *Erlebnisort Kino* (Marburg: Schüren, 2000).

Schuster, Andrea, *Zerfall oder Wandel der Kultur? Eine kultursoziologische Interpretation des deutschen Films* (Wiesbaden: DUV, 1999).

Silberman, Marc, *German Cinema: Texts in Context* (Detroit: Wayne State University Press, 1995).

Strauss, Annette C., *Frauen im deutschen Film* (Frankfurt am Main: Peter Lang, 1996).

Thomas, Hans Alex, *Die deutsche Tonfilmmusik: Von den Anfängen bis 1956* (Gütersloh: Bertelsmann, 1962).

Traub, Hans (ed.), *Die Ufa: ein Beitrag zur Entwicklungsgeschichte des deutschen Filmschaffens* (Berlin: Ufa-Buchverlag, 1943).

Trumpener, Katie, *Divided Screens: Postwar Cinema in East and West* (Princeton, NJ: Princeton University Press, forthcoming).

Vogt, Guntram and Sanke, Philipp, *Die Stadt im Kino: deutsche Spielfilme 1900–2000* (Marburg: Schüren, 2001).

Werner, Paul, *Die Skandalchronik des deutschen Films von 1900 bis 1945* (Frankfurt am Main: Fischer, 1990).

Wollenberg, Hans H., *Fifty Years of German Film* (London: Falcon, 1948).

Zglinicki, Friedrich von, *Der Weg des Films* (Berlin: Rembrandt, 1956).

Regional

Aurich, Rolf, Fuhrmann, Susanne and Müller, Pamela (eds.), *Lichtspielträume: Kino in Hannover 1896–1991* (Hanover: SOAK, 1991).

Berg-Ganschow, Uta and Jacobsen, Wolfgang (eds.), … *Film … Stadt … Kino … Berlin …* (Berlin: Argon, 1987).

Esser, Michael (ed.), *In Berlin produziert: 24 Firmengeschichten* (Berlin: Stiftung Deutsche Kinemathek, 1987).

Fischli, Bruno (ed.), *Vom Sehen im Dunkeln: Kinogeschichten einer Stadt* (Cologne: Prometh, 1990).

Hanisch, Michael, *Auf den Spuren der Filmgeschichte: Berliner Schauplätze* (Berlin: Henschelverlag, 1991).

Henningsen, Wiltrud, *Die Entstehung des Kinos in Münster* (Münster: Wiltrud Henningsen, 1990).

Hoffmann, Detlef and Thiele, Jens (eds.), *Lichtbilder, Lichtspiele: Anfänge der Fotografie und des Kinos in Ostfriesland* (Marburg: Jonas, 1989).

Kosok, Lisa and Jamin, Mathilde (eds.), *Öffentliche Lustbarkeiten im Ruhrgebiet der Jahrhundertwende* (Essen: Ruhrlandmuseum, 1992).

Schaper, Petra, *Kinos in Lübeck: die Geschichte der Lübecker Lichtspieltheater und ihrer unmittelbaren Vorläufer 1896 bis heute* (Lübeck: Graphische Werkstätten, 1987).

Töteberg, Michael, *Filmstadt Hamburg. Von Emil Jannings bis Wim Wenders. Kino-Geschichte(n) einer Grossstadt* (Hamburg: VSA, 1990).

Van Keeken, Nadja, *Kinokultur in der Provinz: am Beispiel von Bad Hersfeld* (Frankfurt am Main, Berlin, Bern and New York: Peter Lang, 1993).

Wolf, Sylvia and Kurowski, Ulrich, *Das Münchner Film-
und Kino-Buch* (Munich: Edition achteinhalb, 1988).

(II) Austria and Switzerland

Aeppli, Felix, *Der Schweizer Film 1929–1964: die Schweiz
als Ritual*, 2 vols (Zurich: Limmet, 1981).

Beckermann, Ruth and Blüminger, Christa (eds.), *Ohne
Untertitel: Fragmente einer Geschichte des
österreichischen Kinos* (Vienna: Sonderzahl, 1996).

Bono, Francesco, Caneppele, Paolo and Kreun, Günter,
*Elektrische Schatten. Beiträge zur österreichischen
Stummfilmgeschichte* (Vienna: FilmArchiv Austria,
1999).

Buache, Freddy, *Le cinéma suisse, 1898–1998* (Lucerne:
L'âge d'homme, 1998).

Büttner, Elisabeth and Dewald, Christian, *Anschluß am
Morgen: eine Geschichte des österreichischen Films von
1945 bis zur Gegenwart* (Salzburg: Residen, 1997).

Cuneo, Anne, *La machine fantaisie: enquête sur le cinéma
suisse* (Vevey: Bertil Galland, 1977).

Dumont, Hervé, *Histoire du cinéma suisse: films de fiction,
1896–1965* (Lucerne: Cinémathèque Suisse, 1987).

Fritz, Walter, *Kino in Österreich*, 3 vols (Vienna:
Österreichischer Bundesverlag, 1981–91).

Fritz, Walter, *Im Kino erlebe ich die Welt …: 100 Jahre Kino
und Film in Österreich* (Vienna: Brandstätten, 1997).

Grafl, Franz, *Praterbude und Filmpalast: wiener Kino
Lesebuch* (Vienna: Verlag für Gesellschaftskritik, 1993).

Jansen, Peter W. and Schütte, Wolfram (eds.), *Film in der
Schweiz* (Munich and Vienna: Hanser, 1978).

Kinematographengesellschaft (ed.), *Film und Filmwirtschaft in der Schweiz: fünfzig Jahre allgemeine Kinematographengesellschaft* (Zurich: Kinematographengesellschaft, 1977).

Kramer, Thomas and Prucha, Martin, *100 Jahre Kino in
Deutschland, Österreich und der Schweiz* (Vienna:
Überreuter, 1996).

Schlappner, Martin and Schaub, Martin, *Vergangenheit und
Gegenwart des Schweizer Films (1896–1987): eine
kritische Wertung* (Zurich: Schweizerisches
Filmmuseum, 1987).

Schlemmer, Gottfried and Mayr, Brigitte (eds.), *Der
österreichische Film: von seinen Anfängen bis heute*
(Vienna: Synema, 1999).

Steiner, Gertraud, *Die Heimat-Macher: Kino in Österreich
1946–1966* (Vienna: Verlag für Gesellschaftskritik,
1987).

Steiner, Gertraud, *Filmbuch Österreich* (Vienna:
Bundespressedienst, 1995).

Part II: Genres, stars, transnational connections

GENRE STUDIES

Belach, Helga and Jacobsen, Wolfgang (eds.), *Wir tanzen
um die Welt: deutsche Revuefilme 1933–1945* (Munich
and Vienna: Hanser, 1979).

Belach, Helga and Jacobsen, Wolfgang (eds.), *Slapstick &
Co.: Early Comedies* (Berlin: Argon, 1995).

Bergfelder, Tim, 'The Nation Vanishes: European Co-
Productions and Popular Genre Formulae in the 1950s
and 1960s', in Hjort, Mette and Mackenzie, Scott (eds.),
Cinema and Nation (London and New York: Routledge,
2000), pp.139–52.

Bergfelder, Tim, 'Exotic Thrills and Bedroom Manuals.
West German B-Film Production in the 1960s', in
McCarthy, Margaret and Halle, Randall (eds.), *Light
Motives: German Popular Film in Perspective* (Detroit:
Wayne State University Press, forthcoming).

Bliersbach, Gerhard, *So grün war die Heide: die gar nicht
so heile Welt im Nachkriegsfilm* (Weinheim: Beltz,
1989).

Bock, Hans-Michael and Jacobsen, Wolfgang (eds.), *Der
komische Kintopp* (Hamburg: CineGraph, 1997).

Gemünden, Gerd, 'Between Karl May and Karl Marx: The
DEFA *Indianerfilme* (1965–85)', in *Film History*, 10,
1998, pp. 399–407.

Habel, Frank-Burkhard, *Goiko Mitic, Mustangs,
Marterpfähle: die DEFA-Indianerfilme* (Berlin:
Schwarzkopf & Schwarzkopf, 1995).

Hagener, Malte (ed.), *Als die Filme singen lernten.
Innovation und Tradition im Musikfilm 1928–1933*
(Munich: edition text+kritik, 1999).

Hagener, Malte (ed.), *Geschlecht in Fesseln: Sexualität
zwischen Aufklärung und Ausbeutung im Weimarer Kino
1918–1933* (Munich: edition text+kritik, 2000).

Hanke, Ken, 'The "Lost" Horror Film Series: The Edgar
Wallace *Krimis*', in Schneider, Steven J., *Fear without
Frontiers: Horror Cinema across the Globe* (Guildford:
FAB Press, forthcoming).

Höfig, Willi, *Der deutsche Heimatfilm 1947–1960*
(Stuttgart: Enke, 1973).

Jörg, Holger, *Die sagen- und märchenhafte Leinwand:
Erzählstoffe, Motive und narrative Strukturen der
Volksprosa im 'klassischen' deutschen Stummfilm
(1910–1930)* (Sinzheim: Pro Universitate, 1994).

Kerekes, David, *Sex – Murder – Art: The Films of Jörg
Buttgereit*, 2nd edn (Manchester: Headpress, 1998).

König, Ingelore, Wiedemann, Dieter and Wolf, Lothar
(eds.), *Zwischen Bluejeans und Blauhemden: Jugendfilm
in Ost und West* (Berlin: Henschelverlag, 1995).

Kramp, Joachim, *Hallo! Hier spricht Edgar Wallace: die
Geschichte der Kriminalfilmserie 1959–1972* (Berlin:
Schwarzkopf & Schwarzkopf, 2001).

Musée du cinéma, *Fantastique et realisme dans le cinéma
allemand, 1912–1933* (Brussels: Musée du cinéma,
1969).

Pauer, Florian, *Die Edgar Wallace Filme* (Munich:
Goldmann, 1982).

Prawer, Siegbert S., *Caligari's Children: The Film as Tale of
Terror* (Oxford: Oxford University Press, 1980).

Rapp, Christian, *Höhenrausch: der deutsche Bergfilm*
(Vienna: Sonderzahl, 1997).

Schacht, Daniel Alexander, *Fluchtpunkt Provinz: der neue
Heimatfilm zwischen 1968 und 1972* (Münster: MakS,
1991).

Scheugl, Hans and Schmidt Jr., Ernst, *Eine Subgeschichte
des Films: Lexikon des Avantgarde-, Experimental-
und Undergroundfilms*, 2 vols (Frankfurt am Main:
suhrkamp, 1974).

Schneider, Tassilo, 'Finding a New *Heimat* in the Wild
West: Karl May and the German Western of the 1960s',
in Buscombe, Edward and Pearson, Roberta E. (eds.),
Back in the Saddle Again: New Essays on the Western
(London: British Film Institute, 1998).

Schöning, Jörg (ed.), *Triviale Tropen: Exotische Reise- und
Abenteuerfilme aus Deutschland 1919–1930* (Munich:
edition text+kritik, 1997).

Tohill, Cathal and Tombs, Pete, *Immoral Tales: Sex and
Horror Cinema in Europe, 1956–1984* (London:
Creation, 1994).

Uhlenbrok, Katja (ed.), *MusikSpektakelFilm. Musiktheater
und Tanztheater im deutschen Film, 1922–1937*
(Munich: edition text+kritik, 1998).

Unucka, Christian (ed.), *Karl May im Film* (Dachau:
Franke, 1980).

Watson, Stephanie and Recht, Alex, 'German Drug
Cinema', in Stevenson, Jack (ed.), *Addicted: The Myth
and Menace of Drugs in Film* (London: Creation, 2000),
pp. 166–75.

Wetzel, Kraft and Hagemann, Peter, *Liebe, Tod und
Technik: Kino des Phantastischen 1933–45* (Berlin:
Volker Spiess, 1977).

Witte, Karsten, 'Visual Pleasure Inhibited. Aspects of the
German Revue Film', in *New German Critique*, 24–5,
1981–2, pp. 228–63.

STARS

Belach, Helga (ed.), *Henny Porten: der erste deutsche
Filmstar 1890–1960* (Berlin: Haude & Spener, 1986).

Beyer, Friedemann, *Die Ufa-Stars im Dritten Reich: Frauen
für Deutschland* (Munich: Heyne, 1991).

Carter, Erica, *Dietrich's Ghosts: Stars in Third Reich Film*
(London: British Film Institute, forthcoming).

Faulstich, Werner and Korte, Helmut (eds.), *Der Star.
Geschichte, Rezeption, Bedeutung* (Munich: Fink,
1997).

Heinzlmeier, Adolf, Schulze, Berndt and Witte, Karsten,
Die Unsterblichen des Kinos, 3 vols (Frankfurt am Main:
Fischer, 1980–82).

Hickethier, Knut, *Grenzgänger zwischen Theater und Kino:
Schauspielerportraits aus dem Berlin der zwanziger Jahre*
(Berlin: Mythos Berlin, 1986).

Hickethier, Knut (ed.), *Schauspielen und Montage.
Schauspielkunst im Film: zweites Symposium (1998)* (St
Augustin: Gardez, 1999).

Koebner, Thomas (ed.), *Idole des deutschen Films: eine
Galerie von Schlüsselfiguren* (Munich: edition
text+kritik, 1997).

Koebner, Thomas (ed.), *Schauspielkunst im Film. Erstes
Symposium (1997)* (St Augustin: Gardez, 1998).

Korte, Helmut and Strake-Behrendt, Gabriele, *Der
Filmstar. Forschungsstand, kommentierte Bibliographie,
Starliste* (Braunschweig: Hochschule für Bildende
Künste, 1990).

Lenssen, Claudia, *Blaue Augen, blauer Fleck. Kino im
Wandel von der Diva zum Girlie* (Berlin:
Parthas/Filmmuseum Potsdam, 1997).

Lowry, Stephen and Korte, Helmut, *Der Filmstar*
(Stuttgart and Weimar: Metzler, 2000).

Möhrmann, Renate (ed.), *Die Schauspielerin. Zur
Kulturgeschichte der weiblichen Bühnenkunst* (Frankfurt
am Main: Insel, 1989).

montage/av, vol. 6, no. 2, 1997. Special issue on stars.

Patalas, Enno, *Sozialgeschichte der Stars* (Hamburg:
Schröder, 1963).

Patalas, Enno, *Stars – Geschichte der Filmidole* (Frankfurt
am Main: Fischer, 1967).

Romani, Cincia, *Tainted Goddesses: Female Film Stars of
the Third Reich* (New York: Sarpedon, 1992 [orig. in
Italian as *Le dive del terzo reich*, 1981]).

Thomsen, Christian W., *Sellers, Stars und Serien. Medien
im Produktverband* (Heidelberg: Reihe Siegen 89, 1989).

Winkler-Mayerhöfer, Andrea, *Starkult als Propagandamittel: Studien zum Unterhaltungsfilm im Dritten
Reich* (Munich: Olschläger, 1992).

MIGRATION, EXILE, TRANSNATIONAL CONNECTIONS

Angst-Nowik, Doris and Sloan, Jane (eds.), *One-Way Ticket to Hollywood: Film Artists of Austrian and German Origin in Los Angeles. Emigration, 1884–1945* (Los Angeles: Max Kade Institute, 1987).

Arnheim, Rudolf, 'Film' [1934], in Kaznelson, Siegmund (ed.), *Juden im deutschen Kulturleben*, 2nd edn (Berlin: Jüdischer Verlag, 1959), pp. 220–41.

Asper, Helmut G., *'Etwas Besseres als der Tod …'. Filmexil in Hollywood* (Marburg: Schüren, 2002).

Baxter, John, *The Hollywood Exiles* (New York: MacDonald and Jane's 1976).

Behn, Manfred (ed.), *Schwarzer Traum und weiße Sklavin: Deutsch-dänische Filmbeziehungen 1910–1930* (Munich: edition text+kritik, 1994).

Belach, Helga and Prinzler, Hans-Helmut (eds.), *Exil. Sechs Schauspieler aus Deutschland: Elisabeth Bergner – Dolly Haas – Hertha Thiele – Curt Bois – Francis Lederer – Wolfgang Zilzer* (Berlin: Stiftung Deutsche Kinemathek, 1983).

Bergfelder, Tim, 'The Production Designer and the *Gesamtkunstwerk*. German Film Technicians in the British Film Industry of the 1930s', in Higson, Andrew (ed.), *Dissolving Views. Key Writings on British Cinema* (London and New York: Cassell, 1996), pp. 20–37.

Blum, Heiko R., *Meine zweite Heimat Hollywood: Deutschsprachige Filmkünstler in den USA* (Berlin: Henschel, 2001).

Cargnelli, Christian and Omasta, Michael, *Aufbruch ins Ungewisse: österreichische Filmschaffende in der Emigration vor 1945* (Vienna: Wespennest, 1993).

Dittrich, Kathinka, 'Spielfilme: die Niederlande und die deutsche Emigration', in Dittrich, Kathinka and Würzner, Hans (eds.), *Die Niederlande und das deutsche Exil* (Amsterdam and Königstein: Athenäum, 1982), pp. 186–214.

Garncarz, Joseph, 'Hollywood in Germany. Die Rolle des amerikanischen Films in Deutschland: 1925–1990', in Jung, Uli (ed.), *Der deutsche Film: Aspekte seiner Geschichte von den Anfängen bis zur Gegenwart* (Trier: Wissenschaftlicher Verlag, 1993), pp. 167–214 (in translation as 'Hollywood in Germany. The Role of American Films in Germany, 1925–1990', in Ellwood, David W. and Kroes, Rob (eds.), *Hollywood in Europe. Experiences of a Cultural Hegemony* [Amsterdam: VU University Press, 1994]).

Ghezzi, Enrico (ed.), *Vienna–Berlino–Hollywood: il cinema della grande emigrazione* (Venice: Bienniale, 1981).

Goethe Institute of North America, *German Film Directors in Hollywood: Film Emigration from Germany and Austria* (San Francisco: Goethe Institute, 1978).

Göktürk, Deniz, *Künstler, Cowboys, Ingenieure: Kultur- und mediengeschichtliche Studien zu deutschen Amerika-Texten 1912–1920* (Munich: Wilhelm Fink, 1998).

Göktürk, Deniz, 'Migration und Kino – Subnationale Mitleidskultur oder transnationale Rollenspiele?', in Chiellino, Carmine (ed.), *Interkulturelle Literatur in Deutschland: ein Handbuch* (Stuttgart: Metzler, 2000), pp. 329–47.

Gough-Yates, Kevin, 'The British Feature Film as a European Concern: Britain and the Émigré Filmmaker 1933–1945', in Berghaus, Günter (ed.), *Theatre and Film in Exile* (Oxford: Oswald Wolff and Berg, 1989), pp.135–66.

Gough-Yates, Kevin, 'Jews and Exiles in British Cinema', in *Leo Baeck Yearbook 37* (1992), pp. 517–43.

Higson, Andrew and Maltby, Richard (eds.), *'Film Europe' and 'Film America'. Cinema, Commerce, and Cultural Exchange 1920–1939* (Exeter: University of Exeter Press, 1998).

Hilchenbach, Maria, *Kino im Exil* (Munich: Saur, 1982).

Horak, Jan-Christopher, *Middle European Emigrés in Hollywood: An American Film Institute Oral History* (Beverly Hills: Louis B. Mayer Foundation, 1977).

Horak, Jan-Christopher, 'The Palm Trees were Gently Swaying: German Refugees from Hitler in Hollywood', in *Image*, vol. 23, no. 1, June 1980, pp. 21–32.

Horak, Jan-Christopher, *Fluchtpunkt Hollywood: eine Dokumentation zur Filmemigration nach 1933* (Münster: MakS, 1984).

Horak, Jan-Christopher, *Anti-Nazi-Filme der deutschsprachigen Emigration von Hollywood 1939–45* (Münster: MakS, 1984).

Horak, Jan-Christopher, 'Rin-Tin-Tin in Berlin or American Cinema in Weimar', in *Film History*, 5 (1993), pp. 49–62.

Horak, Jan-Christopher, 'German Exile Cinema, 1933–1950', in *Film History*, 8, 1996, pp. 373–89.

Hurst, Heike and Gassen, Heiner (eds.), *Kameradschaft/Querelle: Kino zwischen Deutschland und Frankreich* (Munich: Institut Français-CICIM, 1991).

Karpf, Ernst, Kiesel, Doron and Visarius, Karsten (eds.), *'Getürkte Bilder': zur Inszenierung von Fremden im Film* (Marburg: Schüren, 1995).

Koch, Gertrud, *Die Einstellung ist die Einstellung. Visuelle Konstruktionen des Judentums* (Frankfurt am Main: suhrkamp, 1992).

Koepnick, Lutz, *The Dark Mirror: German Cinema between Hitler and Hollywood* (Berkeley: University of California Press, forthcoming).

Kracauer, Siegfried, 'National Types as Hollywood Presents Them', in *Public Opinion Quarterly*, 13, Spring 1949, pp. 53–72.

Kulaoğlu, Tuncay, 'Der neue "deutsche" Film ist "türkisch"? Eine neue Generation bringt Leben in die Filmlandschaft', in *Filmforum*, February/March 1999, pp. 8–11.

Leab, Daniel, 'Deutschland, USA: German Images in American Film', in Miller, Randall M. (ed.), *The Kaleidoscopic Lens: How Hollywood Views Ethnic Groups* (Englewood, NJ: Jerome S. Ozer, 1980), pp. 156–81.

Loacker, Armin and Prucha, Martin (eds.), *Unerwünschtes Kino: der deutschsprachige Emigrantenfilm 1934–1937* (Vienna: Filmarchiv Austria, 2000).

Loewy, Ronny (ed.), *Von Babelsberg nach Hollywood: Filmemigranten aus Nazideutschland* (Frankfurt am Main: Deutsches Filmmuseum, 1987).

Morrison, James, *Passport to Hollywood. Hollywood Films, European Directors* (Albany: SUNY Press, 1998).

Petrie, Graham, *Hollywood Destinies: European Directors in America, 1922–1931* (London: Routledge/Kegan Paul, 1985).

Phillips, Alastair and Vincendeau, Ginette (eds.), *Journeys of Desire: European Actors in Hollywood* (London: British Film Institute, forthcoming).

Phillips, Gene D., *Exiles in Hollywood: Major European Film Directors in America* (Bethlehem, PA: Lehigh University Press, 1998).

Saunders, Thomas J., *Hollywood in Berlin: American Cinema and Weimar Germany* (Berkeley: University of California Press, 1994).

Saunders, Thomas J., 'The German–Russian Film (Mis)alliance (DERUSSA): Commerce and Politics in German–Soviet Cinema Ties', in *Film History*, 9, 1997, pp. 168–88.

Schoenberner, Gerhard and Seifried, Ursula, 'Ausländer unter uns. Ein Filmkatalog', in *Deutsch lernen. Zeitschrift für den Sprachunterricht mit ausländischen Arbeit-nehmern*, vol. 2/3, 1983, pp. 1–273.

Schöning, Jörg, *London Calling: deutsche im britischen Film der dreißiger Jahre* (Munich: edition text+kritik, 1993).

Schöning, Jörg (ed.), *Fantaisies russes: russische Filmemacher in Berlin und Paris 1920–1930* (Munich: edition text+kritik, 1995).

Spieker, Markus, *Hollywood unterm Hakenkreuz: der amerikanische Spielfilm im Dritten Reich* (Trier: Wissenschaftlicher Verlag, 1999).

Sturm, Sibylle and Wohlgemuth, Arthur (eds.), *Hallo? Berlin? Ici Paris! Deutsche-französische Filmbeziehungen 1918–1939* (Munich: edition text+kritik, 1996).

Taylor, John Russell, *Strangers in Paradise: The Hollywood Emigrés 1933–1950* (London: Faber and Faber, 1983).

Thompson, Kristin, *Exporting Entertainment: America in the World Market, 1907–1934* (London: British Film Institute, 1985).

Whittemore, Don and Cecchittini, Philip Alan (eds.), *Passport to Hollywood: Film Immigrants Anthology* (New York: McGraw-Hill, 1976).

Wicclair, Walter, *Von Kreuzberg bis Hollywood* (Berlin [GDR]: Henschelverlag, 1975).

Part III: Periodised bibliography

WILHELMINE CINEMA 1895–1918

Altenloh, Emilie, *Zur Soziologie des Kino: die Kino-Unternehmung und die sozialen Schichten ihrer Besucher* (Jena: Eugen Diederichs, 1914 [partial English translation in *Screen*, vol. 42, no. 3, Autumn 2001, pp. 249–93]).

Birett, Herbert, *Lichtspiele: der Kino in Deutschland bis 1914* (Munich: Q-Verlag, 1994).

Cherchi Usai, Paolo and Codelli, Lorenzo (eds.), *Prima di Caligari. Cinema tedesco, 1895–1920/Before Caligari: German Cinema, 1895–1920* (Pordenone: Biblioteca dell'Immagine, 1990).

Curtis, Scott, 'The Taste of a Nation: Training the Senses and Sensibility of Cinema Audiences in Imperial Germany', in *Film History*, 6, 1994, pp. 445–69.

Dibbets, Karel and Hogenkamp, Bert (eds.), *Film and the First World War* (Amsterdam: Amsterdam University Press, 1995).

Elsaesser, Thomas and Wedel, Michael (eds.), *A Second Life: German Cinema's First Decades* (Amsterdam: Amsterdam University Press, 1996).

Gad, Urban, *Der Film: seine Mittel, seine Ziele* (Berlin: Schuster & Loeffler, 1920 [orig. in Danish as *Filmen*, 1919]).

Garncarz, Joseph, 'Die Entstehung des Kinos aus dem Varieté: ein Plädoyer für ein erweitertes Konzept der Intermedialität', in Helbig, Jörg (ed.), *Intermedialität: Theorie und Praxis eines interdisziplinären Forschungsgebiets* (Berlin: Erich Schmidt, 1998), pp. 244–56.

Hake, Sabine, *Passions and Deceptions: The Early Films of Ernst Lubitsch* (Princeton, NJ: Princeton University Press, 1992).

Hansch, Gabriele and Waz, Gerlinde (eds.), *Filmpionierinnen in Deutschland: ein Beitrag zur Filmgeschichtsschreibung* (Berlin: Frauenforschung des Berliner Senats, 1998).

Hansen, Miriam, 'Early Silent Cinema: Whose Public Sphere?', in *New German Critique*, 29, Spring/Summer 1983, pp. 147–84.

Jochum, Norbert (ed.), *Das wandernde Bild: der Filmpionier Guido Seeber* (Berlin: Stiftung Deutsche Kinemathek/Elefanten Press, 1979).

Kaes, Anton, 'Mass Culture and Modernity: Notes Toward a Social History of Early American and German Cinema', in Trommler, Frank and McVeigh, Joseph (eds.), *America and the Germans: An Assessment of a Three-Hundred-Year History*, vol. 2 (Philadelphia: University of Pennsylvania Press, 1985), pp. 317–31.

Kilchenstein, Gabriele, *Frühe Filmzensur in Deutschland: eine vergleichende Studie zur Prüfungsarbeit in Berlin und München (1906–1914)* (Munich: diskurs film, 1997).

Kullmann, Max, *Die Entwicklung des deutschen Lichtspieltheaters* (Kallmünz: Michael Laßleben, 1935).

Loiperdinger, Martin, *Film und Schokolade: Stollwercks Geschäfte mit lebenden Bildern* (Basel and Frankfurt am Main: Stroemfeld/Roter Stern, 1999).

Mack, Max (ed.), *Die zappelnde Leinwand* (Berlin: Eysler, 1916).

Messter, Oskar, *Mein Weg mit dem Film* (Berlin: Max Hesse, 1936).

Müller, Corinna, *Frühe deutsche Kinematographie: formale, wirtschaftliche und kulturelle Entwicklungen 1907–1912* (Stuttgart and Weimar: Metzler, 1994).

Panofsky, Walter, *Die Geburt des Films*, 2nd edn (Würzburg: Triltsch, 1944).

Rossell, Deac, 'Beyond Messter: Aspects of Early Cinema in Berlin', in *Film History*, 10, 1998, pp. 52–69.

Rossell, Deac, *Faszination der Bewegung: Ottomar Anschütz zwischen Photographie und Kino* (Basel and Frankfurt am Main: Stroemfeld/Roter Stern, 2001).

Schliepmann, Hans, *Lichtspieltheater: eine Sammlung ausgeführter Kinohäuser in Groß-Berlin* (Berlin: Wasmuth, 1914).

Schlüpmann, Heide, 'Melodrama and Social Drama in the Early German Cinema', in *Camera Obscura*, 22, January 1990, pp. 73–85.

Schlüpmann, Heide, *Die Unheimlichkeit des Blicks: das Drama des frühen deutschen Kinos* (Basel and Frankfurt am Main: Stroemfeld/Roter Stern, 1990).

Schlüpmann, Heide 'Cinema as Anti-Theater: Actresses and Female Audiences in Wilhelmine Germany', in Richard Abel (ed.), *Silent Film* (London: Athlone, 1996), pp. 125–41.

Schweinitz, Jörg (ed.), *Prolog vor dem Film: Nachdenken über ein neues Medium 1909–1914* (Leipzig: Reclam, 1992).

Segeberg, Harro (ed.), *Mediengeschichte des deutschen Films*, 3 vols (Munich: Wilhelm Fink, 1996, 1998, 2000).

Stark, Gary D., 'Cinema, Society and the State: Policing the Film Industry in Imperial Germany', in Stark, Gary D. and Lachner, Bede Karl (eds.), *Essays on Culture and Society in Modern Germany* (Arlington: University of Texas Press, 1982), pp. 122–66.

Traub, Hans, *Als man anfing zu filmen: die Erfindung der Kinematographie und ihrer Vorläufer* (Berlin: Ufa-Buchverlag, 1940).

Warstat, Dieter H., *Frühes Kino der Kleinstadt* (Berlin: Volker Spiess, 1982).

WEIMAR CINEMA 1918–33

Aurich, Rolf and Jacobsen, Wolfgang, *Werkstatt Film: Selbstverständnis und Visionen von Filmleuten der zwanziger Jahre* (Munich: edition text+kritik, 1998).

Barlow, John D., *German Expressionist Film* (Boston: Twayne, 1982).

Berger, Jürgen (ed.), *Erobert den Film: Proletariat und Film in der Weimarer Republik* (Berlin: Neue Gesellschaft für Bildende Kunst, 1977).

Beyfuss, E. and Kossowsky, A. (eds.), *Das Kulturfilmbuch* (Berlin: Chryselius, 1924).

Brennicke, Ilona and Hembus, Joe, *Klassiker des deutschen Stummfilms 1910–1930* (Munich: Goldmann, 1983).

Budd, Mike (ed.), *The Cabinet of Dr. Caligari: Texts, Contexts, Histories* (New Brunswick, NJ: Rutgers University Press, 1990).

Calhoon, Kenneth S. (ed.), *Peripheral Visions. The Hidden Stages of Weimar Cinema* (Detroit: Wayne State University Press, 2001).

Coates, Paul, *The Gorgon's Gaze: German Cinema, Expressionism, and the Image of Horror* (Cambridge: Cambridge University Press, 1991).

Courtade, Francis, *Cinéma expressioniste* (Paris: Henri Veyrier, 1984).

Dyer, Richard, 'Weimar: Less and More Like the Others', in *Now You See It: Studies on Lesbian and Gay Film* (London and New York: Routledge, 1990), pp. 7–46.

Eisner, Lotte, *The Haunted Screen: Expressionism in the German Cinema and the Influence of Max Reinhardt* (Berkeley: University of California Press, 1969 [orig. in French as *L'écran démoniaque*, 1952]).

Elsaesser, Thomas, 'Social Mobility and the Fantastic: German Silent Cinema', in Donald James (ed.), *Fantasy and the Cinema* (London: British Film Institute, 1989), pp. 23–38.

Elsaesser, Thomas, 'European Cinema: Germany and Hollywood 1927–1934', in Muscio, Giuliana (ed.), *Before the Hays Code* (Venice: Marsilio, 1991), pp. 201–12.

Elsaesser, Thomas, *Weimar Cinema and After: Germany's Historical Imaginary* (London and New York: Routledge, 2000).

Esser, Michael (ed.), *Gleissende Schatten: Kamerapioniere der zwanziger Jahre* (Berlin: Henschelverlag, 1994).

Gandert, Gero (ed.), *Der Film der Weimarer Republik: ein Handbuch der zeitgenössischen Kritik 1929* (Berlin: De Gruyter, 1993).

Hardt, Ursula, *From Caligari to California: Erich Pommer's Life in the International Film Wars* (Providence, RI, and Oxford: Berghahn, 1996).

Jung, Uli and Schatzberg, Walter (eds.), *Filmkultur zur Zeit der Weimarer Republik* (Munich: Saur, 1992).

Kaes, Anton, *Shell Shock: Film and Trauma in Weimar Germany* (Princeton, NJ: Princeton University Press, 2002).

Kasten, Jürgen, *Der expressionistische Film: Abgefilmtes Theater oder avantgardistisches Erzählkino? Eine stil-, produktions- und rezeptionsgeschichtliche Untersuchung* (Münster: MakS, 1990).

Kaul, Walter (ed.), *Caligari und Caligarismus* (Berlin: Deutsche Kinemathek, 1970).

Keiner, Reihold, *Thea von Harbou und der deutsche Film bis 1933* (Hildesheim: Olms, 1991).

Klaus, Ulrich J., *Deutsche Tonfilme 1929/30* (Berlin: Klaus, 1988).

Korte, Helmut (ed.), *Film und Realität in der Weimarer Republik* (Munich and Vienna: Hanser, 1978).

Korte, Helmut (ed.), *Der Spielfilm und das Ende der Weimarer Republik: ein rezeptionshistorischer Versuch* (Göttingen: Vanderhoeck & Ruprecht, 1998).

Kracauer, Siegfried, *From Caligari to Hitler: A Psychological History of the German Film* (Princeton, NJ: Princeton University Press, 1947).

Kühn, Gertraude, Tümmler, Karl and Wimmer, Walter (eds.), *Film und revolutionäre Arbeiterbewegung in Deutschland 1918–1932*, 2 vols (Berlin [GDR]: Henschelverlag, 1978).

Kurtz, Rudolf, *Expressionismus und Film* (Berlin: Licht-Bild-Bühne, 1926 [reprint Zurich: Rohr, 1965]).

Lüdeke, Willi, *Der Film in Agitation und Propaganda der revolutionären deutschen Arbeiterbewegung (1919–1933)* (Berlin: Oberbaum, 1973).

McCormick, Richard W., 'From *Caligari* to Dietrich: Sexual, Social, and Cinematic Discourses in Weimar Film', in *Signs: Journal of Women in Culture and Society*, vol. 18, no. 3, 1993, pp. 640–68.

McCormick, Richard W., *Emancipation and Crisis: Gender, Sexuality, and 'New Objectivity' in Weimar Film and Literature* (New York: Palgrave/St Martin's Press, 2002).

Meissner, P., *Das große Bilderbuch des Films*, 3 vols (Berlin: Filmkurier, 1920–28).

Monaco, Paul, *Cinema and Society: France and Germany During the Twenties* (New York: Elsevier, 1976).

Mühl-Benninghaus, Wolfgang, *Das Ringen um den Tonfilm: Strategien der Elektro- und der Filmindustrie in den 20er und 30er Jahren* (Düsseldorf: Droste, 1999).

Murray, Bruce, *Film and the German Left in the Weimar Republic* (Austin: University of Texas Press, 1990).

Petro, Patrice, *Joyless Streets: Women and Melodramatic Representation in Weimar Cinema* (Princeton, NJ: Princeton University Press, 1989).

Plummer, Thomas G. and Murray, Bruce (eds.), *Film and Politics in the Weimar Republic* (Minneapolis: University of Minnesota Press, 1982).

Rügner, Ulrich, *Filmmusik in Deutschland zwischen 1924 und 1934* (Hildesheim: Olms, 1988).

Salt, Barry, 'From Caligari to Who?', in *Sight and Sound*, vol. 48, no. 2, 1979, pp. 119–23.

Saunders, Thomas J., *Hollywood in Berlin: American Cinema and Weimar Germany* (Berkeley: University of California Press, 1994).

Schebera, Jürgen, *Damals in Neubabelsberg: Studios, Stars und Kinopaläste im Berlin der zwanziger Jahre* (Leipzig: Edition Leipzig, 1990).

Schwarz, Alexander, *Der geschriebene Film: Drehbücher des deutschen und russischen Stummfilms* (Munich: diskurs film, 1994).

Seidler, Walther (ed.), *Stummfilmmusik gestern und heute* (Berlin: Volker Spiess, 1979).

Silberman, Marc, 'Industry, Text, and Ideology in Expressionist Film', in Bronner, Stephen E. and Kellner, Douglas (eds.), *Passion and Rebellion: The Expressionist Heritage* (South Hadley, MA: J. F. Bergin, 1982), pp. 374–83.

Wager, James B., *Dangerous Dames: Women and Representation in the Weimar Street Film and Film Noir* (Athens: Ohio State University Press, 1999).

Wehling, Will (ed.), *Der Weg ins Dritte Reich: deutscher Film und Weimars Ende* (Oberhausen: Laufen, 1974).

Wilmesmeier, Holger, *Deutsche Avantgarde und Film: die Filmmatinee 'Der absolute Film' 3. Und 10.Mai 1925* (Münster: LIT, 1994).

THIRD REICH CINEMA 1933–45

Ahren, Yizhak, Melchers, Christoph B. and Hornshøj-Møller, Stig, *Der ewige Jude: wie Goebbels hetzte* (Aachen: Alano, 1990).

Albrecht, Gerd, *Nationalsozialistische Filmpolitik: eine soziologische Untersuchung über die Spielfilme des Dritten Reiches* (Stuttgart: Enke, 1969).

Albrecht, Gerd, *Der Film im Dritten Reich* (Karlsruhe: Doku-Verlag, 1979).

Bechdolf, Ute, *Wunsch-Bilder? Frauen im nationalsozialistischen Unterhaltungsfilm* (Tübingen: Vereinigung für Volkskunde, 1992).

Becker, Wolfgang, *Film und Herrschaft: Organisationsprinzipien und Organisationsstrukturen der nationalsozialistischen Filmpropaganda* (Berlin: Volker Spiess, 1973).

Benzenhöfer, Udo and Eckart, Wolfgang U. (eds.), *Medizin im Spielfilm des Nationalsozialismus* (Tecklenburg: Burg, 1990).

Brandt, Hans-Jürgen, *NS-Filmtheorie und dokumentarische Praxis: Hippler, Noldan, Junghans* (Tübingen: Max Niemeyer, 1987).

Carter, Erica, 'The New Third Reich Film History', in *German History,* vol. 17, no. 4, 1999, pp. 565–83.

Courtade, Francis and Cadars, Pierre, *Geschichte des Films im Dritten Reich* (Munich: Hanser, 1975 [orig. in French as *Histoire du cinéma nazi,* 1973]).

Dammeyer, Manfred, *Der Spielfilm im Dritten Reich* (Oberhausen: 1. Arbeitsseminar der Westdeutschen Kurzfilmtage, 1966).

Drewniak, Boguslav, *Der deutsche Film 1938–1945* (Düsseldorf: Droste, 1987).

Ehrlich, Evelyn, *Cinema of Paradox: French Filmmaking Under the German Occupation* (New York: Columbia University Press, 1985).

Fox, Jo, *Filming Women in the Third Reich* (Oxford: Berg, 2000).

Gitlis, Baruch, *Film and Propaganda: The Nazi Anti-Semitic Film* (Tel Aviv: Revivim, 1984).

Grunsky-Peper, Konrad, *Deutsche Volkskunde im Film: gesellschaftliche Leitbilder im Unterrichtsfilm des Dritten Reichs* (Munich: Minerva, 1978).

Hake, Sabine, *Popular Cinema of the Third Reich* (Austin: University of Texas Press, 2002).

Happel, Hans-Gerd, *Der historische Spielfilm im Nationalsozialismus* (Frankfurt am Main: Fischer, 1984).

Hippler, Fritz, *Betrachtungen zum Filmschaffen* (Berlin: Reichsfilmkammer, 1942).

Hoffmann, Hilmar, *The Triumph of Propaganda: Film and National Socialism, 1933–1945* (Providence, RI: Berghahn, 1996).

Hollstein, Dorothea, *Jud Süß und die Deutschen: antisemitische Vorurteile im nationalsozialistischen Spielfilm* (Frankfurt am Main: Ullstein, 1983).

Hull, David Stewart, *Film in the Third Reich* (Berkeley: University of California Press, 1969).

Kanzog, Klaus, *'Staatspolitisch besonders wertvoll': ein Handbuch zu 30 deutschen Spielfilmen der Jahre 1934 bis 1945* (Munich: diskurs film, 1994).

Krah, Hans (ed.), *Geschichte(n) NS-Film – NS-Spuren heute* (Kiel: Ludwig, 1999).

Kramer, Thomas and Siegrist, Dominick, *Terra: Ein Schweizer Filmkonzern im Dritten Reich* (Zurich: Chronos, 1991).

Leiser, Erwin, *Nazi Cinema* (London: Secker and Warburg, 1975 [orig. in German as *Deutschland erwache! Propaganda im Film des Dritten Reichs,* 1968]).

Loiperdinger, Martin (ed.), *Märtyrerlegenden im NS-Film* (Opladen: Leske + Budrich, 1991).

Lowry, Stephen, *Pathos und Politik: Ideologie in Spielfilmen des Nationalsozialismus* (Tübingen: Max Niemeyer, 1991).

Maiwald, Klaus-Jürgen, *Filmzensur im NS-Staat* (Dortmund: Peter Nowotny, 1983).

Mannes, Stefan, *Antisemitismus im nationalsozialistischen Film – Jud Süß und Der Ewige Jude* (Cologne: Teiresias, 1999).

Moeller, Felix, *Der Filmminister: Goebbels und der Film im Dritten Reich* (Berlin: Henschelverlag, 1998).

Nazi Cinema. Special issue of *New German Critique,* 74, 1998.

Oertel, Rudolf, *Filmspiegel: ein Brevier aus der Welt des Films,* 5th edn (Vienna: Frick, 1944).

Osten, Ulrich von der, *NS-Filme im Kontext sehen! 'Staatspolitisch besonders wertvolle' Filme der Jahre 1934–1938* (Munich: diskurs film, 1998).

Petley, Julian, *Capital and Culture: German Cinema 1933–45* (London: British Film Institute, 1979).

Phillips, Baxter, *Swastika: Cinema of Oppression* (London: Lorrimer, 1976).

Prinzler, Hans-Helmut (ed.), *Europa 1939* (Berlin: Stiftung Deutsche Kinemathek, 1989).

Rabenalt, Arthur Maria, *Film im Zwielicht: über den unpolitischen Film des dritten Reiches und die*

Begrenzung des totalitären Anspruchs (Hildesheim and New York: Olms, 1975 [1958]).

Rabenalt, Arthur Maria, *Joseph Goebbels und der 'Großdeutsche' Film* (Munich: Herbig, 1985).

Reeves, Nicholas, *The Power of Film Propaganda: Myth or Reality?* (London and New York: Cassell, 1999).

Reimer, Robert C. (ed.), *Cultural History through a National Socialist Lens: Essays on the Cinema of Nazi Germany* (Rochester, NY: Camden House, 2000).

Rentschler, Eric, *The Ministry of Illusion: Nazi Cinema and its Afterlife* (Cambridge, MA and London: Harvard University Press, 1996).

Sakkara, Michele (ed.), *Die große Zeit des deutschen Films 1933–1945* (Leoni: Druffel, 1980).

Schulte-Sasse, Linda, *Entertaining the Third Reich: Illusions of Wholeness in Nazi Cinema* (Durham and London: Duke University Press, 1996).

Short, K. R. M. (ed.), *Catalogue of Forbidden German Feature and Short Film Productions held in the Zonal Film Archives of Film Section, Information Services Division, Control Commission for Germany (BE)* (Trowbridge: Flicks, 1996).

Spiker, Jürgen, *Film und Kapital: der Weg der deutschen Filmwirtschaft zum nationalsozialistischen Einheitskonzern* (Berlin: Volker Spiess, 1975).

Taylor, Richard, *Film Propaganda: Soviet Russia and Nazi Germany*, 2nd edn (London and New York: I. B. Tauris, 1998).

Traudisch, Dora, *Mutterschaft mit Zuckerguß? Frauenfeindliche Propaganda im NS-Spielfilm* (Pfaffenweiler: Centaurus, 1993).

Vogelsang, Konrad, *Filmmusik im Dritten Reich: eine Dokumentation* (Hamburg: Facta Oblita, 1990).

Welch, David, *Propaganda and German Cinema 1933–1945* (Oxford: Oxford University Press, 1983).

Wetzel, Kraft, *Zensur: verbotene deutsche Filme 1933–1945* (Berlin: Volker Spiess, 1978).

Witte, Karsten, *Lachende Erben, Toller Tag: Filmkomödie im Dritten Reich* (Berlin: Vorwerk 8, 1995).

Wulf, Joseph, *Theater und Film im Dritten Reich* (Gütersloh: Siegbert Mohn, 1964).

Zielinski, Siegfried, *Veit Harlan: Analysen und Materialien zur Auseinandersetzung mit einem Film-Regisseur des deutschen Faschismus* (Frankfurt am Main: Fischer, 1981).

'RUBBLE FILM' (*TRÜMMERFILM*) 1945–49/50

Becker, Wolfgang and Schöll, Norbert, *In jenen Tagen … wie der deutsche Nachkriegsfilm die Vergangenheit bewältigte* (Opladen: Leske + Buderich, 1995).

Berger, Jürgen, Reichmann, Hans-Peter and Worschech,

Rudolf (eds.), *Zwischen Gestern und Morgen – Westdeutscher Nachkriegsfilm 1946–1962* (Frankfurt am Main: Deutsches Filmmuseum, 1989).

Bessen, Ursula, *Trümmer und Träume: Nachkriegszeit und fünfziger Jahre auf Zelluloid. Deutsche Spielfilme als Zeugnisse ihrer Zeit* (Bochum: Brockmeyer, 1989).

Brockmann, Stephen and Trommler, Frank (eds.), *Revisiting Zero Hour: 1945* (Washington, DC: American Institute for Contemporary German Studies, 1996).

Carter, Erica, 'Sweeping up the Past: Gender and History in the Post-War German 'Rubble Film', in Sieglohr, Ulrike (ed.), *Heroines without Heroes. Reconstructing Female and National Identities in European Cinema, 1945–51* (London and New York: Cassell, 2000), pp. 91–112.

Deutscher Filmverlag. *Auf neuen Wegen: 5 Jahre fortschrittlicher Film* (Berlin: Deutscher Filmverlag, 1951).

Fehrenbach, Heide, *Cinema in Democratizing Germany: Reconstructing National Identity after Hitler* (Chapel Hill: University of North Carolina Press, 1995).

Greffrath, Bettina, *Gesellschaftsbilder der Nachkriegszeit 1945–1949* (Pfaffenweiler: Centaurus, 1995).

Hauser, Johannes, *Neuaufbau der westdeutschen Filmwirtschaft 1945–1955 und der Einfluß der US-amerikanischen Filmpolitik* (Pfaffenweiler: Centaurus, 1989).

Jaeger, Klaus and Regel, Helmut (eds.), *Deutschland in Trümmern: Filmdokumente der Jahre 1945–1949* (Oberhausen: Laufen, 1976).

Perinelli, Massimo, *Liebe '47 – Gesellschaft '49. Geschlechterverhältnisse in der deutschen Nachkriegszeit. Eine Analyse des Films Liebe '47* (Hamburg: LIT, 1999).

Pleyer, Peter, *Deutscher Nachkriegsfilm 1946–1948* (Münster: Fahle, 1965).

Prinzler, Hans-Helmut (ed.), *Das Jahr 1945: Filme aus fünfzehn Ländern* (Berlin: Stiftung Deutsche Kinemathek, 1990).

Shandley, Robert R., *Rubble Films: German Cinema in the Shadow of the Third Reich* (Philadelphia: Temple University Press, 2001).

Stettner, Peter, *Vom Trümmerfilm zur Traumfabrik: die 'Junge Film-Union' 1947–1952* (Hildesheim: Olms, 1992).

Theuerkauf, Holger, *Goebbels' Filmerbe: das Geschäft mit unveröffentlichten Ufa-Filmen* (Berlin: Ullstein, 1998).

Wilkening, Albert, *Geschichte der DEFA von 1945–1950* (Potsdam: DEFA, 1981).

GDR / DEFA

Agde, Günter (ed.), *Kahlschlag: Das 11. Plenum des ZK der SED 1965* (Berlin: Aufbau, 1991).

Allan, Seán and Sanford, John (eds.), *DEFA: East German Cinema, 1946–1992* (New York and Oxford: Berghahn, 1999).

Arbeitsgemeinschaft für Jugendfilmarbeit und Medienerziehung. *Der Alltag im DDR-Film der 70er Jahre* (Aachen: Bundesarbeitsgemeinschaft der Jugendfilmclubs, 1981).

Becker, Dorothea, *Zwischen Ideologie und Autonomie: die DDR-Forschung über die deutsche Filmgeschichte* (Münster: LIT, 1999).

Beutelschmidt, Thomas, *Sozialistische Audiovision: zur Geschichte der Medienkultur in der DDR* (Potsdam: Verlag für Berlin-Brandenburg, 1995).

Blunk, Harry, *Die DDR in ihren Spielfilmen: Reproduktion und Konzeption der DDR-Gesellschaft im neueren DEFA-Gegenwartsspielfilm* (Munich: Profil, 1984).

Blunk, Harry and Jungnickel, Dirk (eds.), *Filmland DDR: ein Reader zur Geschichte, Funktion und Wirkung der DEFA* (Cologne: Wissenschaft und Politik, 1990).

Bock, Hans-Michael and Behn, Manfred (eds.), *Film und Gesellschaft in der DDR* (Hamburg: Cinegraph, 1988).

Byg, Barton, 'The Anti-fascist Tradition and GDR Film', in *Proceedings, Purdue University Fifth Annual Conference on Film* (West Lafayette, IN: Purdue University, 1980).

Byg, Barton, 'What Might Have Been: DEFA Films of the Past and the Future of German Cinema', in *Cinéaste*, vol. 17, no. 4 (1990), pp. 9–15.

Byg, Barton, 'Two Approaches to GDR History in DEFA Films', in Gerber, Margy *et al.* (eds.), *Studies in GDR Culture and Society, 10. Selected Papers from the Fifteenth New Hampshire Symposium on the German Democratic Republic* (Lanham, MD, New York and London: University Press of America, 1991), pp. 85–103.

Byg, Barton and Moore, Betheny (eds.), *Moving Images of East Germany: Past and Future of DEFA Film* (Washington DC: John Hopkins University Press, 2002).

DEFA. *Autoren sagen aus: Erfahrungen mit dem Spielfilm. 1946–1976, 30 Jahre DEFA* (Berlin: DEFA, 1976).

Drawer, Christel (ed.), *So viele Träume: DEFA-Film-Kritiken aus drei Jahrzehnten von Heinz Kersten* (Berlin: Vistas, 1996).

Fritzsche, Karin and Löser, Claus (eds.), *Gegenbilder: filmische Subversion in der DDR 1976–1989* (Berlin: Janus, 1996).

Geiss, Axel, *Repression und Freiheit: DEFA-Regisseure zwischen Fremd- und Selbstbestimmung* (Potsdam: Brandenburgische Landeszentrale für politische Bildung, 1992).

Gersch, Wolfgang (ed.), *Film- und Fernsehkunst der DDR: Traditionen, Beispiele, Tendenzen* (Berlin [GDR]: Henschelverlag, 1979).

Giesenfeld, Günter (ed.), *Der DEFA-Film: Erbe oder Episode*. Special issue of *Augen-Blick: Marburger Hefte zur Medienwissenschaft*, no. 14, February 1993.

Glass, Peter, *Kino ist mehr als Film: die Jahre 1976–1990* (Berlin: AG-Verlag, 1999).

Hasenberg, Peter and Thull, Martin (eds.), *Filme in der DDR 1987–90* (Cologne: Katholisches Institut für Medieninformation, 1991).

Heimann, Thomas, *DEFA-Künstler und SED-Kulturpolitik: Verständnis von Kulturpolitik und Filmproduktion in der SBZ/DDR 1945 bis 1959* (Berlin: Vistas, 1994).

Heimann, Thomas, 'Erinnerung als Wandel: Kriegsbilder im frühen DDR-Film', in Sabrow, Martin (ed.), *Geschichte als Herrschaftsdiskurs* (Cologne: Böhlau, 2000), pp. 38–85.

Hoff, Peter and Wiedemann, Dieter (eds.), *Der DEFA-Spielfilm in den 80er Jahren – Chancen für die 90er?* (Berlin: Vistas, 1992).

Hofmann, Heinz (ed.), *DEFA-Spielfilme am Beginn der 80er Jahre* (Berlin [GDR]: VFF, 1982).

Holba, Herbert, Lichtenstein, Manfred and Schulz, Günter, *Filmprogramme in der DDR 1945–1975* (Vienna and Ulm: Action/Knorr, 1976).

Jansen, Peter W. and Schütte, Wolfram (eds.), *Film in der DDR* (Munich and Vienna: Hanser, 1977).

Janssen, Herbert (ed.), *Filme in der DDR 1945–1986: kritische Notizen aus 42 Kinojahren* (Cologne: Katholisches Institut für Medieninformation, 1987).

Jordan, Günter and Schenk, Rolf (eds.), *Schwarzweiß und Farbe: DEFA-Dokumentarfilm 1946–92* (Berlin: Henschelverlag, 1996).

Kannapin, Detlef, *Antifaschismus im Film der DDR: DEFA-Spielfilme 1945–1955/56* (Cologne: PapyRossa, 1997).

Kasjanowa, Ljudmila and Karawaschkin, Anatoli, *Begegnungen mit Regisseuren: Kurt Maetzig, Günter Reisch, Joachim Halser, Konrad Wolf* (Berlin [GDR]: Henschelverlag, 1974).

Klaue, Wolfgang, *Filme contra Faschismus* (Berlin [GDR]: Staatliches Filmarchiv der DDR, 1965).

König, Ingelore, Wiedemann, Dieter and Wolf, Lothar (eds.), *Zwischen Marx und Muck: DEFA-Filme für Kinder* (Berlin: Henschelverlag, 1996).

Landesbildstelle Berlin. *Film-, Bild- und Tondokumente zum 17.Juni 1953 und zum Tag der deutschen Einheit* (Berlin: Landesbildstelle Berlin, 1973).

Leonhardt, Sigrun O., 'Testing the Borders: East German Film between Individualism and Social Commitment', in Goulding, Daniel (ed.), *Post New Wave Cinema in the Soviet Union and Eastern Europe* (Bloomington: Indiana University Press, 1989), pp. 51–101.

Liehm, Mira and Liehm, Antonin J., *The Most Important Art: Soviet and Eastern European Film after 1945* (Berkeley: University of California Press, 1977), pp. 47–75, 259–74, 359–68.

Mückenberger, Christiane (ed.), *Prädikat: besonders schädlich – 'Das Kaninchen bin ich', 'Denk bloß nicht daß ich heule'* (Berlin: Henschelverlag, 1990).

Mückenberger, Christiane and Jordan, Günter (eds.), *'Sie sehen selbst, sie hören selbst': die DEFA von ihren Anfängen bis 1949* (Marburg: Hitzeroth, 1994).

Poss, Ingrid (ed.), *DEFA 50: Gespräche aus acht Filmnächten* (Berlin: Brandenburgische Zentrale für Politische Bildung, 1997).

Richter, Rolf (ed.), *DEFA-Spielfilm-Regisseure und ihre Kritiker*, 2 vols (Berlin [GDR]: Henschelverlag, 1983).

Schenk, Rolf (ed.), *Das zweite Leben der Filmstadt Babelsberg, DEFA 1946–92* (Berlin: Henschelverlag, 1994).

Schenk, Rolf, *Vor der Kamera: fünfzig Schauspieler in Babelsberg* (Berlin: Henschelverlag, 1995).

Spielhagen, Edith (ed.), *So durften wir glauben zu kämpfen …: Erfahrungen mit DDR-Medien* (Berlin: Vistas, 1993).

Watercamp, Rainer (ed.), *Frauenbilder in den DDR-Medien* (Bonn: Schriftenreihe Mediaberatung, 1996).

Wendrin, Lydia Wiehring von and Lehmann, Kirsten (eds.), *Auswahlbibliographie – 50 Jahre DEFA* (Babelsberg: Hochschule für Film und Fernsehen 'Konrad Wolf', 1996).

Wilkening, Albert, *Die DEFA in der Etappe 1950–1953* (Potsdam: DEFA, 1984).

Wolf, Dieter, *Gruppe Babelsberg. Unsere nicht gedrehte Filme* (Berlin: Das neue Berlin, 2000).

Zilinski, Lissi (ed.), *Spielfilme der DEFA im Spiegel der Kritik* (Berlin [GDR]: Henschelverlag, 1970).

Zimmermann, Peter (ed.), *Deutschlandbilder-Ost: Dokumentarfilme der DEFA von der Nachkriegszeit bis zur Wiedervereinigung* (Konstanz: UVK-Medien, 1995).

Zimmermann, Peter and Moldenhauer, Gebhard (eds.), *Der geteilte Himmel. Arbeit, Alltag und Geschichte im ost- und westdeutschen Film* (Stuttgart: UVK Medien, 2000).

WEST GERMAN CINEMA: GENERAL, 1949–90

Barthel, Manfred, *So war es wirklich: der deutsche Nachkriegsfilm* (Munich: Herbig, 1986).

Berger, Jürgen, Reichmann, Hans-Peter and Worschech, Rudolf (eds.), *Zwischen Gestern und Morgen – westdeutscher Nachkriegsfilm 1946–1962* (Frankfurt am Main: Deutsches Filmmuseum, 1989).

Bertram, Thomas (ed.), *Der rote Korsar: Traumwelt Kino der fünfziger und sechziger Jahre* (Essen: Klartext, 1998).

Bongartz, Barbara, *Von Caligari zu Hitler – von Hitler zu Dr. Mabuse? Eine 'psychologische' Geschichte des Films von 1946–1960* (Münster: MAkS, 1992).

Dillmann-Kühn, Claudia, *Artur Brauner und die CCC: Filmgeschäft, Produktionsalltag, Studiogeschichte 1946–1990* (Frankfurt am Main: Deutsches Film-museum, 1990).

Jary, Michaela, *Traumfabrik made in Germany: die Geschichte des deutschen Nachkriegsfilms 1945–1960* (Berlin: edition q, 1993).

Kreimeier, Klaus, *Kino und Filmindustrie in der BRD: Ideologieproduktion und Klassenwirklichkeit nach 1945* (Kronberg: Scriptor, 1973).

Loiperdinger, Martin, 'Amerikanisierung im Kino? Hollywood und das westdeutsche Publikum der fünfziger Jahre', in *Theaterzeitschrift*, 28, Summer 1989, pp. 50–60.

Pleyer, Peter, *Nationale und soziale Stereotypen im gegenwärtigen deutschen Spielfilm* (Munich: Institut für Publizistik, 1968).

Schenk, Irmbert, ' "Derealisierung' oder 'aufregende Modernisierung"? Film und Kino der 50er Jahre in der Bundesrepublik', in Schenk Irmbert (ed.), *Erlebnisort Kino* (Marburg: Schüren, 2000), pp. 112–29.

Schmieding, Walther, *Kunst oder Kasse: der Ärger mit dem deutschen Film* (Hamburg: Rütten & Loening, 1961).

Schneider, Tassilo, 'Somewhere Else: The Popular German Cinema of the 1960s', in *Yearbook of Comparative and General Literature*, no. 40 (Indiana: Indiana University Press, 1992), pp. 75–82.

Seidl, Claudius, *Der deutsche Film der fünfziger Jahre* (Munich: Heyne, 1987).

Sigl, Klaus, Schneider, Werner and Tornow, Ingo, *Jede Menge Kohle? Kunst und Kommerz auf dem deutschen Filmmarkt der Nachkriegszeit* (Munich: Filmland Presse, 1990).

Westermann, Bärbel, *Nationale Identität im Spielfilm der 50er Jahre* (Frankfurt am Main: Peter Lang, 1990).

YOUNG AND NEW GERMAN CINEMA 1962–90

Berg, Jan (ed.), *Am Ende der Rolle: Diskussion über den Autorenfilm* (Marburg: Schüren, 1993).

Blum, Heiko R., *30 Jahre danach: Dokumentation zur Auseinandersetzung mit dem Nationalsozialismus im Film 1945 bis 1975* (Cologne and Berlin: May/Maulwurf, 1975).

Collins, Richard and Porter, Vincent (eds.), *WDR and the Arbeiterfilm: Fassbinder, Ziewer and Others* (London: British Film Institute, 1981).

Corrigan, Timothy, *New German Cinema: The Displaced Image*, 2nd edn (Austin: University of Texas Press, 1994).

Davidson, John E., *Deterritorializing the New German Cinema* (Minneapolis and London: University of Minnesota Press, 1999).

Dost, Michael, Hopf, Florian and Kluge, Alexander (eds.), *Filmwirtschaft in der Bundesrepublik Deutschland und in Europa: Götterdämmerung in Raten* (Munich: Hanser, 1973).

Elsaesser, Thomas, *New German Cinema: A History* (London: British Film Institute and Macmillan, 1989).

Elsaesser, Thomas, *Fassbinder's Germany: History – Identity – Subject* (Amsterdam: Amsterdam University Press, 1996).

Fischer, Robert and Hembus, Joe, *Der neue deutsche Film 1960–1980* (Munich: Goldmann, 1981).

Fischetti, Renate, *Das neue Kino – Filme von Frauen: acht Porträts von deutschen Regisseurinnen* (Dülmen-Hiddengsel: tende, 1992).

Franklin, James, *New German Cinema: From Oberhausen to Hamburg* (Boston: Twayne, 1983).

Grunert-Bronnen, Barbara and Brocher, Corinna (eds.), *Die Filmemacher: zur neuen deutschen Produktion nach Oberhausen* (Munich: Bertelsmann, 1973).

Hembus, Joe, *Der deutsche Film kann gar nicht besser sein: ein Pamphlet von Gestern, eine Abrechnung von heute* (Munich: Rogner & Bernhard, 1981).

Jansen, Peter W., *The New German Film* (Munich: Goethe Institute, 1980).

Joachim, Dierk and Nowotny, Peter, *Kommunale Kinos in der BRD* (Münster and Osnabrück: Becker/Polit-Buchvertrieb, 1978).

Kaes, Anton, *From Hitler to Heimat: The Return of History as Film* (Cambridge, MA: Harvard University Press, 1989).

Kluge, Alexander, *Bestandsaufnahme Utopie Film. zwanzig Jahre neuer deutscher Film* (Frankfurt am Main: Zweitausendeins, 1983).

Knight, Julia, *Women and the New German Cinema* (London and New York: Verso, 1992).

Koch, Krischan, *Die Bedeutung des Oberhausener Manifests für die Filmentwicklung in der BRD* (Frankfurt am Main: Peter Lang, 1985).

Linville, Susan E., *Feminism, Film, Fascism: Women's Autobiographical Film in Postwar Germany* (Austin: University of Texas Press, 1998).

Lukasz-Aden, Gudrun and Strobel, Christel, *Der Frauenfilm. Filme von und für Frauen* (Munich: Heyne, 1985).

McCormick, Richard, *Politics of the Self: Feminism and the Postmodern in West German Literature and Film* (Princeton, NJ: Princeton University Press, 1991).

Möhrmann, Renate, *Die Frau mit der Kamera: Filmemacherinnen in der Bundesrepublik* (Munich: Hanser, 1980).

New German Cinema. Special issue of *New German Critique*, 24/5, Autumn/Winter 1981–2.

New German Cinema. Special issue of *Persistence of Vision*, 3 (Autumn 1985).

New German Cinema. Special issue of *Wide Angle*, vol. 3, no. 4, 1980.

Petermann, Werner and Thoms, Ralph (eds.), *Kino-Fronten: 20 Jahre '68 und das Kino* (Munich: Trickster, 1988).

Pflaum, Hans Günter, *Germany on Film: Theme and Content in Cinema of the Federal Republic of Germany* (Detroit: Wayne State University Press, 1990).

Pflaum, Hans Günter and Prinzler, Hans-Helmut, *Cinema in the Federal Republic of Germany* (Bonn: Inter Nationes, 1983 [orig. in German as *Film in der Bundesrepublik Deutschland*, 1979]).

Phillips, Klaus (ed.), *New German Filmmakers: From Oberhausen through the 1970s* (New York: Ungar, 1984).

Reichmann, Hans-Peter and Worschech, Rudolf (eds.), *Abschied von Gestern: Bundesdeutscher Film der sechziger und siebziger Jahre* (Frankfurt am Main: Deutsches Filmmuseum, 1991).

Reimer, Robert C. and Reimer, Carol J. (eds.), *Nazi-Retro Film: How German Narrative Cinema Remembers the Past* (New York: Twayne, 1992).

Rentschler, Eric, *West German Film in the Course of Time* (New York: Redgrave, 1984).

Rentschler, Eric (ed.), *West German Filmmakers on Film: Visions and Voices* (New York and London: Holmes & Meier, 1988).

Sandford, John, *The New German Cinema* (London: Eyre Methuen, 1980).

Santner, Eric L., *Stranded Objects: Mourning, Memory, and Film in Post-War Germany* (Ithaca, NY: Cornell University Press, 1990).

Schacht, Daniel Alexander, *Fluchtpunkt Provinz: der neue*

Heimatfilm zwischen 1968 und 1972 (Münster: MakS, 1991).

Verband des deutschen Filmclubs. *Neuer deutscher Film: eine Dokumentation* (Frankfurt am Main: Verband des deutschen Filmclubs, 1967).

Verband der Filmarbeiterinnen. *Frauen Film Handbuch* (Berlin: Verband der Filmarbeiterinnen, 1984).

Weinberger, Gabrile, *Nazi Germany and its Aftermath in Women Directors' Autobiographical Films of the Late 1970s: In the Murderer's House* (San Francisco: Mellen Research University Press, 1992).

West German Film in the 1970s. Special issue of *Quarterly Review of Film Studies*, vol. 5, no. 2, Spring 1980.

Zöchbauer, Franz and Strobel, Hans (eds.), *Der deutsche Kurzfilm: Versuch einer Aussagenanalyse der deutschen Kurzfilme Oberhausen* (Munich and Düsseldorf: Wissenschaftliches Institut für Jugend- und Bildungsfragen in Film und Fernsehen, 1970).

POST-UNIFICATION CINEMA: 1990 ONWARD

Amend, Heike and Bütow, Michael (eds.), *Der bewegte Film: Aufbruch zu neuen deutschen Erfolgen* (Berlin: Vistas, 1997).

Brady, Martin and Hughes, Helen, 'German Film After the *Wende*', in Lewis, Derek and McKenzie, John R. P. (eds.), *The New Germany: Social, Political and Cultural Challenges of Unification* (Exeter: Exeter University Press, 1995), pp. 279–85.

Byg, Barton, 'German Unification and the Cinema of the Former German Democratic Republic', in *Michigan German Studies*, vol. 21, nos. 1/2, Autumn 1995, pp. 150–68.

Frankfurter, Bernhard (ed.), *'Offene Bilder': Film, Staat und Gesellschaft in Europa nach der Wende* (Vienna: Promedia, 1995).

Hochmuth, Dieter (ed.), *DEFA NOVA – nach wie vor? Versuch einer Spurensicherung* (Berlin: Vistas, 1993).

Koepnick, Lutz, 'Consuming the Other: Identity, Alterity, and Contemporary German Cinema', in *Camera Obscura*, 44 (2000), pp. 41–72.

Kosta, Barbara, *Recasting Autobiography: Women's Counterfictions in Contemporary German Literature and Film* (Ithaca, NY: Cornell University Press, 1994).

Majer O'Sickey, Ingeborg and Zadow, Ingeborg von (eds.), *Triangulated Visions: Women in Recent German Cinema* (Albany: State University of New York Press, 1998).

Medien der Ex-DDR in der Wende. Special issue of *Beiträge zur Film- und Fernsehwissenschaft*, 40, 1991.

Menge, Marlies, *Zurück nach Babelsberg: Blick auf ein vereintes Land* (Cologne: Kiepenheuer & Witsch, 1992).

Nowell-Smith, Geoffrey and Wollen, Tana (eds.), *After the Wall: Broadcasting in Germany* (London: British Film Institute, 1991).

Post-Wall German Cinema. Special issue of *Camera Obscura*, 44, 2000.

Recent German Film. Special issue of *Seminar: A Journal of Germanic Studies*, vol. 33, no. 4 (1997).

Rentschler, Eric. 'From New German Cinema to the Post-Wall Cinema of Consensus', in Hjort, Mette and MacKenzie, Scott (eds.), *Cinema and Nation* (London and New York: Routledge, 2000), pp. 260–77.

Screen International Special Edition: Germany in the New Millennium, 2000.

Silberman, Marc, 'Post-Wall Documentaries: New Images from a New Germany', in *Cinema Journal*, vol. 33, no. 2, pp. 22–41.

Töteberg, Michael (ed.), *Szenenwechsel: Momentaufnahmen des jungen deutschen Films* (Hamburg: Rowohlt, 1999).

Trumpener, Katie, *Divided Screens: Postwar Cinema in East and West* (Princeton, NJ: Princeton University Press, forthcoming).

Part IV: Film, video (PAL and NTSC) and DVD sources

British Film Institute Video (PAL, mostly 'classics')
21 Stephen Street
London W1T 1LN
Tel: 020 7957 8960
Online catalogue:
http://www.bfi.org.uk/bookvid/videos/index/php3

Facets Video (PAL and NTSC, mainly 'classics')
1517 W. Fullerton Avenue
Chicago
IL 60614
Tel: (00 1+) 800-331-6197
e-mail: sales@facets.org

German Language Video Center (PAL and NTSC, ca. 2,500 titles)
Indianapolis
IN 46226-5298
USA
Tel: (00 1+) 317-547 1247
Online catalogue and ordering:
http://www.germanvideo.com

Goethe-Institut/Inter Nationes (16mm print hire)
British Film Institute
21 Stephen Street
London W1P 1PL
Tel: 020 7957 8938
Online catalogue of available prints:
http://www.goethe.de/gr/lon/film/index.htm

Icestorm International, Inc. (NTSC and DVD-R1: DEFA
specialist)
78 Main Street
Northampton
MA 01060
USA
Tel: (00 1+) 413-587 9334
Online catalogue and ordering:
http://www.icestorm-video.com

International Historic Films (NTSC and DVD-R1: Third
Reich and First World War specialist)
PO Box 29035
Chicago
IL 60629
USA
Tel: (00 1+) 773-927 2900
Online catalogue and ordering: http://ihffilm.com

Mail-Order-Kaiser München (PAL and DVD-R2: mainstream contemporary and 'classics')
80791 München
Germany
Tel: (00 49+) (0)181 5341734
Online catalogue and ordering:
http://www.mail-order-kaiser.de

Sinister Cinema (PAL and NTSC: rare releases 1910s–80s,
including Edgar Wallace)
PO Box 4369
Medford
OR 97501-0168
USA
Tel: (00 1+) 541-773 6860
Online catalogue and ordering:
http://www.sinistercinema.com

World Language Sales (NTSC and DVD R-1 & R-2: over
500 German titles)
2130 Sawtelle Boulevard
Suite 304A
Los Angeles
CA 90025
USA
Online catalogue and ordering:
http://www.worldlanguage.com/ProductTypes/
MoviesVideos.htm

Index